Switzerland

a travel s ◁ S0-AWM-472

Mark Honan

Switzerland – a travel survival kit

1st edition

Published by
Lonely Planet Publications
Head Office: PO Box 617, Hawthorn, Vic 3122, Australia
Branches: 155 Filbert St, Suite 251, Oakland, CA 94607, USA
                 10 Barley Mow Passage, Chiswick, London W4 4PH, UK
                 71 bis rue du Cardinal Lemoine, 75005 Paris, France

Printed by
Singapore National Printers Ltd, Singapore

Photographs by
Mark Honan (MH)
James Lyon (JL)
Tony Wheeler (TW)
Verbier Tourist Office, Mark Shapiro (VTO)
Zermatt Tourist Office (ZTO)
Front cover: Hot-air ballooning over Château d'Oex (Vaud Tourist Office)
Back cover: Eiger from Kleine Scheidegg (MH)

Published
January 1994

Although the authors and publisher have tried to make the information as accurate as possible, they accept no responsibility for any loss, injury or inconvenience sustained by any person using this book.

National Library of Australia Cataloguing in Publication Data

Honan, Mark
    Switzerland – a travel survival kit.

    1st ed.
    Includes index.
    ISBN 0 86442 200 8.

    1. Switzerland – Description and travel – Guidebooks.
    I. Title. (Series: Lonely Planet travel survival kit).

914.940473

text & maps © Lonely Planet 1994
photos © photographers as indicated 1994
climate charts compiled from information supplied by Patrick J Tyson, © Patrick J Tyson, 1994

Mark Honan

After a university degree in Philosophy opened up a glittering career as an office clerk, Mark decided 'the meaning of life' lay elsewhere and set off on a two-year trip around the world. As a freelance travel writer, he then went camper vanning around Europe to write a series of articles for a London magazine. When the magazine went bust Mark joined a travel agent from where he was rescued by Lonely Planet. Mark wrote the Austria, Liechtenstein and Switzerland chapters for Lonely Planet's *Western Europe on a shoestring* and is currently working on *Central America – a travel survival kit*.

From the Author

Thanks to all those people who helped me with my research, especially Heidi Reisz and Evelyn Lafone from the Swiss National Tourist Office in London, and numerous staff in local and regional tourist offices throughout Switzerland. Those particularly worthy of mention are Patrick Walter, Elizabeth Lagger, Fiorenzo Fässler and Daniele Burckhardt. Important help was also received from the Jungfrau Region Railway, the Lake Lucerne Navigation Company, Pro Helvetia and TCS.

Parts of the coverage of Chamonix were adapted from Daniel Robinson's chapter on France in the Lonely Planet guide, *Western Europe on a shoestring*. In the same book, Lynn Seldon wrote the original draft of the Germany chapter, from which stuff on the Black Forest and Lake Constance has been adapted. I also adapted parts of the introductory chapters from the same book, written by the LP editorial team, for the corresponding chapters here.

Ed, Andy and Kevin in London should be mentioned for suggestions and technical help especially with the first version of this work as it appeared in the Western Europe book. Thanks also to my parents for preventing my financial affairs from dissolving into debt-ridden disarray during frequent trips abroad. Within Switzerland, a large debt of gratitude is due to the Donikian family for providing a secure base and home comforts in Zofingen. Thanks also to Jim and Sue for insights into Geneva's attractions.

From the Publisher

This book was edited and proofed by Simone Calderwood. Chris Klep was responsible for the maps, title page and illustrations. Additional illustrations by Melanie Hodis and Margaret Jung. Thanks to Margaret for designing the cover, and to Sally Woodward, Jane Hart, Chris Lee-Ack and Rob van Driesum for their help. Thanks also to the Swiss Consulate in Melbourne for providing an abundant supply of illustrative references.

Warning & Request

Things change – prices go up, schedules change, good places go bad and bad places go bankrupt – nothing stays the same. So if you find things better or worse, recently opened or long since closed, please write and tell us and help make the next edition better.

Your letters will be used to help update future editions and, where possible, important changes will also be included in a Stop Press section in reprints.

We greatly appreciate all information that is sent to us by travellers. Back at Lonely Planet we employ a hard-working readers' letters team to sort through the many letters we receive. The best ones will be rewarded with a free copy of the next edition or another Lonely Planet guide if you prefer. We give away lots of books, but, unfortunately, not every letter/postcard receives one.

Contents

Map Legend

BOUNDARIES

— · — · — · —	.... International Boundary
— · · — · · —	.... Internal Boundary
+·+·+·+·+·+·+	.... National Park or Reserve
- - - - - - - -	.... The Equator
· · · · · · · · · ·	.... The Tropics

SYMBOLS

◉	NATIONAL	.... National Capital
●	PROVINCIAL	.... Provincial or State Capital
●	Major	.... Major Town
●	Minor	.... Minor Town
■		.... Places to Stay
▼		.... Places to Eat
⊠		.... Post Office
✕		.... Airport
i		.... Tourist Information
⊖		.... Bus Station or Terminal
66		.... Highway Route Number
¿ ↓ 🕌 ⛪		...... Mosque, Church, Cathedral
♀		.... Castle
✚		.... Hospital
✳		.... Lookout
⚐		.... Camping Area
⊼		.... Picnic Area
⌂		.... Hut or Chalet
▲		.... Mountain or Hill
↦─■─↤		.... Railway Station
═		.... Road Bridge
┼┼┼┼		.... Railway Bridge
⇒ ⇐		.... Road Tunnel
↦) (↤		.... Railway Tunnel
⌒⌒⌒		.... Escarpment or Cliff
⌣		.... Pass
⊓⊔⊓⊔		.... Ancient or Historic Wall

ROUTES

═══66═══	.... Motorway
───────	.... Major Road or Highway
- - - - - - -	.... Unsealed Major Road
───────	.... Sealed Road
- - - - - - -	..... Unsealed Road or Track
═══════	.... City Street
+·+·+·+·+·+·+	.... Railway
··············	.... Walking Track
- - - - - - -	.... Ferry Route
─┼┼─┼┼─┼┼─	.... Cable Car or Chair Lift

HYDROGRAPHIC FEATURES

∿∿∿	.... River or Creek
- - - - -	.... Intermittent Stream
⬬ ⬭	.... Lake, Intermittent Lake
∿∿∿	.... Coast Line
	.... Spring
	.... Waterfall
ᴠᴡ ᴠᴡ ᴠᴡ	.... Swamp
(hatched box)	.... Salt Lake or Reef
(contour box)	.... Glacier

OTHER FEATURES

(dotted box)	Park, Garden or National Park
(crossed box)	.... Built Up Area
(grid box)	... Market or Pedestrian Mall
(plaza box)	.... Plaza or Town Square
(+ + + box)	.... Cemetery

Note: not all symbols displayed above appear in this book

Introduction

What is it about Switzerland that so fascinates? Is it the idea that 700 years ago a band of woodsmen, a bunch of parochial William Tells, were able to repel the might of the all-conquering Habsburgs and thereby make possible the formation of the Swiss Confederation? Is it that such a militarily efficient nation as this could have avoided international warfare for so long? Could it be that (as Orson Welles/Harry Lime points out in the film *The Third Man*) 500 years of Swiss democracy and peace has produced nothing more than the cuckoo clock?

Actually Orson Welles' character was wrong on more than one count. For one thing, the Swiss didn't invent the cuckoo clock, that came from the German Black Forest. But the Swiss are a brainy lot, and per capita have produced more Nobel Prize winners and registered more patents than any other country. Milk chocolate, DDT, life insurance, the pump-turbine – all are Swiss inventions. They also came up with the Alp horn, an instrument several metres long and about as portable as a posse of elephants – hardly ideal for carrying up and down the sides of mountains.

The Swiss have a way of making the unexpected work. Like successfully knitting together people from four language groups into one small nation. When travelling around the country, the visitor gets a flavour of Germany, France and Italy, but always seasoned with a unique Swissness. The Swiss political system is one of the most complicated in the world, yet citizens dutifully inform themselves of the issues and vote regularly in a whole host of referenda.

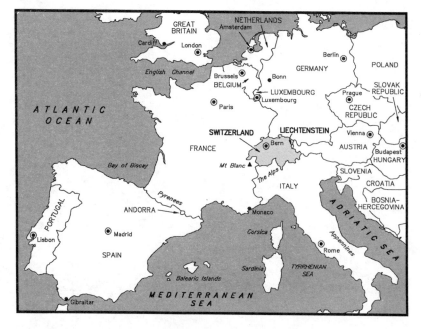

Every adult male has an army rifle at home but nobody goes around blowing people's heads off. British trains are late if a few leaves fall on the line in autumn, yet Swiss trains go over, round, and through the Alps and still generally arrive minute-perfect. Things work in Switzerland – and work well.

And the Alps! They are sufficient reason alone for visiting Switzerland. The countryside is visually stunning. Breathtaking views inspire peace and tranquillity and provide many sporting possibilities for the more adventurous. Skiers and hikers find paradise in the Alps. But you don't have to be a sportsperson to enjoy yourself; dreamers find their niche, and have done for centuries. The Romantics like Byron and Shelley were drawn to the mountains for inspiration, as were many writers, artists and musicians before and since.

Beyond the Alps and the chalet-style mountain resorts there are the towns and cities. Sober, responsible banker's towns like Zürich, Geneva and Lugano, which are nevertheless attractively situated and packed with interesting sights and fine museums. There's the enigmatic capital, Bern, that looks more like a museum piece than a seat of power. And there are many places, such as Lucerne, Murten and Stein am Rhein, that have old town centres so apparently unchanged by time that they could have been preserved under glass, like parts of a watch (yes, they make watches in Switzerland, too).

So here we have the fundamental dichotomy of things Swiss – the untamed, wild and majestic Alpine landscape, set against the tidy, just-so, watch-precision towns and cities. Goethe summed it up succinctly in his description of Switzerland as a combination of 'the colossal and the well-ordered'. It's two different sides of a highly valued coin. Spend it at your leisure.

Facts about the Country

HISTORY

Switzerland is seen as the ultimate neutral state, a paragon of virtue, too pure and too clever to sully its hands in the base conflicts that plague the rest of the world. Yet in 1845 the Austrian Chancellor, Metternich, wrote:

The (Swiss) Confederation staggers from evils into upheavals and represents for itself and for its neighbours an inexhaustible spring of unrest and disturbance.

Maybe that was true. Or maybe Metternich was simply still smarting from the way the Austrians had been booted out of Switzerland centuries before.

Pre-Confederation

The first inhabitants of the region were Celtic tribes. The most important of these were the Helvetii, who lived in the Jura and the Mittelland plain, and the Rhaetians, located in the Alpine region that became Graubünden. The Romans appeared on the scene in 107 BC by way of the St Bernard Pass, but their attempted conquest was indecisive owing to the difficulty of the terrain. Nevertheless, under Julius Ceasar they defeated the Gauls in 58 BC, thereby gaining control of Gaul and present-day Switzerland. Two centuries of prosperity followed, in which Aventicum (now the site of Avenches) was established as the capital of Roman Switzerland.

In 260 AD the Germanic Alemanni tribe began the first of many incursions southwards, and by around 400, succeeded in driving the Romans from the northern side of the Alps altogether. The Alemanni settled in eastern Switzerland, and were joined by another Germanic tribe, the Burgundians, who settled in the west. The latter adopted Christianity and the Latin language, thereby starting the division between what became French-speaking and German-speaking Switzerland. The Franks conquered both tribes in the 6th century, but the two areas were torn asunder when Charlemagne's empire was partitioned in 870.

The territory was united under the Holy Roman Empire in 1032 but central control was never very tight, allowing neighbouring nobles to contest each other for local influence. One of the most successful of these was the Zähringen family, who founded and fortified towns as a means of securing their scattered possessions. In the 1300s they founded Fribourg, Bern and Murten, and built a castle at Thun. They were not alone in this policy; the Savoy family established a ring of castles around Lake Geneva, most notably the Château de Chillon.

The internal fighting of the nobles was all changed by the Austrian Habsburg family, who gradually extended their power throughout central Europe. Habsburg expansion was spearheaded by Rudolph I, who became the Holy Roman Emperor in 1273. He installed heavy-handed bailiffs to take care of the local administration of Swiss territories, and in this way, gradually brought the squabbling dynasties west of Zürich to heel.

The Swiss Confederation

Habsburg domination was deeply resented, and upon the death of Rudolph I in 1291, local leaders saw a chance to gain independence. The forest communities of Uri, Schwyz and Nidwalden formed an alliance on 1 August 1291. Central to the agreement was the assertion that they would not recognise any external judge or law. Their pact of mutual assistance is seen as the origin of the Swiss Confederation and the inaugural document is still preserved in the canton of Schwyz. The efforts of the founding cantons to free themselves from the yoke of the Habsburgs is personified in the tale of William Tell, who in all probability never actually existed as an individual. According to the legend, it was the Habsburg bailiff, Gessler, who compelled Tell to shoot the

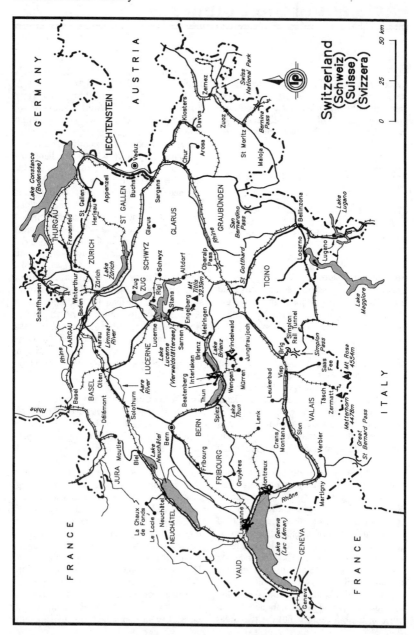

apple off his son's head, in what must be the most famous episode in Swiss history. Tell got his revenge by later murdering Gessler at Kussnacht, by Lake Lucerne.

Duke Leopold responded to the Swiss shenanigans by dispatching a powerful Austrian army in 1315. The duke must have anticipated a straightforward victory against such ill-equipped forest folk, but his army was thoroughly defeated by the Swiss at Morgarten. The effective action of the union soon prompted other communities to join. Lucerne (1332) was followed by Zürich (1351), Glarus and Zug (1352), and Bern (1353). Further defeats of the Habsburgs followed at Sempach (1386) and Näfels (1388).

Encouraged by these successes, the Swiss gradually acquired a taste for territorial expansion themselves. Further land was seized from the Habsburgs. They took on Charles the Bold (the Duke of Burgundy) and defeated him at Grandson and Murten. Fribourg, Solothurn, Basel, Schaffhausen and Appenzell joined the Confederation, and the Swiss gained independence from Holy Roman Emperor Maximilian I after their victory at Dornach in 1499.

In 1513 the Confederation was at the peak of its territorial influence, and even had Milan under its protection but finally the Swiss over-reached themselves. They squared up against a superior combined force of French and Venetians at Marignano in 1515 and lost. The Swiss army in the battle had been compiled without the support of several cantons, most noticeably the all-powerful Bern. This first defeat gave the Swiss cause for thought. In order to ensure that future armies would be full-strength, it would be necessary to curtail the autonomy of the cantons, something they were not prepared to do. Another consideration was that weaponry had advanced – soldiers had to be equipped with the new firearms which was a very expensive proposition as the Swiss fighting reputation had been previously built on the use of the halberd, a combination axe, pick and pike on the end of a long staff.

The Swiss therefore decided to withdraw from the international scene by renouncing expansionist policies and declaring their neutrality. Not being a nation to waste useful skills, Swiss mercenaries continued to serve in other armies for centuries to come, and earned an unrivalled reputation for their skill and courage. (Even today the pope is protected by the Swiss Guard.) The mercenary policy (effectively, exporting war) actually helped to preserve Swiss neutrality, in at least two ways. It provided an outlet for aggression without ever involving the country in international disputes under in its own colours, and it showed the Swiss the economic sense of keeping war beyond its own borders – to feed off war rather than suffer from it. The policy only ceased when Swiss soldiers increasingly found themselves fighting on opposing sides (such as during the War of the Spanish Succession in 1709).

The Reformation in the 16th century caused upheaval throughout Europe. Ulrich Zwingli, from eastern Switzerland, started teaching the Protestant word in Zürich in 1519. The new faith spread rapidly, but central Switzerland remained Catholic. The

Ulrich Zwingli

result was conflict, and Zwingli was killed in fighting between the factions in 1531. But Zwingli's death did not halt the spread of the Reformation in the Confederation, and in the meantime, Calvin and Farel were thumping the Protestant pulpit in neighbouring Geneva and Neuchâtel.

The Catholic church responded with the Counter Reformation, and while the rest of Europe was fighting it out in the Thirty Years' War, the Swiss closed ranks and kept out of trouble. They even prospered during the conflict, trading in food and materials which the fighting nations were unable to provide for themselves. At the end of the war in 1648 they were recognised in the Treaty of Westphalia as a neutral state.

Peasant unrest, fuelled by the burgeoning powers of the urban upper class over the rural areas, was quashed in 1653. However, religious disputes dragged on in Switzerland, in the Villmergen Wars of 1656 and 1712. At this time the Catholic cantons were sucked into a dangerous alliance with France that could have split the Confederation beyond repair had matters really come to a head but the Catholic factions reluctantly agreed to religious freedom and the country was able to get on with the serious business of making money. Switzerland gradually prospered as a financial and intellectual centre; the economic aspect driven to a great extent by the textile industry in the north-east.

The French invaded Switzerland in 1798 and established the Helvetic Republic. The new regime was liberal in many ways – sovereignty was invested in the people and cantonal frontiers were abolished – but the Swiss did not take too kindly to such centralised control. Internal fighting prompted Napoleon (who had now assumed power of France) to restore the former Confederation of cantons in 1803 (the Act of Mediation), but with France retaining overall jurisdiction. Further cantons also joined the Confederation at this time: Aargau, St

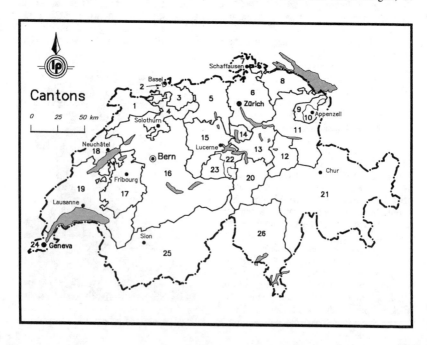

Gallen, Graubünden, Ticino, Thurgau and Vaud. Napoleon was finally sent packing following his defeat by the British and Prussians at Waterloo. The Congress of Vienna established Switzerland as a federation in 1815, and guaranteed its independence and permanent neutrality, as well as adding the cantons of Valais, Geneva, and Neuchâtel. But politically the country had moved backwards, with the aristocrats regaining most of their old powers.

The Modern State

The July Revolution in Paris in 1830 sparked off similar forces in several cantons so that the liberals came to power. Lucerne was particularly volatile; coup was followed by counter-coup, and the liberals were appalled when the Jesuits were invited to take over cantonal education. Civil war broke out in 1847 when the Protestant army led by General Dufour quickly crushed the Catholic cantons (including Lucerne) who had formed a separatist league (the *Sonderbund*).

1	Jura (JU)
2	Basel Town (BS)
3	Basel District (BL)
4	Solothurn (SO)
5	Aargau (AG)
6	Zürich (ZH)
7	Schaffausen (SH)
8	Thurgau (TG)
9	Ausser-Rhoden (AR)
10	Inner-Rhoden (AI)
11	St Gallen (SG)
12	Glarus (GL)
13	Schwyz (SZ)
14	Zug (ZG)
15	Lucerne (LU)
16	Bern (BE)
17	Fribourg (FR)
18	Neuchâtel (NE)
19	Vaud (VD)
20	Uri (UR)
21	Graubünden (GR)
22	Nidwalden (NW)
23	Obwalden (OW)
24	Geneva (GE)
25	Valais (VS)
26	Ticino (TI)

Victory by liberal forces was quickly underlined with the creation of a new federal constitution in 1848, which is largely still in place today. Various civil liberties were granted, such as equality before the law, freedom of association and freedom of place of residence.

The constitution was a neat compromise between advocates of central control, and conservative forces wanting cantonal authority to be retained. Throughout the gradual move towards one nation, each canton remained fiercely independent, even to the extent of controlling their own currency and postal services and levying their own customs duties. All these powers were transferred to federal authority, but cantons nevertheless retained legislative (Grand Council) and executive (State Council) powers to deal with local matters. Furthermore, the federal assembly that was set up to take care of national issues was composed of two chambers, one of which gave the cantons their voice. The consent of both houses was required to pass a federal law (see the Government section later in this chapter). Bern was established as the capital and the seat of power.

Having achieved political stability, Switzerland was able to concentrate on economic and social matters. Relatively poor in mineral resources, it developed industries predominantly dependent on highly skilled labour. Industry was mainly of the cottage type, based upon peasants supplementing dwindling earnings from the land. A network of railways and roads was built, opening up previously inaccessible Alpine regions and helping the development of tourism. Between 1850 and 1860, six new commercial banks were set up. The International Red Cross was founded in Geneva in 1863 by Henri Dunant, and compulsory free education was introduced.

Many of the new political leaders had fingers in various economic pies, and patronage and nepotism became the standard way to conduct government. Movements towards greater democracy soon gathered momentum in the cantons, particularly in Zürich, and made it inevitable that there would be some change at the national level. In 1874 the constitution was revised to enable citizens to partake in direct democracy. In the years that followed, political battle lines gradually moved from struggles between liberals and Catholics to one between workers and the bourgeoisie.

With WW I, Switzerland came close to violating its much vaunted neutrality. German-speaking Switzerland (but not the French or Italian parts) was pro-Germany, and secret military information was passed to the German side. In 1917 Hermann Hoffmann, a federal councillor, even tried to bring about a separate peace between Germany and Russia. He was forced to resign when the plan became public. In physical terms, Switzerland's only involvement in WW I lay in the organising of Red Cross units, although the civilian army was prepared in case it needed to defend the country's borders. After peace was restored, Switzerland joined the League of Nations under the proviso that its involvement would be purely financial and economic rather than entailing any possible military sanctions.

Swiss industry profited during the war, but the rewards did not filter down to the working classes. Mobilisation of the civilian army affected wages, and food prices more than doubled during the period. In November 1918 a general strike brought the country to a halt. The paralysis was only temporary: the army was called in and within three days the strike leaders had capitulated. But the strike was not a waste of time. It eased the passage of a referendum on proportional representation, and some of the strikers' demands were subsequently accepted by the Federal Council: a 48-hour week was introduced, collective contract-bargaining between workers and employers was developed, and the social security system was extended.

The conciliatory mood spread and in 1937 the Swiss Metalworkers and Watchmakers' Union created the *Arbeitsfrieden* with the Federation of Metal and Machine Industry Employers, under which all future disputes would be solved by agreement. One side would abandon strikes, and the other would no longer use such tactics as 'lockouts' and 'scab' labour. This contract has been periodically renewed, and subsequently imitated by other Swiss industries, giving the country an envied industrial relations record ever since. Not one full day was lost to strikes in 1987.

Switzerland was left largely unscathed by WW II. Again the civilian army was mobilised, and Henri Guisan was elected as the general. Surrounded by Axis powers, Switzerland was in a very vulnerable position in 1940. In July of that year, Guisan, in a symbolic but effective move, called all top military personnel to the Rütli meadow (the site of the 1291 Oath of Allegiance), when he instilled in those present and the world at large the Swiss determination to defend its soil at all costs. Swiss neutrality remained unbreached (barring some accidental bombing in 1940, 1944 and 1945), and its territory proved to be a safe haven for escaping Allied prisoners.

Post WW II

While the rest of Europe underwent the painful process of rebuilding from the ravages of war, Switzerland was able to expand from an already powerful commercial, financial and industrial base. Zürich developed as an international banking and insurance centre. The World Health Organisation, the World Council of Churches, and many other international organisations based their headquarters in Geneva. Social reforms were also introduced, such as old-age pensions in 1948.

Post-war prosperity was largely built on the backs of foreign workers, who mostly had menial jobs, while Swiss workers were often elevated to supervisory roles. In 1945 foreigners made up 5% of residents in Switzerland; by 1974 this figure had grown to 17%. Foreign workers had (and have) few political rights, and in theory, could have their residency status rescinded in times of economic hardship. Indeed, tens of thousands left (voluntarily) in the depression of 1974-5.

Afraid that its neutrality would be compromised, Switzerland declined to become a member of the United Nations, NATO or the EEC (European Economic Community as it was then called). It did, however, join UNESCO (the United Nations Educational, Scientific and Cultural Organisation) and EFTA (the European Free Trade Association).

In the face of other EFTA nations applying for EC (European Community) membership, Switzerland finally made its own application in 1992. This was a pre-emptive move by the parliament, because in the meantime, it was necessary to hold a referendum on membership of the EEA (European Economic Area). The EEA was seen as a sort of halfway house towards the EC composed of EFTA members, under which there would be the free trade advantages of the EC without the political commitment. A majority of citizens and a majority of cantons had to vote in favour in order for EEA membership to be ratified.

Despite the strong support of industry and political parties, Swiss citizens were unimpressed, and the motion failed on both counts in the vote in December 1992. Although in percentage terms the defeat was a narrow one (49.7% voted 'yes', 50.3% voted 'no'), only seven cantons were in favour when at least 12 were needed. Those in favour included all the French-speaking cantons (Geneva, Vaud, Neuchâtel, Jura, Fribourg and Valais) and only one German-speaking canton (Basel). Overall, French-speakers were three to one in favour of joining, and there was bitter resentment towards German-speakers for keeping Switzerland isolated.

All this rather upset plans to join the EC.

Defence

Despite the fact that Switzerland has managed to avoid international conflicts for over 400 years, every able-bodied male starts national service at age 20. After 17 weeks of training he is released, but remains attached to a unit and eligible for call-up until the age of 32. From 33 to 50 (55 for officers) he remains in the military reserves, and in the first 10 years has to attend a further three two-week courses. Throughout this period he keeps his rifle, ammunition and full kit (including gas mask) at home, and has to attend target practice sessions. The army is subject to Federal Council control, and a general is only appointed as commander-in-chief of the armed forces in times of national emergency. Within 48 hours over 600,000 civilian soldiers can be mobilised. In 1993 plans were announced to reduce the army to around 400,000, by lowering the upper age limit for reservists from 50 to 42.

In December 1989 a surprisingly large number of people (35.6%) voted in favour of abolishing the army, yet conscientious objectors were still getting sentenced to imprisonment by military courts. Civil service as an alternative to military service for objectors was rejected in an earlier referendum in 1984, but finally got through in 1991. In 1992 conscientious objectors numbered 433.

In the last 40 years, Switzerland has made comprehensive preparations against foreign aggression. Besides the civilian army, a whole infrastructure is in place to repel any invasion. After military service, men then have to undertake civil protection service until age 60, requiring more training courses and assignment of duties in the event of attack. Roads and bridges have built-in recesses at key points so that they can be primed for explosion without delay. All new buildings must have a substantial air-raid capacity, and underground car parks can be instantly converted to bunkers.

Around 90% of the population can currently be sheltered underground; this figure will reach 100% at the end of the decade. Fully equipped emergency hospitals, unused yet maintained, await underneath ordinary hospitals. Food and raw materials have been stockpiled. It's a sobering thought, as you explore the countryside, to realise that those apparently undisturbed mountains and lakes hide a network of military installations and storage depots. The message that comes across today is the same as that dealt out by the country's fearless mercenaries of centuries ago: don't mess with the Swiss. ■

According to the original timetable, Switzerland was expected to be granted EC membership by 1996. In consequence of the EEA vote, Switzerland's EC application has been put on ice, without actually being withdrawn. In the meantime the pro-EEA and EC lobby has not given up hope, and there are thoughts of forcing a second referendum on the EEA issue. The government will also attempt to push through economic reforms that would have been necessary had EEA membership been ratified.

GEOGRAPHY

Above all, Switzerland is known as an Alpine country. The Alps and Pre-Alps make up 60% of Switzerland's 41,295 sq km. The Jura Mountains chain accounts for 10% and the Bernese Mittelland (Central Plateau) accounts for the remaining 30%. The land is 45% meadow and pasture, 24% forest and 6% arable. Farming of cultivated land is intensive and cows graze on the upper slopes in the summer as soon as the retreating snow line permits.

The Alps occupy the central and southern regions of the country. The Dufour summit (4634 metres) of Monte Rosa is the highest point, although the Matterhorn (4478 metres) is more well known. A series of high passes in the south provide overland access into Italy. Glaciers account for an area of 2000 sq km, most notably the Aletsch Glacier which at 169 sq km is the largest valley glacier in Europe.

The St Gotthard Massif in the centre of Switzerland is the source of many lakes and rivers, such as the Rhine and the Rhône. The Jura Mountains straddle the northern border with France. These mountains peak at around 1700 metres and are less steep and less severely eroded than the Alps.

The Bernese Mittelland is between the two mountain systems, running in a band from Lake Geneva in the south-west to Lake Constance in the north-east. It is a region of hills crisscrossed by rivers, ravines and winding valleys. This area has spawned the most populous cities and is where much of the agricultural activity takes place. The one canton entirely south of the Alps is Ticino, home to the northern part of Lake Maggiore: at 193 metres the lake is the lowest point in the country.

Lakes are dotted throughout the country, except in the Jura where the substrata rock is mostly too brittle and porous. The majority of lakes, including all those in the Bernese Mittelland, were created from the depressions and basins left by glacial ice or moraines (the debris from melting glaciers) after the ice age.

The Federal Government has introduced measures to protect forests, lakes and marshland from environment damage. In the mountains, the policy is to contain ski resorts rather than allow them to expand.

CLIMATE

The mountains are mainly responsible for the variety of local and regional microclimates enjoyed (or suffered) by Switzerland. Air currents waft in from the four points of the compass, each bringing a different type of weather. Ticino in the south has a hot, Mediterranean climate. Most of the rest of the country has a central European climate, with temperatures typically around 20° to 25° C in summer and 2° to 6° C in winter, with spring and autumn hovering around the 7° to 14° C mark. Valais in the south-west is noted for being dry. Staldenried in eastern Valais gets just 53 cm per year, as opposed to 257 cm at Rochers de Naye, above Montreux in Vaud. The coldest area is the Jura, and in particular the Brevine Valley, a natural trap for cold air.

Summer tends to bring a lot of sunshine, and most rain falls in the spring and autumn. You will need to be prepared for a range of temperatures dependent on altitude. Look out for the *Föhn*, a hot, dry wind that sweeps down into the valleys and can be oppressively uncomfortable. It can strike at any time of the year. Daily weather reports covering 25 resorts are displayed in major train stations.

Statistics can be used to back up all sorts of meteorological claims. The sun obviously gets about a bit: La Chaux de Fonds, Sierre,

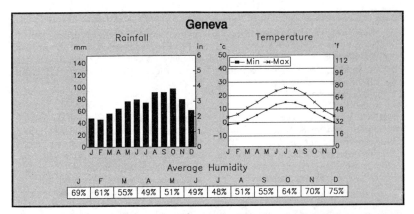

Geneva

Average Humidity

J	F	M	A	M	J	J	A	S	O	N	D
69%	61%	55%	49%	51%	49%	48%	51%	55%	64%	70%	75%

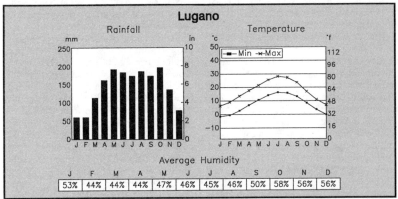

Lugano

Average Humidity

J	F	M	A	M	J	J	A	S	O	N	D
53%	44%	44%	44%	47%	46%	45%	46%	50%	58%	56%	56%

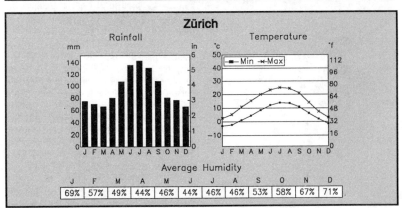

Zürich

Average Humidity

J	F	M	A	M	J	J	A	S	O	N	D
69%	57%	49%	44%	46%	44%	46%	46%	53%	58%	67%	71%

Locarno and Crans-Montana are all said to enjoy the sunniest climate in Switzerland.

FLORA & FAUNA

Climatic variations means that vegetation ranges from palm trees in Ticino to nordic flora in the Alps. Flowers bloom as late as June in the higher regions. In the Bernese Mittelland, trees are a mixture of deciduous and conifers. Above 800 metres conifers become more numerous. Around 2000 metres tall trees are replaced by bushes and scrub, which finally yield to Alpine meadows. Alpine flowers, such as primroses and edelweiss, are usually protected and should not be picked. Like in most of the rest of the continent, forests are being depleted by pollution and acid rain, increasing the risk of avalanches and landslides.

Despite strong environmental legislation, animal life is on the retreat in Switzerland. Eighty-one species of bird are currently threatened with extinction (that doesn't include wooden cuckoos in clocks). One bird that seems to be surviving is the jackdaw (Bergdohle), with its black feathers and yellow peak. They are often seen fluttering around at mountain tops. The most famous and distinctive Alpine animal is the ibex, a mountain goat, the male of which has huge, curved and ridged horns. There are about 12,000 left in Switzerland. The chamois (a horned antelope) also frequents high areas.

Fire Lily

Marmots (chunky rodents related to the squirrel) are other famous residents.

Flora and fauna are carefully preserved in the Swiss National Park in Graubünden (see the Zernez section in the Graubünden chapter).

GOVERNMENT

The modern Swiss Confederation is made up of 23 cantons; three are subdivided bringing the total to 26. Each has its own constitution and legislative body for dealing with local issues, and has a great deal of independent autonomy. The Jura achieved full cantonal status as late as 1979, after a protracted struggle with its former ruler, Bern.

National legislative power is in the hands of the Federal Assembly which consists of two chambers. The lower chamber, the National Council (*Nationalrat*), is elected by proportional representation with one member per 22,000 people. The upper chamber, the States Council (*Ständerat*), is composed of 46 members, two per canton (one per half-canton). The Federal Assembly elects seven members to form the Federal Council, which holds executive power. All elections are for a four-year term except the posts of president and vice-president of the Confederation, which are rotated annually. The holder of these posts has no special authority over the rest of the Federal Council. The vice-president always succeeds the president. In this way the governing body is not dominated by any one individual.

Elected members of parliament are usually part-timers, and receive payment only for expenses. Incredibly, the cost of running the parliament is a mere Sfr7 per person per annum (no wonder they don't want to join the bureaucratic EC). At the last general election, in 1991, the Radical Democrats won the most seats (44 National, 18 States), although this was fewer than in 1987. In descending order, the next most important parties are the Christian Democrats (37 National, 16 States), the Social Democrats (43 National, 3 States) and the Swiss People's Party, formerly the Farmers'

Party (25 National, 4 States). It doesn't take a genius to work out that the Green Party (14 National and none in the States) and the Motorists' Party (8 National and none in the States) tend not to agree with each other. Women were elected to 35 National and 4 States seats. The Social Democrats are the only large left-of-centre party. The composition of the Federal Council adheres to a 'magic formula' unchanged since 1959: two members each from the Radical, Christian and Social Democrats and one from the Swiss People's Party.

Laws can actually be influenced directly by the Swiss people, provided enough signatures can be collected from active citizens: 50,000 to force a full referendum on proposed laws, and 100,000 to initiate legislation. In any case important federal decisions are generally subject to a referendum. The system is known as direct democracy, and is one that tends to lead to a government based on compromise. Surprisingly for such a democratic people, women only won the right to vote in federal elections in 1971. In some cantons women gained a local vote only in the last few years. A few cantons still vote by a show of hands in an open-air parliament (*Landsgemeinde*).

As if these two tiers of government weren't enough, each Swiss citizen is also the member of a commune (*Gemeinde*), the smallest political unit. There are around 3000 in the whole country. Even communes have significant autonomy to act independently. Citizens regularly have to turn out to vote on issues at all three levels: federal, cantonal and communal. The commune has its own councillors with responsibility for finances, fire services, taxes, welfare, schools and civil defence. Most adults get involved in community service in one way or another.

The Swiss political system works from the bottom upwards, and it is actually membership of a commune that invests constituents with Swiss citizenship, rather than vice versa. The electorate (ie private individuals) is viewed as holding ultimate authority, and is often referred to as the 'sovereign', as in 'the sovereign has decided' when a referendum has been accepted or rejected. Subsidiarity (*Subsidiarität*) is the new buzzword that is currently in vogue in EC matters, but it is a principle that has guided Swiss politics for centuries. It describes the view that the lowest level of authority that can effectively perform a task should be left alone to do so.

ECONOMY

Switzerland has a mixed economy with the emphasis on private ownership. The only industries nationalised outright are the telephone, telegraph, post and some railways. Other than municipal enterprises, everything else is in private hands and operates accord-

---

Recent Referenda

Under their direct democracy system, the Swiss regularly turn out to vote on all sorts of issues. The most resounding assent in a Swiss referendum was in 1938 when 91.6% voted in favour of accepting Romansch as a fourth national language. Votes for women was turned down in 1959 before the men had a change of heart in 1971. The introduction of VAT was rejected three times, most recently in 1993. The abolition of nuclear power was rejected twice (1984 and 1991), although in the latter year it was agreed to have a 10-year moratorium on building nuclear power stations.

Recent accepted proposals include: equal rights for men and women (1981), imposition of a motorway tax (1984), protection of marshlands (1987), civic duties for conscientious objectors to military service (1991, after being rejected in 1984), and the lowering of the voting age from 20 to 18 (1991).

Recent rejected proposals include: rights for the unborn child (1985), abolition of vivisection (1985), UN membership (1986), lowering of pension age (1988), introduction of a 40-hour week (1976 and 1988) and abolition of the army (1989). ∎

ing to free-market principles, with the occasional subsidy thrown in. A good proportion of the wealth generated is channelled back into the community via social welfare programmes. The overall result is incredibly efficient and strikes are rare. But even Switzerland is not immune from economic downturns. Like much of the rest of the world, the Swiss economy went into recession in the early 1990s. In early 1993, unemployment was at the unusually high level (for Switzerland) of 4.8% and inflation was at 4.1%.

Agriculture occupies 5.5% of the working population, and Swiss farmers enjoy one of the highest levels of protection in the world (subsidies account for 80% of the value of total output), keeping prices high. Cartel agreements in other sectors of the economy also contribute to general high prices, and restrict competition. Over 60% of workers are employed in service areas as compared to around 34% in industry. In the absence of other raw materials, hydro-electric power

has become the main source of energy (57%). Nuclear energy production (41%) is the highest in Europe, despite a groundswell of opposition. Chemicals, machine tools, watches and clocks are the most important exports. Silks and embroidery, also important, are produced to a high quality.

SMH (Société Suisse de Micro-élelectronique et d'Horlogerie) unleashed the swatch onto the world. This innovative product revitalised the Swiss watchmaking industry which had been taking a battering at the hands of cheap Japanese models. At the top end of the watch market (where watches cost thousands in any currency you care to name) Swiss domination was never broken, and it has a 90% worldwide share. Swiss breakthroughs in science and industry include vitamins, DDT, gas turbines and milk chocolate. They also, for their sins, developed the modern formula for life insurance.

Swiss banks are a magnet for foreign funds attracted by political and monetary

Bank Accounts

Voltaire once said: 'If you see a Swiss banker jump out of a window, follow him. There is surely money to be made.' There's certainly no shortage of bankers to follow: the country has 630 domestic banks and over 200 foreign banks. The Swiss are great savers, storing away an unusually high level of their income. Banks have a long tradition, but really took off after WW II, thanks to their reputation for discretion and secrecy.

Numbered bank accounts are a well-known Swiss institution. These are where the account is identified purely by a number, rather than being linked to a name, so anonymity is assured. The anonymity brings the risk of attracting funds of dubious origin, or money that is simply trying to avoid the attention of the tax inspectors.

Numbered accounts were introduced in WW II, allegedly to provide cover for funds escaping from Nazi control. For years Swiss banks have been a favourite destination for funds spirited away by corrupt African leaders. It is believed that the deposed dictator of Mali, Moussa Traore, deposited at least US$1 billion – this from one of the poorest countries in the world. President Mobutu of Zaïre is estimated to have US$8 billion hidden away.

Perfectly legitimate money flows in too, of course, attracted by the stability of the country. When Iraq invaded Kuwait in 1990 there was a huge influx of money into Switzerland from the Middle East. That was also the year that a new law against money laundering was introduced. There is now an obligation for the banks to identify the true owner of the monies deposited with them in the event of an investigation, and they can be prosecuted if they hinder the identification of suspected 'dirty money' (proceeds from drug or arms trafficking, etc). The legislation was inspired by the arrest in Switzerland in 1988 of two drug traffickers who deposited Sfr1.5 billion in a Zürich bank (the deposit drew attention as it was marginally higher than the average Swiss salary cheque).

In practice, anybody can still open a Swiss bank account, numbered or otherwise. All you have to do is sign a form declaring that the money is rightfully yours. Responding to such a question with an untruth would hardly cause great pangs of conscience in the average underworld boss. ∎

stability. The three biggest banks are the Union Bank of Switzerland, the Swiss Bank Corporation, and Credit Suisse. The country is the fourth most important financial centre in the world, after New York, London and Tokyo. In most cantons there are more banks than dentists, and Switzerland is one of the world leaders for private banking. Tourism is important to the economy – it's the third biggest export with a turnover of over Sfr20 billion. The Swiss aim to make things as easy as possible for visitors. (It's certainly easy to spend money.)

Switzerland's most important trading partner is Germany, responsible for 32% of imports and 23% of exports. France and Italy come next, with EC countries as a whole accounting for 70% of imports and 59% of exports. These figures are significant in view of the uncertainty surrounding Switzerland's membership to the EC; most economists (but not all) agree that there will be an economic cost if Switzerland stays out. The country usually has a negative visible trade balance, which is offset by earnings from investment income and the current account. The average income per inhabitant is Sfr42,349.

POPULATION & PEOPLE

With a population of 6.8 million, Switzerland averages 164 inhabitants per sq km. The Alpine districts are sparsely populated, meaning that the Mittelland is densely settled, especially round the shores of the larger lakes. Zürich is the largest city with 341,000 inhabitants, next comes Basel (191,000), Geneva (167,000) and Bern (145,000). Most of the people are of Germanic origin as indicated by the breakdown of languages spoken in Switzerland. German speakers account for 66% of the population, French 18%, Italian 10% and Romansch just 1%.

As many as 17% of people living in the country are residents but not Swiss citizens – over 1.16 million. This figure does *not* include the many seasonal workers, temporary residents and international civil servants and administrators. Most of the permanent residents arrived after WW II: initially from Italy and Spain, and subsequently from the rest of southern Europe.

The other side of the equation is the Swiss community living abroad, numbering about 500,000. Historically, Swiss left the country

---

The Swiss National Character

Some people believe that the magnificent, untamed Swiss landscape is wasted on the native dwellers. There's an old joke that imagines that heaven and hell are run by a number of European nations. In heaven, the Swiss are the organisers (and the French are the lovers). In hell, the Swiss are the lovers (and the Italians are the organisers). This joke illustrates the oft-expressed view that the people are a dull, colourless, undemonstrative lot, somewhat petty, yet extremely efficient. Like many generalisations, this picture of the Swiss character is an inadequate one. The Swiss people are as varied as the languages they speak. To make a few more generalisations: the French Swiss make a habit of kissing each other on both cheeks upon meeting (a custom the undemonstative British would have a hard time adapting to); the Italian Swiss have a mediterranean complexion and outlook in a canton where *dolce vita* competes with the *Arbeit* ethos; in the valleys of south-east Switzerland, many villagers still speak Romansch, a language with its roots in ancient Latin that well reflects their enduring, rural lifestyle.

But what about the majority, the German Swiss, I hear you ask. They are what we mean by the typical Swiss; efficient and honest yet conventional and lacking in individuality. There is something to be said for this view, but it hardly gives an adequate or complete picture. I know somebody who goes to university in Zürich; she complains the Zürichers are cold and money-oriented, not like the people of Basel who are much more friendly and open.

The people of Appenzellerland have a reputation among other Swiss for being simple folk with intellects that could blunt the sharpest knife. You may encounter many other regional differences if you travel with an open mind. Of course, you may also find that your preconceptions about the Swiss are confirmed, but travel is always more enjoyable if you allow yourself the possibility of being surprised by the people you meet. ■

because of domestic food shortages (thousands died of hunger in 1817) and through mercenary service (halted in 1859). Nowadays emigration is more due to the expansion of Swiss firms abroad.

EDUCATION

Control of education is at the cantonal level, with the consequence that there are 26 different systems in operation. They all adhere to a greater or lesser extent to a national standard, but there are variations in types of schools, curricula, and teaching methods. It wasn't even until the referendum in 1985 that it was agreed to universally start the school year at the end of summer.

Most children attend nursery school from age four. Compulsory schooling starts at age six or seven and continues for eight or (usually) nine years. Towards the end of this period students are eased into different streams: apprenticeship, vocational, or academic. The latter two streams usually continue with two to three years of post-compulsory education, leading to entry into a vocational college (medicine, teaching etc) or a general university or institute. There are eight cantonal universities.

Apprenticeships are given in private companies, and at the same time the trainee usually attends part-time courses in a college. There remains a shortage of skilled labour in the country, forcing some Swiss firms to expand abroad. Switzerland is one of the highest spenders on research and development in the world (3.1% of GDP). Around one third of university expenditure goes in this field.

ARTS

Switzerland does not have a very strong tradition in the arts, even though many foreign writers and artists (such as Voltaire, Byron and Shelley) have visited and settled, attracted by the beauty and tranquillity of the mountains and lakes. The 18th century writings of Rousseau in Geneva played an important part in the development of democracy. Influential artists settled in Zürich in the early 20th century and created the Dada movement.

In contrast, many creative Swiss left the country to make their name abroad, such as Jean-Luc Godard, Paul Klee and Charles Le Corbusier.

Writers & Artists

Few Swiss writers have gained international attention. Hermann Hesse is by far the best known novelist, though he was German born and naturalised Swiss. The linguistic diversity in the country makes it very hard to have a literary tradition. Carl Spitteler (1845-1924) won the Nobel prize for his writings in German.

Paul Klee's work can be seen in the art museum in Bern. He was born in Bern yet he never actually acquired Swiss citizenship and did most of his work in Germany. Klee (1879-1940) created abstract works which used colour, line and form to evoke a variety of sensations.

Alberto Giacometti (1901-66), a sculptor from Graubünden who settled in Paris, dabbled in cubism and and surrealism before developing his distinctive stick-like figures (expressive, apparently, of individual isolation). His father, Giovanni, and his uncle, Augusto, are also well known artists. You can see their work, particularly in the art museums in Chur and Zürich.

The most 'Swiss' artist in lineage, residence and the subject matter of his work is Ferdinand Hodler (see the North West Switzerland for more information about Hodler). The motorised sculptures of Jean Tinguely, mostly cobbled together from discards, can be seen especially in Basel and Fribourg.

Music & Theatre

Until the 17th century, folk music and religious music were the only genres that developed in Switzerland. The country still lacks famous exponents: Arthur Honegger (1892-1955) is the only Swiss composer of note. He settled in Paris and co-founded the avant-garde 'Les Six'. Despite this dearth, music is strongly emphasised with a full symphony orchestra in every main city. Music festivals are held throughout the year: two of the most famous are the Lucerne International Music Festival and the Montreux Jazz Festival.

The theatre scene flourishes, even in English in Geneva and Zürich. Go to Bern to visit small-scale, atmospheric cellar (Keller) theatres, where plays are often performed in dialect.

Architecture

Gothic and Renaissance architecture are evident in urban areas, especially Bern. Rural Swiss houses vary according to region, but the typical chalet-style is generally characterised by ridged roofs with wide, overhanging eaves, and balconies and verandahs which are usually enlivened by colourful floral displays. Anybody interested in regional architecture should visit the Ballenberg Museum outside Brienz (see the Freilichtmuseum Ballenberg section in the Bernese Overland chapter). Ticino offers an architectural itinerary exploring more modern styles. Le Corbusier is the country's best known architectural export (see the La Chaux de Fonds section in the Neuchâtel, Fribourg & Jura chapter).

CULTURE
Traditional Lifestyle

In a few mountain regions such as Valais, people still wear traditional rural costumes, but dressing up is usually reserved for festivals. Every spring, hardy herders climb to Alpine pastures with their cattle and live in summer huts while tending their herds. They gradually descend back to village level as the grassland is grazed. Both the departure and the return is a cause for celebrations and processions. Yodelling and playing the Alp horn are also part of the Alpine tradition. Swiss wresting is another event that is featured in frequent festivals.

Festivals and carnivals crop up in urban as well as rural areas. Sometimes ancient traditions and customs are inherent in the celebrations.

Avoiding Offence

In general the Swiss are a law-abiding nation; even minor transgressions such as littering can cause offence. Always shake hands when being introduced to a Swiss, and again when leaving. Shaking hands is the norm upon meeting, even with young and casual people. Formal titles should also be used (*Herr* for men and *Frau* for women). It is also customary to greet the proprietor upon entering a shop, bar or café, and to say goodbye when leaving. Public displays of affection are fine, but are more common in French Switzerland than in the slightly more formal German-speaking parts. Exchanging kisses upon meeting is a common ritual in French Switzerland.

On the beach, nude bathing is usually limited to restricted areas, but topless bathing is common in many parts. Women should be wary of taking their tops off as a matter of course. The rule is, if nobody else seems to be doing it, don't. You're not there to educate the locals.

Dress codes are pretty relaxed in Switzerland. It's not unusual to see office workers, bank clerks and tourist office staff wearing casual clothes like jeans. But men would be advised to wear a jacket and tie when dining in some of the top restaurants mentioned in this book. It is no problem for men to wear shorts away from the beach.

Sport

The number one activity is walking, with 40% of the population regularly taking walks in the countryside. Skiing is of course very popular, and Swiss competitors usually win a good haul of medals at international winter sports events. Swimming mountaineering, cycling, fishing and football are also favourite pastimes.

Shooting and gymnastic clubs are popular with male adults. The interest in shooting is a spillover from the need to maintain a minimum standard with service weapons while in the reserves. There are 3600 shooting clubs in Switzerland. A strange running race, unique to Switzerland, is called the *Waffenlaufen*, where runners complete a course between 18 and 42 km, dressed in military uniform, complete with rucksack and rifle.

RELIGION

The country is split pretty evenly between Protestantism (in decline since WW II, now down to 44%) and Roman Catholicism (47%). Most of the rest of the population are 'unaffiliated'. The predominant faith varies between cantons. Bern is a Protestant stronghold, followed by Vaud, Zürich, Thurgau and Glarus. Strong Catholic areas are Valais, Ticino, Uri, Unterwalden and Schwyz, followed by Fribourg, Lucerne, Zug and the Jura. Curiously, the two half-cantons of Appenzell are at odds: Ausser-Rhoden is strongly Protestant while nine out of 10 people in Inner-Rhoden are Catholic. Some churches are supported entirely by donations from the public while others receive state subsidies.

LANGUAGE

Located in the corner of Europe where the German, French and Italian language areas meet, the linguistic melting pot that is Switzerland (Schweiz, Suisse, Svizzera) has three official federal languages: German (spoken by about 66% of the population), French (18%) and Italian (10%). A fourth language, Rhaeto-Romanic, or Romansch, is spoken by 1% of the population, mainly in the canton of Graubünden. Derived from Latin, it's a linguistic relic which, along with Friulian and Ladin across the border in Italy, has survived in the isolation of mountain valleys. In 1938, Romansch was recognised as an official national (though not federal) language by referendum.

Being Understood in English

The English language is not a compulsory subject in Swiss schools. That's surprising as generally the Swiss speak English very well, especially in German Switzerland. Ask a German-speaking Swiss if they speak English and you normally get one of two answers: 'a little' means they speak it fluently, but a philosophical discussion on

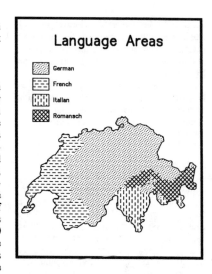

Language Areas

- German
- French
- Italian
- Romansch

etymology and epistemology in English would probably be beyond their grasp; a simple 'yes' means that your ego is about to get a battering – they speak English better than you do, and no doubt know what those obscure 'ology' words mean into the bargain. Most people working in 'service' areas (tourist office staff, telephone operators, hotel and office receptionists, restaurant staff, shopkeepers) speak some English.

Nevertheless, don't automatically assume that everyone you meet does speak English, especially in smaller, less-touristy towns where English has less penetration. It is simple courtesy to greet people with *Grüezi* (hello) and to enquire *Sprechen Sie Englisch?* (Do you speak English?) before launching into English. And don't feel discouraged if your clumsy attempts at speaking German immediately elicit a response in English – your efforts at intergrating yourself will still be appreciated.

In French Switzerland you shouldn't have too many problems being understood either, though the locals' grasp of English is likely to be less complete than that of German speakers. Italian Switzerland is where you will have the greatest difficulty. Most locals speak some French and/or German in addition to Italian, but English has a lower priority. Even so, you will find that the majority of restaurants and hotels have at least one English-speaking staff member.

In the Romansch-speaking parts of Graubünden, those involved in the tourist industry usually speak English, but ordinary country folk probably won't. Instead, they may offer you one of the other three national languages.

Swiss German

Though German-speaking Swiss have no trouble with standard High German, they use Swiss German, or *Schwyzerdütsch*, in private conversation and in most unofficial situations. Contrary to the worldwide trend of erosion of dialects, its usage is actually increasing. Swiss German covers a wide variety of melodic dialects that can differ quite markedly from High German, often more closely resembling the German of hundreds of years ago than the modern version. Swiss German is an oral language, rarely written down, and indeed there is no standard written form. Newspapers and books almost invariably use High German and it is also used in news broadcasts, schools, and the federal parliament. But people are more comfortable with their own Swiss German, and may even attempt a completely different language when speaking to foreigners rather than resort to High German.

Germans themselves often have trouble understanding Schwyzerdütsch. To English-speakers' ears High German sounds like it's full of rasping 'ch' sounds, but even Germans think that Schwyzerdütsch sounds like a lot of throat-clearing. A reason for this is that the Germanic 'k' becomes 'ch' in High German only at the middle and end of words, whereas in Swiss German it also applies at the beginning. Hence the relatively manageable *Küchen-kästchen* (kitchen cupboard) in High German become the almost unpronounceable *chuchichäschtli* in Swiss German.

To make matters even more complicated, regional dialects are strongly differentiated for a small country, thanks to the isolating effect of mountain ranges. In the south, such as in Upper Valais, an older form of dialect has been preserved. Eastern dialects have words in common with all other German vernaculars, whereas in western dialects, some Old Alemannic names have been retained. For example, *meadow* is *Wiese* in High German, *wise* in eastern dialects and *matte* in the west. The letters 'b', 'd' and 'g' are voiceless in Swiss German, and hardened in eastern dialects into an unaspirated 'p', 't' and 'gg', hence the High German *bitte, danke* and *Gans* (please, thank you and goose) become *pitte, tankche* and *ggans. St* is always pronounced as *scht.* Visitors will probably note the frequent use of the suffix *-li* to indicate the diminutive, or as a term of endearment.

As there is no written form and so many dialects, it is impossible to provide a proper vocabulary for Swiss German. Commonly used greetings are *Grüezi* meaning 'Hello' and *UfWiederluege*, meaning 'Goodbye'. 'How are you?' sounds something like *vee guhts?* (phonetic spelling) to which the answer is *guet* (good).

For more information, read *Dialect and High German in German-Speaking Switzerland* (paperback, published by Pro Helvetia).

High German

Following are some High German words and expressions which may be of use. Words that you'll often encounter on maps and throughout this chapter include: *Altstadt* (old city), *Bahnhof* (station), *Brücke* (bridge), *Hauptbahnhof* (main train station), *Markt* (market, often the central square in old towns), *Platz* (square) and *Rathaus* (town hall). One distinctive feature of German is that all nouns are written with a capital letter.

Pronunciation Unlike English or French, German does not have silent letters: you pronounce the **k** at the start of the word *Knie*, 'knee', the **p** at the start of *Psychologie*, 'psychology', and the **e** at the end of *ich habe*, 'I have'.

Vowels As in English, vowels can be pronounced long, like the 'o' in 'pope', or short, like the 'o' in 'pop'. As a rule, German vowels are long before one consonant and short before two consonants: the **o** is long in the word *Dom*, 'cathedral', but short in the word *doch*, 'after all'.

a	short, as the 'u' sound in 'cut', or long, as in 'father'
au	as in 'vow'
ä	short, as in 'act', or long, as in 'hair'
äu	as in 'boy'
e	short, as in 'bet', or long, as in 'day'
ei	as the 'ai' in 'aisle'
eu	as in 'boy'
i	short, as in 'in', or long, as in 'see'
ie	as in 'see'
o	short, as in 'pot', or long, as in 'note'
ö	as the 'er' in 'fern'
u	as the 'u' in 'pull'
ü	like the 'u' in 'pull' but with stretched lips

Consonants Most German consonants sound similar to their English counterparts. One important difference is that **b**, **d** and **g** sound like 'p', 't' and 'k', respectively, at the end of a word.

b	normally the English 'b', but 'p' at end of a word
ch	the *ch* in Scottish *loch*
d	normally as the English 'd', but 't' at end of a word
g	normally as the English 'g', but 'k' at the end of a word, and *ch*, as in the Scottish *loch*, at end of a word and after **i**
j	as the 'y' in 'yet'
qu	'k' plus 'v'
r	as the English 'r', but rolled at the back of the mouth
s	normally as the 's' in 'sun'; as the 'z' in 'zoo' when followed by a vowel
sch	as the 'sh' in 'ship'
sp, st	's' sounds like the 'sh' in 'ship' when at the start of a word
tion	the **t** sounds like the 'ts' in 'hits'

ß	as in 'sun' (written as **ss** in this book)
v	as the 'f' in 'fan'
w	as the 'v' in 'van'
z	as the 'ts' in 'hits'

Greetings & Civilities

Hello (Good day).	*Guten Tag.*
Goodbye.	*Auf Wiedersehen.*
Yes.	*Ja.*
No.	*Nein.*
Please.	*Bitte.*
Thank you.	*Danke.*
That's fine. You're welcome.	*Bitte sehr.*
Sorry. (excuse me, forgive me)	*Entschuldigung.*

Some Useful Phrases

Do you speak English?	*Sprechen Sie Englisch?*
Does anyone here speak English?	*Spricht hier jemand Englisch?*
I (don't) understand.	*Ich verstehe (nicht).*
Just a minute.	*Ein Moment!*
Please write that down.	*Können Sie es bitte aufschreiben?*
How much is it ?	*Wieviel kostet es?*

Useful Signs

Camping Ground	*Campingplatz*
Entrance	*Eingang*
Exit	*Ausgang*
Full, No Vacancies	*Voll, Besetzt*
Guesthouse	*Pension, Gasthaus*
Hotel	*Hotel*
Information	*Auskunft*
Open/Closed	*Offen/Geschlossen*
Police	*Polizei*
Police Station	*Polizeiwache*
Rooms Available	*Zimmer Frei*
Toilets	*Toiletten (toilet)*
Train Station	*Bahnhof (Bf)*
Youth Hostel	*Jugendherberge*

Getting Around

What time does ... leave?	*Wann fährt ...ab?*
What time does ... arrive?	*Wann kommt ...an?*

What time is the next boat?	*Wann fährt das nächste Boot?*
next	*nächste*
first	*erste*
last	*letzte*

the boat	*das Boot*
the bus (city)	*der Bus*
the bus (intercity)	*der (Überland)bus*
the tram	*die Strassenbahn*
the train	*der Zug*

I would like ...	*Ich möchte ...*
a one-way ticket	*eine Einzelkarte*
a return ticket	*eine Rückfahr-karte*
1st class	*erste Klasse*
2nd class	*zweite Klasse*

Where is the bus stop?	*Wo ist die Bushaltestelle?*
Where is the tram stop?	*Wo ist die Strassen-bahnhaltestelle?*
Can you show me (on the map)?	*Können Sie mir (auf der Karte) zeigen?*
I'm looking for ...	*Ich suche ...*

far/near	*weit/nahe*
Go straight ahead.	*Gehen Sie geradeaus.*
Turn left ...	*Biegen Sie ...links ab.*
Turn right ...	*Biegen Sie ...rechts ab.*

Around Town

I'm looking for ...	*Ich suche ...*
a bank	*eine Bank*
the city centre	*die Innenstadt*
the ...embassy	*die ...Botschaft*
my hotel	*mein Hotel*
the market	*den Markt*
the police	*die Polizei*
the post office	*das Postamt*
a public toilet	*eine öffentliche Toilette*
the telephone centre	*die Telefon-zentrale*

the tourist information office	*das Verkehrsamt*
beach	*Strand*
bridge	*Brücke*
castle	*Schloss*
cathedral	*Dom*
church	*Kirche*
hospital	*Krankenhaus*
island	*Insel*
lake	*See*
main square	*Hauptplatz*
market	*Markt*
monastery	*Kloster*
mosque	*Moschee*
old city	*Altstadt*
palace	*Palast*
ruins	*Ruinen*
sea	*Meer*
square	*Platz*
tower	*Turm*

Accommodation

Where is a cheap hotel?	*Wo ist ein billiges Hotel?*
What is the address?	*Was ist die Adresse?*
Could you write the address, please?	*Könnten Sie bitte die Adresse aufschreiben?*
Do you have any rooms available?	*Haben Sie noch freie Zimmer?*

I would like ...	*Ich möchte ...*
a single room	*ein Einzelzimmer*
a double room	*ein Doppelzimmer*
a room with a bathroom	*ein Zimmer mit Bad*
to share a dorm	*einen Schlafsaal teilen*
a bed	*ein Bett*

How much is it per night/per person?	*Wieviel kostet es pro Nacht/pro Person?*
Can I see it?	*Kann ich es sehen?*
Where is the bathroom?	*Wo ist das Bad?*

Food

bakery	*Bäckerei*
grocery	*Lebensmittelgeschäft*
delicatessen	*Delikatessengeschäft*
restaurant	*Restaurant, Gaststätte*
breakfast	*Frühstück*
lunch	*Mittagessen*
dinner	*Abendessen*

I would like the set lunch, please.	*Ich hätte gern das Tagesmenü bitte.*
Is service included in the bill?	*Ist die Bedienung inbegriffen?*
I am a vegetarian.	*Ich bin Vegetarierin (f) Vegetarier. (m)*

Time & Dates

today	*heute*
tomorrow	*morgen*
in the morning	*morgens*
in the afternoon	*nachmittags*
in the evening	*abends*

Monday	*Montag*
Tuesday	*Dienstag*
Wednesday	*Mittwoch*
Thursday	*Donnerstag*
Friday	*Freitag*
Saturday	*Samstag, Sonnabend*
Sunday	*Sonntag*

January	*Januar*
February	*Februar*
March	*März*
April	*April*
May	*Mai*
June	*Juni*
July	*Juli*
August	*August*
September	*September*
October	*Oktober*
November	*November*
December	*Dezember*

Numbers

0	*null*
1	*eins*
2	*zwei* (*zwo* on the telephone)
3	*drei*
4	*vier*
5	*fünf*
6	*sechs*
7	*sieben*
8	*acht*
9	*neun*
10	*zehn*
11	*elf*
12	*zwölf*
13	*dreizehn*
14	*vierzehn*
15	*fünfzehn*
16	*sechzehn*
17	*siebzehn*
18	*achtzehn*
19	*neunzehn*
20	*zwanzig*
21	*einundzwanzig*
22	*zweiundzwanzig*
30	*dreissig*
40	*vierzig*
50	*fünfzig*
60	*sechzig*
70	*siebzig*
80	*achtzig*
90	*neunzig*
100	*hundert*
1000	*tausend*
one million	*eine Million*

Swiss French

Neuchâtel is where the purest form of French is spoken, yet you won't find very much difference from standard French wherever you go. Of course there are some local expressions and regional accents. Suisse Romande is a term used to refer to French-speaking Switzerland.

Pronunciation French has a number of sounds which are notoriously difficult to produce for Anglophones. The main causes of trouble are:

1. The distinction between the 'u' sound (as in *tu*) and 'oo' sound (as in *tout*). For both

sounds, the lips are rounded and projected forward, but for the 'u' the tongue is towards the front of the mouth, its tip against the lower front teeth, whereas for the 'oo' the tongue is towards the back of the mouth, its tip behind the gums of the lower front teeth.

2. The nasal vowels. During the production of nasal vowels the breath escapes partly through the nose and partly through the mouth. There are no nasal vowels in English; in French there are three, as in *bon vin blanc*, 'good white wine'. These sounds occur where a syllable ends in a single 'n' or 'm'; the 'n' or 'm' in this case is not pronounced, but indicates the nasalisation of the preceding vowel.

The standard 'r' of Parisian French is produced by moving the bulk of the tongue backwards to constrict the air flow in the pharynx while the tip of the tongue rests behind the lower front teeth. It is quite similar to the noise made by some people before spitting, but with much less friction.

Greetings & Civilities

Hello.	*Bonjour.*
Goodbye.	*Au revoir.*
Yes.	*Oui.*
No.	*Non.*
Please.	*S'il vous plaît.*
Thank you.	*Merci.*
That's fine. You're welcome.	*Très bien. Je vous en prie.*
Excuse me.	*Excusez-moi.*
Sorry. (excuse me, forgive me)	*Pardon.*

Do you speak English?	*Parlez-vous anglais?*
Does anyone speak English?	*Est-ce qu'il y a quelqu'un qui parle anglais?*
I understand.	*Je comprends.*
I don't understand.	*Je ne comprends pas.*
Just a minute.	*Attendez une minute.*
Please write that down.	*Est-ce-que vous pouvez l'écrire?*
How much is it ?	*C'est combien?*

Signs

Camping Ground	*Camping*
Entrance	*Entrée*
Exit	*Sortie*
Full/No Vacancies	*Complet*
Residential Hotel	*Pension de Famille*
Hotel	*Hôtel*
Information	*Renseignements*
Open/Closed	*Ouvert/Fermé*
Police	*Police*
Police Station	*(Commissariat de) Police*
Prohibited	*Interdit*
Rooms Available	*Chambres Libres*
Toilets	*Toilettes, W.C.*
Train Station	*Gare SNCF*
Youth Hostel	*Auberge de Jeunesse*
Ferry Terminal	*Gare Maritime*
Bus Station	*Gare Routière*

Getting Around

What time does the next boat leave/ arrive?	*À quelle heure part/arrive le prochain train?*
the boat	*le bateau*
the bus (city)	*l'(auto)bus*
the bus (intercity)	*l'(auto)car*
the tram	*le tramway*
the train	*le train*
next	*prochain* (m) *prochaine* (f)
first	*premier* (m) *première* (f)
last	*dernier* (m) *dernière* (f)
I would like ...	*Je voudrais ...*
a one-way ticket	*un billet aller simple*
a return ticket	*un billet aller-retour*
1st class	*Première classe*
2nd class	*Deuxième classe*
Where is the bus/tram stop?	*Où est l'arrêt d'autobus/de tramway?*

I want to go to ...	*Je veux aller à ...*
I am looking for ...	*Je cherche ...*
Can you show it to me (on the map)?	*Est-ce que vous pouvez me le montrer (sur la carte)?*

far/near	*loin/proche*
Go straight ahead.	*Continuez tout droit.*
Turn left ...	*Tournez à gauche ...*
Turn right ...	*Tournez à droite ...*

Around Town

I'm looking for ...	*Je cherche ...*
a bank	*une banque*
the city centre	*le centre-ville*
the ... embassy	*l'ambassade de ...*
my hotel	*mon hôtel*
the market	*le marché*
the police	*la police*
the post office	*le bureau de poste*
a public toilet	*des toilettes*
the railway station	*la gare*
a public telephone	*une cabine téléphonique*
the tourist information office	*l'office de tourisme/le syndicat d'initiative*

Where is (the) ...?	*Où est ...?*
beach	*la plage*
bridge	*le pont*
castle, mansion, vineyard	*le château*
cathedral	*la cathédrale*
church	*l'église*
hospital	*l'hôpital*
island	*l'île*
lake	*le lac*
main square	*la place centrale*
mosque	*la mosquée*
old city	*la vieille ville*
palace	*le palais*
quay/bank	*le quai/la rive*
ruins	*les ruines*

sea	*la mer*
square	*la place*
tower	*la tour*

Accommodation

Where can I find a cheap hotel?	*Où est-ce que je peux trouver un hôtel bon marché?*
What is the address?	*Quelle est l'adresse?*
Could you write the address, please?	*Est-ce vous pouvez écrire l'adresse, s'il vous plaît?*
Do you have any rooms available?	*Est-ce que vous avez des chambres libres?*
I would like ...	*Je voudrais ...*
a single room	*une chambre pour une personne*
a double room	*une chambre double*
a room with a shower and toilet	*une chambre avec douche et W.C.*
to stay in a dormitory	*coucher dans un dortoir*
a bed	*un lit*
How much is it per night/per person?	*Quel est le prix par nuit/par personne?*
Can I see it?	*Je peux la voir?*
Where is the bathroom/shower?	*Où est la salle de bain/douche?*

Food

bakery	*boulangerie*
cake shop	*pâtisserie*
cheese shop	*fromagerie*
delicatessen	*charcuterie*
grocery	*épicerie*
restaurant	*restaurant*
breakfast	*petit déjeuner*
lunch	*déjeuner*
dinner	*dîner*

Top: Chalets, Mürren village, Bernese Oberland (MH)
Bottom Left: Onion market, Bern (MH)
Bottom Right: Blowing the Alp horn, Bärenplatz, Bern (MH)

Top: Ice hockey, St Moritz, Graubünden (MH)
Bottom Left: Powder skiing near Zermatt, Valais (ZTO)
Bottom Right: Para-gliding above Verbier, Valais (VTO)

I would like the set lunch, please.	*Je prends le menu.*	12	*douze*
		13	*treize*
I am a vegetarian.	*Je suis végétarien* (m) *végétarienne* (f).	14	*quatorze*
		15	*quinze*
		16	*seize*
		17	*dix-sept*

Time & Dates

today	*aujourd'hui*	18	*dix-huit*
tomorrow	*demain*	19	*dix-neuf*
yesterday	*hier*	20	*vingt*
in the morning	*le matin*	21	*vingt-et-un*
in the afternoon	*l'après-midi*	22	*vingt-deux*
in the evening	*le soir*	30	*trente*
		40	*quarante*
		50	*cinquante*
		60	*soixante*
Monday	*lundi*	70	*soixante-dix*
Tuesday	*mardi*	80	*quatre-vingts*
Wednesday	*mercredi*	90	*quatre-vingt-dix*
Thursday	*jeudi*	100	*cent*
Friday	*vendredi*	1000	*mille*
Saturday	*samedi*	one million	*un million*
Sunday	*dimanche*		

January	*janvier*
February	*février*
March	*mars*
April	*avril*
May	*mai*
June	*juin*
July	*juillet*
August	*août*
September	*septembre*
October	*octobre*
November	*novembre*
December	*décembre*

Numbers

0	*zéro*
1	*un*
2	*deux*
3	*trois*
4	*quatre*
5	*cinq*
6	*six*
7	*sept*
8	*huit*
9	*neuf*
10	*dix*
11	*onze*

Swiss Italian

There are some differences in Ticinese dialect compared to standard Italian, but they are not very significant. You may come across some people saying *Bun di* instead of *Buon giorno* (Good morning/day) or *Buona noc* (pronounced 'nockh') instead of *Buona notte* (Goodnight).

Pronunciation Italian is not difficult to pronounce once you learn a few easy rules. Although some of the more clipped vowels, and stress on double letters, require careful practice for English speakers, it is easy enough to make yourself understood.

Vowels Vowels are generally more clipped than in English.

a	as the second 'a' in 'camera'
e	as the 'ay' in 'day', but without the 'i' sound
i	as in 'see'
o	as in 'dot'
u	as in 'too'

Consonants The pronunciation of many Italian consonants is similar to that of English. The following sounds depend on certain rules:

c	like 'k' before 'a', 'o' and 'u'. Like the 'ch' in 'choose' before 'e' and 'i'
ch	a hard 'k' sound
g	a hard 'g' as in 'get' before 'a', 'o' and 'u'. Before 'e' and 'i', like the 'j' in 'job'
gh	a hard 'g' as in 'get'
gli	as the 'lli' in 'million'
gn	as the 'ny' in 'canyon'
h	always silent
r	a rolled 'rrr' sound
sc	before 'e' and 'i', like the 'sh' in 'sheep'. Before 'h', 'a', 'o' and 'u', a hard sound as in 'school'
z	as the 'ts' in 'lights' or as the 'ds' in 'beds'

Note that when 'ci', 'gi' and 'sci' are followed by 'a', 'o' or 'u', unless the accent falls on the 'i', it is not pronounced. Thus the name 'Giovanni' is pronounced 'joh-**vahn**-nee', with no 'i' sound after the 'G'.

Stress Double consonants are pronounced as a longer, often more forceful sound than a single consonant.

Stress often falls on the next to last syllable, as in *spaghetti*. When a word has an accent, the stress is on that syllable, as in *città*, 'city'.

Greetings & Civilities

Hello.	*Buon giorno./Ciao.*
Goodbye.	*Arrivederci./Ciao.*
Yes./No.	*Sì./No.*
Please.	*Per favore./Per piacere.*
Thank you.	*Grazie.*
That's fine./You're welcome.	*Prego.*
Excuse me.	*Mi scusi.*
Sorry. (excuse me, forgive me)	*Mi scusi. Mi perdoni.*

Do you speak English?	*Parla (Parli) inglese?*
Does anyone speak English?	*C'è qualcuno che parla inglese?*
I (don't) understand.	*(Non) Capisco.*
Just a minute.	*Un momento.*
How much is it?	*Quanto costa?*

Signs

Camping Ground	*Campeggio*
Youth Hostel	*Ostello per la Gioventù*
Entrance	*Ingresso/ Entrata*
Exit	*Uscita*
Full/no Vacancies	*Completo*
Guest House	*Pensione*
Hotel	*Albergo*
Information	*Informazione*
No Smoking	*Vietato Fumare*
Open/Closed	*Aperto/Chiuso*
Police	*Polizia/Carabinieri*
Police Station	*Questura*
Telephone	*Telefono*
Toilets	*Gabinetti/Bagni*

Getting Around

What time does ... leave/arrive?	*A che ora parte/arriva ...?*
the boat	*la barca*
the bus	*l'autobus*
the train	*il treno*
first	*il primo*
last	*l'ultimo*
I would like ...	*Vorrei ...*
a one-way ticket	*(un biglietto di) solo andata/ un biglietto semplice*
a return ticket	*(un biglietto di) andata e ritorno*
1st class	*prima classe*
2nd class	*seconda classe*
Where is ...?	*Dov'è ...?*
I want to go to ...	*Voglio andare a ...*

Can you show me (on the map)?	*Me lo puo mostrare (sulla carta/ pianta)?*
far/near	*lontano/vicino*
Go straight ahead.	*Si va (vai) sempre diritto.*
Turn left ...	*Gira a sinistra ...*
Turn right ...	*Gira a destra ...*

Around Town

I'm looking for ...	*Sto cercando ...*
a bank	*un banco*
church	*la chiesa*
the city centre	*il centro (città)*
the ... embassy	*l'ambasciata di...*
my hotel	*il mio albergo*
the market	*il mercato*
the museum	*il museo*
the post office	*la posta*
a public toilet	*un gabinetto/ bagno pubblico*
the telephone centre	*il centro telefonico/SIP*
the tourist information office	*l'ufficio di turismo/ d'informazione*
beach	*la spiaggia*
bridge	*il ponte*
castle	*il castello*
cathedral	*il duomo/la cattedrale*
church	*la chiesa*
island	*l'isola*
main square	*la piazza principale*
market	*il mercato*
mosque	*la moschea*
old city	*il centro storico*
palace	*il palazzo*
ruins	*le rovine*
sea	*il mare*
square	*la piazza*
tower	*il torre*

Accommodation

Where is ...?	*Dov'è ...?*
a cheap hotel	*un albergo che costa poco*
What is the address?	*Cos'è l'indirizzo?*
Could you write the address, please?	*Può scrivere l'indirizzo, per favore?*
Do you have any rooms available?	*Ha camere libere?/C'è una camera libera?*
I would like ...	*Vorrei ...*
a single room	*una camera singola*
a double room	*una camera matrimoniale/ per due*
a room with a bathroom	*una camera con bagno*
to share a dorm	*un letto in dormitorio*
a bed	*un letto*
How much is it per night/per person?	*Quanto costa per la notte/ciascuno?*
Can I see it?	*Posso vederla?*
Where is the bathroom?	*Dov'è il bagno?*

Food

breakfast	*prima colazione*
lunch	*pranzo/colazione*
dinner	*cena*
I would like the set lunch.	*Vorrei il menu turistico.*
Is service included in the bill?	*È compreso il servizio?*
I am a vegetarian.	*Sono vegetariano/a. Non mangio carne.*

Time & Dates

What time is it?	*Che ora è? Che ore sono?*
today	*oggi*
tomorrow	*domani*
yesterday	*ieri*
in the morning	*di mattina*

in the afternoon	*di pomeriggio*
in the evening	*di sera*
Monday	*lunedì*
Tuesday	*martedì*
Wednesday	*mercoledì*
Thursday	*giovedì*
Friday	*venerdì*
Saturday	*sabato*
Sunday	*domenica*
January	*gennaio*
February	*febbraio*
March	*marzo*
April	*aprile*
May	*maggio*
June	*giugno*
July	*luglio*
August	*agosto*
September	*settembre*
October	*ottobre*
November	*novembre*
December	*dicembre*

Numbers

0	*zero*
1	*uno*
2	*due*
3	*tre*
4	*quattro*
5	*cinque*
6	*sei*
7	*sette*
8	*otto*
9	*nove*
10	*dieci*
11	*undici*
12	*dodici*
13	*tredici*
14	*quattordici*
15	*quindici*
16	*sedici*
17	*diciassette*
18	*diciotto*
19	*diciannove*
20	*venti*
21	*ventuno*
22	*ventidue*
30	*trenta*

40	*quaranta*
50	*cinquanta*
60	*sessanta*
70	*settanta*
80	*ottanta*
90	*novanta*
100	*cento*
1000	*mille*
one million	*un milione*

Romansch

Romansch dialects tend to be restricted to their own particular mountain valley. Usage is gradually being undermined by the steady encroachment of German, and linguists fear that the language may eventually disappear altogether. There are so many dialects that not all the following words may be universally understood. See the Graubünden chapter for some examples of regional variations. The main street in villages is usually called Via Maistra.

Useful words are:

Tourist office	*societad da traffic*
Please.	*anzi*
Thank you.	*grazia*
Hello.	*allegra*
Good morning.	*bun di*
Good evening.	*buna saira*
Good night.	*buna notg*
Goodbye.	*adieu, or abunansvair*

room	*la chombra*
bed	*il letg*
closed	*serrà*
left	*sanester*
right	*dretg*
woman	*la dunna*
man	*l'um*
cross-country skiing	*il passlung*
food	*mangiar*
bread	*il paun*
cheese	*il chaschiel*
fish	*il pesch*
ham	*il schambun*
drink	*baiver*

		Numbers	
milk	*il Latg*		
wine	*il vin*	1	*in*
		2	*dus*
		3	*trais*
Sunday	*Dumengia*	4	*quatter*
Monday	*Lündeschdi*	5	*tschinch*
Tuesday	*il Mardi*	6	*ses*
Wednesday	*Marculdi*	7	*set*
Thursday	*la Gievgia*	8	*och*
Friday	*Venderdi*	9	*nouv*
Saturday	*Sanda*	10	*diesch*

Facts for the Visitor

VISAS & EMBASSIES

Visas are not required for passport holders of the UK, Ireland, the USA, Canada, Australia, New Zealand or South Africa, whether visiting as a tourist or on business. A maximum three-month stay applies although passports are rarely stamped. With British passports, the following endorsements are all acceptable: 'British Citizen', 'British subject: citizen of the United Kingdom and colonies', 'British protected person', 'British dependent territories citizen', 'British overseas citizen'. The few Third World and Arab nationals who require visas should have a passport valid for at least six months after their intended stay.

Enquire at a Swiss Embassy before departure if you're going to Switzerland to take up employment, as you will need to acquire an 'Assurance of a Residence Permit'. Visa requirements can change, and regardless of the purpose of your trip, you should always check with the embassy or a reputable travel agent before travelling.

Being able to show a return ticket and 'sufficient means of support' are not an entry requirement, but if a border guard has cause to question the purpose of your trip you may have problems if you can't show either or both. No inoculations are required for entry.

Swiss Embassies

Swiss embassies abroad include:

Australia
   7 Melbourne Ave, Forrest, Canberra, ACT 2603
   (☎ (06) 273 3977)
Canada
   5 Ave Marlborough, Ottawa, Ontario K1N 8E6
   (☎ 613-235 /1837/8)
Ireland
   6 Aylesbury Rd, Ballsbridge, Dublin 4 (☎ 01-269 2515)
New Zealand
   22 Panama St, Wellington (☎ (04)721 593/4)
South Africa
   818 George Ave, Arcadia 0083, PO Box 2289, 0001 Pretoria (☎ 012-436 707)

UK
   16-18 Montague Place, London W1H 2BQ
   (☎ 071- 723 0701
USA
   Cathedral Ave NW, Washington, DC 20008-3499
   (☎ 202 745 7900)

Foreign Embassies in Switzerland

These are located in Bern (see the Bern Information section in the Bernese Mittelland chapter for details). Consulates can be found in many other towns. New Zealand doesn't have a full embassy in Switzerland, but there is a consulate and mission in Geneva (see the Geneva chapter).

DOCUMENTS
Passport

The key travel document is your passport which ideally should remain valid until well after your trip. If it's just about to expire, renew it before you go to save hassles and delays.

If you don't already have a passport, or simply need a renewal, applying for one can be a lengthy process, so allow plenty of time. Australian citizens can apply at a post office or the passport office in their state capital; Britons can get application forms from travel agents and major post offices, and the passport is issued by the regional passport office; Canadians can apply at regional passport offices; New Zealanders can apply at any district office of the Department of Internal Affairs; US citizens must apply in person (but may usually renew by mail) at a US Passport Agency office or some courthouses and post offices.

Once you start travelling, carry your passport at all times and guard it carefully. The Swiss are required by law to carry personal identification, so you will need to be able to identify yourself, too.

Europeans Citizens of many European countries don't need a valid passport to travel to Switzerland; a national identity card or expired passport may be sufficient. British citizens may travel on a one-year British Visitors' passport, available from the post office. If you want to exercise any of these options, it is *important* to check with your travel agent or the Swiss Embassy.

There are a number of other documents worth considering. Don't forget travel insurance documentation (see the Health section for medical criteria to consider). You'll need to show an International Health Certificate if you're coming from an infected area, such as Africa and South America, where cholera or yellow fever are prevalent.

International Driving Permit (IDP)

If you hold a non-European driving licence and plan to drive, it's a good idea to obtain one of these permits from your local automobile association before you leave – you'll need a passport photo and a valid licence. They are usually inexpensive and valid for one year only. An IDP helps foreign officials make sense of your unfamiliar local licence (make sure you take that with you, too) and can make life much simpler, especially when hiring cars and motorbikes. Even without an IDP, a foreign licence is sufficient for you to drive for one year in Switzerland.

While you're at it, ask your automobile association for a Card of Introduction. This entitles you to services offered by sister organisations in Europe. (See the Useful Organisations section for information on Swiss motoring clubs.)

Camping Carnet

Your local automobile association also issues a Camping Carnet, which is basically a camping ground ID. Carnets are also issued by your local camping federation, and sometimes on the spot at camping grounds. They incorporate third-party insurance for damage you may cause, and many camping grounds offer a small discount if you sign in with one. Some hostels and hotels also accept carnets for signing-in purposes, but won't give discounts.

International Youth Hostel Card

An IYHF (International Youth Hostel Federation) card is useful if you're staying at youth hostels. It's cheaper to buy this in your home country than to get membership in Switzerland. (See the Youth Hostels section in this chapter for more information.)

Student & Youth Cards

The International Student Identity Card (ISIC) can get the holder all sorts of discounts on admission prices, air and international train tickets, even some ski passes. If you're under 26 years of age but not a student, you can apply for a Federation of International Youth Travel Organisations (FIYTO) card; this is not so useful, but may work for reductions in lieu of an ISIC.

Both cards are issued by student unions and by youth-oriented travel agents.

CUSTOMS

Duty free limits are as follows: visitors arriving from Europe may import 200 cigarettes, 50 cigars or 250 grams of pipe tobacco. Visitors from non-European countries may import twice as much. The allowance for alcohol is the same for everyone: one litre of spirits plus two litres below 15% vol. Tobacco and alcohol may only be brought in by people aged 17 or over. Gifts up to the value of Sfr100 may also be imported, and food provisions for one day.

MONEY

The Swiss make it as easy as they can for you to spend your money. Banks are generally open from Monday to Friday from 8.30 am to 4.30 pm (closed on public holidays), but you can also change money at airports and nearly every train station every day until sometime in the evening. Exchange rates are virtually identical between these places. Rates for travellers' cheques are about 1% better than those for cash.

At present, no commission is charged for changing cash or travellers' cheques, but the big banks have whispered they may soon introduce small charges, which means everyone else will probably follow suit. Big hotels change money too, but avoid using their services as rates are invariably lower. All major currencies are equally acceptable.

Cash

Avoid carrying large amounts of cash, but taking some will allow more flexibility of changing upon arrival and departure. Towards the end of your trip, you don't want to change more than you think you'll need as you will lose out if you have to reconvert the excess. Banks rarely accept coins in currencies other than their own, so spend your last coins on a cup of coffee or fuel if travelling by car.

Travellers' Cheques

All major travellers' cheques are equally acceptable, though you may want to stick to those from American Express, Visa or Thomas Cook because of their 'instant replacement' policies.

Keeping a record of the cheque numbers and the initial purchase details is vital when it comes to replacing lost cheques. Without this, you may well find that 'instant' is a very long time indeed. You should also keep a record of which cheques you have cashed. Keep these details separate from the cheques themselves. American Express has offices in Bern, Basel, Geneva, Lausanne, Lucerne and Zürich; addresses are listed in the appropriate city sections. Buy cheques in your home currency (as long as it's freely convertible and stable), as if you buy too many in Swiss francs you'll lose on the 'spread' of the exchange rate when cashing in the excess back home.

International Transfers

If you need to get money sent from home, it's easiest if you open a bank account in Switzerland to which the money can be credited. The big banks do not charge for setting up an account, or for making withdrawals, and they don't mind if you're only going to use it for the few weeks that you're in the country. All you need to open an account is a passport and a home address. You may even earn some interest. The Union Bank of Switzerland (UBS; Schweizerische Bankgesellschaft, Union de Banques Suisses, Unione di Banche Svizzere) makes no charges for accepting transfers to its account holders; the Swiss Bank Corporation (SBC; Schweizerischer Bankverein, Société de Banque Suisse, Societá di Banca Svizzera) charges about Sfr8. Both banks would be reluctant to accept transfers for a non-account holder, and even if they did, they would make higher handling charges.

There are always charges made by the sending bank – a telegraphic transfer is usually more expensive than an International Money Order (IMO). You sometimes need to allow up to two weeks to effect transfers, or using the 'Swift' system (electronic transfer of funds) within Europe can take just a few hours but from Britain you should allow two to three days.

You can also transfer money through American Express or Thomas Cook. Americans can also use Western Union but there may not be a convenient collecting office. If you have an American Express card, you can cash up to US$1000 of personal cheques at American Express offices in a 21-day period.

Credit Cards & ATMs

Using a credit card can limit or even remove the need to carry travellers' cheques. Not only can you pay for many goods and services by card (eg Swiss train tickets worth over Sfr20), but you can also use them to get cash advances at most banks. Automated teller machines (ATMs) are common and stop you being tied to bank opening times; they're accessible 24 hours a day.

ATMs are linked up internationally and you can shove your credit card in, punch in a personal identification number (PIN) and get instant cash. Check with your credit card company about charges for cash advances through these – there's usually a 1 or 2% flat fee of the total withdrawn plus the usual monthly interest rate starting from the day of withdrawal up to the time the account is settled (although you could leave you account in credit before you depart to avoid this). Not all cards are accepted by ATMs –

Visa and MasterCard (also known as Eurocard or Access) are accepted in ATMs at branches of UBS and SBC, and these machines will accept cards with a PIN of up to six digits.

Similarly, not all shops, hotels or restaurants will accept credit cards, but penetration is fairly widespread and Visa and Master-Card are the most popular. Charge cards like American Express and Diners Club are generally less widely acceptable than ordinary credit cards.

Eurocheques

These guaranteed personal cheques are a convenient way to organise your money if you're a European or have time to set up a European bank account (at least two weeks to apply for the cheques). Getting Eurocheques from a UK bank costs around £6 joining fee plus a charge of around £6 per annum.

Each cheque is guaranteed for up to Sfr300 in Switzerland though you can write more than one if you have a larger purchase. You will need to show your Eurocheque card to the vendor, and sometimes your passport. Many hotels, restaurants and shops accept these cheques, and getting cash withdrawals from banks is easy. The card can also be used in ATMs, open 24 hours.

Post Office Accounts

Opening a postcheque account (Postcheckkonto, compte de cheque postal) is another efficient way to organise your money in Switzerland. There is no charge to open an account or make withdrawals (you even earn a small amount of interest), and post offices are open longer hours than banks. You can open one on arrival (the drawback is that you would have to make your initial deposit in cash). You could also arrange it before departure through your national post office postgiro system (if there is one; it's mostly a European network), which can also transfer funds over for you. Don't ask for the paying bills facility as you would then have to lodge a large deposit as a guarantee. Enquire of your national

system, as it may enable you to make cash withdrawals directly at Swiss post offices. (British Girobank postcheques allow you to do this.)

Currency

Swiss francs are divided into 100 centimes (usually called *Rappen* in German-speaking Switzerland). There are notes for 10, 20, 50, 100, 500 and 1000 francs, and coins for five, 10, 20 and 50 centimes, as well as for one, two and five francs.

If you're driving to Switzerland and intend to use the motorways, you'll have to pay a one-year motorway tax of Sfr30. Have this money ready, since there may not always be an exchange facility at the border.

Exchange Rates

UK£1	=	Sfr2.17
DM1	=	Sfr0.91
FF10	=	Sfr2.70
ASch10	=	Sfr1.30
IL1000	=	Sfr0.92
US$1	=	Sfr1.45
C$1	=	Sfr1.05
A$1	=	Sfr0.97
NZ$1	=	Sfr0.70

Costs

Switzerland, as you will soon discover, is expensive, but you needn't emerge from your trip as a pauper.

The secret to low costs is cheap accommodation. Camping and staying at hostels are the cheapest option and often great places to meet people. A student card can cut the cost of entrance fees (see the previous Documents section) and rail and other transport passes almost invariably save money (see the Getting Around chapter). Don't forget to apply for the consumer tax rebate on large purchases (see the Consumer Taxes section). Hitchhiking, preparing your own meals and avoiding alcohol are other good ways of saving money.

Your budget depends on how you live and travel. If you're moving around fast, going to lots of places, spending time in the big cities, then your day-to-day living costs are going to be quite high; if you stay in one place and get to know your way around, they're likely to come down.

Daily Costs Hotel prices are the biggest variable; expect to pay more than the average in Zürich, Geneva, Bern and plush ski resorts.

Average costs are:

Youth hostel Sfr18
Cheap hotel Sfr40
Cheap restaurant Sfr14 (lunch) or Sfr20 (dinner)
Loaf of bread Sfr3
Glass of draught beer Sfr3 (0.3 litre)
Big Mac Sfr5.60
Petrol Sfr1.30 per litre (super)
100 km by train Sfr29
100 km by local bus Sfr0.80 to Sfr2.40
Local telephone call Sfr0.40
Time magazine Sfr4.50

Admission prices are usually under Sfr10 or can even be free (some museums). An occasional expense that can blow any budget is trips in cable cars; these are rarely covered by travel passes (at best you can expect a 25-50% reduction). A modest ascent can cost Sfr10 to Sfr20. Return trips up Mt Titlis and Schilthorn exceed Sfr60.

Possible Budgets Always allow some extra cash for emergencies. Overall, around Sfr30 (US$20) per day is the *bare* minimum if you spend your time camping, mostly self-catering, hitching, hiking and visiting the occasional museum. This is survival level, leaving no money for non-essentials. After buying a rail pass, Sfr50 (US$33) a day will allow hostel accommodation, picnic lunch, admission to a tourist attraction, cheap dinner and the odd beer. Add about Sfr20 (US$14) a day if you want to stay in a cheap pension instead. You would still need to be very careful with your money at this level: at Sfr100 (US$65) a day you can relax a bit. Under Sfr200 (US$130) a day will get you a comfortable hotel, cheap lunch, a good dinner, and enough left over to visit a range of tourist sights. Sfr350 (US$230) or more will put you in the luxury class.

Tipping & Bargaining

Tipping is not really necessary or expected as hotels, restaurants and bars are required by law to include a 15% service charge in bills. Even taxis normally have a charge included. If you've been very happy with a meal or service you could round up the bill. Bargaining is virtually nonexistent, though you could try haggling on hotel prices in the low season.

Consumer Taxes

A 6.2% 'turnover' or sales tax (*Wust*) is levied on all goods. Nonresidents are eligible for a tax refund on items purchased for export but a form must be signed at the time of purchase. Depending on the shop, a refund will be given immediately or else sent to your home address. Swiss customs will need to see this form upon departure. The authorities want to introduce VAT (*MWST*) to bring Switzerland in line with the rest of Europe, but the people have already rejected this in three referenda.

WHEN TO GO

You can visit Switzerland any time throughout the year. Summer lasts roughly from June to September, and offers the most pleasant climate for outdoor pursuits. Unfortunately, you won't be the only tourist during summer – prices can be high, accommodation fully booked, and the sights packed. You'll find much better deals, and less crowds, in the shoulder seasons either side of summer: in April, May or September, October. In Ticino, flowers are in bloom as early as March and hints of summer warmth are already seeping through.

On the other hand, if you're keen on winter sports, resorts in the Alps begin operating in late November and move into full swing around Christmas, closing down again when the snows begin to melt around April. Nowadays the winter season is the busiest time for Alpine resorts, and they all but shut down in May and November. July and August are their summer high season.

As a rule, spring and autumn are wetter and windier than summer and winter, and the continental climate in the Alps tends to show the greatest extremes between summer and winter.

WHAT TO BRING

As little as possible is the best policy. It's very easy to find almost anything you need along the way, and since you'll inevitably buy things as you go, it's better to start with too little rather than too much. When you decide to go will have a bearing on the clothes you bring along. Insulation works on the principle of trapped air, and several layers of thin clothing are warmer than only a thick one (and will be easier to dry, too). You'll also be much more flexible in responding to temperature changes as you change altitude.

A backpack is still the most popular method of carrying gear as it is convenient and the only way to go if you have to do any walking. On the debit side, a backpack doesn't offer too much protection for your valuables; the straps tend to get caught on things and some airlines may refuse to be responsible if the pack is damaged or broken into.

Travelpacks, a combination of backpack and shoulder bag, have become very popular. The backpack straps zip away inside the pack when not needed so you almost have the best of both worlds. Some packs have sophisticated shoulder-strap adjustment systems and these can be used comfortably even for long hikes. Packs are always much easier to carry than a bag. Another alternative is a large, soft zip-bag with a wide shoulder strap so it can be carried with relative ease if necessary. Backpacks or travelpacks can be reasonably thief-proof with small padlocks. Suitcases are OK if you're travelling by car, but you'll still find them a bit limiting if, for example, you ditch your vehicle for a few days and go hiking.

A minimum packing list could include:

- underwear, socks & swimming gear
- a pair of jeans and maybe a pair of shorts
- a few T-shirts & shirts
- a warm sweater
- a solid pair of shoes
- sandals or thongs for showers
- a coat or jacket
- a raincoat or umbrella, or waterproof jacket
- a medical kit and a sewing kit
- a padlock
- a Swiss Army knife
- soap & towel
- toothpaste, toothbrush & toiletries

Campers obviously need to take a few extras. A sleeping sheet may be worth taking for hostels, though you usually have to use one that's provided. A padlock (and chain) is useful to lock your bag to a train or bus luggage rack, and may also be needed to secure your youth hostel locker. Swiss Army knives are the most versatile pocket knives available; get one with at least a bottle opener and corkscrew. You could need waterproof gear at any time of the year. Tampons and condoms are widely available. A supply of passport photos is useful for visas for onward travel, rail/bus passes, etc.

Other items that might be useful include a compass, a flashlight (torch), an alarm clock (or watch alarm), an adapter plug for electrical appliances (such as a cup water heater to save on expensive tea and coffee), a universal bath/sink plug (a film canister sometimes works, too), sunglasses, a few clothes pegs, and string (impromptu clothes line). During city sightseeing, a small daypack is better than a shoulder bag for deterring bag snatchers (see the Dangers & Annoyances section).

As for clothing, informal gear is fine for normal wear, but men will need proper shoes (not trainers or running shoes), smart trousers (not jeans) and a tie to get into nightclubs; this is also the accepted attire for top restaurants. Being able to present a smart appearance helps when dealing with officialdom (like at border controls).

There are two final considerations. The secret of successful packing is plastic carry bags or garbage bags inside your backpack: they not only keep things separate and clean but also dry if the bag gets soaked. Airlines do lose bags from time to time, but you've got a much better chance of it not being yours if it is tagged with your name and address *inside* the bag as well as outside. Outside tags can always fall off or be removed.

TOURIST OFFICES

The Swiss National Tourist Office (SNTO) abroad and local tourist offices in Switzerland are extremely helpful and have plenty of literature to give out, including maps (nearly always free). Somebody invariably speaks English. Local offices can be found everywhere tourists are likely to go, and will often book hotel rooms and organise excursions. In German-speaking Switzerland they are called *Verkehrsbüro*, or *Kurverein* in some resorts. In French they are *Office du Tourisme* and in Italian, *Ufficio Turistico*.

As if the combination of national and local tourist offices weren't already enough to meet the needs of visitors, the Swiss have made doubly sure that ever angle is covered by dividing the country up into 12 tourist regions, each with its own regional tourist office. Each chapter in this book covers one tourist region, and the address of the regional office is given in the chapter introduction.

Local tourist offices in many resorts organise a Visitor's Card, sometimes called a Guest Card or Resort Card *(Kurkarte)*. The aim is to entice tourists to stay in the locality instead of just breezing in on a day trip. Cards are usually issued by hotels and pensions (sometimes hostels), and they must be stamped where you are staying in order to be valid. Visitor's Cards are good for various discounts, such as for museum and swimming pool entry, or use of cable cars, and is worth asking for if your hotel doesn't supply it spontaneously.

Tourist Offices Abroad

The SNTO headquarters is in Zürich (see the Zürich chapter for details). Offices outside Switzerland include:

Australia
> Swiss Consulate General, 3 Bowen Crescent, Melbourne 3004 (☎ 03-867 2266)
> PO Box 82, Edgecliff, NSW 2027 (☎ 02-328 7925)

Canada
> SNTO, 154 University Ave, Toronto, Ont M5H 3Z4 (☎ 416-971 9734)

South Africa
> SNTO c/o Swissair, Swiss Park, 10 Queens Road, Parktown, POB 3866, Johannesburg 2000, (☎ 011-484 19 86)

UK
> SNTO, Swiss Centre, Swiss Court, London W1V 8EE (☎ 071-734 1921)

USA
> SNTO, Swiss Center, 608 Fifth Ave, New York, NY 10020 (☎ 212-757 59 44)

The SNTO also has offices in Los Angeles, San Francisco, Chicago, Buenos Aires, Tokyo, Tel Aviv and Cairo. Nearly half of foreign visitors hail from Germany, as can be guessed from the distribution of European offices: Amsterdam, Brussels, Düsseldorf, Frankfurt, Hamburg, Paris, Rome, Stockholm, Stuttgart, Madrid, Milan, Munich and Vienna.

USEFUL ORGANISATIONS

SSR-Reisen in German Switzerland or Voyages-SSR in French Switzerland (☎ 01-297 11 11), Postfach, CH-8026, Zürich, is a budget travel agency specialising in student and budget fares. It is the only agency in Switzerland entitled to make changes to tickets issued by STA branches (Sfr40 fee) and to issue ISIC cards. It also issues USIT tickets (cheap tickets mainly oriented to student travellers) and is an agent for Eurotrain. There are branches in Zürich, Geneva, Bern, Basel, Lausanne, Biel, St Gallen, Winterthur, Chur, Fribourg, Lucerne and Neuchâtel; these are listed in the appropriate chapters.

The Swiss Youth Hostel Association is the Schweizerischer Bund für Jugendherbergen (☎ 031-24 55 03), Neufeldstrasse 9, CH-3012, Bern. The travel arm is called Jugi Tours (☎ 031-23 26 21) and is based in the same building. It offers a varied programme (especially in summer) of tours and activities in Switzerland for IYHF members, mainly staying in youth hostels or mountain huts. Write to the above address for brochures. The type of packages available are: one-week's skiing in Grindelwald with a ski school for Sfr680, windsurfing in the Engadine for Sfr390 (three days), scuba-diving in Lake Lucerne for Sfr1010 (seven-day course), one-week's sailing in Spiez from Sfr640, one-week's hiking in Ticino (Sfr580), and six days of mountaineering around Saas Fee (Sfr960).

If you're a traveller with special requirements, the SNTO or local tourist offices can often provide information on facilities and local organisations for particular groups.

Other useful organisations in Switzerland include:

Swiss Hotel Association
    Schweizer Hotelier-Verein (SHV), Monbijoustrasse 130, CH-3001 Bern (☎ 031-50 71 11)
Swiss Camping and Caravanning Federation
    Schweizerischer Camping-und Caravanning-Verband (SCCV), Habsburgerstrasse 35, CH-6004 Lucerne (☎ 041-23 48 22)
Swiss Camping Association
    Verband Schweizer Campings, Seestrasse 119, CH-3800 Interlaken (☎ 036-23 35 23)
Swiss Automobile Club
    Automobil-Club der Schweiz (ACS), Wasserwerkgasse 39, CH-3000 Bern 13 (☎ 031-22 47 22) This is the largest motoring organisation in Switzerland, with affiliations round the world.
Swiss Touring Club
    Touring Club der Schweiz (TCS), 9 Rue Pierre Fatio, CH-1211, Geneva 3 (☎ 737 12 12) Motoring organisation affiliated with the RAC (Britain), AAA (USA) and AAA (Australia)
Swiss Alpine Club
    Schweizer Alpenclub (SAC), Helvetiaplatz 4, CH-3005 Bern (☎ 031-43 36 11)
Swiss Mountain Guide Federation
    c/o Skischule Davos, Promenade 83, CH-7270, Davos Platz (☎ 081-43 71 71)
Swiss Ski School Federation (SSSV)
    Oberalpstrasse, CH-6490, Andermatt (☎ 044-6 73 69)
Swiss Spa Association (SSA)
    Postfach 1456, CH-5400, Baden (☎ 056-22 53 18)
Swiss Invalid Association
    Schweizerischer Invalidenverband, Froburgstrasse 4, CH-4600 Olten (☎ 062-32 12 62)
Arts Council of Switzerland
    Pro Helvetia, Hirschengraben 22, CH-8024, Zürich (☎ 01-251 96 00). Pro Helvetia promotes cultural activities and publishes a range of books covering specific interests such as music, dance ballet, and languages. You pay for its books if you

buy them in Switzerland, but copies are sent to foreigners abroad free of charge.

BUSINESS HOURS & HOLIDAYS

Most shops are open from 8 am to 6.30 pm, Monday to Friday, with a 90-minute or two-hour break for lunch at noon. Some are closed on Monday morning, and in towns, shops often stay open late until 9 pm on Thursday. Closing times on Saturday are usually 4 or 5 pm.

Banks are open Monday to Friday from 8.30 am to 4.30 pm with some local variations.

National holidays are:

New Year's Day, 1 January
Good Friday, Easter Sunday and Monday
Ascension Day
National Day, 1 August
Whit Sunday and Monday
Christmas Day, 25 December
Boxing Day, 26 December

Some cantons observe their own special holidays and extra religious days, eg 2 January, 1 May (Labour Day), and Corpus Christi.

CULTURAL EVENTS

Numerous events take place at a local level throughout the year, so it's worth checking with the local tourist office. Most dates vary from year to year. Following is a brief selection of the main events; more information and further festivals are mentioned in the relevant chapter sections. The SNTO annually brings out a booklet giving an exhaustive list of local events, including cultural, social and sporting occasions.

January
    Costumed sleigh-rides in the Engadine, and the Lauberhorn ski race at Wengen
February
    Carnival time *(Fasnacht)* in many towns, but especially in Basel
March
    Engadine Skiing Marathon, Graubünden. Cow fighting (yes, the cows fight each other!) starts at the end of the month in lower Valais and continues for most of the summer

April

Meetings of the Landsgemeinde in Appenzell, Hundwil (or Trogen), Sarnen and Stans (last Sunday of the month)

May

May Day celebrations, especially in St Gallen and Vaud

June

Geneva Rose Week, and the International June Festival of the Arts in Zürich. The annual performance of *William Tell* starts in Interlaken, and continues until early September.

July

Montreux Jazz Festival

August

National Day (1 August) celebrations and fireworks, and Swiss wrestling in the Emmental. The middle of the month sees the start of the Geneva Festival and the International Festival of Music in Lucerne.

September

Shooting contest (*Knabenschiessen*) in Zürich, and a religious festival in Einsiedeln

October

Vintage festivals in wine-growing regions such as Morges, Neuchâtel and Lugano

November

Open-air festivals on the fourth Monday in November including the onion market (*Zibelmärit*) in Bern

December

St Nicholas Day celebrations on 6 December and the Escalade festival in Geneva

POST & TELECOMMUNICATIONS

As you might expect, the mail and telephone systems are very efficient. Post office opening times vary but typically are Monday to Friday from 8 am to noon and 2 to 6.30 pm, and Saturday from 8 to 11 am. The larger post offices offer services outside normal hours (eg lunch time, evening, Saturday afternoon, Sunday morning), but transactions are subject to a Sfr1 to Sfr2 surcharge. Information on main post offices is given in the city sections in this book.

Postal Rates

Within Switzerland, deliveries are either by A-Post (98% delivered next working day) or B-Post (takes two to three days). Letters and postcards by A-Post cost Sfr0.80, or Sfr1.50 if over 250 grams. By B-Post they cost Sfr0.60 or Sfr1.20.

For international deliveries, the categories are Prioritaire and Non Prioritaire. By the Prioritaire, deliveries to Europe take two to five days, and to elsewhere, four to 10 days. By Non Prioritaire, to Europe takes four to 10 days and to elsewhere takes six to thirty days.

Prioritaire rates are:

Weight	Europe	Elsewhere
Not Over	Sfr	Sfr
20g	1.00	1.80
50g	1.80	3.00
100g	2.80	4.40
200g	5.00	7.70

Non Prioritaire rates are:

Weight	Europe	Elsewhere
Not Over	Sfr	Sfr
20g	0.80	0.90
50g	1.00	1.20
100g	1.30	1.80
200g	2.00	2.90

Prices for countries bordering the Mediterranean are the same as for Europe. For sending parcels, you can buy special cardboard boxes in various sizes from the post office. Paketpost rates are cheaper for heavier items than Briefpost (letter post).

Receiving Mail

Mail can be sent to any town with a post office and is held for 30 days, but you need to show your passport in order to collect it. Unless specified otherwise, it will go to the town's main post office. The international term for this, 'poste restante', is widely understood although you might prefer to use the German term, *Postlagernde Briefe*. Ask people writing to you to print and underline your surname; if an expected letter isn't there, ask if the staff will check under your first name. American Express also holds mail (but not parcels) for one month for people who use its cheques or cards.

Telephones

There are nearly always ordinary telephones

outside post offices, and some of the larger ones have special telephone sections, usually open longer hours than the general post office counters. In these booths you simply make your call and pay the total charge after you've finished at the desk. The call rates are the same as for normal phones but there is a 50c 'connection fee' per call, as opposed to the 20c that applies in normal telephone boxes. This makes the minimum charge per call 70c instead of 40c. Thereafter calls are charged per 10c in either a box or a booth. Hotels can charge as much as they like for telephone calls, so avoid using their telephones to make calls (even if they are direct dial).

Calls within Switzerland are 60% cheaper on weekdays between 5 pm and 7 pm and between 9 pm and 8 am, and throughout the weekend. The length of time you get depends upon the distance; zones are: local, up to 10 km, up to 100 km, and over 100 km. International calls to Europe are cheaper from 9 pm to 8 am on weekdays, and throughout the weekend. USA and Canada can also be called at a lower rate at off-peak times (but not Australia or New Zealand). You can direct dial to just about anywhere worldwide. The normal tariff for one minute is: Sfr1 to Europe (including Britain), Sfr1.80 to USA and Canada, Sfr2.40 to Australia and Japan, and Sfr3.20 to New Zealand. Reverse-charge (collect) calls are not possible to every country, so check with the operator.

Phone cards *(Taxcard)* are available for Sfr10 and Sfr20 and avoid the need to store change. To find a telephone number in Switzerland check the phone book or dial ☎ 111. For Germany dial ☎ 192, for France, ☎ 193, and for anywhere else, ☎ 191. Call ☎ 114 for the international operator.

International Dialling The country code for Switzerland is 41. When telephoning Switzerland from abroad you miss out the initial zero from the area code, hence to call Bern you dial ☎ 41 31, *preceded* by the overseas access code of the country you're dialling from. The overseas access code from Switzerland is 00. So to call Britain (country code 44), you would start dialling with ☎ 00 44. Other country codes are: Australia 61, Canada 1, Hong Kong 853, India 91, Ireland 353, Japan 81, New Zealand 64, Singapore 65, South Africa 27, USA 1.

Fax & Telex Services
Telephone offices in post offices also have fax and telex facilities. If you do it yourself, a fax costs Sfr2 plus the equivalent telephone call; if you get the counter staff to do it, it costs more. The same system applies for sending telexes.

TIME
Swiss time is GMT/UTC plus one hour. If it's noon in Bern it is 11 am in London, 6 am in New York and Toronto, 3 am in San Francisco, 9 pm in Sydney and 11 pm in Auckland. Daylight-saving time comes into effect at midnight on the last Saturday in March, when the clocks are moved forward one hour; they go back again on the last Saturday in September.

ELECTRICITY
In a country where most things are straightforward, plugs are a pain. Plugs sockets vary, even sometimes inside the same building. Pins are round – three is usual, but two is not uncommon. The standard Continental type, with two round pins, can be used in a three-pin socket, but it depends on the shape. Some are recessed, either circular, or more commonly, a six-sided shape, with the top and bottom sides being closer together. Continental plugs are no good for these. Basically this means that you may be able to get by with the standard Continental plug, but it may be easier to buy the six-sided shape once in Switzerland as this also fits into the three-pin round socket. To wire it up, getting the earth wire in the centre pin is crucial. It doesn't matter which way round the other wires go.

Using an adapter is an alternative to rewiring. Most hotels of the tourist class and above have adapters you can use, but they may not fit plugs from your home country.

Try and buy an adapter before you leave home to be sure. There's generally no problem in finding a spare power point, even in hostels or camp grounds.

Voltage & Cycle

The electric current in Switzerland is 220 volts, 50Hz. Most appliances that are set up for 240 V will handle 220 V quite happily without modifications (and vice versa). It's always preferable to adjust your appliance to the exact voltage if you can (some modern battery chargers and radios will do this automatically). Just don't mix 110/125 with 220 V without a transformer, which will be built in if the appliance can be adjusted.

Several countries such as the USA and Canada have 60 Hz AC, which will affect the speed of electric motors even after the voltage has been adjusted to Swiss values, so record players and tape recorders (where motor speed is all-important) will be useless. But things like electric razors, hair driers, irons and radios will be fine.

Video Systems

If you want to record or buy video tapes to play back home, you won't get a picture if the image registration systems are different. Switzerland uses PAL (as do Britain and Australia), which is incompatible with North American and Japanese NTSC system.

LAUNDRY

There is no shortage of coin-operated or service launderettes (*Waschanstalt, laverie, lavanderia*) in cities. Expect to pay around Sfr10 to wash and dry a five-kg load. Many youth hostels also have washing machines, and prices are usually slightly cheaper. Ask the tourist office or look in the phone book if they aren't listed in the book. Tourist class hotels always have a laundry service, but prices are high.

WEIGHTS & MEASURES

The metric system is used. Like other Continental Europeans, the Swiss indicate decimals with commas and thousands with points.

BOOKS & MAPS
Special Interest Guides

The SNTO sells camping and hiking guides in English, and other books and maps on Switzerland. The TCS and the SCCV both publish comprehensive guides to Swiss campsites. The TCS guide has more detail, but annoyingly for backpackers, it's printed on very heavy paper.

A useful guide for hikers is *On Foot Through Europe – Austria, Switzerland and Liechtenstein* by Craig Evans (paperback). *Off the Beaten Track – Switzerland* (various authors, paperback) concentrates, as the name suggests, on lesser known destinations, while missing out places like Geneva altogether. *Living and Working in Switzerland* by David Hampshire (paperback) is an excellent practical guide for those doing what the title suggests.

Switzerland: A Phaidon Cultural Guide, edited by Niklaus Flüeler, gives a vast amount of detail on art and architecture.

Nonfiction

The ultimately authoritative tome about the Swiss armed forces, national defence and foreign policy is *Swiss Neutrality and Security* (hardback), edited by Marko Milivojevic and Pierre Maurer, but it's hardly light reading. The best book for people wanting to understand the social and political side of Switzerland is *Why Switzerland?* by Jonathan Steinberg (paperback). His enthusiasm for Switzerland leaps off the page and he manages to answer the questions *What Makes Switzerland Tick?* and *What Makes Switzerland Unique?* rather more successfully than the author of those two hardback volumes, Richard Wildblood. Both Wildblood's trawls through Swiss political institutions are competent but dull and dogged, and as humourless as visitors suppose the Swiss themselves to be. Believe it or not, the Swiss do have a sense of humour, as the book *Tell me a Swiss joke* by René Hildbrand indicates.

A collection of essays covering all aspects of Swiss life has been put together under the title *George Mikes Introduces Switzerland* (hardback). It's all a bit dry, except for the opening article by the humorous Mr Mikes. Two entertaining anecdotal travel books about Europe, where the author spent a fair amount of time in Switzerland, are Mark Twain's *A Tramp Abroad* and Bill Bryson's *Neither Here Nor There*. What's the best way to make a Swiss roll? Take him to a mountaintop and give him a push (Bryson's joke, not mine).

Pro Helvetia (see the Useful Organisations section) can send books on all aspects of Swiss culture free of charge.

Fiction

Good fiction on Switzerland is surprisingly hard to track down. Many books describe the Swiss scenery but fewer describe the Swiss themselves. Thomas Mann's *The Magic Mountain* is a weighty, reflective novel set in the Alps. The mountains also influenced the work of John Ruskin and Leslie Stephen. Mary Shelley wrote *Frankenstein* in Switzerland and set much of the action around Lake Geneva. This was when she was a neighbour of Lord Byron who wrote the poem *The Prisoner of Chillon* about the unfortunate fate of Bonivard, chained to a pillar in Chillon Castle. Sherlock Holmes met his death in Switzerland, in a struggle with Moriarty at Reichenbach Falls. This episode is recounted by Sexton Blake in the short story *The Adventure of the Final Problem*.

Heidi, the famous story for children by Johanna Spyri, is set in the Maienfeld region, just north of the Graubünden capital of Chur.

Maps

Once you're in Switzerland, tourist office maps and the maps in this book will be sufficient for most purposes. It usually pays to go directly to the local tourist information office to stock up on maps and brochures. Another excellent source of free maps is the Swiss Bank Corporation (SBC), which has free detailed maps of most towns and cities

(not, surprisingly, Lucerne), including a street index. It also gives out a general map of Switzerland, with some town plans on the reverse. Other banks, such as the Union Bank of Switzerland (UBS) occasionally have maps.

Other than perhaps a decent country map at the outset to aid planning, you'll probably only need to buy a map if you're driving, cycling, or hiking. Good detail is essential in these instances to prevent you getting lost. Michelin covers the whole country with four maps. The Topographical Survey of Switzerland (*Landeskarte der Schweiz*) series is larger in scale and especially useful for hiking. These maps are widely available in Switzerland. Kümmerly & Frey also publish excellent maps on Switzerland, including a series for hikers.

MEDIA
Newspapers & Magazines

English-language newspapers are widely available on the evening of the same day or a day late (depending on where you are) and cost around Sfr2.50 for tabloids or Sfr4 for the serious broadsheets. The best British 'quality' paper to buy is the *Guardian*; it has good news content and as it's printed in Frankfurt it hits the stands a day earlier than most of its rivals, and is cheaper (Sfr2.50). The *Financial Times* also arrives early (Sfr3.20), as do the American papers, the passably interesting *Herald Tribune* and the colourful but superficial *USA Today* (both Sfr3).

In the news-magazine category, *Time*, *Newsweek* and the *Economist* are widely available. A local English-language magazine worth looking at is *Swiss News* (Sfr6 monthly). Its layout is somewhat staid and dated and it dwells rather a lot on business news, but it still has good cultural features and illuminating news snippets, as well as a comprehensive *What's on in Switzerland* section.

Radio & TV

The BBC World Service broadcasts on medium wave (1296 and 648 KHz), and on short wave at 6195, 9410, 12095, 15070 and 15575 kHz (but not all at the same time). The American Forces Network is on the FM band (101.8 MHz) and The Voice of America (VOA) can usually be found on 1197 kHz.

Swiss Radio International broadcasts in English at 6 to 6.30 am, 8 to 8.30 am, and 1 to 1.30 pm. Pick it up on 3985 kHz, 6165 kHz or 9535 kHz. Hotels with three or more stars invariably have radios in the room and these are usually automatically tuned into six subscriber channels of the Swiss Broadcasting Corporation. Channel 1 is predominantly in English, with news, features and pop music.

If you have a TV in your hotel room it usually offers cable or satellite viewing, meaning you can pick up one or all of CNN (the American Cable News Network), MTV (music channel), Eurosport and Super Channel (a British general entertainment channel with ITN world news at 10 pm and 8 am). The British Sky channel is less common. The Swiss complain their national TV is boring. It's highly information-oriented, designed to clue-in the populace on current affairs. The Swiss tune in to the networks of neighbouring countries for their entertainment.

FILM & PHOTOGRAPHY

Film is cheaper than in Austria and comparable to Germany, at around Sfr7 for Kodak Gold and Sfr16 for Kodachrome (36 exposures). *Inter Discount* is one of the cheapest places to buy in Switzerland.

HEALTH

No inoculations are required for entry into Switzerland, but you'll need an International Health Certificate entry requirement if you're coming from an infected area, such as Africa or South America, where cholera and yellow fever are prevalent. A tetanus jab is a good idea. There is no state health service in Switzerland and all treatment must be paid for; there are no reciprocal agreements for free treatment with any other country. Medication and consultations are expensive; costs vary, but you can expect the briefest

consultation to cost a minimum of Sfr35, or Sfr70 at weekends. The local tourist office can tell you where to get treatment if no contact is given in this book.

Pre-departure Preparations
Health Insurance Good travel insurance is essential, and you should enquire about the claims procedure in the event medical treatment is required. A few insurers require notification *before* treatment is sought in order to meet the claim – tricky in an emergency situation. Other things to look out for are whether the policy covers 'dangerous' sports (such as skiing and mountaineering) and if ambulances, helicopter rescue or emergency repatriation are included. Whatever your insurance, you will probably have to pay initial costs yourself (which you can claim back later) and the insurers will issue guarantees for subsequent charges.

Medical Kit A small, straightforward medical kit is a wise thing to carry. A possible kit list includes:

• Aspirin or Panadol – for pain or fever
• Antihistamine (such as Benadryl) – useful as a decongestant for colds, allergies, to ease the itch from insect bites or stings or to help prevent motion sickness
• Kaolin preparation (Pepto-Bismol),
• Imodium or Lomotil – simply a change in your usual diet may be enough to cause stomach upsets
• Antiseptic, Mercurochrome and antibiotic powder or similar 'dry' spray – for cuts and grazes
• Calamine lotion – to ease irritation from bites or stings
• Bandages and Band-aids – for minor injuries
• Scissors, tweezers and a thermometer (note that mercury thermometers are prohibited by airlines)
• Insect repellent, sunscreen, suntan lotion, chapstick

You can buy all these things in Switzerland, but they will probably be more expensive. A local product I've found excellent for clearing up blisters is *Hirschtalg* (Stag Fat). If you wear glasses, take a spare pair and your prescription. If you're taking medication, bring prescriptions with the generic rather than the brand name (which may not be locally available), as it will make getting replacements easier. It's a wise idea to have a letter from your doctor to show you legally use the medication – you can't be sure that over-the-counter drugs in your home country won't be illegal without a prescription in Switzerland, or even banned altogether. Keep the medication in its original container. If you're carrying a syringe for some reason, have a note from your doctor to explain why you're doing so.

A Medic Alert tag is a good idea if your medical condition is not always easily recognisable (heart trouble, diabetes, asthma, allergic reactions to antibiotics etc).

Basic Rules

Switzerland is a healthy place, but it still pays to take care in what you eat and drink.

Tap water is safe to drink but always beware of natural water, even crystal clear Alpine streams. Take a water bottle with you if you're going on long walking trips. If you need to resort to natural water, it should be boiled for 10 minutes; and remember that at high altitude water boils at a lower temperature, so germs are less likely to be killed. Iodine is very effective in purifying water and is available in tablet form (such as Potable Aqua), but follow the directions carefully and remember that too much iodine can be harmful.

Food should not really cause any health problem – salads, fruit and dairy products are all fine but try to vary your diet. Be careful with food that has been cooked and left to go cold, which might happen in some self-service places.

Potential Hazards

Sunburn On water, ice, snow or sand, you can get sunburnt surprisingly quickly, even through cloud. Use a sunscreen and take extra care to cover areas that don't normally see sun – eg your feet. A hat provides added protection, and it may be a good idea to use zinc cream or some other barrier cream for your nose and lips. Calamine lotion is good for mild sunburn.

Remember that too much sunlight can damage your eyes, whether it's direct or reflected (glare). If your plans include water, ice, snow or sand, then good sunglasses are doubly important. Make sure they're treated to absorb ultraviolet radiation – if not, they'll actually do more harm than good by dilating your pupils and making it easier for ultraviolet light to damage the retina.

Cold Too much cold is just as dangerous as too much heat, particularly if it leads to hypothermia. Cold combined with wind and moisture (ie soaking rain) is particularly risky. If you are trekking at high altitudes or in a cool, wet environment, be prepared.

Hypothermia occurs when the body loses heat faster than it can produce it and the core temperature of the body falls. It is surprisingly easy to progress from very cold to dangerously cold due to a combination of wind, wet clothing, fatigue and hunger, even if the air temperature is above freezing. It is best to dress in layers – silk, wool and some of the new artificial fibres are all good insulating materials. A hat is important, as a lot of heat is lost through the head. A strong, waterproof outer layer is essential, as keeping dry is vital. Carry basic supplies, including food that contains simple sugars to generate heat quickly, and lots of fluid to drink.

Symptoms of hypothermia are exhaustion, numb skin (particularly toes and fingers), shivering, slurred speech, irrational or violent behaviour, lethargy, stumbling, dizzy spells, muscle cramps and violent bursts of energy. Irrationality may take the form of sufferers claiming they are warm and trying to take off their clothes.

To treat hypothermia, first get the patient out of the wind and/or rain, remove their clothing if it's wet and replace it with dry, warm clothing. Give them hot liquids – not alcohol – and some high-kilojoule, easily digestible food. This should be enough for the early stages of hypothermia, but if it has gone further, it may be necessary to place victims in warm sleeping bags and get in with them. Do not rub patients, place them near a fire or remove their wet clothes in the wind. If possible, place a sufferer in a warm (not hot) bath.

Altitude Sickness The higher you go, the thinner the air and the easier you need to take things (and the quicker you get drunk!). Acute Mountain Sickness or AMS occurs at high altitude and can be fatal. There is no hard and fast rule as to how high is too high; AMS can strike at altitudes of 3000 metres, although 3500 to 4500 metres is the usual range.

Headaches, nausea, dizziness, a dry cough, insomnia, breathlessness and loss of appetite are all signs to heed. Mild altitude problems will generally abate after a day or so, but if the symptoms persist or become worse the only treatment is to descend – even 500 metres can help.

Motion Sickness Eating lightly before and during a trip will reduce the chances of motion sickness. If you are prone to motion sickness, try to find a place that minimises disturbance – near the wing on aircraft, close to midships on boats, near the centre on buses. Fresh air and a steady reference point like the horizon usually help, whereas reading or cigarette smoke don't. Commercial antimotion-sickness preparations, which can cause drowsiness, have to be taken before the trip commences – when you're feeling sick, it's too late. Ginger is a natural preventative and is available in capsule form.

Diarrhoea A change of water, food or climate can all cause the runs; diarrhoea caused by contaminated food or water is more serious, but unlikely in Switzerland. A few rushed toilet trips with no other symptoms is not indicative of a serious problem. Moderate diarrhoea, involving half-a-dozen loose movements in a day, is more of a nuisance. Dehydration is the main danger

with any diarrhoea, particularly for children, so fluid replenishment is the number one treatment. Weak black tea with a little sugar, soda water, or soft drinks allowed to go flat and diluted 50% with water are all good.

With any diarrhoea more severe than this, go straight to the casualty ward of the nearest hospital and have yourself checked. You may need a rehydrating solution to replace minerals and salts. Stick to a bland diet as you recover.

Viral Gastroenteritis This is caused not by bacteria but, as the name suggests, by a virus. It is characterised by stomach cramps, diarrhoea, and sometimes by vomiting and/or a slight fever. All you can do is rest and drink lots of fluids.

Rabies Though rare in Europe, rabies occasionally crops up. Dogs are a noted carrier, but cats, foxes and bats can also be affected. Any bite, scratch or even lick from a mammal should be cleaned immediately and thoroughly. Scrub with soap and running water, and then clean with an alcohol solution. If there is any possibility that the animal is infected, particularly if it froths at the mouth and behaves strangely, medical help should be sought immediately. Even if it is not rabid, all bites should be treated seriously as they can become infected or can result in tetanus.

Sexually Transmitted Diseases (STDs) While abstinence is the only 100% preventative, using condoms is also effective. Gonorrhoea and syphilis are the most common of these diseases: sores, blisters or rashes around the genitals, discharges, or pain when urinating are common symptoms. Symptoms may be less marked or not observed at all in women. Syphilis symptoms eventually disappear completely but the disease continues and can cause severe problems in later years. The treatment of gonorrhoea and syphilis is by antibiotics.

The most dangerous STD is of course HIV (Human Immunodeficiency Virus), which may develop into AIDS (Acquired Immune

Deficiency Syndrome). It can also be spread by dirty needles used for purposes of vaccinations, acupuncture, tattooing and ear or nose piercing or drug abuse.

Snakes Snakes tend to keep a very low profile, but to minimise your chances of being bitten, always wear boots, socks and long trousers when walking through undergrowth where snakes may be present. Tramp heavily and they'll usually slither away before you come near. Don't put your hands into holes and crevices, and be careful when collecting firewood.

Switzerland is home to several types of snakes, a couple of which can deliver a nasty although not fatal bite. They are more prevalent in the mountains. If the worst happens, keep the victim calm and still, wrap the bitten limb tightly, as you would for a sprained ankle, and then attach a splint to immobilise it. Then seek medical help. Tourniquets and sucking out the poison are now comprehensively discredited.

WOMEN TRAVELLERS

Women travellers should experience no special problems. Swiss men generally believe that a woman's place is in the home (under Swiss marriage laws, wives weren't granted equal rights until 1988!), but the independence of female travellers is respected. A wedding ring (on the left ring finger) sometimes helps to deter unwanted advances, along with talk about 'my husband'. Slightly conservative dress and toned-down make-up can help to avoid attention, and dark sunglasses help to reduce eye contact from others. Common sense is the best guide to dealing with potentially dangerous situations like hitchhiking, walking alone at night etc.

Some women experience irregular periods when travelling, due to the upset in routine. Don't forget to take time zones into account if you're on the pill; if you run into intestinal problems, the pill may not be absorbed. Ask your physician about these matters.

STUDENT TRAVELLERS

Students are eligible for all sorts of discounts, which are detailed in this book when possible. An ISIC will need to be shown (see the earlier Documents section in this chapter).

TRAVELLING WITH CHILDREN

Successful travel with young children can require some special effort. Don't try to overdo things; even for adults, packing too much into the time available can cause problems. And make sure the activities include the kids as well – balance that day sightseeing Lugano's churches with a day at in the miniature fun park (Swissminiatur) at nearby Melide. Include children in the trip planning; if they have helped to work out where you will be going, they will be much more interested when they get there. See Lonely Planet's *Travel with Children* by Maureen Wheeler for much more information.

DISABLED TRAVELLERS

If you have a physical disability, get in touch with your national support organisation (preferably the travel officer if there is one). You'll be surprised how much they can tell you about travelling independently or on package tours. They often have complete libraries devoted to travel, and can put you in touch with travel agents who specialise in tours for the disabled.

The British-based Royal Association for Disability and Rehabilitation (RADAR) publishes a useful guide titled *Holidays and Travel Abroad: A Guide for Disabled People*, which gives a good overview of facilities available to disabled travellers in Europe. Contact RADAR (☎ 071-637 5400) at 25 Mortimer St, London W1N 8AB.

Within Switzerland, hotels with three stars and above invariably have a lift in addition to stairs. More basic places often don't. The SNTO produces a booklet *Swiss Hotel Guide for the Disabled* that categorises hotels according to ease of access for wheelchair users and those with walking difficulties. Criteria assessed include width of doorways and accessibility of toilets. The same booklets also lists which health spas and other resorts are suitable for a variety of medical complaints.

GAY & LESBIAN TRAVELLERS

Gays and lesbians should also get in touch with their national organisation. This book lists several contact addresses and gay and lesbian venues in the main towns, but your organisation should be able to give you much more comprehensive information. The *Spartacus International Gay Guide*, published by Bruno Gmünder (Berlin), is a good international directory of gay entertainment venues worldwide (mainly for men). The same publisher also puts out *Stuttgart & Zürich Von Hinten*, with comprehensive information for those cities and it covers most of Switzerland. For lesbians, the international *Gaia's Guide* and *Places of Interest for Women* is recommended. Within Switzerland, contact the Schweizerische Organisation der Homosexuellen (☎ 01-271 70 11), Sihlquai 67, PO Box 70 88, CH-8023 Zürich; or the Lesbian Organisation of Switzerland (LOS/OSL) (☎ 061-25 40 95), c/o LIBS, Frauenzimmer, Klingentalgraben 2, CH-4000, Basel.

Public attitudes to homosexuality in Switzerland are reasonably tolerant. The revision of the criminal code on sexual offences, granting equality of treatment under the law for homosexuals, was approved by referendum in May 1992. That means, among other things, that the age of consent for gay sex is the same as for heterosexuals: 16. The Swiss gay scene, according to the Spartacus guide, is 'renown for its high standards of service, cleanliness and friendliness'. There are a number of gay bars and saunas in all the main cities.

SENIOR TRAVELLERS

Senior citizens are entitled to many discounts in Europe on things like public transport (but no longer on Swiss railways), museum admission fees etc, provided they show proof of their age. The minimum qualifying age for Swiss people is 65 for men, and 62 for women. Legislation has been proposed that will raise the age for women to 64.

In your home country, a lower age may already entitle you to all sorts of interesting travel packages and discounts (on car hire, for instance) through organisations and travel agents that cater for senior travellers. Start hunting at your local senior citizens advice bureau.

SPECIAL DIETS

If you have dietary restrictions, tourist offices should be able to help with lists of suitable restaurants. Information on vegetarian places is given in this book for all major towns. See also the Food section later in this chapter. The *Jewish Travel Guide* published by Jewish Chronicle Publications details kosher restaurants, synagogues, and relevant institutions. There are seven pages just on Switzerland in its worldwide listings.

DANGERS & ANNOYANCES

The average Swiss person's idea of living-on-the-edge law-breaking is to drop a sweet-wrapper on the pavement, or maybe if they're feeling really anarchic, a bit of jay-walking (for which a fine is theoretically possible, but unlikely). That's not to knock the Swiss – rather that than the situation in somewhere like New York, where trading gunshots is a polite way to say hello. The Swiss are very rule-oriented, and the average person will have no qualms about pointing out to you any transgression you might make. Crime may be relatively uncommon but it's not unknown, so don't become too casual about security. The recent rise in unemployment and the growing drug problem among the young can only make matters worse.

Emergency telephone numbers you can call if you have a problem are police, ☎ 117, fire brigade, ☎ 118, motoring assistance, ☎ 140, and ambulance, ☎ 144 (most areas).

Theft

You're never more vulnerable to theft than when travelling. Guard your most important possessions – passport, papers, tickets and money – next to your skin in a money belt or in a sturdy leather pouch on your belt. Train station lockers or luggage storage counters are useful places to store your luggage (but not valuables) while you get your bearings in a new town. Be very suspicious about people who offer to help you operate your locker. Carry your own padlock for hostel lockers.

You can further lessen the risks by being careful of snatch thieves. Cameras or shoulder bags are great for these people – a small daypack is more secure. Pickpockets are most active in dense crowds, especially in busy train stations and peak-hour public transport. A common ploy is for one person to distract you while another zips through your pockets. (Some of these types would make great magicians!)

Be careful even in hotels; don't leave valuables lying around in your room. Also be wary of sudden friendships – you never know what they may be after. Parked cars are prime targets for petty criminals in most cities, and cars with foreign number plates and/or rental agency stickers in particular. Don't ever leave valuables in the car, and remove all luggage overnight, even (some would say especially) if it's in a parking garage. Another ploy (though rare in Switzerland), is for muggers to pull up alongside your car and point to the wheel; when you get out to have a look, you become one more robbery statistic. While driving in cities, beware of snatch thieves when you pull up at the lights – keep doors locked and windows rolled up high. In case of theft or loss, always report the incident to the police and ask for a statement, or your travel insurance won't pay out.

Generally, keep your wits about you, and be wary of any scam that seems too good to be true. Sadly, other travellers are sometimes the people you most have to guard against.

Photocopies The loss of your passport is a real hassle, but it can be made a little easier if, somewhere else, you've got a record of its number and issue date, or even better, photocopies of the relevant data pages. A photocopy of your birth certificate can also be useful.

While you're compiling that information, add the serial numbers of your travellers' cheques (cross them off as you cash them in) and photocopies of your credit cards, airline ticket and other travel documents. Keep all this emergency material totally separate from your passport, cheques and other cash, and leave extra copies with someone you can rely on back home. Add some emergency money, say US$50, to this separate stash as well. If you do lose your passport, notify the police immediately to get a statement, and contact your nearest consulate.

Drugs
Always treat drugs with a great deal of caution. Don't ever think about trying to carry drugs across the border. There is a fair bit of dope available, and young Swiss in places like Geneva aren't particularly shy about smoking it in public parks. It's illegal of course, but the police tend not to do much about it. If you're unlucky and get caught with a small amount of dope you might just get a small fine, say around Sfr100 to Sfr200. Possession of over about 30 grams and you may be looked upon as a dealer, and possibly liable for a large fine and jail or deportation. The police spend more time trying to solve the heroin problem, possession of which can get you in real trouble.

Local Laws
There are 26 different cantons, and each has its own cantonal laws. Generally the rules and regulations are the same, but there may be some variation in specifics. In Zürich, for example, women are not allowed to use or carry a pepper spray *(Pfefferspray)* to deter attackers, whereas in neighbouring Aargau they are. Similarly, busking (playing music in the streets) may be allowed in some places and not in others. Very confusing for a visitor, but all you can do is ask the local police or tourist office if you're unsure about anything.

WORK

It's not impossible to find legal work. Obviously your chances are vastly improved if you're fluent in at least one of the local languages. The trick is to start writing or asking around early. September is almost too late for the winter season and April the latest for the summer (many places close in May). If you do find a temporary job, the pay is likely to be less than that offered to locals, but the rates will still be good.

Work Permits

Officially, only foreigners with special skills can work legally and the job offer and paperwork should be sorted out before departure. Getting a work permit in this way can be tough, but in practice people manage to find work upon arrival just by asking around. Although it's beyond their brief, tourist offices can often be helpful. Employers sometimes have unallocated work permits that they can assign to you, or there's always the possibility of undeclared cash-in-hand work. If you get caught working illegally you can be fined and deported.

The seasonal 'A' permit *(Permis A, Saisonbewilligung)* is valid for up to nine months, and the elusive and much sought-after 'B' permit *(Permis B, Aufenthalts-bewilligung)* is renewable and valid for a year.

The situation should ease for Europeans if Switzerland eventually joins the EC.

Types of Work

Language skills are particularly crucial for any type of work in service industries. Wages are about the highest in Europe, even for casual workers. Generally, the ski resorts are the most likely places for people to find work. *Working in Ski Resorts – Europe* (paperback) by Victoria Pybus and Charles James provides specific information and case histories. Potentially all sorts of jobs are available during the season, ranging from snow clearing to washing dishes. Hotel work has the advantage of including meals and accommodation. Within Switzerland, check the ads for hotel and restaurant staff in the weekly newspaper, *hotel & touristik revue*.

In October, work is available in vineyards in Vaud and Valais. Rates are good and the quality of accommodation and food offered to grape-pickers is usually better than in other countries.

Work Your Way Around the World by Susan Griffith (paperback) gives good, practical advice on a wide range of issues. The same publisher, Vacation Work, has a book titled *The Au Pair and Nanny's Guide to Working Abroad* by Susan Griffith & Sharon Legg (paperback), which may also help. Busking (playing music in the street) is not uncommon in Switzerland and may make

---

26 Countries in One.

Switzerland is viewed as being a single country since the Rütli meadow oath in 1291. Yet up to 1848 the cantons were more-or-less independent states with separate armies, currencies and customs duties between each border. Even now they have their own constitution, government, police force, laws, courts and schools. Some cantons even describe themselves as a republic to emphasise their independence (eg Jura, Neuchâtel). Income tax levels vary between the cantons, and the fees charged for obtaining Swiss citizenship varies enormously too (Sfr75,000 for some communes in Geneva, down to purely administrative costs in Glarus).

Four categories of control have been identified in the the sharing of power between country and canton. In the first category, the federal government has absolute authority: customs, currency, post and telecommunications, railways and navigation. In the second, the cantons are in charge: police, social services, housing and religion. In the third, the legislative powers belong to the Confederation, but the cantons are responsible for implementation: weights and measures, road traffic, military affairs, unemployment, social insurance, and civil and criminal courts. In the fourth category, powers are shared: taxation, road construction, hunting and fishing, health insurance, education and training. ∎

you a few francs if you have the required skills. Check with the local police if you plan to do this, as there are usually regulations on where and for how long you can play.

ACTIVITIES

The outdoor life is a bigger draw than the cities in Switzerland. The mountains and lakes make more than just a pretty picture; they're a natural playground for sporty types.

Various activity programmes are offered by travel agents. SSR has various summer and winter options, including high-altitude ski touring, ski safaris, trekking and climbing. Prices vary, but are in the region of Sfr600 for a weekend and Sfr1000 to Sfr1300 for a week. Jugi Tours is a travel agent for youth hostel members and is generally cheaper. Most packages include some level of tuition. (See the Useful Organisations section for more information about SSR and Jugi Tours.)

Skiing

There are dozens of ski resorts throughout the Alps, the Pre-Alps and the Jura. Those resorts favoured by the package-holiday companies do not necessarily have better skiing facilities, but they do tend to have more diversions off the slopes, in terms of sightseeing and nightlife. Make sure your travel insurance covers you for winter sports.

The skiing season generally lasts from early December to late March, though at higher altitudes, skiing is possible until way into the summer. Snow conditions can vary greatly from one year to another, so telephone ahead to the tourist office to ask about the state of the runs. January can get cold on the slopes. Christmas and February tend to be the best (and busiest!) months, and most resorts are fairly dead in May and November.

Ski passes provide transport to the slopes, but it might be cheaper for beginners to buy ski coupons where available if they only want to try a couple of experimental runs. Prices for ski passes are usually quoted in this book for one day (and sometimes one week to give an idea of the relative cost) but

you can invariably specify the exact number of days you want, or even buy segments of one day. Expect to pay around Sfr40 to Sfr50 for a one-day pass, reducing over longer periods.

Equipment can always be hired at resorts; charges average about Sfr35/20 per day for downhill/cross-country gear. You can buy new equipment at reasonable prices. It's also worth looking around for ski dumps, as the Swiss are so affluent they tend to throw away perfectly usable equipment.

Cross-country skiing *(Langlauf, ski de fond)* is nearly as popular as downhill skiing, and Switzerland's trails compare to the best in Scandinavia. It works out much cheaper than downhill skiing, as lift tickets are rarely required.

Switzerland has some of the best downhill skiing in Europe, but it's no surprise to discover that it is also about the most expensive. If you're contemplating nipping across the border to look for cheaper skiing, France is almost as expensive, Austria and Germany a bit cheaper, and Italy cheaper still. But price isn't everything. There's not many places that can compare with Swiss resorts such as Zermatt and Verbier for the combination of great skiing, great scenery, and great nightlife.

There are also many schools where you can learn to ski in Switzerland. All the ski resorts listed in this book have at least one ski school (there are around 200 in total), and you can join a group class or pay for individual tuition on a per lesson basis. It shouldn't be necessary to arrange these in advance.

Hiking

There are 50,000 km of designated footpaths (*Wanderweg*) with regular refreshment stops en route. Bright yellow direction signs along the trail make it difficult to get lost; each usually gives an average walking time to the next destination. Yellow markers are often painted on trees alongside the path. At higher altitudes, signs and markers for mountain paths (*Bergweg*) are red. Not surprisingly, the best trails are away from the towns and in the hills. If you can afford it, take a cable car to get you started. A good guide for hiking in the Swiss Alps is *Walking in Switzerland* by Brian Spencer (paperback).

Try and go on one of the 'planetary paths', conceived as a scale version of the solar system with information boards and mini planets. The one in the Anniviers Valley in Valais has the best models of the planets and higher mountain peaks at which to gaze. See also Emmental, Doubs Basins and Zürich.

An organisation that promotes hiking in Switzerland is Schweizer Wanderwege (☎ 061-601 15 35), Im Hirshalm 49, CH-4125, Riehen.

Mountaineering

Mountaineering is not for the uninitiated and you should never climb on your own. There are well-established mountaineering schools in Pontresina and Meiringen, and in many other locations. Zermatt is perhaps the most famous destination for experienced mountaineers, and has a Mountain Guides Office to help organise climbs in the region. For information also contact the Swiss Alpine Club (which maintains huts for overnight stays at altitude) or the Mountain Guides Federation. Addresses are given in the Useful Organisations section earlier in this chapter.

Ski mountaineering is popular along the Haute Route in Valais. See Verbier, Zermatt and Saas Fee for more information.

Aerial Sports

Mountains are made for paragliding and hang-gliding. Both are popular, especially the former, and the equipment is more portable. Many resorts have places where you can hire the gear, get tuition, or simply go as a passenger on a flight. Ballooning is also taking off, despite the high costs. Château d'Oex is one of the best-known locations.

Water Sports

The lakes are equally as developed for sports as the mountains. Water-skiing, sailing and windsurfing are common on most lakes, especially the latter two activities. Courses

are usually available, especially in Graubünden and central Switzerland.

There are over 350 beaches in the country, most of which are private and require an entrance fee (around Sfr5 per day). Anglers should contact the local tourist office for a fishing permit valid for lakes and rivers.

The Rotsee, near Lucerne, is a favourite place for rowing. Rafting is possible on many Alpine rivers including the Rhine (see the Graubünden chapter) and the Saane (see the Bernese Oberland chapter). Canoeing is mainly centred on the Muota in the Schwyz canton and on the Doubs River in the Jura. Paddleboats (*Pedalos*) are usually waiting for hire in lakeside resorts.

Courses

Apart from learning new physical skills, you can enrich your mind in a variety of structured ways. Probably the best organisation for adult education courses in Switzerland is the Migros klubschule (école-club, scuola club). It has schools in all the large towns and cities, and offers a huge number of courses, including mainstream and marginal subjects as astrology, astronomy, bonsai, cooking, dance, karate, photography, politics and music. It also has comprehensive coverage of languages, including Swiss-German.

Most courses last for 10 weeks to one year, and prices tend to be lower than in other institutions. Studying French in French-speaking Switzerland, for example, would cost Sfr510 for 60-hour tuition over 10 weeks. An intensive course is also offered: 15 or 20 hours per week over two weeks, costing Sfr142.50 or Sfr190 per week. There are three terms a year, starting in mid-August, mid-January and mid-April. Write in advance for information at the schools mentioned in the sections on Bern, Zürich, Geneva and Lugano. The language school, Inlingua, also has many outlets in Switzerland.

HIGHLIGHTS
Castles & Churches

There are many interesting castles scattered through the country. The Château de Chillon is one of the most famous (see the Montreux section in the Lake Geneva chapter). Also try and take a day tour of the castles around Lake Thun. Basel and Bern both have fine cathedrals. The most impressive abbey churches in the country, quite breathtaking in their scale, are those in Einsiedeln and St Gallen.

Museums & Galleries

Basel and Zürich each has an excellent art museum, the Kunstmuseum and the Kunsthaus. Getting away from the mainstream, my personal favourite is the bizarre l'Art Brut collection in Lausanne. Zürich's national museum (Schweizerisches Landesmuseum) gives the most complete rundown of Swiss life and times, making all but redundant equivalent regional museums. The sprawling Art and History Museum in Geneva covers a bit of everything. The best clock and watch museum is probably the Museum of Horology in La Chaux de Fonds.

Picturesque Town Centres

Rathausplatz in Stein am Rhein is harmonious and perfectly preserved; the main street in Gruyères is almost as photogenic. Lucerne is worthy of its fame. Schaffhausen and St Gallen sport fine centres bristling with oriel windows. Bern is unbelievably quaint for a capital city. Murten, and to a lesser extent, Estavayer-le-Lac, proudly display ancient centres ringed by fortifications, virtually unchanged by time.

Scenery & Ski Resorts

In a country so blessed with beautiful vistas it is difficult to select favourites. You can't get much better than the view from Schilthorn, or from its neighbour across the valley, Jungfrau. The three or four-pass tour (see the Meiringen section in the Bernese Oberland chapter) is unforgettable on a fine day. The mountains and lakes combination seen from one of the summits round Lake Lucerne (Mt Pilatus, Mt Rigi, Mt Stanserhorn) is as seductive as views from higher peaks. The ski resorts invariably provide great panoramas to go with the pistes. Zermatt has excellent skiing and inspiring views of the

Matterhorn. Davos and Verbier offer some of the best skiing in the world.

ACCOMMODATION

Accommodation is efficiently classified and graded according to the type of establishment and level of comfort. Tourist offices invariably have extensive lists of everything available, usually listing prices and facilities on-site. Often the office will find and book hotels and pensions for little or no commission. They tend not to find the really budget places, but this service could save you a lot of time and effort, especially in somewhere like Zürich where finding a place to stay can be a problem. It's wise to book ahead where possible anyway: sometimes a deposit is required, sometimes a phone call is sufficient.

Hotels, pensions and hostels almost always include breakfast as standard. This can range from a couple of rolls and a beverage in cheaper places to a fully-fledged breakfast buffet in three-star places and above. Unless stated otherwise, you can assume that the places listed in this book do *include* breakfast in the price per night.

Except in some towns and cities, it is normal to have a low, middle and high season. Prices in budget hotels tend not to change very much, but the price difference in higher-rated hotels can be quite marked, especially in mountain resorts. In this book, prices are usually quoted as 'starting from...', in other words the *low season* price. You may therefore have to pay more than you anticipate, but the relative increase should be consistent between rival hotels. Another thing to bear in mind is that most hotels have a range of rooms available. Price is dependent on size, facilities and fittings. You may not always be able to get the cheapest rooms. The more you pay, the better it gets. At the budget level, the IYHF youth hostel in Lugano and Balmer's Herberge in Interlaken definitely stand out. Palazzo Salis in Soglio offers palatial trappings while only charging minimal prices. Teufelhof in Basel (mid-price) gives the unique opportunity to sleep in a piece of art. The ultimate in top-class accommodation is Badrutt's Palace in St Moritz.

Camping

There are about 450 camp sites, which are classified from one to five stars depending upon their amenities and convenience of location. They are often scenically situated in an out-of-the-way place by a river or lake. Fine if you're exploring the countryside, but a bit of a pain if you want to sightsee in a town. For this reason, and because you have so much extra gear to carry, camping is more viable if you have your own transport. Hostels, especially for solo travellers, don't work out much more expensive. Charges per night are around Sfr5 per person plus Sfr3 to Sfr5 for a tent, and the same for a car. Many sites offer a slight discount if you have a Camping Carnet. Camping Gaz replacement canisters are widely available.

Free camping *(Wildes camping)* is not strictly allowed and should be discreet, but it is perfectly viable in the wide open mountain spaces, and is fairly common in places like Ticino. If the police come across you, they may not do anything (especially if you've been responsible with your rubbish) or they may move you on. A fine is theoretically possible. Farmers might let you pitch on their land – but ask first.

Youth Hostels

Staying in dormitories is easily the cheapest way to get a roof over your head. Youth hostel dorms usually have four to six beds but are sometimes much larger. Family rooms or double rooms for couples are sometimes available. A major pain with youth hostels is the tendency for the doors and reception to be closed during the day, usually from 9 am to 5 pm. Occasionally keys are available to avoid the equally annoying night-time curfew (usually between 10 pm and midnight). Youth hostels have some communal facilities but rarely, unfortunately, use of a kitchen.

Youth hostel is *Jugendherberge* in German, *Auberge de jeunesse* in French, and *Alloggio per giovanni* in Italian. There is a

good network of hostels (about 80) spread throughout the country which are members of the Swiss Youth Hostel Association. They are therefore automatically affiliated with the International Youth Hostel Federation (IYHF). Membership cards must be shown, and precedence is given to those aged over 25. Prices are in the range of Sfr10 to Sfr22. Nonmembers pay a Sfr7 'guest fee', but that's not as bad as it sounds, as six guest fees add up to a full membership card. However, you're better off paying a one-off fee of Sfr30 for international membership, and becoming a member in your country of residence is even cheaper.

National YHA offices include:

Australia
Each state has its own Youth Hostel Association. The National Administration Office is at Australian Youth Hostels Association, Level 3, 10 Mallett St, Camperdown, NSW 2050 (☎ 02-565 1699)
Canada
Canadian Hostelling Association, 1600 James Naismith Drive, Suite 608, Gloucester, Ontario K1B 5N4 (☎ 613-748 5638)
England & Wales
Youth Hostels Association, Trevelyan House, 8 St Stephen's Hill, St Albans, Herts AL1 2DY (☎ 0727-55215)
New Zealand
Youth Hostels Association of New Zealand, PO Box 436, 173 Gloucester St, Christchurch 1 (☎ 03-799 970)
Northern Ireland
Youth Hostel Association of Northern Ireland, 56 Bradbury Place, Belfast BT7 1RU (☎ 0232-324733)
Scotland
Scottish Youth Hostels Association, 7 Glebe Crescent, Stirling FK8 2JA (☎ 0786-51181)
USA
American Youth Hostels Inc, PO Box 37613, Washington, DC 200013-7613 (☎ 202-783 6161)

Hostels do get full, and telephone reservations are not accepted. Write, or use the excellent telefax service. Under this system, Swiss hostels will reserve ahead to the next hostel for you but you must give specific dates. The cost is only Sfr1 plus a Sfr9 refundable deposit, and you must claim your bed by 7 pm. Hostels sell a worthwhile guide called *Discover Switzerland*, giving sightseeing highlights in the vicinity of most youth hostels. It also includes an excellent map giving full details of all hostels on the reverse, including their fax numbers. The price of the book varies depending on where you buy it: Chur youth hostel charges Sfr2.50; other hostels up to Sfr4. The map is available free of charge by itself from SNTO.

It is rare to be asked to do chores in hostels, other than simply clearing away your meal things and returning bed sheets to the laundry basket. In busy times a three-day maximum stay may apply. Sheets are nearly always provided in hostels at no extra cost (or rather, there is a cost, but you must use theirs anyway) so you will only save money on the odd occasion by bringing your own.

Other Hostels & Dormitories

Private hostels of the 'backpacker' type are quite rare, but dormitory accommodation in ski resorts definitely isn't. Take care in studying accommodation lists, as the dormitory *(Touristenlager, Massenlager)* may only take groups. It's not unusual for mattresses to be crammed side by side in massive bunks in these places; to compensate, there is usually no curfew restrictions or the hassle of the doors being locked during the day. They are usually run by an adjoining hotel or a restaurant.

Alpine huts tend to be dormitory-style. These are maintained by the Swiss Alpine Club, and there are around 150 of them at higher altitudes. Some are only accessible to experienced climbers. Look out also for Naturfreundehaus (Friends of Nature) hostels. You may come across non-IYHF hostels that are not (or no longer) members because they simply haven't got enough facilities.

Hotels & Pensions

Swiss accommodation is geared towards value for money rather than low cost, so even bottom-of-the-range rooms are fairly comfortable. High-season prices can be 10% to 40% higher than in the low season, but exactly when the high season occurs varies from region to region. In ski resorts in winter, terms may be on a half-board basis, and there may be a minimum stay stipulation.

Pensions tend to be smaller-scale, more personal, and cheaper than hotels. The majority are simple affairs, yet there are more expensive ones where you will find attached bathrooms and other luxuries. Prices start at around Sfr40/60 for a basic single/double room in a small town or village. Count on at least Sfr10 more per person for a room with a shower. Places in cities and the top resorts may be much more expensive. Hotels can also be fairly basic, but more often they are geared towards affluent tourists and business people.

Swiss levels of service are renowned throughout the world. Hotels and pensions are star rated according to an efficient and standardised system, and almost invariably, you get the level of comfort you're prepared to pay for. The ratings are reliable, but don't be afraid to check the room and the bathroom if you have any doubts, or to compare the quality with other hotels nearby. In older hotels the rooms may vary in size, yet cost the same, so it could be worth asking to view several rooms in the same place.

Ask if there are discounts for longer stays or if anything costs extra (such as breakfast, room service etc). If you discover anything wrong with the room after you've paid – complain right away. Check where the fire exits are. If you can't afford what's offered, ask for something cheaper – there may be a smaller/older room they haven't told you about. If you're with a group or plan to stay for a reasonable length of time, it's always worth trying to negotiate a special rate. Don't be afraid to haggle for a reduction in low season even if you're only staying a couple of nights; it often works.

The top hotels in Switzerland are among the top hotels in the world. Apart from meticulous service, in these places you can expect pristine fixtures and fittings, all the comforts of home, and facilities on site such as a swimming pool, sauna, fitness room (gym), nightclub, bars, elegant boutiques and a gourmet restaurant.

Other

The classification 'Country Inn' denotes a smaller scale establishment, usually in a scenic location. 'Hotel Garni' means bed and breakfast without any extra meals being available. Private houses in rural areas sometimes offer inexpensive rooms; look out for signs saying *Zimmer frei* ('room(s) vacant'). Some farms also take paying guests. Self-catering accommodation is available in holiday chalets, apartments or bungalows. These are often booked out well in advance. Tourist offices will send lists if requested.

Student rooms may be offered during holidays in university towns (such as in Geneva), which can be very good value.

FOOD

The Swiss emphasis on quality extends to meals. Basic restaurants provide simple but well-cooked food, and prices are generally high. Many budget travellers rely on picnic provisions from supermarkets, but even here prices can be a shock with cheese costing over Sfr2 a kilo! The main supermarket chains are Migros and Coop.

In the larger Migros and Coop outlets, and in many department stores (especially the EPA chain) there are inexpensive self-service restaurants which are rarely licensed for alcohol. These are great value and the food is always fairly palatable, sometimes downright tasty. Usually these restaurants are open to around 6.30 pm on weekdays (sometimes with late opening on Thursday) and until 4 or 5 pm on Saturdays. In most towns they are the cheapest place for a hot meal, with dishes starting at around Sfr7.

University restaurants (*mensas*) are a real bargain, even if the food tends to be fairly bland. Some (eg in Bern and Zürich) are freely open to everyone. Others are supposed to be restricted to ISIC-carrying students or local students, but controls are rarely tight and you can usually get away with it if you're determined.

Buffet-style restaurant chains, like Manora and Inova, offer good food at low prices. Don't be put off by the description 'self-service' – they are comfortable inside, the food is freshly cooked in front of you, and you can sometimes select the ingredients yourself. Some wine bars *(Weinstübli)* and beer taverns *(Bierstübli)* serve meals.

The *Weltwoche* newspaper annually compiles a list of the 100 best restaurants in Switzerland. It draws on existing well-respected guides as well as local information from testers and regional media. In 1992 the top three restaurants held on to their 1991 rating. They are:

Girardet (☎ 021-634 05 05), 1 Rue d'Yverdon, Crissier, near Lausanne, Vaud.
Petermann's Kunststuben (☎ 01-910 07 15), Mittlere Bahnhofstrasse 4, Küsnacht, near Zürich.
Le Pont de Brent (☎ 021-964 52 30), Brent, near Blonay, Vaud.

Many of the other restaurants in the top 100 are listed in the appropriate town sections. In the mid-price territory, dining at Speranza in Bellinzona is a memorable experience.

The best value is a fixed-menu dish of the day *(Tagesteller, plat du jour,* or *piatto del giorno)*, frequently available at midday only. Fast-food joints are proliferating. McDonald's are popping up everywhere (even in restaurant cars). Kiosks often sell cheap snacks that, like sausage and bread in St Gallen, are as much a regional speciality as the fancy dishes.

Main meals in Switzerland are eaten at noon. Cheaper restaurants tend to be fairly rigid in when they serve; lunch is noon to around 1.30pm and dinner about 6.30 to 9 or 9.30 pm. Don't be fooled if some of the closing times given in this book are much later; the place may stay open several hours after the kitchen closes, catering for drinkers. Go to a hotel or more up-market restaurant for more flexible, later eating. Pizzerias are an inexpensive yet flexible option; it's not unusual for the ovens to be kept glowing straight through from around 11 am to 11 pm. The self-service places are normally flexible during the day, too.

Dedicated vegetarian restaurants can be hard to come by, but it's common nowadays for restaurants to offer one or two non-meat choices. *Fitness Tellers* for the calorie counters are a growing phenomenon, especially in ski resorts.

The classier restaurants tend to have pretensions towards *nouvelle cuisine*, with beautifully presented but fairly insubstantial courses. Carbohydrates are anathema in these places, as if they're trying to distance themselves from the filling meat-and-potatoes fare of earthier joints.

Monday and Tuesday are the quietest nights in restaurants, and some places take the opportunity to have a rest day *(Ruhetag)*. Weekends are the busiest times, yet surprisingly some of the very top restaurants in the towns close on Saturday and/or Sunday, probably because they get a lot of their trade from expense-account business people.

Swiss Cuisine

Switzerland hasn't got a great indigenous gastronomic tradition – instead, Swiss dishes borrow from the best of German and French cuisine. In addition, Zürich and particularly Geneva have loads of restaurants of all sorts of nationalities. Ticino has its own interesting specialities. You don't have to spend a fortune to enjoy a meal; lunch on a mountain top or by a lake with a fresh stick of bread, some local cheese and salami and a tomato or two, washed down with a cheap bottle of local wine, can be one of the recurring highlights of any trip.

The typical breakfast is of the continental variety. *Müsli* (sometimes spelled Muesli) was invented in Switzerland at the end of the 19th century but few people seem to eat it in its country of origin – *Birchermüsli* is the most common variety. Soups are popular and often very filling, and sometimes contain small dumplings *(Knöpfli)*.

Cheeses form an important part of the Swiss diet. Emmentaler and Gruyère are combined with white wine to create *fondue*, which is served up in a vast pot and eaten with bread cubes. According to tradition, if your cube leaps off your fork and disappears in the pot, you have to buy a round of drinks. *Raclette* is another melted cheese dish, usually served with potatoes and small onions.

Rösti (crispy, fried, shredded potatoes) is German Switzerland's national dish. A wide variety of *Wurst* (sausage) is available. Veal is highly rated throughout Switzerland. In Zürich it is thinly sliced and served in a cream sauce *(Geschnetzeltes Kalbsfleisch)*. *Bündnerfleisch* is air-dried beef, smoked and thinly sliced. Fresh fish from the numerous lakes frequently crop up on menus, especially perch and trout. Swiss chocolate, excellent by itself, is often used in desserts and cakes. Local specialities are usually mentioned in the main chapters.

Food Glossary These are some food terms you may come across in German (G), French (F) and Italian (I):

Soup
    Suppe (G), Potage or consommé (F), Brodo (I)
Shrimp cocktail
    Krevetten Cocktail (G), Cocktail de crevettes (F), Cocktail di gamberi (I)
Butter-fried trout
    Forelle Müllerinart (G), Truite à la meunière (F), Trota fritata al burro (I)
Whitefish fillets (with almonds)
    Felchenfilets (mit Mandeln) (G), Filets de féra (aux amandes) (F), Filetti di coregone (alla mandorle) (I)
Grilled Salmon
    Grillierter Salm (G), Saumon grillé (F), Trota salmonata alla griglia (I)
Veal
    Kalb (G), Veau (F), Vitello (I)
Fillet of beef
    Rindsfilet (G), Filet de boeuf (F), Filetto di manzo (I)
Sirloin steak
    Zwischenrippenstück (G), Entrecôte (F), Costata di manzo (I)
Pork
    Schwein (G), Porc (F), Maiale (I)

Lamb cultlets
Lammkoteletten (G), Côte d'agneau (F),
Entrecôte d'agnello (I)
Boiled potatoes
Salzkartoffeln (G), Pommes nature (F),
Patate bollite (I)
Rice
Reis (G), Riz (F), Riso bianco (I)
Vegetables
Gemüse (G), Légumes (F), Vedura (I)
Noodles
Nudeln (G), Nouilles (F), Tagiatelle (I)
Ice cream
Rahmeis (G), Glace (F), Gelato (I)
Fruit salad
Fruchsalat (G), Macédoine de fruits (F)
Macedonia di frutta

DRINK

Mineral water is readily available but tap
water is fine to drink. Coffee is more popular
than tea – the latter will come without milk
unless you ask specially for it. Hot chocolate
is also popular. The health-conscious should
be aware that milk from Alpine cows contains a high level of fat.

Some restaurants are alcohol free but otherwise alcohol licensing laws are not very
restrictive. You're more likely to be
restricted by the cost. Beer and wine prices
in basic beer halls or café aren't too bad
(comparatively speaking), but chic bars can
be very expensive. Spirits are expensive
everywhere. Happily, beer and wine prices
in supermarkets are fairly low.

In bars, lager beer comes in 0.3 or 0.5-litre
bottles, or on draught *(Bier vom Fass, bière
à la pression, birra alla pressione)* with measures ranging from 0.2 to 0.5 litre. There isn't
the tradition of beer-drinking as there is in

Müsli

It's a funny thing about müsli (müseli). It was invented in Switzerland at the end of the 19th century but few people seem to eat it in its country of origin. Go into any supermarket in Italy and half the shelves will be taken up with a thousand different varieties of pasta. In Swiss supermarkets you find maybe a couple of müsli packets tucked away in the corner and that's it. You're hardly force-fed the stuff as a visitor – it usually appears at lavish breakfast-buffets in the higher-class hotels, but the basic hotel breakfast is rolls, cheese, meat and jam, and that reflects national eating patterns.

So what's the story? Could it be an invidious modern invention that the Swiss created largely to inflict upon the rest of humanity, like life insurance salesmen? (the Swiss developed the modern formula for life insurance); something that nobody really likes but feels compelled to put up with for reasons of health or security? The official tale is that Dr Bircher-Benner created the stuff as a nutritious and healthy food to serve to patients in his private clinic in Zürich. But I think it could have been invented something like this:

Mr and Mrs Müsli, hard-up farm folk, awoke one morning at the crack of dawn to find no food in the house for breakfast – no bread, butter, meat, cheese or jam. The shops wouldn't be open for ages, so they searched the farm for stuff they normally spread on the fields, or gave to the farm animals.

'Here's some chicken feed,' cried Mrs Müsli triumphantly.

'And some bonemeal,' yelled Mr Müsli.

'And what about this old bag of oats?'

More leftovers were discovered, and everything they found was thrown into a big basin and mixed together. Unfortunately the whole thing looked like an unappetising stodge, so in desper-ation they turned to the fruit bowl. There was an old apple, shrivelled to the core, that was chopped up and chucked in.

'What about these old grapes?'

'But they're wizened and rock hard!'

'Never mind. In they go!'

They could find nothing else, and before they dared try the concoction, they drowned it in rich Alpine milk to try to disguise the taste. It didn't work.

'This is terrible,' said Mrs Müsli.

'I know,' said Mr Müsli, 'but we've got a whole vat full of the stuff now. I wonder if we can sell it?' ■

Top Left: Electric taxis, Zermatt, Valais (MH)
Top Right: Mt Pilatus funicular, Lake Lucerne, Central Switzerland (MH)
Bottom Left: Cable car, Lake Lucerne, Central Switzerland (MH)
Bottom Right: Milk urn transport, Klewenalp, Central Switzerland (MH)

Top: The Aare River, Bern (MH)
Bottom Left: Fountain of Justice, Bern (MH)
Bottom Right: Clock tower (Zeitglockenturm), Bern (TW)

neighbouring Germany, but the many small breweries dotted round the country testify to the popularity of the beverage.

Wine is considered an important part of the meal even though it is rather expensive. Local wines are generally good but you may not have heard of them before, as output can not even meet domestic demand so they are rarely exported. The main growing region is the French-speaking part of the country, particularly in Valais and by Lake Neuchâtel and Lake Geneva (Lac Léman in French). Both red and white wines are produced, and each region has its own speciality. Ticino is known for Merlot. See the introductions of the Valais and Ticino chapters for more information. There is also a choice of locally produced fruit brandies, often served with or in coffee.

ENTERTAINMENT

So how do the restrained Swiss entertain themselves? An image of a Swiss party is half-a-dozen people seated in front of a bowl of peanuts, passing around a carton of orange juice and humming along to *Heidi Yodels Richard Clayderman's Greatest Hits*. Luckily, it's not that bad, although many people go to bed early. (Let's face it, *Richard Clayderman's Greatest Hits* must be a short record.)

The Swiss read more newspapers and watch less TV than any other European nation. Listening to music is popular throughout the country, meaning that classical, folk, jazz and rock concerts can be found in many towns and cities. Two of Switzerland's best known orchestras are the *Tonhalle* in Zürich and the *Suisse Romande* in Geneva. Most headline rock bands eventually find their way to Switzerland. Bern has several good jazz venues.

In German Switzerland, cinemas nearly always show films in the original language. To confirm this, check the advertisements for the upper-case letter: E/f/g means that the film is in English with French and German subtitles. In French Switzerland, look for *VO*, which signifies 'original version'.

Nightlife is not all it could be in the cities, and where it does exist, it is expensive. Geneva is the best place for late nightclubs *(boîtes)*, but Zürich is also lively. Alternative arts flourish in many towns, usually centred in one main venue. Two of the best places are l'Usine in Geneva and Rote Fabrik in Zürich – music, art, theatre, dance and cinema are

---

Tourism Figures

Based on the number of overnight stays in hotels (a total of 20 million per annum), one third of all foreign visitors are German. Next in line (but at only 25% of the German figure) come Britons, followed by Americans, French and Italians. The most popular tourist region by some margin is Graubünden: its mountains and ski resorts attract three million hotel overnighters. Fighting it out for second place with very similar figures are Valais, Central Switzerland and the Bernese Oberland. Zürich actually gets slightly more visitors (2.4 million) than these areas, but a much higher proportion are business visitors.

The northern regions are less visited by foreigners, recording under one million stays. The Bernese Mittelland is surprisingly low in the list, with 0.5 million overnighters. Languishing at the bottom of the table is Fribourg, Neuchâtel and Jura, with just 0.3 million. Across the country, the summer season (May to October) brings nearly 50% more hotel overnighters than the winter.

Foreign tourists staying in holiday apartments, hostels and camp sites add 16 million overnight stays. The breakdown of visitors per nationality is more-or-less the same as for hotels, except that the Benelux countries show a higher proportion. In these categories of accommodation, summer is still the most important season, with around 20% more visitors than the winter.

Foreign visitors staying in hotels spend an average of Sfr114 on lodgings, Sfr55 on meals and Sfr72 on incidentals, giving a total per day of Sfr241.Those in holiday apartments spend respectively Sfr23, Sfr27 and Sfr24, in a daily total of Sfr74. Campers spend Sfr9, Sfr23 and Sfr22 (total Sfr54) and youth hostellers spend Sfr19, Sfr22 and Sfr12 (total Sfr53). Under 'incidentals', the greatest expenditure is on petrol, followed by tobacco and sweets. ■

featured. Zürich and Geneva are also the best places to catch up on English-language theatre.

Football is a popular spectator sport, with most towns having their own professional team. Alpine festivals are common in the summer in rural villages, whereas tourists in the towns have to make do with folklore shows. A listing of local events is invariably available from tourist offices.

Ski resorts have an atmosphere all their own. 'Après ski' entertainment seems to consist of drinking large amounts in bars and then dancing or falling over in clubs.

THINGS TO BUY

Watches, penknives, textiles and embroidery are all popular buys. Swiss knives range from simple blades (Sfr10) to mini toolboxes (Sfr100 or more). A grotesquely tacky cuckoo clock with a girl bouncing on a spring will set you back at least Sfr20, a musical box anything upwards of Sfr25. Should you want a cowbell to warn people of your arrival, one with a decorative band will cost Sfr14 to Sfr25.

Most of these goods are available in numerous souvenir shops in all tourist centres. Heimat or Heimatwerk shops tend to sell hand-made goods which can be pricey but are generally good quality. Department stores often sell similar products (eg Swiss knives) at more competitive prices. Video and cassette tapes, records and CDs, photographic film and tape recorders are all reasonably priced by European standards. A cheap outlet (especially for film) is Inter Discount, with branches all over Switzerland. EPA is an inexpensive department store.

Getting There & Away

Air travel is the quickest, easiest, and sometimes cheapest means of trans-continental travel. If you're visiting Switzerland from afar, don't overlook the possibility of flying to a European 'gateway' city and overlanding from there. Basel, for example, is only three hours and Sfr76 from Frankfurt by rail. Paris is only four hours and Sfr78 from Geneva by the TGV train. There are some great fares available on certain routes thanks to severe competition between the airlines.

Don't forget that travel insurance usually covers for cancellation or delays in your travel arrangements, as well as ticket loss. Make a point of taking a separate record of all your ticket details, or better still, a photocopy. Buy travel insurance as early as possible, or you may find that you're not covered for delays to your flight caused by strikes or other industrial action that may have been in force before you took out the insurance.

Paying for your ticket with a credit card often provides limited travel accident insurance, and you may be able to reclaim the payment if the operator doesn't deliver. In the UK, for instance, credit card providers are required by law to reimburse consumers if a company goes into liquidation and the amount in contention is more than £100. Ask your credit card company what it's prepared to cover.

AIR

The main entry points for international flights are Zürich and Geneva. Both airports are linked directly to the Swiss rail network. Basel airport is another busy centre, even though it is actually on the French side of the border in Mulhouse. Bern and Lugano airports also take some international flights. There are Swissair luggage check-in facilities at many Swiss train stations.

Remember always to reconfirm your onward or return bookings by the specified time – usually 72 hours before departure on international flights. Otherwise there's a real risk that you'll turn up at the airport only to find that you've missed your flight because it was rescheduled, or that you've been reclassified as a 'no show' (see the Air Travel Glossary later in this chapter), with all the problems that involves if your flight happens to be full.

There is no airport departure tax to pay when flying out of Switzerland.

Buying a Plane Ticket

Acquiring one of these valuable bits of paper can be an intimidating business. There is likely to be a multitude of airlines and travel agents hoping to separate you from your money, and it's always worth putting aside some time to research the current state of the market. Start early: some of the cheapest tickets have to be bought months in advance, and some popular flights sell out early. Look out for special offers that crop up from time to time.

Cheap tickets are available in two distinct categories: official and unofficial. Official ones are advance-purchase tickets, budget fares, Apex, super-Apex or whatever other brand name the airlines may invent as a marketing tool.

Unofficial tickets are simply discounted tickets that the airlines release through selected travel agents. Don't go looking for discounted tickets straight from the airlines; they are only available through travel agents. Airlines can, however, supply information on routes and timetables, and their low-season, student and senior citizens' fares can be very competitive.

Return tickets usually work out cheaper than two one-ways – often *much* cheaper. In some cases, a well-planned return ticket can even be cheaper than a one-way. Open Jaw returns, by which you can travel into one city and out of another, provide some measure of flexibility. In London, Trailfinders (☎ 071-937 5400) and STA (☎ 071-937 9921) can both give you tailor-made versions of these tickets. Your chosen cities needn't necessarily be in the same country.

Round-the-World (RTW) tickets have become very popular in recent years. The airline RTW tickets are often real bargains, and can work out to be no more expensive or even cheaper than an ordinary return ticket. Prices start at about UK£850, A$1800 or US$1300 depending on the season. The official airline RTW tickets are usually put together by a combination of two airlines, and permit you to fly anywhere you want on their route systems so long as you don't backtrack. Other restrictions are that you (usually) must book the first sector in advance and cancellation penalties then apply. There may be restrictions on how many stops you are permitted, and usually the tickets are valid for 90 days up to a year.

Air Travel Glossary

Apex Apex, or 'advance purchase excursion' is a discounted ticket which must be paid for in advance. There are penalties if you wish to change it.

Baggage Allowance This will be written on your ticket; usually one 20 kg item to go in the hold, plus one item of hand luggage.

Bucket Shop An unbonded travel agency specialising in discounted airline tickets.

Bumped Just because you have a confirmed seat doesn't mean you're going to get on the plane – see Overbooking.

Cancellation Penalties If you have to cancel or change an Apex ticket there are often heavy penalties involved, insurance can sometimes be taken out against these penalties. Some airlines impose penalties on regular tickets as well, particularly against 'no show' passengers.

Check In Airlines ask you to check in a certain time ahead of the flight departure (usually 1½ hours on international flights). If you fail to check in on time and the flight is overbooked the airline can cancel your booking and give your seat to somebody else.

Confirmation Having a ticket written out with the flight and date you want doesn't mean you have a seat until the agent has checked with the airline that your status is 'OK' or confirmed. Meanwhile you could just be 'on request'.

Discounted Tickets There are two types of discounted fares – officially discounted (see Promotional Fares) and unofficially discounted. The lowest prices often impose drawbacks like flying with unpopular airlines, inconvenient schedules, or unpleasant routes and connections. A discounted ticket can save you other things than money – you may be able to pay Apex prices without the associated Apex advance booking and other requirements. Discounted tickets only exist where there is fierce competition.

Full Fares Airlines traditionally offer first class (coded F), business class (coded J) and economy class (coded Y) tickets. These days there are so many promotional and discounted fares available from the regular economy class that few passengers pay full economy fare.

Lost Tickets If you lose your airline ticket an airline will usually treat it like a travellers' cheque and, after inquiries, issue you with another one. Legally, however, an airline is entitled to treat it like cash and if you lose it then it's gone forever. Take good care of your tickets.

No Shows No shows are passengers who fail to show up for their flight, sometimes due to unexpected delays or disasters, sometimes due to simply forgetting, sometimes because they made more than one booking and didn't bother to cancel the one they didn't want. Full fare passengers who fail to turn up are sometimes entitled to travel on a later flight. The rest of us are penalised (see Cancellation Penalties).

On Request An unconfirmed booking for a flight, see Confirmation.

An alternative type of RTW ticket is one put together by a travel agent using a combination of discounted tickets.

Generally, you can find discounted tickets at prices as low as or lower than the Apex or budget tickets. Phone around the travel agents for bargains, and don't necessarily believe someone who says they have the last two tickets available to Zürich this year. Find out the fare, the route, the duration of the journey, the stopovers allowed, and any restrictions on the ticket (see Restrictions in the Air Travel Glossary). Ask about cancellation penalties.

If you are travelling from the USA, UK or south-east Asia, you will probably find that the cheapest flights are being advertised by obscure agencies whose names haven't yet reached the telephone directory. Many such firms are honest and solvent, but there are a

---

Open Jaws A return ticket where you fly out to one place but return from another. If available this can save you backtracking to your arrival point.

Overbooking Airlines hate to fly empty seats and since every flight has some passengers who fail to show up (see No Shows) airlines often book more passengers than they have seats. Usually the excess passengers balance those who fail to show up but occasionally somebody gets bumped. If this happens guess who it is most likely to be? The passengers who check in late.

Promotional Fares Officially discounted fares like Apex fares which are available from travel agents or direct from the airline.

Reconfirmation At least 72 hours prior to departure time of an onward or return flight you must contact the airline and 'reconfirm' that you intend to be on the flight. If you don't do this the airline can delete your name from the passenger list and you could lose your seat. You don't have to reconfirm the first flight on your itinerary or if your stopover is less than 72 hours. It doesn't hurt to reconfirm more than once.

Restrictions Discounted tickets often have various restrictions on them – advance purchase is the most usual one (see Apex). Others are restrictions on the minimum and maximum period you must be away, such as a minimum of 14 days or a maximum of one year. See Cancellation Penalties.

Standby A discounted ticket where you only fly if there is a seat free at the last moment. Standby fares are usually only available on domestic routes.

Tickets Out An entry requirement for many countries is that you have an onward or return ticket, in other words, a ticket out of the country. If you're not sure what you intend to do next, the easiest solution is to buy the cheapest onward ticket to a neighbouring country or a ticket from a reliable airline which can later be refunded if you do not use it.

Transferred Tickets Airline tickets cannot be transferred from one person to another. Travellers sometimes try to sell the return half of their ticket, but officials can ask you to prove that you are the person named on the ticket. This is unlikely to happen on domestic flights; on an international flight tickets may be compared with passports.

Travel Agencies Travel agencies vary widely and you should ensure you use one that suits your needs. Some simply handle tours while full-service agencies handle everything from tours and tickets to car rental and hotel bookings. A good one will do all these things and can save you a lot of money but if all you want is a ticket at the lowest possible price, then you really need an agency specialising in discounted tickets. A discounted ticket agency, however, may not be useful for other things, like hotel bookings.

Travel Periods Some officially discounted fares, Apex fares in particular, vary with the time of year. There is often a low (off-peak) season and a high (peak) season. Sometimes there's an intermediate or shoulder season as well. At peak times, when everyone wants to fly, not only will the officially discounted fares be higher but so will unofficially discounted fares or there may simply be no discounted tickets available. Usually the fare depends on your outward flight – if you depart in the high season and return in the low season, you pay the high-season fare. ■

few rogues who will take your money and disappear, to reopen elsewhere a month or two later under a new name. If you feel suspicious about a firm, don't give them all the money at once – leave a deposit of 20% or so and pay the balance when you get the ticket. If they insist on cash in advance, go somewhere else or be prepared to take a very big risk. And once you have the ticket, ring the airline to confirm that you are actually booked onto the flight.

You may decide to pay more than the rock-bottom fare by opting for the safety of a better-known travel agent. Firms such as STA, which has offices worldwide, Council Travel in the USA or Travel CUTS in Canada offer good prices to most destinations, and are unlikely to disappear overnight leaving you clutching a receipt for a nonexistent ticket. One of the best travel agencies for long-haul flights out of Switzerland is Globetrotter (see the Zürich chapter). It also has a branch in Baden, Basel, Bern, Lucerne, St Gallen and Winterthur. Owing to high costs in Switzerland, its fares aren't as competitive as those in Europe's discount centres, but it can put together a RTW ticket out of Zürich starting at around Sfr2250.

Courier fares, where you get cheap passage in return for accompanying an urgent package through customs, offer incredibly low prices but I know of no courier companies that operate to Switzerland. It might be worth ringing around, though.

Fares quoted in this book should be used as a guide only, as they are particularly subject to change.

Travellers with Special Needs

If you have special needs of any sort – you've broken a leg, you're vegetarian or require a special diet, travelling in a wheelchair, taking the baby, terrified of flying, whatever – let the airline people know as soon as possible so that they can make arrangements. Remind them when you reconfirm your booking (at least 72 hours before departure) and again when you check in at the airport. It may also be worth ringing around the airlines before you make your booking, to find out how they can handle your particular needs.

Children aged under two travel for 10% of the standard fare (or free on some airlines) as long as they don't occupy a seat. They don't get a baggage allowance either. 'Skycots', baby food and diapers should be provided by the airline if requested in advance. Children aged between two and 12 can usually occupy a seat for half to two-thirds of the full fare, and do get a baggage allowance.

Fly-Rail Programme

Most world airlines (except American and British carriers for outward flights) are part of this programme. It allows you to wave goodbye to your luggage when you check-in at your departure airport and pick it up again at your choice of any Swiss railway station. This saves you having to wait for your luggage at the arrival airport or accompany them through customs. Similarly upon departure, you can check-in your luggage at any of the 110 Swiss railway stations up to 24 hours before your flight and pick it up at your destination airport. The charge is Sfr15 per item of luggage.

The following Swiss railway stations provide a complete check-in service for Swissair, including issuing boarding passes: Aarau, Arosa, Basel SBB, Bern, Biel/Bienne, Davos Platz and Dorf, Fribourg, Geneva, Interlaken Ost and West, Lausanne, Locarno, Lugano, Lucerne, Montreux, Neuchâtel, St Gallen, St Moritz, Solothurn, Thun, Zug and Zürich.

To/From the UK

London is one of the world's major centres for discounted fares. You should be able to find a flight that beats the equivalent fare by rail (London to Zürich return is £123). In London, look for ads in *Time Out*, *City Limits*, the *Evening Standard* and *Exchange & Mart*. Also pick up the free magazines and newspapers available outside many tube stations, especially *TNT* (recommended),

Southern Cross and *Trailfinder*. In the rest of the country, check the Sunday national papers.

Trailfinders' head office (☎ 071-938 3999), 194 Kensington High St, London W8, has competitive fares, plus they have a travel library, bookshop, visa service and immunisation centre. The Manchester branch (☎ 061-839 6969), is at 58 Deansgate. STA (☎ 071-937 9962) is at 74 Old Brompton Rd, London SW7, also with an office in Manchester (061-834 0668). Campus Travel (☎ 071-938 2188) 174 Kensington High St, London W8 has many interesting deals and very cheap travel insurance. Council Travel (071-437 7767, 28A Poland St, London W1, is the USA's largest student and budget travel agency.

Most British travel agents are registered with the ABTA (Association of British Travel Agents). If you have paid for your flight with an ABTA-registered agent who then goes out of business, ABTA will guarantee a refund or an alternative. Unregistered bucket shops are riskier but sometimes cheaper. Always ask about possible restrictions in the validity of the ticket. A bucket shop that often has the most competitive price for flights to Switzerland is Bluewheel Limited (081-202 0111), 417 Hendon Way, London, NW4 3LH. This ABTA travel agent can also arrange good deals on travel insurance and car hire.

You may have to pay a bit more for an airline with a reliable track record. British Airways return fares are rarely available for less than £130, Swissair offers a high season London/Zürich return ticket for £176. This fare only applies if you book and pay at least 14 days ahead; it is valid for three months and the return flight is fixed.

For short stays in Switzerland, a charter flight may be the most economical option. Prices can be as low as £70 return to Zürich or Geneva. Usually there are restrictive conditions attached, such as your stay must include a Saturday night but may not exceed 12 days.

Scheduled flights into Switzerland are liable for a tax of around Sfr5 which is included in the ticket price. It does not apply to chartered flights.

To/From Continental Europe

Though London is the discount capital of Europe, there are several other cities in the region where you'll find a wide range of good deals. Athens is a good centre for cheap fares; shop around the travel agents in the backstreets between Syntagma and Omonia Squares. Amsterdam is another recognised centre for cheap tickets: try Budget Air (☎ 020-627 12 51), ICL Reizen (☎ 020-620 51 21) Malibu Travel (☎ (020-623 68 14) or the student agency, NBBS (☎ 020-624 09 89).

Across Europe, many travel agents have ties with STA, where cheap tickets can be purchased and STA tickets can be altered free of charge (first change only). Outlets in important transport hubs include: Voyages et Découvertes (☎ 1-42 61 00 01), 21 Rue Cambon, Paris; SRID Reisen (☎ 069-43 01 91), Berger Strasse 118, Frankfurt; and ISYTS (☎ 01-32 21 267), 2nd Floor, 11 Nikis St, Syntagma Square, Athens.

Zürich and Geneva have several nonstop fights a day to major transport hubs like Paris and Frankfurt. Getting between airports and city centres is rarely a problem in Europe thanks to the ever improving subway networks and good bus services. But if you're already in continental Europe and not in a tearing hurry, taking the train is a more sensible option.

To/From the USA

The North Atlantic is the world's busiest long-haul air corridor and the flight options are bewildering. The *New York Times*, the *LA Times*, the *Chicago Tribune* and the *San Francisco Chronicle Examiner* all produce weekly travel sections in which you'll find any number of travel agents' ads. Council Travel and STA Travel have offices in major cities nationwide. Access International in New York offers discounts to Europe from 50 cities in the USA. You should be able to fly New York to a European gateway city and return for US$350 to US$450 low season, US$550 to US$650 high season.

One-way fares can work out to about half this on a stand-by basis. Airhitch (☎ 212-864 2000) specialises in this sort of thing, and can get you from the east coast/west coast/elsewhere in the USA to Europe one-way for US$160/269/229. Swissair flies daily except Tuesday from Los Angeles to both Zürich and Geneva; flights from New York are daily. The minimum you can expect to pay on Swissair (a 'seat sale' fare) is around US$620 return. American Airlines, TWA and Delta also fly direct into Switzerland. An interesting option is with Icelandair (☎ 800-223 5500), flying from New York to Luxembourg, via Reykjavík. This may end up one of the cheapest deals.

The *Travel Unlimited* newsletter, PO Box 1058, Allston, MA 02134, publishes details of the cheapest air fares and courier possibilities for destinations all over the world from the USA and other countries including the UK. It's a treasure trove of information. A single monthly issue costs US$5, and a year's subscription, US$25 (US$35 abroad).

To/From Canada

Travel CUTS has offices in all major cities. Scan the budget travel agents' ads in the *Toronto Globe & Mail*, the *Toronto Star* and the *Vancouver Province*. Swissair flies daily except Monday and Tuesday from Toronto and Montreal to Zürich.

To/From Australia

STA and Flight Centres International are major dealers in cheap air fares. Check the travel agents' ads in the Yellow Pages and ring around.

The Saturday travel sections of Sydney's *Sydney Morning Herald* and Melbourne's the *Age* newspapers have many ads offering cheap fares to Europe, but don't be surprised if they happen to be 'sold out' when you contact the agents: they're usually low-season fares on obscure airlines with conditions attached. With Australia's large and well-organised ethnic populations, it pays to check special deals in the ethnic press.

No airline flies direct into Switzerland from Australia. Return fares to Europe on mainstream airlines through a reputable agent like the Flight Centre cost between A$1600 (low season) and A$2500 (high season). Flights to/from Perth are a couple of hundred dollars cheaper.

To/From New Zealand

As in Australia, STA and Flight Centres International are popular travel agents in New Zealand, and no airline flies directly into Switzerland. Not surprisingly, the cheapest fares to Europe are routed through the USA, and a RTW ticket can be cheaper than a return.

To/From Africa

Nairobi is probably the best place in Africa to buy tickets to Europe, thanks to the many bucket shops and the strong competition between them. A typical one-way/return fare to London would be about US$550/800. Alternatively, a direct flight to Zürich (Tuesday, Thursday and Saturday) on Swissair will start at around US$860 for a return 75-day excursion fare.

Swissair flies directly to Zürich from a number of other places in Africa, including Johannesburg (Monday, Wednesday and Saturday). Several West African countries such as Burkina Faso and the Gambia offer cheap charter flights to France, and charter fares from Morocco can be incredibly cheap if you're lucky enough to find a seat. If you intend departing from Cairo, it's often cheaper to fly to Athens and to proceed with a budget bus or train from there.

To/From Asia

Hong Kong is the discount plane-ticket capital of Asia, and its bucket shops are at least as unreliable as those of other cities. Ask the advice of other travellers before buying a ticket. Many of the cheapest fares from south-east Asia to Europe are offered by Eastern European carriers. STA has branches in Hong Kong, Tokyo, Singapore, Bangkok and Kuala Lumpur.

To/from India, the cheapest flights tend to be with eastern European carriers like LOT and Aeroflot, or with Middle Eastern airlines such as Syrian Arab Airlines and Iran Air. Bombay is the air transport hub, with many transit options to/from south-east Asia, but tickets are slightly cheaper in Delhi. Try Delhi Student Travel Services in the Imperial Hotel, Janpath.

Swissair flies to/from Geneva and/or Zürich to Karachi, Bombay, Delhi, Bangkok, Singapore, Hong Kong, Beijing, Seoul, Tokyo and Manila.

BUS

For getting across Europe, bus travel tends to take second place to going by train. The bus has the edge in terms of cost, sometimes quite substantially, but is generally slower, less comfortable and more cramped. Eurolines (☎ 071-730 0202), 52 Grosvenor Gardens, Victoria, London SW1, is the main international carrier. Eurolines' European representatives include: Eurolines/Budgetbus (☎ 020-627 51 51), Rokin 10, Amsterdam; Eurolines (☎ 1-43.54.11.99), 55 Rue Saint Jacques, 75005 Paris; Deutsche Touring (☎ 089-59 18 24), Arnulfstrasse 3, Munich; and Lazzi Express (☎ 06841 74 58), via Tagliamento 27R, Rome. These may also be able to advise you on other bus companies and deals.

On ordinary return trips, youth fares are around 10% less than the ordinary full fare, eg a London-Zürich return ticket (valid six months) costs £98 for adults or £88 for youths up to 25 years old. The London-Geneva return fare is £94 and £86 respectively. There are four departures per week from London's Victoria Coach Station for each service and the journey takes 21 hours. Onward or return journeys must be reserved prior to departure for all tickets. Geneva also has international bus routes heading to Rome, the south of France, and along the eastern coast of Spain (see also the Geneva chapter).

Europabus is the motor coach system of the European railways and has information offices in Brussels (☎ 02-217 66 60), Frankfurt (☎ 069-7 90 30), Paris (☎ 1-40.38. 93.93), Rome (☎ (06-481 82 77), and Vienna (☎ 0222-501 80).

TRAIN

Trains are a popular and convenient way to travel, and are more environmentally-friendly than cars or buses. They are good meeting places, comfortable and reasonably frequent. Nevertheless, always be aware of the need for security. Everyone seems to know or has heard of someone who has been robbed of their gear on trains, sometimes involving elaborate gassing or drugging of passengers. This sort of thing can happen, although it's not nearly as widespread as some people make out. The overwhelming chances are that you will only have fond memories of being on the train. Despite this, it pays to take basic precautions. Don't leave your stuff unattended, and make sure you lock compartment doors overnight. Some people make a point of leaving a window open to maintain a flow of fresh air (possibly to protect themselves against less sinister gaseous emissions than those mentioned above!).

To/From Europe

European railpasses make train travel affordable, even for backpackers, despite the fact that prices leapt in 1993 to prevent certain countries dropping out of the scheme. Unless you actually want to explore other countries in Europe as well, it may work out cheaper to pay the normal fare to Switzerland then use a national railpass to explore the country (see the Getting Around chapter). Within Switzerland, Swiss railpasses are valid on more private rail lines than the European passes, and you can get discounts on mountain transport, which the European passes tend not to include. Supplements and reservation costs are not covered by any railpasses, and pass holders must always carry their passport on the train for identification purposes.

If do you plan to travel extensively in

Europe by train, it might be worth getting hold of the *Thomas Cook European Timetable*, which gives a complete listing of train schedules and indicates where supplements apply or where reservations are necessary. It is updated monthly and is available from Thomas Cook outlets worldwide.

Paris, Amsterdam, Munich, Milan and Vienna are all important hubs for international rail connections. Switzerland, located at the heart of Europe, has excellent services to/from these hubs and the rest of the continent. Zürich is the busiest international terminus. It has five trains daily to Vienna, with a journey time of eight hours. There are several trains a day to both Geneva and Lausanne from Paris, and journey time is three to four hours by the super-fast TGV. Paris to Bern takes 4½ hours by TGV. Most connections from Germany pass though Zürich or Basel. Nearly all connections from Italy pass through Milan before branching off to Zürich, Lucerne, Bern or Lausanne.

Express Trains Fast trains can be identified by the symbols EC (EuroCity) or IC (Inter-City). The French TGV and the German ICE are even faster trains. Supplements can apply on fast trains, and it is a good idea (sometimes obligatory) to make seat reservations at peak times and on certain lines. Reservations made in Switzerland are subject to a Sfr4 to Sfr22 surcharge depending upon the day and/or the service.

Overnight Trains Overnight trains will usually offer a choice of couchette or sleeper if you don't fancy sleeping in your seat with somebody else's elbow in your ear. Again, reservations are advisable as sleeping options are allocated on a first-come, first-served basis. Couchettes are bunks numbering four (1st class) or six (2nd class) per compartment and are comfortable enough, if lacking a bit in privacy. A bunk costs a fixed price of around US$16 for international travel, irrespective of the length of the journey.

Sleepers are the most comfortable option, offering beds for one or two passengers in 1st class, and two or three passengers in 2nd class. Charges vary depending upon the journey but they tend to be significantly more expensive than couchettes. Most long-distance trains have a dining car or an attendant who wheels a drink-and-snack-laden trolley through carriages, but prices tend to be steep.

Eurail Passes These passes can only be bought by residents of non-European countries, and are supposed to be purchased before arriving in Europe. However, Eurail passes can be purchased within Europe so long as your passport proves you've been there for less than six months, but the outlets where you can do this are limited. French National Railways (071-493 9731), 179 Piccadilly, London, is one such outlet. You can also buy them in Zürich train station, and in other major Swiss cities. If you've lived in Europe for more than six months, you are eligible for an Inter-Rail pass, which is a better buy.

Eurail passes are valid for unlimited travel on national railways and some private lines in Austria, Belgium, Denmark, Finland, France (including Monaco), Germany, Greece, Hungary, Italy, Luxembourg, the Netherlands, Norway, Portugal, Ireland, Spain, Sweden and Switzerland (including Liechtenstein). Britain is not covered.

Eurail is also valid for ferries between Ireland and France (but not between Britain and France), between Italy and Greece, and from Sweden to Finland, Denmark or Germany. In addition, reductions are given on steamer services in various countries.

Eurail passes offer reasonable value to people aged under 26. A Youthpass is valid for 2nd-class travel for 15 days (£294 or Sfr790), one month (£435 or Sfr825) or two months (£614 or Sfr1165). The Youth Flexipass, also for 2nd class, is valid for a number of freely-chosen days' travel in two months and comes in four versions, eg seven days for £215 (Sfr410) or 15 days for £404 (Sfr765).

The corresponding passes for those aged over 26 are available in 1st class only. The

Flexipass (four versions within two months) costs from £254 (Sfr490) for five days up to £577 (Sfr1100) for 15 days. The standard Eurail Pass (five versions) costs from £418 (Sfr790) for 15 days' unlimited travel up to £1130 (Sfr2150) for three months. Two or more people travelling together (minimum three people between 1 April and 30 September) can get good discounts on a Saverpass, which works like the standard Eurail Pass. Child passes are valid in the same class and categories as the adult passes.

If you lose your Eurail pass before you get to Europe, you cannot claim a refund. If your pass is lost or stolen once you are in Europe, you may apply for a duplicate, but only after you meet certain conditions. The above prices are applicable in London and Zürich; buying in Zürich may seem better value, but that can change as exchange rates alter. However, as already mentioned, you'll be much better off buying a Swiss railpass instead, unless your plans include travelling elsewhere in Europe.

Inter-Rail Passes Inter-Rail passes are available to residents of European countries. The normal Inter-Rail card is limited to travellers under 26 years of age and costs £249 for one month. Terms and conditions may vary slightly from country to country but in all cases it applies that in the country of origin there is only a discount of around 50% on normal fares. Within the UK, Inter-Rail passes can only be purchased by people who have been resident in Britain for at least six months, and passport identification is required. Inter-Rail cards should be treated like cash, as you can make no claims in the event of loss or theft. You can buy Inter-Rail in Switzerland as long as you have a work permit and are under 26; the price is Sfr530.

Cards are valid for free 2nd-class rail travel in all countries covered by Eurail, plus Bulgaria, the Czech and Slovak Republics, Morocco, Poland, Romania, Turkey and former Yugoslavia. If bought in Britain, the card is also valid for 34% to 50% discounts on train travel in Britain and Northern Ireland, as well as 30% to 50% discounts on

various ferry routes (many more than covered by Eurail) and certain river and lake services. It also gives free travel (barring port tax) on shipping routes from Brindisi (Italy) to Patras (Greece).

There is also an Inter-Rail card for people aged 26 or over, but it is no longer valid for travel in western Europe or Switzerland.

Discount Tickets Travellers aged under 26 can pick up BIJ (Billet International de Jeunesse) tickets which cut fares by up to 50%. Unfortunately, you can't always bank on a substantial reduction; the £115 return from London to Zürich represents just an £8 saving on the normal fare. Various agents issue BIJ tickets in Europe, including Eurotrain (071-730 3402), 52 Grosvenor Gardens, London SW1. British Rail International (071-834 2345) and Wasteels (071-834 7066) also sell BIJ tickets in London. They are also available from agents in all major European cities, such as Council Travel (☎ 42 66 20 87) in Paris. (See the previous Air travel section for details about other travel agents.)

Some fare discounts only apply if you have already bought a travel pass; the Rail Europe Family Card and the Rail Europe Senior Card are worth investigating for families or travellers aged over 60.

To/from Asia

It takes 49 hours on the direct train from Basel to Moscow (via Frankfurt) and costs Sfr291, plus Sfr128 for a compulsory sleeper. From there you can take four different trains for onwards eastern travel. Three of them (the trans-Siberian, trans-Mongolian and trans-Manchurian) follow the same route to/from Moscow across Siberia but have different eastern railheads. The fourth, the trans-Kazakhstan, runs between Moscow and Ürümqi (north-western China) across central Asia. Prices can vary enormously, depending on where you buy the ticket and what is included, but you won't save money compared to flying. If you have time (between six and nine days minimum) they are an interesting option, but only really worthwhile if you want to stop off and explore China and Russia on the way through. They could become more popular as tourism expands in the region.

CAR & MOTORBIKE

Getting to Switzerland by road is simple, as there are fast, well-maintained motorways (freeways) through all surrounding countries. German motorways (Autobahn) have no tolls or speed limits, whereas Austrian, French (Autoroute) and Italian (Autostrada) motorways have both. The Alps present a natural hazard to entering Switzerland, but main highways tend to blast straight through such immovable objects. An important tunnel if approaching from the south is the Grand St Bernard between Aosta (Italy) and Bourg St Pierre (toll Sfr16 to Sfr32 for cars and Sfr16 for motorbikes). The minor roads are more fun and scenically more interesting but special care is needed when negotiating mountain passes. Some, such as the N5 (E21) route from Champagnole (in France) to Geneva are not recommended if you have not had previous experience of driving in the mountains.

If you're driving from Italy to Switzerland, don't fill up with petrol before crossing the border, as fuel is much cheaper on the Swiss side. It's also cheaper than in France and virtually the same as in Germany and Austria, despite the fact that in 1993 Swiss citizens voted for the imposition of a 20c per litre tax.

Paperwork & Preparations

Proof of ownership of a private vehicle should always be carried (Vehicle Registration Document for British-registered cars). You can drive a vehicle registered abroad for up to 12 months within Switzerland. Foreign driving licences are also valid for a period of one year, but you may find it useful to obtain an International Driving Permit from your motoring organisation (see Documents in the Facts for the Visitor chapter).

The Green Card, the international third-party insurance certificate, is not compulsory in Switzerland as long as you already have third-party insurance. But it is a good idea to get a Green Card anyway if you're driving across Europe to get to Switzerland. It will ease problems in the event of an accident and is actually compulsory in some countries (eg Germany). It is issued by your vehicle insurer in your home country, often free of charge. Also ask your insurer for a European Accident Statement form, which can simplify things if worst comes to worst. Never sign statements you can't read or understand – insist on a translation and sign that only if it's acceptable.

If you want to insure a vehicle and have a good insurance record, you might be eligible for considerable premium discounts if you can show a letter to this effect from your insurance company back home.

Taking out a European breakdown assistance policy is a good investment, such as the AA Five Star Service or the RAC Eurocover Motoring Assistance. Ask your motoring organisation for a Card of Introduction, which entitles you to free services offered by sister organisations around Europe. (See the Documents section in the Facts for the Visitor chapter.)

Every vehicle travelling across an international border should display a nationality plate of its country of registration. A warning triangle, to be used in the event of breakdown, is compulsory almost everywhere, including Switzerland. Recommended accessories are a first-aid kit, a spare bulb kit, and a fire extinguisher. Contact the RAC (☎ 081-686 0088) or the AA (☎ 0256-20123) in the UK for more information. (See the Getting Around chapter for information on road rules in Switzerland.) The RAC annually brings out its *European Motoring Guide*, which gives an excellent summary of regulations in each country in Europe, including parking rules. Motoring organisations in other countries have similar publications.

If you're from outside Europe and want to buy a vehicle to tour around, you'll find that most European countries have a restriction that only residents may buy and register a vehicle within their borders. This doesn't apply in Britain, and Britain is also one of the cheapest places for buying secondhand cars. Continental Europeans drive on the right. Vehicles brought over from Britain or Ireland should have their headlights adjusted to avoid blinding oncoming traffic at night. (A simple solution on older headlight lenses is to cover up the triangular section of the lens with tape.)

Camper Van

Travelling in a camper van can be a surprisingly economical option for budget travellers, especially in Switzerland where you can save on the high cost of eating and sleeping by doing both those things in the van. London is a good place to buy: look in *TNT* magazine, *Loot* newspaper and go to the Van Market in Market Rd, London N7. Expect to spend at least £1000 to £1500 (US$1600 to US$2400). The most common camper van is the VW based on the 1600 cc or 2000 cc Transporter, and spares are widely available in Europe. Free camping, such as in Autobahn rest areas, is rarely a problem.

A drawback with camper vans is that they're expensive to buy in spring and hard to sell in autumn. A car and tent might do just as well instead.

Motorcycle Touring

Europe and Switzerland are ideal for motorcycle touring, with winding roads of good quality, stunning scenery to stimulate the senses, and an active motorcycling scene. Just make sure your wet-weather gear is up to scratch. The wearing of crash helmets for rider and passenger is compulsory everywhere in Europe nowadays. Austria, Belgium, France, Germany, Luxembourg and Spain as well as Scandinavian countries also require that motorcyclists use headlights during the day; in other countries it is recommended. However it's illegal to drive with headlights on during the day in Italy.

Motorway Tax

Upon entering Switzerland you will need to decide whether you wish to use the motorways and semi-motorways (identified by green signs). There is a one-off charge of Sfr30 if you do. Organise this money beforehand, since you might not always be able to change money at the border – or try to buy it in advance from a SNTO office or a motoring organisation such as the AA. The tax is payable if using either the St Gotthard or the San Bernardino tunnel. Officials at some major crossings may insist you pay the charge even if you declare you only want to use minor roads, in which case backtrack and re-approach via a smaller road, where you should have no trouble getting in. The sticker (called a *vignette*) you receive upon paying the motorway tax must be displayed on the windscreen. It is valid for a calendar year with a month's leeway either side (ie if you visit on 1 December you can buy the following year's tax, or up to 31 January you can visit on the previous year's tax). If you're caught on the motorways without the vignette you pay a fine of Sfr100 plus the tax.

BICYCLE

This is one of the best ways to travel in terms of your bank balance, your health, and the environment. But it does require a high level of commitment to see it through.

To/From Europe

Cycling to Switzerland from elsewhere in Europe is certainly viable. One organisation that can help is the Cyclists' Touring Club (☎ 0483-417 217), Cotterell House, 69 Meadrow, Godalming, Surrey GU7 3HS, Britain. It can supply information to members on cycling conditions in Europe as well as detailed routes, itineraries and cheap insurance. Membership costs £24 per annum, or £12 to people aged under 18. If you're taking in Switzerland as part of a more general bike tour, consider investing in *Europe by Bike* by Karen & Terry Whitehall (paperback), available in the USA or selected outlets in the UK.

A primary consideration on long cycling trips is to travel light, but you should take a few tools and spares including a puncture repair kit and and a spare inner tube. Panniers are essential to balance your possessions on either side of the bike frame. A bike helmet is also a very good idea. Take a good bike lock and always use it when you leave your machine unattended. Seasoned cyclists can average 80 km a day but there's no point in overdoing it. The slower you travel, the more locals you're likely to meet. If you get weary of pedalling or simply want to skip a boring transport section, you can put your feet up on the train. On slower trains, bikes can usually be taken on board as luggage, subject to a small supplementary fee. Fast trains (IC, EC etc) can rarely accommodate bikes; they need to be sent as registered luggage and may end up on a different train from the one you take (the cost varies, from London to Zürich it is £7).

Bicycles are not allowed on European motorways – not that you would want to pedal on those tedious bits of concrete anyway. Stick to small roads or dedicated bike tracks where possible. Good routes into the country from the north are through the German Black Forest or around Lake Constance. Access from the south is difficult because of the Alps. Coming from the west you need to negotiate the Jura Mountains chain to get into French Switzerland. The approach from Austria in the east is also mountainous but scenically rewarding.

To/From Elsewhere

Transporting your bike by plane is relatively easy. You can either take it to pieces and pack everything in a bike bag or box, or simply wheel it to the check-in desk, where it should be treated as a piece of baggage. You may have to remove the pedals and turn the handlebars sideways so that it takes up less space in the aircraft's hold; check all this with the airline well in advance, preferably before you pay for your ticket. If your bicycle and other luggage exceed the allowable weight limit, ask about alternatives or you may suddenly find yourself being charged a fortune for excess baggage.

HITCHING

Hitchers can end up making good time, but obviously your plans need to be flexible in case a trick of the light makes you appear invisible to passing motorists. A man and woman travelling together is probably the best combination. Two or more men must expect some delays; two women together will make good time and will be reasonably safe. A woman hitching on her own is taking a risk. Dedicated hitchers may wish to invest in *Europe – a Manual for Hitchhikers* by Simon Calder (paperback), even though it's getting a bit ancient by now. It is sometimes possible to arrange a lift in advance; scan student notice boards in colleges, or contact car-sharing agencies. Such agencies are particularly popular in France (Allostop-Provoya) and Germany (Mitfahrzentrale).

Don't try to hitch from city centres; take public transport to suburban exit routes. Hitching is usually illegal on motorways (freeways) in Europe – stand on the slip roads, or approach drivers at petrol stations and truck stops. Look presentable and cheerful and make a cardboard sign indicating your intended destination in the local language. Never hitch where drivers can't stop in good time or without causing an obstruction. At dusk, give up and think about finding somewhere to stay.

Hitchers should make average progress through Austria and Italy, and probably slower progress through France. The quickest and best approach is through Germany, where hitching is an accepted method of getting around. If coming from Britain, try waving your thumb at cars as they embark onto the ferry; you may score a free ride as fares for vehicle sometimes cost the same irrespective of the number of passengers.

Although many travellers hitchhike, it's not a totally safe way of getting around. How and where to hitchhike is discussed in this book but it isn't necessarily recommended.

MOUNTAIN ESCAPES

The most dramatic way to arrive or leave Switzerland is over the Alps. This is straightforward by car, but there are more exciting ways to do it. By skis is one, on the Ventina route to Italy (see the Zermatt section in the Valais chapter for details). Ski mountaineers traverse the Valais Alps on the Haute Route to Chamonix in France. There are also various hiking trails. A famous route is over the Great St Bernard Pass, via the historic hospice, towards Mont Blanc (see the Great St Bernard Pass section also in the Valais chapter).

BOAT

This is a pleasurable if not time or price-efficient way to get to/from Switzerland. It is possible to take a cruise down the Rhine all the way from Basel to Amsterdam but you'll need a boatload of money to do so. The main operator along the Rhine is the German Köln-Düsseldorfer (KD) Line (☎ 0221-2 08 82 88), 15 Frankenwerft, 5000 Cologne 1, Germany. Its agent in Britain is GA Clubb Rhine Cruise Agency Ltd (☎ 0372 742 033), 28 South St, Epsom, Surrey. The trip takes five days, operates between April and October, and costs upwards of £578 per person. A cheaper option is to do the stretch Basel-Nijmegen by boat, then transfer by coach to Amsterdam. The price including coach travel starts at £318 departing from Basel (takes 4 days) or £365 departing from Amsterdam (takes 5 days). (See Basel for more information.)

Switzerland can also be reached by steamer from several lakes: from Germany via Lake Constance (Bodensee in German); from Italy via Lake Maggiore; and from France via Lake Geneva. (See the relevant sections.)

TOURS

All-in skiing holidays are the most popular way to visit Switzerland using a tour operator. All the large companies, such as Thomson, Bladon and Kuoni, include Swiss ski resorts in their brochures. Enquire at travel agents or look in the national press for details of these and other special interest holidays.

Young people who like travelling in a group with like-minded revellers may consider joining one of the youth-oriented tour buses which are based on hotel or camping accommodation. In London, Contiki (☎ 081-290 6422) offers a variety of tours starting from 14 days for £420 (plus food fund). Tracks (☎ 071-937 3028) can work out slightly cheaper. Top Deck (☎ 071-370 6487) has the added novelty of tours where you travel and sleep in a converted doubledecker bus. All these operators converge on Lauterbrunnen, in the Jungfrau Region, for the Swiss leg of the European itinerary. Student or youth travel agencies in other countries have similar deals.

For people aged over 60, Saga Holidays (☎ 0800-300 500), Saga Building, Middelburg Square, Folkstone, Kent CT20 1AZ, Britain, offers an 11-day coach tour of Switzerland including a trip on the Glacier Express. Saga also operates in the USA (☎ 617-451 6808), 120 Boyleston St, Boston, MA 02116; and Australia (☎ 02-957 4222), Level 4, 20 Alfred St, Milsons Point, Sydney 2061.

Getting Around

Swiss public transport is a fully integrated and comprehensive system incorporating trains, buses, boats, funiculars and cable cars. It can claim to be one of the most efficient transport networks in the world. It is a rare luxury to travel on a system that works so well. The Swiss think nothing of co-ordinating schedules where there may be only a few minutes leeway between arrivals and departures. Missing a connection through a late arrival is very rare. Various special tickets are available to the tourist to make the system even more attractive.

Information is readily available as and when you need it, but if you like to plan things down to the very last detail, pick up the complete timetable of trains, boats, buses and mountain transport that covers the whole country (Sfr14), and is sold at most Swiss train stations.

European railpasses (Inter-Rail and Eurail) will get you free travel to most places you might want to go, but rarely on mountain transport. Generally, where they are valid for boats or private railways, Inter-Rail gets a 50% discount and Eurail is good for free travel.

SWISS TRAVEL PASSES

The best deal for people planning to travel extensively is the Swiss Pass, entitling the holder to unlimited travel on Swiss Federal Railways, boats, most Alpine postbuses and also on trams and buses in 30 towns. Reductions of 25% apply on funiculars and mountain railways. Passes are valid for four days (Sfr200), eight days (Sfr250), 15 days (Sfr290) and one month (Sfr400) – prices are for 2nd-class tickets, 1st class is about 40% higher.

The Swiss Card allows a free return journey from your arrival point to any destination in Switzerland, 50% off rail, boat and bus excursions, and reductions on mountain railways. The cost is Sfr130 (2nd class) or Sfr160 (1st class) and it is valid for a month.

The Half-Fare Card is a similar deal minus the free return trip. The cost is Sfr85 for one month or Sfr150 for one year. The Swiss Flexi Pass allows free, unlimited trips for three days out of 15. The cost for 2nd class is Sfr200.

All these cards are best purchased before arrival in Switzerland from SNTO, as they are only available from a few major transport centres once within the country. If you buy any of these cards or the Swiss Transfer Ticket from SNTO you can get a free Family Card, good for free travel for minors accompanied by at least one parent. Once within Switzerland, the Family Card can be purchased by any family for Sfr20. The Swiss Transfer Ticket is only available from SNTO and is a flat-rate return ticket (Sfr35 in 2nd class, Sfr54 in 1st class) from frontier stations or airports to your destination in Switzerland.

Regional passes are available for free travel on certain days and for half-price travel on other days within a seven or 15-day period, but they are only valid within that particular region. Details are given at the beginning of the relevant chapters. Buy these passes in the region or at major stations before you get there.

Another option worth considering is a Euro Domino Freedom Pass, valid for free travel on freely chosen days within one month. They are sold by European national railways *outside* Switzerland. Prices from British Rail Continental are: three days for £68, 5 days for £100, and 10 days for £132 (£52, £75, £100 respectively for people under 26). Bear in mind that validity is not as extensive as for the Swiss Pass.

AIR

Internal flights are not of great interest to the visitor, owing to the excellent ground transport. Swissair has flights between Zürich and Geneva, but it is Crossair, a subsidiary of Swissair, that is the major carrier. It has

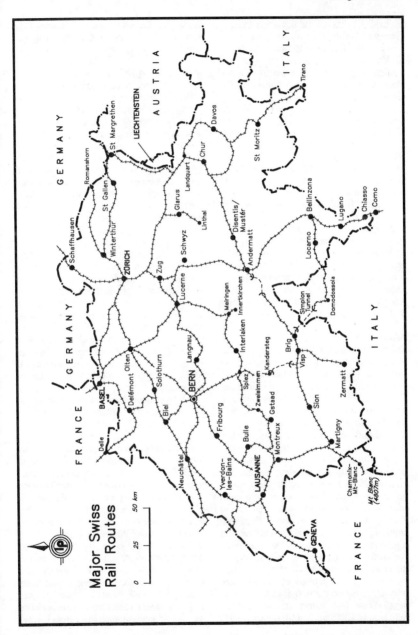

Major Swiss Rail Routes

several flights daily between Zürich, Geneva, Basel (Mulhouse), Bern and Lugano. The fare from Zürich to Geneva is Sfr350 return or Sfr198 one-way. Swissair is a sales agent for Crossair. See the Getting There & Away chapter for information on the Fly-Rail programme.

Some mountain resorts have helicopter operators which offer hugely enjoyable but highly expensive cruises around the Alps.

BUS

Yellow postbuses are a supplement to the rail network, following postal routes and linking towns to the more inaccessible regions in the mountains. In all, routes cover some 8000 km of terrain. They are extremely regular, and departures tie in with train arrivals. Postbus stations are almost invariably next to train stations. Tickets are usually purchased from the driver, although on some routes over the Alps (for example, the Lugano-St Moritz service) it is necessary to reserve a place in advance. Details are given in the relevant chapters.

TRAIN

The Swiss rail network covers 5000 km and is a combination of state-run and private lines. The Swiss Federal Railway is abbreviated to SBB in German, CFF in French and FFS in Italian. All major stations are connected to each other by hourly departures, and the normal operating time is between 6 am and midnight. Trains are clean, reliable, frequent and as fast as the terrain will allow.

On railtracks with severe gradients, a rack and pinion (cogwheel) system is utilised to help propel the trains along; the passenger is not aware of any change except for a slight increase in noise. An example is the line to Zermatt. Carriages are always divided into smoking and non-smoking sections and long-distance trains usually have a dining car. In fact, Switzerland is the first country in the world to have a McDonald's restaurant on board. (If you feel ill you don't know whether to blame the burger or travel sickness.) These two restaurants (McDonald's paid around US$5 million for them in 1992)

are on the Basel-Geneva and Geneva-Brig service and prices are the same as in a normal McDonald's restaurant.

Information & Tickets

Larger stations have separate information offices that can help you plan your route and give you a computerised print-out of your itinerary. Even small stations can usually give advice in English. Free timetable booklets are invariably available.

Single train tickets for longer journeys are often valid for two days and it is possible to break the journey on the same ticket, but tell the conductor of your intentions. Train schedules are revised yearly, so you should double-check all fares and frequencies quoted. Ordinary fares are expensive, meaning that one of the special passes mentioned will almost certainly save you money. But if you have a specific and pre-planned itinerary then a *Rundfarht* (*Billet Circular* in French) ticket might do the job instead. This is a return ticket that allows you to take a circuitous route, with stops along the way, and the price depends on the km covered. For example, starting from Zürich and calling at Lucerne, Lugano, Lausanne, Geneva and Bern, before returning to Zürich would cost Sfr162. Like all return tickets, it is valid for one month.

All fares quoted are for 2nd class unless stated otherwise, and fares for 1st class average about 65% higher.

Fare Warning Prices usually go up in May by a set percentage across the board. In May 1993, SBB opted for a complicated re-structuring of the method for calculating fares, so it's no longer purely a matter of the number of km travelled. Or rather it is, but the km values are now nominal: eg the km between Schaffhausen and Winterthur hasn't changed so the fare is the same, but the fare from Schaffhausen to Zürich (via Winterthur) is now 'longer', so the fare has gone up. The general picture is that although some fares didn't go up at all, others increased by over 10%. The busiest routes tended to experience the highest increase, such as services involving Zürich, Bern, Lucerne and Geneva. Some private railways (eg the Rhätische Bahn) undertook the same exercise. You may therefore come across some fare disparities but I hope I've given you fair warning.

Luggage

Train stations invariably offer luggage storage, either at a special counter (Sfr2 to Sfr5 per piece) or in 24-hour lockers (Sfr2 or Sfr3 small, Sfr3 or Sfr5 large). Nearly every station allows you the option to send your luggage ahead by train where you can pick it up at your destination station in the evening. This is especially useful if you're on a tight schedule and are visiting several different locations in the course of the day before your overnight stop. The charge is Sfr9 per piece (Sfr7 for skis).

First Class

Seats are comfortable and spacious in SBB trains, usually a single and a pair across the width of the carriage. A few private lines are less generous with space. It is rare for 1st class to be full; often it's virtually empty. The placement of 1st-class sections is usually announced over the loudspeaker in stations, or shown in a diagram on the platform. As the train approaches, look for the easy-to-see horizontal yellow stripe on SBB trains rather than going cross-eyed scanning for a small '1' between the windows.

Second Class

SBB trains are comfortable by international standards and have two seats either side of the aisle. Carriages are sometimes fairly full, especially when the army is on the move, but it is rare that you'll have to stand.

CAR & MOTORBIKE

Driving is an enjoyable experience in Switzerland. Roads are well maintained, well signposted and generally not too congested. You may find it frustrating to have to concentrate on the road while magnificent scenery unfolds all around, but at least you can stop at frequent parking bays to take it all in.

Travelling in your own vehicle gives you the most flexibility, and compared to most other countries, it is not necessary to spend very long on the road between places of interest. Unfortunately, the independence you enjoy does tend to isolate you to some extent from the local people. Cars are usually inconvenient in city centres, where it is generally worth ditching your trusty chariot and relying on public transport.

You generally have a choice when driving in mountainous areas. Principal routes are as direct as the terrain will allow, often ploughing through mountains via long tunnels. Smaller roads go over the mountains. They take much longer to negotiate and add miles to your journey, but are scenically much more rewarding. Some of these minor passes are closed from November to May (see the Alpine Passes section later in this chapter) and you should stay in low gear on steep stretches. Carrying snow chains is recommended in winter.

The Swiss Touring Club (TCS) operates a 24-hour breakdown service on ☎ 022-3 58 00. The TCS or the ACS (see Useful Organisations in the Facts for the Visitor chapter) can provide detailed information about motoring in Switzerland.

Road Rules & Signs

An inexpensive handbook on Swiss traffic regulations (in English) is available from cantonal registration offices and at some customs posts. The minimum driving age is 18.

Like the rest of continental Europe, the Swiss drive on the right, and if in doubt, always give priority to traffic approaching from the right. Vehicles on roundabouts have priority over those about to enter it. On mountain roads, the ascending vehicle has priority, unless a postbus is involved, which always has right of way. Postbus drivers let rip a multi-tone bugle that sounds like a call to a cavalry charge when approaching blind corners.

Many driving infringements are subject to an on-the-spot fine, and you should always ask for a receipt. Speed limits are 50 km/h in towns, 120 km/h on motorways and 80 km/h on other roads. The driver and front seat passenger are required to wear a seat belt, and vehicles must carry a breakdown warning triangle which must be readily accessible (ie not in the boot). Dipped headlights must be used in all tunnels, and is recommended for motorcyclists during the day. Motorcyclists and passengers must wear crash helmets.

Switzerland is tough on drink-driving, so don't risk it; the BAC limit is 0.08%, and if caught exceeding this limit, you may face a heavy fine, a ban from driving in Switzerland for two months, or even imprisonment.

Road signs are straightforward, easy to follow, and adopt internationally recognised conventions. Triangular signs with a red border warn of dangers and circular signs with a red border illustrate prohibitions. Signs you may not have come across before are: a criss-crossed white tyre on a blue circular background means snow chains are compulsory, and a yellow bugle on a square blue background means it is a mountain postal road and you must obey indications given by postbus drivers.

As in most other European countries, motorways and principal routes are designated by two different numbering systems: the national one (N) and the pan-European one (E). Both versions are usually listed in the text. A motorway is identified by the sign showing a white dual-carriageway on a rectangular green background, and a semi-motorway by one showing a white car on a rectangular green background. This is important if you don't want to stray onto a motorway without a vignette (See Motorway Tax in the Getting There & Away chapter).

For parking in blue zones in cities, you need to display a parking disc, obtainable free from offices of the Swiss motoring organisations (TCS and ACS), and sometimes from the tourist office.

Alpine Passes

Some minor Alpine passes are closed from November to the end of May. Most of the major ones are negotiable year-round,

depending on the weather. Where they aren't (eg the St Bernard, St Gotthard, San Bernardino), there's usually a tunnel to take instead. Other passes that are closed in winter are Albula, Furka, Grimsel, Klausen, Nufenen (open June to September only), Oberalp, Susten and Splügen. Passes that are open year-round are Bernina, Brünig, Flüela, Forclaz, Il Fuorn (Ofen) Julier, Maloja, Mosses, Pillon and Simplon.

More information on important passes is given throughout the book. A motoring organisation should be able to supply greater detail (gradients, altitudes etc), and a decent road map will also have that information. The local tourist office can tell you if passes are open, or you can ring ☎ 163 for road reports.

Trains can sometimes carry cars, such as through the Lötschberg tunnel south of Kandersteg.

Car Rental

The variety of special deals and terms and conditions attached to car rental can be mind-boggling. However, there are a few pointers that can help you through. The multinationals – Hertz, Avis, Budget Car, and Europe's largest rental agency, Europcar – will give you reliable service and a good standard of vehicle. Usually you will have the option of returning the car to a different outlet at the end of the rental period.

Unfortunately, if you walk into an office and ask for a car on the spot, you will pay over the odds, even allowing for special weekend deals. If you want an on-the-spot deal like this, look to national or local firms, which can often undercut the big companies by significant margins.

If you plan ahead, the multinationals might have the deal for you. Pre-booked and pre-paid rates are always cheaper, and there are fly/drive combinations and other special offers that are worth looking into. No matter where you rent, make sure you understand what is included in the price (unlimited km, tax, insurance, collision damage waiver etc) and what your liabilities are. The minimum rental age varies from 20 to 25 depending upon the company and category of vehicle, and you'll probably need a credit card (life will certainly be easier with one). Be wary of signing anything in a language you can't read and if you're dealing with a local, cut-price operator it might be worth looking over the car before you agree to the terms.

Local firms are the cheapest operators. Sixt-Alsa is convenient because it allows one-way rentals between Zürich and Geneva. However, it recently hiked its prices to be comparable with Budget and Europcar, which have many more outlets for one-way drop-offs (no charge within Switzerland). These companies only marginally undercut Hertz and Avis, which have the same rates as each other: the cheapest models for one day are Sfr63 plus Sfr0.86 per km, or Sfr191 with unlimited km. On weekend rates, Hertz beats Avis by just Sfr5 with its unlimited km price of Sfr199. Collision Damage Waiver (if required) is extra and costs around Sfr20 per day.

Motorbike and moped rental is not very common in Switzerland, but there are a few places that do this (see the Geneva chapter).

Purchase

The price of new and used cars in Switzerland is not bad compared to the rest of Europe; unfortunately you must be a Swiss resident to buy one. The TCS publishes a monthly guide to used car prices. All Swiss-registered cars must undergo an annual emission test and a serviceability control test every three years. Car registration plates are issued to the owner, so whether you buy new or secondhand the vehicle will come without plates. Likewise, if you sell a vehicle, you remove the plates and return them to the cantonal motor registration office (or transfer them to your new car).

Importing a vehicle into Switzerland is a long and tediously bureaucratic process, and all newly registered cars must be fitted with a catalytic converter. You can drive for one year in a vehicle registered abroad.

BICYCLE

Despite the hilly countryside, cycling is popular in Switzerland. Cycles can be hired from most train stations and returned to any other station with a rental counter. The rental charge for ordinary bikes (seven-speed) is Sfr14 for half a day, Sfr18 for a full day or Sfr64 per week. Counters are open daily, usually from the crack of dawn until some time in the evening. The larger stations also have mountain bikes (Sfr29 for one day). Bikes can be transported on normal trains but not on InterCity or EuroCity trains. On slow trains a bike can go in the luggage carriage for Sfr6; on direct trains it needs to go as unaccompanied luggage (Sfr12), and may end up on a different train to the one you take. The SNTO issues three free, useful booklets on cycling holidays, concentrating on the Pre-Alps, the Midlands, and from the Rhine to Ticino.

HITCHING

Although illegal on motorways, hitching is allowed on other roads and can be fairly easy. At other times it can be quite slow. Indigenous Swiss are not all that sympathetic towards hitchers, and you'll find that most of your lifts will come from foreigners. A sign is helpful. Make sure you stand in a place where vehicles can stop. This in itself can be a problem, as rural roads are rarely wide enough to allow stopping (except for passing bays), and there's often no pedestrian walkway beside the road. In other words, you can't really walk between lifts; find a good spot and stay there. To try to get a ride on a truck, ask around the customs post at border towns (also see the Hitching section in the Getting There & Away chapter).

WALKING

Many city centres are compact enough to enable major tourist sights to be seen on a walking tour, but walking really comes into its own in rural areas. Hikes are an excellent way to leave behind the wail of car horns and the opaque logic of train schedules. (For more information, see the Activities section in the Facts for the Visitor chapter, as well as the individual regional chapters.) The SNTO shows the way with its *Switzerland*

Step by Step booklets detailing 100 walks to mountain lakes, over mountain passes, and from town to town.

BOAT

All the larger lakes are serviced by steamers operated by Swiss Federal Railways (SBB), or allied private companies for which national travel passes are valid. Lakes covered include Geneva, Constance, Lucerne, Lugano, Neuchâtel, Biel, Murten, Thun, Brienz and Zug, but not Lake Maggiore. Rail passes are not valid for cruises offered by smaller companies on these lakes. A Swiss Navigation Boat Pass costs Sfr30 and entitles the bearer to 50% off fares of all services operated by SBB. It is valid for a calendar year, but only a few services operate in winter. The pass is well worth buying for those who aren't covered by a railpass (eg car drivers).

MOUNTAIN TRANSPORT

There are five main modes of transport used in steep Alpine regions. A funicular *(Standseilbahn, funiculaire, funicolare)* is a pair of counter-balancing cars drawn by cables along an inclined track. A cable car *(Luftseilbahn, téléphérique, funivia)* is a cabin dramatically suspended from a cable high over a valley, also with a twin that goes down when it goes up. A gondola *(Gondelbahn, télécabine)* is a smaller version of a cable car except that the gondola is hitched onto a continuously running cable once the passengers are inside. Nowadays the terms gondola and cable car are interchangeable and I haven't been pedantic about the distinction. A cable chair *(Sesselbahn, télésiège, seggiovia)* is likewise hitched onto a cable but is unenclosed. A ski lift *(Schlepplift, téléski, sciovia)* is a T-bar hanging from a cable, which the skiers hold or sit onto while their ski-clad feet slide along the snow. T-bars aren't as safe as modern cable cars (as they are vulnerable to careless skiers letting go) and are being gradually phased out.

LOCAL TRANSPORT
Public Transport

All local city transport is linked together on the same ticketing system. You should buy tickets before boarding from ticket dispensers by stops. In some towns, tickets are valid for one trip or for a limited time (eg one-hour's travel) within a particular zone. Multi-strip tickets are often available at a discount, or one-day passes are even better value. There are regular checks for people travelling without tickets; those found wanting, pay an on-the-spot fine of Sfr40 to Sfr50.

Taxi

Good bus, rail and underground railway networks make the taking of taxis all but unnecessary, but if you need one in a hurry they can usually be found idling like a gang of street urchins by train stations, or you can telephone. They are always metered and work on the basis of a starting flat fee plus a charge per km. Prices are high.

TOURS

Tours are booked through local tourist offices. The country is so compact that excursions to the major national attractions are offered from most towns. A trip up to Jungfraujoch, for example, is available from Zürich, Geneva, Bern, Lucerne and Interlaken. Most tours represent reasonable value. They work out more expensively than going it alone, but can be the best option if you are pressed for time. A short city tour will give you a quick overview of the place and can be a good way to begin your visit.

Bernese Mittelland

The main focus of the Bernese Mittelland region is the Swiss capital, Bern, an enticing city with a provincial feel that belies its status. The Bernese Mittelland is also known as the home of the famous cheese, Emmental.

History

In the 12th century the Dukes of Zähringen were the most powerful family in the localty, and in 1191, founded the fortified town of Bern. Shortly after it became established, Bern independently proceeded to conclude alliances with lesser nobles and gradually extended its own sovereignty in the region. In 1218 it managed to win the status of an imperial city under the direct responsibility of the Habsburgs. Meanwhile, it continued its territorial ambitions and entered into a

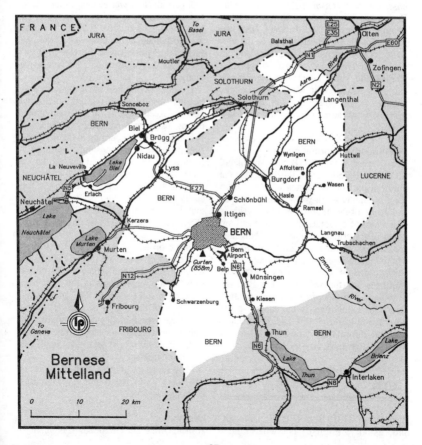

Bernese Mittelland

series of alliances known as the Burgundian Confederation.

Bern joined the Swiss Confederation in 1353, as it was concerned with protecting itself in the east while it expanded in other directions. In 1415 Bern gained control of Aargau in the north, and in the 16th century, most of the territory around Lake Geneva fell under Bernese rule, largely at the expense of the House of Savoy. At this stage, Bern had reached the peak of its power and influence, a situation that continued until 1798.

In 1798, the French invaded Switzerland and completely destroyed Bern's power base. Under the ensuing Helvetic Republic, Bern was chopped down to size and lost control of the Oberland. In 1803, Bern was reunited with the Oberland but, in the new Switzerland that emerged from the Congress of Vienna (1814-15), it was stripped of Aargau and Vaud, which became separate cantons. Although it was chosen as the capital of Switzerland in 1848, more land was lost when the canton of Jura was created in 1979.

Orientation & Information

The Bernese Mittelland (Berner Mittelland, Le Plateau Bernois) is the fertile plain in the northern part of the canton of Bern. Bern itself is slightly south-west of the geographical centre of the region. The countryside is characterised by small villages and rolling, green hills. German is the principal language spoken, except for a small area round Biel where French is on an equal footing.

The tourist office for Bern handles tourist enquiries for the whole of the Bernese Mittelland, but there is also an information centre for exhibitions in the canton in the Bern prison tower (☎ 031-22 23 06), and a cantonal information office (☎ 031-64 40 91) at Postgasse 68, also in Bern.

Bern

Founded in 1191, Bern (Berne in French, and, usually, English) is Switzerland's

capital and fourth-largest city with a population of 145,000. The name of the city, so the story goes, is in honour of the first animal killed by the founder, Berthold V, when hunting in the area. That animal was a bear (*Bär* in German, and *Bärn* in local dialect), and even today the bear remains the heraldic mascot of the city.

In 1405 the predominantly wood-built town was all but destroyed by a devastating fire. It was rebuilt using sandstone, and although most of the houses were replaced in the 16th and 17th centuries, the structure of the centre remains largely unaltered from that period. Bern was elected as the seat of federal authority upon the adoption of the new Swiss Constitution in 1848. The other main candidate at the time was Zürich, but French-speakers swayed the vote in Bern's favour as they considered Zürich too Germanic.

Despite playing host to the nation's politicians, Bern retains a relaxed, small-town charm. Except, that is, in the train station during rush hour, where you feel like a cork bobbing in a sea of surging humanity; mere flotsam in a tide of purposeful commuters. A picturesque old town contains six km of covered arcades and 11 historic fountains, as well as the descendants of the city's first casualty (the bear) who perform tricks for tourists. The world's largest Paul Klee collection is housed in the Museum of Fine Arts.

Orientation

The compact centre of town is contained within a sharp U-bend of the Aare River, and some of the main streets in this part have pedestrian access only. The main train station is in the mouth of this 'U' and is within easy reach of all the main sights. The station has luggage lockers (Sfr2), bicycle rental (daily from 6.10 am to 11.45 pm) and Swissair check-in.

Most shops are shut on Monday morning and have extended hours on Thursday evening until 9 pm.

Information

Tourist Office The Offizielles Verkehrsbüro

Bern (☎ 031-311 66 11) is in the train station and is open daily from 9 am to 8.30 pm. From 1 October to 31 May it shuts two hours earlier and Sunday hours are reduced to 10 am to 5 pm. Services include hotel reservations (Sfr3 service charge) and excursions. Its free booklet, *This Week in Bern*, contains much practical and recreational information. The tourist office map is fine for the centre, but if you need to go into the suburbs, pick up a free map with a street index from the Swiss Bank Corporation. The train information office is just opposite the tourist office, open Monday to Friday from 8 am to 7.30 pm and Saturday and Sunday from 8 am to 5 pm.

Money Exchange facilities, including cash advances with Visa, Eurocard, American Express and Diners Card, can be found in the lower level of the train station. The office is open daily from 6.15 am to 9.45 pm, except from mid-October to May when it closes at 8.45 pm.

Post & Telecommunications The main post office (Schanzenpost 1) is at Schanzenstrasse; it is open Monday to Friday from 7.30 am to 6.30 pm and on Saturday from 7.30 to 11 am.

The telephone code for Bern is 031.

Warning By 1994 all Bern telephone numbers will have seven digits. The system was not yet finalised when this book went to press, but for numbers in the central district you can *usually* substitute the initial 22 with 311.

Foreign Embassies Most embassies can be found south-east of the Kirchenfeldbrücke.

Australia
    Alpenstrasse 29 (☎ 43 01 43)
Canada
    Kirchenfeldstrasse 88 (☎ 44 63 81)
Eire
    Eigerstrasse 71, west of the Monbijoubrücke (☎ 46 23 53)

France
    Schosshaldenstrasse 46, south-east of the Nydeggbrücke (☎ 43 24 24)
Germany
    farther south at Willadingweg 83 (☎ 44 08 31)
South Africa
    Jungfraustrasse 1 (☎ 44 20 11)
UK
    Thunstrasse 50 (☎ 44 50 21)
USA
    Jubiläumsstrasse 93 (☎ 43 70 11)

As Bern is Switzerland's capital, dozens of other embassies are also located here. The tourist office has a full list.

Travel Agencies American Express (☎ 22 94 01) is at Bubenbergplatz 11; it is open Monday to Friday from 8.30 am to 12.30 pm and 1.30 to 6 pm and Saturday from 9 am to noon. The Swiss budget travel agency SSR has two offices: a branch at Falkenplatz 9 (☎ 24 03 12), and one at Rathausgasse 64 (☎ 21 07 22). Both are open Monday to Friday from 9.30 am to 6 pm (8 pm on Thursday).

Bookshops Stauffacher AG (☎ 22 14 23), Neuengasse 25, has a whole room of English-language books, both fiction and nonfiction. Travel books are in the annex down the adjoining Von Werdt Passage. Atlas (☎ 22 90 44), Schauplatzgasse 31, specialises in travel books.

Emergency There is a police station (☎ 68 41 11) and a chemist in the train station. For medical emergencies, call ☎ 22 92 11. The national emergency numbers can also be used: for police, ☎ 117; for the fire brigade, ☎ 118; for an ambulance, ☎ 144; and for car breakdown service, ☎ 140.

Gay & Lesbian HAB (☎ 22 63 53), Brunngasse 17, is a gay counselling and information centre. There is a women's centre in the Reithalle.

Dangers & Annoyances There is a drug problem in this otherwise idyllic town, which the authorities try to contain within

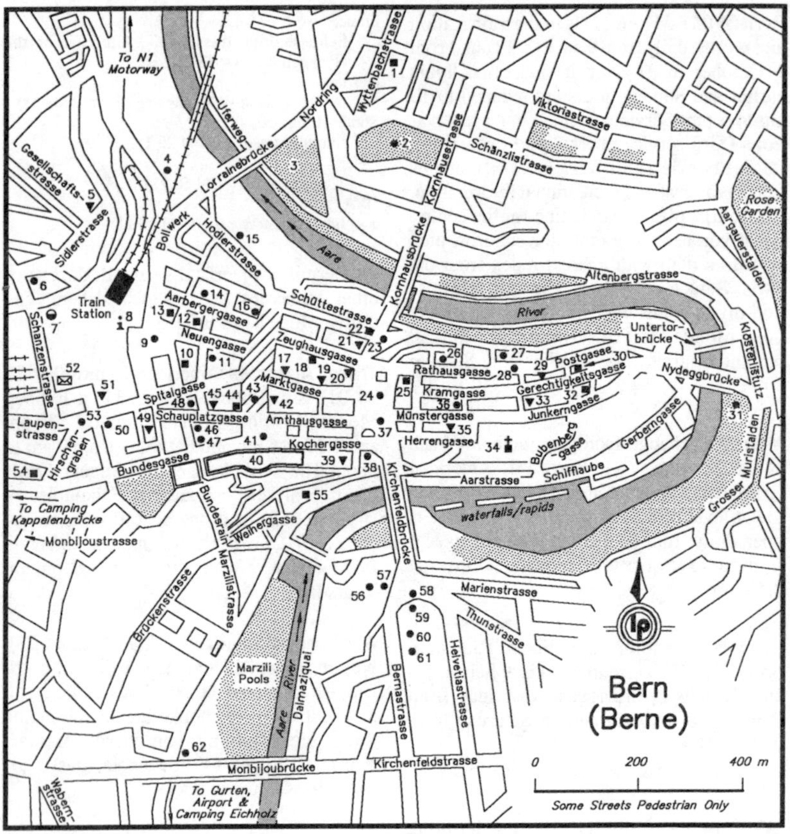

Bern (Berne)

0   200   400 m

Some Streets Pedestrian Only

one area. The location changes periodically, but it's not a pleasant thing to stumble upon; you find youngsters openly injecting themselves, and the area littered with needles and bloody swabs. It's not a pretty sight. There has been the occasional violent incident in the area around the Reithalle (see the Entertainment section) so be careful if you're in this area on your own.

Laundry In the lower level of the station there's a laundry room next to the place where there are showers. Self-service machines cost Sfr3 or Sfr4 to wash and Sfr1 per 15 minutes to dry. It's open weekdays from 7 am to 7 pm, Saturday from 7 am to 6 pm, and Sunday from 10 am to 1 pm and 2 to 6 pm.

Walking Tour

The city map from the tourist office details a picturesque walk through the old town. The core of the walk is Marktgasse and Kramgasse with their covered arcades and colourful fountains. The statues appear every 150 metres and were constructed in approximately 1545. The **Ogre Fountain** on Kornhausplatz, dividing the two streets,

■ **PLACES TO STAY**

1	Marthahaus Garni
10	Hotel Gauer Schweizerhof
12	Hotel Savoy
13	Hotel Wächter & Hotel Krebs
18	Hotel Bern
25	Hotel Glocke & Swiss Restaurant Chalet
30	Hospiz zur Heimat
32	Hotel Goldener Adler
44	Hotel Bären & Hotel Bristol
54	Hotel National
55	Youth Hostel

▼ **PLACES TO EAT**

5	Mensa
17	Migros Supermarket & GD Restaurant
19	EPA Department Store
20	Restaurant Brasserie Anker
21	Kornhauskeller
29	Klötzlikeller
33	Ratskeller
35	Menuetto
39	Bellevue-Grill & Bellevue Palace
42	Gfeller & Chinese Restaurant
45	Della Casa
49	Manora
51	Café Bubenberg Vegi

OTHER

2	Kursaal
3	Botanical Gardens
4	Reithalle

6	SSR (Travel Agency)
7	Bus Station
8	Tourist Office
9	Bahnhofplatz
11	Stauffacher AG Bookshop
14	Aarbergerhof
15	Museum of Fine Arts
16	Inlingua Sprachschule
22	Stadttheater
23	Kornhausplatz
24	Zeitglockenturm
26	SSR (Travel Agency)
27	Town Hall (Rathaus)
28	Rathausplatz
31	Bear Pits
34	Cathedral
36	Einstein House
37	Theaterplatz
38	Hertz (Car Rental)
40	Parliament
41	Bundesplatz
43	Bärenplatz
46	Atlas Bookshop
47	Babalu
48	Swiss Bank Corporation
50	American Express (Travel Agency)
52	Main Post Office
53	Bubenbergplatz
56	Swiss PTT Museum
57	Swiss Alpine Museum
58	Helvetiaplatz
59	Bern Historical Museum
60	Swiss Rifle Museum
61	Natural History Museum
62	Dampfzentale (Music Venue)

depicts the unusual subject matter of an ogre devouring small children.

Nearby is the **Zeitglockenturm**, a clock tower on which revolving figures herald the chiming hour. Congregate on the Kramgasse side at least four minutes before the hour on the east side to see them twirl. Originally a city gate, the clock was installed in 1530. The next fountain along shows a bear holding a shield bearing the Zähringen coat of arms – this appears in many a postcard.

Just over the Aare River are the **bear pits** *(Bärengraben)*, open daily to 6 pm (4 pm October to March). Bears have been at this site since 1857, although records show that as far back as 1441 the city council bought acorns to feed the ancestors of these overgrown pets. Up the hill is the **Rose Garden**, which has 200 varieties of roses and an excellent view of the city. Another good place to wander is the **Botanical Gardens** (free entry), on the north side of the Lorrainebrücke. Near the town is the hilltop, **Gurten**, where you can hike and enjoy the fine views. Get there by tram No 9 to Gurtenbahn then the funicular (total fare Sfr6).

Cathedral The unmistakably Gothic, 15th century cathedral (Münster) stands tall with the highest spire (100 metres) in Switzerland. The tower gives a fine view extending to the Bernese Alps, with the reddish rooftops of Bern itself scattered below. The best feature of the church is the **main portal**, with an elaborate tympanum depicting the Last Judgement. It was recently repainted; notice one pope ascending to heaven and another cast into the fires of hell. The cathedral was Catholic until the Reformation, at which point many of the statues were thrown out (hence the empty recesses in the chancel), but the Catholic saints on the ceiling remain as they were too high to get at.

Other features to notice are the stained-glass windows (mostly built in 1421 to 1450) and the carved choir stalls (1523). The cathedral is open daily from 10 am (11 am Sunday) to noon and 2 to 5 pm, except from November to Easter Sunday when it's closed on Sunday afternoon and Monday. The tower closes half an hour earlier each day at 11.30 am for lunch and at 4.30 pm at the end of the day, and costs Sfr3 or Sfr1 for children.

Parliament Well worth a visit is the Bundeshäuser, home of the Swiss Federal Assembly. There are free daily tours when the parliament is not in session. Arrive early and reserve a place for later in the day. A multilingual guide takes you through the impressive chambers. This grand, domed building was built in 1902, and on the glass of the dome are displayed the coats of arms of 22 cantons. (The canton of Jura wasn't yet inaugurated.) Inside are other plaques, pictures and statues that reflect important events in Swiss history. There are two main chambers, the National Council and the Council of States; the latter has a huge chandelier, a tangled mess of wrought iron weighing 1½ tonnes and sprouting 214 bulbs.

Museums
There is no shortage of museums. Many are grouped together on the south side of the Kirchenfeldbrücke.

Museum of Fine Arts The Kunstmuseum, Hodlerstrasse 8-12, holds the Paul Klee collection, a total of over 2000 works (mostly drawings), although it is not possible to show all of them at once. The museum also displays canvasses by Italian masters from the 14th, 15th and 16th centuries, such as Fra Angelico *(Madonna and Child)* and Duccio. Swiss artists since the 15th century are well represented, particularly Ferdinand Hodler. More modern schools of art are not overlooked, either, with paintings by Cézanne, Matisse and Picasso, and works by contemporary artists. It is open Tuesday from 10 am to 9 pm, and Wednesday to Sunday from 10 am to 5 pm; entry costs Sfr4 (students Sfr3, children free).

Bern Historical Museum This fine museum (Bernisches Historisches Museum) is on Helvetiaplatz, open Tuesday to Sunday from 10 am to 5 pm (admission Sfr5, or Sfr3 for students). Highlights include the original sculptures from the Münster doorway depicting the Last Judgement, Niklaus Manuel's macabre *Dance of Death* panels, and the ridiculous codpiece on the William Tell statue upstairs. Elsewhere, the museum contains Habsburg Church treasures (from the Königsfelden Abbey), and tapestries captured from the Burgundian troops of Charles the Bold. Various rooms show how life was lived in the canton of Bern in the last two centuries, and, somewhat tangentially, there is the Islamic collection of Henri Moser-Charlottenfels.

Natural History Museum This museum (Naturhistorisches Museum) on Bernastrasse, has eye-catching and extensive displays of animals depicted in realistic dioramas. Near the entrance are the stuffed remains of Barry, the most famous of the 40 St Bernard dogs who between them rescued an estimated 2000 travellers stranded in the Alps. Such moth-eaten preservation is a dubious reward for sterling service. It is open Monday from 2 pm to 5 pm, Tuesday to Saturday from 9 am to 5 pm, and Sunday from 10 am to 5 pm. Entry is Sfr3, or Sfr1.50 for students and senior citizens.

Other Museums The **Einstein House**, Kramgasse 49, is where the physicist developed his special theory of relativity in 1905, while working as a clerk in the patents office (free entry). There's not a vast amount to see, but it's worth allocating a few minutes (although time being what it is, it may seem longer). The **Swiss Alpine Museum**, Helvetiaplatz 4, will whet your appetite for the mountains if you haven't yet headed into the Alps. It details the history of Alpine mountaineering and cartography and has an impressively comprehensive collection of relief maps.

Philatelists will stamp their feet with joy at the **Swiss PTT Museum**, Helvetiastrasse 16, where countless postage stamps are displayed on endless panels. Afterwards, shoot over to the **Swiss Rifle Museum**, Bernastrasse 5, for a collection of firearms made since 1817.

Markets
An open-air vegetable, fruit and flower market can be found at Bundesplatz in the morning on Tuesday and Saturday. On the first Saturday of the month there's a craft market in front of the cathedral.

Festivals
On the 4th Monday in November, Bern hosts its famous onion market (Zibelmärit), where traders take over the whole of the centre of town. According to tradition, the origin of the market dates back to 1405 and the great fire. The farmers of the canton of Fribourg helped the Bernese to recover from the resulting devastation and were allowed to sell their produce in Bern as a reward. But it's more than just a market – people walk around throwing confetti and hitting each other on the head with plastic hammers, and many street performers (particularly South American bands) add to the carnival atmosphere.

Bern also hosts an important jazz festival in early May. Prices for events are between Sfr20 and Sfr50 and tickets are available in advance from the Ticket Corner, Schweizerischer Bankverein (☎ 66 25 39), Bärenplatz 8, Bern.

Courses
Inlingua Sprachschule (☎ 22 24 13) is at Waisenhausplatz 28. Volkshochschule Bern (☎ 22 41 92), Bollwerk 15, Postfach has adult education courses (10 week minimum) for all sorts of disciplines ranging from languages to gymnastics. The administration for the Migrosschule (Migros school; ☎ 21 15 01) is on the 1st floor at Marktgasse 46.

Organised Tours
There is a daily (Saturday only in winter) two-hour city tour by coach, which costs Sfr19 and departs from outside the tourist office. You can walk to all the places yourself without bothering with a tour, but the multilingual commentary is informative. Departures are at 10 am (except winter) and

---

Police State
In the late 1980s Switzerland was rocked by several political scandals. Confidence was hit when the then Justice Minister, Mrs Kopp, was accused of breaching secrecy rules and warning her husband that his company was under investigation for money laundering. She was later acquitted, a judgement that was greeted with disbelief by many Swiss.

A greater furore erupted when it was discovered that the federal police had kept 900,000 secret files on Swiss citizens and foreigners. That's nearly one person in seven. Violent street demonstrations broke out in Bern, and the government pledged to destroy all files, except those relating to terrorism, espionage, or organised crime. Shortly afterwards there was the discovery of a secret army, set up under the auspices of organising resistance against an occupying power, but which was actually indulging in all sorts of fringe activities, with scant official control. The army was soon disbanded (a secret army that is no secret is no use as a secret army).

Public opinion was further disgruntled in 1990 by the revelation in a study published by Geneva University, that ultimate political and economic power in Switzerland is wielded by a closely linked network of less than 100 people. ■

2 pm (except Sunday). Tours also depart daily to all the main attractions in the Bernese Oberland, central Switzerland and to some lesser-known local destinations. Prices are from Sfr21.20 to Sfr154, and are worth considering if you're on a lightning visit.

A trip by bus to the Emmental Cheese Dairy (see the Emmental section in this chapter) costs Sfr28. To reserve or get more information go to the tourist office.

Places to Stay – bottom end
Camping To get to *Camping Kappelen-brücke* (☎ 901 10 07), take postbus No 3 or 4 from the train station to Eymatt. The site is open year-round; reception is shut from 1 to 4 pm and the gates close at 11 pm. Overnight charges are Sfr6 per adult, Sfr7 per car and Sfr4 per tent. Near the river but to the south of town is *Camping Eichholz* (☎ 961 26 02), Strandweg 49. Take tram No 9 from the station. The site is open from late April to the end of September, and costs are Sfr4.80 per person, tents Sfr3, cars Sfr2, and vans Sfr8. It also has two-bed rooms for Sfr12 plus Sfr4.80 per person.

Hostel The IYHF *youth hostel* (☎ 22 63 16), Weihergasse 4, is open year-round and in a good location below the parliament. The paths down the hill are signposted to the hostel. It is usually full in summer, when a three-day maximum stay applies. Reception is shut from 9.30 am to 4 or 5 pm, but bags can be left in the common room during the day. Beds are Sfr14, breakfast Sfr5, and lunch and dinner are Sfr9 each. There are free lockers, a midnight curfew, and washing machines at Sfr3 per load.

Hotels There's a limited choice of budget rooms in Bern. *Bahnhof-Süd* (☎ 992 51 11), Bümplizstrasse 189, to the west of town beyond the autobahn, has singles/doubles from Sfr50/80 without breakfast (shower and toilet out in the corridor). To get there, take bus No 13 from the city centre. Conveniently close to the train station is the hotel,

National (☎ 381 19 88), Hirschengraben 24. It has good-for-the-price singles/doubles without shower from Sfr47/84, or Sfr 85/110 with shower and toilet.

Within the old town in an 18th century building is *Hospiz zur Heimat* (☎ 311 04 36), Gerechtigkeitsgasse 50. Features include clean, spacious rooms and a wonderfully rude and impatient proprietor who presumably went to the Basil Fawlty school of hotel management. Singles/doubles are Sfr58/84, and triples/quads are Sfr111/148. Rooms with shower are around Sfr22 more expensive, otherwise there are showers in the hall. The hotel also has a restaurant with a cheap lunch-time menu.

Also ideally situated is *Glocke* (☎ 311 37 71), Rathausgasse 75. Singles/doubles are Sfr82/120 with private shower, or Sfr60/96 without. Another place in the old town is *Wächter* (☎ 311 08 66), Genfergasse 4, with a restaurant belonging to the Mövenpick chain. Rooms come in various sizes and levels of comfort, but you're never without a TV. Prices start at Sfr54/128.

Take bus No 20 from Bahnhofplatz for *Marthahaus Garni* (☎ 332 41 35), Wyttenbachstrasse 22A. It's a friendly place with comfortable rooms and two TV lounges. Singles/doubles/triples with breakfast start from Sfr55/85/120, although prices go up slightly in the summer.

Places to Stay – middle
Opposite and to the left of Hospiz zur Heimat is the more upmarket *Goldener Adler* (☎ 311 17 25) at Gerechtigkeitsgasse 7, which has singles/doubles for Sfr95/150. Another good choice for mid-price accommodation is *Hotel Krebs* (☎ 311 49 42), Genfergasse 8, near the train station. Singles with shower, toilet, TV and breakfast buffet are expensive at Sfr118, but the corresponding doubles are a much better deal at Sfr145; the family room for four costs Sfr235. There are a few singles with showers in the hall for Sfr85.

Hotel Alfa (☎ 381 38 66), Laupenstrasse 15, has adequate rooms for Sfr125/175 with all the requisite amenities. But it hasn't much character, and the bare concrete in the hallways hardly adds to the ambience.

Places to Stay – top end

Hotel Bären (☎ 311 33 67), Schauplatzgasse 4, and the adjoining *Hotel Bristol* (☎ 311 01 01), at No 10, are effectively the same hotel. They're part of the Best Western chain and have comfortable if uninspiring rooms from Sfr150/210. *Hotel Bern* (☎ 312 10 21), Zeughausgasse 9, is the same standard and price. The best place to stay without jumping to the luxury class is the *Hotel Savoy* (☎ 311 44 05), Neuengasse 26, where prices start at Sfr160/230. The rooms are bigger, better furnished, and have an overall more welcoming feel than those of its rivals.

There are only two five-star hotels in town: the *Bellevue Palace* (☎ 320 45 45) is at Kochergasse 3-5 and the *Gauer Schweizerhof* (☎ 311 45 01) is at Bahnofplatz 11. Prices at both start at Sfr190/300 for singles/doubles.

Places to Eat

Self-Service *Migros* supermarket at Marktgasse 46 is open Monday from 2 to 6.30 pm; Tuesday, Wednesday and Friday from 8 am to 6.30 pm; Thursday from 8 am to 9 pm and Saturday from 7 am to 4 pm. It has a cheap self-service restaurant on the 1st floor. On the same floor is *G D Restaurant* with a good selection of local dishes from Sfr9, open Monday to Friday from 8.30 am to 7.30 pm (closes 9.30 pm on Thursday), and Saturday from 8 am to 4 pm.

The best value in town is at the university *Mensa*, Gesellschaftsstrasse 2, on the 1st floor. Menus cost around Sfr6, and there are reductions for students. It is open Monday to Friday from 11.30 am to 1.45 pm and 5.45 to 7.30 pm. (It closes at 1.45 pm on Friday.) The café downstairs keeps longer hours for drinks and snacks.

The *EPA* department store, straddling Zeughausgasse and Marktgasse, has a restaurant on the 1st floor where meals cost between Sfr6 and Sfr10. *Manora* (☎ 22 37 55), Bubenbergplatz 5a, is a busy and sometimes hectic restaurant, but usually has the tastiest food of the self-service bunch. Meals are Sfr9 to Sfr16, and the pile-it-on-yourself salad is Sfr4.50 to Sfr9.50 per plate. It is open daily from 7 am (9 am Sunday) until 10.45 pm.

Cheap Restaurants *Apero*, on the top floor in the train station, has daily specials from Sfr8 to Sfr15, and terraced seating overlooking the square. Nearby is *Café Bubenberg Vegi* (☎ 22 75 76), Bubenbergplatz 8, which has terrace seating and good vegetarian food for Sfr11 to Sfr19. It is open Monday to Friday from 7 am to 10 pm and Saturday from 7 am to 5 pm. Slightly more expensive but recommended for vegetarian food is *Menuetto* (☎ 22 14 48), Münstergasse 47, open daily except Sunday from 9 am to 10 pm.

Several pleasant restaurants with outside seating line Bärenplatz. There's little difference between them – study menus to make your choice. On the 1st floor above *Gfeller* is a *Chinese* self-service restaurant. *Mazot* at No 5 is a good place for Swiss food.

Kornhauskeller (☎ 22 11 33), Kornhausplatz 17, is a traditional beer hall with live music nightly (entry is free but the music can yield more pain than pleasure, depending on the band) and a jazz matinée on Sunday (entry Sfr15 to Sfr20). Food is around Sfr12 to Sfr30; perhaps the best option is the well-prepared, two-course menu (lunch and evening), which is good value for around Sfr15. It is open Tuesday to Saturday from 6 am to around midnight, and Sunday from 11.15 am to 11 pm.

Around the corner, the *Restaurant Brasserie Anker* (☎ 22 11 13) at Zeughausgasse 1 has fondues from Sfr17.50. Its relaxed atmosphere is as popular with drinkers as its low beer prices – just Sfr3.80 for half a litre. It is open until 11.30 pm except on Sunday when it shuts at 6 pm.

Mid-Price & Expensive Restaurants The dingy exterior of *Della Casa* (☎ 311 21 42), Schauplatzgasse 16, hides a good-quality restaurant within. The local speciality, *Bärner Platte* (a selection of meats also including sauerkraut and beans), is served here but it is expensive (Sfr34). If you're lucky, you can find it on the excellent three-course daily menu for Sfr19 (different menu for lunch and dinner). It is open Monday to Friday from 8.30 am to 11.30 pm but the daily menu stops at 9 pm. The upstairs section is slightly more expensive.

For good-quality fish and meat dishes (Sfr17 to Sfr46) in a calm setting, try the *Ratskeller* at Gerechtigkeitsgasse 81 (open daily). More lively and atmospheric is *Klötzlikeller* (☎ 22 74 56), a wine cellar at Gerechtigkeitsgasse 62. It has interesting dishes ranging from snails to tripe and costing Sfr16 to Sfr35. It is open Tuesday to Saturday from 4 pm till after midnight.

Bellevue-Grill in the Bellevue Palace Hotel (☎ 320 45 45), Kochergasse 3-5, is considered the best restaurant in Bern. Reserve ahead, as despite the high prices, it is often full. Main courses start at Sfr36 but the most people go for the creative menu for Sfr98. The food is presented with a flourish here; the servers troop out in file, each bearing the main course for each guest around the table. When all the plates are carefully placed before the appropriate diner, they simultaneously whip off the metal cover to reveal the feast beneath. They then stand reverently in a circle, covers held aloft, as the head server recites a short spiel describing each dish. It's almost a religious ceremony and has to be seen to be believed.

Entertainment

On Mondays, cinemas cost Sfr9 instead of the usual Sfr13 to Sfr15. There are a couple of cinemas on Laupenstrasse.

The *Kursaal* (☎ 42 54 66), Schänzlistrasse 71-77 (take tram No 9 from Kornhausplatz), has gambling from 9pm, and live music with a cover charge of about Sfr5 to Sfr12. There's also a disco which is free for women on Thursday. A few late venues in the city centre keep going until around 3 am (except Sunday) but they can get expensive. *Babalu*, Gurtengasse 3, is a nightclub with live music and different themes each night, including a gay night on Wednesday. Cover charge is

Sfr13 to Sfr23. *Ursus Club*, Junkerngasse 1, is a gay bar and disco open every night except Tuesday (and Sunday in the summer).

A place popular with young locals is the bright bar/café *Aarbergerhof*, Aarbergergasse 40. The rather noisier and darker *Interview*, down the Ryffligässchen passage between Neuengasse and Spitalgasse, attracts a regular and youthful clientele.

Reithalle, Shuttzenmattestrasse, a former riding school, is a fascinating place to spend time. It's a semi-legal centre for alternative arts housed in several graffiti-splattered, derelict-looking buildings under the railway line. The faint-hearted may be deterred by the rotting caravans, the piles of junk in the courtyard and the bedraggled punters openly smoking dope, and unfortunately there have been occasional safety problems. On site there is a music venue, theatre, library, café and cheap restaurant. There's also a women's-only disco upstairs on the first Friday of the month. The philosophy of the place dictates that there's no set entry fee for events – just pay what you can afford. For information call ☎ 42 01 42 or ☎ 24 63 17.

If your tastes lean more toward the traditional, go to the *Swiss Restaurant Chalet* at the Hotel Glocke (see Places to Stay). A folklore show starts at 8.30 pm from June to October (closed Sunday). Inevitably these places are a bit touristy but it's free (you pay for it in the drink prices) and the music goes on until at least 1 am.

Bärenplatz is a great place to linger on a sunny day. There's always something happening, whether it be buskers, giant chess games, or demonstrations outside the parliament building. Something else the Bernese enjoy on a sunny day is floating down the Aare River. They take the plunge in the Sandrain district and float downstream to the free open-air pools at Marzili, just north of Montbijoubrücke. Near to the Marzili pools is Dampfzentrale, a venue for jazz, soul, funk and art exhibitions. Jazz is also on the agenda at *Marian's Jazzroom* (☎ 309 61 11), Engestrasse 54.

The *Stadttheater* has productions almost every day and tickets are available from the

Top Left: Staubbach Falls, Lauterbrunnen, Bernese Oberland (MH)
Top Right: Country house, near Brienz, Bernese Oberland (MH)
Bottom: View of the Aletsch Glacier from Jungfraujoch, Bernese Oberland (MH)

Top Left: Giessbach Falls, Lake Brienz, Bernese Oberland (MH)
Top Right: Breithorn and Lauberhorn from Männlichen, Bernese Oberland (MH)
Bottom Left: Leading herd through village, Interlaken, Bernese Oberland (MH)
Bottom Right: Lake Brienz from Harder Kulm, Bernese Oberland (MH)

Theaterkasse (☎ 22 07 77), Kornhausplatz 18. There are also a number of small theatre groups (including a puppet theatre) which perform in the cellars along Kramgasse and Gerechtigkeitsgasse. Bern has a symphony orchestra, and there's always something going on in the classical music field. Concerts are often held in the large hall of the Casino, Herrengasse 25. Check *This Week in Bern* for details.

North of the centre is the Wankdorf football and athletics stadium. Nearby is the more famous ice-hockey stadium; it's one of the biggest in Europe and Bern has one of the best teams in the country.

Things to Buy

The Swiss Craft Centre (Heimatwerk) on Kramgasse 61 offers handmade but expensive souvenirs, such as wood-carvings, jewellery and Bernese pottery. There are many other souvenir shops on Kramgasse and Gerechtigkeitsgasse. *Klözli*, Rathausgasse 84, boasts a huge selection of Swiss army knives.

Getting There & Away

Air There are daily flights by Crossair (☎ 961 55 33) to/from Paris, Lugano, Florence, Nice, Venice and Brussels. The Swissair check-in counter in the train station (☎ 22 95 11) will take your luggage and get it on your flight from Zürich or Geneva. See the Getting There & Away chapter for details.

Train Bern has excellent train connections. Departures are at least hourly to most destinations, including Geneva (Sfr45, takes 1¾ hours), Basel (Sfr32, takes 70 minutes), Interlaken (Sfr21, takes 50 minutes), and Zürich (Sfr38, takes 1½ hours). The train information office is opposite the tourist office

Bus Postbuses depart from the Schanzenstrasse side of the train station, although the train service should meet the needs of most visitors.

Car & Motorbike There are three motorways which intersect at the northern part of the city. The N1 is the route from Neuchâtel in the west and Basel and Zürich in the northeast. The N6 connects Bern with Thun and the Interlaken region in the south. The N12 is the route from Geneva and Lausanne in the south-west.

There are several underground parking spots in the city centre, including one at the train station. The tourist office map lists locations.

Rental Hertz (☎ 311 33 61) is in the old town at Kasinoplatz, and Avis (☎ 46 13 13) is at Wabernstrasse 41. Both have an office at the airport. Europcar (☎ 25 75 55) is at Laupenstrasse 22.

Getting Around

To/From the Airport The small Bern/Belp airport is 10 km south-east of the city centre. A bus run by Crossair links the airport to the train station (Sfr 12). It takes 20 minutes and is coordinated with flight arrivals and departures.

Bus & Tram Getting around on foot is easy enough if you're staying near the city centre, although buses and trams are cheap and frequent. Tickets cost Sfr1.10 to Sfr1.70, but you're better off buying daily tourist cards valid for unlimited travel. One, two or three-day passes cost Sfr4, Sfr6 or Sfr9. A 24-hour card costs Sfr5 and is valid from first use. Buy single-journey tickets at stops and daily cards from the tourist office or the public transport office (☎ 22 14 44) at Bubenbergplatz 5. Special night buses run at 12.35 am and 1.40 am; the fare is Sfr3 and passes are not valid.

Taxi Many taxis wait by the station. The cost is Sfr6 plus Sfr2.20 to Sfr2.80 per km depending on the number of passengers and the time of day.

Biel

Biel (or Bienne in French), is one of those Swiss towns nonchalantly spanning the linguistic divide. The town has expanded greatly since the end of the 19th century, thanks in part to cashing in on the burgeoning watch and clock-making industry. Some of the biggest names – Omega, Rolex and Swatch – are based in Biel. The town now has a population of 53,000. Its lake and old town centre are the main attractions.

Orientation & Information

Biel is at the northern end of Lake Biel (Bielersee, Lac de Bienne). It's a bilingual city and all street names are shown in both languages. The main train station is between the lake and the old town and has bike-rental and money-exchange counters open daily. The tourist office (☎ 032-22 75 75) and bus information are in a shack by the bicycle park in front of the station. Opening hours are 8.30 am to noon and 2 to 6 pm, and from May to October on Saturday from 9 am to noon and 2 to 5 pm. The main post office is also by the train station. To reach the old town,

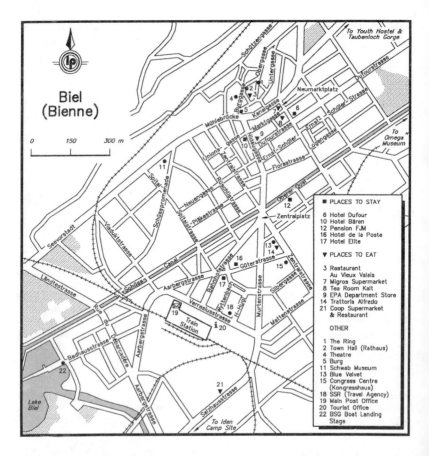

Biel (Bienne)

0   150   300 m

■ PLACES TO STAY

6 Hotel Dufour
10 Hotel Bären
12 Pension FJM
16 Hotel de la Poste
17 Hotel Elite

▼ PLACES TO EAT

3 Restaurant
   Au Vieux Valais
7 Migros Supermarket
8 Tea Room Kalt
9 EPA Department Store
14 Trattoria Alfredo
21 Coop Supermarket
   & Restaurant

OTHER

1 The Ring
2 Town Hall (Rathaus)
4 Theatre
5 Burg
11 Schwab Museum
13 Blue Velvet
15 Congress Centre
   (Kongresshaus)
18 SSR (Travel Agency)
19 Main Post Office
20 Tourist Office
22 BSG Boat Landing
   Stage

walk down Bahnhofstrasse to Zentralplatz then take Nidaugasse to the end (15 minutes).

SSR (☎ 032-22 58 88), the budget travel agency, is at Hugistrasse 3.

The telephone code for Biel is 032.

Things to See & Do

The old town has as its centrepiece the **Ring**, a picturesque square with a 16th century fountain. The name harks back to bygone days when justice was dispensed in the square. The community big-wigs would sit in an intimidatory semicircle to pass judgement upon unfortunate miscreants who were brought before them.

Adjoining the Ring on Obergasse (Rue Haute) is another 16th century fountain, depicting an angel with a leering devil at her shoulder. Leading from the opposite side of the Ring is Burggasse (Rue de Bourg), where you can see the step-gabled town hall and the Fountain of Justice (1744). The centre doesn't take long to explore. If you have time to kill, drop into a café and indulge in some eavesdropping, but only to admire the lingual ability of the locals to switch between French and German with barely a break in the rhythm of their conversations.

The **Schwab Museum**, Seevorstadt 50 (Faubourg du Lac 50), is a museum of prehistory and archaeology, named after the 19th century colonel who was instrumental in unearthing the secrets of the ancient lakedwellers of the region. Many of the more interesting finds from around the lakes of Biel, Murten and Neuchâtel are on display. The 6000-year-old settlements were revealed when the level of the lakes fell by some two metres following measures introduced to control the water flow in the Jura. The museum is open from Tuesday to Sunday from 10 am to noon and 2 to 5 pm, and entry costs Sfr2.

The **Omega Museum** (☎ 42 92 11), Stämpflistrasse 96, gives a free glimpse of the company's watch-making activities, past and present (open on request).

The town puts on a weekend **carnival** starting the Friday after Ash Wednesday.

Places to Stay – bottom end

Camping There are four camp sites clustered round the southern end of Lake Biel. Much nearer Biel and also by the lake is *Iden* (☎ 57 13 45) at Sutz-Lattrigen. The train to Sutz runs every 30 minutes (Sfr3) and brings you to within one km of the site. It's open from Easter to mid-October and costs Sfr5.50 per person and from Sfr4 per tent.

Hostel There is an IYHF *youth hostel* (☎ 41 29 65), Solothurnstrasse 137, but it's nowhere near the centre; take trolley bus No 1 from the station, get off at Zollhaus then walk for 15 minutes. To compensate, beds are just Sfr9 without breakfast. Reception is closed from 9 am to 5 pm and the hostel is closed from 1 November to mid-March.

Hotels & Pensions *Pension FJM* (☎ 22 04 32), Oberer Quai 12, is really a student's home with mainly long-term guests. If there's space they're happy to take shortterm visitors, so phone from the station. (They don't accept advance reservations.) All rooms are single for Sfr42 with use of hall shower. Reception shuts at 8 pm and you get your own key. It's on the 2nd floor and says 'Pension Farel' on the front door. The only other cheapish place is *Hotel de la Poste* (☎ 22 25 44), Güterstrasse 3, off Bahnhofstrasse, with singles/doubles for Sfr50/90.

Places to Stay – middle

Hotel Bären (☎ 22 45 73), Nidaugasse 22, near the old town, has singles/doubles for Sfr85/130 and triples for Sfr210, all with shower or bath, toilet, radio and telephone. Rooms are a bit plain but reasonably large. Solid metal lights in the corridor seem specially designed to cave-in the forehead of the inattentive guest. Reception is at a small counter in the busy restaurant. Rooms are comparable in the *Hotel Dufour* (☎ 42 22 61) on Neumarktplatz (Place du Marché), except each room has a TV. Prices start at Sfr85/130.

Places to Stay – top end

At the *Hotel Elite* (☎ 22 54 41), Bahnhofstrasse 14, you'll pay at least Sfr150/220, but the attentive service makes it worthwhile.

Place to Eat

Self-Service There's a large *Coop* with a restaurant round the back of the station on Salzhausstrasse. More convenient for the centre is *EPA* on Nidaugasse, or the *Migros* on Neumarktplatz. All offer similar quality and prices (meals for under Sfr10) and are open until 6.30 pm on weekdays (except late till 9 pm on Thursday) and to 4 pm on Saturday.

Restaurants Tea rooms are a budget option in the daytime. *Tea Room Kalt*, Marktgasse, off Neumaktplatz, has several menus including soup from Sfr11. For a more relaxing ambience, explore the typical and fairly inexpensive places in the old centre. Look for the *Restaurant Au Vieux Valais* (☎ 22 34 55), off the Ring at Untergässli 9, which has lunches with soup from Sfr12, fondue for Sfr16.50 and meat dishes from Sfr18 (closed Monday). *Hotel Dufour* (see Places to Stay) has a couple of vegetarian dishes for around Sfr12, smallish portions of pizza/pasta from Sfr8, and grills and fish from Sfr22. It's closed on Saturday evening. *Trattoria Alfredo*, Zentralstrasse 56, has cheery décor and pizzas from Sfr9.50 (closed Sunday).

Gourmet's heaven is at the restaurant of the *Hotel Elite* (see Places to Stay). The food is mainly French style although it periodically has festivals featuring different culinary themes. Main dishes top Sfr35 and multi-course menus are around the Sfr80 mark. It is open daily. The attention to presentation is meticulous, even down to the waiters or chefs carefully constructing patterns from the dessert sauces.

Entertainment

Blue Velvet (☎ 23 28 18), Zentralstrasse 54, is a live music and disco venue, open from 10 pm on the weekends. Nearby is the *Kongresshaus* (☎ 23 33 11) where concerts and cultural events are held. Biel has its own orchestra and municipal theatre; productions are usually in German.

Getting There & Away

Biel is just 30 minutes from Bern by train (Sfr9.80). Solothurn (Sfr7.80, 50 minutes), Neuchâtel (Sfr9, 20 minutes), and Murten (Sfr10.60, 40 minutes) are also close by train, but a more enjoyable way to get to these towns is by boat. Ferries are run by BSG (see the following Around Biel section). Getting to Murten by boat takes two hours 40 minutes and costs Sfr22 one-way or Sfr36 return. Neuchâtel takes a similar time and has two departures a day in season. Solothurn can be reached by boat along the Aare River; there are five departures a day in summer and it takes less than 2½ hours (Sfr21 one-way, Sfr34 return).

AROUND BIEL

Flora and fauna abound in **St Peter's Island** (St Peterinsel, Île de St Pierre) a nature reserve at the south-west end of Lake Biel. Rousseau spent, in his own words, the happiest time of his life here, and his carefully preserved residence can be viewed. The island became connected to the shore when the level of the lake dropped, exposing a natural causeway. It's a relaxing 1½-hour stroll to the island along this causeway from the town of Erlach on the shore. Get to the island by boat from Biel (Sfr7.20, takes 50 minutes) or several other towns round the lake. From Biel, a train runs to La Neuveville and an infrequent bus continues to Erlach, but the journey is easier by boat.

The southern shore of **Lake Biel** offers the best swimming spots. The northern shore is noted for a string of wine-growing villages. The tourist office has a leaflet describing (in French) a walking path connecting these villages, including information on several wine cellars *(caveaux)* where produce can be purchased and sampled.

The BSG boat company (☎ 22 33 22) offers various tours on the lake between early April and late October, but services are only regular between the end of May and late September. The departure point on the lake from Biel is near the Schüss Canal. The neighbouring lakes of Neuchâtel and Murten are connected by canal; a day-long tour of all three lakes leaves Biel harbour at 9.50 am every day in the season. A special bus runs from the train station. Some packages include lunch in Murten (Sfr41 to Sfr56).

About a 30-minute walk on the road to Solothurn (or take trolley bus No 1) is the **Taubenloch Gorge**. A path runs along its two-km length (Sfr0.50 entry).

Emmental Region

Emmental is the region to the east of the towns of Langenthal, Bern and Thun. The core of the area is the valley of the Emme River, from which the name is derived (valley in German is *Tal*). A tour along the banks of the river yields picturesque towns and villages, and many buildings display architecture typical of the area. The angled roof is the most distinctive feature; it hangs very low over the sides of the house and usually has a section over the front façade, forming a triangular covering. Below this triangle there is often a semicircular trim framing the upper windows.

Things to See & Do
The local tourist offices promote hiking, and an interesting path is the Plantenenweg from **Burgdorf** to **Wynigen**, on which tiny models of the planets allow you to pretend you're marching through the universe on a scale of one: 1000 million (US billion). It takes about three hours to walk from the sun to Pluto. Afterwards, you can get the train back to Burgdorf which has a castle, bearing a large representation of the emblem of the canton. There is a historical museum inside the castle (open daily from April to October).

The town of **Langnau** is known for its ornamental crockery; the production process may be viewed at a pottery (Schautöpferei) (☎ 035-6 60 29), in nearby **Trubschachen**, reached by rail. For more details contact the tourist office for the Emmental (☎ 035-2 42

52) in Langnau. Ask the office about dates of local markets (Märit) and traditional fairs (Chilbi).

The best known product of the area is **Emmental cheese**. The Emmental Dairy Show (Emmentaler Schaukäserei) gives you the chance to see the stuff being made into huge wheels (60 to 130 kg – a bit bulky to take on a picnic). It is at Affoltern, six km east of Burgdorf. From Burgdorf, take the train to Hasle then the postbus. The dairy is open from 8.30 am to 6.30 pm every day, but it's better to get there between 9 to 11 am and 2 to 4 pm when the various production stages are being instigated. **Kiesen**, on the rail route running south-east of Bern (Sfr6.80), has a museum of dairy products that can provide more background information (open daily from 2 to 5 pm between 1 April and 31 October).

Places to Stay
There are only a few camp sites in the area. There's a TCS (Touring Club Schweiz) site, *Waldegg* (☎ 034-22 79 43), by the river in Burgdorf, (open 1 April to 1 October) and another site, *Mettlen* (035-2 36 58), at Gohl, near Langnau (open year-round).

Langnau has an IYHF *youth hostel* (☎ 035-2 45 26), 10 minutes' walk from the station at Mooseggstrasse 32. Beds cost just Sfr9 without breakfast and the hostel is closed for a few weeks in early February and late September.

Tourist offices can help you find somewhere to stay. Accommodation is mostly in small-scale country inns and pensions which are very reasonably priced (around Sfr30 to Sfr70 per person).

Getting There & Away
Every hour from Bern to Burgdorf there's a fast train (takes 15 minutes) and a local train, and the fare is Sfr6.80. Langnau can be reached by direct train from Bern (Sfr11.60) or Burgdorf.

Bernese Oberland

The Bernese Oberland (Berner Oberland) is where the scenic wonders of Switzerland come into their own. People often end up staying longer than they planned, such are the toe-twitching hikes and eye-spinning sights on offer. Good weather is essential to fully enjoy the stunning landscape, so if the sun shines, flee the cities and head for here. From Bern, a train will get you to Interlaken in less than an hour.

Orientation & Information

The Bernese Oberland tourist region covers the southern part of the canton of Bern, stretching from Gstaad in the west to the Susten Pass (2224 metres) in the east. The regional tourist office for the whole area is the Verkehrsverband Berner Oberland (☎ 036-22 26 21) at Centralstrasse Jungfraustrasse 38, CH-3800, Interlaken. It's on the first floor without a recognisable office front, and the opening hours are Monday to Saturday from 8.00 am to noon, and Monday to Friday from 2 to 6.00 pm. Pick up the detailed *Summer Info* or *Winter Info* brochures covering sights and sports in the whole region. (See the Bernese Mittelland chapter for information on the history of the canton.)

Getting Around

The Bernese Oberland Regional travel pass is one of the most useful regional passes available. It is also one of the most expensive: Sfr155 for 2nd class and Sfr198 for 1st class, with reductions for holders of Swiss travel passes (around 20% off). It gives free travel on five days out of 15 on certain routes, such as cruises on Lake Brienz and Lake Thun, and trains as far as Gstaad, Kleine Scheidegg, Thun and Meiringen. On the other days there is a 50% reduction. Many other routes (including to Bern, Zermatt, Mt Titlis, and the three pass bus tour) get 50% off for all 15 days, and mountain transport (Jungfraujoch. Schilthorn,

Gornergrat, etc) get 25% off. The pass is available from 1 May and 31 October.

Interlaken

Interlaken, flanked by Lake Thun and Lake Brienz and within striking distance of the mighty peaks of the Jungfrau, Mönch and Eiger, is an ideal centre from which to explore the surrounding delights. But if time allows, an overnight stay farther inside the Jungfrau region is even more rewarding.

Orientation & Information

Most of Interlaken is coupled between its two train stations: Interlaken West and Interlaken Ost. Each station offers bike rental and daily money-exchange facilities, and behind each is a boat landing for boat services on the lakes. The main shopping street, Höheweg, runs between the two stations. You can walk from one to the other in 20 minutes.

The tourist office (☎ 036-22 21 21), Höheweg 37, is nearer to Interlaken West train station and it's open Monday to Friday from 8 am to noon and 2 to 6 pm, and Saturday from 8 am to noon. During July and August, hours are extended to Saturday from 2 to 4 pm and Sunday from 5 to 7 pm. The office charges Sfr5 for hotel reservations and has lists of private rooms from Sfr30 per night, but the minimum stay for these is three days; the minimum for apartments is one week.

The main post office (Interlaken 3800, Postplatz) is near the Interlaken West station at Marktgasse 1. It is open for postal services from Monday to Friday from 7.30 am to noon and from 1.45 to 6.30 pm, and Saturday from 7.30 to 11 am. There are telephones and stamp machines outside. The telephone code for Interlaken is 036.

Call ☎ 23 23 23 if you have a medical emergency.

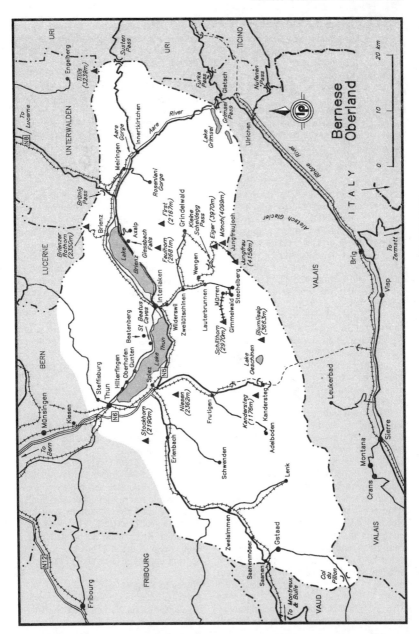

Bernese Oberland

URI

TICINO

Tillis (3239m) • Engelberg

UNTERWALDEN

To Lucerne

N8

Susten Pass

Furka Pass

Gletsch

Nufenen Pass

Grimsel Pass

Innertkirchen

Aare River

Aare Gorge

Lake Grimsel

Ulrichen

Meiringen

ITALY

Rhône River

Brünig Pass

Rosenlani Gorge

Brienzer Rothorn (2350m)

Brienz

Axalp

First (2167m)

Giessbach Falls

Faulhorn (2681m)

Grindelwald

Kleine Scheidegg Pass

Eiger (3970m)

Mönch (4099m)

Jungfraujoch

VALAIS

Aletsch Glacier

Brig

To Zermatt

Visp

LUCERNE

Lake Brienz

Interlaken

Wengen

Jungfrau (4158m)

St Beatus Caves

Beatenberg

Wilderswil

Zweilütschinen

Lauterbrunnen

Mürren

Stechelberg

Gimmelwald

Schilthorn (2970m)

Blumlisalp (3565m)

BERN

Steffisburg

Thun

Hilterfingen

Oberhofen

Gunten

Spiez

Lake Thun

N6

Lake Oeschinen

Leukerbad

Münsingen

Kiesen

To Bern

Niesen (2362m)

Frutigen

Kandersteg (1176m)

Kandersteg

Stockhorn (2190m)

Erlenbach

Adelboden

Montana

Crans

Sierre

N6

Schwenden

Lenk

VALAIS

Zweisimmen

Saanenmöser

Gstaad

FRIBOURG

To Montreux & Bulle

Saanen

Col du Pillon

VAUD

Fribourg

N12

To Bern

20 km   10   0

Things to See & Do

Most of the points of interest are around Interlaken rather than in the town itself. All the following attractions mentioned in the Jungfrau Region, Lake Thun and Lake Brienz sections can be reached on a day trip from Interlaken.

A good circular orientation walk is to wander down Höheweg, glancing at the souvenir shops and grand hotels, and at either station, cut back to the tree-lined footpaths along the Aare River. The prettiest area of Interlaken is around the **Stadthaus** dating from 1471, on the north side of the Aare in Unterseen. There's a large cobbled square bordered by attractive old buildings with a church tower at two opposite corners. One of the old buildings is the **Tourist Museum**, Obere Gasse 26. It gives a rundown of the development of tourism and transport in the region, displaying models, old posters and photos, skis and chair lifts. Explanations are in German but you can pick up a summary in English, and it's worth spending up to an hour in here. Entry costs Sfr3 (Sfr2 with Guest Card, Sfr1 for children), and it's open May to mid-October, Tuesday to Sunday from 2 to 5 pm.

Just off Höheweg there is **Chäsdorfli**, a touristy enclave where there are free cheese-making demonstrations from May to September.

If you're a train enthusiast or travelling with children, the **Model Railway Exhibition** (Modelleisenbahn-Treff) by Interlaken West train station on Rugenparkstrasse, could take up another hour of your time. There are model trains whizzing all over the place on perimeter tracks (you can even get a train to serve you coffee) and elaborate representations of famous railway routes. Not to suggest that they're biased or anything, but it's funny that, while the trains chug along freely, most of the cars shown are either held up by roadworks, passing cows, or being towed out of a ditch. It's open from the end of April to mid-October, daily from 10 am to noon and 1.30 to 6 pm. Entry costs Sfr6 or Sfr3 for children. The model railway exhibition is expensive for what it is, but still

better value than the 15-minute model railway show at **Heimwehfluh** that costs Sfr5.80 (children for Sfr3.60). Heimwehfluh does at least have a play area outside that's quite fun (free, or Sfr3.50 for the Bob-Run) and a good view of the town and lakes from the tower by the pricey restaurant. Don't bother taking the expensive funicular (Sfr7.40 return, children Sfr5.20) as the signposted walk up takes only 20 minutes, and leads to further walking trails. There's an even shorter route up (unsignposted) that starts 10 metres to the right of the base funicular station as you face it.

The village of Wilderswil can be reached in eight minutes by bus No 5 from Interlaken West (see the Jungfrau Region map). It's a good deal quieter than Interlaken, and many of the wooden houses there retain a traditional, rural ambience. Wilderswil is also the starting point for a cog-wheel train (closed November to May) that runs up to **Schynige Platte** at 2001 metres. The views are terrific from here and there is also an Alpine garden with 500 types of flora. At this altitude, many flowers are just beginning to bloom in June or July. There is a great hike from here to Faulhorn (2681 metres), Lake Bach (featured in many tourist brochures) and on to First, Grindel and Grindelwald. The whole thing takes six hours one-way and treats hikers to excellent unfolding panoramas of the Jungfrau massif.

Numerous hiking trails dot the area surrounding Interlaken, all with signposts giving average walking times. The funicular up to **Harder Kulm** (Sfr11.40 up, Sfr18.40 return, closed November to May) yields a memorable panorama and further prepared paths. While you're waiting for the funicular, wander around the enclosures containing ibexes and marmots (free). The restaurant up at Harder Kulm with the pointed roof is another regular in tourist brochures. To walk up from Interlaken takes about 2¼ hours.

Places to Stay

Ask your hotel for the Visitor's Card, which is valid for useful discounts (see the Tourist Offices section in the introductory Facts for

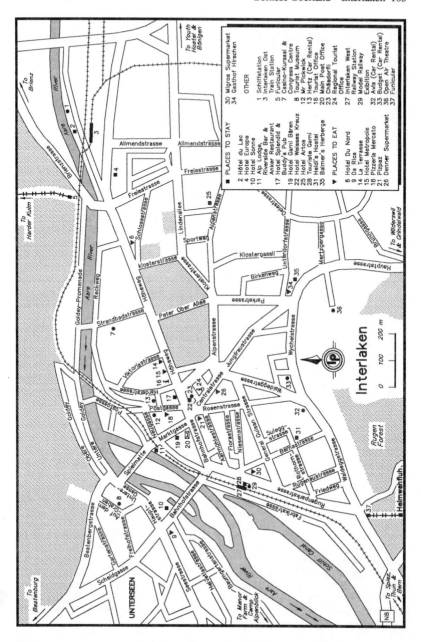

PLACES TO STAY
2 Hôtel du Lac
4 Hotel Europe
10 Hotel Sonne
11 Alp Lodge,
   Riverside Bar &
   Anker Restaurant
17 Hotel Splendid &
   Buddy's Pub
19 Hotel Garni Bären
22 Hotel Weisses Kreuz
25 Hotel Artos
28 Touriste Garni
31 Heidi's Hostel
35 Balmer's Herberge

PLACES TO EAT
6 Hotel Du Nord
9 Da Rico
14 La Terrasse
15 Hotel Metropole
18 Pizzeria Mercato
21 Pizpaz
26 Denner Supermarket
30 Migros Supermarket
34 Gasthof Hirschen

OTHER
1 Schifistation
3 Interlaken Ost
   Train Station
5 Funicular
7 Casino-Kursaal &
   Congress Centre
8 Tourist Museum
12 Mr Pickwick
13 Hertz (Car Rental)
16 Tourist Office
20 Main Post Office
23 Chäsdörfli
24 Regional Tourist
   Office
27 Interlaken West
   Railway Station
29 Model Railway
   Exbition
32 Avis (Car Rental)
33 Budget (Car Rental)
36 Open Air Theatre
37 Funicular

Interlaken

0   100   200 m

the Visitor section). By the Interlaken West train station there's a hotel board with a free telephone.

Places to Stay – bottom end

Camping There are five camp sites close together north-west of Interlaken West. *Camp Alpenblick* (☎ 22 77 57), on See-strasse by the Lombach River, costs Sfr4.50 per person, from Sfr3 per tent and Sfr4 for a car. Just along the road by the lake is *Manor Farm* (☎ 22 22 64), which is more expensive in the high season. Both sites are open all year.

Hostels The IYHF *youth hostel* (☎ 22 43 53), Aareweg 21, am See, Bönigen, is a 25-minute walk around the lake from Interlaken Ost, or you can take bus No 1. It has an excellent location by the lake, with swimming facilities, but the petty regulations can be annoying. Beds in large dorms are Sfr18.60, a lunch packet is Sfr8.50 and dinner is Sfr9. The reception shuts between 9.30 am and 5 pm, there is an 11 pm curfew, and the hostel is closed from 1 November to 31 January.

More central and much more sociable is *Balmer's Herberge* (☎ 22 19 61), Hauptstrasse 23, a 15-minute walk (signposted) from either station. Excellent communal facilities include a kitchen, reading room, games room, music room and videos every night, plus a good book-exchange in the store (Sfr5 to buy, free to swap).

The staff also organises various excursions and rents bikes. There is a great atmosphere and it's a refreshing change of style from youth hostels. Somebody even escorts you to your dorm in quiet periods. During the high season, however, the American summer-camp atmosphere and queuing for showers and breakfast can get a bit too much for some people.

Beds are Sfr15 including breakfast, showers are Sfr1, optional sheet rental is Sfr4, and there is a choice of dinners nightly in the price range of Sfr5 to Sfr10. Sign for a bed during the day and check in at 5 pm.

During busy periods, people aged over 30 are charged Sfr18 in dorms. Doubles (Sfr26 per person) and triples and quads (Sfr21 per person) are also available, and it is open all year.

Hotels & Pensions Basic but cheap is *Heidi's Hostel* (☎ 22 90 30), Bernastrasse 37, sometimes called Beyeler Garni. Singles/doubles for Sfr33/60 have a private shower; those rooms for Sfr25/50 have no access to a shower at all. These are low season prices without breakfast; when things get busier breakfast is included and prices rise.

The *Alp Lodge* (☎ 22 47 48) at Marktgasse 59, is a low-budget annex of the Bellevue, a mid-price hotel. It's good value in the low season: singles/doubles with hall facilities are Sfr35/50 and doubles/quads with private shower/toilet are Sfr70/88. Unfortunately the prices take a hike in high season; the single, for example, leaps to Sfr63 from mid-June to mid-September.

A few metres on the right from Interlaken West train station is *Touriste Garni* (☎ 22 28 31); standard singles/doubles start at Sfr36/65 and prices are Sfr10 higher in the high season. Another good choice is *Hotel Sonne* (☎ 22 88 35), Bahnhofstrasse 9. The furnishings are a bit old, but the rooms are more spacious than in a modern place, and there is a shower and toilet on every floor. Singles/doubles are around Sfr38/72 rising only marginally in high season. The Tagesmenu in the restaurant costs Sfr14 with soup. It closes in November.

Hotel Garni Bären (☎ 22 76 76) on Marktgasse has singles/doubles for Sfr40/80 with use of hall showers. Doubles are especially spacious and have a sofa. The best place for those wanting a quiet life is *Hotel Artos* (☎ 23 34 34), Alpenstrasse 45, as it's a Methodist organisation, alcohol-free, with a home for the aged upstairs. The large, gleaming singles are the best deal, starting at Sfr52 with shower or Sfr46 without. Full pension rates are very favourable for stays of three days or more.

Places to Stay – middle

Hotel Splendid (☎ 22 76 12), Höheweg 33, offers three-star comfort and a central location. Singles and doubles with private shower/toilet start at Sfr 78/115 and Sfr52/82 for those using hall facilities. Less central but convenient if you're taking the Jungfrau train is *Hotel Europe* (☎ 22 71 41) at Höheweg 94. Rooms are a similar price and standard, and there is ample free parking.

Places to Stay – top end

The plush choice without spending vast sums of money is *Hôtel du Lac* (☎ 22 29 22), Höheweg 225, overlooking the Lake Brienz boat-landing stage. Singles/doubles start at Sfr90/150 with private bath/toilet, cable TV and (usually) a balcony. The restaurant has tempting Tagestellers for Sfr17 to Sfr21.

Places to Eat

The *Migros* restaurant, above the supermarket on Bahnhofstrasse by Interlaken West, is open Monday to Friday from 7.30 am to 6.30 pm, Saturday to 4 pm. There are a number of *Denner* supermarkets around town, good for picnic provisions. The Migros supermarket doesn't sell alcohol; the Denner on Centralstrasse does.

Anker Restaurant, Marktgasse 57, has a varied menu from Sfr11 to Sfr33, and good portions. The tasty goulash soup with bread for Sfr6 is sufficient for lunch. It's open daily except Thursday evening. There is a games room around the back, but the restaurant section is fairly civilised. Vegetarians can choose the special section in the restaurant of the *Weisses Kreuz* hotel on Höheweg next to the Chäsdorfli. Meals are Sfr14 to Sfr19 and it's closed on Wednesday in the low season.

A good place for reasonable Italian food is *Pizzeria Mercato*, off Höheweg around the back of the Chalet restaurant, open to at least midnight (closed Tuesday). There are other decent pizzerias around town including *Pizpaz* on Centralstrasse (closed Monday) and *Da Rica* on Seestrasse north of the Aare in Unterseen (though the waiters here look like spaghetti-western extras in their black

sombreros). Prices for all of them start at Sfr9 for smallish pizzas.

The *Hotel Europe* (see the previous Places to Stay section) has comfortable surroundings and a comprehensive selection of Swiss wines from Sfr18 a bottle. Despite approaching mid-price ambience and quality, it has a good two-course menu for just Sfr13 (not Sunday), which represents one of the best eating deals in Interlaken. Beer is Sfr3.80 for half a litre, and the kitchen closes at 9 pm. There's often a cheapish vegetarian menu, and other dishes cost Sfr15 to Sfr25. A good place for traditional food in rustic yet comfortable surroundings is *Gasthof Hirschen*, on the corner of Hauptstrasse and Parkstrasse. Main courses start from around Sfr30 and it's closed on Tuesday.

The *Hotel Metropole*, by the tourist office on Höheweg, is more up-market, but it still has lunch-time specials from Sfr13, and a three-course menu for around Sfr30 (lunch time only). Evening dining is more formal and more expensive: *à-la-carte* dishes start at around Sfr30, and multi-course menus at Sfr70 (open daily). The hotel also has the *Panoramic Bar/Café* on the 15th floor – it's worth going up for a beer or a coffee to admire the view and to walk around the balcony.

The restaurant in the *Hotel Du Nord* on Höheweg (☎ 22 26 31), offers Swiss food, seafood and vegetarian dishes, mostly in the range of Sfr30 to Sfr40. There's also a five-course gourmet menu for Sfr65. It's open daily. For splendid surroundings and attentive service you can't beat *La Terrasse* in the Victoria-Jungfrau Hotel (☎ 21 21 71), Höheweg 41. Soothing piano music helps you digest excellent French cuisine (full menus above Sfr75).

Entertainment

Evening entertainment in Interlaken encompasses the Casino-Kursaal with its folklore show, and several discos around town. Inside the Kursaal, entering from either Höheweg or Reckweg, is the Spycher restaurant which offers several 'folklore menus' for around Sfr43, or it's Sfr15 just for the show and late dancing. Shows are year-round but much more frequent in the summer; check with the tourist office for schedules or call ☎ 22 25 21.

Most of the young English-speakers (particularly the Balmer's contingent) head for the *Riverside Bar* (closed Monday and Tuesday) on Marktgasse, which features voluble conversation and a raunchy, sweaty piano player. There are two adjoining bars, Ost (open daily from 3 pm) and West (open Wednesday to Sunday from 9.30 pm with live music nightly). The place closes at 1 am or later and drinks are more expensive in the West bar. Next door is *Anker* (see Places to Eat), which often has live music on Saturday night. Other good places for a drink are *Buddy's Pub* in the Hotel Splendid, Höheweg 33 (draught beer at Sfr2.70 for a 0.3 litre glass), and *Mr Pickwick* on Postgasse.

Between mid-June and mid-September there are at least weekly performances of Schiller's *Wilhelm Tell* in the *open-air theatre* in the Rugen forest, near Balmer's. The first performance was in 1912 and it's now an annual event. Over 250 amateur actors take part in the production, not to mention the many horses, cows and goats who wander around and add sound effects as appropriate. It is staged in German but an English synopsis is available for Sfr1. Get tickets (Sfr12 to Sfr32) from Tellspielbüro (☎ 22 37 23), Bahnhofstrasse 5.

The biggest local event, with over 2500 participants, is the Unspunnen Festival. Unfortunately it's only every 12 years, and the next one isn't until 2005.

Things to Buy
There are plenty of souvenir shops along Höheweg, many with a good selection of Swiss army knives. If you're interested in wood carvings, it's better to buy directly in Brienz.

Getting There & Away
Trains to Lucerne depart hourly from Interlaken Ost train station. Trains to Brig (Sfr33, via Spiez and Lötschberg) and to Montreux (via Bern or Zweisimmen) depart from Interlaken West or Ost. Main roads go to Lucerne, Bern and to the west via Zweisimmen. For vehicles, the only way south through the mountains without a big detour is to take the car-carrying train from Kandersteg, south of Spiez.

Car Rental All reasonably central are Avis (☎ 22 12 14), Waldeggstrasse 34a, Hertz (☎ 22 61 72), Harderstrasse 44, and Budget (☎ 22 22 41), Wychelstrasse 1.

Getting Around
Interlaken taxis cost Sfr5 plus around Sfr2.50 per km, depending upon the number of passengers. There are usually some waiting by the railway stations, or call ☎ 22 00 88. Bus fares start at Sfr2.

Jungfrau Region

Some of the best scenery in the whole of Switzerland can be found in the Jungfrau region. Marvellous views and hikes compete for attention from various vantage points, usually accessible by railway or cable car. Attention is wrested by the towering triplets: the Jungfrau (4158 metres), Mönch (4099 metres) and Eiger (3970 metres), which head a series of 3000-plus metre mountains that undulate to the south. But the shimmering peaks of these snow-topped giants are only half the story; the white and grey of their rugged flanks are made all the more beautiful by the green, gold and brown of the nearer hills and valleys. It's a hard place to leave.

Orientation & Information
There are two valleys branching southwards from Interlaken. The valley that curves to the east is dominated by Grindelwald, a well-established skiing and hiking centre. The valley that runs more directly south leads first to Lauterbrunnen, a leaping-off point for the car-free resorts nestled on the hills above. Above Lauterbrunnen (via funicular) on the western ridge is Grütschalp. Walking or

Jungfrau Region

taking the train along the ridge yields tremendous views across the valley to the Jungfrau, Mönch and Eiger peaks, and brings you to the ski resort of Mürren (fare from Lauterbrunnen Sfr7.80). A 40-minute walk down the hill from Mürren is tiny Gimmelwald, virtually undisturbed by tourists.

Gimmelwald and Mürren can also be reached from the valley floor by the Stechelberg cable car, which runs all the way up to Schilthorn at 2970 metres (Sfr64 return). Wengen perches on the eastern ridge of the Lauterbrunnen Valley.

One or two trains depart for the region per hour from Interlaken Ost train station; sit in the front half of the train for Lauterbrunnen or the back half for Grindelwald. The two sections of the train split up where the two valleys diverge at Zweilütschinen. The railtracks loop around and meet up again at Kleine Scheidegg, at the foot of the Eiger. Many cable cars close briefly for servicing at the end of April and the end of November. On transport in the region, Eurail rarely earns any reduction, and Inter-Rail usually gets 50% off (not on buses).

Skiing is a major activity in the winter months, with a good variety of intermediate runs plus the demanding run down from the Schilthorn. In all there are 150 km of prepared runs and 46 ski lifts. Ski passes for different areas cost Sfr43 or Sfr45 per day, or Sfr126 for a minimum three days in the whole Jungfrau region (children half-price). A season pass costs Sfr700.

Just about every resort has its own Visitor's Card, which is good for a number of discounts throughout the Jungfrau region. Tourist offices can invariably provide details, or enquire at hotels.

The telephone code for the Jungfrau region is the same as that for Interlaken: 036.

GRINDELWALD

Grindelwald is the largest ski village in the

Jungfrau, and occupies a marvellous position under the north face of the Eiger. It is also a great base for hiking, especially in the First region where there are 90 km of paths above 1200 metres. Of these, 48 km stay open in winter.

Orientation & Information

The main village is to the east of the train station (which changes money). At either end of the village, Terrassenweg branches off the main street and takes a scenic, elevated east-west course to the north. Below and south of the main street is the Schwarze Lütschine River. The tourist office (☎ 53 12 12) is in the centre by the Sportzentrum; it's open daily in summer, and weekdays and Saturday morning from October to June. It is 200 metres up from the train station – only follow the more visible information sign down the hill if you can read Japanese.

Postbus depart from the train station, and there are several car parks nearby. Many sports shops down the main street rent ski equipment.

Activities

Skiing The gondola from Grindelwald to First is in three sections and takes 20 minutes (Sfr23 up, Sfr39 return). This is the main skiing area, with a variety of runs (mostly intermediate or difficult) stretching from Oberjoch at 2486 metres, right down to the village at 1050 metres. From Kleine Scheidegg or Männlichen there are long, easy runs back to Grindelwald. The ski school (☎ 53 20 21) has had good reports for its instruction to children. Grindelwald is also a good base for cross-country skiing (33 km of trails).

Hiking From First, you can hike to Schwarzhorn (2 hours 50 minutes), Grosse Scheidegg (1½ hours) the Upper Glacier (1½ hours), Grindelwald (2½ hours), Lake Bach (1 hour), Faulhorn (2 hours 20 minutes) and Schynige Platte (5½ hours). The scenery from up here is breathtaking.

The Upper Glacier (Oberegletscher) is well worth a visit. It's a 1½ hour hike from

the village, or a postbus goes to the Hotel restaurant, Wetterhorn, from where it's just 15 minutes. It costs Sfr4 to get in to see the ice grottoes (open June to October). The sculptures themselves are pretty pathetic, but notice the air bubbles and the stones trapped in the ice that create kaleidoscopic patterns.

From here it's a few minutes' walk up to the Milchbach restaurant where a further track, incorporating wooden ladders, climbs up alongside the ice. It's a good route but it's annoying to have to pay to use it (Sfr3, allow around 1½ hours return). There's a viewpoint up there looking over the sea of ice (Eismeer), but if you carry on along a less well-defined path to where there's a 'skull and crossbones' glacier avalanche warning, there's an even better perspective looking up to the top.

A cable car glides up to **Pfingstegg** (Sfr7.80 or Sfr12 return) from May to October. Apart from enjoying the view, you can take short hiking trails to Stieregg, near the Lower Glacier, and to the Restaurant Milchbach, near the Upper Glacier. Along this route you pass the **Breitlouwina**, a sloping terrace of rock billed as a geologist's paradise. You can see pot-holes, scratches on the rock caused by stones inside moving ice, and places where two different types of rock (40 million years and 120 million years old) have fused together.

The Glacier Gorge (Gletscherschlucht) is a 30-minute walk from the village centre. It's open from May to October between 9 am and 6 pm and entry costs Sfr5 (with Visitor's Card Sfr4, children Sfr2.50). It's not a bad spectacle, but you can get a good idea of what it looks like from the entrance and it doesn't really get any better further in.

Mountaineering The Mountaineering Centre (☎ 53 52 00) has a climbing programme in summer and winter. It also organises events such as abseiling and guided hikes that are geared towards adults and children.

Festivals

In July, Grindelwald has a yodelling festival

and later in the month there's Swiss wrestling at nearby Grosse Scheidegg.

Places to Stay

There are many holiday chalets in this village, especially up on Terrassenweg and down near the glacier gorge.

The tourist office has prices (Sfr20 to Sfr35 per person) and availability logged on its computer. The chalets are usually available per week, Saturday to Saturday. Write to the tourist office at least six months in advance giving dates and requirements. If you can't plan that far ahead, look in the hotel information hut upon arrival. There's a notice board in there listing chalets that are still available; you may be lucky in low season.

There are also various hotels (many with dorms) outside the village, such as the Wetterhorn (☎ 53 12 18) at the bottom of the Upper Glacier, the *Glecksteinhütte SAC* (☎ 53 25 00) high up on the mountain overlooking the glacier (experienced climbers only), and the *Berghaus Bort* (☎ 53 17 62), by the Bort station on the First.

Camping Grindelwald has several camp sites. The most convenient is *Gletscherdorf* (☎ 53 14 29), near the Pfingstegg cable car, open May to late October for tents or year-round for caravans. On the far side of the

---

Thomas Cook: the First Conducted Tour of Switzerland

Thomas Cook, the excursionist who spawned the world-wide travel company, was instrumental in opening up Switzerland to mass tourism in the 19th century. He embarked on his first conducted tour of Switzerland in 1863. Previously Mr Cook had concentrated on Scotland for excursions into lake and highland scenery, but in frustration at the refusal of the English and Scottish Railway to renew a cheap excursion ticket to that country (a frustration familiar to 20th century British Rail travellers), he decided to look further afield. Switzerland seemed the ideal substitute. Various notices subsequently appeared about his plans in the regular newsletter written and produced by Mr Cook, *Cook's Excursionist and Advertiser.*

Public interest was immediate and extensive. Cook initially wanted a party of 25, but ultimately in excess of 130 people set off from London on 26 June 1863. They travelled by ferry to Dieppe and then took the train to Paris. The original party was whittled down to 62 who were scheduled to continue the whole way to Switzerland, and included in that number were many independently-minded Victorian ladies. One of these, Miss Jemima Morrell, wrote a book about their experiences *(Miss Jemima's Swiss Journal* – now out of print but still available in some libraries). Various locations in Switzerland were included in the tour, with the main focus of the trip being the Jungfrau region. This was in the days before the mountains had been tamed by funiculars and cable cars, yet these hardy ladies were undaunted as they negotiated steep mountain passes. Some trails, Miss Jemima wrote, were 'a mere groove cut in the face of (a) huge cliff, just wide enough for a mule to pass'.

The trip proved to be a great success, even though not everything about foreign countries appealed to the tourists (French tea, Miss Jemima considered, was 'truly peculiar'). It's worth noting, in our current climate of supposedly free movement between European nations, that these Victorian British travellers did not need a passport to enter France and Switzerland. Mr Cook followed up his success with regular subsequent trips, but not everybody appreciated the influx of masses: the English gentry, who had previously made the Swiss Alps their private playground, were particularly miffed.

In those days, Switzerland was relatively cheap. The exchange rate was around £1 = Sfr24. Mr Cook's personal bill for tea, bed and attendance in the Hotel Clerc, Martigny where the treatment was 'kind and liberal' was Sfr4.50. Costs for mules and guides over the mountain passes were less than Sfr8 per person. Mr Cook reckoned that with careful spending, all-in costs for a 14-day jaunt to Switzerland could be as little as £10 to £12, or £20 for a month. Nevertheless, £20 was still a substantial amount of money for the average Victorian. But not, apparently, for Mr Cook, because he wrote in his *Excursionist* (21 July 1863) that £20 was 'a sum often spent at home, in fashion and folly, in a single night, leaving little for the disbursement but aching heads, wearied limbs and restless ennui'. Mr Cook himself was teetotal, but it seems, was in the habit of indulging in wild nights out in the company of dissolute spendthrifts! ■

river near Grindelwald Grund is *Eigernordwand* (☎ 53 12 42), open year-round.

Hostels The IYHF *youth hostel* (☎ 53 10 09), is at Terrassenweg, 15-minutes' climb from the train station, taking the road that follows the tracks on the north side. If you're walking, don't miss the small sign on the brown and white house indicating the steep footpath up to the right. Dorm beds (including local tax for the guest card) are Sfr18.50 with breakfast, or Sfr13.50 in summer when breakfast is an optional extra. Kitchen facilities are available. It's housed in a typical old chalet which must have accounted for a couple of forests' worth of wood all by itself. The view is fantastic and there is an open fire and musical instruments. Reception is shut from 9 am to 5 pm (though you can gain access to the communal areas during that time) and the hostel closes completely from one week after Easter for five weeks, and from the end of October to mid-December.

A 10-minute walk from the youth hostel along Terrassenweg is the *Naturfreundehaus* (☎ 53 13 33), which has dorms for Sfr19 and breakfast for Sfr7. In the high season you must take a half-pension for Sfr40. Slight reductions apply for students and youth hostel members, and it's open from the end of May to mid-October and from December to after Easter. A bus runs from the bus station if you don't fancy the walk. Other dorms are listed in the tourist office leaflet.

Hotels & Pensions *Lehmann's Herberge* (☎ 53 31 41) costs just Sfr35 per person, and that's irrespective of whether you want a two, four or six-bed room, or the one single (book ahead). It's in the centre of the village just off the main road (signposted). If you can't get in there, the best place to stay is 50 metres away: the *Hotel Tschuggen* (53 17 81), with attractive singles/doubles for Sfr50/100 with hall shower or Sfr60/100 with private bath/shower.

At the eastern end of the village is *Alpenblick* (☎ 53 11 05), with basic but pleasant singles/doubles from Sfr50/84 with

use of a hall shower. It also has a dormitory with good, wide beds for Sfr35. *Gydidorf* (☎ 53 13 03), by the bottom First cable station, is a small place with a nice flower garden that's often booked ahead by regulars: singles/doubles start at Sfr50/96.

Moving upmarket a bit, try *Fiescherblick* (☎ 53 44 53), in a flower-stewn chalet towards the east of the village on the main street. Rooms start at Sfr95 or Sfr160 for single occupancy. *Sunstar-Hotel* (☎ 54 54 17), starts at Sfr110 per person and has good facilities including a swimming pool, sauna and tennis court.

Places to Eat
For eating, just follow your nose. Most hotels have reasonable restaurants but they can be a bit pricey. On the main street is the Hotel Spinne which has the *Ristorante Mercado*, about the cheapest place to eat. Pizza and pasta start from Sfr10 and lunch specials are around Sfr14. Along the road, *Restaurant Rendez-vous* also has decent daily specials from around Sfr11.50. Fondue costs Sfr34 for two (closed Tuesday).

Nearby, the alcohol-free *Tea-Room Ringenberg* offers cheap hamburgers and Italian food (closed Monday). *Hirschen Restaurant*, also on the main street, has a good selection of daily specials for around Sfr15 plus a couple of vegetarian dishes (closed Thursday). *Fiescherblick* (see the previous Places to Stay section) has two restaurants with a tempting array of dishes from Sfr15. It also has the 'Swiss Menu' for Sfr29 comprising a starter, Zürich-style Geschnetzeltes with Rösti, followed by blueberries and cream (closed Wednesday lunch time and Tuesday).

There's a *Coop* supermarket opposite the tourist office, with half-day closing on Wednesday.

Entertainment
The most popular watering-hole in the centre is the *Espresso Bar*, where draught light (hell) or dark (dunkel) beer costs Sfr3.50 for 0.3 of a litre. Next door, the *Spider Nightclub* offers dancing 'til late but only in the winter.

Entry may be free depending upon whether Charley (a highly-charged South African woman) recognises you as a regular.

Alpenblick (see Places to Stay) has another popular bar. Beer costs Sfr3 for 0.3 of a litre and there's a pool table.

Getting There & Away

Grindelwald is only 40 minutes by train from Interlaken Ost (Sfr8.40 one-way, Sfr16.80 return). It can also be reached by a good road from Interlaken. A smaller road continues from the village over the Grosse Scheidegg Pass (1960 metres). This is a great way to get to Meiringen – the hillside is very desolate-looking with many rocks half-overgrown with grass and shrubs, and the views are excellent. The army performs manoeuvres here twice a year. I've been assured that this has no relevance to the fact that private traffic is banned from using the road. Postbuses use this route from the end of May to mid-October to get to Meiringen (takes two hours). It's possible to make a round trip, including bus to Meiringen, a train to Brienz, a boat to Interlaken and a train back to Grindelwald, with stops en route allowed. The validity is two days and the adult fare is Sfr46.20.

LAUTERBRUNNEN

This village at 806 metres can be reached by car or rail. It's a suitable base for a number of excursions, although many people simply use it as a car park before visiting the nearby car-free resorts. There is a multi-storey car park by the station with space for 900 cars; summer rates are slightly cheaper than in winter: Sfr7 per day (one to eight days) reducing over longer periods. There is also a car park (free, but unenclosed) by the Stechelberg cable-car station.

Spare a glance for the Staubbach Falls just outside the village, where wispy threads of spray cascade down the sheer face of the western ridge. It's just one of many water-falls in the valley. Lauterbrunnen has the small **Heimat Museum** featuring historical exhibits and mountain-related stuff. Its open from 2 to 5.30 pm, on Tuesday, Thursday,

Saturday and Sunday, and costs Sfr2.50 (Sfr2 with Guest Card, Sfr0.60 for children).

Find out about other attractions from the tourist office (☎ 55 19 55) on the main street above the train station. Its opening hours in winter are Monday to Friday from 8 am to noon and 2 to 6 pm. At other times of the year it is open on Saturday depending upon demand, and even on Sunday afternoon in July and August. The post office and nearly all the shops and hotels are along this same street. *Crystal Sport* (☎ 55 20 80) rents mountain bikes (Sfr35 for one day), ski equipment and mountaineering gear. The valley floor is good for cross-country skiing in the winter.

A short bus ride or a 50-minute walk down the valley are the **Trümmelbach Falls**, which drains the detritus from 24 sq km of Alpine glaciers and snow deposits. It's viewed mainly from inside the mountain (illuminated), and as you get quite damp anyway, it's something to do if the weather is poor. The water generates incredible power – up to 20,000 litres of water is pro-pelled down per second, and the noise is unceasing. The fissures of rock have been sculptured into dramatic shapes by the swirl-ing waters over the 10 stages of the falls. It's worth seeing, but Sfr8 (Sfr3 for children) is a lot to charge to view a natural phenomenon, even if they did build a few staircases and install a lift. An hour is ample time to see the whole thing. The falls are open from April to November, daily between 9 am and 5 pm (8 am to 6 pm June to September).

Places to Stay

Lauterbrunnen is well fixed for self-catering dormitory accommodation. *Camping Schützenbach* (☎ 55 12 68) and *Camping Jungfrau* (☎ 55 20 10) both have kitchen facilities and dorms for around Sfr10. The sites are on either side of the river a few minutes' walk to the south of the village. Camping Jungfrau is used by Contiki tour buses, although their parties in the 'Bombshelter' don't disrupt the rest of the site too much. Schützenbach is used by Top Deck tours. For campers, Jungfrau costs Sfr5 per person (Sfr5.60 in winter), Sfr2 for a car and Sfr2 to Sfr7 for a tent.

The best budget place to bed down is *Matratzenlager Stocki* (☎ 55 17 54). To get there from the station, follow the white signs that take you around the right side of the multi-storey car park and over the river. It's about 200 metres down the road on the right; see Frau Graf in the next house along for check-in. She's a trusting soul and runs free-and-easy lodgings for Sfr10 a night (no breakfast). Mattresses in the dorms are side-by-side and there's only one shower, but there are good kitchen facilities (no meters) and the open communal area generates a sociable atmosphere.

Chalet im Rohr (☎ 55 15 07), by the church, has singles/doubles for Sfr24 per person without breakfast, although there are kitchen facilities. *Pension Bären* (☎ 55 16 54) has singles/doubles from Sfr28/50. *Hotel Jungfrau* (☎ 55 34 34) is the mid-price choice. Comfortable singles/doubles with private shower/toilet are Sfr60/100, or more depending upon the season. The hotel has a swimming pool and a solarium on the premises.

In Stechelberg at the end of the valley there are various Zimmer-frei (room(s) free) possibilities. Just past *Camping Breithorn* (☎ 55 12 25), *Theo von Allmen* (☎ 55 18 21) has two rooms for two to three people, sharing a kitchen and a shower. The price per room is Sfr50 or Sfr60 per night, with a minimum stay of four days. Stechelberg has its own *Coop* supermarket.

Places to Eat

There is less choice when it comes to cheap eating in Lauterbrunnen. Go to the *Coop* near the tourist office for provisions if picnicking or self-catering. When this is closed on Tuesday afternoon there are other shops open in the village, that sell bread and groceries. The *Metzg-hus* meat store offers Bratwurst and bread for Sfr3.50, chips for Sfr3, and usually has spit-roast chickens cooking outside (Sfr8, or Sfr4.50 for a half). It closes at 6.30 pm except Wednesday (noon), Saturday (4 pm) and Sunday.

Go to the *Hotel Jungfrau* (see Places to Stay) for salads (Sfr4 to Sfr6.50), spaghetti bolognese (Sfr11.50) and a daily dish with soup for around Sfr13. The *Hotel Oberland* serves fondue for Sfr17 and Raclette for Sfr10. The *Hotel Silberhorn* is another good choice for food. *Hotel Horner* has a bar-disco open 'til late, but small beers or soft drinks are expensive at Sfr6.

GIMMELWALD

There's nothing to do in Gimmelwald except relax, enjoy the view and keep away from the crowds. Various hiking trails lead up and around the mountains from the village. In winter, it's perfectly viable to enjoy the ski runs around Mürren and to retreat back down here for the night. It's cheaper to stay here than in Mürren, and you still get the same Guest Card benefits (See Mürren for more details).

The steep hike down from Gimmelwald to Stechelberg takes around two hours, taking the trail to the right of the cable car as you're facing the valley.

Places to Stay & Eat

The diminutive, decaying, regulation-free *Mountain Hostel* (☎ 55 17 04) has dusty dorms for Sfr7, with kitchen facilities. Not all the kitchen hotplates work and the Sfr1 showers tend to run out of hot water. People end up showering in the Mürren sports centre (Sfr3) The Mountain Hostel is by the cable-car station. Up the hill a bit is *Mittaghorn* (☎ 55 16 58), where singles/doubles are Sfr54/59 and triples/quads are Sfr78/96. In the summer there are dormitory beds in the loft for Sfr22. The food is great in the small café downstairs, but you must pre-order unless you just want beer (Sfr3.60 for an 0.6-litre bottle). There's another café by the Mountain Hostel, and an adjoining shop open just a few mornings a week.

In the village you could also try *Pension Gimmelwald* (☎ 55 17 30).

MÜRREN

Mürren is a car-free, skiing and hiking resort that claims to be the birthplace of skiing in the Alps. There are 50 km of prepared ski-runs in the vicinity (mainly for intermediates), as well as a ski school (☎ 55 12 47) and a children's ski nursery (☎ 55 16 16). The village is long on views and pretty chalets and short on nightlife. It puts on a yodelling festival every year in late July. Mürren has two versions of the Guest Card; the 'normal' one and the 'Passepartout', available in hotels and selected apartments. Extra benefits include free entry to the swimming pool, ice-skating rink and curling rinks.

The tourist office (☎ 55 16 16) is in the sports centre, and its low-season opening hours are Monday to Friday from 9 am to noon and 2 to 5 pm. In the high season it's open daily except Sunday morning from 9 am to noon and 1 to 6 pm. Write in advance (Verkehrsbüro, CH-3825 Mürren) if you're interested in the various all-in summer or winter activity packages it organises. Prices are in the range of Sfr121 for two days to Sfr617 for one week.

Places to Stay & Eat

Mürren is more touristy and therefore more expensive than either Lauterbrunnen or Gimmelwald. Staying in the village costs around Sfr80 per person. There are two cheaper pensions close together; about a 30-minutes' walk up the hill, though you can take the Allmendhubel funicular from the village to save your legs. *Pension Suppenalp* (☎ 55 17 26) has dorms for Sfr29 and rooms for Sfr39 per person. *Pension Sonnenberg* (☎ 55 11 27) usually only does half-pension: Sfr45 in dorms or Sfr55 in rooms.

If you stay for five days or more, you do at least get 10% off the Jungfrau Regional ski pass (but you can get this by staying in Gimmelwald, too). One of the cheapest places to stay in the village is *Hotel Edelweiss* (☎ 55 26 12), which also has reasonable food from Sfr12, and good views from the south-facing terrace (closed Tuesday).

The small *Staegerstübli*, next to the Coop supermarket, has daily specials from Sfr10, salad plates for Sfr11 and fondue from Sfr17.50. It's open daily.

SCHILTHORN

This 2970-metre peak provides a perfect viewing platform from which to gaze at the mountains across the valley. It's easily (if expensively) reached from the Stechelberg cable car, via Gimmelwald and Mürren. From the top there's a fantastic 360° panorama, and the film shows in the **Touristorama** will remind you that James Bond performed several stunts here in *On Her Majesty's Secret Service*. The view is more spectacular than that from Jungfraujoch in some ways, as you see a broader expanse of peaks, and you get a real sense of the height of the mountains across the valley. The view from Birg (2677 metres), the station after Mürren, is well worth stopping off for; the 'big three' are closer than from the summit and you get a great perspective of the dark ridge of the Männlichen.

The high cost of the trip by cable car can sometimes be reduced by special offers. Ask if there are lower prices in the spring, autumn, or for the first/last ascent of the day. The Swiss Half-Fare Card and the Swiss Pass are also good for reductions.

The hike up is a strength-sapping four hours from Mürren, often very steep, and you're likely to encounter snow above Birg. The walk down is more manageable, and you're facing the mountains across the

Mountain Goats

valley, rather than climbing with your back to them. About halfway between Mürren and Birg there's a grassy knoll to the valley-side of the path which is an ideal place to break for a picnic. At the top, refreshment is provided by the *Piz Gloria* restaurant (meals from Sfr17) or the cheaper self-service section.

Ever since 1928, Schilthorn has welcomed amateur skiers eager to take on the difficult course down to Mürren, known as the inferno run. It takes place in mid-January and attracts around 1000 participants – the largest event of its kind in the world. Skiing is possible on Schilthorn until June.

WENGEN

This car-free, chalet-style ski resort at 1350 metres is slightly more developed than Mürren, across the valley, and is popular with British skiers. As with most places in this region, the views are wonderful. The high point of its year is when it hosts the international Lauberhorn downhill ski race in late January: it costs Sfr20 to watch the race or Sfr10 for just the training. Expect price hikes and accommodation problems at this time.

Wengen has a ski school (☎ 55 20 22) where half-day classes cost Sfr25 or Sfr98 for five. The ski runs are reached by gondola to Männlichen, or by railway to Allmend, Wengernalp or Kleine Scheidegg. The same areas are also excellent for hiking in the summer, and 20 km of paths stay open in winter, too. The hike down to Lauterbrunnen takes about an hour, or the frequent train does it in 15 minutes (Sfr5). Other attractions include a natural and an artificial ice rink, and tennis courts. There's also a cinema, with a pool hall next door.

From the train station, take a left at Hotel Silberhorn and walk for two minutes to get to the tourist office (☎ 55 14 14). Opening hours in the low season are Monday to Friday from 8 am to noon and 2 to 6 pm, and Saturday from 8.30 am to 11.30 pm. In the high season it is also open from 4 to 6 pm on both Saturday and Sunday. Next door is the post office. The train station changes money

daily, but the rates aren't as good as in the bank. Yellow and brown signs around town indicate the way to hotels.

Places to Stay & Eat

There's a fair selection of dormitory accommodation available in the village. The best is at the *Bergheim YMCA* (☎ 55 27 55) where a place in the mixed six-bed dorm costs Sfr18 (Sfr21 in winter, Sfr23 during the Lauberhorn race) without breakfast. It's run by the Hotel Jungfraublick so check there first for vacancies. Rooms in the comfortable main *Bergheim* are around Sfr100 but dorm-users can use the common room there, or even the library in the Jungfraublick.

That's in favourable contrast to the *Bernerhof* (☎ 55 27 21) where dorms are a couple of francs cheaper in the low season but the users are treated like pariahs, shunted off around the back and excluded from hotel amenities. The dorm is a large room, partitioned into unappealing two-person boxes. Optional breakfast costs Sfr12. The hotel also has quite acceptable 'tourist rooms' from Sfr65, and better-quality rooms from Sfr86 (both per person, half-board). The best thing about its restaurant is the salad bar, which costs Sfr6.50, Sfr8.80, or Sfr11.50 for a plate the size of a Mexican's sombrero. The restaurant also has other dishes from Sfr15 and fondue for Sfr35 for two.

The worst dorm deal is in the *Garni Hotel Bären* (☎ 55 14 19). The 12-bed dorms cost Sfr25 with breakfast, but there are no showers, only one ancient trough-type sink between 24 people. The rooms here are better value, starting at Sfr50 per person with showers down the hall. Rooms with bunk-beds start at Sfr45. The restaurant is also good value. Pasta and pizza start at Sfr9 and other dishes from Sfr15. The Rugenbräu bottled beer is cheap but somewhat without flavour. Around the back of this place, the *Hotel Edelweiss* (☎ 55 23 88) has reasonable rooms and the best prices for stays of three days or more: from Sfr47/74 in singles/ doubles and from Sfr26 per person in multi-bed rooms in the basement. To get to both these hotels, take the road passing under the railtracks and look for the signs.

There are dozens of chalets scattered around the village, normally requiring a stay of one week or more, starting at Sfr20 per person. The tourist office has lists.

Few eating options are open apart from eating in the hotel restaurants. The large *Coop* across from the station provides budget provisions. *Da Mario* by the cinema has mid-price Italian food, and is open daily until 11.30 pm. Part of the same building is the bar-restaurant *Sina's Pub*, open daily from 7 pm to 2.30 am.

MÄNNLICHEN

Männlichen (2230 metres) is up on the ridge dividing the two valleys. Take the gondola (Sfr16.20 up, Sfr26 return) from Wengen or make the pleasant three-hour hike up through the trees.

From the top station, walk 10 minutes up to the crown of the hill for a fantastic panorama. To the south is the dark conical shape of the Lauberhorn (2472 metres), with the snow-capped giants looming impressively in the background. These are flanked by the two valleys, and their different characteristics are particularly evident from here; the broad expanse of the Grindelwald Valley to the left and the glacier-formed Lauterbrunnen Valley to the right with its severe square sides. To the north you can see gentler green hills and a stretch of Lake Thun. The hike from here to Kleine Scheidegg is an extremely rewarding gradual descent on the Grindelwald side, and takes a little over an hour. By foot, Grindelwald itself can be reached in three hours, or you can take the thirty-minute cable car down to Grindelwald-Grund (Sfr42.20 one-way, Sfr66.80 return). It is the longest gondola cableway in Europe, traversing 6.2 km.

KLEINE SCHEIDEGG

This small place is little more than a few buildings grouped around the train station, yet it occupies such a wonderful position at the base of the Eiger that it's surprising that it is not more developed than it is. It looks like a toy village against the backdrop of soaring peaks. Most people only linger a few minutes while changing trains for Jungfraujoch (see the following section), but Kleine Scheidegg (2061 metres) is a good base for a longer exploration of this scenic area. There are short (one hour apiece) undemanding hiking trails to Eigergletscher, down to Wengernalp, and up the Lauberhorn (green in summer, red-brown in autumn) behind the village. These areas become intermediate ski runs from mid-November up until May. A one-day ski pass for the Kleine Scheidegg/Männlichen region costs Sfr45 (Sfr23 for children).

Find out local information and change money in the train station. The small post office is also in the train station. The *Bahnhof Restaurant* (☎ 55 11 51) offers dormitory accommodation year-round for Sfr30 with breakfast or Sfr48 with half-pension. *Restaurant Grindelwaldblick* (☎ 53 30 43) has slightly cheaper dorms but it closes in the off-season. There's only one hotel in Kleine Scheidegg (☎ 55 12 12). It's in two buildings by the station, and singles/doubles with private shower and half-pension start at Sfr150/220.

Eat in one of the restaurants mentioned already or pick up cheap snacks at the outside kiosk by the station.

JUNGFRAUJOCH

The trip to Jungfraujoch by railway (the highest in Europe) is excellent. Unfortunately, the price is as steep as the track and is hardly worth it unless you have good weather – call ☎ 55 10 22 for forecasts in German, French and English. From Interlaken Ost, trains go via Grindelwald or Lauterbrunnen to Kleine Scheidegg. From here, the line is less than 10-km long but took 16 years to build. Opened in 1912, the track powers through both the Eiger and the Mönch with wonderful views from windows from the mountain side, before terminating at 3454 metres at Jungfraujoch.

On the summit, there is free entry to the **ice palace**, a gallery cut in the glacier, featuring disparate sculptures carved in ice, such as Sherlock Holmes and a sumo wrestler. From the terrace of the Sphinx Research Institute (a weather station) the panorama of peaks is unforgettable, including the Aletsch Glacier to the south, and mountains as distant as the Jura and the Black Forest in the north. Expect to queue up to an hour for the terrace in the peak of summer. You can walk across the glacier behind the Mönch on a marked path, but remember to keep a leisurely pace because of the high altitude. The views keep getting better. Along the way you pass a tame summer skiing area (Sfr25 for rental and lift). Husky dogs and sleds are also to be found up here: rides cost Sfr4 for adults or Sfr2 for children.

In fine weather you can take a helicopter ride around the peaks, with Bohag (☎ 22 92 30). The views are incredible, especially when you fly around the north face of the peaks, but it's over all too quickly. An eight-minute trip costs Sfr60 and it's worth doing if your budget can handle it: longer flights cost Sfr100 and Sfr140. The same company also offers a number of flights departing from Gsteigwiler, Grindelwald and Männlichen, and this may even be a viable alternative to taking the railway up.

There's also a small exhibition in the complex giving an erudite rundown of the work of the weather station, including various facts about the atmosphere (there's one-third less oxygen in the air at Jungfrau compared to at sea-level, for example).

Take warm clothing any time of the year, and sunglasses if you're going to walk on the glacier. Bringing your own food will help to cut costs, although the self-service restaurant in the complex is quite reasonable, with spaghetti bolognaise for Sfr11.50 and other meals for around Sfr14. There is also another, more expensive, restaurant upstairs. If you walk the full way across the glacier along the prepared path (45 minutes) you reach the *Möchsjochhutte* (☎ 71 34 72) at 3650 metres. This mountain hut offers dormitory accommodation for Sfr24 and a great view across the mountains fringing the glacier. Breakfast costs Sfr8 and dinner is Sfr17. Other meals and snacks are also avail-

able, and it's open April to the end of September (except June).

Getting There & Away

From Interlaken, journey time is 2½ hours each way and the fare is Sfr140 (Eurail no reduction, Inter-Rail Sfr70, Swiss Pass Sfr97). If you depart at 6.34 am or 7.37 am, the fare is reduced to Sfr97 (Inter-Rail still Sfr70, Swiss Pass Sfr74). From 1 May to 31 October these reductions (so-called 'excursion fares') apply only on the first train and at any time of year you must leave the summit by noon. The last train back in the summer is at 6 pm. Allow at least three hours at the site.

Getting these early trains is not such an effort if you start from farther down the track. If you stay overnight at Kleine Scheidegg, you can pick up the excursion-fare train at 8.02 am in the summer and at 8.02 and 9.02 am in the winter. From here, the full return is Sfr86 and the excursion return is Sfr43. Ordinary return fares are valid for one month.

The Lakes

A boat tour of Lake Thun *(Thunersee)* or Lake Brienz *(Brienzersee)* is a popular and enjoyable excursion. Lake Thun has the greater number of resorts and villages clustered around it, and has more facilities to offer water sports enthusiasts. Lake Brienz, in contrast, has a more rugged shoreline and fewer diversions. It claims to be the cleanest lake in Switzerland, ideal for angling. No fishing permit is needed for the shore of the lakes; if you go out on a boat you need to get a permit from the tourist office (Sfr30 for one day or Sfr95 for one week, valid for the whole canton). At one time the lakes were one great waterway, but deposits from the Lütschine in the south and the Lombach in the north gradually formed a plain (the Bödeli, upon which Interlaken now stands) that divided it in two. The lakes are still linked by the Aare River, but boats can't navigate this stretch.

Steamers sail year around and are more frequent from the end of May to late September. A day pass valid for both lakes costs Sfr26 (Sfr40 in 1st class) or Sfr34 (Sfr50) in July and August. Children travel half price and those with a Half-Fare Card pay Sfr17 (Sfr25 in 1st class) any time of the year. Passes are also available for seven and 15 days, or even longer. Eurail passes are valid on all boats and Inter-Rail and the Swiss Half-Fare Card are good for 50% off the fare of individual rides. The Regional Pass and the Swiss Pass are valid on all boat rides.

The most famous ferry on Lake Thun is the *Blümlisalp*, a paddle-steamer built in 1906. It started operating again in 1992 after plans to scrap it were overturned in a public referendum. A 'steam supplement' of Sfr5 is payable on top of the normal ferry ticket if you travel on this boat, and it sails daily except Monday in summer.

THUN

Evidence of habitation in Thun date back to 2500 BC. Its name is derived from the Latin, *Dunum* (meaning fortified hill), and its castle remains its most dominant feature today. The town was acquired by the canton of Bern in 1384.

Orientation & Information

Thun (pronounced Toohn) is the largest town on the lake and has a population of 36,500. The Aare River separates the train station (with bike rental and money-exchange counters) from the medieval centre around the castle. The river itself is split by a sliver of land which has the important street of Bälliz running along its length. This island is laced to the mainland by several roads and footpaths. The central area can easily be covered on foot.

The tourist office is in the train station (☎ 22 23 40). Opening hours are Monday to Friday from 8.30 am to noon and 1 to 6 pm, and Saturday from 9 am to noon. If it's shut, the train information counter usually has a hotel list. The main post office is on Bälliz,

open Monday to Friday from 7.30 am to noon and 1.30 to 6.15 pm, and Saturday from 7.30 to 11 am, although the international telephone section is open extended hours.

The telephone code for Thun is 033.

Things to See & Do

Roaming around the river and the old town, enjoying the views, is an attraction in itself. Be sure to walk down **Obere Hauptstrasse**, where the street is in two tiers. The roofs of the shops on the lower level provide the walkways for the upper level. Wherever you are in the town, attention is drawn to the 12th century **castle** (Schloss Thun), up on the hill. It contains the **Historical Museum** for which entry costs Sfr4 (students Sfr2, children Sfr1). It's open from April to October from 10 am to 5 pm (9 am to 6 pm from June to September). The museum contains several interesting exhibits, encompassing weapons, toys, ancient coins, and pottery-making. It also provides access to the Romanesque tower with its four corner turrets, yielding fine views. The parish church, that shares the skyline with the castle, is fairly nondescript inside.

In June, Thun has its International Barrel Organ Festival, followed a month later by a rock festival.

Places to Stay

The best deal in the centre is at *Bio Pic* (☎ 22 99 52), Bälliz 54. It has singles/doubles/triples for Sfr30/56/86 on the fifth floor, which is dominated by huge pot plants but lacks a shower. That's not a big problem as there are showers on lower floors where rooms are Sfr38/68. For rooms with private shower/toilet the charge is Sfr50/64/100. Not surprisingly, it's nearly always full, so reserve ahead.

Rathaus Platz is an attractive cobbled square in the medieval part of town, below the castle. At one side of it is *Hotel Metzgern* (☎ 22 21 41), with basic singles/doubles from Sfr45/90. On the other side of the square, with its own pointed tower, is *Hotel Krone* (☎ 22 82 82), with spacious but not-particularly-plush-for-the-price rooms with

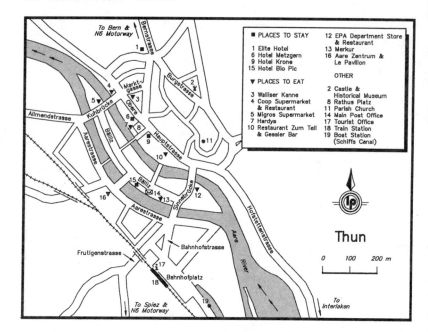

PLACES TO STAY
- 1 Elite Hotel
- 6 Hotel Metzgern
- 9 Hotel Krone
- 15 Hotel Bio Pic

PLACES TO EAT
- 3 Walliser Kanne
- 4 Coop Supermarket & Restaurant
- 5 Migros Supermarket
- 7 Hardys
- 10 Restaurant Zum Tell & Gessler Bar

- 12 EPA Department Store & Restaurant
- 13 Merkur
- 16 Aare Zentrum & Le Pavillon

OTHER
- 2 Castle & Historical Museum
- 8 Rathus Platz
- 11 Parish Church
- 14 Main Post Office
- 17 Tourist Office
- 18 Train Station
- 19 Boat Station (Schiffs Canal)

Thun

radio, telephone, mini-bar, and own shower/toilet. Singles/doubles start at Sfr85/140. The Hotel Krone's restaurant is highly regarded. The *Elite Hotel* (☎ 23 28 23), Bernstrasse 1, is not so comely as Krone from the outside, but has similar standard rooms (plus TV) for the same price.

Places to Eat

Thun is a great place to eat well and cheaply. There are dozens of restaurants clustered around the old town, offering all types of cuisine. Pizzerias are particularly numerous, with pizzas starting at Sfr10.

Self-service The old favourites are here, offering daily specials from around Sfr7.50. A *Migros* restaurant and supermarket is on the island by Kuhbrücke (open weekdays to 6.30 pm, Saturday to 4 pm). Across the river from it is a *Coop* supermarket and restaurant. On the other side of the island by Sinnebrücke is an *EPA* department store and

restaurant. But perhaps the best place to go is to *Le Pavillon* in the Aare Zentrum shopping centre on Aarestrasse (same closing hours as Migros). You can browse among the different counters offering Italian food (from Sfr8.80), Asian food (from Sfr7.50), or coffee and confectionery. There's an excellent salad buffet as well: a large plate costs Sfr9.50 but you can pile enough in the Sfr6.80 bowl to make a full meal.

Restaurants A small place with friendly service is *Restaurant Zum Tell* on Obere Hauptstrasse. It has tasty two-course menus for around Sfr12 and the usual selection of meats and grills. It's closed Sunday, and Saturday evening in summer. Downstairs is the *Gessler Bar*, open to 1.30 am except Sunday. Another small and cosy restaurant is *Walliser Kanne*, Marktgasse 3, with a good selection of fondues (from Sfr17) and Röstis (from Sfr13.50). It's closed on Sunday, and Monday lunch time.

Hardys is a pub-style place on Rathaus Platz, mainly attracting young people. It has weekday menus for Sfr11, rising to around Sfr16 on the weekend. The *Merkur* restaurant at Bälliz 62 also has a good array of daily and weekly specials. Vegetarians can eat here, or feast themselves in the restaurant at *Bio Pic* (see Places to Stay section), which is open from 7 am to 8 pm on weekdays and 7 am to 4 pm on Saturday. Menus start at Sfr9.50.

Getting There & Away

Thun is on the main north-south rail route from Frankfurt to Milan and beyond. From Interlaken, Thun is Sfr24.40 return by steamer or train.

SPIEZ

Spiez (pronounced 'Schpee-its') is a pretty little town hunched around a horseshoe-shaped bay. Its medieval castle and lakeside views are the main attractions. Don't expect to party here; in the low season, Spiez has all the vitality of a walk-in freezer.

Orientation & Information

The tower of the castle makes orientation easy. The train station is about a 10-minute walk uphill from the bay and 15 minutes from the castle. The main street in the resort is Seestrasse, which intersects with Thunstrasse and Oberlandstrasse downhill to the left from the station. The tourist office (☎ 033-54 21 92) is outside the train station, open Monday to Friday from 8 am to noon and 2 to 5 pm. In the summer season it's open longer hours in the afternoon and on Saturday.

The telephone code for Spiez is 033.

Things to See & Do

The castle, **Schloss Spiez** was the home of the influential von Bubenburg and von Erlach families. Many of the portraits hang on the walls. It's amusing to note how the children have no childlike quality at all; they all look like midget adults, especially the dour grandchildren of Franz Ludwig von Erlach (1645). The castle tower was con-structed in the 16th to 17th centuries and provides a fetching view of the town and the bay. Elsewhere, the castle contains weapons, period furniture, and impressive wooden doorway surrounds and stucco ceilings. The Romanesque **church** by the castle dates from the 10th century. It is open from May to October, 10 am to 5 pm except Monday morning, and entry costs Sfr4 or Sfr1 for children.

Near the castle is the small **Heimat and Rebbaumuseum** with exhibits on wine cultivation; it's free and open Wednesday, Saturday and Sunday from 2 to 5 pm.

Spiez has a heated swimming pool at Schachenstrasse 19, and a well-known **sailing school** (☎ 54 21 38). In October there's a Vintage Wine Festival, the Läsetsunntig, with a fair, parades and music.

Places to Stay & Eat

It is viable to use Faulensee youth hostel as a base for Spiez (see Around Lake Thun), or you could ask the tourist office about cheap private rooms.

Cheap singles/doubles are available south-west of the Bahnhof at *Bären* (☎ 54 38 15), Simmentalstrasse 21 (Sfr40/70), and nearby *Rössli* (☎ 54 34 34) on Frutigenstrasse (Sfr45/80, or from Sfr65/118 with private shower). More convenient is *Krone* (☎ 54 41 31), with rooms for Sfr43/80 using hall shower. It's down to the left from the station near the junction of Thunstrasse and Oberlandstrasse.

There's a good view from the four-star *Strandhotel Belvédère* (☎ 54 33 33), on Schbachenstrasse, where rooms start from Sfr110 per person, and there's a garden for lakeside strolls. It also has a renowned restaurant with a number of sumptuous dining areas. À-la-carte main courses nudge the Sfr40 mark.

Dining elsewhere in Spiez is also dependent upon hotel restaurants. There are a couple of places to try on Seestrasse, or head for the *Pizzeria al Porto* by the harbour on Schachenstrasse 3; it serves pizza from Sfr11, plus pasta and fish dishes.

There's a large *Coop* (without restaurant)

at the junction of Bahnhofstrasse and Thunstrasse which closes at 12.15 pm on Wednesday.

Getting There & Away

From Interlaken, Spiez is Sfr17.60 return by steamer or train. Spiez is also the rail start for the car-carrying train to Brig (see Brig in the Valais chapter for more details) and the MOB line south-west to the Vaud Alps and Montreux.

CASTLES

One of the best castles around the lake is **Schloss Oberhofen**. It looms over Oberhofen boat-landing stage and dates from the 13th century. It was held by the Habsburgs for a while before Bernese troops wrested control after the Battle of Sempach (1386). The castle contains a good collection of grand furniture, portraits, weapons, children's toys, and even a Turkish smoking room. The gardens were landscaped in the 19th century and are a fine place for a stroll. The castle and grounds are open from May to mid-October, and combined entry costs Sfr4 (Sfr1 children) or Sfr1 just for the garden. Opening hours for the garden are from 9.30 am to 6 pm, and for the castle are 10 am to noon and 2 to 5 pm every day.

In Oberhofen, compile a picnic at the *Coop* on the main street (half-day Wednesday), or chomp cheap meals in the *Zaugg tea room* (open daily). *Hotel Restaurant Kreuz* (☎ 033-43 16 76) by the castle has rooms from Sfr35 (closed Monday and Tuesday in winter).

Another interesting castle is **Schloss Hünegg**, one boat-stop down the lake at Hilterfingen. The interior illustrates the comfortable lifestyle of the 19th century elite. Particularly evocative is the main bedroom with adjoining Lady's Dressing Room, Master's Dressing Room, and split-level bathroom complete with a gleaming nickel-plated bathtub and complicated taps. It was built in the 1860s and renovated in 1900, and provides a fascinating mix of Neo-Renaissance and art nouveau (Jugendstil) styles. It's also open from May to October, daily from

2 to 5 pm, plus Sunday morning from 10 am to noon. Entry costs Sfr4 (children Sfr1.50). Hilterfingen also has a free concrete-and-grass 'beach', the **Strandbad Hünegg**, open daily from 9 am to 7 pm.

There's time enough to fit in a visit to all the castles at Spiez, Thun, Oberhofen and Hilterfingen, in a single day trip by boat. They're all worth seeing, but that's probably a bit of overkill, especially as the first three collections cover similar ground. Keep your sanity by skipping an interior, probably Spiez or Thun, as they contain fewer and less diverse exhibits. On the other hand, if your appetite is insatiable, you can also digest the **Swiss Museum of Gastronomy**. It's in the castle at Schadau, on the outskirts of Thun, where the Aare River meets the lake. On display are 4000 cookery books dating from the 16th century, plus crockery and pottery. It is open from the end of March to the end of October, daily except Monday; hours are 1 to 5 pm except from June to August when they are 10 am to 6 pm. Only a few boats stop here, though you can walk from Thun centre in 20 minutes. Entry costs Sfr4 (children Sfr2). All the castles offer a discount with a Guest Card.

AROUND LAKE THUN

A short, Sfr4.60 boat ride from Interlaken are the St Beatus Caves (**St Beatus Höhlen**) , with some impressive stalagmite and stalactite formations, and a small museum. Combined entry is Sfr8.50, or Sfr7.50 for students. The department store dummies in a 'realistic reconstruction of a prehistoric settlement' are a laugh. Photography is prohibited in the caves as it holds up the guided tour – not that this stops anybody. The caves can also be reached from Interlaken by bus or a 90-minute walk, and are open daily from 9.30 am to 5 pm.

The loudest sound in quiet **Faulensee** is the wind rustling in the sails of the windsurfers. Get on board by calling Maluco Sportferien (☎ 033-54 54 68), which rents equipment and organises outings. Contact the tourist office (☎ 033-54 32 64) for more information. There is also a water-skiing school (☎ 033-37 79 91). Faulensee has an IYHF *youth hostel* (☎ 033-54 19 88), Quellenhofweg, a 35-minute walk from Spiez train station. The hostel is closed from mid-November to the end of February and costs Sfr16.

Därligen, towards Interlaken, is another water sports centre. It has windsurfing, water-skiing and diving, all arranged at the Hôtel du Lac (☎ 036-21 61 51). The same activities are offered at **Gunten**, on the north shore. Its tourist office (☎ 033-51 11 46) has details. On the hill above Gunten is **Sigriswil**, where there are two folklore-related festivals in July.

GIESSBACH FALLS

These falls by Lake Brienz are a popular excursion, one hour from Interlaken Ost by boat (Sfr8.20 each way). The water spills down over several stages and makes an attractive rather than a spectacular sight. A funicular runs up from the boat station (Sfr3) but the walk doesn't take long. The sun is at a better angle for photography in the afternoon. Various footpaths traverse the surrounding hillside. It takes a little over an hour to walk around the lake to Brienz; unfortunately the route is along the road rather than on a separate footpath.

BRIENZ

Brienz (population 2750) is the centre of the Swiss wood-carving industry and the main town on the shores of Lake Brienz. It is a convenient base for visiting the Ballenberg museum.

Orientation & Information

Orientation in Brienz is easy. The train station, boat station, Rothorn Bahn lower terminal, post office and a Coop supermarket are all within a stone's throw of each other in the centre of town. The tourist office (☎ 036 51 32 42) is also here; opening hours are Monday to Friday from 8 am to noon and from 2 to 6 pm. From April to June it is also open Saturday from 8 am to noon, and in July and August, hours are extended to Monday

to Friday from 8 am to 7 pm and Saturday from 8 am to noon and 2 to 6 pm.

The telephone code for Brienz is 036.

Things to See & Do

There are many touristy shops and boutiques along Hauptstrasse, selling locally-carved statues and mememtos. Linden is a popular wood to use for sculpting as it is so soft; a 20-centimetre high statue of a bear would take about 18 hours to carve. Some shops have factories attached where you can take a quick tour and see the crafts people at work. Have a look in **Jobin** which has been in business since 1835; maybe you can afford to buy its replica grandfather clock for Sfr198,000. **Walter Stähli** at No 41 has a small museum adjacent to the shop.

The **Woodcarving School** (Schnitzlerschule) is open for free visits on weekday mornings during term time (check dates with the tourist office), and has an exhibition room packed with finished work. The tourist office books courses with a local crafts person: five days including materials, hotel accommodation and full board is around Sfr740.

The **Rothorn Bahn** is the only cog-wheel steam train still operating in Switzerland; check with the station as some of the journeys are performed by a standard electric train. It hauls passengers up to 2350 metres for fine views and hikes. The fare is Sfr36 single or Sfr58 return (25% discount with Swiss Pass, no reductions Eurail or Inter-Rail). As always, there's a hotel and restaurant at the summit. Walking to the top from Brienz takes around five hours.

Brienz gives access to Axalp, where **skiing** is neither extensive nor expensive: a one-day pass costs Sfr28 (Sfr17 for children).

Places to Stay

Camping Aaregg (☎ 51 18 42) is by the lake, 15-minutes' walk east of the centre, and is open from 1 April to 31 October. The IYHF *youth hostel* (☎ 51 11 52), Strandweg 10 is nearby, in a brown and white house by the railway tracks. It costs Sfr17 and it is closed from December to March and for two weeks in early May. The reception is closed from 9 am to 5 pm.

Most hotels close for at least a couple of weeks around the end of November. The cheapest beds are at *Bären am See* (☎ 51 24 12), Hauptstrasse 72. It has a good range of rooms costing from Sfr35 to Sfr140 per person depending upon the time of year or whether you need a private shower/toilet, balcony or lake view (closed for Christmas and New Year). A few minutes east of the station on Hauptstrasse is *Schültzen am See* (☎ 51 16 91), with singles/doubles for Sfr50/100 with private shower or Sfr40/80 without. Prices don't go up in the summer and it is closed in October.

Places to Eat

All the restaurants are ranged along Hauptstrasse, and there are some reasonable places with seating overlooking the lake. One of these is *Walz* at No 102. It has a Tagesmenu for Sfr12.50, weekly specials, and pizza/pasta from Sfr9. It's open daily from 8 am to 8 pm (10 pm in summer). Double rooms with private shower start at Sfr86 (Sfr106 in summer). *Seerestaurant Löwen* at No 8 also overlooks the water; fresh perch and trout costs Sfr20 to Sfr30 (closed Tuesday).

Restaurant Steinbock at No 123 has meticulously arranged pink tablecloths and violet napkins. Similar care is devoted to the food; most dishes cost Sfr9 to Sfr24, but grills are more expensive.

Whizz into *Wydi* at No 110 for cheap fast food, or linger and play a game of pool.

Getting There & Away

From Interlaken, Brienz is Sfr18.80 return by steamer, or Sfr11.20 return by train. The scenic Brünig Pass (1008 metres) is the road route to Lucerne.

FREILICHTMUSEUM BALLENBERG

This open-air park is east of Brienz, and displays traditional Swiss crafts and houses from all over the country. The wide diversity of architectural styles between different regions is clearly shown. It's too big to absorb the whole thing in one visit so don't even try. Instead, pick up a plan at the entrance (Sfr2), check the times of special demonstrations on the board, and work out an itinerary. According to the plan, the park is four km across; by my calculations that scale is exaggerated, but it still takes a lot of walking to get round. It's set in parkland and there are often big gaps between groups of buildings.

Most of the properties were slated for demolition before they were moved brick-by-brick to the park. The Geneva Farmhouse (No 551) contains an exhibition outlining its own history; it took eight months and Sfr1.88 million to move it in 1984. Statistics like that, I suppose, justify the admission price of Sfr12 (students Sfr10, children Sfr6). The park is open daily from mid-April to the end of October, from 10 am to 5 pm (6 pm in fine weather from July to September), and entry is half-price after 4 pm. There are restaurants on site or you can buy sausages and cheese and make use of the barbeque areas (free firewood).

Getting There & Away

From Brienz, take the hourly bus (Sfr2.80) or walk for one hour. There are car parks at each of the two entrances; take the east entrance if coming from Lucerne or Meiringen.

East Bernese Oberland

East of the Jungfrau region is the Hasli Valley (Haslital), with its main town of Meiringen.

MEIRINGEN

Meiringen (population 4000, altitude 595 metres) is a suitable base for exploration of the Hasli Valley.

Orientation & Information

The town is on the north bank of the Aare River. The train station is in the centre, with

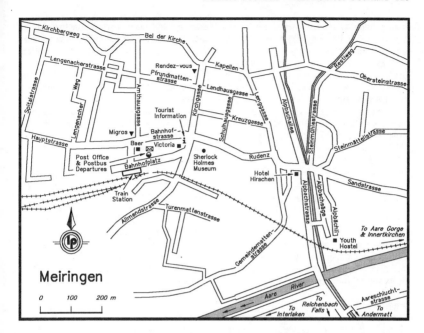

Meiringen

0   100   200 m

postbuses and the main post office opposite. Exiting the train station (bike rental available), go right down Bahnhofplatz as it veers left and turn left for the tourist office (☎ 036 71 43 22) on the main thoroughfare, Bahnhofstrasse. Its opening hours are Monday to Friday from 8 am to noon and 2 to 6 pm, and Saturday from 8 am to noon.

The telephone code for Meiringen is 036.

Things to See & Do
The **Reichenbach Falls** achieved notoriety when Arthur Conan Doyle allowed his famous hero, Sherlock Holmes, to tumble down from them to his death in a struggle with the evil Moriarty. Eccentric fans of the fictional detective still make an annual pilgrimage to the site in the summer (his 'death' was the 4th May) A funicular makes the journey up from Willigen, south of the Aare River, from mid-May to late September, and the fare is Sfr4, or Sfr6 return (children half-price). In winter the Reichenbach Falls are a

mere trickle, as most of the water upstream is diverted for hydro-electricity production. It takes 50 minutes to walk back down to Meiringen from the top.

The **Rosenlaui Valley**, the route to Grindelwald, is certainly worthy of exploration. The views of the mountains (particularly the Welhorn and the Wetterhorn) and the glacier are tremendous, and a path leads to the glacier gorge (Gletscherschlucht), which is open from May to October (Sfr5, Sfr3 for students and children). Buses somehow negotiate the dramatically winding road along the valley from the end of May to mid-October, and the walk back to Meiringen takes two hours.

Less than two km from the town in the direction of Innertkirchen is the **Aare Gorge** (Aareschlucht). The sides are precipitous, narrow (as little as one metre apart in places) and worn smooth by thousands of years of erosion. The gorge is open from April to October, but buses only make the trip (hourly, takes 12 minutes) from late June to late September. Entry to the gorge costs Sfr5 (students and children Sfr3).

Meiringen really milks its tenuous Sherlock Holmes connection; a statue of the detective reclines in Conan Doyle Place, and the Sherlock Pub is in 'Baker St' (the real Baker St in London was never like this!). There's also the **Sherlock Holmes Museum**, featuring a replica of the study at 221b Baker St. It's a nice idea but they need to extend the theme somehow to make it worthwhile – a visit doesn't take more than 10 or 15 minutes. It's open daily from 10 am to 6 pm between May and September, and Wednesday to Sunday from 3 to 7 pm for the rest of the year. Entry costs Sfr3.50 or Sfr1.50 for children.

Meiringen has a famous mountaineering school, the *Bergsteigerschule Rosenlaui* (☎ 71 35 37), 3860 Meiringen. Write away for its special programme.

Organised Tours

The Threee Alpine Pass Tour is a wonderful all-day excursion if the weather is clear. Starting from Meiringen, you can make a circular trip crossing the Susten, Furka and Grimsel passes before returning to Meiringen. The views are excellent all the way round, with the mountain ranges showing great variations in colour and profile. From the Susten Pass there's a great view over the Stein Glacier and lake. The Furka Pass has the Rhône Glacier, which looks stupendous between rocky shoulders of brown and green. There's an ice grotto (Sfr4), and if you take the Panoramaweg and cut down over the rocks you'll enter the closed-off area without realising you were supposed to pay. On the south-west side of the pass the landscape looks browner and more parched, and the road twists away into the distance like lengths of unfurled ribbon. The bus departs from the post office on Bahnhofplatz. If travelling by car, take Alpbachstrasse and cross the river.

At the Grimsel Pass, to the south you can see tufts of snowy peaks above the lake, and to the north there are two more lakes, dammed by the power station that barely disturbs the view of the valley beyond. The pass marks the cantonal border between Bern and Valais.

By making a larger loop south, you can take in the Gotthard Pass and the Nurfenen Pass at the cost of missing the Furka Pass (or if you have your own car you can detour and double-back at Gletsch to include that as well). If you don't have a car, or simply want your eyes free to take in the views, the three or four-pass tour can be taken by postbus. It is necessary to reserve a seat the day before, either in person in Meiringen or by telephoning ☎ 71 32 05. As the road constantly winds back on itself, it doesn't really matter which side of the bus you sit, except for the stretch between Susten and Furka, where the left side is better. On the three-pass tour, there's a break at Andermatt for lunch.

The tours only operate from mid-June to mid-October as the passes are closed for most of the rest of the year.

Places to Stay

Camp at *Aareschult* (☎ 71 19 66), near the Aare Gorge. It's open year-round and costs Sfr3 for an adult and from Sfr4 for a tent.

The IYHF *youth hostel* (☎ 71 17 15) is a signposted 10-minute walk east of the station near the tracks. The signposts leave you in the dark at the last lap; immediately after crossing the stream turn right and the hostel is the last building. Dorms cost Sfr17 (plus Sfr1.10 tax) in communal bunks and there are too few showers. The hostel closes from late April to the end of May and from 1 November to late December. Reception is closed from 9 am to 5 pm although you can gain access to the building during this time.

Prices are reasonably low for hotel rooms. The *Victoria* (☎ 71 10 33) on Bahnhofplatz is a good place to stay, despite the strange wooden phallic shapes in the garden. It has a choice of old-style or more modern rooms starting from Sfr33 per person using hall shower, or Sfr40 with private shower. The *Hotel Hirschen* (☎ 71 18 12) also has some old rooms, with excellent huge cast-iron radiators. It's along the main road towards the youth hostel, and singles/doubles start at Sfr35/58. The three-star *Baer* (☎ 71 46 46) has modern, comfortable rooms bang in the centre of town next to the post office. Singles/doubles with own shower start at Sfr50/90.

Places to Eat

Fifty metres in front of the station awaits a *Migros* supermarket and restaurant. Meals from Sfr7.50 are available until 6.30 pm weekdays and 4 pm Saturday. *Rendez-vous* at Kirchgasse 17 has dull decor in shades of brown, but at least the food is OK. It has pizzas from Sfr9, meat dishes from Sfr15, fondue for Sfr17 and various Swiss wines. Unusually, there's plenty of sauce with the spaghetti carbonara (Sfr12). It is closed on Tuesday during winter.

Hirschen (see Places to Stay) is also a good place to eat, with a Tagesmenu with soup for Sfr14 and other dishes around Sfr15 to Sfr25. Draught beer is Sfr3.80 for half a litre. *Baer*, also mentioned, has a good, informal restaurant with meals starting at Sfr9.50.

Getting There & Away

Meiringen has frequent trains to Lucerne (Sfr28; takes one hour 20 minutes), and Interlaken Ost (Sfr9, takes 30 minutes), stopping at Brienz en route. In summer, buses and cars can take the pass road south-east (Andermatt) but the road south-west over Grosse Scheidegg (to Grindelwald) is closed to private vehicles.

West Bernese Oberland

At the western side of the Jungfrau are Simmental and Frutigland, dominated by two river valleys, the Simme and the Kander. In the extreme west of the Bernese Oberland is Saanenland, known mainly for the ski resort of Gstaad.

STOCKHORN

This summit (2190 metres) offers a heart-pumping view of mountains and lakes. Mont Blanc is visible on a clear day, and you can watch the hang-gliders leaping off into space. There are 70 km of mountain and hiking trails; you can walk to/from the summit but the path is fairly steep. The cable car to the top operates from June to mid-April and costs Sfr29 return. The lower station is 15-minutes' walk from Erlenbach train station, easily reached from Spiez (Sfr5, takes 15 minutes).

Erlenbach is the starting point for **white-water rafting** on the Simme River, organised by River Express (☎ 033-43 39 87). In season (May to September) participants meet at Erlenbach train station at 9.30 am and 1.30 pm. The cost is Sfr50, including equipment and a snack. Reservations aren't necessary but telephone to make sure they're operating that day.

NIESEN

This ascent is from the Mülenen station in the Kander Valley. Niesen (2362 metres) offers views comparable to those from better-known peaks. The cable car runs from May to October and costs Sfr26 return.

KANDERSTEG

Kandersteg (1176 metres) is a good base for **hiking** excursions. The trip to the **Blue Lake** (Blausee) and the **Klus Gorge** are well worth considering. Contact the tourist office (☎ 033-75 12 34) for advice. Its office is in the village centre, ahead and to the left of the train station. Opening times are Monday to Friday from 8 am to noon and 2 to 6 pm, plus Saturday in high season. It closes altogether from after Easter to early June and from the end of October to mid-December, indicating that not much happens in the village during those times.

The Blue Lake is open from late April to early October and entry costs Sfr4 (families Sfr9). The best outing is to the **Lake Oeschinen** (Oeschinensee). This is superbly situated with sturdy mountains crowding its shores and in summer, its waters are sparkling blue. The ancient chair lift up costs Sfr8, or Sfr12 return. It leaves you about a 20-minute walk away from the lake.

Once at the lake, it only takes an hour to walk directly back to Kandersteg.

In winter there are 75 km of cross-country skiing trails, and 20 km of hiking tracks stay open. The downhill skiing is suited to beginners and passes cost only Sfr28 for one day.

Places to Stay & Eat

The *Rendez-vous* (☎ 033-75 15 34) camp site is open year-round. It costs Sfr3 per adult and Sfr3 for a tent, but prices rise slightly in the summer and winter high season. Reception is in the Chalet Felsehus, near to the Lake Oeschinen chair lift.

Right by the chair lift is the *Restaurant Rendezvous* (☎ 033-75 13 54), which has dorms for Sfr15. Showers are Sfr1 and breakfast, if required, is Sfr10. The restaurant itself has Swiss and Italian food from Sfr9.50 and closes on Tuesday during low season. *National* (☎ 033-75 10 85) also has dorms from Sfr10 to Sfr20, depending on whether you need sheets and/or breakfast. Singles/doubles are Sfr42/64, and breakfast is an extra Sfr8 per person. To get there from the station, take a right once you're on the main street.

In the centre, *Hotel zur Post* (☎ 033-75 12 58) offers compact rooms for Sfr37/70 with use of the hall showers, and doubles with private shower cost Sfr92. Swiss food in the restaurant costs Sfr12 to Sfr27 (closed Monday and Tuesday). Nearby is *Chalet-Hotel Adler* (☎ 033-75 11 21), where good rooms start at Sfr75 per person. The restaurant is mid-price (open daily) but has many cheaper options for vegetarians.

Italian, Spanish and Swiss food (from Sfr9.50) are available at the inexpensive *Bahnhofbuffet*. The *Rösti Bahnhof* – shredded potato with gorgonzola, ham and egg is a filling and satisfying plateful for Sfr14.50. In front of the station is a *Coop* supermarket with early closing on Wednesday.

Getting There & Away

Kandersteg is at the north end of the Lötschberg tunnel, through which car-carrying trains trundle south to Brig (see Brig for details). The traditional way to head south is

to hike; it takes a little over five hours to get to the Gemmi Pass and a further one hour and 40 minutes to reach Leukerbad.

GSTAAD (1100 metres)

This resort is an understudy for St Moritz in that it aspires to the same aura of affluence. It's smaller and not quite so elitist, but still attracts many fur-lined celebrities who come to pose on the slopes and in the chic bars.

Orientation & Information

The train station is in the centre, just off the main street, Hauptstrasse, and has bike rental, luggage storage and money-exchange counters. Turn right on Hauptstrasse and walk 200 metres to the tourist office (☎ 030-4 71 71). Opening hours are Monday to Friday from 8.30 am to noon and 2 to 6 pm, and Saturday from 8.30 am to noon. In the season it's also open Saturday afternoon from 2 to 5 pm.

The post office is just to the left of the station and the telephone code for Gstaad is 030.

Activities

There's reasonable **skiing** for intermediates but little for anybody else, and the fact that the lifts around the village only go up around 2000 metres is also limiting. To enjoy more varied skiing you need to take the train or bus to neighbouring resorts such as Saanen, Saanenmöser, Zweisimmen and St Stephan. These are only some of the places that are included in the Gstaad Super Ski Region, totalling 250 km of ski runs. In all, 69 lifts are covered, some as far afield as Château d'Oex and the Diablerets Glacier (see the Vaud chapter) A day pass costs Sfr42 (children Sfr25) for one day, and ski coupons are available.

Four main valleys radiate out from Gstaad, allowing a good variety of **hikes**. The tourist office sells two versions of hiking maps. Take the cable car up to Wispile (Sfr16 up, Sfr21 return) and walk down to the valley on either side. From Lauenen or Feutersoey a bus runs back to Gstaad. A long but undemanding excursion is to walk to Turbach,

Top: Eiger and Mönch from Schilthorn, Bernese Oberland (MH)
Bottom: Grimsel Pass, Bernese Oberland (MH)

Top: Kapellbrücke, Lucerne, Central Switzerland (MH)
Bottom Left: Decorated house, Lucerne, Central Switzerland (TW)
Bottom Right: Lion Monument, Lucerne, Central Switzerland (MH)

over the Reulisenpass, and down to St Stephan or Lenk in the adjoining Simmen Valley (around 4½ hours total). From either resort, a train runs back to Gstaad (change at Zweisimmen).

Various other **sports** are on offer, such as swimming, tennis (Sfr20 per hour) and horse-riding. Just to the left of the station on Hauptstrasse is a curling hall (Eislauf) where games costs Sfr12 per person per hour. River-rafting on the Saane' River happens between the end of April and August, and costs Sfr90. Book at the tourist office.

Every year at the beginning of July, Gstaad hosts the **Swiss Open** tennis tournament. Nearby Saanen is a pretty little village which is the location for the **Yehudi Menuhin Festival** of classical music. It's held every August, in the 15th century Mauritius church.

The après-ski scene can get expensive. (So what's new!)

Places to Stay & Eat

There is year-round camping in the west of the village at *Bellerive* (☎ 4 63 30), by the river. The IYHF *youth hostel* (☎ 4 13 43) is at Chalet Rüblihorn in nearby Saanen, just four minutes away by train. It is closed in May and November and costs Sfr18.

Saanen also has the cheapest hotels, such as *Bahnhof* (☎ 4 14 22), costing from Sfr40 per person. Gstaad itself is bristling with hotels sporting three or more stars. On Hauptstrasse by the station is the *Sporthotel Victoria* (☎ 4 14 31). Rooms with rustic wooden furniture and private shower/toilet start at Sfr60 per person. The restaurant has pizzas from Sfr11, weekly specials from Sfr12 and other meat and fish dishes above Sfr14 (open daily).

Fairly similar is the *Sporthotel Rüti* (☎ 4

29 21), near the Wispile cable car, with singles/doubles starting at Sfr18/140. It also has a restaurant, and in season there is live folk music in the evenings.

Right outside the station stands *Bernerhof* (☎ 8 33 66). Good rooms start at Sfr85 per person, and the hotel swimming pool and sauna are free for guests. The busy restaurant is open daily and offers a lunch special for around Sfr16, fondue for Sfr20 and has a section for Chinese food. The cheapest eating is at the *Coop* supermarket and restaurant, where menus are about Sfr10. It is on Hauptstrasse to the left of the station, and the restaurant section is open daily: weekdays from 7.30 am to 7 pm (2 pm Wednesday), Saturday from 7.30 am to 5 pm and Sunday from 10 am to 6 pm.

The top of the pile, literally and figuratively, is the *Gstaad Palace* (☎ 8 31 31), which despite its hefty price tag of at least Sfr300/490 for half-pension still gives good value for money. You can't miss its turrets up on the hill. Comparable quality for eating is *Chesery* (☎ 4 24 51), near the tourist office on Lauenenstrasse. Expect to pay between Sfr40 and Sfr60 for a main course or over Sfr100 for a multi-course menu. It's small and cosy, so reserve ahead in season (closed Tuesday). There's a piano bar downstairs.

Getting There & Away

Gstaad is on the Panoramic Express rail link between Montreux (Sfr28, takes 1½ hours) and Spiez (Sfr22, takes one hour 20 minutes; change at Zweisimmen). There is also a regular postbus that runs year-round to Les Diablerets (Sfr10.60) and takes 50 minutes. The principal road is highway 11 connecting Aigle and Spiez, which passes close to Gstaad at Saanen.

Central Switzerland

This region sums up what many visitors believe to be the 'true' Switzerland. Not only is it rich in typical Swiss features – mountains, lakes, tinkling cowbells, and Alpine villages – but it is also where Switzerland began as a nation 700 years ago. The original pact of 1291, signed by the communities of Uri, Schwyz and Nidwalden, can be viewed today in the Bundesbriefarchiv building in the Schwyz town centre. It was Schwyz that gave the country both its name and its flag but the focus for tourism in the region is Lucerne, and the convoluted contours of the lake that links the founding cantons.

Orientation & Information

The tourist region that is central Switzerland has at its heart Lake Lucerne (Vierwaldstättersee in German). The German name translated literally means

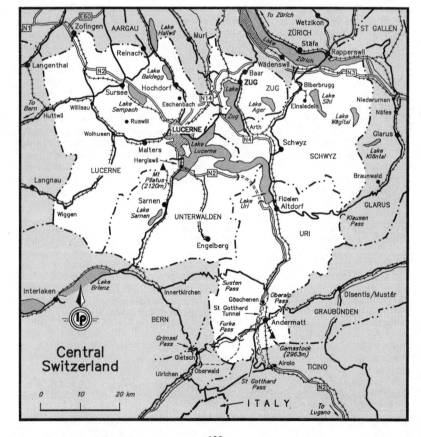

'lake of the four forest cantons'. The four cantons in descending order of size are Lucerne, Uri, Schwyz and Unterwalden. Unterwalden is sub-divided into two half-cantons, Nidwalden and Obwalden. Also included in this region is Zug: at just 239 sq km it's the smallest rural canton in Switzerland.

In the north and west, central Switzerland is fairly flat, but a southern tongue of territory reaches deep into the Alps, as far as the St Gotthard Pass. Lake Lucerne is ringed by other large lakes, notably Lake Zug (Zugersee) to the north. There are also several mountains thrusting up from its irregular shoreline, providing good hiking and excellent views. The regional tourist office is: Verkehrsverband Zentralschweiz (☎ 041-51 18 91), Alpenstrasse 1, Ch-6002 Lucerne. It's on the 5th floor and opening times are Monday to Friday from 8 am to noon and 2 to 5 pm.

The half-canton of Obwalden (including Engelberg) has a religious holiday on the 25th of September.

Getting There & Away

The nearest airport is at Zürich. Road and rail connections are excellent in all directions. An interesting way to leave the region is by the William Tell Express, which runs from mid-May to late October. Departing from Lucerne, it includes 1st-class passage on a paddlesteamer to Flüelen, with multilingual commentary and a gourmet meal along the way, then a train ride (in 1st class) through the St Gotthard Tunnel to either Lugano or Locarno. The fare is Sfr145 or Sfr93 with the Swiss Half-Fare Pass. Reservations are advised; contact the Lake Lucerne Navigation Company SGV, Werftestrasse 5, PO Box 4265, CH-6002, Lucerne (☎ 041-44 05 47).

Getting Around

The Central Switzerland Regional Pass is a good buy if you want to spend a lot of time exploring Lake Lucerne (unless you have a Eurail Pass or a Swiss Pass, both of which get free passage on paddlesteamers). It is valid for seven or 15 days, and gives half-price fares on public transport for the whole period, and unlimited free travel for two or five days on selected routes, including Lake Lucerne steamers, most of the way up to Mt Titlis, the cogwheel railway up to Mt Pilatus and both routes up to Rigi. The seven-day pass costs Sfr116, or Sfr58 for children (six to 16 years), and the 15-day pass costs Sfr160 (Sfr128 with Swiss travel passes) or Sfr80 for children. Prices are slightly higher if you want 1st-class boat travel, and it is available from 1 April to 31 October.

Lucerne

Lucerne (Luzern in German), once a small fishing village, increased in size and importance when the St Gotthard Pass became a trade route around 1220. As late as the 19th century, merchandise had to be sent to Lucerne before being transported by barge to Flüelen, and thence over the pass. In 1332, Lucerne was the first town to join forces with the original three forest cantons, and was one of the few Swiss cities to remain Catholic during the Reformation. Ideally situated in the historic and scenic heart of Switzerland, it is an excellent base for a variety of excursions, yet also has a great deal of charm in its own right, particularly the medieval town centre. Indeed, it is one of the main tourist destinations in the whole of Switzerland, as indicated by the myriad of souvenir shops.

Orientation

Lucerne is on the western edge of Lake Lucerne, on both sides of the Reuss River. The train station is on the south bank within walking distance of the medieval town centre. Extensive station facilities below the ground level include bike rental (from 7 am to 7.45 pm daily) and money-exchange (open daily to 6 pm or later).

City buses leave from in front of the train station at Bahnhofplatz. Boats for excursions on Lake Lucerne depart from the quays around Bahnhofplatz. The old part of town

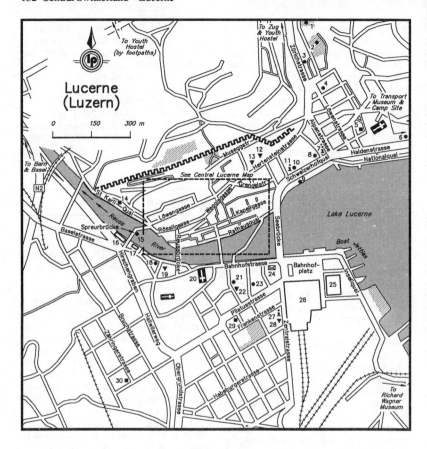

and the city towers and ramparts are on the north bank.

Information

Tourist Offices Take the left exit of the train station for the tourist office (☎ 041-51 71 71) at Frankenstrasse 1. Between April and October, it is open Monday to Friday from 8.30 am to 6 pm and Saturday from 9 am to 5 pm. Between November and March, it is open Monday to Friday from 8.30 am to noon and 2 to 6 pm, and Saturday from 9 am to 1 pm. Pick up a copy of the useful *Official*

Guide. The office has a room-booking service for Sfr3 (one person) or Sfr4 (two people) commission, and sells tickets for mountain excursions. Its return price of Sfr69 to Mt Titlis by rail and cable car is cheaper than anywhere else (further reductions with travel passes). The office also sells guided tours by coach to Mt Titlis and Mt Pilatus for Sfr75 each. Two-hour guided tours of the old town cost Sfr12. Many other excursions are available, all detailed in the tourist office brochure.

In the summer, another tourist office opens up in the bank on Schweizerhofquai.

■ PLACES TO STAY	3	Avis (Car Rental)
	4	Bourbaki Panorama
5 Wirtshaus zum Rebstock	6	Casino
14 SSR Touristenhotel	7	Regional Tourist Office
29 Schiller Hotel	8	American Express
30 Pension Pro Filia	9	SNG (Boat Rental)
	10	Robert Räber Bookshop
▼ PLACES TO EAT	11	Summer Tourist Office
	15	Spreuerbrücke
12 Migros Supermarket & Restaurant	16	Museum of Natural History
13 Moderama Department Store & Coop		& Archaeology
Restaurant	17	Historical Museum
19 Wilden Mann Hotel	18	Flea Market
22 Bistro du Theatre	20	Jesuit Church
28 Hotel/Restaurant Waldstätterhof	21	Atelier (Cinema)
	23	Club Flora
OTHER	24	Post Office
	25	Fine Arts Museum (Kunstmuseum)
1 Glacier Garden	26	Train Station (Bahnhof)
2 Lion Monument	27	Tourist Office

Post & Telecommunications The most convenient post office (Luzern 2, Bahnhof) is at the south end of Seebrücke, open Monday to Friday from 7.30 am to 6.30 pm and Saturday from 8 to 11 am.

The telephone code for Lucerne is 041.

Consulates The Austrian Consulate (☎ 23 41 82) is at Hirschengraben 13 and the Italian Consulate (☎ 41 40 56) is at Obergrundstrasse 92.

Travel Agencies On the north side of the river is American Express (☎ 041-50 11 77) at Schweizerhofquai 4, open Monday to Friday from 8.30 am to 6 pm (5 pm for financial services), and Saturday from 8.30 am to noon. SSR (☎ 51 13 02), in the old town at Mariahilfgasse 3, is open Monday from 1.30 to 6 pm and Tuesday to Friday from 10 am to 6 pm.

Bookshops Robert Räber, by the summer tourist office on Schweizerhofquai, sells English-language books, as do branches of Raeber in the old town.

Emergency Call the police on ☎ 117. Phar-

macies operate an emergency service on a rota system, listed in the *Official Guide*.

Dangers & Annoyances Eisengasse, off Kapellgasse in the old town, is a small street with seedy bars where local youngsters consume their hard drugs, but they're in too much of a world of their own to really hassle anyone.

Walking Tour

The tourist office sells *A short city guide* detailing several walking tours of the centre. The picturesque old town centre certainly merits a leisurely stroll. There are many 15th century buildings with painted façades, particularly in the vicinity of Weinmarkt and Kornmarkt. The **town hall** (Rathaus) is Renaissance in style and was built in the early 17th century. Overlooking the centre are the **city towers**, some of which can be climbed for good views of the town and the lake.

On the 17 August 1993, one of Lucerne's famous covered bridges, **Kapellbrücke**, caught on fire destroying the span although the watertower remained intact. The fire started when a small boat, moored to one of the pylons, caught on fire. Plans are underway to rebuild the bridge which should be completed by early next 1994. The Kapellbrücke was built in 1333 and appears in just about every photograph of Lucerne.

The **Spreuerbrücke** dates from 1408 and likewise features pictorial scenes, completed from 1625 to 1635. The artist, Caspar Meglinger, chose a rather more macabre theme, *The Dance of Death*. The eaves under the roof of both bridges also host an impressive collection of spiders that look even more enormous when illuminated by the strip lights at night. Between the bridges on the south bank is the **Jesuit Church**, the oldest Baroque church in Switzerland, consecrated in 1677. The interior is characteristically ornate.

The poignant **Lion Monument** near Glacier Garden was carved out of natural rock in 1820. It is dedicated to the Swiss soldiers who died in the French Revolution in 1792. They were slaughtered on the steps of the Tuileries Palace while defending Louis XVI and French royal family. Next to the monument is the fascinating **Glacier Garden** (Gletschergarten), Denkmalstrasse 4, where giant glacial potholes prove that Lucerne was a subtropical palm beach 20 million years ago. The potholes can be perused from Tuesday to Sunday, and admission costs Sfr6.50 (students 4.50). It includes a mirror maze that is incredibly disorientating.

Also worth a look is the nearby **Bourbaki Panorama**, Löwenstrasse 18, an 1100-sq metre circular painting of the Franco-Prussian war. The scene is brought to life with recorded commentary (in English). Entry is Sfr 3, or half price for students.

Lucerne is a good base for exploring the lake. See the Lake Lucerne section for more details. You can either take round trips with smaller operators, or use the scheduled services from Bahnhofplatz.

Museums The biggest and best museum in Lucerne is the **Transport Museum** (Verkehrshaus) at Lidostrasse 5. This museum receives more visitors than any other museum – over half a million a year. Bus No 2 from Bahnhofplatz drops you right outside. It has large halls filled with old trains, cars, aeroplanes and boats, plus a planetarium and a gallery devoted to the artist, Hans Erni.

There are several hourly shows, the best of which is the Swissorama, a 20-minute, 360° film which whizzes you around the sights of Switzerland as if you were travelling by air, sea, road and foot. You get a real sense of motion as your 'aircraft' banks between the mountains. Also great fun, especially for kids, is the communications section, where there are lots of toys and machines to play with. Explanations are in English. Opening hours are: 1 March to 31 October, daily from 9 am to 6 pm; and the rest of the year, Monday to Saturday from 10 am to 4 pm and Sundays and holidays from 10 am to 5 pm. Inter-Railers and small children get in free; everyone else pays Sfr15 (adults), Sfr11 (students), Sfr8 (children aged six to 16), or Sfr36 (family pass).

The **Picasso Collection** in the Ann Rhyn House on Furrengasse demands an hour of your time. There are some paintings and graphics by the man himself, but the best part is nearly 200 photographs taken by David Douglas Duncan. They show Picasso at work and at play in the clutter of his house, 'La Californie', in Cannes, over the last 17 years of his life. Admission costs Sfr5 (Sfr3 for students and senior citizens), and it is open daily: from 10 am to 6 pm in the summer and 11 am to 1 pm and 2 to 4 pm from November to March.

The **Historical Museum**, with its exhibits and short film (in English), successfully places the city and region in their historical context. The **Fine Arts Museum** (Kunstmuseum) by the train station mainly displays local art, from the Middle Ages to the present. Natural history and archaeology are combined in the **Museum of Natural History and Archaeology** (Naturmuseum). Interesting for music lovers is the **Richard Wagner Museum** in Tribschen, on the southern shore of the lake. All four museums are closed on Monday.

Markets There are daily fruit and vegetable

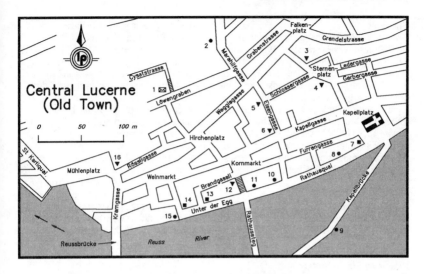

Central Lucerne (Old Town)

0   50   100 m

■ PLACES TO STAY

7   Hotel des Alpes
13 Hotel Schiff
14 Hotel Linde

▼ PLACES TO EAT

3   Bistrettino
4   Restaurant Stadtkeller
5   Spycher
6   Goldener Löwen

12 Zum Raben
16 EPA Department Store

OTHER

1   Post Office
2   SSR (Travel Agency)
8   Pickwick Pub
9   Wasserturm
10 Picasso Collection
11 Town Hall (Rathaus)
15 Movie (Bar)

---

markets along the river quays, and there's a flea market at Unter Burgerstrasse/Reusssteg every Saturday.

Activities

Water pursuits are important in the summer. The Rotsee is a favoured place for rowers; contact the Regattaverein Lucerne (☎ 26 15 15) for details. SNG (☎ 44 45 44) at the north side of Seebrücke rents rowing boats (up to three people, Sfr15 for one hour, Sfr50 for five hours), motorboats (up to four people, around Sfr30 an hour), and pedalboats (for two people, around Sfr15 an hour). You can try kayaking on the lake through Eurotrek (☎ 01-462 02 02), a travel company based in Zürich, at Malzstrasse 17-21. It also organises river-rafting on the Reuss River. There is swimming in the confines of the Lidostrandbad (☎ 31 38 06), near the camp site, for which entry costs Sfr4. Save money by swimming for free on the other bank of the lake by Seepark, off Alpenquai.

If you like the idea of paragliding off Pilatus, telephone ☎ 05 11 41. Information on further paragliding possibilities is available on ☎ 51 58 49. Call the same number for ballooning information.

Festivals

Five days of **Fasnacht** celebrations begin on the Thursday before Ash Wednesday. Lucerne hosts the annual **International Festival of Music** from mid-August to mid-September, one of the most important classical music events in Switzerland. Details are available from the International Festival of Music (☎ 23 35 62), Hirschmattstrasse 13, CH-6002 Lucerne. Prices for concerts are anything between Sfr10 and Sfr180. The programme is published in late March, after which individual ticket applications are processed.

Places to Stay

Get your hotel to stamp your *Official Guide*; this entitles you to discounts on entry fees to most attractions.

Places to Stay – bottom end

Camping *Camp Lido* (☎ 31 21 46), Lidostrasse 8, is on the north shore of the lake and east of the town. It is open all year and charges Sfr4 per person, Sfr2 per tent and Sfr3 per car. To get there take bus No 2 from Bahnhofplatz.

Hostel The modern IYHF *youth hostel* (☎ 36 88 00) is at Sedelstrasse 12, north of the centre. Bus No 18 from the train station gets you closest (stop: Goplismoos) but after 7.40 pm you'll have to take bus No 1 (stop: Schlossberg). The hostel is actually less than a 15-minute walk from the city walls, but you'll need a detailed map to pick out the footpaths and avoid the long walk by road. Beds with free lockers are Sfr21, including breakfast. Dinners are not too bad and cost Sfr9. Reception is shut from 9.30 am to 4 pm when the doors are also locked. Curfew is at 11.30 pm.

Pensions & Hotels The small *Linde* hotel (☎ 51 31 93; see the Central Lucerne map), Metzgerrainle 3, off Weinmarkt, has fairly spartan singles/doubles for Sfr39/78 with free use of showers in the hall. The walls are paper-thin and the streets outside can be noisy, but it has an excellent central location

and it's the best place for those with low budgets. Breakfast is not included.

SSR Touristenhotel (☎ 51 24 74), St Karli Quai 12, has large dorms for Sfr33, and doubles for Sfr98 with shower and toilet, or Sfr76 without. Single occupancy of double rooms is possible in winter for Sfr59 with shower, Sfr48 without. From 1 April to 31 October, prices go up Sfr20 per double. The dorms are overpriced, despite the 10% discount for students which applies on all the rooms. Triples and quads are also available, and breakfast is included.

Spartan but amenable is *Pension Pro Filia*, (☎ 22 42 80), Zähringerstrasse 24, with two lounges. Singles/doubles for Sfr50/95 with use of hall showers, and doubles for Sfr95 have private showers. Triples and quads are an extra Sfr20 per person, and Sfr15 buys a three-course dinner.

Places to Stay – middle

Out of the centre towards the transport museum is *Pension Villa Maria* (☎ 31 21 19), at Haldenstrasse 36, in a residential part of town. Doubles are Sfr117 with private shower or Sfr97 using hall facilities. There are a few triples but no singles. Telephone ahead to reserve.

Overlooking the river is the comfortable *Hotel des Alpes* (☎ 51 58 25; see the Central Lucerne map), Rathausquai 5. It has decent-sized rooms, all with shower, toilet, TV and buffet breakfast. Singles/doubles start at Sfr75/120, rising by about 20% from 1 April to 31 October. *Hotel Schiff* (☎ 51 38 51; see the Central Lucerne map), Unter der Egg 8, is similar in price, situation and standard, except that it also has rooms from Sfr54/86 with use of hall shower.

Places to Stay – top end

Wirtshaus zum Rebstock (☎ 51 35 81) St Leodegar-Strasse 3, has rooms from Sfr130/210 decorated with flair and more than a touch of modern art. All have shower/bath, toilet, TV, radio and telephone. *Schiller Hotel* (☎ 23 51 55), Pilatusstrasse 15, starts at Sfr120/150 and has similar facilities. The cheaper rooms have modern fittings and stuccowork around the ceilings. Pay a bit more and you'll get a larger room with elaborate stylised decor, ranging from Thai to nautical.

Places to Eat

Lucerne is bursting with restaurants of all types. Eating can get pricey but there are still plenty of places with a Tagesmenu in the range of Sfr13 to Sfr15. Local speciality is the *Kügelipasteti*, a giant vol-au-vent stuffed with meat and mushrooms and served with a rich sauce.

For the cheapest chomping, look to the self-service places. *Migros* supermarket and restaurant is at Hertensteinstrasse 44. Next door is the Moderama department store with a *Coop* restaurant on the first floor. *EPA* department store, Mühlenplatz, (see the Central Lucerne map) has an excellent self-service restaurant with unbelievable prices for Switzerland: soup Sfr1.50, salad buffet Sfr4.50 and Sfr5.80, lunch-time specials from Sfr6, and tea or coffee for Sfr1.60.

Wirtshaus zum Rebstock (see Places to Stay), has several eating areas, including a sociable café and a potato-speciality place upstairs. Daily specials cost Sfr10 to Sfr30, and there are always vegetarian dishes. A mainly young hang-out is *Bistro du Theatre*, Theaterstrasse 5. It is a French-style bar and restaurant which has a studentlike feel with posters on the wall. Midday menus with soup are Sfr12.50 and Sfr14.50 and evening dining starts at Sfr11.50.

Goldener Löwen, Eisengasse 1, (see the Central Lucerne map) is small, fairly untouristy and open daily. Main courses, including Swiss specialities, start at around Sfr12. Around the corner is *Spycher* (☎ 52 85 29), the place to go for cheese specialities. It is small and rustic and has a special section for Raclette. Fondue starts at Sfr21.50 (closed Sunday lunch time).

The widest choice for vegetarian food is *Hotel-Restaurant Waldstätterhof* (☎ 23 54 93), Zentralstrasse 4, next to the tourist office. It has a daily menu (Sfr14.50) and serves meat dishes too. *Bistrettino*, Theilinggasse 4, is one of the reliable if fairly

unspectacular Bistretto chain. Pizza and pasta starts at Sfr9.30 and there is a Sfr1 surcharge after 6 pm when self-service stops. Plates from the salad bar cost between Sfr4.30 and Sfr9.80.

The restaurant in the *Hotel Schiff* (see Places to Stay) has lunch specials with soup from Sfr13, and it's also a good place to shed some francs and gain some pounds on quality evening dining (starting from Sfr17). Cuisine from different nationalities is featured in winter festivals, and in summer, there's a gourmet menu for around Sfr60. The local speciality, here called *Aechti Lozärner Chögelipastete*, costs Sfr23.50. The nearby *Zum Raben* (☎ 51 51 35; see the Central Lucerne map). Kornmarkt 5, is also good, and has meals starting at Sfr20.

The *Wilden Mann Hotel* (☎ 23 16 66), Bahnhofstrasse 30, has a gourmet restaurant where main courses start at Sfr30 and multi-course menus at Sfr65. It has good fish specialities, and is open daily.

Entertainment

Restaurant Stadtkeller (☎ 51 47 33; see the Central Lucerne map), Sternenplatz 3, has two folklore shows a day to allow you to yodel with your mouth full. A full meal with the show and wine or beer will cost around Sfr65 per person, and reservations are usually necessary. It works out to be quite expensive, but it is one of the best folklore shows around, and most guests eagerly participate in the party mood. Lunch is cheaper but there's less atmosphere. If you don't eat, the show costs Sfr12. From November to mid-March, live music replaces the full show.

Sedel, near the youth hostel, behind Rotsee at Emmenbrücke, is a former women's prison which holds rock concerts at the weekend. Concerts are advertised under the name 'The Club', Kulturzentrum (☎ 36 63 06). Local bands practice in the cells during the week, so it can be fun to just walk around the corridors, absorbing the clashing sounds and the vivid colours of the graffiti-covered walls.

There are several decent bars in the centre

and most close around midnight or just after. The Schiller Hotel (see Places to Stay) shelters three good places clustered around its noisy lobby: *Casablanca* is a bar with a good if slightly claustrophobic atmosphere (mind your head on the unfurled rolls of film dangling from the ceiling); *Grand Café* is a café with huge Greek-style statues and strange metal grids on the ceiling; *Cucaracha* is a Mexican bar and restaurant.

On the north side of the river is the *Pickwick Pub* near the Kapellbrücke (see the Central Lucerne map), a pseudo-English bar where the punters overflow onto the quayside. On Weinmarkt is *Movie*, a bar with film star pics and movie promos on the walls. If you go through the section around the side where they serve food, the premises opens out into a terrace overlooking the river.

The *Club Flora*, on Seidenhofstrasse, is a disco where the cover charge is Sfr10 (free Sunday to Thursday with a stamped *Official Guide)* and the drinks are Sfr10 or more. Dress standards are fairly casual and there are occasional 'theme' evenings. The *Casino* on Haldenstrasse caters for gamblers, dancers, and has a summer folklore show.

There are many cinemas where admission costs Sfr9 to Sfr13. *Atelier* (☎ 23 12 30) on Theaterstrasse has some interesting non-mainstream offerings.

Barstube Zur Gerbern at Sternenplatz 7 in the old town, is a well-known bar for gay men.

Things to Buy

Some shops are shut on Monday morning but most stay open until 9 pm on Thursday. Gift stalls at the boat quays even open up on Sunday. You can buy anything you could possibly want (and lots of things you couldn't), such as Swiss knives, cuckoo clocks, beer tankards and pug-faced dolls. More practical stuff can be bought in the many department stores.

Getting There & Away

Call ☎ 23 66 77 for train information. Hourly trains connect Lucerne to Interlaken (Sfr23), Bern (Sfr29), Zürich (Sfr17), Lugano (Sfr54) and Geneva (via Interlaken or Langnau). The N2 (E9) motorway connecting Basel and Lugano passes by Lucerne, and the N14 provides the road link to Zürich.

Car Rental Europcar (☎ 41 14 33) has a rental office at Garage Epper, Horwerstrasse 81. Hertz (☎ 36 02 77) is at Maihofstrasse 101 and Avis (☎ 51 32 51) is at Zürichstrasse 35. Local firm Miecar (☎ 23 00 44), at Neuweg 4, has weekend (Friday 8 am to Monday 6 pm) prices starting at just Sfr128, including 1000 km.

For information on boat transport see the following Lake Lucerne section.

Getting Around

Walking is the best way to explore the centre where many of the streets are pedestrian-only anyway. Bus tickets cost Sfr1 for one zone, Sfr1.50 for two and Sfr1.90 for three. Ticket dispensers state the number of zones to each destination, or tickets are also available from the driver. For longer journeys you're better off getting a day card for Sfr5.

Lake Lucerne

You could spend several days exploring the historic locations and the scenic mountains around this lake (Vierwaldstättersee in German). The views are constantly changing around its twisting coastline and there are many typical villages and attractive resorts to enjoy along the way.

Always ask if there is a guest card if you stay anywhere around the lake, as not all hotels and pensions provide these spontaneously. It is definitely worth having. The *Gästekarte Schwyzerland* in Brunnen, for example, entitles the bearer to various discounts on sporting facilities in Brunnen, 20% to 25% off certain cable cars, and reductions on some admission prices in Lucerne and elsewhere.

If contemplating ascending Mt Pilatus or Rigi, inquire about weather conditions from

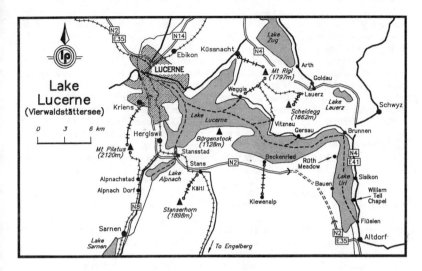

the Lucerne tourist office. In winter, also ask about special low-season prices.

Getting Around

Old-fashioned paddlesteamers operate at certain times of the day, more frequently in summer, although any of the boats provide a fun day out. Boats sail year round. Longer trips are relatively much cheaper than short ones, and you can alight from the boat as often as you want. Swiss Pass and Eurail Pass are valid on all boat trips and Inter-Rail gets you half price. All passes are valid or get discounts only on selected mountain railways and cable cars.

Examples of return boat fares from Lucerne are: Alpnachstad Sfr23, Weggis Sfr17.80, Vitznau Sfr23, Brunnen Sfr33, and Flüelen Sfr36. Return fares are about 60% more than singles, and 1st-class prices (less crowded, but otherwise not particularly more comfortable) is about 50% more than 2nd-class prices. Some single fares from Flüelen are: Brunnen Sfr9.60, Weggis Sfr20 and Lucerne Sfr22. Lake Lucerne attracts more boat passengers than any other lake – almost 2.2 million per year. (Next in order come the lakes of Geneva, Zürich and Thun.)

Driving around the lake is perfectly viable. Roads run close to the shoreline all the way around, with the exception of the stretch from Flüelen to Stansstad. Here there is a motorway (N2) that ploughs a fairly straight line, sometimes underground, usually away from the water.

Mt Pilatus

The rugged contours of Mt Pilatus (2120 metres) overlooks Lucerne from the south. According to tradition it was named after Pontius Pilate, who apparently haunted its heights; any climber with the temerity to approach the summit would cause his spirit to unleash storms onto the populace below. Foolhardy tourists ignore this ancient wisdom and regularly ascend for panoramic views of the lake and the Alpine range. The inspiring vistas make it worth risking Pilate's wrath.

A popular route from Lucerne is to take the lakesteamer to Alpnachstad, the cog railway up Mt Pilatus, the cable car down to Kriens and bus No 1 back to Lucerne. The total cost for this jaunt is Sfr66.20. Kriens-Pilatus return or Alpnachstad-Pilatus return is Sfr53. The Swiss Pass and the Half-Fare card get 50% off, Eurail gets 35% off and there's no reduction with Inter-Rail. Children (six to 16) can go half-price.

This cog railway is the steepest of its kind in the world, reaching a gradient of 48%; it's closed from late November to mid-May. The cable car is closed for maintenance from mid-October to mid-November.

The cog railway is an all-or-nothing trip but the cable car is in several stages, allowing you to ride some of the way and walk the rest. The last stage to the summit is the steepest. Walking up from Alpnachstad takes around four hours and from Kriens about five hours. From the summit, it's three hours down to Alpnachstad, 3½ hours to Kriens or three hours down to Hergiswil boat station. The cable station of Fräkmüntegg is about halfway up in walking terms, so you could ride Alpnachstad-Mt Pilatus-Fräkmüntegg for Sfr40 and take the easy walk down from there.

At the top of Mt Pilatus are two hotels, *Pilatus Kulm* and *Hotel Bellevue*. They share the same reception (☎ 041-96 12 55) in the circular building. Singles/doubles cost Sfr90/160 with private shower or Sfr60/100 without. Prices in the self-service restaurant are reasonable, with hot meals starting from Sfr13.50.

If you want to stay in Alpnachstad, look for the private B&B run by Frau Schnider (☎ 041-96 19 32) at Brünigstrasse 23. Singles/doubles are Sfr40/70. There is a better selection of restaurants a couple of km down the road in Alpnach Dorf than in Alpnachstad itself.

Mt Rigi

From the top there is a great view of tiers of mountain peaks to the south and east; on a clear day Mt Titlis and the Jungfrau region giants are visible. The view to the north and west is also good, with an aeroplane-eye view of Arth-Goldau below, and Lake Zug (Zugersee in German) curving around until it almost joins Küssnacht and an arm of Lake Lucerne. The green slopes of Mt Rigi itself, the swathes of conifers and the constantly tinkling cowbells all add to the scene. Seeing

the sunrise from the summit is a popular activity with a long precedent.

The mountain can be ascended in a number of ways. Hiking is of course the cheapest, but it's at least a four-hour slog from Weggis. Walking can be made more manageable by taking the cable car from Küssnacht up to Seeboldenalp (Sfr11 up, Sfr7.50 down, Sfr15 return). There are two paths from there, the shortest takes a little over two hours, and the last section is quite steep. The lazy, rushed and infirm can take the rack railway to within 200 metres of the summit in 40 minutes. Two rival tracks were built in the 1870s: one from Arth-Goldau (Sfr24 up, Sfr48 return) and the other from Vitznau (Sfr34 up, Sfr48 return) The Arth-Goldau service closes for two weeks in late May but Vitznau operates year round.

The Vitznau track gives the further option of diverting at Rigi Kaltbad and taking instead the cable car to/from Weggis. The whole thing can be done from Lucerne for Sfr62.80 (reductions with railpasses).

Being at the top for the sunrise is made easier by the presence of the *Rigi Kulm Hotel* (☎ 041-83 13 12), just five minutes' walk from the summit. South-facing singles/doubles with private shower and toilet cost Sfr70/130, and with a bath, Sfr80/150. North-facing rooms cost Sfr80/45 with use of hall shower, and rooms in the annex cost Sfr60/35. There are even dorms for Sfr20 per person. The restaurant is OK considering it has a captive market; light meals start at Sfr10 but most dishes are closer to Sfr20. A half litre bottle of beer is Sfr4.30. An outside kiosk is open during the day.

Weggis

This south-facing, lakeside resort enjoys plenty of sunshine, meaning that the quayside parades a palette of colours from its flowerbeds, magnolias, palm trees and fig trees. Musicians play in the Kurplatz most summer mornings, and there's a couple of churches worth peeking into, plus a monument to Mark Twain who stayed here. It's also the base for the cable car up to Rigi Kaltbad. There is swimming in the Lido-

Mt Rigi & 19th century Tourism

Everything works so well in Switzerland. The people are affluent, well-dressed, courteous, unflappable.... and above all, in command. It's not hard as a tourist to get the feeling that you're the poor relation from an underdeveloped country visiting a successful cousin. The balance of power is definitely with the Swiss.

But it wasn't always like that. The picture that emerges from 19th century texts is that tourists were like visiting royalty, with the Swiss scurrying around attending their needs and desperately hoping to make a few coins to eke out a meagre lifestyle. Many locals – men and boys bearing mules and eager grins – would offer their services as guides for tourists walking in the hills. Always there would be people determinedly trying to sell snacks and trinkets. Mark Twain in his travel reminiscences reported being plagued by Alp horn players at Mt Rigi. He paid them generously to get rid of them, only to find their number had doubled at the next village, hoping for a similar pay-off. Such scenes ring bells with any traveller to the Third World.

Jemima Morrell, writing in 1863 (*Miss Jemima's Swiss Journal*), describes being surrounded by dozens of would-be guides at Weggis: 'We were literally infested by, dogged and danced around by these importunates. Our efforts to evade them were numerous and varied.' They ignored the throng and proceeded to walk up Mt Rigi. Unaccompanied – but not for long: 'Again, we are reminded that tourists are the staple commodity in the twenty-two cantons of Switzerland as another band of parasites would feed upon us, or rather feed us, as they dangled branches of cherries in our faces with the cry 'Vingt centimes, vingt centimes!' These cherry vendors regarded us as their legitimate prey – they industriously reap a good harvest in their Rigi farms as they try every art and device to make us purchasers.'

The party of British tourists eventually left behind even the most persistent vendors, and continued climbing towards the summit. They attained a promontory and were standing around admiring the view towards Uri, when: 'Vingt centimes! Vingt centimes!' again rings in our ears. putting to flight our dreams of history, or valour, of poetry and beauty.'

The cherry vendors may have been unlucky with Miss Morrell's party, but they had plenty of other tourists to pester instead. Morrell reported that there were as many as 150 early risers congregated at the summit of Mt Rigi the next morning, all there to enjoy the view at sunrise. ■

Hallenbad (Sfr5) to the west of the centre, and bikes can be hired through the tourist office. Don't expect much nightlife – it's a quiet resort favoured mainly by older visitors.

The tourist office (☎ 041-93 11 55) is next to the boat station, open Monday to Friday from 8 am to noon and 2 to 6 pm in winter, and Monday to Friday from 8 am to noon and 1.30 to 6.30 pm, and Saturday from 8 am to noon and 2 to 4 pm in summer.

Places to Stay & Eat The best deal is at the *Hotel-Restaurant Viktoria* (☎ 041-93 11 28), overlooking the lake promenade. Reasonably spacious rooms, some with balconies, are Sfr40 per person, with use of hall shower. The restaurant has daily menus including soup, salad and main course for Sfr14.50 and Sfr18.50. Fish dishes are around Sfr20. The place is closed in December and January, and

the restaurant also closes on Wednesday in winter.

Just 100 metres to the east along the promenade is *Hotel Gotthard am See* (☎ 041-93 21 14). The room aren't really that much better than the Viktoria's, except they do have private shower/toilet. Singles/doubles start at Sfr70/130, rising in the summer. Guests can use the private pool of the *Beau Rivage* (☎ 041-93 14 22), opposite which sports four stars and has rooms starting at Sfr75 per person. The Gotthard's restaurant has a shaded, open-air section overlooking the lake where pizzas start at Sfr10.50. The hotel and restaurant are closed mid-October to mid-December.

Stans

The capital of Nidwalden, Stans is noteworthy as one of only four Swiss communities to still hold the show-of-hands vote, the *Landsgemeinde* (open-air parliament). It takes place on the last Sunday in April, and is worth watching if you're in the area. Stans is also the starting point for the excellent excursion up the **Stanserhorn** mountain (1898 metres). It is not as popular as the trip up to Mt Rigi, which faces it across the lake, but it provides at least as good a view. The big ranges to the south (including Mt Titlis and the Jungfrau Massif) is closer and seems to surround you more, yet you still have the lakes and hills panorama to the north, including a wide expanse of Lake Lucerne and Lake Zug, plus Lake Sarnen, squeezed between the mountains in the south-west. There are plenty of viewing boards at the top so you can identify what you're seeing. From the cable station it's just 10 minutes' hike to the summit, and you can return by a different circular route. As always, a restaurant awaits by the top cable station; this one has outside seating.

The journey up – by funicular to Kälti then a cable car – costs Sfr20 each way or Sfr36 return, and the base station is five minutes' walk (signposted) from the train station. It operates from mid-April to mid-November. The hike up from the town takes around 4½ hours to ascend the grassy slopes, or if you have a car you can save almost an hour by driving up to Kälti and parking there.

In the main town, the central Dorfplatz is worth a stroll. It has a fountain and attractive 18th century buildings, as well as essentials such as hotels (around Sfr50 per person), supermarkets and a pharmacy. Its centre-piece is the early Baroque **Parish Church**, tastefully decorated inside in white and black, rather than the usual overdose of gold gilding. Adjoining the church is a Roman-esque belltower with a 16th century spire. There's a *pizzeria* by the base funicular station for cheapish fodder (from Sfr11).

Stans is on the Lucerne-Engelberg railway, or it can be reached by hourly bus from Buochs boat station.

Brunnen

This resort is at the dog-leg where Lake Uri (Urnersee) and Lake Lucerne meet. It's worth visiting if only for the view, with the two stretches of the lake shimmering either side of the spit of land on the opposite shore: the green patch to the left of that promontory is the famous Rütli meadow where the 1291 pact was signed. It's one of the livelier resorts on the lake (which, to be honest, isn't saying very much), and it's a good base for explor-ing in either direction, or for visiting Schwyz. Brunnen offers sailing, water-skiing and windsurfing, and there are schools for each of these activities. There's also swimming in the lake or in the Hallenbad heated pool. Contact the Outdoor sports centre (☎ 043-31 54 31), Gersauer-strasse 25, for river rafting and sea kayaking. The sports centre is also the place for surfing, roller-skating and mountain biking.

Contact the tourist office (☎ 043-31 17 77) at Bahnhofstrasse 32 for more details. Opening hours are Monday to Saturday from 8.30 am to noon and 1.30 to 6 pm (closes 5 pm Saturday). Between October and April it is closed Saturday afternoon and opens half an hour later for all other sessions. Don't forget to ask about the guest card; discounts are listed in the *Gäste Information* booklet.

Places to Stay & Eat There are two camp-sites overlooking the lake at Brunnen: *Camping Urmiberg* (☎ 043-31 33 27), open May to September, and *Camping Hopfreben* (☎ 043-31 18 73), open April to October. Both have similar facilities and cost Sfr4 per person (plus Sfr1.20 tax). In addition, Urmiberg costs Sfr3 to Sfr5 per tent and Sfr2.50 per car, and Hopfreben costs Sfr8 to Sfr14 per site.

In Brunnen you must pay at least Sfr50 per person for any hotel overlooking the water. *National* (☎ 043-31 18 78), at Bahnhof-strasse 47, is more affordable, starting at Sfr40/65 for singles doubles using hall facil-ities, or Sfr50/85 with private shower/toilet per person. It has a restaurant with outside seating, is family-friendly, and has adequate parking. It is also convenient for the train station which has money-exchange counters and bike rental available daily.

Nearer the lakefront is *Brunnerhof* (☎ 043-31 17 57) at Kapellplatz, with singles/doubles starting at Sfr65/110. Some slightly more expensive rooms have TV and/or balcony. Brunnerhof is also a good place to eat, with meals starting from Sfr9 and daily menus including soup and dessert starting at Sfr15.50. It is open daily from 8 am to midnight except between December and February when it closes down. Not far away is the busy *Pizzeria Bacco* at Gersauerstrasse 21. Great pizzas start from Sfr10.50 and there's a wide range of more expensive fish and meat dishes (closed Tuesday).

Entertainment Opposite Pizzeria Bacco on Gersauerstrasse is the *Kingfisher Pub*, a popular English-style drinking place (open daily, Sfr5 for half a litre of beer). *Bierhalle Kleinstadt*, Kleinstadt 8, is a more traditional drinking den. Beer costs just Sfr3.50 for half a litre. There are a couple of disco places on the waterfront, such as the *Beach Club* of the Hotel Bellevue. Across the road is the *Casino Brunnen*, where you can bet up to Sfr5 on Boule (open daily from 10 pm to 2 am, casual dress OK).

Lake Uri
There are several historic sights on this section. If you take the ferry from Brunnen towards Flüelen, the first sight you pass is a natural obelisk protruding from the water to a height of nearly 26 metres. The gold lettering inscribed thereon is a dedication to Schiller, the author of the play *Wilhelm Tell* in 1859, who was so instrumental in creating the Tell legend.

Next stop is the **Rütli Meadow**, where the Oath of Eternal Alliance was signed by the three cantons of Uri, Schwyz and Nidwalden. You can see it well enough from the boat, but if you want to alight, all you will find is a flagpole, a grassy field, and (inevitably) a souvenir shop which doubles as a café and post office.

To commemorate the 700th anniversary of the 1291 pact, the **Swiss Path** was built, which runs all the way round Lake Uri from Rütli to Brunnen. It is in 26 sections, each representing one of the 26 cantons, starting

with the first three to sign up and concluding with Jura (1979). Right at the end in Brunnen is a square dedicated to the Swiss living abroad, featuring a surprisingly ugly metal structure. The length of each section is determined by the population of the canton, with every five mm representing one person. Surprisingly, the Swiss haven't been so meticulous as to inscribe the name of every individual person along the path, but they have marked off each section with a stone plaque. It would take some dedication to walk the whole 36 km, but one or two sections (for example between boat stops) are easily manageable and worth undertaking. The hilliest stretches are from Rütli to Bauen and from Sisikon to Brunnen. Bauen to Flüelen (around 270 minutes in total) is almost flat and Flüelen to Sisikon (145 minutes) isn't too up-and-down either.

One of the boat stops on the lake is the **William Tell Chapel** (Tellskapell). The walls are covered in murals depicting four episodes in the Tell legend, including the one supposed to have occurred on this spot. He was being taken to prison in Gessler's boat, when a storm whipped up, causing his keepers to lose control. Tell leapt onto the rock, at the same time pushing the boat away from him and back into the stormy waves. He was thus able to make good his escape.

The last port of call on the lake is Flüelen. Its main importance is that it's on the main road and rail route through the St Gotthard Pass, and historically it was a staging post for the mule trains making this crossing. There is a cheap snack bar at Flüelen boat station, with food from Sfr4 to Sfr11.50. Near the town is **Altdorf**, where William Tell is reputed to have performed his apple-shooting stunt. A statue of the man himself stands in the main square, and Schiller's play is sometimes performed in the Tellspielhaus in Altdorf.

Between Vitznau and Brunnen on the north bank is **Gersau** (population 1700). Remarkably, this tiny place was an independent republic between 1390 and 1817 (the world's smallest) before joining the canton of Schwyz. There is an IYHF *youth hostel*

(☎ 041-84 12 77) between Vitznau and Gersau at Rotschuo. It's open from March to November and costs Sfr10 without sheets or breakfast. The reception is closed from 10 am to 4.30 pm.

On the opposite bank is **Beckenried**. A few minutes' walk from the boat station, a cable car makes the 10-minute ascent to **Klewenalp** (Sfr10 single or Sfr16 return). The views across the lake are good, and there are a number of hiking trails heading into the hills and valleys beyond. A map up there outlines the options. There are two mountain huts to aim for (altitude 1600 metres): *Klewen* (☎ 041-64 29 22) and *Klewenstock* (☎ 041-64 17 84). Both serve food, have dorms for Sfr25 with breakfast, and are open year-round except during cable car maintenance in May and November.

Engelberg

This sunny resort (1050 metres) at the foot of Mt Titlis is an ideal day trip from Lucerne, or a base for a longer stay. In summer, the hills above Engelberg sing with the melodic yet insistent sound of cowbells – it sounds like there's a never-ending procession of Hare Krishna devotees up there.

Orientation & Information
Engelberg (population 3000) is a popular summer and winter resort in the canton of Unterwalden. The main street is Dorfstrasse. This runs west-east along the railway track, past the train station (the terminus of the line), and on to the large monastery. Most of the shops and restaurants are ranged either side of this road, or on the intersecting Bahnhofstrasse. The Mt Titlis base station is south of the rail tracks, about one km from the centre. The post office is next to the train station and the tourist office (☎ 041-94 11 61) is just round the corner at Dorfstrasse 34.

The tourist office opening hours are Monday to Friday from 8 am to noon and from 2 to 5.45 pm and Saturday from 9 am to noon. During the summer and winter high season it is also open on Saturday afternoon depending upon demand. There is a low, middle, and high season in both summer and winter, which affects hotel prices. Peak times are early-February to late-March, and mid-July to mid-September. In November most of Engelberg closes down. The tourist office has a free room-booking service for hotels, but not B&Bs. Pick up the list of private rooms (from Sfr13 per person) and cheap mountain lodgings (from Sfr15 per person).

The guest card (obtainable from your hotel) is good for various discounts, including 20% off the Mt Titlis cable car in summer only. Mind you, the benefits are off-set by the Kurtaxe for staying in the resort, which ranges from Sfr2.20 to Sfr2.90 per day.

The telephone code for Engelberg is 041.

Things to See & Do
The **Engelberg Monastery** is one of only five such Benedictine monasteries in Switzerland. The original building dated from 1120 but was burnt down three times before finally being rebuilt in stone. There is a guided tour from Monday to Saturday at 10 am and 4 pm. It costs Sfr2 and lasts around 45 minutes. You're taken around several rooms decorated with incredibly detailed wood inlays – all done by one of the monks who continued doing this work until he was well into his seventies. A typical panel measuring around 50 cm by 20 cm contains 300 pieces of wood, and he spent years on each room. The Baroque monastery church is also impressive (free entry), with numerous side-altars. It even has a one-handed clock above the main altar so parishioners can time the sermon.

The **Tal Museum**, Dorfstrasse 6, is just of passing interest. One floor is a representation of a typical late 18th century dwelling. It is open most afternoons and costs Sfr5 (Sfr4 with guest card).

Mt Titlis The trip to the top cable station at 3020 metres is the most spectacular excursion in Engelberg. First there is the ascent to Gerschnialp (1300 metres), then there's a

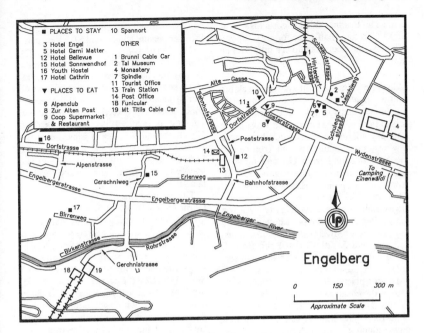

Engelberg

PLACES TO STAY	10 Spannort
3 Hotel Engel	OTHER
5 Hotel Garni Matter	
12 Hotel Bellevue	1 Brunni Cable Car
15 Hotel Sonnwendhof	2 Tal Museum
16 Youth Hostel	4 Monastery
17 Hotel Cathrin	7 Spindle
	11 Tourist Office
PLACES TO EAT	13 Train Station
	14 Post Office
6 Alpenclub	18 Funicular
8 Zur Alten Post	19 Mt Titlis Cable Car
9 Coop Supermarket	
& Restaurant	

0   150   300 m

Approximate Scale

horizontal passage over cow pastures, before rising again to Trübsee (1800 metres). From here you transfer to a gondola which goes to Stand (2450 metres) and provides a fine view back down to the lake and the valley below. Finally you board the world's first revolving gondola (completed in December 1992) for the passage over the Titlis Glacier, a dazzling expanse of ice with ridges, hollows and hints of blue. From Mt Titlis station to the 3229-metre summit it's about a 45-minute hike (wear sturdy shoes) in the summer. The station complex provides a sun terrace, restaurant, south-facing windows reached through a tunnel in the ice, and an ice grotto.

The whole journey is rather expensive, and if you go up in cloud you've wasted your money. Single/return prices from Engelberg are: Gerschnialp (Sfr5/7), Trübsee (Sfr15/21), Stand (Sfr29/41), and Titlis (Sfr43/60). The Swiss Half-Fare Card and the Regional Pass get 50% off, and the Swiss Pass, Eurail and Inter-Rail get a 25% reduc-

tion. From Engelberg to the Mt Titlis station takes around 45 minutes.

As ever, you can save on the cost and walk some sections. Between Stand and Trübsee the panoramaweg is open from July to September; it takes about 1¾ hours up and 1¼ hours down. From Trübsee up to Jochpass takes about 1½ hours, or down to Engelberg takes around the same time.

The cable cars run year round, except for the Stand-Titlis section which closes for maintenance from late October to early December. From Trübsee you have the option of walking round the lake and taking the chair lift up to Jochpass.

Brunni The Brunni cable car, on the opposite side of the valley, goes up 1600 metres and provides access to a number of hiking trails. A traveller complained to me that the 5½-hour Benediktusweg went up and down too many hills – but I suppose that's what happens when you go hiking in the mountains! The Brunni cable car costs Sfr8.60 or Sfr13.60 return (half-price for kids), or you can make the steep hike up in a little over an hour.

Skiing Engelberg is well-known as a skiing centre. In addition to the lifts previously mentioned, there are also cable cars or chair lifts to Fürenalp and Obertrüsee. Most of the runs are intermediate although there are a few easy ones, mainly around Trübsee and the lift branching from Gerschnialp. The main season is from mid-December to mid-April and a one-day pass costs Sfr45 for adults or Sfr23 for children. Part-day passes are available and rates are slightly higher on the weekends and holidays. Limited validity day passes cost Sfr25 (kids Sfr12.50) for just Trübsee and Sfr29 (Sfr 16) for Brunni. Multi-day passes are cheaper and transferable. Make use of the free ski buses.

Lots of places hire out skiing equipment. One of the cheapest is Amstutz Sport (☎ 94 12 68), Dorfstrasse 39. Skis, poles and ski boots for Alpine skiing cost Sfr33 for the first day, reducing with each subsequent day. Cross-country equipment starts at Sfr20 for the first day. There is a ski school (☎ 94 30 40) with an information office opposite the tourist office, open daily to 6 pm.

Bungy Jumping The seriously insane can contemplate bungy jumping off Mt Titlis. The 120-metre jump (from a cable car) costs Sfr169, or the trifling 70-metre jump, Sfr119. For information and reservations contact Freizeit Aktiv AG (☎ 036-22 73 07), Postgasse 16, CH-3800 Interlaken.

Mountain Biking There are routes up both sides of the valley. Many sports shops in the village rent bikes for around Sfr30 a day.

Places to Stay
Camping Einenwäldli (☎ 94 19 49) is about a 25-minute walk from the train station. Go down Klosterstrasse until it becomes Wydenstrasse, then take the right fork. In the winter you can take the ski bus instead. It's

open year-round and costs from Sfr4.50 to Sfr6 per person, and around Sfr5 for a car.

The IYHF *youth hostel* (☎ 94 12 92), Dorfstrasse 80, is 10 minutes back down the railway line on the north side of the tracks. Dorm beds are Sfr20 and the dinners are well worth the extra Sfr9.50 – if things aren't chock-a-block you keep getting refills until you beg for mercy. It is closed in October, November and for most of May. There is a 10.30 pm curfew and the main doors are locked between 9 am and 5 pm (you can leave your bags in the ski room and check-in later).

The cheapest place in the centre is *Hotel Garni Matter* (☎ 94 15 56), on Dorfstrasse towards the monastery. It only has a few basic singles/doubles for Sfr50/80 (Sfr55/90 in high season). *Hotel Engel* (☎ 94 11 82), in front of the monastery church, has singles/doubles with private shower from Sfr55/110. *Hotel Bellevue* (☎ 94 12 13), overlooking the station, has a deceptively majestic lobby, with pseudo-marble pillars and a grand piano. The rooms, in contrast, are fairly plain, varying in size from very spacious to difficult-to-swing-a-cat-in. Prices start at Sfr80/120 with private shower and toilet or Sfr60/100 using those down the corridor. It closes in November, May and June.

A good choice for personal service is *Hotel Cathrin* (☎ 94 44 66), on Birrenweg near the base of the Mt Titlis cable car. Singles/doubles with private shower start at Sfr67/114 and great four-course dinners are an extra Sfr20. Book ahead as this smallish place is used by the Kuoni tour group. *Sonnwendhof* (☎ 94 45 75), Gerschiweg 1, is convenient for both Mt Titlis and the centre. Sparkling new rooms (it was built in 1990) are neatly laid-out with all required amenities. Prices start at Sfr90/140, rising to Sfr110/180 in high season.

Places to Eat
Engelberg is not cheap for food, but if you study menus carefully down Dorfstrasse you may find Tagestellers from around Sfr13. The budget place to go is the *Coop* super-

market and restaurant on Klosterstrasse. Meals start at Sfr9; it has a salad bar and it's open Monday to Saturday from 8 am to 6.30 pm. There are restaurants at all the cable car stations. The restaurant in the *Hotel Bellevue* (see Places to Stay) is not too bad – it has soup from Sfr4.50 and other dishes from Sfr12 to Sfr30. It's open daily, except on Wednesday in low season.

The café-restaurant *Zur alten Post*, opposite the tourist office, has some interesting dishes from Sfr13. It is open Friday to Wednesday from 7.15 am to 6.30 pm.

There are several places to eat at *Alpenclub* on Dorfstrasse. Downstairs is a pizzeria, open from 5 pm daily with pizzas starting at Sfr13.50. Also open from the afternoon onwards are the ground floor restaurant serving Swiss food from Sfr28, and the first-floor section serving fondue from Sfr17. *Spannort* (☎ 94 26 26), Dorfstrasse, is a gourmet restaurant serving Swiss and French food (from Sfr30). It is closed on Monday and noon on Tuesday.

Entertainment

The *Angel Pub* of the Hotel Engel (see Places to Stay), by the monastery, is an English-style pub with darts and pool. An un-English touch is the tree trunk in the corner of the bar. This is a German game where you try and hammer in a nail using the reverse end of the hammer (the thin end). The last person to succeed buys the drinks. It is open daily from 9 am to midnight, and beer (half a litre) is Sfr3.70. The *Casino* on Dorfstrasse offers drinking, dancing and gambling on Boule (open daily). *Spindle*, on Dorfstrasse next to the Alpenclub pizzeria, has dancing from 9 pm to 3 am.

Getting There & Away

Engelberg is an hour away from Lucerne by train – on one steep stretch the train engages a cogwheel mechanism to help it along. The journey takes an hour and costs Sfr10.60. Seeing Engelberg and Mt Titlis in a day trip from Lucerne is easily viable; the first train leaves Lucerne at 6.19 am and the last one back leaves Engelberg at 9.50 pm. The

Lucerne tourist office sells special excursion tickets. (See the Getting Around section at the beginning of this chapter for details.)

Hiking Unless travelling by road from Lucerne or Stans, the only other way to leave or reach Engelberg is by foot, and the passes are only accessible in the summer. The Surenen Pass (2291 metres) is the route to Attinghausen, and from there a bus can take you to Altdorf and the southern end of the Urnersee. It takes around seven hours to get to Attinghausen; taking a cable car along the route can save two hours. From Jochpass a path goes to Meiringen via Engstenalp and Tannalp. The highest point you reach is 2245 metres. From Meiringen it is easy to get to Lake Brienz. Acquire a decent map and check on snow conditions before you try one of these routes.

Schwyz

The fame of Schwyz rests upon the fact that it gave Switzerland both its name and flag. Together with the communities of Uri and Nidwalden, it was signatory to the Oath of Eternal Alliance of 1291. This charter is seen as the birth of the Swiss Confederation and the document has been preserved, together with subsequent historic agreements, in the town's Archives building. There is little else to detain the visitor in this quiet place, although the nearby resort of Brunnen may demand some attention.

Orientation & Information

Schwyz is the capital of its canton and has a population of 12,000. Rising above the town are the twin peaks of the Mythen (1898 metres and 1811 metres). The train station is two km away from the town centre in Seewen. To get to the centre, take any bus outside the station marked Schwyz Post, and get off at Postplatz. The tourist office (☎ 043-21 34 46) is inside the post office, and is open Monday to Friday from 9 am to noon and from 1.30 to 5 pm. Pick up the

Gäste Information booklet which also covers Brunnen and Morscharch, and ask about the guest card if you plan to stay overnight in the area. Postplatz is on the corner of the central square, Hauptplatz.

The telephone code for Schwyz and the surrounding resorts is 043.

Federal Archives

Historic charters and other agreements are collected in the **Bundesbriefarchiv** building on Bahnhofstrasse in the town centre. Entry is free and it is open daily from 9.30 to 11.30 am and from 2 to 5 pm. The federal charters are in the circular cabinet in the centre of the room. The inaugural 1291 charter displayed here is the only copy in existence. It is written in Latin and bears only the seals of Uri and Nidwalden – Schwyz's own seal has been lost. In the document, the partners agreed to work for mutual defence and security and formulated their own legal system. They successfully defended this pact in 1315 by defeating the Habsburg force at Morgarten. The second charter marks this victory by restating the original agreement

(in German) and making provision for a common foreign policy.

The other charters mark the acceptance of further cantons to the Confederation, with a corresponding increase in the number of heavy seals attached to each document. The last charter proclaims the entry of Appenzell in 1513 and resolves not to admit any other members to its elite circle. The Confederates kept this resolution intact until the French marched onto the scene in 1798.

Also on display round the outside of the room are charters relating to privileges won by Schwyz through the years, and flags and banners carried in important battles.

Other Attractions

In Hauptplatz there is the 17th century **Town Hall**, complete with 19th century murals depicting famous events in Swiss history, particularly the Battle of Morgarten. On the other side of the square is **St Martin's Church**, with Baroque fixtures and a marble pulpit. Schwyz was the home of many of the 16th and 17th century mercenaries who fought in foreign armies. Those who

---

The Swiss Flag

Soldiers from the canton of Schwyz went to the aid of the excommunicated Emperor Frederick II in 1240, during his campaign in Italy. As a reward Schwyz was granted freedom from sovereign overlords and the right to use a red flag, the blood banner of the Holy Roman Empire, complete with heraldic cross. But a subsequent Diet in Nuremberg declared Frederick's dispensation invalid, so Schwyz pitched in behind Rudolf I of Habsburg in a battle against the Burgundians in 1289, and were rewarded by having their privileges confirmed.

The different Swiss cantons all had their own flags, yet they soon accepted the use of the white cross as a common emblem for Swiss mercenary soldiers. When Napoleon created the Helvetic Republic in 1798 he gave the country its first official national flag, a green, red and yellow tricolour. This flag was ditched in 1803, but it wasn't until 1841 that the cantons agreed to accept the free-standing white cross on the red field as a federal flag. Tireless campaigning by General Henri Dufour was instrumental in getting the flag accepted.

But the matter did not end. People got very excited about whether the cross should consist of four equal squares arranged around a central square, or whether the bars of the cross should be one-sixth longer than their width. The federal constitutions of 1848 and 1874 neglected to settle this burning issue. Finally, the Federal parliament tried to put an end to the argument by deciding in favour of the latter in 1889. Even so, debate raged on this crucial matter for years to come.

The federal decision seemed to be vindicated when in 1906 the international community honoured the Swiss flag by choosing to reverse its colours (to make a red cross on white) as a universal emblem for army medical corps. Nowadays the Swiss seem to have forgotten the passions aroused by the extra one-sixth, and seem content in the knowledge that they have the only square national flag in the world, along with that of the Vatican. ■

returned with body and fortune intact built some of the grand houses that can still be seen round the town today. At the rear of Seewen train station is a building that looks like a block of cheese. This is the **Schau-käserie Schwyzerland** (☎ 21 61 61), where the different stages in making cheese are explained and illustrated. Entry costs Sfr1 and it's open Tuesday to Saturday from 9 am to 6 pm.

Hiking and skiing is possible on the surrounding mountains, accessible by cable car or funicular. For information on the Mythen ski region call its tourist office on ☎ 21 34 46. There is also skiing at Stoos (1300 metres). From Schwyz, take bus No 3 to Schlattli then the funicular (Sfr11 up, Sfr11 down, Sfr18 return). A cable car goes up from Stoos to Frontalpstock (1922 metres). A good, if steep, circular hike from Stoos around the Frontalpstock area takes three to four hours.

Schwyz is near Lake Lauerzer, and it's also within reach of the Lake Lucerne resort of Brunnen (see the Lake Lucerne section for details). From Brunnen, you can get to Stoos via bus No 4 to Morscharch, then a cable car (Sfr10.80 up, Sfr17 return).

Places to Stay & Eat
Some pension receptions are closed on Monday. For budget rooms, explore the vicinity of Seewen station. Other than that, the cheaper places are up the mountains, such as the *Berggasthaus* (☎ 21 17 74) on Haggenegg (Sfr35 per person). In the middle of Schwyz, try *Drei Königen* (☎ 21 24 10), by St Martin's Church on Schulgasse. Rooms are Sfr50 per person, or Sfr60 with private shower. The food is not bad value either, with spaghetti starting at Sfr9 and other meat dishes from Sfr14 (closed Sunday evening and Monday).

Hirschen Garni (☎ 21 12 76), Hinterdorfstrasse 9, is good too, with comfortable singles/doubles starting at Sfr45/78. *Restaurant Löwen*, near Hirschen Garni, has a three-course menu for Sfr14 (closed Tuesday evening and Wednesday).

The best restaurant in Schwyz is *Ratskeller* (☎ 21 10 87) at Strehlgasse 3. It is closed Sunday evening, Monday, and for two weeks from mid-February (no credit cards accepted). Not so bank-breaking is *Restaurant Hofmatt,* Zeughausstrasse 7, with a lunch and evening menu including soup for Sfr14 (closed Sunday).

Getting There & Away
Schwyz is just 30 minutes away from Zug on the main north-south rail route. It is also only a few kms detour off the N4 which passes through Brunnen. (See the Zug and Einsiedeln Getting There & Away sections for more information.)

Zug

Many multinational companies are registered in affluent Zug, thanks to the canton's status as a tax haven. The canton is easily the richest is Switzerland, earning an incredible Sfr70,532 per inhabitant per year; over 60% higher than the national average. Tourists, however, will be attracted more by its delightful medieval town centre and the nearby lake. Maybe the lake is a little too nearby – parts of the town sank in it in 1435, 1594 and 1887.

Orientation & Information
Zug (pronounced Tzoogk) hugs the northeast shore of Lake Zug (Zugersee). The train station is one km north of the old town centre, and there are bike rental and money-exchange counters. Exit the station on the east side of the tracks and walk 500 metres south down Baarerstrasse until it becomes Bahnhofstrasse. The tourist office (☎ 042-21 00 78) is here at No 23. It's only a desk in Cityzug Reisebüro (a travel agent) but has various brochures and a city map to give out. Opening hours are Monday to Friday from 9.30 am to noon and 1 to 6 pm, and Saturday from 9.30 am to noon. Continue down

Bahnhofstrasse for the main post office and the Altstadt (old town).

The telephone code for Zug is 042.

Things to See & Do

The medieval town centre can easily be explored on foot. Start with the **clocktower** (Zytturm) in Kolinplatz. It's the symbol of the town and its distinctive tiled roof is painted in the blue and white of the cantonal colours. The shields below the 1557 clockface are those of the first eight cantons to join the Confederation (Zug was the seventh in 1352). The fountain in Kolinplatz was built in honour of Wolfgang Kolin, the flag bearer of the Swiss army that was defeated in the Battle of Arbedo (1422) by a vastly superior force led by the Duke of Milan.

Leading off from Kolinplatz are the medieval streets of Fischmarkt, Oberaltstadt and Unteraltstadt. The old step-gabled houses are notable for their overhanging balconies. Nearby is Landsgemeindeplatz where there's a free aviary containing a number of feathered inmates, such as owls, peacocks, ibises and parakeets.

Off Kolinplatz to the other side is Kirchenstrasse which leads to the 13th century castle, now containing the **Museum in der Burg**. It exhibits a collection of archaeological, art, and historical implements. Opening hours are Saturday and Sunday from 10 am to noon, and daily except Monday from 2 to 5 pm; admission is Sfr3 (students Sfr1) except on Sundays and holidays when it's free. Almost opposite is **St Oswald's Church**, built in late-Gothic style from the 15th and 16th centuries. It has a number of interesting features including a trio of carved wooden altars.

There are paddleboats available by Landsgemeindeplatz for trips on the lake (Sfr17 per hour), and various beaches, including one just round the shore from the youth hostel. The funicular from Schönegg will take you up the Zugerberg (988 metres), where there are hiking trails and an unobstructed view.

A good excursion from Zug is to the **Sta-lactite Grottoes** (Höllgrotten) near Baar, about eight km to the north-east. These limestone caves are open 1 April to 31 October, every day from 9 am to noon and 1 to 5.30 pm. Entry costs Sfr6 (Sfr3 for students and children) and they take about an hour to get around. To get there by public transport, take the Menzingen bus and get off at Tobelbrücke-Höllgrotten.

Places to Stay

There is *camping* (☎ 31 50 34) on the shore of the lake, two km west of the centre, along Chamer Fussweg. Charges are Sfr5 per person and Sfr5 per tent. The spanking new IYHF *youth hostel* (☎ 21 53 54) is at Allmendstrasse 8, a 10-minute walk west of the station along Gubel Strasse. Beds including breakfast cost Sfr21, and there are kitchen facilities and evening dinners (Sfr9). The hostel is closed from 10 am to 5 pm and has an 11.30 pm curfew.

Other accommodation is on the expensive side. The best value in the centre is *Hotel Löwen* (☎ 21 77 22) at Landsgemeindeplatz, a good location near the lake. Smallish singles/doubles with private shower and toilet are Sfr95/145 or Sfr70/125 with free use of hall facilities. All rooms have a radio. The only cheap place is two km south of Zug at Oberwil. Take the bus heading south down Bahnhofstrasse (which become Artherstrasse) and, at No 119 on Bahnhofstrasse, is *Adler* (☎ 21 16 94), with singles/doubles from Sfr46/80.

People with more money to spend should head for *City-Hotel Ochsen* (☎ 21 32 32) at Kolinplatz. This quiet place has singles/doubles from Sfr130/195. Dating from 1480, it's the oldest inn in central Switzerland; Goethe once stayed here.

Places to Eat

Cherry trees are grown locally, so look out for the speciality, Zug cherry cake (*Zuger Kirschtorte*). It's a diet-busting combination of pastry, biscuit, almond paste, and butter cream with cherry brandy.

There's no shortage of self-service places

in town – all the old standbys are here. Across Baarstrasse from the train station there's a *Migros* supermarket and restaurant in the Metalti arcade, open Monday to Friday from 8 am to 6.30 pm (9 pm on Thursday) and Saturday from 8 am to 5 pm. Just down the street there's a large *Coop* restaurant and supermarket in the arcade opposite Bundesplatz. On Bundesplatz itself there's an *EPA* department store with menus for Sfr6.50 and Sfr8.50, tea and coffee for Sfr1.60, and other dishes for Sfr6 to Sfr12. Opening hours are as for Migros.

Try typical Swiss food where the locals eat (no English spoken) in *Restaurant Kreuz* on Aageristrasse 28 by the Kaperzinerkloster Church. Meals are Sfr8.50 to Sfr15, salads are Sfr3.50 to Sfr10, and beer is Sfr3.50 for half a litre. It is closed on Saturday.

There are two top restaurants in this small town. The *Rathauskeller* (☎ 21 00 58) has the best reputation. It's at Oberaltstadt 1, right in the centre of town, and it closes on Sunday and Monday. Also highly regarded is *Aklin* (☎ 21 18 66), a few paces away, next to the clocktower in an old guild house. French-style gourmet menus are above Sfr60, and it also has a cheaper restaurant (closed Sunday and Monday).

Getting There & Away

Train connections are excellent. Zug is on the main north-south rail route from Zürich to Lugano, and it is also the station at which trains from Zürich branch off to Lucerne and the Bernese Oberland.

By road, the north-south N4 (E31) runs from Zürich, sweeps round the western shore of Lake Zug and joins the N2 (E35), which continues through the St Gotthard Pass and on to Lugano and Italy. Highway 25 peels off the N4 north of Zug at Sihlbrugg, completes the corset round the eastern shore of the lake, then rejoins the N4 at Goldau.

Boats depart from Zug's Schiffsstation Bahnhof and chug south to Arth (Swiss Pass and Half-Fare Card valid) in the summer, and to many other destinations round the lake. Some outings include meals and music on board. Reserve on ☎ 26 24 26.

Einsiedeln

Einsiedeln is the most important pilgrimage destination in Switzerland, and its church is worth visiting simply for its sumptuous interior. Einsiedeln's reputation stems from 964, when the Bishop of Constance attempted to consecrate the original monastery. He was halted in his tracks by a heavenly voice declaring, 'Desist – God Himself has consecrated this building'. Presumably somebody checked the premises for ventriloquists, because a papal bull subsequently acknowledged the miracle as genuine.

Orientation & Information

Einsiedeln is south of Lake Zürich and by the western shore of Lake Sihl. The train station and the post office are together in the centre of town. In front of them is Dorfplatz, from which leads the main street, Hauptstrasse. The church is at the end of this street, overlooking Klosterplatz. The tourist office (☎ 055-53 44 88) at Hauptstrasse 85, is open Monday to Friday from 9 am noon and 2 to 5.30 pm and Saturday from 9 am to noon and 2 to 4 pm.

Things to See & Do

The main focus of activity is the **Abbey Church**. This majestic Baroque edifice was built from 1719 to 1735 by the architect, Caspar Moosbrugger. Much of the interior of the church is the work of the Asam brothers, who were also responsible for the remarkable Asamkirch in Munich. The frescoes and stucco embellishments are exceptional, even if the newly restored colours are a bit overpowering. (Which misguided soul chose that salmon pink?) It slightly pre-dates and obviously influenced the design of the similarly lavish St Gallen Cathedral which is rather appropriate, as the original monastery here was based on the original monastery in St Gallen.

The main prize for pilgrims is the **Black Madonna**, housed in a chapel by the entrance to the church; it is to this that most of the prayers are directed. It's only a small statue, but one that has somehow survived three fires. The chapel is built on the spot where St Meinrad was murdered in 861.

In front of the church is a large square (plenty of parking) where stalls sell kitsch religious souvenirs. Continuing the religious theme, there's a **diorama** of Bethlehem, featuring 500 figures, and a **panorama** painting of Calvary. These are in Benzigerstrasse; entry for each costs Sfr3.50 (children Sfr1.50) and they are open from Easter to the end of October.

Every year on the 14 September there is the **Festival of the Miraculous Dedication** involving a torchlit procession. At five-yearly intervals in the summer (the next one is in 1997) is the formidable production of *The Great Theatre of the World*, a religious drama by Calderón de la Barca. Over 600 villagers act in the event.

Activities in the surrounding area include winter cross-country skiing, hiking, and boating and bathing in nearby **Lake Sihl**. Fishing permits for the lake cost Sfr14 per day and Sfr40 per week. There are suggestions for hikes in the free *Gäste Information* booklet from the tourist office. Walk beside the church through the monastery buildings (pausing to pat the horses in the paddock) and continue along the path for 15 minutes for a good viewpoint of the church, green hills, the lake and the adjoining mountains.

Places to Stay & Eat

There's *camping* (☎ 055-53 17 37) on the far shore of Lake Sihl at Willerzell.

If you decide to stay overnight in Einsiedeln, *Storchen* (☎ 055-53 37 60), Hauptstrasse 79, has largish singles/doubles with own shower/toilet and TV from Sfr70/114, and a mid-price restaurant. A couple of doors down, *Schweizerhof* (☎ 055-53 28 85), is a fascinating place to stay. It's an ancient, creaking place with decaying fittings and period knick-knacks, and is run by a charming old woman who probably thinks that hula hoops are still the latest teen craze to hit town. There's a great old curio shop downstairs, too. You need to be pre-

pared to rough it, as the one shower is usually out of commission; singles/doubles are Sfr35/60. A similar price is *Meinradsberg* (☎ 055-53 28 56), in front of the church at Igenweidstrasse.

Get basic food at the *Coop* supermarket, off Dorfplatz, or in the snack bar in the Bahnhof. *Pizzeria zia Teresa* and café-restaurant *Central*, both on Dorfplatz, are reasonable choices for an inexpensive meal. *Restaurant Sihlsee*, Hauptstrasse 28, has lunch menus for Sfr12.50 and Sfr14.50 including soup, and grills from Sfr17. Speciality of the house is the tasty half chicken in a basket for Sfr12 (closed Wednesday).

Getting There & Away

Einsiedeln is in a rail cul-de-sac so getting there usually involves changing at Biberbrugg, but this is rarely a problem as arrivals/departures coincide. It is also within range of the canton of Zürich's S-Bahn system transport. Zürich itself (Sfr14) is less than one hour away (via Wädenswil). To Lucerne (Sfr18.60) takes 1½ to two hours, depending upon connections. From Einsiedeln to Schwyz, you can take the scenic 'back route' in the summer: postbus to Oberiberg, then private bus (Swiss Pass not valid) from there.

By car, Einsiedeln is five km off highway 8 between Schwyz and Rapperswil.

Andermatt

Andermatt (1447 metres) is a skiing resort at the crossroads of four major Alpine passes: Susten, Oberalp, St Gotthard and Grimsel. The views from the town itself are surprisingly unspectacular given the mountain ranges all around – but that changes as soon as you gain some altitude.

Orientation & Information

Andermatt is at the southern end of the canton of Uri, and was formerly an important staging-post on the north-south St Gotthard route. Nowadays the town has been bypassed by the St Gotthard tunnel, but it still remains an important transport junction. In appearance Andermatt is borderline dull, with too many featureless concrete blocks, saved only by a couple of church spires breaking up the skyline, and the small river, the Unteralpreuss, running through the centre. The train station is 400 metres north of the core of the village. Postbuses stop by the station, and the tourist office (☎ 044-6 74 54) is in the postbus ticket office. Its opening hours are Monday to Friday from 9 am to noon and 2 to 6 pm, and Saturday from 9 am to noon. From mid-June to late September and early December to mid-May it is also open on Saturday from 2 to 6 pm.

The post office is on the main street, Gotthardstrasse (PTT, 6490, Andermatt). Some hotels and restaurants close from early November to mid-December and from late April to early June. The resort has newly introduced a Visitor's Card, available from hotels, that's good for various discounts.

The telephone code for Andermatt is 044.

Things to See & Do

The **skiing** is between 1438 and 2963 metres, with runs mostly for experts and intermediates. One-day ski passes range from Sfr25 (Sfr17 for children) valid for one lift, to Sfr88 (Sfr59) for a two-day general pass. There is cross-country skiing along the broad, flat valley towards Realp. Realp also has a small ski lift where beginners can hone their skills (Sfr18 for one day, children half-price).

From **Realp**, steam trains run to Tiefenbach (an 18-minute ride) on weekends between early June and early October. The return fare is Sfr18 for adults and Sfr9 for children.

The passes on all four sides make for excellent driving tours, and can also be visited on a circular tour by postbus (see Meiringen for details). It's also fun to watch the trains winding their way backwards and forwards over the mountains. The **St Gotthard Museum** (☎ 094-88 15 25), on the St Gotthard Pass (2109 metres), is open from 9 am to 6 pm daily, but only between June

and October when the pass itself is open. The museum uses reliefs, models, documents and weapons to tell the story of the history of the pass, highlighting mule drivers, stage-coaches, and the new tunnel. The St Gotthard tunnel now takes the brunt of most Alp crossings.

The tourist office has information on walking tours to/from the passes and other points of interest, taking one to six hours. From **Gemsstock** (2963 metres), there's a panorama of 600 Alpine peaks. The journey to the top by cable car from Andermatt is in two sections and costs Sfr11.60 up or Sfr16.80 return (children half-price, reductions with Swiss rail passes).

Places to Stay & Eat

Lager Zgraggen (☎ 6 76 58) offers dorm beds year round, with kitchen facilities, for Sfr19. It's near the station on the west side of the Unteralpreuss, on Bodenstrasse. Otherwise, accommodation in the village is expensive. *Bergidyll* (☎ 6 74 55), Gotthard-strasse 39, is probably the best value. It has pleasant, reasonably spacious rooms for Sfr55 per person with private shower, or Sfr5 less using one in the hall. There's also a lounge with easy chairs and an open fire.

Löwen (☎ 6 72 23), just down the road at No 51, has singles doubles from Sfr41/78, and breakfast is Sfr5 per person. Between the two, the *Hotel Monopol* (☎ 6 75 75) has better-appointed rooms from Sfr60 per person with private shower.

For eating, check the hotel restaurants for daily specials. Most restaurants are on Gotthardstrasse near where the road crosses the river. *Badus*, close to the station on Gotthardstrasse, usually has two-course lunch specials for Sfr13.50 and Sfr17, and a three-course evening menu for around Sfr28. It also offers some vegetarian dishes. *Hotel Löwen* has pizzas and pasta from Sfr12. *Postillion Snack-Restaurant*, has a salad buffet (albeit fairly limited) for Sfr7.50/10 for a small/large plate.

There is a *Coop* on Gotthardstrasse in the south of the village. You could also check out

Bonetti House, near the gondola station, where there is a self-service restaurant.

Getting There & Away

If you travel extensively in Switzerland you're almost certain to end up in or near Andermatt. It is a stop on the Glacier Express from Zermatt to St Moritz, and on the William Tell Express from Lucerne to Lugano. If you take the three or four pass tour (see the Meiringen section in the Bernese Oberland chapter) you will stop for lunch in Andermatt. The St Gotthard tunnel (N2/E35) is one of the busiest north-south routes across the Alps. The tunnel (17 km) is the world's longest, and opened in 1980. It extends from Göschenen to close to Airolo, bypassing Andermatt. Each weekend *30 tonnes* of nitrogen is emitted into the atmosphere by traffic on the St Gotthard route.

Zürich Canton

The canton of Zürich is the most populous in Switzerland with 1,150,000 inhabitants and one of the most affluent. It is a hub of industry and the financial centre of the country. Heavy industry (metals and machines) are particularly important for a number of towns. As a tourist centre it is not so pre-eminent. Zürich itself welcomes many visitors – tourists and business people – who can enjoy the old centre, museums and galleries, and lakeside setting. Otherwise, there's little in the canton to detain the visitor, except perhaps a visit to Winterthur, highly-regarded for its art collections, or a tour on Lake Zürich.

Information
The tourist office in Zürich city handles enquiries for the whole Zürich tourist region, and has racks of brochures on many towns throughout Switzerland. The headquarters of the Swiss National Tourist Office is also in Zürich (see the Zürich Information section for details).

Zürich

The city of Zürich started life as a Roman customs post with the name of Turicum. Expansion thereafter was slow, but merchants trading in textiles slowly increased the financial clout of the town until, in 1218, it graduated to the status of a free city under the Holy Roman Empire. In 1336 the increasingly powerful merchants and artisans formed guilds which took over the governing of the city.

Zürich's reputation as a cultural and intellectual centre began after it joined the Swiss Confederation in 1351. Zwingli helped things along with his teachings during the Reformation, from 1519, and became a key figure in the running of the city. Zürich's intellectual and artistic tradition continued during WW I with the influx of luminaries such as Lenin, Trotsky, Tristan Tzara, Hans Arp and James Joyce. The Dada art movement was born in 1916 in the Cabaret Voltaire on Spiegelgasse 1. Around the same time, Carl Jung was honing his psychoanalytical theories in the city. Heinrich Pestalozzi (1746-1827), seminal educationalist, was also a citizen of Zürich, and his statue stands on Bahnhofstrasse.

On the financial side, Zürich's status as an international industrial and business centre is thanks in no small part to the efforts of the energetic administrator and railway magnate, Alfred Escher, in the 19th century. His statute is in front of the station. Zürich's stock exchange was founded in 1877 and is most important in the country.

Switzerland's most populous city by far (341,300 people, over twice the number living in Geneva) offers an ambience of affluence and plenty of cultural diversions. Banks and art galleries will greet you almost at every turn in a strange marriage of finance and aesthetics. In 1993, the Social Democrats were at the helm of the Zürich's administration, but the guilds retain a powerful, if behind closed doors, voice in the running of the city.

Orientation
Zürich is 409 metres above sea level at the northern end of Lake Zürich. The city centre is on both sides of the Limmat River which heads north from the lake before sweeping round to the west. Like many Swiss cities, it is compact and conveniently laid out. The main train station (Hauptbahnhof) is on the west bank of the river.

Information
Tourist Office The main tourist office (☎ 01-211 40 00) is at the Hauptbahnhof, Bahnhofplatz 15, and arranges hotel reservations (Sfr5 commission), car rentals and excursions. The opening hours change

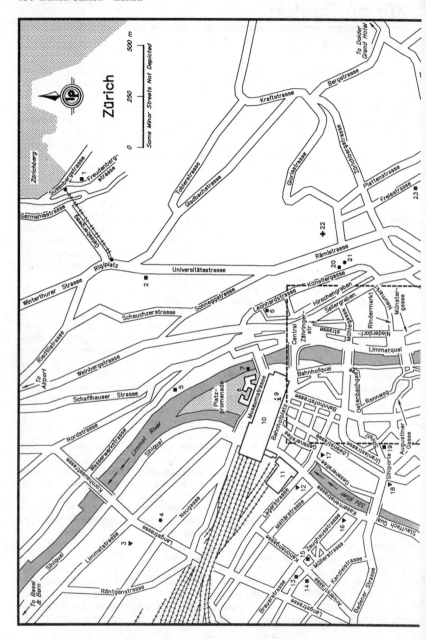

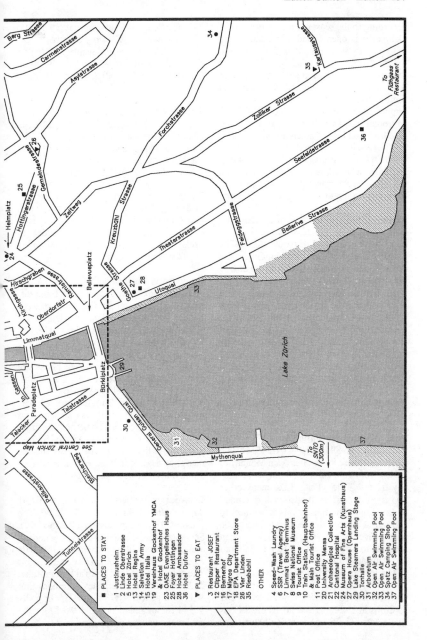

according to the season. From 1 April to 31 October it is open Monday to Friday from 8.30 am to 9.30 pm, and Saturday and Sunday from 8.30 am to 8.30 pm. The rest of the year it is open Monday to Friday from 8.30 am to 7.30 pm, and Saturday and Sunday from 8.30 am to 6.30 pm. There's an airport branch in Terminal B (☎ 01-816 40 81), open daily from 10 am to 7.00 pm. Maps of Zürich and lists of hotels are Sfr1 to Sfr3.

The Swiss National Tourist Office (SNTO) headquarters (☎ 01-288 11 11) is at Bellariastrasse 38, and has information on the whole of Switzerland. It's open Monday to Friday from 8 to 11.45 am and 1 to 5 pm.

Money There's no shortage of choice when exchanging money in this banking city. Visa cash advances and Eurocheque ATM machines are widely available. Banks are open Monday to Friday from 8.15 am to 4.30 pm, except Thursday when they are open until 6 pm. The big three banks have branches near the station open until at least 6.30 pm weekdays and 4 pm Saturday: Union Bank of Switzerland in Bahnhof Passage, in the Shop Ville, Underground by the station (closes 9 pm Thursday), Swiss Bank Corporation at Bahnhofstrasse 70, and Credit Suisse at Bahnhofstrasse 89 (closes 9 pm Thursday). The exchange office in the Hauptbahnhof is open daily from 6.15 am to 10.45 pm, and it's by platform 16.

Post & Telecommunications The main post office is Sihlpost (☎ 01-245 41 11), Kasernenstrasse 95-99. It is open Monday to Friday from 7.30 am to 6.30 pm, and Saturday from 7.30 to 11 am. Like many other Swiss post offices, it also has extended trading hours but transactions are subject to a small surcharge during these times. The post office in the Hauptbahnhof is open Monday to Friday from 7.30 am to 6.30 pm and Saturday from 7.30 to 11 am.

The telephone code for Zürich is 01.

Consulates The British Consulate (☎ 261 15 20) is at Dufourstrasse 56. The US Consulate (☎ 422 25 66) is at Zollikerstrasse 141. The South African Consulate (☎ 911 06 60) is south-east of Zürich at Seestrasse 221, Küsnacht. The German Consulate (☎ 265 65 65) is at Kirchgasse 48, and the Austrian Consulate (☎ 383 72 00) is at Minervastrasse 116.

Travel Agents SSR (☎ 261 29 56), Leonhardstrasse 5 and 10, is a specialist in student and youth fares. The SSR administration headquarters (☎ 242 30 00) is at Bäckerstrasse 52; there's another branch at Bäckerstrasse 40. Globetrotter (☎ 211 77 80), Rennweg 35, concentrates on non-European destinations; it's open Monday to Friday from 9 am to 12.30 pm and 1.30 to 6 pm. American Express (☎ 219 61 11) is at Bahnhofstrasse 20; it's open Monday to Friday from 8.30 am to 5.30 pm and Saturday from 9 am to noon.

Bookshops Buchhandlung Stäheli (☎ 201 33 02; see the Central Zürich map), Bahnhofstrasse 70, has many English-language books: fiction, nonfiction, travel, and old stock (during May only) from Sfr1. It is open Monday to Friday from 9 am to 6.30 pm and Saturday from 9 am to 4 pm.

English and French-language books are also available at Librairie Poyot, Bahnhofstrasse 11. The Travel Book Shop (☎ 252 38 83; see the Central Zürich map), Rindermarkt 20, has an enormous selection of English-language travel books and can order anything you want (expect to pay Sfr2 to Sfr10 above the cover price). It also runs the map shop next door. It's open Monday from 1 pm, otherwise hours are as above.

Emergency For medical help, ring ☎ 261 61 00; for dental help, ring ☎ 257 32 69. The Cantonal University Hospital (☎ 255 11 11), Schmelzbergstrasse 8, has a casualty department. There is a 24-hour chemist at Bellevue Apotheke (☎ 252 56 00), Theaterstrasse 14. The police (☎ 216 71 11) are at Bahnhofquai 3. The national emergency numbers are: ☎ 117 for police, ☎ 118 for the fire brigade, ☎ 144 for an ambulance and ☎ 140 for the car breakdown service.

Gay & Lesbian The gay switchboard (☎ 271 70 11), is open Tuesday only between 8 to 10 pm. There's a lesbian phone line at the same hours on ☎ 272 73 71. Haz (☎ 242 98 44), Begegnungszentrum, 3rd floor, Sihlquai 67, is a gay and lesbian centre. The gay and lesbian newspaper *Cruiser* has extensive listings and maps of Swiss towns.

Women Travellers Frauenzentrum (☎ 272 85 03), Mattengasse 27, is a women's centre which has a health centre (☎ 272 77 50) and a bar on the premises.

Dangers & Annoyances Zürich has a large contingent of hard drug users. They used to congregate in the infamous 'needle park' behind the Schweizerisches Landesmuseum. They're now dispersed in the city but the problem is still there: you may be hassled if you come across them.

Laundry Speed-Wash at the corner of Mattengasse and Josef-Strasse near Neugasse, is self-service. Machines cost from Sfr5 to wash and Sfr1.50 per 10 minutes for drying. It's open daily until 10 pm.

Walking Tour
Pick up the tourist office brochure *Walks through Zürich* detailing (in English) four walks in the city centre.

The pedestrian streets of the old town on either side of the Limmat River contain most of the major sights. Features to notice are winding alleyways, 16th and 17th century houses and guildhalls, courtyards and fountains. Zürich has 1030 fountains and the locals insist the water is drinkable in them all. Don't be surprised if a waiter heads for the nearest fountain if you ask for tap water in a restaurant!

Lindenhof, a raised terrace on the west bank, has trees, gravel and giant chess games. This is the spot where the Romans founded their customs post in 15 BC. The elegant **Bahnhofstrasse** was built on the site of the city walls which were torn down 150 years ago. Underfoot are bank vaults crammed full of gold and silver. Zürich is one of the world's premier precious metals markets but the vaults (for some reason) aren't open to the public. The 13th century tower of **St Peter's Church**, St Peterhofstatt, has the largest clock face in Europe (8.7 metres in diameter). The

---

Crime & Drugs
Switzerland may not have a high crime rate, but it doesn't pay to be too blasé about security. In the city of Zürich alone there were 925 armed robberies in 1992, a jump from 333 in 1980. Admittedly, crime is more of a problem in Zürich than anywhere else in Switzerland. There would seem to be a correlation between the rising crime figures and the rise in drug addicts in the city. Dealers and users (all drugs) known to the police numbered 7532 in '92. Zürich is in danger of becoming an international drugs market: the products dirty the streets and the proceeds get laundered in the banks.

Crime and drug deaths in Zürich peaked in '91 during the operation of the infamous 'Needle Park' where heroin addicts were supplied with sterilised needles. Since the park closed in early '92 both figures have come down, but there were still 82 drug-related deaths in 1992 in the canton. Switzerland as a whole has the highest number of drug deaths in Europe per capita.

Switzerland hasn't yet worked out how to combat the drug problem. The drug culture was slow in catching up with the country, but now seems fully entrenched. In 1975 the authorities took a hard line on drug abuse, imposing sentences for dealing of up to 20 years imprisonment and a fine of up to Sfr1 million.

The heavy-handed policy didn't work. In 1989 a narcotics commission recommended a soft approach, advocating legalisation of consumption. Drugs remain illegal, though some cantons now have 'fixer rooms' where addicts can inject themselves safely. But as Zürich's experience shows, a liberal policy is not necessarily the answer either. One thing is certain, however. The pushers won't go away – not when, to quote the narcotics commission, prices for heroin, cocaine and cannabis in Switzerland are 'among the highest in the world'. ■

Fraumünster Church nearby is noted for the distinctive stained glass windows in the choir created by Marc Chagall in 1970, completed when he was 83. The building itself dates from the 13th century. Augusto Giacometti also made a window here, as well as in the **Grossmünster Cathedral** across the river, where Zwingli preached his message of 'pray and work' in the 16th century. The figure glowering from the south tower of the Grossmünster is Charlemagne, who founded the church that was originally at this location. This part of Zürich was once an island, said to be the burial site of the town's patron saints, Felix and Regula, who carried their heads here after they were decapitated by the Romans.

These sights are covered in the guided walking tour (see Organised Tours). Don't neglect a stroll round the shores of Lake Zürich (Zürichsee). The concrete walkways

Church in Zürich

give way to trees and lawns in the Arboretum on the west bank. Look out for the flower clockface at nearby Bürkliplatz.

Locations for outdoor swimming and sunbathing are open from May to September, and entry costs around Sfr3. Well-known places are Utoquai, Utoquai 49, on the west shore of the lake and Mythenquai, Mythenquai 95, on the east shore. Other sports are listed in the *Sport Für Alle* booklet available from the tourist office.

Museums

Museum of Fine Arts This is one of the most important of Zürich's many museums. Known as the Kunsthaus (☎ 251 67 65), it's at Heimplatz 1. The large permanent collection ranges from 15th century religious art to the various schools of modern art. Most big names have works on display, such as Dali, Arp, Man Ray, Hockney, Bacon, Cézanne, Renoir, Manet, Monet and Gauguin. There's a fair sprinkling of Picassos, a whole room devoted to Marc Chagall and the largest Edvard Munch collection outside Scandinavia. Franz Gertsch's *Franz und Luciano* (1973) is a remarkable image, capturing seventies fashion with photographic clarity (even giving the face and hands a faint blanching, as if shot using an overpowerful flash).

Swiss artists are well represented, too. Johan Heinrich Füssli (1741-1825) favours waif-like, pale figures against dark backgrounds. Ferdinand Hodler's *Einmutigkeit* depicts a show-of-hands vote and dominates the stairway. On the 1st floor are many sculptures by Alberto Giacometti (pin-headed, lumpy, skinny figures with seven-league boots) and some of his paintings. The gallery is open Tuesday to Thursday from 10 am to 9 pm, and Friday to Sunday from 10 am to 5 pm. Entry costs Sfr4 (students Sfr3) except on Sundays when it's free. Temporary exhibitions always cost extra.

Swiss National Museum This museum (Schweizerisches Landesmuseum), is at Museumstrasse 2, housed in a pseudo-castle built in 1898. It gives the ultimate rundown

Top: The city of Zürich from Utoquai, Zürich Canton (MH)
Bottom Left: Window by Chagall, Fraumünster, Zürich, Zürich Canton (MH)
Bottom Right: Grossmünster, Zürich, Zürich Canton (MH)

Top: Town hall (Rathaus), Basel, North-West Switzerland (MH)
Bottom Left: Clock tower, Solothurn, North-West Switzerland (MH)
Bottom Right: Old town centre, Basel, North-West Switzerland (MH)

on Swiss life and times from the prehistoric to the present. It exhibits a good selection of church art, plus weapons, coins, room interiors, costumes and utensils. The fresco in the Hall of Arms, the *Retreat of the Swiss Confederates at Marignano* is by Ferdinand Hodler. In the basement there's an interesting section on book-inscribing in the Middle Ages (the colour purple was extracted from snails), with some fine 14th century facsimiles to leaf through.

Opening hours are Tuesday to Sunday from 10 am to 5 pm and entry is free. Some signs are in English. There are sometimes free guided tours: enquire at the museum (☎ 218 65 65) or the tourist office.

Other Museums The tourist office has information on many other museums, covering a range of interests. The **Zur Meisen** guildhall (see the Central Zürich map) was built in the 18th century and houses a collection of ceramics. It is at Münsterhof 20, admission is free and it's closed on Monday. Also free is the **Zürich Toy Museum** (Züricher Spielzeugmuseum) at Fortunagasse 15 (closed Saturday morning and Sunday). The measurement of time is the theme in the **Beyer Museum** at Bahnhofstrasse 31, open Monday to Friday from 10 am to noon and 2 to 4 pm (free entry). In the university on Rämistrasse 73, is an **Archaeological Collection**, mainly from southern Europe and the Middle East. It is open Tuesday to Friday from 1 to 6 pm and weekends from 11 am to 5 pm and entry is free. Look out also for the numerous private galleries around the city.

Zoo

Zoo Dolder, Zürichbergstrasse 221, vies with that in Basel for the status of the most important in the country. Whereas Basel's is in the city centre, this one is on the Zürichberg, allowing it to spread out more. It has 250 animal species from all around the world, in all about 2000 animals. It's open daily from 8 am to 6 pm (to 5 pm November to February). Entry costs Sfr8.50 (students Sfr4) and you can get there by tram No 5 or

6. The zoo backs on to Zürichberg, a large wood ideal for walks away from the noise of the city.

Courses

Perhaps the best organisation for education courses, including language courses, is the Migros Klubschule (☎ 277 27 44), Limmatstrasse 152.

Organised Tours

Informative guided walks around the old town, organised by the tourist office from June to September, last around 2½ hours and cost Sfr16 (or Sfr14 for students and senior citizens). The tourist office books tours ranging from a two-hour coach tour of Zürich (Sfr22) to day trips to Mt Titlis (Sfr96) and Lucerne (Sfr40). These are available year-round.

Festivals

Most shops are shut in the afternoon on the third Monday in April when Zürich's spring festival, **Sechseläuten**, is held. Guild members parade down the main streets in historical costume and then adjourn to the local pubs. Another local holiday is **Knabenschiessen**, celebrated during the second weekend of September. Events revolve around a shooting competition for 12 to 16-year-old boys.

The Zürich Carnival, **Fasnacht**, is noted for mobile bands of lively musicians and a large, costumed procession. The carnival commences with typical Swiss precision at 11.11 am on 11 November, but big parades and the liveliest atmosphere is the climax of the festival in February. The **International June Festival** concentrates on music and the arts, and the **International Jazz Festival** takes place at the end of October.

Places to Stay

Accommodation can be a problem, particularly from June to August. Cheaper hotels fill early. A few, such as *Alpha Hotel*, Gertrudstrasse 48, are full all the time with residents who can't find or can't afford apartments. (Renting a two-bedroom flat in Zürich costs

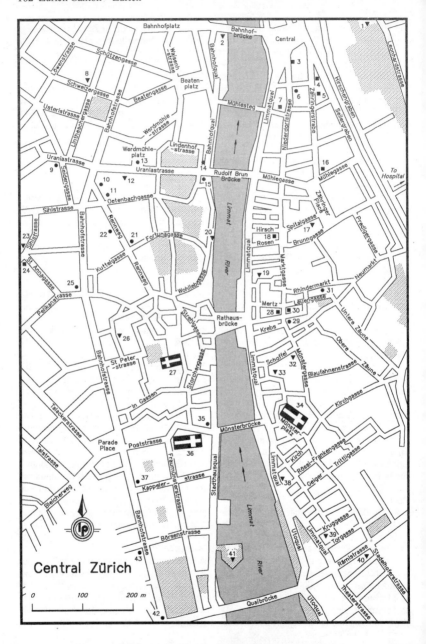

Central Zürich

0   100   200 m

■	PLACES TO STAY	39	Bistretto
		40	EPA Department Store
3	Hotel Limmathof	41	Bauschänzli
4	Du Théâtre		
5	Hotel Martahaus		OTHER
7	Hotel Leonhard		
16	Hotel Scheuble	6	Rheinfelder Bierhalle
18	Hotel Hirschen	9	Jelmoli Department Store
24	Hotel Glockenhof	10	Swiss Bank Corporation
28	Hotel Rothus	11	Buchhandlung Stäheli Bookshop
30	Hotel Goldenes Schwert	13	Billettzentrale Ticket Office
		14	Police Station
▼	PLACES TO EAT	15	Heimatwerk
		21	Zürich Toy Museum
1	Mensa Polyterrace	22	Globetrotter Travel Agency
2	Coop Supermarket	25	Beyer Museum
8	Bistretto	27	St Peter's Church
12	Brasserie Lipp	29	Casa Bar
17	Café Zähringer	31	The Travel Bookshop
19	Königstuhl	34	Grossmünster Cathedral
20	Stadtküche	35	Zur Meisen Guildhall
23	Hilti Vegi	36	Fraumünster Church
26	Café Munz	37	American Express
32	Bodega Española	42	Bürkliplatz
33	Mère Catherine	43	Librairie Poyot
38	Café Select		

Sfr2000 to Sfr3000 a month!) Book ahead if you can. Private rooms are virtually nonexistent and boarding houses generally require a stay of at least a week.

Places to Stay – bottom end

Camping *Camping Seebucht* (☎ 482 16 12) is on the west shore of the lake, four km from the city centre, at Seestrasse 559. It is well signposted and can be reached by bus No 161 or 165 from Bürkliplatz. It has good facilities including a shop and café, but it is only open from 1 May to 30 September. Prices are Sfr5 per person (20% discount with Camping Carnet), Sfr8 for a tent or Sfr10 for a camper van.

Hostels The IYHF *youth hostel* (☎ 482 35 44) is at Mutschellenstrasse 114, Wollishofen, in a 25-year-old building with a faded pink paint job. Take tram No 6 or 7 to the Morgental stop. Reception is closed from noon to 12.30 pm, but the doors are always open during the day, with check-in

from 10.30 am. Curfew is at 1 am and beds are Sfr22 and you get your own locker. Dinner costs Sfr9 and there are laundry facilities available (Sfr8 to wash and dry).

Vereinhaus Glockenhof YMCA (☎ 221 36 73), Sihlstrasse 33, takes men only, and singles cost from Sfr40 without breakfast. Reception closes at 7.45 pm weekdays, 3.45 pm Saturday and 1.30 pm on Sunday. It has a cheap café open to all, with daily menus, and breakfast for Sfr5.50. You have your best chance (almost your *only* chance) of getting a room here from June to September, when students are on holiday.

Foyer Hottingen (☎ 261 93 15), Hottingerstrasse 31, is run by nuns. The sisters of the cloth believe that single men always cause problems, so they only accept women, married couples and families. Such people reckon this is a very nice place to stay, an opinion that is probably not totally uninfluenced by the absence of noisy young men. Reception hours are from 8 am to midnight. Singles/doubles are Sfr45/75 (Sfr50/80 for single night's stay), and triples/quads are Sfr81/96. Dorms (with lockers) start from Sfr20. Breakfast is included but showers cost Sfr1. Telephone reservations are accepted.

OASE Evangelisches Haus (☎ 252 39 81) is at Freiestrasse 38, off Hottingerstrasse. It's mainly geared towards students and those between 18 and 28 years old, although older people can stay. Expect a not-so-subtle purveying of Christian faith and values, but at least it's cheap: singles/doubles for Sfr59/98, and dorms for Sfr25.

If you're really stuck consider staying at the Salvation Army *(Heilsarmee)* (☎ 242 90 00), Molkenstrasse 6. Bed and breakfast in two to four-bed rooms is Sfr21 and half-pension is Sfr33, but it's a depressing atmosphere, with more than a hint of down-and-out territory.

Justinusheim (☎ 361 38 06), Freuden-bergstrasse 146, is a student home which has up to 30 beds available from mid-July to mid-October and during March and April. The rest of the year there are only a few vacancies. The staff are friendly and you get your own key in case you wish to return late at night. Singles/doubles vary in size and price, starting at Sfr35/65. Just a few paces away from the woods of Zürichberg, it's an attractive old building with balconies, a terrace and good views of Zürich and the lake. Take tram No 10 from the Hauptbahnhof to Rigiplatz and then the Seilbahn to the top. (It runs every few minutes and city network tickets are valid.)

Hotels *Martahaus* (☎ 251 45 50; see the Central Zürich map), Zähringerstrasse 36, is in an excellent location in the old town. Singles/doubles cost Sfr60/90, and Sfr30 gets you a place in a six-bed dorm which is separated into individual cubicles by partitions and curtains. There is a comfortable lounge and breakfast room, and a shower on each floor. Book ahead (telephone reservations OK), particularly for single rooms.

Hirschen (☎ 251 42 52; see the Central Zürich map), Niederdorfstrasse 13, is in a 600-year-old building. Low ceilings and sloping floors add character (except when you're inebriated!). It's also in an ideal central location. Newly renovated singles/doubles/triples are Sfr60/100/120 with breakfast. Rooms with private shower are available, and the reception is open 24 hours a day.

Regina (☎ 242 65 50), Hohlstrasse 18 near Müllerstrasse, is in a noisy and lively area of the red-light district. The reception is open 24 hours. Singles/doubles start from Sfr40/60, although the cheaper rooms in the decaying old wing are usually full, so expect to pay Sfr60/100, or more if you want a room with shower. If you're a light sleeper or have strong moral values steer clear; one traveller reported being kept awake by a prostitute plying her trade in an adjoining room.

Dufour (☎ 422 36 55), Seefeldstrasse 188, is in a calmer location, and has acceptable singles/doubles for Sfr55/70. Reception at the bar downstairs is open daily from 8 am to midnight. Get there by tram No 2 or 4.

Hotel Italia (☎ 241 05 55), Zeughaus-strasse 61, is a welcoming, if ageing, hotel and has singles/doubles for Sfr60/80 with free hall showers. Prices rise by Sfr5 in the summer. *Linde Oberstrass* (☎ 363 21 09) Universitätsstrasse 91, is a quiet place north of the centre, offering rooms from Sfr60/85, also using hall showers.

Places to Stay – middle
As even budget hotels are in effect mid-price in Zürich, the following two-star hotels are only slightly more expensive than those listed previously. In the city centre, *Hotel Limmathof* (☎ 261 42 20; see the Central Zürich map), Limmatquai 142 , has modern fittings but it's a bit stingy with space. Singles/doubles with bath or shower are from 95/110, and triples/quads are Sfr180. Nearby is *Leonhard* (☎ 251 30 80; see the Central Zürich map), Limmatquai 136, with singles/doubles from Sfr100/140, or Sfr130/160 in summer. The rooms are better but the staff can occasionally be abrupt.

Goldenes Schwert (☎ 252 59 40; see the Central Zürich map), Marktgasse 14, has singles/doubles from Sfr100/140, with bath and toilet. The staff thoughtfully (and significantly) lay out ear plugs in each room. Reception is opposite in the *Hotel Rothus*, which is the same price, but also has cheaper rooms: from Sfr52/95 using hall shower or Sfr75/115 with private shower.

The three-star *Hotel Scheuble* (☎ 251 87 95; see the Central Zürich map), is also in the old town at Mühlegasse 17, and has singles/doubles starting at Sfr80/140 in winter and Sfr110/170 in summer. Rooms are a reasonable size and have all the required amenities. Also good is the *Du Théâtre* (☎ 252 60 62), nearby at Seilergraben 69, with singles/doubles from Sfr100/130. It also has some singles without shower for Sfr65 and Sfr70.

Places to Stay – top end

All rooms mentioned in this section have private shower, toilet, TV, and other luxuries. The four-star *Hotel Glockenhof* (☎ 211 56 50), Sihlstrasse 31, has singles/doubles from Sfr172/250, and a pleasant garden restaurant and terrace. The rooms are quiet and there is good disabled access. *Ambassador* (☎ 261 76 00), Falkenstrasse 6, overlooks the lake and is a similar standard and price.

The top hotels in Zürich are very nearly the top hotels in the world. The pick of them all is perhaps the *Dolder Grand Hotel* (☎ 251 62 31), Kurhausstrasse 65. This architecturally interesting place occupies a quiet and panoramic position on the edge of the Zürichberg. It has a whole heap of facilities including a nine-hole golf course, tennis courts, swimming pool, and ice rink (in winter), all of which are free to guests. Its restaurant is also highly rated, especially for its French cuisine. There is private parking, or to get there by public transport take tram No 3, 8 or 15 to Römerhof and the Dolderbahn from there. Rooms cost upwards of Sfr290/430 for singles/doubles.

Slightly more affordable luxury comes from the modern *Hotel Zürich* (☎ 363 63 63), Neumühlequai 42, overlooking the Limmat River. Extensive facilities include an indoor swimming pool, a sauna and a bowling alley. Singles/doubles start at Sfr255/295.

Near the Airport It shouldn't really be necessary to stay in an airport hotel as train connections to/from the city are so good, and even the airport hotels are a bus ride or at least a 15-minute walk away from the terminal. However, if you do need to stay in the vicinity, places to try are: *Löwen* (☎ 810 73 33), Schaffhauserstrasse 116, Glattbrugg, with basic singles/doubles for Sfr70/95; *Welcome-Inn* (☎ 814 07 27), Holbergstrasse 1, Kloten, with singles/doubles with private shower and TV from Sfr106/152; and the plush *Airport* (☎ 810 44 44), Oberhauserstrasse 30, Glattbrugg, with singles/doubles from Sfr150/190, likewise with private shower and TV.

Places to Eat – bottom end

Zürich has hundreds of restaurants serving all types of local and international cuisine. The Zürich speciality, *Geschnetzeltes Kalbsfleisch* (thinly sliced veal in a cream sauce), will probably set you back at least Sfr20. Fast-food stands offer bratwurst and bread from around Sfr4.50. There is a large *Coop* opposite the Hauptbahnhof (see the Central Zürich map), open Monday to Friday from 7 am to 6.30 pm and Saturday from 7 am to 4 pm. Beer halls (see the Entertainment

Clocktower

section) are often good places for an inexpensive meal. *Zürich News* from the tourist office lists a variety of restaurants according to style of cuisine.

Self-service *Mensa Polyterrace*, Leonhardstrasse 34 (see the Central Zürich map), is next to the Polylbahn (funicular) exit, overlooking the city. Large and busy, it has good meals for around Sfr9 (Sfr5 for students) including vegetarian options. The self-service counters are open Monday to Friday from 11.15 am to 1.30 pm and 5.30 to 7.15 pm, and every second Saturday from 11.30 am to 1 pm. From mid-July to the end of September, the mensa is open for lunch only. There is a café upstairs which is also popular. Just along the road, there is another mensa in the university building, Rämistrasse 71, open Monday to Friday from 7.30 am to 8 pm, and alternative Saturdays to the Polyterrace.

Other bargain eateries are the subsidised kitchens run by the government, the *Stadtküche*. There are 17 of these dotted round the city, but the most convenient is the one at Schipfe 16, overlooking the Limmat. It adjoins the Limmat-Club Zürich, and has meals from around Sfr8. Opening times are Monday to Friday from 11.30 am to 1 pm.

The underground area by the station is called Shop Ville, and it's a good place to find cheap food. *Silberkugel* is a cheap café and takeaway, open daily until 10 pm (7.30 pm Sunday). Nearby is *Restaurant Marché Mövenpick*, where well-presented buffet-style food costs around Sfr10 to Sfr13. Salad plates are Sfr3.50 to Sfr8.20, and it's open daily from 6.30 am to 11 pm.

The *EPA* department stores on Sihlporte and at Stadelhoferstrasse each have a very cheap self-service restaurant. There is a *Migros* restaurant in the Migros City shopping centre at Löwenstrasse 35.

Bistretto, Schweizergasse 6 (see the Central Zürich map), has spaghetti and pasta dishes from Sfr9.30 to Sfr12.80 which must be ordered at the counter. Build salad tower blocks at the help-yourself salad bar where different plate sizes cost from Sfr4.30 to

Sfr9.30. Opening hours are Monday to Saturday from 6.15 am to 8.00 pm (10 pm Thursday) and Sunday from 8.30 am to 5.30 pm. There is another branch with the same prices and setup on the corner of Schifflände and Kruggasse; this one closes at 11.30 daily.

East Bank In the centre, explore the smaller streets off the main thoroughfares for the best value. *Vier Linden*, Gemeindestrasse 48, has a wide choice of vegetarian food including menus from Sfr13.70. It is open Monday to Friday from 11.30 am to 8.30 pm. An alternative café, run by a collective, is *Café Zähringer* on Spitalgasse (see the Central Zürich map). It serves up healthy, vegetarian food, and is a good place for a coffee and a game of chess in the evenings (closed Monday).

Also popular is *Café Select*, Limmatquai 16 (see the Central Zürich map), with outside tables overlooking the square. The service is not the swiftest but the food is fine. It serves Italian and Swiss dishes, and there is a games area upstairs.

Mère Catherine (☎ 262 22 50; see the Central Zürich map), Nägelhof 3 near Schoffelgasse, is a popular French restaurant in a small courtyard, open daily from 11 am to midnight. The food is mostly mid-price (Sfr16.50 to Sfr33), unless you choose the lunch-time menus for Sfr12.50 or Sfr13.50 (not on Sunday).

West Bank *Clipper Restaurant* (☎ 242 63 20), Lagerstrasse 1, is basic and busy with good-value if simple food. Seating opens on to the pavement making it nice and cool in the summer. Most main dishes cost as little as Sfr9 to Sfr12.50. The cheap beer (Sfr4 for half a litre) attracts many local drinkers. It is open daily from 10 am to 11.30 pm.

Bernerhof (☎ 241 73 06), Zeughausstrasse 1, has satisfying, filling food in an unpretentious environment. Several daily menus from Sfr10.80 (including soup) are available midday and evening. The restaurant closes at midnight and opens on weekdays at 8 am. On Saturday they have a lie-in until 3 pm, and on Sunday they open at 9.30 am. Food stops around 9 pm, after which time you will find the locals sitting around drinking and playing board and card games.

Vegetarians will have a field day in the meat-free environment of *Hiltl Vegi* (☎ 221 38 71; see the Central Zürich map), Sihlstrasse 28, on two floors. It has a wide menu including tofu steak, curry (from Sfr16.20), spaghetti bolognese (made with soya) for Sfr14.50, salads from Sfr9.50 and varying lunch-time specials. It is open Monday to Saturday from 6.30 am to 9 pm (10 pm on Thursday), and Sunday from 11 am to 9 pm.

Zürich is well-known for its cafés where you can linger over a coffee, soak up the atmosphere and maybe take a light meal. Try the entertaining *Café Münz* (☎ 221 30 27; see the Central Zürich map), Münzplatz 3 near Bahnhofstrasse, where Jean Tinguely mobiles hang from the ceiling. It is open Monday to Friday from 6.30 am to 7 pm (9 pm on Thursday), and Saturday from 8 am to 5 pm.

Places to Eat – middle

Splurge on French food amid the mirrors and gleaming metal of *Brasserie Lipp Restaurant* (☎ 211 11 55; see the Central Zürich map), Uraniastrasse 9. The decor reflects the Parisien Belle Epoque period. A clientele of all ages is attracted by the wide choice of sumptuous dishes in the Sfr20 to Sfr40 range (open daily). Servings are generous and there are English menus.

Restaurant JOSEF (☎ 271 65 95), Gasometerstrasse 24 near Limmatstrasse, caters to a casual, voluble crowd; borderline yuppies. There are five main dishes chalked on the wall that cost from Sfr20 to Sfr30. These change daily, and may include Swiss, Italian or Chinese food, depending on the whims of the chef. There's always something interesting on the list. Reservations are usually necessary in this small place, and it's closed Saturday and Sunday lunch time.

To sample quality Spanish fare (Sfr17 to Sfr45) go to *Bodega Española* (☎ 251 23 10;

see the Central Zürich map), on the 1st floor at Münstergasse 15. The paella (Sfr34 per person) is a popular choice here, and rightly so. There is a good selection of Spanish wines from Sfr31 a bottle. Reserve ahead.

Bauschänzli, Stadthausquai, is worth visiting on a sunny summer's day. It is open-air and often has live music (middle-of-the-road). Meals are around Sfr14 to Sfr35.

Places to Eat – top end

As you might expect, there are plenty of these. *Königstuhl* (☎ 261 76 18; see the Central Zürich map) Stüssihofstatt 3, near the river on the east bank, has an excellent reputation (closed Sunday). The food is undeniably good in this old guild house, but the prices are steep in the gourmet restaurant upstairs. The bistro downstairs is cheaper (different menu, same kitchen), less formal, and open daily. *Flühgass* (☎ 381 12 15), Zollikerstrasse 214, two km from the centre on the east bank, is the gourmet's choice for French food.

Other top restaurants you might try are *Tübli* (☎ 251 24 71), Schneggengasse 8, in the centre, and *Riesbächli* (☎ 422 23 24), a little out of the way at Zollikerstrasse 157.

Entertainment

Many late-night pubs, clubs and discos are in Niederdorfstrasse and adjoining streets in the old town. This area is also a red-light district. On Sundays you might come across devout parishioners parading through the sin-sodden streets chanting hymns to anyone who can't avoid listening. Another red-light district is south-west of the Hauptbahnhof around Brauerstrasse.

If you're making a night of it in Niederdorfstrasse, kick off with a few cheap beers (Sfr3.60 for half a litre) at *Rheinfelder Bierhalle* at No 76 (see the Central Zürich map). The food isn't bad either, with all-day menus including soup starting from Sfr12.50. Opening hours are 9 am to midnight daily. There are many other beer halls in this part of town. Down the road is the *Casa Bar*, Münstergasse 30 (see the Central

Zürich map), is a lively, crowded pub with live jazz from 8 pm daily.

Alternative arts are centred in *Rote Fabrik* (☎ 481 65 64), Seestrasse 395, not far from the IYHF youth hostel. It has concerts most nights ranging from rock and jazz to avant-garde (Sfr15 to Sfr20), original-language films (Sfr10), plus theatre and dance. It's worth going along simply to enjoy the laid-back atmosphere in the bar area.

Tickets for most events in the city can be obtained from the *Billettzentrale* (☎ 221 22 83), Werdmühleplatz, off Bahnhofstrasse; it's open Monday to Friday from 10 am to 6.30 pm, Saturday to 4 pm. It is a government agency, so commission charges are minimal. It's closed in July and August when activities in the arts die down. Zürich has a famous orchestra, the *Tonhalle*, which performs in the venue of the same name (☎ 201 15 81), at Claridenstrasse 7 near General Guisan Quai, as does the Zürich Chamber Orchestra. Prices are anything from Sfr10 to Sfr120, depending on the seat and the event. The *Opernhaus* (Opera House; ☎ 251 15 81), Falkenstrasse 1, also has a world-wide reputation.

During summer, the *Comedy Club* performs plays in English. Venues vary, but the *Theater am Hechplatz* (☎ 252 32 34) is a regular. The ticket office on the 3rd floor of the Jelmoli department store, Uraniastrasse, has information and sells tickets.

Cinema prices are reduced to Sfr9.90 every Monday from their normal price of around Sfr15. Films are nearly always in the original language.

Bafüsser (☎ 251 40 64), Spitalgasse 14, is Switzerland's oldest gay bar, open daily from 3 pm to midnight. Lesbians prefer the *Riverside* bar and restaurant at Schifflände 18, Beim Hecktplatz, open 9 pm to 2 am. *Club Hey* (☎ 252 32 10), Rämistrasse 6 (enter from Freieckgasse), has a gay and lesbian disco on Saturday from 10.30 pm to 5 am. There are also women-only nights, and you can bring your own alcohol.

Spectator Sports Zürich has two football teams, which means there's a match in the city every weekend during the season. Ice hockey is played at the Hallenstadion in the district of Oerlikon. In early August, Zürich hosts an important international athletics meeting at the Letzigrund stadium (take tram Nos 2 or 10).

Things to Buy

Bahnhofstrasse is a famous shopping street, and has large department stores, such as Vilan, and specialist shops. Many places have late opening on Thursday. Heimatwerk is where you can get hand-made Swiss souvenirs, and the good quality is reflected in the prices. There's a large store on the west side of the Rudolf Brun bridge, and branches in the train station and airport. At Rosenhof, in the old town on the east bank, there's a crafts market on Thursday and Saturday.

For camping and trekking equipment, go to Spatz Camping (☎ 383 38 38), Hedwigstrasse 25. Take tram No 11 from the Hauptbahnhof.

Getting There & Away

Air The major gateway of Kloten Airport is 10 km north of the city centre and has several daily flights to/from all important destinations. Swissair has an office in the Hauptbahnhof (☎ 258 33 11) which is open Monday to Friday from 8 am to 6 pm, Saturday to 4 pm. For Swissair reservations around the clock, ring ☎ 251 34 34. The airport has two terminals: terminal A is for flights by Swissair, Crossair, Austrian Airlines and SAS; all other airlines use terminal B. Parking is available and costs Sfr4 for one hour and Sfr24 for 24 hours.

Train The busy Hauptbahnhof has direct trains to Stuttgart (Sfr57), Munich (Sfr83), Innsbruck (Sfr61) and Milan (Sfr66) as well as to many other international destinations. There are also hourly departures to most Swiss towns, eg Lucerne (50 minutes, Sfr16.60), Bern (70 minutes, Sfr38) and Basel (65 minutes, Sfr26). Winterthur (Sfr9) is just 20 minutes away by train and there are four to five departures an hour.

Car & Motorbike The N3 approaches Zürich from the south along the shore of Lake Zürich. The N1 is the fastest route from Bern and Basel and the main entry point from the west. The N1 also services routes to the north and east of Zürich.

Car Rental Sixt AG car rental (☎ 201 13 13) is at Tödistrasse 9; one-way rentals to Geneva are possible. Europcar (☎ 271 56 56), Josef-Strasse 53, is only slightly more expensive and has many more outlets for one-way drop-offs. The airport branch is on ☎ 813 20 44. Hertz (☎ 242 25 86) is at Mortgartenstrasse 5 and Avis (☎ 242 20 40) is at Gertenhofstrasse; both also have airport branches. See the introductory Getting Around chapter for rates.

Hitching Zürich's Mitfahrzentrale (☎ 261 68 93) is at Leonhardstrasse 15. This agency links drivers and hitchers; hitchers end up paying about half the equivalent train fare.

Getting Around
To/From the Airport Don't take a taxi if you can help it. Trains are about a tenth of the price at Sfr4.20. On average, five trains an hour depart from the Hauptbahnhof between around 6 am and midnight, and the journey takes 10 minutes.

Bus, Tram & Train There is a comprehensive and unified bus, tram and S-Bahn service in the city. Operating times are approximately 5.30 am to midnight. Tickets are also valid for boats on the Limmat River and should be bought in advance from dispensers at stops. The variety of tickets and zones available can be confusing. Short trips (up to five stops) cost Sfr1.80, but it's worth getting a 24-hour pass for Sfr6 (press the blue key and return symbol). This covers only travel in the central zone, which is sufficient for most purposes, including for very short trips on the lake. Seek advice from the counter staff in the train station if you want to take longer lake trips. Getting to the airport

---

Zürich's Transport System.
In the 1970's Zürich's citizens voted against constructing an underground system, thereby forcing a re-introduction of the old city trams. Environmental concerns were paramount in this decision. It was backed up by the introduction of a non-profit ticket in the late '80s for use on the city's public transport network. Zürich was anxious to avoid the situation in cities like Los Angeles where an unbelievable 70% of ground space is devoted to the motor car – in the form of roads, car parks, driveways and petrol stations. In contrast, thanks to Zürich's forward-looking transport policy, car-parking spaces have been gradually converted over to pedestrian areas with seating and planted shrubs. Motorists have been enticed and persuaded to use public transport for commuting.

For the most part, ex-motorists are happy to use the tram network. The Swiss have studied the problem of how to make public transport an acceptable option, and they have concluded that what is psychologically crucial is not how long the journey takes, but how long one expects it to take. Reliability is therefore the key. The progress of trams in Zürich is monitored by a series of ultra-sound beacons at the roadside (those inconspicuous little boxes at junctions) which are triggered by passing trams but are unaffected by normal traffic. The signals are relayed back to transport headquarters which then passes instructions to the appropriate driver to either speed up or slow down. If a rogue tram route is shown to be consistently behind time, the schedule is adjusted accordingly. Zürich trams, therefore, should always be on time.

But reliability isn't the only criterion: waiting time is important too. Studies also showed that the average limit of acceptability for waiting is 10 minutes. Most Zürich trams run to six-minute intervals.

It is a pity that more cities worldwide don't follow Zürich's lead. Zürich's streets have always been clean, but now the air is cleaner too – trams are much more environmentally friendly than cars. Road junctions are safer as well – everybody knows who has the right of way as trams *always* have priority over cars. And the greening of the city is another positive effect – I'd rather spend time in a tree-lined pedestrian cul-de-sac than in a concrete car park. ■

involves travel in two zones (Sfr9 for a 24-hour pass).

A 24-hour pass valid for unlimited travel within the whole canton of Zürich costs Sfr24, including access to virtually all the lake. Zürich's suburban trains (S-Bahn) reach Baden, Schaffhausen, Stein am Rhein, Zug and Einsiedeln, but these places are just beyond the validity area of the cantonal ticket.

Taxi Taxis in Zürich are expensive even by Swiss standards, at Sfr6 plus Sfr2.80 per km.

Car & Motorbike The tourist office has a list of car-parking garages (around Sfr24 per 24 hours) near the central pedestrian zone. Parking on the street in the centre is a bit of a problem; many streets have a one hour maximum and rates can be high (Sfr1 to Sfr3.50 per hour).

Bicycle Rental in the Hauptbahnhof is open from 6 am to 11.30 pm. Bikes may be borrowed free of charge (100 available) between 8.30 am and 9.30 pm from 1 May to 31 October, from the bike depots at Paradeplatz or Bellevue. A passport or identity card must be left as a deposit.

Boat Lake steamers leave from Bürkliplatz, departing hourly between 29 March and 20 October. There are only limited services in winter. For boat information, ring ☎ 482 10 33.

AROUND ZÜRICH
Uetliberg
One of the best short excursions to take from Zürich starts off with the train (line S10) to Uetliberg at 813 metres (takes 23 minutes, departures every 30 minutes). From here, there is a panoramic two-hour **Planetary Path** (Planetenweg) running along the mountain ridge overlooking the lake to Felsenegg. En route you pass models of the planets in the solar system: these and the distances between them are on a scale of one to one billion (US billion). At Felsenegg, a cable car descends every 10 minutes to

Adliswil, from where frequent trains return to Zürich (line S4, takes 16 minutes).

Maur
The village of Maur is close to Lake Greifensee where swimming, boating and hiking is possible.

A good possibility for accommodation is in the farming village of Maur, 10 km southeast of the city. Reinhard Lüder (☎ 01-980 22 48), Kehlhof 518, Maur, offers bed and breakfast in his 200-year old country house. In this health-conscious place there are vegetarian meals (Sfr6) and bike rental for only Sfr2 per day, and smoking is not allowed on the premises. The first night's stay costs Sfr40/66 for singles/doubles and Sfr90 for triples, and there is a Sfr5 reduction per person for each subsequent night. Use of the washing machine costs Sfr3 per load.

Get to Maur from Zürich by taking tram No 3, 8 or 15 to Klusplatz, then a 20-minute bus ride on No 747 to Maur Dorf. The whole journey can be undertaken on a Sfr6 ticket.

Winterthur

Although a mechanical engineering and textiles centre, Winterthur attracts visitors with its fine museums and art galleries.

Orientation & Information
Winterthur is less than 20 km north-east of Zürich and in the same canton. The train station is on the western edge of the compact old town centre. Exit on the platform 1 side for the tourist office (☎ 212 00 88), Bahnhofplatz 12. Opening hours are Monday to Saturday from 8 am to noon and 2 pm to 6 pm (4 pm Saturday).

The budget travel agency, SSR (☎ 052-213 81 25, is at Neustadtgasse 1a, with late opening on Thursday (closed weekends and Monday morning).

The telephone code for Winterthur is 052.

Things to See & Do
Winterthur owes much of its eminence as an

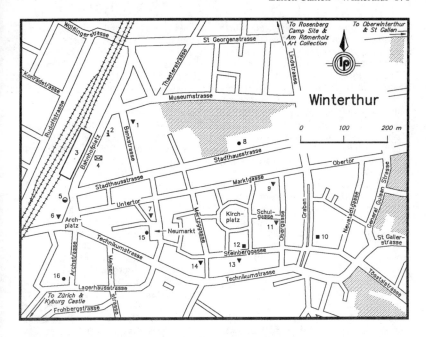

art centre to Oskar Reinhart, who turned his back on the banking and insurance enterprises of his powerful family and collected art instead. Upon his death in 1965, the whole collection was bequeathed to the nation and entrusted to his home town. The **'Am Römerholz' Oskar Reinhart Collection** is sited in his former home at Haldenstrasse 95, a 20-minute hike or short bus ride (No 3 to Spital) from the centre. The extensive impressionist section includes works by Van Gogh, Renoir, Manet, Monet and Cézanne, plus there are other impressive paintings by Rubens, Rembrandt, Greco and Goya. It will be closed for around six months from the end of 1994.

Less important but still well worth viewing is the collection of Swiss, German and Austrian art at the **Oskar Reinhart Foundation** which he established during his lifetime. It's at Stadthausstrasse 6 in the centre, and is due to re-open in February 1995 after two year's closure. Entry for each gallery costs around Sfr3 (Sfr1.50 or Sfr1 for students and children) and they are open daily (except Monday) from 10 am to 5 pm. The Foundation backs on to a relaxing park graced by several naked ladies (in statue form only).

Practical concerns aren't overlooked, either. The **Swiss Technorama**, Technoramastrasse 1 in Oberwinterthur, has hands-on exhibits and creative displays that de-mystify science and technology. It's open daily from 10 am to 5 pm (9 pm Tuesday) and costs Sfr12 (Sfr6 for children). To get there, take bus No 1 from the train station.

Winterthur also has four castles, including one that houses the youth hostel. The best is the **Kyburg Castle**, six km south of town over Töss River. Dating from the 10th century, it was occupied by the Habsburgs for several centuries until possession was won by the city of Zürich in 1452. It has an interesting Romanesque chapel and makes a good starting place for a number of hikes. Admission costs Sfr4 (students and children Sfr3) and it's closed on Monday.

When walking around, notice the surprising number of specialist shops selling designer lights. The ridiculous prices – Sfr100 to Sfr1200 or more – makes one speculate with envy at the size of the average Swiss disposable income (or cringe with horror at Swiss concepts of interior design).

Places to Stay

Finding accommodation can be difficult in spring and autumn when there are many trade conventions, but the tourist office can help with its free room-booking service for personal callers.

The camping site *Rosenberg* (☎ 212 52 60), open year-round, is on the outskirts of Winterthur in an area of woodland. Get there by taking bus No 3 and getting off one stop before the terminus at Rosenberg (Sfr1.70).

The IYHF *youth hostel* (☎ 242 38 40) is at Schloss Hegi, Hegifeldstrasse 125. It's a friendly place in a 15th century castle and receives no school groups, so it invariably has space. Reception is closed from 10 am to 2 pm (5 pm Monday and Friday) and the hostel is open from 1 March until 31 October. From Winterthur train station, take bus No 1 to Oberwinterthur (Sfr2.80) and then it's 10 to 15-minutes' walk to the castle. Beds are just Sfr10 without breakfast.

Hotel prices are sky high in the centre. The cheapest is at *Albani* (☎ 212 69 96), Steinberggasse 16, with singles/doubles without shower from Sfr70/100. It's ideal if you like jazz (see the following Entertainment section). Convenient rooms with private facilities are at *Loge* (☎ 213 91 21), Graben 6, and cost from Sfr100/160.

You get better value to the east of the town centre: *Grüntal* (☎ 232 25 52), Im Grüntal 1, Oberseen, offers singles/doubles with private shower from Sfr75/100, and some showerless singles for Sfr50; *Hotel Römertor* (☎ 242 69 21), Guggenbühlstrasse 6, has singles/doubles from Sfr90/130 with private shower.

The best hotel is the four-star *Garten-Hotel* (☎ 212 1919), Stadthausstrasse 4, with convenient parking and good facilities. Singles/doubles start at Sfr 130/170.

Places to Eat

There is a *Coop* supermarket and restaurant near the tourist office at Bankstrasse. Salad buffets costs Sfr1.60 per 100 grams. An *EPA* department store beckons by the bus station on Bahnhofplatz. Hot food costs from Sfr4.50 to Sfr13.50, including vegetarian dishes. Look out also for the open-air markets in the centre on Tuesday and Friday morning.

Elsewhere, cheap eating can be hard to come by. *Pizzeria Don Camillo*, Steinberggasse 51, is popular but the quality is only so-so. Pasta/pizza starts at Sfr10 (closed Sunday and Monday). Café-Restaurant *Obergasse*, on the corner of Obergasse and

Schulgasse is a lively place with a young clientele. It serves good-sized plates of spaghetti and various salads, with most dishes in the range of Sfr11 to Sfr23. The beer is tempting at Sfr4 for half a litre.

More staid but quite cosy is the *Walliser Kanne* (☎ 212 81 71), Steinberggasse 25, which specialises in fondues from Sfr19.50. Other dishes start at Sfr24, except for the cheaper 'lunch-karte' range (between 11.30 am and 2 pm and 6 to 8.30 pm only). The restaurant is closed on Sunday and Monday.

Restaurant Zur Sonne, Marktgasse 15, offers cheap lunch menus, other meals for around Sfr15 to Sfr32, and Swiss wines from Sfr22 a bottle. There is outside seating around the back and it is closed on Sunday. For top quality dining go to *Trübli* (☎ 212 55 36) on Bosshardengässe 5, just near Untertor. Main dishes start at Sfr20 or you can go for the three to six-course menus for Sfr60 to Sfr98 (closed Sunday and Monday).

Entertainment

A good area for a lively time is Neumarkt, off Untertor in the old town. There are several bars grouped together, and it's fairly chaotic with people spilling out into the street. *City Saloon* at No 5 has free live rock music. Live jazz can be heard most nights at the *Albani Bar*, Steinberggasse 16 (entry Sfr15 to Sfr28). *Planet Maxx*, Archstrasse 8, is a new entertainment complex containing various bars, clubs and discos (entry free or up to Sfr12).

Getting There & Away

There are several trains an hour to Zürich airport (takes 15 minutes, Sfr6.80) and Zürich itself. Many trains also run to Schaffhausen and Lake Constance. By road, the N1 (E60) motorway goes from Zürich, skirts Winterthur and continues to St Gallen and Austria. There are also main roads to Constance and Schaffhausen.

Getting Around

The bus station is next to the train station. Single bus journeys in the town are pricey at Sfr1.70 or Sfr2.80, although the 24-hour pass for Sfr5.60 is a reasonable deal. Rent bicycles from the train station.

North-West Switzerland

The north-west is a densely populated area, where affluent towns fill the landscape as opposed to the scenic vistas of the rest of the country. Coincidentally, four out of Switzerland's five nuclear power stations are in this region. To enjoy the countryside you need to nip over to Germany and the Black Forest, easily accessible from Basel.

The relative dearth of scenic attractions does not mean that the region is not worth a visit. There are some fine old town centres and some particularly diverting museums and art galleries. In any case, Basel is such an important transport hub that you're almost certain to spend some time here, one way or another.

The north-west comprises the cantons of Basel (split into two half-cantons, Town and District, in 1833), Aargau, and Solothurn. Although the Basel tourist office is nominally the regional office, and has information on the whole area (including the Black Forest), administrative functions have largely been devolved to the local tourist offices.

Basel

Basel (Bâle in French, sometimes Basle in English) is Switzerland's second largest city (population 191,000). It is a major centre for commerce, particularly the chemical and pharmaceutical industry, yet retains an attractive old town and offers many interesting museums. Influences from neighbouring France and Germany and a large student population make Basel a vibrant and creative city. It is also the home of the liveliest carnival in Switzerland. Don't miss it if you're in the country on the Monday after Ash Wednesday.

Basel had its origins as a Roman settlement in 44 BC, and was successively occupied by the Alemanni, Franks and Burgundians until it became part of the Germanic Empire in 1032. By this time the Bishop of Basel has already been granted secular authority over the town by the Emperor Henry II. It hosted the Council of Basel (1431-48) which attempted (unsuccessfully) to avoid a schism in the Catholic church. In 1460, under the patronage of Pope Pius II, the University of Basel was opened, the oldest in Switzerland. Basel joined the Swiss Confederation in 1501 and 28 years later adopted the Reformation. The famous Renaissance humanist, Erasmus of Rotterdam, was associated with the city and his tomb rests in the cathedral. Basel reached the peak of its influence in the 18th century.

Orientation

Basel's strategic position on the Rhine River at the dual border with France and Germany has been instrumental in its development as a commercial and cultural centre. On the north bank of the Rhine is Kleinbasel (Lesser Basel), surrounded by German territory. The old town and most of the sights are on the south bank in Grossbasel (Greater Basel). Historically, the 'Klein' tag was partially a denigrating term as it was a working-class locality. The *Lälle Keenig*, or 'Tongue King' (at the crossroads at the southern end of the Mittlere Brücke) sticking his tongue out at the northern section, just about sums up the old attitude.

Grossbasel has the SBB Bahnhof, the train station for travel in Switzerland. Tram Nos 1 and 8 go from here to the old town centre. In Kleinbasel is the BBF Bahnhof, the station for travel to Germany.

Information

Tourist Offices The main tourist office (☎ 061-261 50 50) is by the Mittlere Brücke (bridge) at Blumenrain 2, Schifflände. It has good free city maps and is open Monday to Friday from 8.30 am to 6 pm, and Saturday from 8.30 am to 1 pm. One km south is the

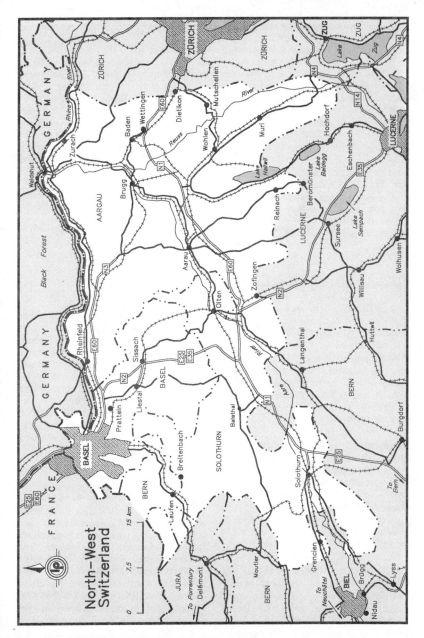

main SBB Bahnhof which has bike rental (6 am to 10 pm daily), money exchange (6 am to 9.45 pm daily) and another tourist office (☎ 061-271 36 84), open Monday to Friday from 8.30 am to 6 pm, and Saturday from 8.30 am to 12.30 pm. This tourist office is open additional hours during parts of the year: between April and September, it is open to 7 pm weekdays and from 1.30 to 6 pm Saturdays; between June and September, it is also open on Sunday from 10 am to 2 pm.

Post & Telecommunications The main post office (Hauptpost) is on Kirschgartenstrasse, not far from the Stadttheatre. The large post office just outside the SBB train station is probably more convenient; its address for poste restante is: Basel 2, Gartenstrasse, CH-4002 Basel.

The telephone code for Basel is 061

Consulates The German Consulate (☎ 693 33 03) is at Schwarzwaldallee 200, a long road parallel to the BBF station. The French Consulate (☎ 272 63 18) is at Elisabethenstrasse 33, not far from the SBB station.

Travel Agencies SSR (☎ 261 71 71) has an office at Schmeidenhof, open Monday to Friday from 10 am to 6 pm and Saturday from 10 am to 2 pm. American Express (☎ 288 66 90) is at Reisebüro Kuendig, Aeschengraben 10.

Bookshop Jäggi Buchhandlung, Freie Strasse 32, is a large store with English books. Specialising only in English texts is Tanner on Streitgasse.

Medical & Emergency The Cantonal Hospital (☎ 265 25 25) is at Petersgraben 2. Telephone ☎ 117 for the police and ☎ 144 for an ambulance.

Gay & Lesbian Arcados (☎ 681 31 32), Rheingasse 69, has an information service and also distributes the free local guide *Come Out!* It is closed on Monday. There's even a gay radio station on FM104.6 MHz.

Walking Tour
The tourist office hands out free do-it-yourself guides to walks through the old town, taking in cobbled streets, colourful fountains and 16th century buildings. The **Fischmarkt** is the core of the old town, and is graced by a Gothic fountain. The **Spalentor** gate tower is 700 years old, a remnant from the time when the city was encircled by a protective wall. The **town hall** (Rathaus) was built in the 16th century and has been impressively restored. It looks very patrician with a vivid red façade, embellished with shields, painted figures and a golden spire. Don't omit to peek into the frescoed courtyard; the statue here depicts Munatius Plancus, the founder of the town.

The 12th century **cathedral** (Münster) is an unmistakable landmark with its Gothic spires built in red sandstone. Take in the view of the Rhine from the rear. Also noteworthy is its Romanesque St Gallus doorway, fringed by a scene showing the Judgement of the Dead.

Be sure to take a look at the **Tinguely Fountain** on Theaterplatz. It's a typical display by the Swiss sculptor, Jean Tinguely, with madcap machinery playing water games with hoses – art with a juvenile heart. If you arrived in the SBB train station you will have seen a sample of his work. He was responsible for the massive mobile in the entrance hall, incorporating steel girders, wheels, coloured lights and animal heads. He died shortly after finishing it, before it was even officially opened in late 1991.

Museums
Of the 27 fine museums, the most important is the **Museum of Fine Arts** (Kunstmuseum), St Albangraben 16, with a good selection of religious, Swiss and modern art. It's the largest art collection in Switzerland. Important German artists represented include Konrad Witz and Holbein the Younger. Rodin's *The Burghers of Calais* stands in the courtyard. It is open Tuesday to Saturday from 10 am to 5 pm, and costs Sfr6 (students Sfr4), except on the first Sunday in the month when it's free. It has an excellent

collection of Picasso's work. The artist was so gratified when the people of Basel paid a large sum for two of his paintings that he donated a further four from his own collection.

Depending upon taste and inclination, you could spend days in the other museums. Contemporary arts, history, ethnography, natural history, musical instruments, cinema, paper and pharmaceuticals are just some of the fields explored. Ask for the museums booklet in English from the tourist office. Most museums are closed on Monday (but not all); a few are free, and most of the others are free on the first Sunday of the month.

Zoo

Basel's zoo rivals Zürich's in importance. It's laid out in a large rectangular park near the SBB station, and has a varied collection from around the world. Some of the rare and highly prized species on display include Indian rhinos, pygmy hippos, golden lion tamarins and king penguins. Feeding times *(Fütterungen)* are displayed by the entrance and are fun to watch. The big cats devour bloody slabs of meat at 4 pm daily. It is open daily from 8 am to 6.30 pm (5 pm winter, 6 pm March, April, September and October) and costs Sfr9 for adults, Sfr7 for students and senior citizens, and Sfr3.50 for children.

Markets

There's a daily fruit and vegetable market in Marktplatz. Barfüsserplatz is the venue for the flea market every 2nd and 4th Wednesday in the month (except November and December), the Christmas Market, and the Autumn Fair (Saturday preceding 30 October, continues for over two weeks).

Festivals

Basel is a carnival town. At the end of January, **Vogel Gryff** is when winter is chased away from Kleinbasel. The three key figures are the griffin *(Vogel Gryff)*, the savage *(Wilde Mann)* and the lion *(Leu)*.

On the Monday after Ash Wednesday, Basel commences a three-day celebration, the **Fasnacht** spring carnival. It kicks off

exactly at 4 am with the **Morgestraich**, when the street lights are suddenly extinguished and the procession starts to wend its way through the central district. All the participants wear elaborate costumes and masks. Some carry large painted lanterns, others have lights dangling from their heads, and in between the marchers are musicians in alternating sections playing flutes or drums. Bars and cafés stay open all night to ensure the celebrations don't flag. SBB puts on special night trains from other towns for this event. The main parades are on the Monday and Wednesday afternoon, when the large floats get wheeled out and fruit, flowers, confetti and candies are thrown into the crowd. On Tuesday afternoon is the children's parade. Speciality food for the carnival is *Ziblewaaire*, an onion flan.

Trade fairs play an important part in the Basel calendar, and have done so ever since the city was granted its licence to stage such events in 1471. The **Autumn Fair** at the end of October and the **Swiss Industries Fair** (MUBA), held every spring, are the most important ones.

Organised Tours

Contact the main tourist office for details. Most tours are from mid-March to mid-October. Options include city tours by foot (Sfr10) or bus (Sfr18), Black Forest tours (Sfr38) or the three-countries tour (Sfr55).

Places to Stay

Hotels are expensive and liable to be full during the numerous trade fairs and conventions. Be sure to book ahead. The tourist office in the SBB Bahnhof reserves rooms for Sfr10 commission. The same service is undertaken in the Schifflände office for Sfr5.

Places to Stay – bottom end

Camping Six km south of the SBB train station is *Camp Waldhort* (☎ 711 64 29) at Heideweg 16, Reinach. To get there, take tram No 11 to Landhof. It's open from March to October.

Youth Hostel The IYHF *youth hostel*

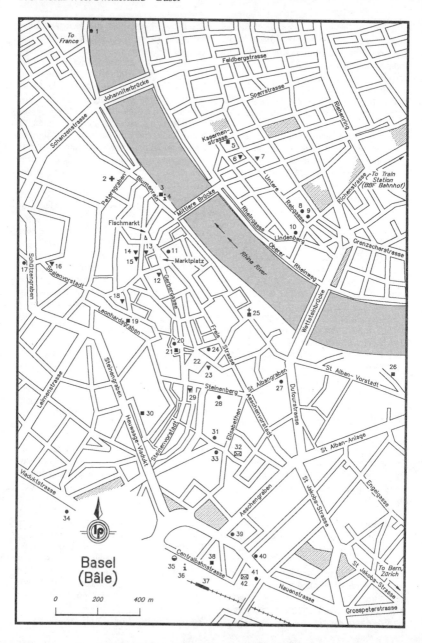

Basel
(Bâle)

0   200   400 m

■ PLACES TO STAY

3 Hotel Drei Könige
5 Klingental Garni
19 Kunsthotel Teufelhof
21 Hotel Stadthof
26 Youth Hostel
30 Hotel Steinenschanze
38 Hotel Bristol

▼ PLACES TO EAT

6 EPA Department Store
7 Migros Supermarket
12 EPA Department Store
13 Weinstube Gifthüttli
14 Café zum Roten Engel
15 Hasenburg Château Lapin
16 Restaurant Wilhelm Tell
18 Löwenzorn
23 Les Quatres Saisons
29 Mister Wong

OTHER

1 Main Boat Landing Stage
2 Cantonal Hospital
4 Tourist Office
8 Elle et Lui
9 Dupf
10 Hirscheneck (Beer Hall)
11 Town Hall (Rathaus)
17 Spalentor Gate Tower
20 Babalabar
22 Barfüsserplatz
24 Tanner Bookshop
25 Cathedral (Münster)
27 Museum of Fine Arts (Kunstmuseum)
28 Tinguely Fountain
31 Theatre (Stadttheater)
32 Main Post Office
33 Atlantis Music Venue
34 Zoo
35 Swissair & Airport Bus
36 Tourist Office
37 Train Station (SBB Bahnhof)
39 Avis (Car Rental)
40 Hertz (Car Rental)
41 Europcar (Car Rental)
42 Post Office

when the doors are also locked. The 1 am curfew is brought forward to midnight in winter.

Budget Hotels Rooms at the cheaper end are generally rather small. In the old town, *Stadthof* (☎ 261 87 11), Gerbergasse 84, has singles/doubles from Sfr54/90 without breakfast. Reception is in the restaurant on the 1st floor. In Kleinbasel, try *Klingental Garni* (☎ 681 62 48), Kasernenstrasse 20, not far from the Mittlere Brücke. This bar and restaurant has rooms for Sfr60 per person. In both places the shower and toilet are on the corridor.

Not far from the SBB Bahnhof is *Steinenschanze* (☎ 272 53 53), Steinengraben 69, which has newly renovated singles/doubles from Sfr90/125 with private shower and toilet. The price for students is reduced to Sfr45 per person for the first three nights, irrespective of the room.

Hotel Bristol (☎ 271 38 22), Centralbahnstrasse 15, is a welcoming place right outside the SBB station. Rooms are fair sized, non-standardised and comfortable. Singles/doubles are Sfr85/120, reduced by Sfr10 in the off season. Doubles with own bathroom are Sfr140, triples are Sfr135, and there are showers in the hall. There are some small singles (so-called 'B Zimmer') for Sfr65 but these can be hard to get.

Places to Stay – middle
The most interesting hotel in Basel is the *Kunsthotel Teufelhof* (☎ 261 10 10), Leonhardsgraben 47. Each of the rooms was assigned to a different artist to create a piece of environmental art. All rooms will stay intact for just two years before being reassigned to a new artist. The shock of waking up in a piece of art is quite something. The rooms have private bath and shower, and prices start at Sfr155/180 for single/double occupancy. Some rooms are more elaborately kitted out than others, but all are a welcome respite from standard hotel fixtures. Its expensive restaurant has an excellent reputation, and there is also a bar and theatre on site.

(☎ 272 05 72) is conveniently near the centre of town at St Alban Kirchrain 10. Beds cost Sfr20 per night with breakfast. Reception is shut from 10 am to 2 pm (3 pm in winter),

Places to Stay – top end

If you can afford to really splash out on accommodation, make for the *Drei Könige* (☎ 261 52 52), Blumenrain 8. It has welcomed luminaries through its portals since 1026 – royals such as Princess (later Queen) Victoria, and the likes of Napoleon, Voltaire and Dickens. You can join them, but only if you can afford the king's ransom of at least Sfr230/375 for a single/double. Breakfast buffet is Sfr28 extra. The three kings in question were Emperor Conrad II, his son, the future Henry III, and the last king of Burgundy, Rudolf III, who met in the inn in the year it was founded. As a result of their meeting the territory that became Switzerland was incorporated into the Germanic Empire. The present building dates from 1844, and the three kings on the façade are now the three wise men.

Places to Eat

Eating is generally a better deal in Basel than accommodation.

Self Service Cross the bridge over the tracks by the SBB post office to get to Güterstrasse. Here you will find *Migros* at No 180 and *Coop* at No 190. Both have a restaurant with meals from Sfr7 and a salad bar. The *EPA* department store, Gerbergasse 4, near the town hall (Rathaus), is cheap and conveniently central. Main dishes start at Sfr7 and soup is Sfr1.50. *Mister Wong*, Steinenvorstadt 1a, offers a reasonable choice of Asian dishes with heaped portions on smallish plates from Sfr8.00. It has a salad bar and is open daily to 10 pm except on Friday and Saturday when it closes at 11 pm.

There is also an *EPA* which is opposite a *Migros* store on Untere Rebgasse, in Kleinbasel, and both have restaurants.

Other Restaurants *Restaurant Wilhelm Tell*, Spalenvorstadt 38, by the Spalentor city gate, is small and busy. In other words it's claustrophobic, but it's still worth paying a visit for tasty local and Italian dishes from Sfr9.50. Opening hours are Monday to Saturday from 7 am to midnight.

For Basel specialities in a typical ambience, try *Weinstube Gifthüttli* (☎ 25 16 56), Schneidergasse 11. It has daily menus from Sfr13 to Sfr30. Opposite is the slightly more down-to-earth *Hasenburg Château Lapin*, with snacks and meals from Sfr5 to Sfr32. Drinkers mostly fill the tables in the evening. Vegetarians should check the environmentally sound *Café Zum Roten Engel* in the adjoining courtyard, with outside tables. It serves only organic vegetarian food (plus some fish dishes) for around Sfr12.50 to Sfr14. Good breakfasts are available and it's open until 8 pm in the week and to 6 pm on weekends. *Löwenzorn*, Gemsberg 2, another typical place, is something of a local secret, and not too expensive (closed Sunday). Speciality of the house is liver and Rösti. Elaborate preparations are around Sfr25 to Sfr35 and light meals start from Sfr9.50.

Stucki (☎ 35 82 22), Bruderholzallee 42, in the suburbs south of the SBB station, is rated in the top five restaurants in all Switzerland. You have to pay for the reputation, of course, with à la carte main courses costing Sfr40 to Sfr70 and menus above Sfr100, but its creative concoctions merit a taste. Duck (*le canard* in French) is a speciality at Sfr110 for two (closed Sunday and Monday). *Les Quatres Saisons* (☎ 691 80 44) in the Hotel Europe, Clarastrasse 43, is similarly plush and pricey (closed Sunday).

Entertainment

Basel has a busy cultural scene, with many theatre groups and two symphony orchestras. *Basel Live*, free from the tourist office, comes out every two weeks and contains full listings.

For more basic evening entertainment, explore the beer halls, especially in Kleinbasel. A good place that attracts an 'alternative' crowd is *Hirscheneck* (☎ 692 73 33), Lindenberg 23. At the weekend it has a disco (entry around Sfr5) or live music, and beer is Sfr4.50 for a 0.58-litre bottle.

Atlantis (☎ 272 20 38), Klosterbergstrasse 13, is one of the best venues in town. It has live music daily (mainly rock, R & B and jazz), and entry costs between Sfr5 and

Sfr25. Another good place is *Babalabar* (☎ 261 48 49), Gerbergasse 76. It has a section where there is a nightly disco with different musical themes, for which entry costs around Sfr5 or Sfr7 on weekends. Beer is Sfr4.50 for 0.30 litre. As it shuts early (midnight or 1 am) it tends to get busy as early as 9 pm.

Gay bars are *Dupf* at Rebgasse 43, and *Elle et Lui*, two doors down at No 39.

Getting There & Away
Air The airport serving Basel is Mulhouse in France. Telephone the Basel number (☎ 325 25 11) for information. There are several flights daily to main European destinations. Contact Swissair (☎ 284 54 80) at the SBB station for reservations on Crossair flights.

Train Basel is a major European rail hub. All trains to France go from SBB Bahnhof where you pass the border controls in the station. There are three to four trains a day to Paris (Sfr65) and connections to Brussels and Strasbourg. Trains to Germany (border controls on the train or in the station) stop at BBF Bahnhof on the north bank although all IC and EC services also pass through the SBB train station. Main destinations along this route are Frankfurt (Sfr70), Cologne, Hamburg and Amsterdam. Local trains to the Black Forest go only from BBF. There are two to three trains an hour to Freiburg (takes 40 minutes). Train services within Switzerland go from SBB: there are fast trains to Geneva via Bern (one minute past the hour) and Zürich (27 and 54 minutes past the hour).

Car & Motorbike By motorway, the E25/E60 heads down from Strasbourg and passes by Mulhouse Airport, and the E35/A5 hugs the German side of the Rhine.

Car Rental Various offices are near the SBB station, such as Hertz (☎ 271 58 22), Nauenstrasse 33, Avis (☎ 271 22 62), in the Hilton Hotel, Aeschengraben 31, and Europcar (☎ 272 85 55), Peter Merianstrasse 58. All three have a branch at the airport.

Boat An enjoyable if expensive way to travel north is to take a boat down the Rhine. The landing stage is between Johanniterbrücke and Dreirosenbrücke. A major operator is KD (☎ 01-363 56 56) which has an office at Kinkelstrasse 10, Zürich. The tourist office has a list of operators with an office in Basel. Circular tours by Basler Personenschiffahrt (☎ 261 24 00) depart from near the tourist office. Prices start at Sfr16, and tours are more frequent in the summer.

The First Hippie
The first man ever to take an LSD 'trip' was Swiss. In 1943 Albert Hofmann was a chemist working for the Sandoz drug company in Basel. While conducting tests during a search for a migraine cure he synthesised lysergic acid diethylamide (LSD), and the chemical was accidentally absorbed through his fingertips. Shortly afterwards the mind-bending sensations began, and he experienced a powerful series of psychedelic pictures and a dreamlike state.

Hofmann's next excursion with the drug, a deliberate experiment, produced the first 'bad trip', in which he thought a demon had invaded him and his neighbour was a witch. Heavy, man!

The drug was soon taken up by writers and artists, such as Aldous Huxley, who saw it as a creative and elevating force. It was later crucial in the evolution of the '60s flower generation, who believed it could be an instrument for world peace. From 1953 the CIA conducted extensive tests, lasting many years, to establish its usefulness as a truth drug. Tests on whether LSD had any clinical value were curtailed when the drug was outlawed in 1966.

Fifty years after his discovery, Mr Hofmann (then 87) defended the drug in an interview with a British newspaper *(The Independent)*, saying medical tests should be carried out to establish its potential. He went on to express the hope that LSD may one day become part of our mainstream culture, with the same acceptability as alcohol.

In the meantime, mine's a pint. ■

Getting Around

Buses run every 20 to 30 minutes between 5 am and midnight between the airport and the SBB station. It's the yellow bus that goes from outside the Swissair office (Sfr2, takes 20 minutes) at the station. The trip by taxi costs around Sfr25.

In the city, buses and trains run every six to 12 minutes. Tickets cost Sfr1.20 for up to four stops, or Sfr2 for the whole central zone. Multi-journey cards are available, but you're better off with a day card for Sfr6.60. Cars are no use for exploring the central pedestrian area – park in one of the spots indicated on the tourist office map. There are several places round SBB station. Small ferries cross the Rhine at various points in the centre (Sfr1), a pleasant alternative to using the bridges.

If you need a taxi, look outside the train stations or ring ☎ 321 44 44 or ☎ 271 11 11.

Around Basel

THE BLACK FOREST

This region in Germany (called Schwarzwald in German) is an ideal excursion from any of the northern border towns between Basel and Schaffhausen. There are plenty of tourists – Germans and foreigners – roaming its hills, but it's easy to leave the busy areas far behind. It is actually the home of the cuckoo clock, for so long associated with Switzerland itself. The epithet 'Black Forest' comes from the darkness enveloping from the canopy of evergreens. It's an ideal hiking region. Hansel and Gretel of childhood fiction encountered their wicked witch here, but 20th century hazards are rather more ominous. The Black Forest looks as lush as ever, yet experts will tell you it is slowly being destroyed by acid rain. Enjoy it while you can.

Orientation & Information

The Black Forest lies east of the Rhine between Basel and Karlsruhe. It's roughly triangular in shape, about 160 km long and 50 km wide. Freiburg is the unofficial capital of the southern Black Forest, although many other small towns in the area have excellent tourist information offices. Freiburg's tourist office (☎ 0761-36 89 00), Rotteckring 14, is open Monday to Saturday from 9 am to 9.30 pm and Sunday and holidays from 10 am to 2 pm. Closure times from 1 November to 30 April are brought forward to 6 pm weekdays, 3 pm Saturday and noon on Sunday. All tourist offices will be able to provide information about accommodation and restaurants.

All the prices in this section are quoted in Deutschmarks. The exchange rate is around Sfr1 to DM1.10. Money exchange is available at banks, train stations and post offices. The post office makes no charge for exchanging cash and takes the lowest commission for travellers' cheque transactions. Some shops and restaurants will accept Swiss francs directly.

The country telephone code for Germany is 49.

Things to See

Though taking advantage of the countryside will be the main focus, there's still lots of history and culture to explore in the region.

Freiburg's main tourist sight is the **cathedral** (Münster), a classic example of high and late-Gothic architecture. It's red pinnacles loom over Münsterplatz, an active market square. Of particular interest are the stone and wood carvings, stained-glass windows, the west porch and the pierced spire. The pedestrian area of the town is great for walking tours, and the many resident students make this place both relaxed and lively.

The area between Freudenstadt and Freiburg is cuckoo clock country, and a few popular stops are **Triberg**, **Schramberg** and **Furtwangen**. If you simply must have a cuckoo clock, this is the area in which to buy one. Prices here are generally lower than in Switzerland. The history and traditional lifestyle of the region are well documented in the **Deutsches Uhrenmuseum** (German Clock Museum) in Furtwagen and the **Schwarzwald Museum** (Black Forest

Museum) in Triberg. Triberg also has a famous **Wasserfall** (waterfall), which hurtles down 162 metres over seven stages. In the summer they charge DM2 to see it, but you can avoid this by entering from the hiking trails above and to the sides.

The Danube

The Danube (Donau) rises in the Black Forest and flows all the way to the Black Sea. It's ideal for hiking, biking and motoring tours. Donaueschingen is recognised as being the source of the river, and this town is the start of the cycle track (*Donauradweg*) that runs most of the way along the river right into Austria. The two tributary rivers that rise even deeper in the Black Forest, the Brigach and the Breg, are also worth exploring.

Activities

Four-season outdoor sports are as organised here as anywhere in Europe, and tourist offices are invaluable for providing maps and further information.

Hiking The southern Black Forest is best in the Feldberg area. Small hiking towns dot the landscape and many are used as bases by knowledgeable Germans getting off the well-worn Black Forest trails. Head for Todtmoos or Bonndorf for a true Black Forest hiking holiday. The 10-km gorge, the Wutachschlucht, outside of Bonndorf, is justifiably famous. If you haven't time to explore the Black Forest thoroughly, take the Schauinslandbahn, on the outskirts of Freiburg, up to the 1284-metre Schauinsland peak (DM14 return). It's a good setting for one-day and half-day hikes.

Skiing The area around the Titisee is a major centre for winter sports. The Feldberg (1493 metres) features fairly uncrowded downhill skiing (day pass DM30). There are currently 18 lifts in the area. Cross-country skiing is basically anywhere you can find snow, but many Germans take cable cars to higher ground and then start from there. For skiing information, contact the tourist information office in Feldberg (☎ 07655-80 19) at

Kirchgasse 1. If you just need area conditions and understand German, call ☎ 07676-12 14.

Getting There & Away

The north-south train route makes entering and leaving the region very easy. Trains run hourly between Basel and Karlsruhe, calling at Freiburg en route. There is also a scenic rail line between Freiburg and Constance.

Road access is good too, with the A5 skirting the western side of the forest and the A81 the eastern side. The A5 is the route that links Basel and Frankfurt. This is an easy hitching route, though you could also resort to the Mitfahrzentale (☎ 0761-367 49) at Belfortstrasse 55, Freiburg.

Getting Around

Rail connections are excellent for a mountainous area. Lines run north and east from Freiburg. The prettiest stretch (called the Höllental route) runs from Freiburg to the lake (Titisee). The Germans rave about this but it's nothing compared to most Swiss train journeys. Where the rail fails to go, the bus system usually provides the way, although services can be fairly infrequent in off-peak times. There is an excellent 'environmental protection ticket' valid for a calendar month on transport in the Freiburg region of the Black Forest. It costs just DM49; and it's transferable.

Drivers enjoy flexibility in an area that rewards it. The main tourist road, the Schwarzwald-Hochstrasse (B500), runs from Baden-Baden to Freudenstadt and Triberg to Waldshut, on the Swiss border. Cycling is a good way to get about, despite the hills (look for rental in Baden-Baden and Freiburg train stations).

Solothurn

Solothurn, originally a Celtic settlement, grew in importance when the Romans built a fort here in 370 AD. In 1481 it was the 11th canton to join the Swiss Confederation. The people of Solothurn took this number to their hearts: the town features 11 towers, 11 churches and chapels, 11 guilds and 11 historic fountains. Despite this evident strong allegiance to the Confederation, the town maintained close links with France, and sent many mercenaries to fight for French kings. It rejected the Reformation, choosing to remain Catholic, thereby placing itself in opposition to nearby Bern and Basel and strengthening the affinity with France. The town was the residence of French ambassadors from 1530 to 1792.

Orientation & Information

The train station is south of the Aare River and has an information office, money-exchange counters and bike rental, all open daily. There's also left luggage and 24-hour lockers. The main post office (Solothurn 1) is just to the left of the station as you exit.

Across the river lies the old town, less than 10-minute walk away. The core of the centre is Kronenplatz, dominated by the cathedral. The tourist office (☎ 065-22 19 24) is on this square, open Monday to Friday from 8.30 am to noon and 1.30 to 6 pm, and Saturday from 9 am to noon, and makes hotel reservations. It also organises guided walking tours of the centre which are illuminating and worth attending. They take place on Saturday afternoon in summer, last one to two hours, and cost Sfr5 per person.

Things to See & Do

Despite the French influences in its history, the centre of town is dominated by an Italianate church, the 18th century **Cathedral of St Ursus**. It was designed and overseen by the Ticino architect, Gaetano Matteo Pisoni, with help from his nephew. The cathedral is dedicated to the two patron saints of Solothurn, Ursus and Victor, who were beheaded in the town during Roman times for refusing to worship the Roman gods. Inside it features a fine pink marble pulpit. A stone's throw down Hauptgasse is the **Jesuit Church**. It's unprepossessing on the outside yet inside it displays magnificent Baroque embellishments and stucco work. The coats

of arms of the families who funded the building can be seen at the back of the church. Incidentally, all the 'marble' in here is fake, just spruced up wood and plaster. It's a common deception in Baroque churches.

A little further down Hauptgasse you reach the **Zeitglockenturm**, a 12th century astronomical clock where the figures do a little turn on the hour. Don't be confused by the clock hands – the smaller one shows the minutes. It was added centuries later than the large hour hand; it only became necessary when modern life dictated that people become yoked to the tyranny of timetables.

The rest of the old centre merits an exploration. There are a couple of city gates to see and several old fountains. One of the most entertaining fountains is the **Justice Fountain** in Hauptgasse, built in 1561. It shows a blindfolded representation of Justice, holding aloft a pair of scales, and at her feet are the four most important figures in Europe at that time. Firstly, the Holy Roman Emperor (in red and white robes), then proceeding anticlockwise: the Pope, the Turkish Sultan, and... the mayor of Solothurn!

Museums The **Old Arsenal** is essential viewing in Solothurn. It contains armour for 400 men, canons, guns and uniforms, and well illustrates the town's past status as a centre for mercenaries. The only exhibit you can touch is the small suit of armour near the entrance: lift up the visor and the dwarf inside will 'spit' on you. Not, thankfully, a typical Solothurn welcome. The Arsenal is free and open Tuesday to Sunday from 10 am to noon and 2 to 5 pm. From November to February it stays closed on weekday mornings.

For a provincial museum, the **Museum of Fine Arts** (Kunstmuseum), Werkhofstrasse 30, holds some impressive works. The *Madonna of Solothurn* (1522) by Holbein the Younger is the most striking, along with *Virgin in the Strawberries* (1425) by the Master of the Garden of Paradise. Swiss artists are strongly represented, especially Ferdinand Hodler, whose famous portrait of William Tell is here. It is open Tuesday to

Ferdinand Hodler

Ferdinand Hodler is perhaps the most important turn-of-the-century Swiss painter. He was born in Bern in 1853 and was influenced early on by the landscape works of Sommer and Calame. He produced many landscapes of his own, right up to the end of his life, with Lake Thun and Alpine scenes cropping up frequently. Hodler embraced the art nouveau style and particularly explored the use of allegory and symbolism. He spent most of his working life in Geneva, despite the fact that its climate of Calvinistic rectitude was often hostile towards him. He died in Geneva in 1918.

Historical themes were also important in his paintings. Some Hodler works hark back to the early days of the Swiss Confederation, when ill-equipped rural villages pitted themselves against the might of the Habsburgs. His famous picture of William Tell is in the Kunstmuseum in Solothurn. Hodler re-worked the scene of the show-of-hand vote several times (eg the *Einmütigkeit* in Zürich's Fine Arts Museum), where villagers stand in a cohesive group listening to an orator. All are rugged he-man types with physiques carved out of granite – the sort who cut their razors when shaving. The lack of three dimensional perspective makes them seem like a solid wall. All the men are about the same height and all have a hand raised in seamless unison. The line of heads and the line of hands create two intimidating tiers of defiance that make it seem plausible that such men could take on the Habsburgs – and win. ■

Sunday from 10 am to noon and 2 to 5 pm (9 pm Thursday) and entry is free.

Places to Stay & Eat

The cheapest place in the centre is *Hotel Kreuz* (☎ 065-22 20 20) on Kronengasse, by the cathedral. Singles/doubles start at Sfr30/50 and it has a restaurant. *Solothurner Hof* (☎ 065-22 04 22), Rossmarktplatz, by the north side of the Wengibrücke, has doubles with private shower starting at Sfr65 and singles without from Sfr35, without breakfast. But its standards of cleanliness are a bit suspect and reservations are not always honoured.

Baseltor (☎ 065-22 34 22), Hauptgasse 79, by the tourist office, is a newly opened restaurant and hotel. Rooms with private shower, toilet and telephone start at Sfr70/120. The restaurant has an interestingly diverse if not extensive menu, with meals costing from about Sfr10 to Sfr22 (closed Sunday). *Hotel Krone* (☎ 065-22 44 12), Hauptgasse 64, opposite the tourist office, is a Best Western hotel with prices starting at Sfr140/170. Rooms are decked out in several different styles and its pricey restaurant is open daily.

The impecunious can find fodder at the *Coop* supermarket and restaurant, 200 metres left of the station at Dornacherplatz.

Menus are Sfr8.50 and Sfr9.50 and it's open to 6.30 pm weekdays with late opening (9 pm) on Thursday, and Saturday to 5 pm. *Rebstock*, Kronengasse 9, is a simple café with daily menus for Sfr12.50 and Sfr14.50 and other meals from Sfr12.

Getting There & Away

Solothurn has hourly trains to Bern on the private RBS line (takes 45 minutes, rail passes valid). Regular trains also run to Basel (Sfr24, takes one hour or more, change at Olten), and Biel (Sfr7.80, 20 minutes). A more enjoyable way to get to and from Biel is to take the boat along the Aare River (see Biel for details). By road, the Weissenstein mountain impedes access directly north, but the N1/E25 motorway passes a few km east of town, providing a fast route to Bern, Basel and Zürich. Take highway 5 for Biel.

AROUND SOLOTHURN

The grand **Castle Waldegg**, a few km north of town, was built in the 17th century and displays period furniture and paintings. The design betrays French and Italian influences and it is open mid-April to the end of October. Take bus No 4 from the station to St Niklaus. The nearby **Weissenstein** (1279 metres), to the north, is a hiking and cross-country skiing centre.

Baden

Baden is the main (virtually the only) tourist destination in the canton of Aargau. It has a dual reputation, as an electro-mechanical engineering centre and as a leading spa town (population 14,000).

Orientation & Information

Baden is split into two localities about 15 minutes' walk apart: the Altstadt (old town centre) to the south and the spa centre to the north, with the train station positioned conveniently between the two. By the station is the main post office (Baden 1, CH-5400) and the postbus departure point. A few metres further on down Bahnhofstrasse at No 50 is the tourist office (☎ 056-22 53 18), open Monday to Friday from 8.30 am to noon and 2 to 6 pm and Saturday from 10 am to noon.

Things to See & Do

Baden's status as a health spa is thanks to the presence of 19 hot **sulphur springs**, with the highest mineral content of any Swiss spa. Their curative properties have been known for 2000 years and are believed to be effective in the treatment of rheumatism, respiratory and cardiovascular complaints, and even some neurological disorders. Alternatively, the springs may be of interest if you simply like wallowing in a 47°C bath. Pools are open to everyone in all the major hotels. Entry costs between Sfr7 and Sfr13, or much more if you want special treatments such as mudpacks or a massage.

The old town centre has some interesting features, including a **covered bridge** (Holzbrücke), step-gabled houses and the city tower. The **Bailiff's Castle** (Landvogtei-schloss) is on the east side of the Limmat River. Inside is a historical museum that's free and closed on Monday. Continue up the hill for 15 minutes to gain a bird's-eye view of the town. Between the Altstadt and the station is the **Swiss Children's Museum** (Schweizer Kindermuseum), Ölrainstrasse 29, featuring all sorts of games (ancient and

modern) that can be viewed and played. It is only open on Wednesday and Saturday from 2 to 5 pm and Sunday from 10 am to 5 pm; entry costs Sfr4 for adults, Sfr3 for students and Sfr2 for children.

Places to Stay

Campingplatz Aue (☎ 056-26 45 00) is a 15-minute walk from the station: turn right for the Altstadt, cross the Limmat River at Hochbrücke, then first right into Kanalstrasse. It's overlooking the river and is open from 1 April to 31 October.

The IYHF *youth hostel* (☎ 056-21 67 96) is nearby at Kanalstrasse 7. It is closed from January to mid-March, costs Sfr18, and reception is closed from 9.30 am to 5 pm.

Staying in hotels, *Hirschen* (☎ 056-22 69 66), Badstrasse, on the opposite side of the Limmat River from the spa, is the cheapest place. Singles/doubles are Sfr35/70 but they are unrenovated. If you can afford it, stay at *Atrium-Hotel Blume* (☎ 056-22 55 69), Am Kurplatz 4, in the spa centre. It's a cheery place featuring an excellent Romanesque inner courtyard with a fountain and plenty of foliage. Singles/doubles with private shower/toilet start at Sfr98/160, or Sfr65/125 using hall facilities. Breakfast is buffet-style and the hotel has its own (small) thermal pool.

Places to Eat

Below ground level in the station are market stalls and takeaway shops. Above ground is an *EPA* department store with a self-service restaurant and menus for Sfr6 and Sfr8. It is open until 6.30 pm on weekdays and 5 pm on Saturday. Nearby, opposite the post office, is a *Migros* supermarket and restaurant, with menus from Sfr7.50. Hours are similar to EPA's, except for late opening on Wednesday (8 pm). In the old town, try *Chen Lay*, Untere Halde 2, for Chinese food; it has special midday menus from Sfr12.50 (closed Monday). *Rebstock*, down the road at No 21, is more traditional and more expensive (closed Sunday and Monday).

Getting There & Away

Baden is just 15 minutes away from Zürich by rail (Sfr6.80). It is also within Zürich's S-Bahn network (lines S6 and S12). By road, it is simple to get to Zürich (N1/E60 motorway) and the German Black Forest town of Waldshut (highway 5).

Neuchâtel, Fribourg & Jura

This region includes the cantons of Neuchâtel (population 156,800), Fribourg (population 185,900) and Jura (population 64,000) as well as the north-west tip of the canton of Bern.

The Neuchâtel canton produces both red and white wine. The first vineyard in Neuchâtel was planted by monks in the 10th century, under the auspices of providing communion wine. Locally-produced brandies include Marc, Prune and Kirsch.

The canton of Fribourg is also tacked on to a tourist region that is otherwise dominated by the long chain of the Jura Mountains. It is this canton that provides many of the highlights: the historic town of Murten, the delightful cheese-making centre of Gruyères, and Fribourg itself. On the other hand, don't neglect a visit to the watch-making towns, merrily ticking away in the Jura mountains. The most important of these are Neuchâtel and La Chaux de Fonds in the canton of Neuchâtel.

Most towns in the canton of Jura have a street named after the 23 June. It was on this day in 1974 that a popular vote supported its creation as a separate canton. Previously it had been part of the canton of Bern, despite tensions and grievances dating back to the 19th century. The Federal Constitution was accordingly amended and, on 1 January 1979, the new canton came into being. It is strange, therefore, that the Jura region should still be lumped within the same tourist region as part of its former ruler.

Orientation & Information

This region is all in French-speaking Switzerland, except for the eastward edge of Fribourg canton where German is spoken. The area north and west of Lake Neuchâtel includes the relatively gentle slopes of the Jura Mountain range, a range which extends all the way along the French border almost to Geneva (see also the Vaud (Lake Geneva Region) chapter). In contrast, the Fribourg area south-east of the lake is mostly in the Mittelland plain. Four regional tourist offices serve the region, each covering its respective canton:

Union Fribourgeoise du Tourisme
  Route de la Glâane 107, Case postale 921 CH-1701 Fribourg (tel-24 56 44)
Fédération Neuchâteloise du Tourisme
  6 Rue du Trésor (Place des Halles), CH-2001 Neuchâtel (☎ 038-25 17 89)
Fédération du tourisme de la République et Canton de Jura
  8 Rue de la Gare, CH-2726 Saignelégier (☎ 039-51 26 26). Open Monday to Friday from 7.30 am to noon and 1.30 to 5 pm
Office du tourisme du Jura bernois
  Ave de la Poste 26, Case postale 127, CH-2740, Moutier. (☎ 032-93 64 66)

Some of the information is available only in French or German.

Getting Around

There is a special 'billet 2 jours' ticket for postbus travel on two consecutive days. It covers only selected routes in the area between Neuchâtel, La Chaux de Fonds, and Ste Croix (see Vaud chapter). It's a good deal if you want to explore the lesser-known destinations in the region. The price is just Sfr20 or Sfr10 for children or those with a Half-Fare Card. The Neuchâtel regional office sells a booklet (Sfr4.50, in French and German) describing different cycling routes within the canton, including showing variations in elevation for each trip. It also sells a detailed walking map. There are no motorways in the Jura region, but other main roads make getting around by car easy, even in winter.

Neuchâtel Canton

The first inhabitants were lake dwellers who settled as early as 3000 BC. The 2nd Iron Age

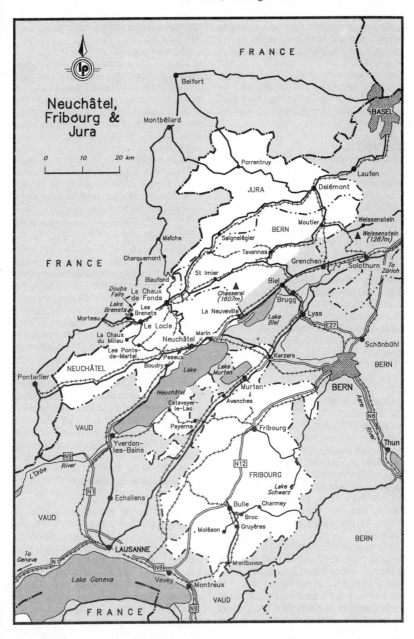

Neuchâtel,
Fribourg &
Jura

0   10   20 km

FRANCE
Belfort
Montbéliard
Porrentruy
JURA
Delémont
Laufen
BASEL
Matche
Salgnelégier
BERN
Moutier
Weissenstein
Weissenstein
(1287m)
Charquemont
Tavannes
Grenchen
Solothurn
To
Zürich
FRANCE
Blaufond
St Imier
Biel
Doubs
Falls
La Chaux
de Fonds
Chasseral
(1607m)
Brugg
Lake
Brenets
Les
Brenets
La Neuveville
Lyss
Morteau
Le Locle
Lake
Biel
E27
La Chaux
du Milieu
Neuchâtel
Marin
Les Ponts-
de-Martel
Peseux
Kerzers
Schönbühl
Boudry
Lake
Lake
Murten
BERN
NEUCHÂTEL
Neuchâtel
Murten
BERN
Pontarlier
Neuchâtel
Estavayer-
le-Lac
Avenches
Aare
VAUD
Payerne
Fribourg
N6
River
Yverdon-
les-Bains
Thun
L'Orbe
River
N9
N12
FRIBOURG
N1
Lake
Schwarz
Echallens
Bulle
Charmey
VAUD
Broc
Moléson
Gruyères
BERN
LAUSANNE
To
Geneva
N1
N9
Montbovon
Lake Geneva
Vevey
Montreux
VAUD
FRANCE

in Europe is referred to as the 'La Tène Period', after the settlement on the eastern end of Lake Neuchâtel where a store of weapons and utensils were discovered. Modern industries include watch-making, precision engineering and printing and publishing. The observatory in Neuchâtel town gives the official time-check for the whole of Switzerland.

NEUCHÂTEL
Neuchâtel (population 32,800) is the capital of its canton. It's a relaxing town, on the north-west shore of the largest lake totally within Swiss territory, Lake Neuchâtel.

The descendants of Ulrich II became known as the Counts of Neuchâtel from the early 12th century. The territory was elevated to a principality at the beginning of the 17th century, with Henry II of Orléans-Longueville as its head. The title of Prince ultimately devolved to Frederick-William III of Prussia, who allowed it to join the Swiss Confederation in 1815. Yet, curiously and incompatibly, the canton remained a principality under Prussia until 1848, when a bloodless revolution won it the status of a republic.

The French spoken in Neuchâtel is the purest in Switzerland.

Orientation & Information
The train station (Gare CFF) changes money daily from 5.30 am to 10 pm and rents bikes. It also has lockers (Sfr2 and Sfr5), luggage storage and a train information office (open weekdays and Saturday morning).

The old part of town is one km away, down the hill along Ave de la Gare. The hub of the town is Place Pury; to get there from the station, take bus No 6. The commercial centre is the pedestrian-only Rue de l'Hôpital.

The tourist office (☎ 038-25 42 42) is between Place Pury and the port, at Rue de la Place d'Armes 7, and is open Monday to Friday from 9 am to noon and 1.30 to 5.30 pm, and Saturday from 9 am to noon (hours are extended in summer). Pick up a copy of its walking tour of the town centre. The

cantonal office is nearby (see the chapter's introduction).

The main post office (Poste Principal) is at Place du Port, overlooking the harbour. Post counters are open weekdays from 7.30 am to 6.30 pm and Saturday until 11 am; the telephone section is open daily until 9.30 pm (9 pm Sunday). There's another post office just opposite the train station (Poste, 2002 Neuchâtel 2). Normal opening hours are weekdays and Saturday morning, but services are available daily for a Sfr1 surcharge.

There is a branch of the budget travel ageny, SSR (☎ 24 48 08) at Fausses-Brayes 1, off Rue de l'Hôpital, open Monday afternoon to Saturday morning.

The telephone code for Neuchâtel is 038.

Things to See & Do
The centrepiece of the old town is the **castle** and the adjoining **Collegiate Church**. The castle dates from the 12th century and now houses cantonal offices. Walk along the ramparts for a view over the town. The church combines Gothic and Romanesque elements. Its most striking feature is a cenotaph of 15 statues dating from 1372. This depicts medieval knights and ladies (most of whom have been identified) standing in suitably pious postures. Nearby, the **Prison Tower** (entry Sfr0.50) offers a good view of the area and has interesting models showing the town as it was in the 15th and 18th centuries. While roaming around the centre, look out for the six historic fountains which were built around the turn of the 16th century. They were all the work of Laurent Perroud and have recently been restored.

Museums The best, and an essential visit, is the **Museum of Art and History** (Musée d'Art et d'Histoire), Quai Léopold Robert 2, which is especially noted for three 18th century clockwork figures. They were built from 1764 to 1774 by Jaquet Droz who was formerly a watchmaker based in La Chaux de Fonds. The technical achievement in constructing these automata was incredible for the time, and they were performed before

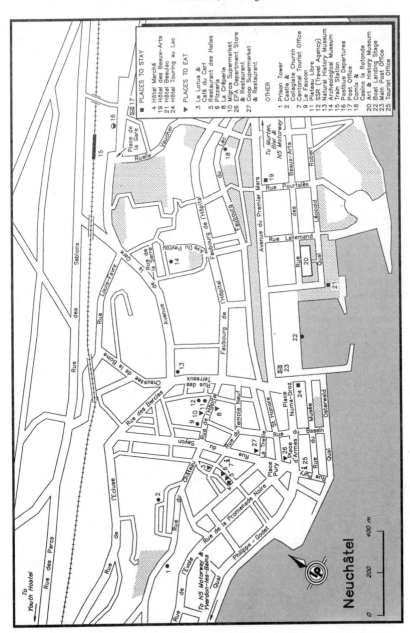

PLACES TO STAY

17 Hôtel Marché
4 Hôtel des Beaux-Arts
19 Hôtel Beaulac
21 Hôtel Touring au Lac
24

PLACES TO EAT

3 Le Lotus &
Café du Cerf
5 Restaurant des Halles
6 Pizzeria
8 La Crêperie
10 Migros Supermarket
26 EPA Department Store
& Restaurant
27 Coop Supermarket
& Restaurant

OTHER

1 Prison Tower
2 Castle &
Collegiate Church
7 Cantonal Tourist Office
9 Le Faxon
11 Plateau Libre
12 SSR (Travel Agency)
13 Natural History Museum
14 Archeological Museum
15 Train Station
16 Postbus Departures
17 Post Office
18 Comix &
Casino la Rotonde
20 Art & History Museum
22 Boat Landing Stage
23 Main Post Office
25 Tourist Office

Neuchâtel

0   200   400 m

admiring crowds in the fairs and royal courts of Europe.

The most elaborate is the **Writer** who can be programmed to write up to 40 characters, including dipping his pen in an inkpot. This is achieved via 120 internal revolving discs; the adjustment of these is so fine – to within 0.1 mm – that if the room gets too hot the expansion of the metal can cause him to make spelling mistakes! The **Musician** can play up to five tunes; it's a real organ she plays, not a disguised musical box, and she breathes and moves her eyes as her fingers strike the keys. The **Draughtsman** is technically the simplest, but he still has a repertoire of six drawings. They were purchased for the museum in 1909 for Sfr75,000, and it is so protective of them that they are only activated on the first Sunday of each month. On other days you can see them at rest and watch a film (in English) explaining their history and functions. Elsewhere in the museum are clocks, coins, decorative arts, and works by Swiss painters. Entry is Sfr7, or Sfr4 for students and children; the museum is open on Tuesday to Sunday from 10 am to 5 pm (9 pm on Thursday from April to October).

Also interesting is the **Museum of Ethnography** (Musée d'ethnographie), Rue St Nicolas 4, which concentrates mainly on exhibits from Africa, Bhutan and Oceania (closed Monday; Sfr7 or Sfr4 for students and children). Go west along Rue du Château until it becomes Rue St Nicholas. The **Natural History Museum** (Musée d'histoire naturelle), 14 Rue des Terreaux (Sfr5, students Sfr3, children free) and the **Archaeological Museum** (Musée cantonal d'archéologie), 7 Ave du Peyrou (free) are also closed on Monday.

Papiliorama This is a hot and humid tropical garden within a large dome. Inside are over 1000 butterflies of all sizes and hues, and a hatchery where, if you're lucky, you'll see chrysalises breaking out of their cocoons. There's also numerous colourful and exotic birds flying around, plus tropical plants, fish, tortoises and an insectarium. You wouldn't need to spend more than an hour in the dome,

so it's rather expensive at Sfr8 for adults (no student reductions) and Sfr4 for children. It's good fun, though. It is open daily from 10 am to 6 pm except October and March when it closes at 5 pm. It's in Marin, six km to the east of town by the Marin Centre, a huge shopping complex with a Migros supermarket and restaurant. Take bus No 1 from Place Pury and get off after Marin village at Bellevue, or take the local train to Marin Epagnier. If driving, go eastwards along Ave du Premier Mars.

Other Attractions Cruises on the lake are well worth considering in the summer. All places of interest around Lake Neuchâtel can be reached, and the neighbouring lakes of Biel and Murten are also accessible via a canal. Trips can be a relaxing day out with meals on board or simply a means to continue onward travel. For more information contact Navigation Neuchâtel et Morat (☎ 25 40 12) at the harbour. See also the Biel Getting There & Away section in the Bernese Mittelland chapter. A one-day pass for free travel on the lake costs Sfr34 or Sfr22 with a Half-Fare Card.

Fishing is allowed on the shores of the lake without a permit, but to do this on a boat you need to get a permit from the cantonal police (☎ 24 24 24), Balance 4.

The best view of the Alps and the lakes can be achieved from **Chaumont** (1087 metres). It's just 30 minutes by car (heading north-east) from the centre, or take bus No 7 to La Coudre (direction: Hauterive) then a short funicular ride.

Vineyards clothe the hills on the northern shore of Lake Neuchâtel. Families have been making wines here for many generations, and most producers are still small-scale concerns. The tourist office has a list of cellars where the output can be sampled. Red wines come from the Pinot Noir grape and white wines from the Chasselas. The white wine, by the way, must be poured from a height of at least six inches above the glass for the best results. A bit of a problem if you're just swigging it from the bottle.

Neuchâtel hosts the Grape Harvest Festi-

Top Left: Castle Garden, Gruyères, Fribourg Canton (MH)
Top Right: Gruyères Church, Fribourg Canton (MH)
Bottom: Castle and Collegiate church, Neuchâtel, Neuchâtel Canton (MH)

Top: Grand Theatre, Geneva (MH)
Bottom: Jardin Anglais, Geneva (MH)

val (Fête des Vendanges) on the last weekend in September. It includes parades and costumes, and a fair amount of drunken revelling.

Places to Stay

Camping There are camp sites a few km away either side of Neuchâtel. *La Tène Plage* (☎ 33 73 40) in Marin is open from April to September and costs just Sfr3 per person, Sfr2.50 for a tent and Sfr2 for parking. It's by the lake, a short walk from Marin Epagnier train station. *Paradis Plage*, by the lake in Colombier, has loads of facilities but it's more expensive (open March to October). Bus No 5 goes to Colombier from Place Pury in Neuchâtel. By car, you can take either the N5 or Quai Philippe-Godet.

Hostel The IYHF *youth hostel* (☎ 31 31 90), Rue du Suchiez 35, is two km from the town centre. It's a long, dull walk so take bus No 6 to Place Pury then Nos 1 or 4 to Vauseyon and follow the signs. It is a small, pleasant, family-run place with good evening meals and a laundry service. Beds are Sfr16 per night; reception is closed from 9 am to 5 pm and the hostel closes from mid-December to mid-February. Get a key to avoid the curfew.

Hotels *Marché* (☎ 24 58 00) is ideally placed in the town centre at Place des Halles 4. Ask for a room overlooking the square. Rooms vary in size, each has a TV but showers are in the hall. Singles/doubles are Sfr 65/90, and an extra bed in the room costs Sfr25. *Hôtel des Beaux-Arts* (☎ 24 01 51), Rue Pourtalès 3, is friendly but not quite so central. Rooms with private shower/toilet start at Sfr75/125 and the inexpensive restaurant is open daily.

Hôtel-Restaurant du Poisson (☎ 33 30 31), Ave Bachelin 7, Marin, has singles/doubles for Sfr38/70 with private shower and toilet.

Hôtel Touring au Lac (☎ 25 55 01), Place Numa-Droz 1, is by the harbour. It has good rooms from Sfr100/160 with shower/toilet, TV, radio, mini bar and telephone. There are a few cheaper rooms in a less salubrious

section of the building. The airy restaurant is a good place to sit and watch the boats, and consume mid-price food. Top of the range in Neuchâtel is *Beaulac* (☎ 25 60 35), Quai Léopold Robert, overlooking the harbour. Large rooms from Sfr145/205 have all the expected amenities. The cable TV picks up 26 channels and there are three restaurants on site.

Places to Eat

Local specialities include tripe, and *tomme Nechâteloise chaude*, a baked cheese starter. Fish from the lake, especially trout *(truite)* is another treat.

Self-service Opposite the tourist office is an *EPA* department store with a restaurant offering menus for as low as Sfr6. It's open to 6.30 pm weekdays and 5 pm on Saturday. Nearby in the town centre is a *Coop* with a self-service restaurant at Rue de la Treille 4. There is also a *Migros* supermarket on Rue de l'Hôpital. Another budget option is the refectory in the Cité Universitaire. Weekday lunches are around Sfr8 but you may be required to show some student identification.

Other Restaurants Opposite Migros at Rue de l'Hôpital 7 is *La Crêperie*, which is popular with mainly youngish locals. There is no name sign outside. If you don't like thin pancakes you'll think this place is a load of crêpe, because that's all it serves. The price is between Sfr2.50 and Sfr9.30, depending on the filling, which covers a wide choice ranging from the exotic to the mundane. A savoury one followed by a sweet one is just about enough for a meal. Have one as a dessert if nothing else.

The *Buffet de la Gare* at the station has a lunch-time *assiette du jour* for Sfr15 but really it's a mid-price, quality restaurant (open daily to midnight). The gourmet's choice is *Restaurant des Halles*, (☎ 24 31 41) in the historic 16th century building with a turret on Place des Halles. The cooking is French in style with main courses starting at Sfr35 and multi-course menus at Sfr65 or more. It's on the 1st floor and closes on Sunday and Monday. Downstairs is a pizzeria where good-sized tasty pizzas cost Sfr12 to Sfr17.

In a small street around the back is *Le Lotus* (☎ 24 27 44), 1st floor, Rue de l'Ancien 4 near Rue du Château. It serves excellent oriental food (mainly Thai) for around Sfr30. The lunchtime assiettes du jour (from Sfr12) and three-course menus (Sfr18 to Sfr25) are good value. At ground level is the *Café du Cerf* where the same daily specials are available for lunch and dinner, but it's mainly used as a drinking venue. It attracts a young crowd with its beer on draught (bier pression, Sfr3.70 for half a litre) and in bottles from around the world (about Sfr6 for 0.3 litre).

Entertainment

Downstairs from the Casino la Rotonde (where dancing girls cavort) on Faubourg du Lac is *Comix*, a student-type bar that's closed on Sunday. Next to McDonald's on Rue de L'Hôpital is *Le Faucon*, a bar with pool tables that stays open as late as 3 am on Friday and Saturday. A few metres down the road at No 4 is *Plateau Libre*, a music venue where a wide range of bands play after 10 pm, every night except Sunday. There's no entry charge but drink prices double at 10 pm (a 0.3-litre beer becomes Sfr7). *La Case a Chocs* (☎ 30 20 56), Rue de Tivoli 30 (take bus No 7 to Tivoli) is an 'alternative' venue where there is live music most weekends and occasional cinema and art shows. It's in the old factory under the bridge, but may have to shift premises sometime in 1994.

Getting There & Away

There are hourly fast trains to Geneva (70 minutes, Sfr37), Bern via Kerzers (35 minutes, Sfr15.80), Basel (35 minutes, Sfr33), Biel (20 minutes, Sfr9), and many other destinations. Around two an hour run to Yverdon (20 minutes, Sfr10.60). Neuchâtel is also the hub for buses and trains into the Neuchâtel Jura. Postbuses leave from outside the station. The bus to Le Loche (sfr15) via La Chaux du Milieu departs

hourly and takes one hour. The bus information office is on Place Pury and train information is at the Hotel Touring au Lac; both are open weekdays and Saturday morning.

Avis car rental (☎ 25 99 91), is at Rue de la Pierre-à-Mazel 51, and Hertz (☎ 30 32 32) is less central at Rue de Bourgogne 12.

Boat Boat services on the lake are most frequent from the end of May to late September. There are several departures a day (except Monday) to Murten (takes 1½ hours, Sfr11.60), Estavayer-le-Lac (1½ hours, Sfr13.20) and Yverdon (3 hours, Sfr15).

Getting Around

Local buses cost Sfr1.40 to Sfr2.20, depending upon the length of the journey (colour-coding on dispensers tell you what you need). Sfr7 gets you a 24-hour ticket. All local buses hit the main transport hub, Place Pury. The free timetable booklet shows the different departure points from the square.

LA CHAUX DE FONDS

This is the largest town in the region (population 40,000) and the highest in Switzerland (1000 metres). It's an important centre for watch and clock-making and the impressive horology museum is the main reason for a visit. Le Corbusier was born in the town in 1887 and fans of this architect can view various examples of his innovative work around the town.

Orientation & Information

La Chaux de Fonds is 20 km north-west of Neuchâtel. Walk straight for Ave Léopold Robert, a long, straight, tree-lined thoroughfare. Turn left and walk 10 minutes until it becomes Rue Neuve. The tourist office (☎ 039-28 13 13) is here at Rue Neuve 11, by an attractive fountain. Opening hours are Monday to Friday from 9 am to 5.30 pm and Saturday from 9 am to noon (December to March) or 10 am to 2 pm (April to November). Sometime in 1994 it is due to transfer to the Espacité, a new office building 100

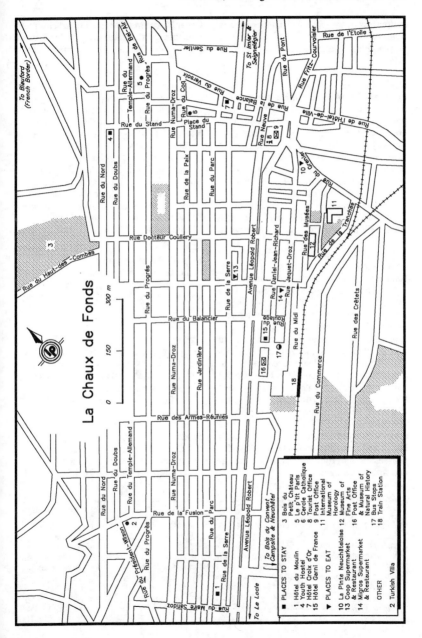

La Chaux de Fonds

PLACES TO STAY
1 Hôtel du Moulin
4 Youth Hostel
7 Hôtel Croix d'Or
15 Hôtel Garni de France

PLACES TO EAT
10 La Pinte Neuchâteloise
13 Coop Supermarket
    & Restaurant
14 Migros Supermarket
    & Restaurant

OTHER
2 Turkish Villa
3 Bois du
   Petit Château
5 Le p'tit Paris
6 Cercle Catholique
8 Tourist Office
9 Post Office
11 International
   Museum of
   Horology
12 Museum of
   Fine Arts
16 Post Office
   & Museum of
   Natural History
17 Bus Stops
18 Train Station

metres towards the station from the old location.

The telephone code for La Chaux de Fonds is 039.

Museums

International Museum of Horology

It was the technical expertise of Huguenot refugees, who settled in Geneva at the end of the 16th century, which started Switzerland on the way to its current annual production of over 100 million watches. The craft soon spread throughout the Jura which quickly established itself as the centre of the industry. This Musée International D'Horlogerie tells you everything you need to know about watch and clock-making. Many signs are in English. It includes information about ways of telling the time in the ancient world and displays clocks and watches from the earliest constructed to many from the 19th century, some extremely elaborate and beautiful.

In subsequent sections it goes on to explain and illustrate all aspects of watch-making, including the constructing and assembling of components, and decorative aspects such as engraving and enamelling. In the car park is a 15-tonne carillon that chimes every 15 minutes. Allow one to two hours to get around; if children get bored they can amuse themselves with the machine that tests reaction times. Admission costs Sfr8 (Sfr7 for senior citizens, Sfr4 for children and students, Sfr18 for families) and it is open Tuesday to Sunday from 10 am to noon and 2 to 5 pm. The museum is at Rue des Musées 29; turn right out of the train station and follow the signs.

Other Museums Next door to the Horology museum is the **Museum of Fine Arts** (Musée des Beaux-Arts; same opening times; Sfr2 for adults, Sfr1 for children and students, and Sfr4 for families). It has an interesting contemporary art section plus many works by Swiss painters. Local boys Léopold Robert, Le Corbusier and Edouard Kaiser are well represented. The **Museum of Natural History** (Musée d'histoire naturelle) is on the 2nd floor of the main post office; it's free and closed on Monday.

Thirteen buildings that relate to Le Corbusier's early life or work are described in an itinerary available from the tourist office. The interior of the Turkish Villa (Villa Schwob) can be view by telephoning in advance on ☎ 23 52 32.

Bois du Petit Château

In this small park is a zoological garden and a vivarium. Entry is free; walk to the north-west end of Rue Docteur Coullery or take bus No 4.

Places to Stay

Camping *Bois du Couvent* (☎ 23 25 55) is on the edge of a wood two km behind the main station, off Boulevard de la Liberté. It's open from May to September.

The IYHF *youth hostel* (☎ 28 43 15), Rue de Doubs 34, has beds for Sfr16. Reception is closed from 9 am to 5 pm (6 pm on Sunday) and the hostel closes in November and December. It's a 15-minute walk from the station; turn right upon reaching Ave Léopold Robert then look for the signs on the

---

Le Corbusier

He was born Charles Edouard Jeanneret on 6 October 1887 at Rue de la Serre 38. His adopted name was derived from that of his maternal grandfather. In 1917 he moved to Paris where his career began in earnest. Le Corbusier was one of the key innovators behind the development of the International Style of Architecture which achieved dominance in the 20th century, and especially since the 1950's. Characteristic features of this style are the use of modern materials (particularly reinforced concrete and steel) to create functional buildings with pure, straight lines. Aesthetic considerations weren't overlooked, although today's boring office complexes and blocks of flats are clear descendants of this genre. Some of Le Corbusier's own creations, however, explore spatial relations in a much more dynamic way. He died in 1965. ■

left. Alternatively, take bus No 4 which becomes No 22 after 7 pm.

Opposite and to the right of the station, on Rue Daniel Richard, is *Garni de France* (☎ 039-23 11 16). It has basic singles/doubles from Sfr25/50 but you need to reserve well ahead for these. Doubles with a shower cubicle cost Sfr70 or Sfr120 with a proper bathroom. The decor is unsubtle and the bar downstairs a bit noisy, but it's not bad value. If you want a quieter life, go to *Croix d'Or* (☎ 28 43 53), Rue de la Balance 15. It's off Rue Neuve, the continuation of Ave Léopold Robert to the right of the station. Rooms with hall shower are Sfr35/70.

Hôtel du Moulin (☎ 26 42 26), Rue de la Serre 130, has comfortable, nicely decorated rooms with TV and shower for Sfr75/135. Some cheaper rooms are available using the hall showers. The hotel has a car park and even a 10-pin bowling alley.

Places to Eat

There's a *Migros* supermarket and restaurant in a new metal and glass structure, 200 metres to the right of the station on Rue Daniel Jean-Richard. Menus cost Sfr6.90 and Sfr8.20. On the other side of Ave Léopold Robert is a *Coop*, Rue de la Serre 37. It's not self-service but it's as cheap as those that are. In a big shopping complex to the south-west of town is *Manora*, Blvd des Eplatures 20, with good buffet-style food for around Sfr11. It's open daily to 10 pm. Take bus No 2 (or No 44 after 7 pm) and get off at Eplatures.

Croix d'Or, already recommended under Places to Stay, has filets de perch for Sfr17 and fondue. The pizza are cheap (Sfr8.50 to Sfr12.20) and good, and you get a bowl of chopped chillis in oil into the bargain. It's open daily to midnight.

Restaurant *La Pinte Neuchâteloise* (☎ 23 38 64), at Rue du Grenier 8, has a lunch menu for Sfr12 including soup or salad. There's a special room for fondue (Sfr15 to Sfr22) where the atmosphere is so thick with bubbling cheese that people on a diet can dine on the smell alone. Meat and fish dishes are Sfr20 or more, and there's a room where a well-dressed clientele consume the *menu degustation*: Sfr62 for five courses (closed Tuesday).

Entertainment

Le p'tit Paris (☎ 28 65 33), is not far from the youth hostel at Rue du Progrès 4. It has a cellar called *La Cave* where there's live music (usually jazz-rock) every Friday and Saturday. Entry is free or up to Sfr12 and beers are not expensive. Next door it has a mid-price restaurant. Also nearby is *Cercle Catholique* on the corner of Rue du Coq and Place du Strand. The main novelty of this place is that it stays open to 6 am – supposedly continuing the local cercle tradition of serving factory night-workers who want refreshments after knocking off their shift. Nowadays it mainly serves beer, pizza and coffee to young clubbers and insomniacs.

Bikini Test (☎ 28 06 66), Joux Perret 3, is a venue which has live music and occasional dance and alternative films. It's on the edge of town to the north-east: take either bus Nos 2 or 22.

Getting There & Away

Trains run to Neuchâtel every hour (Sfr9, takes 30 to 60 minutes). Local trains run to Basel via Saignelégier and Delémont, but this is a slow journey: travelling via Neuchâtel is quicker. Postbuses connect the smaller places; schedules are available from the tourist office. By car, stop off at Vue des Alpes (1283 metres), enroute to Neuchâtel by highway 20. It provides a fine view of the mighty peaks of the Alps. From here, detour a couple of km to the Tête de Ran Hotel, then climb a steep path for 15 minutes. The panorama at this belvedere (1422 metres) is even better.

There is a postbus service running northwards into France to Charquemont, crossing the border at Biaufond. The road is in good condition, if rather winding.

Hertz (☎ 28 52 28) has a car rental office at Charrière 15.

Getting Around

Buses become less frequent at around 7 pm

when it is normal for two routes to combine to form a circular route under a new number. Rides cost Sfr1.60 or Sfr6.50 for a strip of five. There's a major bus hub just to the right of the train station.

NEUCHÂTEL MONTAGNES

Less rugged than the Alps, these mountains make fewer demands on hikers (1500 km of maintained and marked footpaths, some accessible in winter) and cyclists (1760 km of bike paths). In winter, there is some downhill skiing (30 ski lifts), but of greater importance is cross-country skiing. In all there are 400 km of cross-country trails; some of these are groomed regularly and a few are even lit. For a taped snow report (in French), ring ☎ 039-28 75 75, or better still, ask the La Chaux de Fonds tourist office. For equipment rental, try Calame Sports (☎ 039-28 24 40), Neuve 3, La Chaux de Fonds. Ice skating on frozen lakes is also popular, particularly on the Lake of Taillères.

In addition to watch-making, agriculture and milk production are important to the local economy. A network of postbuses connects the smaller towns and villages in the region, although departures can be infrequent.

Le Locle

Le Locle is another important watch-making centre. It was in the late 18th century that Daniel Jean-Richard introduced this skill to the Neuchâtel Jura, practising his craft in Le Locle. The town's **Museum of Horology** is located in 18th century Château des Monts. There are some grand period rooms as well as numerous timepieces that span the centuries from the earliest devices to the latest technological innovations. An unusual automation in the Maurice Sandoz room depicts an old woman with a stooped gait supporting herself on two walking sticks. The museum is open Tuesday to Sunday from 10 am to noon and from 2 to 5 pm (afternoons only between November and April). Admission costs Sfr5 adults, Sfr4 senior citizens, Sfr3 students, Sfr2 children, and Sfr12 families.

Near the town are the **Col-des-Roches**

Underground Mills. These mills exploit the underwater flow of the Bied River on its way to join the Doubs River. It was Jonas Sandoz who started the work of widening existing fissures in the rock and creating waterfalls and wells, until by the end of the 17th century the underground complex included a thresher, two flour mills, an oil mill and a saw mill. The building on the surface dates from 1844. The mills were gradually allowed to fall into disuse and for much of the 20th century were used as a slaughterhouse. It wasn't until 1973 that work began to restore them to their former glory and open them to the public. There's an exhibition in the entrance hall and large pieces of machinery in the underground caves. The site is open May to October from 10 am to noon and 2 to 5.30 pm every day; entry costs Sfr7 for adults, Sfr6 for senior citizens, Sfr4 for students and children, and Sfr15 for families.

For more information, contact the Le Loche tourist office (☎ 039-31 43 30), Daniel Jean-Richard 31.

Getting There & Away Le Loche is only seven minutes from La Chaux de Fonds (Sfr2.80) by hourly train (the same train that goes on to/from Neuchâtel). Trains also run into France to Morteau and beyond. The Col-des-Roches Underground Mills are reached by postbus on the more-or-less hourly Le Loche-La Brévine service (takes 30 minutes; Sfr7.20 each way). For postbus information ring ☎ 039-31 32 31.

Doubs Basins

The Doubs Basins is the area on the French border where the River Doubs broadens into Lake Brenets (Lac des Brenets, or Lac de Chaillexon on the French side of the border). Along part of its length, the shapes of the limestone cliffs are reputed to resemble famous historical figures such as Louis-Philippe (hardly flattering – gives a new significance to the description 'craggy features'). There's also the **Doubs Falls** (Saut du Doubs) which hurtles down from a height of 27 metres. Contact the boat operator, NLB (☎ 039-32 14 14), for short cruises of the lake in the summer. Boats sail between the village of Les Brenets and the waterfall; to walk between these two points takes an hour. There is also the **Chemin des Planètes** between Le Loche and Saut du Doubs, a path reflecting the distance between the planets in the solar system. You could also try bungy jumping at the Falls, courtesy of Oliver's Organisation (☎ 039-31 58 65), which is based in Le Locle.

Getting There & Away Les Brenets is just two km from Le Locle. Train run frequently and cost Sfr2 each way.

Jura Canton

FRANCHES MONTAGNES

This is the part of the Jura mountain chain that is within the canton of Jura. It is usually overlooked by foreign visitors, which means that relatively inexpensive accommodation can be found. It's an area of pastures and woodlands where there are 1500 km of hiking trails and 200 km of prepared cross-country ski trails. Horse-riding is another popular activity; the horses in the area are known for their gentleness and calm disposition. There are equestrian centres in over 30 towns and villages offering all-in weeks, weekends, or simple hourly rides. *Chez Cindy* (☎ 039-51 61 85), La Theurre 1, Saignelégier, charges Sfr22 per hour and Sfr35 for an overnight stay. The weekend rate for kids including rides is Sfr80.

The main town in the region is **Saignelégier**, which is the location for the annual national horse show in early August. Get more information from the canton of Jura tourist office (see the introduction to this chapter) or from the tourist office specifically for the Franches Montagnes (☎ 039-51 21 51), Place du 23 June 1, Saignelégier.

Getting There & Away

Saignelégier is on the rail line between La Chaux de Fonds (takes 40 minutes, Sfr11.60) and Basel (2½ hours, Sfr26). By car, there

are two famous viewpoints you can detour to on the way to this part of the Jura. The northernmost one is at Weissenstein (make for the Kurhaus Weissenstein at 1287 metres), 10 km from Solothurn. The road continues to Moutier where it branches to either Delémont or Tavannes. The more southern of the two routes starts at La Neuveville, on the shore of Lake Biel. A minor road winds up from here to St Imier (33 km). This road is usually impassable in winter and spring. Stop off at the Hôtel du Chasseral, where there is a viewing table, then walk 30 minutes to the telecommunications tower for a 360° panorama. From either Weissenstein or Chasseral you can see the broad expanse of the Alps spread out before you. Chasseral encompasses the hotel viewing point as well as the telecommunications viewpoint, both of which are on the Chasseral (1607 metres) peak.

Fribourg Canton

In the 15th and 16th centuries Fribourg was protected from Bern's expansionist policies by a treaty of association signed in 1403. This alliance held firm despite Fribourg remaining Catholic in the face of the Reformation. The town even managed to extend its own territory during this period, and gobbled up several regions to the south and west, such as Gruyères and Broye.

FRIBOURG

Built on the hilly banks of a river bend and with a skyline dominated by a cathedral, Fribourg (Freiburg in German) is a little reminiscent of Bern. This is not too surprising as it was founded in 1157 by Duke Berchtold IV of Zähringen, father of the bear hunter who founded Bern, Berchtold V. It became a free imperial city in 1478 at the end of the Burgundy Wars. Three years later it joined the Swiss Confederation, the first French-speaking town to do so. Fribourg's prosperity in the Middle Ages was based on manufacturing; affluent artisans were drawn

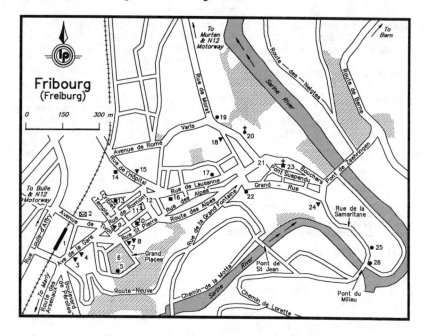

to the city and many of their Gothic houses still survive in the medieval town centre. Other main attractions are its churches and art galleries. The entrepreneur Georges Python was the founder of the Catholic university in 1889.

Orientation

Fribourg is the cantonal capital and has a population of 40,000. The Sarine River (Saane in German) winds its way through the centre of the city. It's a bilingual place; the inhabitants on the west bank of the river mostly speak French, and those on the east bank, German. Street names may differ dependent upon the language used; 4 Rue de Morat and Murtengasse 4, for example, are two versions of the same address. Both versions usually appear on street signs.

Much of the old town is on the west bank of the river, with the main focal point being the Cathedral of St Nicholas. The train station (Gare CFF) is conveniently central.

Leading from it is the shopping street, Ave de la Gare; this becomes Rue de Romont and opens out into the hub of the town, Place Georges-Python.

Information

The tourist information office (☎ 037-81 31 75), is at Square-des-Places 1, on Place Georges-Python. The opening hours are Monday to Friday from 8 am to noon and 2 to 6 pm, and Saturday from 9 am to noon (and 2 to 4 pm from May to September). It can help with room reservations, or visitors can make use of the information board and free telephone outside the station. The station also has money-exchange facilities every day from 6 am to 9.30 pm, plus storage lockers and bike rental.

The main post office (PTT) is close to the station on Ave de Tivoli, and the telephone code for Fribourg is 037.

SSR Voyages (☎ 22 61 61), the budget travel agency, is at Rue de Lausanne 35, open

■ PLACES TO STAY

5 Eurotel
10 Hotel Central
13 Hotel Elite
14 Youth Hostel
16 Hotel Faucon

▼ PLACES TO EAT

3 EPA Department Store
4 Café des Alpes
7 Migros Supermarket
8 Coop Supermarket &
    Department Store
9 Placette Department Store
15 La Chaumière
18 Hotel Musée
24 Auberge de Zaehringen

OTHER

1 Train Station
2 Post Office
6 Grand-Places
11 Tourist Office
12 Place Georges-Python
17 SSR Voyages (Travel Agency)
19 Museum of Art & History
20 Franciscan Church
21 Place de Notre-Dame
22 Town Hall
23 Cathedral of St Nicholas
25 La Spirate
26 Swiss Puppet Museum

Monday to Friday from 9.30 am to 12.30 pm and 1.30 to 6 pm.

Things to See

A walking tour of the old town centre is enlivened by several historic fountains, mostly constructed in the 16th century. They depict figures as varied as St George (outside the Town Hall), Sampson (Place de Notre-Dame) and Christ with the Samaritan woman (Rue de la Samaritane). These are copies; the originals are in the Museum of Art and History. There are a number of good spots for panoramic views of the town, particularly Grandes-Places, Chemin de Loret on the south of the river, and the two bridges, Pont de Zaehringen and Pont du Milieu. The latter

yields the classic view of the town that appears on many tourist posters.

Town Hall The 16th century Town Hall (Hôtel de Ville) features a clock tower and a fine double staircase. In front of the building is the **Morat Linden Tree**. According to folklore, this was planted in 1476 to celebrate the defeat of Charles the Bold at Murten (Morat). The messenger who conveyed the good news to the people of Fribourg promptly died of exhaustion immediately after uttering his announcement. As even the Swiss hadn't sorted out proper compensation for death or injury at work in those days, by way of scant recompense they planted the linden twig decorating his hat, and it was from this that the present tree grew. The messenger's journey from Murten is retraced in a popular race on the first Sunday in October.

Cathedral of St Nicholas Construction of this Gothic cathedral was started in 1283. Around the main portal is a representation of heaven and hell and the Last Judgement. Inside, notice the distinctive organ that took six years to build in the 19th century. The stained glass windows (by Mehoffer) are bright and lively, except those in the **Chapel of the Holy Sepulchre** near the entrance, where the blue and purple tones put together by Alfred Manessier in 1977 create a suitably sombre mood in which to view the sculptural group, *The Entombment* (1433). The 74-metre-high **Tower** (completed in 1490) affords a great view but it's only open from mid-June to the end of September (Sfr3, students and children Sfr1). Hours are 10 am to 5.30 pm daily, except lunch times and Sunday morning.

Franciscan Church This church (Église des Cordeliers) on Rue de Morat dates from the 13th century but was much modified 500 years later. On the right upon entering is an impressive wooden triptych which was carved and gilded around 1513. Yet what really grabs the attention is the **High Altar**, and above it the huge triptych painted in

1480 by two different anonymous artists, who signed their work by drawing a red and white carnation. The triptych depicts a crucifixion and other religious scenes.

Museum of Art & History The Musée d'Art et d'Histoire, Rue de Morat, has an excellent collection of late-Gothic sculpture and painting. It is housed in the Renaissance Hôtel Ratzé, with annexes in the former slaughterhouse and armoury. The underground corridors and rooms are atmospherically lit. Particularly effective is the cavernous chamber where religious statues are juxtaposed with moving sculptures that eerily combine animal skulls with rusted-metal machine components. These mobiles were constructed by Jean Tinguely (1925-91), who was born in Fribourg. Tinguely is also responsible for the mobile fountain in Grand-Places, but it's not as impressive as his similar effort in Basel.

Also look out for the wooden relief panels that were carved around 1600. These show biblical scenes in fantastic detail, especially the *Flight in Egypt* panel. The museum is open Tuesday to Sunday from 10 am to 5 pm, plus Thursday evening from 8 to 10 pm, and entry is free.

Other Museums The **Swiss Puppet Museum** (Musée Suisse de la Marionnette), is at Derrière-les Jardins 2, and entry costs Sfr4 (students Sfr3, children Sfr2). There is also a **Beer Museum** in the large brewery just south of the station entrance in Passage du Cardinal. Appointments must be made on (☎ 82 11 51).

Places to Stay
Camping The nearest *camping site* is five

A view from the Saane River (Fribourg)

km south of town in the village of Marly (☎ 037-46 30 60), overlooking a river. It is open from early April to the end of October. There's another site north of Fribourg by Lake Schiffenen, at Düdingen (☎ 037-43 19 17). This one is open year round.

Hostel The IYHF *youth hostel* (Auberge de la Jeunesse in French; ☎ 23 19 16) is at 2 Rue de l'Hôpital, in an off-white wing of a former hospital. Inside it is comfortable enough, with an adjoining self-service café area. Beds in the mostly six-bed dorms cost Sfr19 and the hostel is closed from 9 am to 5 pm. The curfew is at 10 pm.

Hotels The cheapest hotel in the centre is *Faucon* (☎ 22 13 17), 76 Rue de Lausanne. The walls in the rooms are a bit grubby, otherwise it is clean if functional. Prices vary depending upon the length of the stay. Rates start at Sfr60/110 for singles/doubles with private shower or Sfr50/90 without. Triples start at Sfr140. *Jura*, (☎ 26 32 28), 20 Route du Jura, a continuation of Rue de l'Hôpital, is west of the centre (take bus No 3). It has singles/doubles with use of hall shower for Sfr38/76.

Central (☎ 22 21 19), Rue St Pierre 3, has good-value rooms for Sfr60/90, all with private shower and toilet. These are often snapped up so telephone ahead. The restaurant offers a three-course midday menu for around Sfr13, and in the evening its taken over by drinkers.

Hotel Elite (☎ 22 38 36) at 7 Rue du Criblet, near Place Georges-Python, offers three-star comfort and parking facilities, and two bars. Singles/doubles with private shower and TV start at Sfr80/120. *Eurotel* (☎ 81 31 31) is the soaring block at Grand-Places 14. Prices start at Sfr115/200 in large, smart rooms. Parking costs Sfr16.

Places to Eat

The *EPA* department store opposite the station has lunch menus for Sfr9 with soup. Down the road, the *Placette* department store by Grand-Places, has a supermarket in the basement and a self-service restaurant on the

5th floor, with well-prepared dishes for around Sfr10 (open daily for lunch). Round the back on Rue St Pierre is a *Coop* self-service restaurant with menus for Sfr8.50 and Sfr11. Next door to that is a *Migros* supermarket. The youth hostel has a good self-service café which is open Monday to Friday from 9 am to 5 pm and dinners are Sfr9.50.

The restaurant in the *Hotel Musée*, Rue Pierre-Aeby 205, is a good place for fondues at around Sfr17. Grilled meats and salads are also served in this somewhat bare café environment (closed Sunday). Another place with a French feel is *Café des Alpes*, near the station at 20 Ave des Alpes. It has a fairly limited range of meals such as spaghetti (Sfr12), horse steak (Sfr16) and a lunch-time special (around Sfr14). It is closed on Sunday. The restaurant at the Eurotel (see Places to Stay) has a weekday three-course lunch menu for just Sfr16, and a vegetarian plate for Sfr12.50.

La Chaumière, 25 Rue de l'Hôpital, is decked out in fish nets and plastic fruit, but it's the place to head for decent Italian food from Sfr10.50 and meat and fish dishes for around Sfr25 (closed Sunday). The best restaurant in Fribourg is reckoned to be the *Auberge de Zaehringen* (☎ 22 42 36), at the intersection of Grand-Rue and Zaehringen bridge (Pont de Zaehringen) the restaurant is closed on Sunday evening and Monday. It specialises in expensive fish dishes. The *Buffet de la Gare* (☎ 22 28 16) on the 1st floor of the train station also has good quality food (closed on Sunday and mid-July to mid-August).

Entertainment

Fri-son (☎ 24 36 25), Route de la Fonderie 13, south of the station, is a young and lively music venue for rap, reggae, soul and house music. *La Spirale* (☎ 22 66 39), Petit St Jean, welcomes jazz and blues musicians.

Getting There & Away

Fribourg is on the north/south N12 (E27) which connects Lake Geneva to Bern and beyond. Trains run hourly to Neuchâtel (takes one hour), and even more frequently to Geneva (Sfr38, one hour 40 minutes) and Bern (Sfr9.80, 30 minutes). Interlaken Ost (takes two hours) is reached via Bern or Bulle. Buses are run by GFM and bear a green and orange stripe (Swiss Pass valid); they depart from the train station and go to nearby destinations such as Avenches and Bulle. A side trip to consider by bus is to Lake Schwarz.

A local car rental firm is Garage Lehmann (☎ 24 26 26), Ave Beauregard 16. Hertz (☎ 22 37 69) is at Rue de Locarno 6.

Getting Around
Walking is fine in the centre, although those hills can get a bit wearing. Bus tickets are Sfr1 to Sfr1.50 or it costs Sfr4.50 for a day pass. All the city bus lines stop by the station and Place Georges-Python.

ESTAVAYER-LE-LAC
Frogs are the unique attraction of this lakeside resort. They're all 130 years old and inside glass cases in the museum. Much of the medieval town centre looks like it has been preserved under glass too, because this is another of those Swiss towns that the ravages of time seems to have all but ignored.

Orientation & Information
The small train station has minimal facilities (bike rental but no lockers) and the ticket office is often shut. It's just outside the old centre; orient yourself using the map outside. The tourist office (☎ 037-63 12 37) is in a travel agent, Inter Voyages SA, by the Swiss Bank on Place du Midi. It's open Monday to Friday from 9 am to noon and 2 to 5 pm; in the summer, afternoon hours change to 3 to 6 pm.

Things to See & Do
François Perrier, an eccentric 19th century military man, spent much of his leisure hours killing frogs, preserving their skins, and filling them with sand. He would then arrange them in parodies of human situations, complete with props. The **Regional**

Museum displays 108 of his stuffed frogs engaged in courting, studying, playing games and much more. The result is halfway between the bizarre and the cute. Kids are fascinated by it. Less unusual museum exhibits include weapons and kitchen utensils, and a surprisingly extensive collection of railway lanterns and signs. Also notice the novel three-faces-in-one portraits on the right wall just before you go downstairs. It is open Tuesday to Saturday from 9 to 11 am and 2 to 5 pm between March and October and the same hours daily in July and August. The rest of the year it's only open Saturday and Sunday from 2 to 5 pm. Entry costs Sfr3 for adults, Sfr2 for senior citizens and students, and Sfr1 for children.

When you tire of amphibians you can get aquatic yourself in the pleasure boat harbour, or try water-skiing, windsurfing and sailing. The old Gothic centre is well worth a wander. The 13th century **castle** is well preserved and is now the home of the cantonal police. Also peek into the **St Laurent Church** for a look at the fresh stained-glass and the heavily barred altar.

Places to Stay & Eat
Camp at *Nouvelle Plage* (☎ 037-63 16 93), by the lake to the right of the harbour. It's open from mid-April to early October and costs Sfr4.20 per person and Sfr5 per tent; rates are slightly higher in July and August.

Hotel de Ville (☎ 037-63 12 62) is on the street of the same name in the centre. Rooms are good value and include use of hall showers. The price is Sfr35 per person in winter and Sfr40 in summer. There's a good quality restaurant on the first floor. Nearby at No 5 is the *Tea Room Carmen* where you can consume cheap snacks and pizzas. It closes at midnight from Tuesday to Saturday and 6.30 pm on Sunday. *Fleur de Lys* (☎ 037-63 12 37), Rue de la Gare 12, costs Sfr50 per person for rooms with private shower/toilet or Sfr40 using hall facilities. Breakfast is Sfr10 extra and taken downstairs in the *Sherlock Bar*, a busy place for a beer later in the day.

Café-Restaurant du Cerf, Grand Rue 11,

has pizza and pasta from Sfr10, good house specialities for around Sfr30 and other meat and fish dishes from Sfr19 (closed Monday). Also good is the *Gerbe d'Or*, Rue du Camus, opposite the Denner supermarket. This café-restaurant has a lunch-time special for Sfr14, except on Sunday when there's a three-course menu for Sfr25. Fondue is Sfr16.50 and other meat and fish dishes start at Sfr15. It closes on Sunday evening and Monday.

Getting There & Away

Estavayer-le-Lac is on the direct road and rail route between Fribourg and Yverdon, or it's a short detour off the northbound highway 1 (E4) from Lausanne. Estavayer is also a stop on boat services on Lake Neuchâtel. It takes 1½ hours to Neuchâtel and 1¼ hours to Yverdon, and there are around three departures a day from late May to late September except on Monday. Enquire at the tourist office or telephone Navigation Neuchâtel et Morat (☎ 038-25 40 12) in Neuchâtel for more information.

MURTEN (MORAT)

In May 1476, Charles the Bold (the Duke of Burgundy), still smarting from his recent defeat by the Swiss Confederates at Grandson, set off from Lausanne to lay siege on Murten. Two weeks after his arrival in the town the Swiss army arrived in force and trapped the Burgundians on the shore of the lake. The Duke fled with his life, but 8000 of his men were butchered or drowned.

Murten retains a strong sense of history and has much of its medieval fortifications still intact. The lake provides added attractions.

Orientation & Information

French speakers call this place Morat; German speakers call it Murten. You can take your pick as it's right on the linguistic divide. Most of the inhabitants speak German. It is on the eastern shore of Lake Murten (Lac de Morat, Murtensee) and Bern is 20 km to the east. The train station is 300 metres outside the city walls and has money-exchange daily to midnight and bike rental.

There's a map outside so you can orient yourself. The post office is opposite. The tourist office (☎ 037-71 51 12) is in the centre at Französische Kirchgasse 6 near the Bern Tower. In the winter (approximately October to March) it's open Monday to Friday from 9 am to noon and 2 to 5.30 pm. In the summer it's open to at least 6 pm plus Saturday morning. It has a useful booklet giving information on activities, excursions, and biking and hiking tours. Most hotels and restaurants close for part of the winter; the tourist office compiles a list.

The telephone code for Murten is 037.

Things to See & Do

Spend an hour or so roaming around the walled centre and admiring the ancient, arcaded houses. Dwellings in the centre were rebuilt in stone after being destroyed in a fire in 1416. The **castle** dates from the 13th century and offers a view of the lake from the courtyard. At the north-east end of Hauptgasse is the distinctive **Bern Tower**, also 13th century. The best view of the centre is from the city walls themselves. Ascend at the tower behind the German church on Deutsche Kirchgasse and walk around to the tower at Pfisterplatz, where you get the best view. The rows of brown-tiled roofs form an attractive arrangement from this elevated perspective. You could also stroll around Stadtgraben, a path circling the outside of the walls, where you might see locals toiling in their garden allotments beside the ancient fortifications.

Outside the walls near the castle is the **Historical Museum**, housed in the old water mill. In 1829 the dredging of the Broye canal and the drawing of the marshes caused a lowering of the lakes at the foot of the Jura. This uncovered evidence of ancient dwellings dating from 4000 BC, and these archaeological finds were just lying there for any wanderer to pick up. Fortunately, many found their way to this museum. In addition to these relics, there are various other oddities: a huge bullet that killed an elephant, dated and decorated leather fire buckets – a compulsory household utensil after the 1416 fire, and some surprisingly suggestive pewter council flagons (with an arm caressing the spout). Opening hours from May to September are Tuesday to Sunday from 10 am to noon and 2 to 5 pm. In the winter it's open the same hours in the afternoon only, except in January and February when it's open just on Sunday afternoon. Admission costs Sfr3 for adults, Sfr2 for students and senior citizens, and Sfr1 for children. Ask at the desk for the informative notes in English.

Lake Murten provides numerous recreational possibilities. The harbour is by the walled centre. Circular tours of the lake depart summer and winter. Contact the tourist office, the harbour (☎ 72 62 65) or the train station (☎ 71 26 46) for details. Fishing permits can be obtained from the Préfecture (☎ 71 22 57) in the castle. The beach (and a swimming pool) are near the Historical Museum. For the sailing school and boat hire contact Pierre Tschachtli (☎ 71 48 17). The windsurfing school (☎ 22 25 21) is at Marktgasse 27.

At the beginning of March, Murten celebrates its carnival, comprising three days of fun and parades. At the beginning of October there's the Murten-Fribourg race; up to 12,000 participants retrace the 17-km route of the messenger who relayed news of the Battle of Murten. Participants are not expected to re-enact the journey too faithfully – the man died upon arrival!

Avenches This village is eight km south of Morat along highway 1 (E4). It was built on the site of the old capital of the Helvetii, a Celtic tribe who were the first inhabitants of the region. Later it became a flourishing Roman town and reached the peak of its influence in the 1st and 2nd centuries. At this time its population was around 10 times greater than its present total of 2000. The town's defences – a high wall and ring of fortified observation towers – were not sufficient to prevent it being destroyed in 259 by the Germanic Alemanni tribe. Little remains of its former glory except a large amphitheatre (seating 12,000), a Roman Museum (closed Monday) and the occa-

sional turret. Ask the tourist office (☎ 75 11 59), in the town centre at Place de l'Eglise 3, for directions to outlying ruins.

Payerne If you're driving along the Lausanne-Murten highway 1, it's worth stopping off for a brief look at the 11th century Abbey Church in this small town, 10 km south of Avenches. The abbey itself is no more, but its Romanesque church has been extensively restored (open daily, entry Sfr3).

Places to Stay
Camping Löwenberg (☎ 71 37 30) is three km around the lake from Murten, beyond Muntelier (a five minute walk from Muntelier train station). It's open from Easter to the end of October and costs Sfr5 per person and Sfr4.50 for a tent.

There's an IYHF *youth hostel* (☎ 75 26 66) in nearby Avenches, Rue du Lavoir 5. Dorms cost Sfr16 and the hostel closes from December to February. It's situated about a 15-minute walk from Avenches train station; take Ave General Guisan and walk to the far south-west corner of the old centre (or take the bus to 'Cinéma').

The cheapest and possibly the best value choice in the centre is the small and welcoming *Hotel Ringmauer* (☎ 71 11 01), Deutsche Kirchgasse 2. Singles/doubles are Sfr50/90 with hall showers. *Hotel Krone* (☎ 71 52 52), Rathausgasse 5, has rooms from Sfr55/115 or Sfr75/120 with private shower. Next door is the *Hotel Murtenhof* (☎ 71 56 56) with good rooms from Sfr90/120, all with private facilities including TV. Most rooms have interesting decor with patches of old brickwork showing through the modern plaster (intentionally!). It also has some apartments from Sfr200. *Weisses Kreuz* (☎ 71 26 41), also on Rathausgasse, has rooms from Sfr85/140 decked out in a variety of styles, but they are always elegant. All these last three places have more expensive rooms overlooking the lake.

Places to Eat
There's a *Coop* supermarket with a restaurant on Bahnhofstrasse near the castle. It has

menus for around Sfr9 and is open Monday morning and Tuesday to Thursday until 6.30 pm, Friday until 8 pm, and Saturday to 4 pm. Other than that, it's probably best to stick to the hotels already mentioned. *Krone* is the best place to eat, if all the gastronomic plaques outside are to be believed. *Ringmauer* has a fairly limited but tempting choice of hot food from Sfr15.

Murtenhof has a good if pricey salad buffet (Sfr14 for a smallish plate) and views of the lake. There are special menus from Sfr14 and other dishes starting at Sfr15 (closed Monday). *Weisses Kreuz* is a bit more expensive and has many fish specialities (closed Sunday evening and Monday in low season).

Getting There & Away
There are hourly trains to/from Fribourg (Sfr9) and Bern (via Kerzers, Sfr10.80). Avenches (Sfr2.80) is just two stops and eight minutes away on the hourly train to Payerne, which is also on the route to Lausanne (Sfr24). Neuchâtel is just 30 minutes away (Sfr9.80).

Murten is on highway 1, which runs from Lausanne in the south and links with the motorway to Bern. Neuchâtel and Biel can be reached by boat on the 'three lake tour' in the summer; contact the harbour or the tourist office for details (see also the Biel section in the Bernese Mittelland chapter).

Getting Around
The centre is small enough for walking. Although cars can come into the centre and park on Rathausgasse and Hauptgasse, it's just as easy to park in the free spaces just outside the walls.

GRUYÈRES
This picturesque town attracts busloads of tourists with its fine 15th and 17th century houses and commanding castle. Visitors can catch the odd scent of cheese in the air, too.

Orientation & Information
Gruyères is on the western edge of the Pre-Alps in the canton of Fribourg. The small

train station will hold baggage behind the counter for Sfr1 per piece but opening hours are limited. The main village is a 10-minute walk up the hill. Buses and cars must be left in the free car park at the entrance to the village.

The tourist office (☎ 029-6 10 30) is in the middle of the main street in the chapel. It is open Monday to Friday from 8 am to noon and 1.30 to 5 pm, and additionally in July and August from 11 am to 4.30 pm on Saturday and Sunday. It changes money at only marginally worse rates than standard, a useful service as the sole bank is open just weekday afternoons in summer and Wednesday afternoon in winter. There are no street names in this tiny place.

Things to See
If you can avoid the tour buses, Gruyères is a great place to linger and enjoy the harmonious setting and relaxed atmosphere. The main street is extremely photogenic. The impact is immediate upon entering the village; you see the road dipping down to a central fountain, flanked on either side with fine old buildings with hanging signs, and all dominated in the distance by the rising turrets of the castle.

Castle The Château de Gruyères offers an expansive view from its 13th century ramparts. The dungeon is also 13th century but much of the rest of the castle dates from after the fire in 1493. It was the home of the Counts of Gruyères who held sway over the whole Sarine Valley from the 11th to the 16th century. Inside there are various items on display, such as ecclesiastical vestments (booty from the battle of Murten), tapestries, and period furniture. Look out for representations of the crane (grue in French), the heraldic emblem of the Counts of Gruyères. Allow an hour to get around, or more if there's a good temporary exhibition on the ground floor. The castle is open daily: 1 May to 30 September from 9 am to 6 pm, and the rest of the year from 9 am to noon and 1 pm to 4.30 pm (5 pm during March, April, May and October). Admission costs Sfr4 or Sfr2 for students and children.

Wax Museum The tiny Wax Museum is just off the main street, and recreates influential figures from Swiss history such as Henri Dunant (creator of the Red Cross). It is open limited hours in the summer only, and entry costs Sfr3 (Sfr2 for children and students).

Cheese-making Gruyère cheese is one of the best known of Swiss cheeses, and it's one of the main cheeses used in fondue. It takes nearly 12 litres of milk to make one kg of Gruyère and there are 12 different stages in the three-month production process. Two local dairies allow you to see cheese-making in action and try and buy the finished product. The most convenient is the dairy in Gruyères (☎ 029-6 14 10), opposite the train station, where the cheese is made into 'wheels' weighing 35 kg. It is open daily from 8 am to 6.30 pm but the best time to go is when the cheese is actually in production, from 9 to 11.30 am and 1 to 3.30 pm. The most active phase is when the cheese is pumped from the vat to the moulds, about 1½ hours after the start. The dairy gets through 13,000 litres of milk per day. There's a slide show and commentary in English that's informative but rather overstresses the 'harmony with nature' aspect (this has more to do with 'bull' than 'cow', despite the many references to the latter).

There's another dairy in a 17th century chalet in Moléson five km south-west of Gruyères. It is open 15 May to 15 October, every day from 9.30 am to 6.30 pm, but again you should try and visit during cheese production hours. Contact the Moléson tourist office (☎ 029-6 24 34) for information and reservations.

Places to Stay & Eat

There are only four small hotels in the centre of Gruyères so it's a good idea to book ahead. Don't even think of staying overnight if you're on a tight budget, unless you wish to camp at *Haute Gruyère* (☎ 029-6 22 60), five km south of Gruyères at Enney. The cheapest

place in the village is *Hôtel de Ville* (☎ 029-6 24 24) where all rooms have private shower/toilet and singles/doubles cost Sfr70/100 and triples/quads Sfr130/150. Also in the main street, *Fleur de Lys* (☎ 029-6 21 08) costs Sfr90/130 and *Hostellerie St Georges* (☎ 029-6 22 46) at least Sfr80/100. *Hostellerie des Chevaliers* (☎ 029-6 19 33), by the car park, is the biggest and classiest hotel and has a quality restaurant. Singles/doubles start at Sfr135/145.

Inevitably, cheesy creations figure strongly when contemplating a bite to eat. As well as looking at the hotel restaurants, try *Auberge de la Halle* which has pork specialities such as pig's trotters in madeira sauce (Sfr15.50) and big slabs of suckling pig (Sfr28). English menus are available. *Gruyères*, on the other side of the main road, serves the cheapest light meals: spaghetti bolognese for Sfr10, omelettes from Sfr8 and salads below Sfr9.50. It also has fondue (Sfr18), Raclette (Sfr22) and meat and fish dishes.

Getting There & Away

Bulle is the main transport hub for the Gruyère region. From Fribourg, Gruyères is reached by taking the hourly bus (Sfr12.40) or train (same prices) to Bulle and the train (Sfr3.40) or occasional bus from there. Buses depart from the train station in Fribourg, Bulle and Gruyères. Broc is also reached via Bulle, by train Sfr2.80. Gruyères can be reached without going via Bulle on the train from Montreux, changing at Montbovon (Sfr15, takes 1¼ hours).

The main road route is the north-south N12 (E27) motorway from Vevey to Fribourg and Bern, which passes by Bulle. There are also good roads heading south and east through the mountains from Gruyères and Broc.

AROUND GRUYÈRES

Bulle, five km to the north-west, has the Gruyère Region Museum (Musée Gruérien), with a reasonable collection including paintings, furniture, costumes, room interiors and animal dioramas. It is open Tuesday to Saturday from 10 am to noon and 2 to 5 pm, and Sunday and holidays in the afternoon only. Entry costs Sfr4. The town also has a 13th century castle. Broc, a couple of km north of Gruyères, is known mainly for the **Caillers Chocolate factory** (☎ 029-6 51 51). This factory could formerly be visited by guided tour, but the tours were stopped for reasons of hygiene. Nowadays you have to be content with a film presentation and free samples, and you need to phone first to make arrangements. It takes around 40 minutes and is available from early May to late October (except July), on weekdays except Monday morning.

A new attraction is **Electrobroc**, a power station and energy information centre, outside Broc by Lake Gruyère. Free tours (usually in French) are conducted on Saturday between March and December, and take two hours. For information, telephone ☎ 029-6 27 74.

Activities

Just north of Broc there is swimming in Lake Gruyère. In the Gruyère region there is some winter cross-country skiing, plus a few medium and easy downhill runs, particularly at Charmey and Moléson. The 2002-metre Moléson peak also yields a good panorama of the taller peaks further south. Signposted walking trails can be found everywhere, including on Moléson and on neighbouring Vudalla (1668 metres).

Geneva

Geneva (Genève in French) is Switzerland's third-largest city, comfortably encamped on the shores of Lake Geneva (Lac Léman). But Geneva belongs not so much to French-speaking Switzerland as to the whole world. Whether the problem is one of limiting superpower armaments or ethnic cleansing in Bosnia, the negotiators rush to the neutral territory of Geneva to try to seek common ground. It is truly an international city. One in three residents are non-Swiss and over 200 international organisations are based here. Among the most important are the European headquarters of the United Nations, the International Red Cross and the World Health Organisation.

For the administrators, secondment to Geneva must seem more like a holiday than hard work. The city enjoys a fine location. Strolls around the lake on a sunny day (and there are many of those) are hugely enjoyable, as are boat excursions. The cuisine is excellent and varied, and the same applies to the cultural diversions. Geneva is a city in pristine condition: it is clean, efficient and safe. Some say it is too successful in these respects, and complain the city is sterile. Some people wouldn't recognise a good thing if it waved a dozen flags and shouted in their ear.

History

Geneva was occupied successively by Romans and Burgundians and became a powerful bishopric from the 5th century. It was partially subservient to the Imperial Emperor, but that did not prevent the House of Savoy from making repeated attempts to gain control of the city, which was becoming increasingly affluent through its fairs and markets.

Under pressure from the Swiss Confederation, the Duke of Savoy agreed in 1530 to leave Geneva alone. A couple of years later the Reformation was introduced to the city by Guillaume Farel, who was followed and superseded by John Calvin. Calvin's teachings were so effective in Geneva that it became known as the 'Protestant Rome', a time of austerity in which fun became frowned upon. Corrupting habits like dancing and wearing jewels were actually forbidden (yet interestingly, around the same time the taking of interest on a loan was legalised). Such a repressive environment might be expected to deter visitors, but over the ensuing centuries, Geneva earned a reputation as an intellectual centre and attracted many free thinkers.

In the meantime Geneva had to put up with another incursion from Savoy. Led by the duke, Charles Emmanuel, an attempt was made to take the city on the night of 11 December 1602. An advance guard scaled the city walls with the intention of opening the gates and letting in the main force. The Savoyards were spotted by a sentry just in time, and the whole force was routed with the loss of only 18 Genevan lives. An event from this victory is commemorated in the annual Escalade festival (see the Festivals section later in this chapter).

After this success in 1602, Geneva had no further trouble with Savoy, but in 1798 the French annexed the city and held it for nearly 16 years. During this period it was the capital of the French Léman Department. Geneva was freed on 1 June 1814 and within a year it was admitted to the Swiss Confederation.

Orientation

Geneva and the small enclave of Swiss territory around the south-west lip of Lake Geneva constitutes both a separate canton and a distinct tourist region. The canton is home to 376,000 people, half of whom live within the confines of the city. The centre of the city hugs the shore of the lake and is split through the middle by the westward progress of the Rhône. Conveniently in the centre of town on the north side of the river is the main train station, Gare de Cornavin. To the south of the river lies the old part of town (vieille ville), with the pedestrian-only Grand Rue at its core. Most of the museums skirt the old section. East of the old town is Gare des Eaux-Vives, the rail head for trains running south-east into France.

You may come across locals referring to the two parts of the city as *rive droit* (right bank, ie north of the Rhône) and *rive gauche* (left bank, ie the south). Geneva's most visible landmark is the Jet d'Eau, a 140-metre-high fountain spouting water into the lake from a pier on the southern shore.

International organisations are mostly north of the station, and the main shopping area is around Rue du Rhône, on the south bank.

Unfortunately, the presence of so many businesspeople, bankers and diplomats means that prices for food and accommodation can be high.

Information

Tourist Offices The busy tourist office (☎ 022-738 52 00; see the Geneva Station Area map) is in the railway station, and is open Monday to Saturday from 9 am to 6 pm. From mid-June to mid-September, opening hours are extended and from Monday to Friday it's open from 8 am to 8 pm, and Saturday and Sunday from 8 am to 6 pm. Hotel reservations cost Sfr5.

The Centre d'Accueil et de Recontres (CAR) (☎ 022-731 46 47; see the Geneva Station Area map) has tourist and accommodation information. It is based in a yellow bus at the entrance to the Gare de Cornavin and is open daily between 8.30 am and 11 pm, but only between 15 June and 15 September.

Information on the city is also dispensed in the old town at Information de la Ville de Genève (☎ 022-311 99 70; see the Geneva Old Town map), 4 Place du Molard. It is open Tuesday to Friday from 12.30 to 6.30 pm and Saturday from 10.30 am to 4.30 pm. Counselling and information for young people is at Centre d'Information pour Jeunes (☎ 022-311 44 22), 13 Rue Verdaine, between 10 am and 10 pm (6 pm on weekends).

The best map of the city (with a street index) is the free one at the Swiss Bank Corporation (Société de Banque Suisse). There's a branch opposite the station.

Money Exchange counters in Gare de Cornavin are open daily from 6 am to 9.45 pm. Banque Migros at 16 Rue du Mont Blanc is open Monday to Friday from 8.30 to 6.30 pm, and Saturday from 8 am to 5 pm.

Post & Telecommunications There is a post office (☎ 022-739 24 58) by the Gare de Cornavin at Cornavin Dépôt, Genève 2, 16 Rue des Gares, 1211 Genève 2. Look for the yellow PTT signs. It is open Monday to Friday from 6 am to 10.45 pm, Saturday from 6 am to 8 pm, and Sunday from 9 am to 12.30 pm and 3 to 10 pm. There is another large post office at 18 Rue du Mont Blanc, 1211 Genève 1. It is open Monday to Friday from 7.30 am to 6 pm, and Saturday from 7.30 to 11 am. Both post offices will accept poste restante, but unless you specify the office, it will end up at Mont Blanc.

The post code for Geneva is 1201 and the telephone code is 022.

Consulates Among the foreign consulates in Geneva are:

Australia
    56-58 Rue de Moillebeau (☎ 734 62 00)
Canada
    1 Pré de la Bichette (☎ 733 90 00)
France
    11 Rue J Imbert Galliox (☎ 311 34 41)
Italy
    14 Rue Charles Galland.(☎ 346 47 44)
New Zealand
    28A Chemin du Petit-Saconnex; there is no full embassy in Switzerland (☎ 734 95 30)
UK
    37-39 Rue de Vermont (☎ 734 38 00)
USA
    1-3 Ave de la Paix (☎ 738 76 13)

Travel Agencies American Express (☎ 731 76 00; see the Geneva Station Area map) is at 7 Rue du Mont Blanc, open Monday to Friday from 8.30 am to 5.30 pm and Saturday from 9 am to noon. The student and

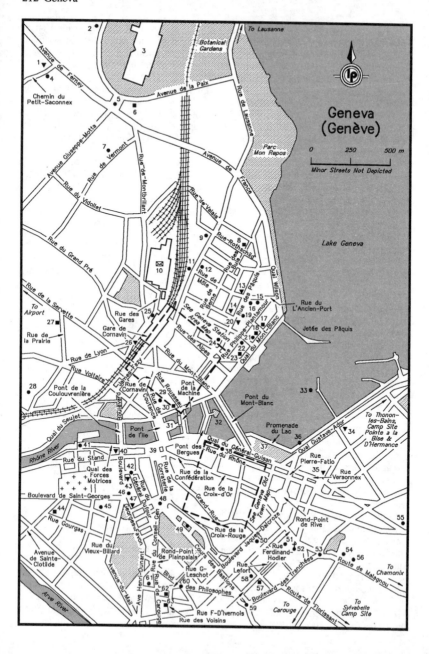

Geneva
(Genève)

0   250   500 m

Minor Streets Not Depicted

Lake Geneva

Rhône River

Arve River

	PLACES TO STAY		11	Budget (Car Rental)
			12	Avis (Car Rental)
6	Centre Masaryk		15	Edelweiss Manotel
8	IYHF Youth Hostel		16	Sixt Alsa (Car Rental)
17	Hôtel de la Cloche		19	Horizon Motos (Motorbikes)
18	Noga Hilton Hôtel		21	Casino
23	Hôtel Beau Rivage		22	American Library
27	Pension de la Servette		24	Permanence Médicale (Medical
30	Hôtel Ambassador			Centre)
44	Hôtel le Grenil		25	Place du Reculet
57	Hôtel Saint Victor		28	Voltaire Museum
62	Centre Universitaire Zofingen		29	Fruit & Vegetable Market
63	Hôtel le Prince		31	Tour d'Île
			32	Île Rousseau
	PLACES TO EAT		33	Jet d'Eau
			36	CGN Boat Station
1	Les Continents		37	Jardin Anglais
13	Migros Supermarket		38	Place du Lac
14	Le Blason		39	Place Bell Air
20	Auberge de Savièse		41	l'Usine
26	l'Oasis Bleu		42	Place de la Synagogue
34	l'Amiral		45	Le Bleu Nuit
35	Dent de Lion		46	Victoria Hall
40	Le Béarn		48	Place Neuve
43	Le Potager		49	Promenade des Bastions
47	Cave Valaisanne et Chalet Suisse			& Reformation Monument
			50	Museum of Art & History
	OTHER		51	Museum of Old Musical Instruments
			52	Russian Church
2	International Red Cross		53	Place Emile Guyénot
	& Red Cresent Museum		54	Museum of Natural History
3	Palais des Nations		55	Gare des Eaux Vives
4	New Zealand Consulate		56	Horology Museum
5	Place des Nations		58	Petit Palais
7	UK Consulate		59	Place Edouard Claparéde
9	Europcar (Car Rental)		60	Place des Philosophes
10	Post Office (Genéve 2)		61	SSR (Travel Agency)

budget travel agency SSR (☎ 617 58 11), 3 Rue Vignier, is open Monday to Friday from 9.30 am to 6 pm. Many other travel agents and airline offices are concentrated along Rue Chantepoulet and Rue du Mont Blanc.

Bookshops Elm Book Shop (☎ 736 09 45), 5 Rue Versonnex, sells English-language books and has lists of city restaurants. Librairie des Amateurs, 15 Grand Rue (see the Geneva Old Town map), sells second-hand books at around Sfr2 to Sfr4 for a paperback. The Book Worm (☎ 731 87 65), 5 Rue Sismondi, of Rue des Pâquis, also has second-hand English books. Artou (☎ 311 45 44), 8 Rue de Rive, is a good place for travel books.

Emergency Permanence Médicale is open 24 hours a day with branches at 21 Rue de Chantepoulet (☎ 731 21 20) and 7 Rue des Pâquis (☎ 731 21 80). The Cantonal Hospital (☎ 382 33 11) is at 24 Rue Micheli du Crest. Dental treatment (☎ 733 98 00) can be obtained between 7.30 am and 8 pm at 60 Ave Wendt.

Rosa Canina (☎ 738 66 66), 4 Rue de Môle, is a health centre for women. There's a rape hotline on ☎ 733 63 63. Ring ☎ 735 81 83 for a legal advice service.

The national emergency numbers can also be used: ☎ 117 for police, ☎ 118 for the fire brigade, ☎ 144 for an ambulance and ☎ 140 for the car breakdown service.

Gay & Lesbian Organisations An information line is run day and night by Dialogai (☎ 731 84 46). This organisation also publishes a guide to the gay scene in Switzerland, and runs a bar at 5 Rue Rossi, open from 8 pm (closed Monday and Tuesday).

Dangers & Annoyances On sunny days youngsters smoke dope in the Jardin Anglais and along the pier of the Jet d'Eau (some may consider this an opportunity rather than an annoyance). Like in most other Swiss cities, there's a growing problem with hard drug users; they tend to congregate between the Anglais Jardin and Place du Molard. It would be wise to exercise caution around this area at night.

Cultural Centres Numerous social and cultural organisations are listed in the free paper, *Guide to the English-speaking Community in Geneva*, available in the tourist office and some hotels. The American Library (☎ 732 80 97), 3 Rue de Monthoux, is a place to browse among stacks of English-language books. Radio 74 (88.8 MHz FM) broadcasts news from the BBC.

Laundry There's a self-service launderette open daily from 7 am to 10 pm at 29 Rue de Monthoux, just north of Place des Alpes.

Walking Tour

Take advantage of the recorded commentary available from the tourist office (Sfr50, refundable deposit) that details 26 points of interest in the old town (duration around 2½ hours).

A good starting point for a scenic walk is the **Île Rousseau**, spanning the Rhône. It is noted for a statue in honour of the celebrated free thinker, who formulated his seminal thoughts on democracy while, in his own words, a 'citizen of Geneva'.

Turn right along the south side of the Rhône until you reach the 13th century **Tour d'Île**, once part of the medieval city fortifications. Walk south down the narrow, cobbled Rue de la Cité until it becomes Grand Rue. On each side are a variety of interesting buildings, including Rousseau's birthplace at No 40. Grand Rue terminates at **Place du Bourg-de-Four**, the oldest square in Geneva. It was once a Roman forum, evolved into a medieval marketplace, and now has a fountain and touristy shops.

The centre of town is dominated by the partially Romanesque, partially Gothic, **Cathedral St Pierre** (Cathédrale de St Pierre). John Calvin preached here from 1536 to 1564; his seat outlasted him and can be seen in the north aisle. The body of the church still matches the austerity of Calvin's teaching in its lack of ostentation. This is in contrast to the small side chapel, first on the right after entering, with its ornate walls, windows and hanging light. Back in the main church, notice the aisle ceilings and the stained glass windows. There is a good view from the tower, which is open daily to 5.30 pm (entry Sfr2).

The cathedral is on an important archaeological site which is of only limited general appeal (entry Sfr5, students Sfr3, closed Monday), but there are some fine 4th century mosaics amid the crumbling foundations.

Nearby, the **Promenade des Bastions** is a pleasant park which contains a massive monument to the Reformation. The giant figures of Bèze, Calvin, Farel and Knox are flanked by smaller statues of other important figures and carved depictions of events instrumental in the spread of the movement. It was created in 1917. The scale is deceptively large; Calvin and his chums stand 4½ metres tall, and it is over 100 metres long.

Perhaps the best walk is along the shores of the lake. At weekends in the summer the water is alive with the bobbing white sails of sailing boats. On the lakefront near the old town, the **Jardin Anglais** features a large clock composed of flowers. Close by is the **Jet d'Eau**, the waters of which shoot up with

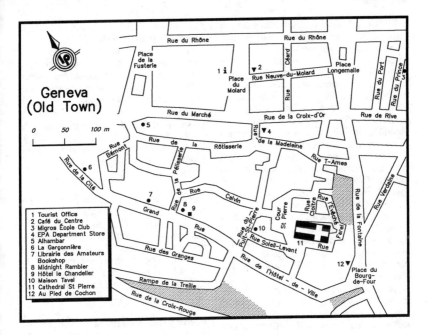

Geneva
(Old Town)

1 Tourist Office
2 Café du Centre
3 Migros École Club
4 EPA Department Store
5 Alhambar
6 La Garçonnière
7 Librairie des Amateurs Bookshop
8 Midnight Rambler
9 Hôtel le Chandelier
10 Maison Tavel
11 Cathedral St Pierre
12 Au Pied de Cochon

incredible force (200 km/h, 1360 horse-power) and, according to the whims of the wind, spray spectators who venture out on the pier. Colourful flower gardens and the occasional statue line the promenade on the north shore of the lake leading to two relaxing parks.

Well worth a visit is the **Botanical Gardens** (Jardin Botanique) which, among other attractions, features exotic plants, llamas and an aviary. Entry is free and it is open daily from 7 am to 7.30 pm. It is near the north of town, off Rue de Lausanne.

Museums & Galleries
Geneva is not a bad place to get stuck on a rainy day as there are plenty of museums, many of which are free.

Museum of Art & History The Musée d'Art et d'Histoire, 2 Rue Charles Galland is one of the most important museums. The vast and varied collection comprises some 500,000 items, including paintings, sculpture, room interiors, weapons and archaeology. A highly-prized exhibit is *La Pêche Miraculeuse* by Konrad Witz. It was painted as an altarpiece for the cathedral and shows fishermen distracted from tending their catch, looking on in awe and astonishment as Christ walks on the water. What is remarkable about the composition is that Witz transposed the scene onto Lake Geneva, and in the background you can see Genevan houses, Mont Blanc and the foothills of Mt Salève.

Elsewhere there is a room of paintings by Ferdinand Hodler, particularly showing Alpine scenes, and several important works by Quentin de la Tour. The museum is open Tuesday to Sunday from 10 am to 5 pm and entry is free.

International Red Cross & Red Crescent Museum The Musée International de la Croix-Rouge et du Croissant-Rouge, 17 Ave de la Paix, is a compelling multi-media trawl through atrocities perpetuated by humanity in recent history. The message is supposed to be one of hope (as proclaimed by the banner above the reception counter, 'Each person has a shared responsibility to humanity'), but the horrors etch deeper in the mind than the palliative. The carnage of the Battle of Solferino (1859) was the event that caused Henri Dunant, a businessman who witnessed the scene, to agitate for an international body to care for wounded soldiers. In 1863 the organisation that was to evolve into the International Committee of the Red Cross was formed, with Dunant as secretary and Henri Dufour as the first president.

The subsequent achievements of the Red Cross (and the Moslem adjunct, the Red Crescent) are well documented; but people keep fighting, as the films, photos, sculptures and soundtracks vividly illustrate. The scale of the problem is bought home in the section containing the records maintained by the Red Cross during WW II to keep track of prisoners. Row upon row of shelves store *seven million* index cards. Allow around 1½ hours to see the 11 areas of the museum, arranged in chronological order. Admission costs Sfr8 (Sfr4 for students and senior citizens, free for children under 12) and it is open Wednesday to Monday from 10 am to 5 pm. Buses 8 and F from Place de Cornavin drop you outside.

Petit Palais This compact gallery at 2 Terrace Saint Victor is expertly presented. The art sometimes encompasses the room decor in which the paintings and sculptures are displayed, creating a powerful overall effect. The gallery covers modern art, including Impressionist, Surrealist and Abstract works, and among the famous names represented are Picasso, Chagall, Renoir, Cézanne and Monet. The section on the Paris School is particularly good. It is a privately-owned gallery so unfortunately admission prices are high: Sfr 10 for adults, Sfr5 for senior citizens and Sfr3.50 for students (up to 25 years). It is open from Tuesday to Sunday

from 10 am to noon and 2 to 6 pm, and on Monday in the afternoons only.

While you're in the area, wander down Rue Lefort to look at the **Russian church**, with gold domes that shimmer from afar on a sunny day. The small interior is a clutter of marble and religious images.

Museum of Old Musical Instruments At 23 Rue Lefort, the Musée des Instruments Anciens de Musique can be both seen and heard (limited opening times; Sfr2, free for students).

Museum of Natural History The nearby Museum of Natural History (Musée d'Histoire Naturelle), 1 Route de Malagnou, has dioramas, minerals and anthropological displays. Living species are displayed in the aquarium and vivarium sections, but the dinosaurs, shown in the their natural environment, are not alive. Entry is free, and it's open Tuesday to Sunday from 10 am to 5 pm.

Horology Museum Down the road from the Museum of Natural History, at No 15, the Horology Museum (Musée de l'Horlogerie et de l'Emaillerie) hints at the importance of clocks and watches to the Genevan economy, and shows some fine examples of expertise in enamel on timepieces and other objects. It's free and open Wednesday to Monday from 10 am to 5 pm.

Maison Tavel The oldest private house in the old town, is Maison Tavel, at 6 Rue du Puits St-Pierre. It is notable for a detailed relief map of Geneva covering 35 sq metres that took the architect, August Magnin, 18 years to construct. The museum also gives a good account of life in Geneva from the 14th to the 19th century. Once again, entry is free, and it is open Tuesday to Sunday from 10 am to 5 pm.

Voltaire Museum Voltaire's residency in Geneva is celebrated in the Voltaire Museum at 25 Rue des Délices (admission free; open Monday to Friday from 2 to 5 pm).

United Nations

The Palais des Nations at the Place des Nations was once the headquarters of the defunct League of Nations. It is now the home of the offspring of that organisation, the United Nations (UN), and the focal point for a resident population of 3000 international civil servants. Fairly interesting but not essential is the hour-long tour of the interior, comparatively expensive at Sfr8 (students Sfr6). There is no charge to walk around the gardens. Among other attractions in the grounds is a towering grey monument coated with heat-resistant titanium, donated by the USSR to commemorate the conquest of space.

The gardens are open Monday to Friday from November to March and daily from April to October. Guided tours are from 10 am to noon and 2 to 4 pm, and from 9 am to noon and 2 to 6 pm during July and August. You need to show your passport to gain admittance.

Mont Salève Cable Car

A popular outing is the cable car up Mont Salève (1100 metres) for an excellent view of the city and Lake Geneva. Take bus No 8 to Veyrier and walk across the border into France. It's just a few minutes to the cable car which costs Sfr14.30 return, Sfr7.90 for students, and operates daily from May to September, Tuesday to Sunday during April, October and mid-November, and only weekends and holidays during winter (closed mid-November to mid-December). A trip to Mont Blanc is also viable – see the Valais chapter for transport details, or take an organised tour.

Courses

The Migros École Club (☎ 310 65 55; see the Geneva Old Town map), 3 Rue du Prince, has all sorts of courses taught in French (including language classes), and a few in English. From mid-July to early October the University of Geneva (☎ 705 71 11) has French language classes lasting three weeks.

Organised Tours

A two-hour bus tour of the city centre in English departs at 2 pm daily from the bus station at Place Dorcière. The price is Sfr23 and tickets are available on the bus or in advance from the tourist office. The tourist office has a leaflet detailing many other tours of city and regional attractions, including boat trips organised by CGN (see the Boat section in Getting There & Away in this chapter). Some of the land trips are organised by Key Tours (☎ 731 41 40), 7 Rue des Alpes. One of these is a day trip to Mont Blanc starting at Sfr120.

Activities

There are several sports centres in the city. Geneva Sports des Vernets (☎ 343 88 50), 4 Rue Hans Wilsdorf, has swimming (Sfr4) and ice skating and is open daily except Monday from 9 am. Swimming in the lake is possible at Genève Plage on the south shore and Jetée des Pâquis on the north shore.

Festivals

The celebration of l'**Escalade** on 11 December is Geneva's best known festival. In 1602, during Savoy's unsuccessful attempt to take Geneva, one of the Savoyard soldiers on the wall was repelled by a housewife, who poured her boiling soup over him, and proceeded to smash the cauldron over his head. This event has been adapted and is commemorated in the annual Escalade festival. In many Genevan homes, as part of the traditional celebrations, a chocolate cauldron is filled with marzipan which represents the vegetables of the soup. The cauldron is smashed by the youngest member of the family, and the cauldron and its contents are quickly consumed with un-Calvinistic eagerness.

As well as the ritual of the soup pot, there are torch-lit processions in historic costumes and a huge bonfire in the cathedral square. On the second weekend in August the **Fêtes de Genève** is a time of jollity, concerts and fireworks.

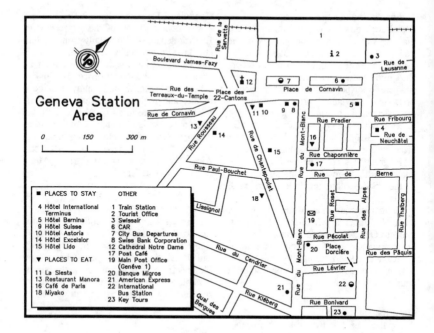

Geneva Station Area

0   150   300 m

■ PLACES TO STAY   OTHER

4 Hôtel International
  Terminus
5 Hôtel Bernina
9 Hôtel Suisse
10 Hôtel Astoria
14 Hôtel Excelsior
15 Hôtel Lido

▼ PLACES TO EAT

11 La Siesta
13 Restaurant Manora
16 Café de Paris
18 Miyako

1 Train Station
2 Tourist Office
3 Swissair
6 CAR
7 City Bus Departures
8 Swiss Bank Corporation
12 Cathedral Notre Dame
17 Post Café
19 Main Post Office
   (Genève 1)
20 Banque Migros
21 American Express
22 International
   Bus Station
23 Key Tours

Places to Stay

As befits an international city that receives many important visitors on unlimited expense accounts, there is no lack of high-class, high-cost hotels. Happily, the city also has an excellent selection of places offering dormitory accommodation, and various religious and university institutions have youth-oriented singles/doubles at low rates. These are listed in the *Young People Info* leaflet issued by the tourist office, which also gives out the comprehensive *Hotels* booklet. Outside the tourist office in the station is an accommodation board with a free telephone.

Places to Stay – bottom end

Camping The most central camp site is *Sylvabelle* (☎ 347 06 03), at 10 Chemin de Conches, south-east of town. Four-person bungalows are available and camping is Sfr4 per person, Sfr3 per tent and Sfr3 per car. It is open from 1 April to 31 October. To get

there, take bus No 8 from Gare de Cornavin or Rond-Point de Rive.

Seven km north-east of the city centre on the south side of the lake is *Camping Pointe a la Bise* (☎ 752 12 96), 1222 Vesenaz. It's open from 1 April to 30 September, and costs Sfr5 per person, tents from Sfr5. Take bus E from Rive de Rond-Pointe. Reception shuts at 10 pm. Seven km farther away from the city in the same direction and a five-minute walk from the last stop on bus E is *Camping D'Hermance* (☎ 751 14 83), Chemin des Glerrets. It is open from 1 April to 30 September and costs Sfr6 per person, Sfr2.50 per tent and Sfr0.50 for showers. People without tents are accepted, and there is free entry to the beach and free car parking outside the site. Reception shuts at midnight.

Camping du Val de l'Allondon (☎ 753 15 15), Route des Granges, Peissy Satigny, is 15 km west of the city centre and only accessible by private transport. It's open from 1

April to 30 October and charges are Sfr3.20 per person (Sfr4 in July and August), tent Sfr2, motorcycle Sfr1, car Sfr6 and parking Sfr2 (free outside the camp). There is a 20% reduction with a Camping Carnet. Reception shuts at 10 pm and facilities include a grocery shop on site.

Hostels This is only a small selection of the places listed in *Young People Info*. In particular, there are seven places not mentioned here that take women only.

North of the Rhône The IYHF *youth hostel* (or Auberge de Jeunesse; ☎ 732 62 60), 28-30 Rue Rothschild, is big, modern and busy, with helpful and knowledgeable staff. Dorms are Sfr18 and there are a few family rooms and doubles (Sfr66) for couples. Dinners are reasonable value (Sfr9.50), even if they are served with all the grace of a decapitated ballet dancer. A TV room, laundry and kitchen facilities are all available. The hostel is closed from 10 am to 5 pm (to 4 pm from 15 June to 15 September) and there is a midnight curfew. If you tire of eating at the hostel, try the cheap university café next door on the other side of Rue des Buis.

Centre Masaryk (☎ 733 07 72), 11 Ave de la Paix, has dorms for Sfr23.50 with an 11 pm curfew. Singles/doubles/triples cost Sfr36/62/87 and you can get your own key for late access. Breakfast is included. Get there by bus No 5 or 8 from Gare de Cornavin.

South of the Rhône Cité Universitaire (☎ 346 23 55), 46 Ave Miremont, has 500 beds available. Take bus No 3 from Cornavin to the terminus at Champel, south of the city centre. Dorms cost Sfr13 without breakfast. Rooms are subject to a three-night minimum stay: singles/doubles cost Sfr34/47 or Sfr28/41 for students, likewise without breakfast. A double studio with kitchen, toilet and shower costs Sfr56. Reception is open from 8 am to noon and 2 to 10 pm (but 6 pm on weekends).

Centre Universitaire Zofingen (☎ 329 11 40), 6 Rue des Voisins, has well-equipped rooms which are excellent value even if they are slightly cramped. Each room has a toilet, shower, sink and small cooker. Singles/doubles/triples are Sfr48/72/90 with breakfast included.

Budget Hotels Choice in this category is extremely limited, and at busy times you may be forced to move up or down-market.

North of the Rhône Hôtel de la Cloche (☎ 732 94 81), 6 Rue de la Cloche, is small, friendly, and liable to be full unless you call ahead. Singles/doubles without shower or breakfast start at Sfr40/65; breakfast and hall showers cost a couple of francs each.

Pension de la Servette (☎ 734 02 30), 31 Rue de la Prairie, is a touch old and dilapidated but the rooms are spacious enough. Singles/doubles/triples are Sfr35/50/75. Farther towards the airport, *Hôtel Luserna* (☎ 344 16 00), 12 Ave Luserna, has singles/doubles for Sfr46/70 and triples/quads for Sfr96/116. Take bus No 10 to Servette.

Hôtel Lido (☎ 731 55 30; see the Geneva Station Area map) 8 Rue de Chantepoulet, has decent-sized rooms compared to the Geneva average; genial staff, too. Singles/doubles with private shower, toilet, TV and radio start at Sfr70/120, and there are a couple of rooms for Sfr60/100 using hall shower.

South of the Rhône To get to *Hôtel Saint Victor* (☎ 346 17 18), 1 Rue Lefort, take bus No 8 or 3 from Cornavin. The entrance is opposite the hairdresser's shop at the far end of the square from the Russian church. It's convenient for the museums and is in a building that's a little bit past its prime. Singles/doubles are available from Sfr45/70.

Hôtel le Grenil (☎ 328 30 55) is at 7 Ave Sainte Clotilde. Singles/doubles are overpriced at Sfr90/120 using hall shower, but there are also triples/quads for Sfr126/140. Singles/doubles with private shower are Sfr110/140. Dormitory beds at Sfr25 are only for people 25 years old or less, and night owls will appreciate the reception being open 24 hours.

Hôtel le Prince (☎ 329 84 44/5), 16 Rue des Voisins, has comfortable if smallish rooms with TV, telephone and shower. Singles/doubles are Sfr75/95, or Sfr10 less using hall shower, and breakfast costs Sfr6. The restaurant is open Monday to Saturday from 7 pm to 10 pm and has meals from Sfr12 to Sfr20.

Places to Stay – middle

There's not much to choose between the tourist-class hotels clustered around the train station. The three-star *International Terminus* (☎ 732 80 95) is at 20 Rue des Alpes. Singles/doubles without shower are Sfr75/105, but these cheaper doubles are usually booked out by companies. Rooms with private shower cost around Sfr45 extra. *Bernina* (☎ 731 49 50), 22 Place de Cornavin, is comparable in price and quality.

Astoria (☎ 732 10 25), 6 Place de Cornavin, and *Excelsior* (☎ 732 09 45), 32 Rue Rousseau, both have reasonably comfortable singles/doubles with shower and toilet for around Sfr100/140. *Hotel Suisse* (☎ 732 66 30), 10 Place de Cornavin, is slightly nicer, with a swirling staircase and better appointed rooms, but it's also more expensive, starting at Sfr125/165.

Hôtel le Chandelier (☎ 311 56 88; see the Geneva Old Town map), 23 Grand Rue, has all the same amenities plus the added character of a 300-year-old building. Singles are Sfr80 to Sfr140, doubles Sfr130 to Sfr190, and it's Sfr30 for an extra bed. The more expensive rooms are very spacious. It's just inside the pedestrian area of the old town, so parking can be a bit of a problem.

Places to Stay – top end

Dozens of four and five-star hotels will allow you to spend a fortune on accommodation if you wish. Count on anything between Sfr100 to Sfr320 per person in four star and Sfr150 to Sfr420 in five star. The lobbies of some of these places are so plush that you feel practically naked if you're not wearing formal dress. One such place is the *Beau-*

Rivage (☎ 731 02 21), 13 Quai du Mont Blanc, an atmospheric 19th century hotel dripping with the opulence of the era. More modern but similarly lavish is the *Noga Hilton* (☎ 731 98 11), 19 Quai du Mont Blanc. It's slightly cheaper (singles/doubles from Sfr300/440) and has its own swimming pool. Both places have top-notch restaurants (see Places to Eat).

At the more affordable end of the scale and conveniently located is *Hotel Ambassador* (☎ 731 72 00), 21 Rive Droite. Prices start at Sfr135/190; the rooms are well fitted-out but not exactly overflowing with space. Breakfast is Sfr13 extra and parking costs Sfr16 for 24 hours.

Places to Eat

Geneva is the cuisine capital of Switzerland. There is a staggering choice in styles and regional specialities. All price ranges are catered for, but as with hotels, getting what you want is easier if you have more money to spend. Eating is generally cheaper north or west of Gare de Cornavin, or south of the old town in the vicinity of the university. The whole range of restaurants are listed in the Genève *Restaurants* booklet, given out free of charge at the tourist office.

Fondue and Raclette are widely available. Also popular is locally-caught perch, which typically costs upwards of Sfr20 unless you can find it as a plat du jour. There is a small fruit-and-vegetable market open daily (except Sunday) on Rue de Coutance.

Self-Service The *Migros* supermarket on the corner of Rue des Pâquis and Rue du Môle has a self-service restaurant. Numerous other Migros and Coop restaurants are listed in the back of the Genève Restaurant booklet. For cheap eating in the old town, make for the restaurant in the *EPA* department store on Rue de la Croix d'Or, opposite Place du Molard. Meals are Sfr8 to Sfr10.

Restaurant Manora, 4 Rue de Cornavin (see the Geneva Station Area Map), is a buffet-style restaurant with tasty daily dishes from Sfr10 and an extensive salad bar. Always popular, it is open daily to 9 pm.

North of the Rhône *La Siesta* is opposite and to the right of the station on the corner of Place de Cornavin and Rue de Chantepoulet. It has a good range of Italian (Sfr8 to Sfr13) and local (Sfr12 to Sfr26) dishes, and a lunch-time plat du jour for Sfr12.50. Opening hours for hot food are 11.30 am to 11.30 pm every day. Around the back of the station is *l'Oasis Bleu*, 4 Place de Montbrillant, a café open daily from 9 am to midnight. It's ideal for a quick chomp between trains, or for more leisurely consumption of snacks, Mediterranean food and vegetarian specialities. Main meals are Sfr14 to Sfr20.

Two informal bistro-style restaurants face each other on Rue des Pâquis. *Le Blason* (☎ 731 91 73) at No 23 has plats du jour for Sfr12 and Sfr14 and a wide selection of salads. It is open Monday to Friday from noon to 11 pm. *Auberge de Savièse* (☎ 732 83 30) at No 20 has lunch-time plats du jour from Sfr13, and Swiss specialities such as fondue from Sfr16.50. Opening hours are Monday to Friday from 8.30 am to midnight, and Saturday from 5.30 pm to midnight.

Café de Paris (☎ 732 84 50; see the Geneva Station Area map), 26 Rue du Mont Blanc, serves up one dish only – succulent entrecôte steak with a special herb and butter sauce, chips and salad (Sfr29.50). It's well-established and very busy, and the harassed table servers can be a bit abrupt at times (open daily until 11 pm).

Take advantage of the international flavour of Geneva to vary your diet. Rue Chaponnière, off Rue du Mont Blanc, is a good street to explore for cheapish Mexican, Chinese and Oriental food. *Miyako* (☎ 738 01 20), 11 Rue de Chantepoulet, is expensive but the quality is excellent. This Japanese restaurant has three-course business lunches for Sfr23 to Sfr35, and a full evening meal will cost around Sfr50.

South of the Rhône The very cheap *Le Zofage* restaurant, downstairs in the Centre Universitaire Zofingen (see Places to Stay), has a choice of plats du jour for Sfr 950 (Sfr8 for students) and is open daily from 7 am to

midnight. *Café du Centre* (☎ 311 85 86; see the Geneva Old Town map), 5 Place du Molard, has outside seating in a pleasant square near the old town. Office staff relax here after work over a coffee or a beer. The lunch-time plat du jour costs around Sfr14 and the café is open daily from 6 am to 2 am. *Le Potager* (☎ 311 75 24), 2 Place de la Synagogue, has plats du jour from Sfr14. It specialises in creative salad concoctions and is closed on Sunday.

Dent de Lion, 25 Rue des Eaux-Vives , is a café with background classical music, a healthy aura (non-alcoholic) and large platefuls. Vegetarian dishes are around Sfr15, and there is a lunch-time plat du jour (Sfr14) and three-course menu (Sfr20). It is open Monday to Friday from 10 am to 2.30 pm and 6 to 10 pm, and is situated right next to the Rue de Lac trolley bus stop (Nos 7 and 2). A self-service branch has recently opened at No 14.

Au Pied de Cochon (☎ 310 47 97; see the Geneva Old Town map), 4 Place du Bourg-de-Four, specialises, as the name suggests, in pig's trotters. These appear in several styles and sauces (from Sfr20), and there are various other porcine products to choose. The weekday lunch menu costs Sfr14.50, and it is open daily.

The large and popular *Cave Valaisanne et Chalet Suisse* (☎ 28 12 36) is at 23 Blvd Georges-Favon. It's an excellent place to try fondue (starting at Sfr16.90); the scent of bubbling cheese inside could give a mouse palpitations at 20 paces. It's open from 7 am to 1 am daily.

Another good place for those with slightly larger budgets is *l'Amiral* (☎ 735 18 08), 24 Quai Gustave Ador, near the Jet d'Eau. Try the fillets of perch here.

Expensive Restaurants Reserve ahead for all these places. *Le Béarn* (☎ 321 00 28), 4 Quai de la Poste, is arguably the best restaurant in Geneva. It serves sumptuous fish specialities and creative cuisine. The restaurant is closed weekends (except Saturday evening in summer) and from mid-July to late August. Close on its heels is *Le Cygne*

(☎ 731 98 11) in the Noga Hilton hotel, 19 Quai du Mont Blanc. The cooking is French-style; main course are in the Sfr35 to Sfr70 price range and there are over 400 different wines on the wine list. It is open daily.

Also very highly rated are *Le Chat Botté* (☎ 731 65 32) in Hotel Beau-Rivage, 13 Quai du Mont-Blanc (closed weekends), and *Les Continents* (734 60 91) in the Hotel Intercontinental, 7-9 Chemin du Petit Saconnex (closed Sunday evening and Saturday).

If you make it to Carouge, try *La Casolette* (☎ 342 03 18), 31 Rue Jaques-Dalphin, near Place de Sardaigne (closed weekends), and *Auberge de Pinchat* (☎ 342 30 77), 33 Chemin Pinchat. Carouge, which was formerly a separate town, is a southern suburb and is reached by tram No 12 from Place Bell Air.

Entertainment

Different genres of music are covered in various festivals through the year. The monthly *Spectacles and Manifestations* leaflet from the tourist office covers classical concerts, opera, theatre, dance, spectator sports and exhibitions. Geneva is the home of the Orchestra of the Swiss Romande; it and other orchestras often perform at the Victoria Hall, 14 Rue du Général Dufour. English-speaking theatre thrives in Geneva on an amateur level. Contact Theatre in English (☎ 301 06 08) for information and tickets. In cinemas, films usually retain their original soundtrack: look for V.O. (version original) to make sure.

Geneva has a good selection of nightclubs but they are expensive. Popular with the money-to-burn brigade are *Arthur's* (☎ 788 16 00), 20 Route de Pré Bois, and *Le Milliardaire* (☎ 788 21 22), 26 Voie de Moëns. *Midnight Rambler* (☎ 311 70 09), 21 Grand Rue, has alternating theme evenings ranging from Gothic and rock to soul and rap.

The main place for alternative arts and highly recommended is *l'Usine* (☎ 781 34 90), 4 Place de Volontaires. A converted old factory, it is now a centre for cinema, cabaret, theatre, concerts and impromptu art objects. It has a good restaurant with menus for Sfr10, Sfr12 and Sfr14 which are available daily from noon to 2 pm and from 7.30 to 10.30 pm. There is also a cheap bar open to 2 am, with beer at around Sfr3.50 for half a litre. Look out also for the semi-legal squats in the city. Some, like the *Cave Douze*, 24 Blvd des Philosophes, are really getting their act together in terms of organising musical and arts events.

Au Chat Noir (☎ 343 49 98), 13 Rue Vautier, Carouge, is a jazz and rock club with interesting murals and music every night. In a similar vein is *Alhambar* (☎ 312 30 11; see the Geneva Old Town map), on the 1st floor of the Alhambra cinema, 10 Rue de la Rôtisserie. There is a lunch-time plat du jour (Sfr12) and food in the evenings. The place is open from Tuesday to Sunday until midnight or later.

A lively bar and café is *Le Bleu Nuit* (☎ 328 34 44), 4 Rue des Vieux Billard. Lunch and evening plats du jour are Sfr13 and Sfr14. Open from 7 am weekdays and 6 pm weekends, it closes around 1 am or later. A good British/Irish meeting place is *Post Café*, 7 Rue de Berne. It's the only place in town with draught cider.

La Garçonnière (☎ 310 21 61; see the Geneva Old Town map), 22 Place Bémont, 15 Rue de la Cité, is a mainly gay bar and disco, although many heterosexuals turn up for the transvestite shows on Friday and Saturday. It's open daily from 10 pm to 4 am. Popular with younger gay people is the bar and disco *Le Musicol*, 5 Rue Richemont. (open daily). It plays house music and has light shows. *Le 1900* 6 Rue Pradier has two bars – one 'straight' and one for lesbians (look for the red lights). It's open daily except Sunday from 9 pm to 2 am and it gets very busy on Friday and Saturday.

The *Casino* at 19 Quai du Mont-Blanc is open daily from noon. Go there to play Boule (the tame Swiss version of roulette) slot machines, and to dance after 9 pm. Folklore shows are not to everybody's taste, but *Edelweiss Manotel* (☎ 731 36 58), 2 Place de la Navigation, believes it has a 'genuine Alpine village in downtown Geneva'. Students of kitsch may want to see for themselves; a meal with the show costs around Sfr30 to Sfr50.

Things to Buy

Geneva is well known as a place to buy watches, jewellery and enamel work. Less expensively, there are several places on Rue Mont Blanc with a good selection of Swiss knives. Various shops, such as the one opposite the Jardin Anglais, sell folklorish things.

Getting There & Away

Air Ceneva airport is an important transport hub and has frequent connections to every major city. Youth-fare bargains are possible on Swissair but there are usually purchasing and validity restrictions. The one-way fare for people aged 24 years or less to Amsterdam is Sfr262 (buy within a week of departure) and to Zürich is Sfr110 (buy anytime). Enquire at the Swissair office (☎ 799 59 99; see the Geneva Station Area map) just to the left of Gare de Cornavin on Rue de Lausanne, open Monday to Friday from 8.30 am to 6 pm. Fares may be higher depending on the time of year.

Swissair is the booking agent for Crossair, which flies daily at least six times to Lugano, twice to Basel and a dozen times to Zürich. Internal flights are expensive.

Train TGV trains depart five or six times a day to Paris-Lyon (Sfr78), and the journey takes 3½ hours. Reservations are essential and cost Sfr4 to Sfr19 (Sfr4 to Sfr24 in 1st class) depending upon the time and day of travel. There are also regular international trains to Hamburg (Sfr246), Milan (Sfr75) and Barcelona (Sfr100).

There are more-or-less hourly connections to most Swiss towns. To Zürich via Bern takes 3½ hours and costs Sfr68. To Interlaken Ost takes three hours and 20 minutes by fast train (Sfr58), also via Bern. Gare des Eaux-Vives is the station for Annecy and Chamonix. To get there from Gare de Cornavin, take bus Nos 8 or 1 to Rond-Point de Rive and then tram No 12.

Bus International buses depart from the Gare Routière (☎ 732 02 30; see the Geneva Station Area map) on Place Dorcière off Rue des Alpes. There are three buses a week to both London (Sfr150) and Barcelona (Sfr99). There are several buses a day to Chamonix (Sfr30).

Car & Motorbike Lyons is 130 km by motorway to the west. The N1/E4 from Lausanne and the north, and the E21 from the southeast, also lead directly into Geneva. Toll-free main roads follow the course of these motorways. A new autoroute bypass around Geneva has recently opened. It takes drivers through the Rhône Valley to the Riveria.

Car Rental Sixt-Alsa (☎ 738 13 13), 1 Place de la Navigation, offers one-way car rentals to Zürich (see the Getting Around chapter for rates). Slightly cheaper on weekend deals is Léman (☎ 732 01 43), nearby at 6 Rue Jean-Charles Amat. Europcar (☎ 731 51 50), is at 65 Rue de Lausanne, and has a branch (☎ 798 11 10) in the airport arrivals hall. Hertz (☎ 343 79 20), 21 Rue Eugène Marziano, Avis (☎ 731 90 00), 44 Rue de Lausanne, and Budget (☎ 732 52 52), 37 Rue de Lausanne, also all have an airport branch.

Horizon Motos (☎ 731 23 39), 22 Rue des Pâquis, rents motorbikes ranging from 125 cc to 1200 cc, and weekend rates (unlimited mileage) are Sfr110 to Sfr480. Monthly rates are very reasonable; a 500 cc machine would cost Sfr1740 with unlimited mileage.

Boat Compagnie Générale de Navigation (CGN) (☎ 311 25 21) by the Jardin Anglais operates a steamer service to all towns and major villages bordering Lake Geneva, including those in France. Most boats only operate between May and September, such as those to Lausanne-Ouchy (3½ hours, Sfr27 one-way or Sfr43 return) and Montreux (4½ hours, Sfr32 one-way or Sfr51 return). CGN also has excursions on the lake lasting one hour (Sfr19) and two hours (Sfr26), operating from the end of March to the end of September. Both Eurail and Swiss railpasses are valid on these trips.

A CGN one-day pass costs Sfr43 (Sfr58 in 1st class).

Another option is the Swiss Boat Pass (Sfr35); it's valid for one year and gets 50% off fares by the major carriers on all Swiss lakes.

Getting Around
To/From the Airport Getting from Cointrin Airport couldn't be easier. There are 100 trains a day into Gare de Cornavin. The trip takes six minutes and costs Sfr4. Alternatively, take bus No 10 to Gare de Cornavin for Sfr2.

Bus A combination of buses, trolley buses and trams makes getting around just as easy. There are ticket dispensers at bus stops. A ticket for multiple rides within one hour costs Sfr2, a book of six such tickets costs Sfr11, and a book of 12 tickets costs Sfr20. Day passes are also available for the city and canton network. One, two or three-day passes cost Sfr8.50, Sfr15 or Sfr19. Passes are available from the tourist office or from Transports Publics Genevois at the lower level of Gare de Cornavin (by the yellow escalators) or at Rond-Point de Rive.

Taxi The cost for taxis is Sfr5 per person plus Sfr2.50 per km. Get one by the station or ring ☎ 141.

Bicycle The bike rental office at Gare de Cornavin is open daily from 6.20 am to 8 pm. It has a leaflet showing cycle routes in and around the city.

Boat In addition to CGN smaller companies operate excursions on the lake between April and October but no passes are valid. Ticket offices and departures are along Quai du Mont Blanc in front of the Grand Casino. Trips range from half an hour (Sfr10 several departures a day) to two hours (Sfr25), with commentary in English.

Is Mountain Air Good for the Brain?
Switzerland has won more Nobel Prizes (and also makes more patent applications) per capita than anywhere else. To date there have been 19 winners – not including awards to Swiss firms or Swiss people resident abroad.

The first winner was Jean Henri Dunant in 1901, founder of the International Red Cross. No prizes for guessing it was the Peace Prize he won (the first ever). In the following year, peace campaigners Elie Ducommun and Charles Albert Gobat won the same prize. Hermann Hesse won the Nobel Prize for Literature in 1946 for *The Glass-Bead Game*, an award previously won by Carl Spitteler in 1919.

Most awards have been won in the field of Physiology and Medicine, with successes for Theodor Kocker (1909), Paul Müller (1948), Walter Hess (1949), Tadeus Reichstein (1950), Daniel Bovet (1957) and Werner Arber (1979).

Chemists have also done well, with five winners. Alfred Werner won in 1913 for his formulation of the coordination theory of valency. Also successful were Paul Karrer (1937), Leopold Ruzicka (1939), Vladimir Prelog (1975) and Richard Ernst (1991). Physicists have netted three awards: Wolfgang Pauli for his work on atomic structure (1945), and more recently, Heinrich Rohrer (1986) and Alexander Müller (1987). ■

Top: Leysin ski area, Vaud (JL)
Bottom Left: Russian Church, Geneva (MH)
Bottom Right: Reformation Monument, Geneva (MH)

Top Left: Matterhorn, Valais (MH)
Top Right: Homes and barns, Hinter Dorf, Zermatt, Valais (MH)
Bottom: Parade participants, Brig, Valais (MH)

Vaud (Lake Geneva Region)

The tourist area known as the Lake Geneva Region comprises the canton of Vaud (pronounced Voh, Waadt in German). In the 1980s the tourist authorities decided they wanted to establish a separate identity for the region, instead of simply being viewed as a mere adjunct to Geneva and the lake. Consequently, they renamed the tourist region after the canton. But then they had a new problem. Previously the territory was easily located on the mental map of most visitors to Switzerland, but few people confronted with the name 'Vaud' had any idea where or what it was. Finally in 1993 those responsible for Vaud tourism marketing accepted the inevitable, and the area again became known as the Lake Geneva Region, or Région du Léman in French.

The canton of Vaud covers the area south of the cantons of Neuchâtel and Fribourg; in

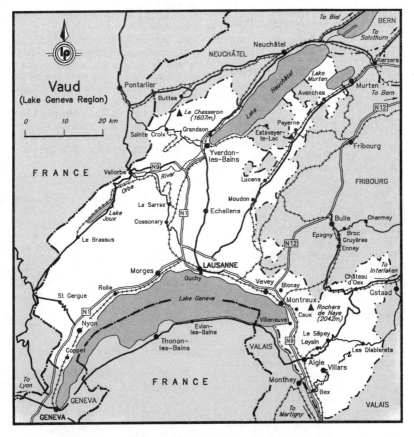

fact, not to overstress the point, the region around Lake Geneva (Lac Léman). It is the towns on the shores of Lake Geneva that provide the most compelling reasons to visit the canton. If you see nothing else, at least make it to the l'art Brut collection in Lausanne and the Château de Chillon outside Montreux.

Vaud is well-known for its wines. A tour of the nearby wine-growers' cellars (caveaux des vignerons) is easy if you have your own transport. The communities bordering the lake to the west and the east produce wines with their own distinctive flavours, and these are discussed in the vineyard guide from the tourist office. A different tourist office booklet details the opening times of the cellars.

History

In 1229 Vaud became a vassal territory of Savoy. In 1536 Bern declared war on Savoy and successfully took over the region. As Bern had an existing treaty of fellowship signed with Lausanne, the people of Vaud naturally thought this might result in them gaining more autonomy. But Bern thought different; it installed a bailiff in the bishop's castle in Lausanne and proceeded to siphon off the city's wealth.

The situation was endured until January 1798 when Fréderic César de la Harpe, leader of the Libèral Party, declared Lausanne and Vaud independent under the title of the Lemanic Republic. Not surprisingly, Bern did not wholly go along with this assertion but the matter was settled in 1803 by Napoleon in his Act of Mediation, in which Vaud became an independent canton within the Swiss Confederation, and Lausanne was installed as the capital.

Orientation & Information

Vaud is almost exclusively French-speaking, and encompasses the three main geographical regions of Switzerland: the Jura Mountains in the west, the relatively flat plain of the Mittelland, and a section of the Alps south-east of Montreux.

The regional tourist office (☎ 021-617 72

02) is at 60 Ave d'Ouchy, CH-1000, Ouchy, Lausanne. Opening times are Monday to Friday from 8 am to noon and 1.30 to 5.30 pm. It gives out the detailed *Guide Touristique Canton de Vaud* which is in three languages, including English, and sells for Sfr5 a good map of the canton showing different walking routes accompanied by a brief description (in French). It also has a couple of guides to vineyards in the Vaud.

For information on Avenches and Payerne see Murten in the Neuchâtel, Fribourg & Jura chapter.

Getting Around

There are two regional transport passes that cover part of the canton and overlap to a small degree. The Montreux/Vevey Region pass gives free travel on three days in seven around the eastern half of Lake Geneva (including boat rides to French resorts) and on buses and trains on routes extending to Gruyères, Château d'Oex, and Gstaad, among other places. These trips get a 50% reduction on the other four days, and there are other routes (as far apart as Geneva and Interlaken) that get 50% off on the whole seven days.

The price is Sfr73 (Sfr58 if already holding a Swiss railpass) or Sfr86 (Sfr69) in first class. The other pass covers a smaller area, the Chablais Region to the south-east of Lake Geneva, and extends to parts of the Vaud Alps. It has the same rules as the Montreux/Vevey pass regarding three days travel in seven and routes at 50% reduction, and costs Sfr50 in second class only, or Sfr40 for holders of a Swiss railpass. The passes are only issued from 1 April to 31 October.

Lausanne

This hilly city is Switzerland's fifth-largest, with 127,000 inhabitants. It enjoys a thriving arts scene, as well as offering a fine cathedral, Alpine scenery and water sports. Lausanne also has one of Europe's most unusual art collections, which should on no account be missed.

The Romans used to have a military camp called Lousonna, on the shores of the lake at Vidy. This was an important stop on the route from Italy to Gaul, via the St Bernard Pass. With the invasion of the Alemanni, the inhabitants abandoned this settlement and joined the people who had settled on the site of the present old city. The commercial and religious importance of Lausanne began to develop hand-in-hand, helped by its first bishop, St Marius, who was previously based in Aventicum and came to live in the city in the 6th century. The Reformation arrived in 1529, thanks to the preaching of Guillaume Farel, a cohort of Calvin. But the conversion wasn't underlined until the invading forces from Bern took over the city in 1536 and proceeded to ransack the Catholic churches.

Lausanne flourished in the following centuries despite its period of subservience to Bern, and welcomed important literary figures such as Voltaire, Dickens, Byron and T S Eliot (who wrote *The Waste Land* here). The city retains a fair measure of status; it is the location of the Federal Tribunal, the highest court in the country, and has been the headquarters of the International Olympic Committee since 1915.

Orientation

The old town and its winding streets, topped by the cathedral, is above and north of the train station. Place St François is the main hub for local transport, and leading off it is Rue de Bourg, the main shopping street. Just west of Place St François is Flon, an intriguing area where formerly derelict warehouses have been taken over by art galleries, trendy shops and restaurants. The city has grown to include the former fishing village of Ouchy, now a picturesque harbour sporting a cluster of hotels.

Information

Tourist Offices There is a tourist office in the train station, open daily between 1 May and 30 June from 2 to 8 pm, between 1 July to 15 October from 10 am to 9 pm, and

between 16 October and 30 April from 3 to 7 pm. The main tourist office (☎ 021-617 73 21), 2 Ave de Rhodanie, is by the harbour in Ouchy. Opening hours are: Easter to mid-October, Monday to Saturday from 8 am to 7 pm, and Sunday from 9 am to noon and 1 to 6 pm; mid-October to Easter, Monday to Friday from 8 am to 6 pm, and Saturday from 8.30 am to 12.15 pm and 1.15 to 5 pm. Pick up a free copy of the excellent *Lausanne Official Guide*, which lists everything from consulates to local walking tours.

The tourist office for the canton de Vaud is also in Ouchy: see the introduction to this chapter.

Consulates The French Consulate (☎ 021-311 41 91), 30 Ave Ruchonnet, is open on weekdays and the Italian Consulate (☎ 021-20 12 91), 12-14 Rue Centrale, is open from Tuesday to Saturday morning.

Train Station The main station (Gare CFF) has luggage lockers (Sfr2 and Sfr3), and a train information office (☎ 320 80 71) open daily from 7 am to 8.45 pm. Money-exchange counters are open from 6.10 am to 8.50 pm weekdays, and 6.10 am to 7.50 pm on weekends. Bicycle rental in the station is open from 6.30 am to 10.30 pm every day.

Post & Telecommunications The large post office at 15 Place St François is open Monday to Friday from 7.30 am to 6 pm and Saturday from 7.30 to 11 am; telephone, telex and fax services are open to 7 pm weekdays and 4 pm on Saturday. The other main post office, by the station at 43 Ave de la Gare, has an emergency counter open daily.

The telephone code for Lausanne is 021.

Travel Agencies SSR (☎ 617 58 11), the specialist student travel agency, is at 20 Blvd de Grancy, open Monday to Friday from 9.30 am to 5.30 pm. American Express (☎ 320 74 25), is at 14 Ave Mon Repos. Swissair (☎ 320 50 11) has an office at 4 Rue du Grand Chêne.

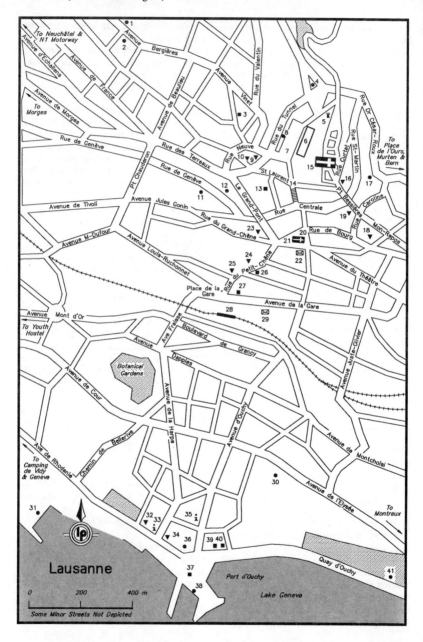

Lausanne

0   200   400 m

Some Minor Streets Not Depicted

■ PLACES TO STAY

3 Du Marché
13 Des Voyageurs
26 Elite
27 Continental Hotel
37 Le Château d'Ouchy
39 Hôtel du Port
40 Hôtel d'Angleterre

▼ PLACES TO EAT

9 Migros Supermarket
10 Coop Supermarket & Restaurant
16 Café de l'Everche
18 Restaurant Au Couscous
19 La Grappe d'Or
23 Manora
24 Paradiso
25 Calèche
32 Mövenpick Radisson Hotel
34 Sherlock's Burger

OTHER

1 Palais de Beaulieu
2 Musée de l'Art Brut
4 Place du Tunnel
5 Castle St Marie
6 Palais de Rumine
  & Museum of Fine Arts
7 Place de la Riponne
8 Europcar (Car Rental)
11 MAD
12 Edelweiss
14 Place de la Palad
15 Cathedral
17 Dolce Vita
20 Place St François
21 St François Church
22 Post Office
28 Main Train Station
29 Main Post Office
30 Musée de l'Elysée
31 CGN Head Office
33 Tourist Office
35 Regional Tourist Office
36 Ouchy Metro
38 CGN Boat Departure Point
41 Olympic Museum

Things to See & Do

Cathedral This is considered one of the finest medieval Gothic churches in Switzerland. It was built in the 12th and 13th centuries, and was consecrated by Pope Gregory X in 1275, in the presence of Rudolph of Habsburg, Emperor of the Holy Roman Empire. Its most striking decoration is the acclaimed **rose window** from the 13th century in the south transept. Also worthy of study are the main portals with their tiers of adorning statues, and the 16th century stalls in the north aisle. The cathedral has recently been extensively restored and is open daily until 7 pm in the summer and until 5.30 pm in winter (October to February); don't try to visit during Sunday morning services. Ascend the tower for a view worthy of a deity (Sfr2); it's open Monday to Saturday from 9 to 11 am and 1.30 to 5.30 pm (4.30 pm in winter) and Sunday from 2 to 5.30 pm (4.30 pm in winter).

The tradition of the nightwatch is still maintained in Lausanne; the hour is called from the cathedral tower between 10 pm and 2 am every night.

Old Town Place St François has a **church** (Eglise St François) that was once part of a 13th century monastery. From the north-east corner, Rue St François becomes Rue du Pont and leads into Place de la Palad, which has a **Fountain of Justice**. This square is taken over by a market every Wednesday and Saturday morning. The 17th century building with the clock tower and the protruding winged dragons is the **Town Hall**, which sometimes has exhibitions in the foyer. The covered stairway leading up from the fountain climbs to the cathedral. Two hundred metres north of the cathedral is the Castle St Maire (Château St Marie). This 15th century building was once the residence of the bishops of Lausanne, and is now the seat of government of the Vaud canton. There's little to see except the view from the terrace.

Musée de l'Art Brut This is a fantastic (in both the literal and colloquial meaning of the word) collection at 11 Ave de Bergières. It was put together by the French artist, Jean Dubuffet, and was opened in Lausanne in 1976. 'Brut' means raw, crude, or rough, and that's exactly what you get.

None of the artists featured is properly trained or part of any artistic circle. On the contrary, many can't even take their place in normal society. Some are criminally insane, others are simply eccentric; most have spent at least some time in a mental institution. Some were so impaired that drawing was just about the only thing they could do; Philipp Schöpke was discharged from the army 'unable to even lace his shoes' (according to the military doctor) and went on to draw figures with the raw impact of primitive tribal icons. Often the people exhibiting started creating art only late in their lives, perhaps led to it following a crisis, after which they would draw or paint obsessively.

The work they produce breaks all the rules. It is vivid, startling, or just plain strange. There are sculptures made out of broken plates and discarded rags, faces made out of shells. Some insisted their drawings originated directly from the spirit world. One woman who believed she was a medium drew on long scrolls of paper in near darkness. As she unrolled fresh areas of paper she rolled up the sections she had completed, and therefore never had any idea what her work looked like in its entirety. A wooden wall shown upstairs was taken from an asylum; it's from a bare cell where Clément Fraisse was incarcerated for two years. The carved designs were done using a broken spoon, and after that was confiscated, the handle of his chamberpot.

Edmund Monseil found it hard to communicate with other people, especially women, and he spent most of WW II hiding from the Germans in an attic. His drawings are cramped, claustrophobic creations on small bits of paper, filled with glaring eyes surrounding the central figure (or figures).

A potted biography of each artist (in English) is displayed alongside the work. This greatly adds to the fascination, but also runs the risk of undermining the art on display; the viewer is sucked into becoming an amateur psychoanalyst and starts looking for specific themes or symbols in the work – phallic shapes in the output of the sexual obsessive, internal conflict in the schizo-phrenic, or portents of doom in the manic depressive. There is the danger of forgetting that art is a work of imagination, and can perhaps provide an escape from a tormented life rather than merely reflecting it. But sometimes the comparison between the life and the work is inevitable. Read the biographies, but be careful not to close your mind to the unexpected.

The gallery is open Tuesday to Friday from 10 am to noon and 2 to 6 pm, and on Saturday and Sunday from 2 to 6 pm. The collection is not huge, but if you see and read everything you could easily be there for three to four hours. Entry costs Sfr5 for adults, Sfr3 for students, and it is free for children. It is close to the Jomini stop on bus Nos 2 and 3.

Palais de Rumine This grand building overlooking the Place de la Riponne holds several museums. The main one is the **Museum of Fine Arts** (Musée cantonal des Beaux-Arts) with many works by Swiss and foreign artists. Only a fraction of the works in the collection may be displayed, however, depending upon the frequent temporary exhibitions. Admission averages around Sfr7, with reductions for students. It's open daily except Monday from 11 am until 5 pm (Friday to Sunday), 6 pm (Tuesday and Wednesday) or 8 pm (Thursday). The other museum collections in the building are all free and open daily from 10 am to noon and 2 pm to 5 pm. Subjects covered include natural history, anatomy, zoology, mineralogy, archaeology and history.

Other Attractions Given that Lausanne is the base for the International Olympic Committee, it is perhaps inevitable that there's a museum devoted to the games. The **Olympic Museum** (Musée Olympique) moved into a lavish new building in June 1993, in the Petit Ouchy park, 1 Quai d'Ouchy. Other museums in the city cover topics as diverse as photography (Musée de l'Elysée), pipes and tobacco, archive films and contemporary art. Opening times and entry fees are listed in the *Lausanne Official Guide*.

The lake provides plenty of sporting opportunities. Vidy Sailing School (☎ 617 90 00) offers courses on windsurfing, water-skiing and sailing, as well as equipment rental. Various boat tours are organised by CGN (see the Getting There & Away section). The boat for the night cruise has an orchestra and restaurant on board (from Sfr20). Lausanne's Botanical Garden (free, open daily) is just south-west of the station by Ave W Fraisse, and there are large woods to the north and east of the city.

Places to Stay – bottom end

Camping Year-round camping is possible at *Camping de Vidy* (☎ 624 20 31), 3 Chemin du Camping, just to the west of the Vidy sports complex. It has a lakeside location, stacks of facilities, and costs Sfr6 per person and Sfr5 to Sfr8 for a tent. Bungalows are also available. To get there, take bus No 2 from Place St François. Get off at Bois de Vaux and walk under the Autoroute towards the lake.

Hostel The IYHF *youth hostel* (☎ 616 57 82), 1 Chemin du Muguet, Ouchy, can be reached by bus No 1 from the train station (direction: Maladière, stop: Batelière), or it's a 20-minute walk if you get on the lake side of the station and head right down Ave Mont d'Or. Dorms cost Sfr16.75 per night and dinners are Sfr9. Reception is closed from 9 am to 5 pm and a curfew comes into effect at 11.30 pm. The lounge has some comfortable sofas but the TV can only pick up one channel. The showers are OK, and washing machines cost Sfr5.

Hotels & Pensions Half-way between a hostel and a hotel is the *Jeunotel* (☎ 626 02 22), 36 Chemin du Bois de Vaud, not far from the camp site, Camping de Vidy. It was newly opened in 1993 and offers dorms (Sfr18), singles (Sfr50), doubles (Sfr50), and triples/quads for Sfr20 per person. Singles/doubles with private shower are Sfr60/62. For breakfast, add Sfr6 per person. Studio apartments are available on a monthly basis (Sfr650).

Villa Cherokee (☎ 647 57 20), 4 Chemin des Charmilles, is a family-run pension with good-sized if slightly shabby rooms – telephone ahead as there aren't many. Singles/doubles from Sfr35/50 include use of a hall shower and breakfast is Sfr5 extra if required. To get there, take bus No 2 from the train station (direction: Désert), get off at Presbytère, backtrack a few steps and walk up Chemin du Presbytére, take the second left then first right (five minutes). *Du Marché* (☎ 647 99 00), Pré du Marché 42, has singles/doubles from Sfr50/70, and studios available for longer stays. It's more central but not as friendly.

Hôtel du Port (☎ 616 49 30), 5 Place du Port in Ouchy, has singles/doubles from Sfr50/90 above a restaurant (closed Tuesday except in July and August).

Places to Stay – middle

Elite (☎ 320 23 61), 1 Ave Ste Luce, and *Des Voyageurs* (☎ 323 19 02), 19 Grand St Jean, are both convenient, comfortable hotels with rooms starting at Sfr100/150. Elite has its own grounds and easier parking.

The best mid-price deal is *Hôtel d'Angleterre* (☎ 617 21 11) on the Quai d'Ouchy in Ouchy, just a couple of doors away from Hôtel du Port. It's a stately old building (no lift) and has large, comfortable rooms with TV and views of the lake. Singles/doubles start at Sfr95/130 with shower or Sfr60/95 without. Byron wrote the *Prisoner of Chillon* here in 1816.

Places to Stay – top end

The *Continental Hotel* (☎ 320 15 51), has more stylish rooms and is right opposite the station at 2 Place de la Gare. Prices start at Sfr125/200 without breakfast. Breakfast-buffet, if required, costs Sfr18.

Enjoy the luxurious setting of *Le Château d'Ouchy* (☎ 616 74 51), a castle dating from the 12th century in Ouchy. Rooms are nicely furnished in Louis XIII style, and all have TV, toilet and bath or shower. Prices start at Sfr152/230 and rooms differ markedly in size. The hotel also has a good-quality restaurant and private parking.

Places to Eat

Self Service There is a *Migros* restaurant below Place de la Riponne at Rue Chaucrau, and it's open Monday from 9 am to 7 pm, Tuesday to Friday from 8 am to 7 pm, and Saturday from 7.30 am to 5 pm. A better bet is probably the buffet-style *Manora*, 17 Place St François, open daily to 10.30 pm. Main dishes are around Sfr10, and there's an excellent choice at the salad buffet (Sfr4.20 to Sfr9.50 per plate), which includes meat and fish offerings. Inexpensive self-service restaurants are also in two department stores on Rue St Laurent: *Coop* and *Placette*.

Other Restaurants Restaurant *Au Couscous* (☎ 312 20 17), 2 Rue Enning, on the 1st floor, has a wide menu including Tunisian, vegetarian and macrobiotic food. Specials start at Sfr12 and it's open daily to 1 am. The vivid red curtains and screens may make you think you've stumbled into some sultan's harem by mistake.

Café de l'Everche, 4 Rue Louis Curtat, by the cathedral, has a lunch and evening two-course menu for Sfr13 and a pleasant garden around the back. It is a small place, open daily from 7 am to midnight. *Calèche* (☎ 323 01 31), in the Hotel Alpha, Petit-Chêne 34, offers plats du jour from Sfr12, a three-course menu for Sfr22 (all available lunch and evening), and fondues and grills for Sfr16 to Sfr35. It is open daily. Just up the road is *Paradiso*, with Italian food and reasonable pizzas from Sfr9. It is closed on Sunday and has a sunny terrace on the roof which is open in summer.

La Grappe d'Or (☎ 323 07 60), Cheneau de Bourg 3, is excellent if very expensive. The food is mainly French, but there are interesting additional flavours, developed by the chef, Peter Baermann, after a recent tour of China. Expect to pay upwards of Sfr20 for a starter and between Sfr40 to Sfr65 for a main course. The service is very attentive in this small restaurant (closed Saturday noon and Sunday). Advance reservations are usually necessary.

In Ouchy, for cheap filler food by the lakeside try *Sherlock's Burger*, next to the

post office on Place de la Navigation. It has an eat-in and takeaway menu covering burgers, kebabs and Italian food (closed Monday).

Just along the road is the *Mövenpick Radisson Hotel* (☎ 617 21 21) which has several restaurants on the ground floor. There's always a good selection of fish dishes and a salad buffet starting at Sfr14. Prices range from main meals for Sfr15 to gourmet menus topping Sfr55. There are many other restaurants around the port, most with good fish specialities.

Entertainment

Concerts, operas and ballets are staged at the *Palais de Beaulieu* (☎ 643 21 11), 10 Ave des Bergières. Lausanne has its own chamber orchestra, and a famous ballet troupe directed by Maurice Béjart, called the Rudra Béjart Ballet. Reservations for these and other performances can be made at the Ouchy tourist office. The theatre scene flourishes at several venues in town, all listed in the Official Guide. Every year at the beginning of July is the City Festival – a week long celebration of music, dance and theatre.

Dolce Vita (☎ 323 09 43), 30 Rue Dr César Roux, is a place that can be a bar, disco, or live music sweat-box depending on the night. The music ranges from jazz to blues to rap, and beers are reasonably priced. Entry to see bands is around Sfr20. It's usually closed Monday and Tuesday, otherwise it's open to at least 2 am. Less alternative, more trendy, is *MAD* (☎ 312 11 22), 23 Rue de Genève, an interesting venue where events include live music, discos, theatre, cinema, and art shows. On Friday and Saturday there are discos with top DJs from 11 pm to 4 am; only members can get in on these nights, but as members can bring two guests (free), people just wait outside until they can get someone to sign them in.

If you want to get a flavour of a Swiss folklore show without having to pay the usual high prices, try *Edelweiss* (☎ 23 37 73), 10 Rue de Genève. The show starts around 8 pm nightly (closed Sunday) and is free, which is just as well, because it's not terribly good. The fairground rhythms of Jacky's organ playing and Patrizia's restrained yodelling struck me as being as typically Swiss as chicken chow mein. But at least it's a change from the usual. The food is reasonable: fondue from Sfr17, meat dishes from Sfr14, and a weekday lunchtime special with soup for Sfr13. Draught beer is Sfr4.50 for 0.3 litre.

Café des Négotiants (☎ 312 97 66), 10 Place du Tunnel, is a bar for gay men (closed Monday); lesbians prefer *La Narcose*, (☎ 320 22 61) 1 Place de l'Ours.

Getting There & Away

Train Lausanne is on the direct TGV route to/from Paris (Sfr76, four departures a day), which stops at Vallorbe before continuing to France (border checks on the train). Advance reservations are compulsory, and cost Sfr8 to Sfr21 depending upon the time and the day. The normal service to Vallorbe is by hourly regional train.

There are three trains an hour from Geneva, the journey takes 40 to 50 minutes and costs Sfr18. Most trains from Bern to Geneva go via Lausanne. Trains to Interlaken go either via Bern (Sfr44) or the scenic route via Montreux (Sfr48). Fast trains run every hour to Yverdon-les-Bains (Sfr11.60, takes 25 minutes).

Car & Motorbike There are motorways linking Lausanne to Geneva and Yverdon (N1), Martigny (N9/E62), and Bern (N9 then N12).

Car Rental There are a dozen different car rental companies in the city, including Avis (☎ 320 66 81), 50 Ave de la Gare, Hertz (☎ 312 53 11), 17 Place du Tunnel, and Europcar (☎ 323 71 42), 12 Place de la Riponne.

Boat Frequent boats sail around the lake in the summer, departing from Ouchy. Contact the head office of CGN (☎ 617 06 66), 17 Ave de Rhodanie, for information. The summer season is from the end of May to late September. There are many departures a day

and boats take in all resorts around the lake, including the French side. Bicycles can only be taken on board the larger boats, and there are no car ferries. Lausanne has direct crossings over to Thonon-les-Bains and Evians-les-Bains with departures every one to three hours. The boat fare to Montreux is Sfr15. If you want to do a lot of cruising buy a day pass: Sfr43 or Sfr58 in 1st class.

Even in winter, nine ferries a day cross over to Evian-les-Bains in France; it takes 35 minutes and costs Sfr11. A boat also goes around the coast of the Swiss Riviera (stopping at Vevey, Montreux and the Château de Chillon) all the way to St Gingolph on the French border, before turning around again. It departs daily in September and October and Sunday only from November to March.

Getting Around

Buses and trolley buses service most destinations, but there are also metro lines from Ouchy up to the main station (every seven

Main Portal (Lausanne Cathedral)

minutes or so) and an almost non-stop service between the station and the Flon area. Another metro line goes from Flon to the western suburbs. Short trips on city transport of up to three stops cost Sfr1, and tickets are valid for 30 minutes. Unlimited journeys for one hour cost Sfr2 or Sfr1 for children. Passes for 24 hours unlimited transport cost Sfr5 and a three-day tourist card is Sfr12; child rates are half-price.

Parking garages can get expensive; the largest is at Place de la Riponne. Parking on streets in blue zones is allowed for up to 1½ hours and is free; red zones have a (free) limit of 15 hours. Parking on streets with metres will have a time limit indicated.

AROUND LAUSANNE
La Côte District
The district west of Lausanne is called La Côte. **Morges** is a wine-growing centre with its own castle, built in 1286 by Louis of Savoy. Inside is a military museum containing weapons, uniforms, and 8000 toy soldiers (Sfr5, students Sfr4, open daily from February to mid-December). The town hosts a tulip festival from April to May. **Rolle** also has a castle built by the Savoy dynasty in the 13th century. Like the one at Morges, it is right on the shores of the lake.

The town of **Nyon** is of Roman origin. It has several museums and (surprise, surprise) a castle that was home to the dukes of Savoy. The quintuple-towered château was started in the 12th century and extensively modified in the 16th century; its elevated perspective allows a fine view from the terrace. One of the town's museum recalls the Roman era, another collects pieces of porcelain, and a third evokes life as it was and is lived around the lake. One ticket (Sfr5) gains entry to all three. The Porcelain Museum is open daily from April to October; the Roman and Lake Geneva Museums are likewise open daily from April to October, and also the rest of the year except Monday.

The town of **Coppet** is halfway between Nyon and Geneva. It too has a castle, which can be visited by guided tour between March and October (Sfr6, or Sfr4.50 for students

and senior citizens; closed Monday). The interior contains furniture in the Louis XVI and Directoire styles. It became the home of Madame de Staël after she was exiled from Paris by Napoleon. She soon presided over a court that was visited by some of the literary élite of the day – Edward Gibbon and Byron among them.

Getting There & Away
All the towns mentioned are on the rail route between Lausanne and Geneva, although only the local trains stop at Coppet and Rolle. All of them can be reached by boat on Lake Geneva steamers run by CGN (☎ 021h617 06 66). Fares from Lausanne are: Morges Sfr8, Rolle Sfr14, and Nyon Sfr20.

Swiss Riviera

The Swiss Riviera rivals its French counterpart in its ability to attract rich and famous residents. The name describes the stretch of the shore roughly between Lausanne and Villeneuve.

VEVEY
Montreux's sister resort on the Swiss Riviera, Vevey, exudes a comparable swanky ambience. The town has welcomed numerous celebrities in the past; a famous recent resident was Charlie Chaplin, who spent 25 years here until his death in 1977, and is buried in the Corsier cemetery. If staying in Vevey or Montreux, the *Tourist Info Pass*, can get you some very useful benefits, such as free entry to swimming pools and the food museum.

Orientation & Information
The hub of the town is Grande Place, 200 metres directly ahead from the train station. The tourist office (☎ 021-921 48 25) is on this large square in the La Grenette building. It collaborates closely with the office in Montreux, and shares much of the same tourist literature. Opening times are Monday to Friday from 8 am to noon and 1.30 to 6.30

pm and Saturday from 8 am to noon. The main post office (1800 Vevey 1) is 100 metres to the right of the station. The telephone code for Vevey is 021

Things to See & Do

There's a good view from the 15th century St Martin's Church, up the hill behind the station. The old streets east of Grande Place and the lakeside promenades are worth exploring – a tourist office brochure details points of interest. Apart from that, the main entertainment comes from several museums.

The **Swiss Museum of Games** (Musée Suisse du Jeu) is certainly the most fun. The games are arranged according to various themes – educational, strategic, simulation, skill and chance, and there are many that you can play as you go around. It's just a pity the explanations are only in French. Admission costs Sfr6 (senior citizens and students Sfr3, children free). It's open daily except Monday from 2 to 6 pm. The museum is in the Château de la Tour de Peilz: take trolley bus No 1 and get off at Place du Temple.

The **Swiss Camera Museum**, 6 Ruelle des Anciens Fossés, near Grande Place, is exactly as the name suggests. Cameras from the last 150 years are displayed, but the museum misses an opportunity by not enhancing the rows of instruments with some actual photographic images. It's open daily except Monday: March to October from 10.30 am to noon and 2 to 5.30 pm, and in the winter, afternoons only. Admission costs Sfr4 for adults, Sfr3 for students and senior citizens, and it's free for children.

The head office of the huge Nestlé food company is in Vevey. It is responsible for the **Food Museum** (Musée de l'Alimentation), Rue du Léman, open daily except Monday from 10 am to noon and 2 to 5 pm. It looks at food and nutrition in historical, scientific and sociological terms in such a didactic way that you almost expect to have to pass a written exam before you're allowed to leave. Entry costs Sfr4, or Sfr2 for students, senior citizens and children. Other museums in Vevey cover art, wine-growing, and the history of the town (all closed Monday).

Vevey is the capital of the Lavaux wine-growing region, and every 25 years the growers congregate on the town for an elaborate and exuberant festival that is years in the planning. The next one occurs in 1999. Film-makers arrive every July for the annual International Comedy Film Festival. There's a folklore market every Saturday morning in July and August.

Places to Stay

Camp by the lake at *La Pichette*, west of the centre towards St Saphorin. The site is open from 1 April to 30 September.

In the centre of Vevey, the best budget option is *Pension Buergle* (☎ 921 40 23), 16 Rue Louis Meyer. It's an ageing building with large rooms and plenty of hall showers. The price is just Sfr30 per person and it's open year-round. It's often full in summer with long-term guests, so check for vacancies by telephone (reservations not accepted).

Opposite the station at Place de la Gare is *Hotel du 10 Aout* (☎ 921 16 82). Singles/doubles cost Sfr45/80 using hall shower and there are a couple of doubles with private shower for Sfr90. Breakfast is not included and the restaurant and reception are closed on Wednesday. Also on Place de la Gare is the *Hotel De Famille* (☎ 921 39 31) which has an indoor swimming pool and a sauna. Rooms start at Sfr75/130, although there are a few cheaper singles without private shower. Just off Grande Place at 27 Rue du Conseil is *Des Négociants* (☎ 922 70 11), with rooms from Sfr70/100, with private facilities.

Places to Eat

Opposite the post office is the Centre Commercial, containing a supermarket and a *Manora* buffet restaurant, open until 6.30 pm weekdays and 5 pm on Saturday. It has a salad bar (Sfr3.80 to Sfr9.50), dessert bar, and main meals for Sfr8 to Sfr15.

A *Migros* supermarket and restaurant has entrances on both Ave Paul Cérésole and Rue de Lausanne. It's open the same hours as the Manora except it stays open late until 8 pm on Thursday. Cheap self-service food is also available at *EPA* department store at Place Ste Claire.

For traditional local fare, explore the centre of town east of Grande Place. *Le Mazot*, 7 Rue du Conseil, is a typical place, offering fondue and horse steaks (closed Sunday lunch and Wednesday). Many restaurants have good daily specials but these are usually only available at lunch time. If you can afford it, go to *Café-Restaurant du Raisin* (☎ 921 10 28), 3 Place du Marché. The plat du jour (lunch and evening) is around Sfr19; otherwise you need to pay Sfr28 or more but the food merits it. Try the lobster (homard) for Sfr32. The restaurant is closed on Sunday evening and Monday.

Getting There & Away

Two or more trains an hour travel around the lake: Vevey is 15 minutes from Lausanne (Sfr5.60) and five minutes from Montreux (Sfr2.80). Trolley bus No 1 also runs from Vevey to Montreux and beyond to Villeneuve (Sfr1.90).

By boat, the fare to Lausanne is Sfr11 and to Montreux, Sfr5. Boats depart from the Débarcadère by Grande Place. For more information, see Getting There & Away in the Lausanne section.

AROUND VEVEY

A steam train chugs along the three-km track from Blonay to Chamby, where a railway museum houses some steam engines and machinery. Sfr10 (children Sfr5) gets entry and the return trip, but it only operates between mid-May and the end of October, on Saturday afternoon and Sunday. Spots near to Vevey for good views and walks are Les Pléiades (1397 metres) and Mont Pèlerin (1080 metres).

MONTREUX

Centrepiece of the Swiss Riviera, Montreux offers marvellous lakeside walks and access to the ever-popular Château de Chillon (pronounced Sheehyon). The town's reputation grew in the 19th century as many artists, writers and musicians discovered the beauties of the area. Lord Byron, Peter Shelley and Mary Shelley (who wrote *Frankenstein* by the lake) were among the first of the literary influx – themselves following in the earlier footsteps of Jean Jacques Rousseau.

Montreux retains a strong musical tradition. It has hosted the jazz festival annually since 1967 and a classical music festival since WW II. Montreux was also the site of a famous event in rock history. On 4 December 1971 the Casino Theatre in Montreux caught fire during a gig by Frank Zappa. The fire raged all night, casting a great pall of smoke over the placid waters of Lake Geneva. The burning building was watched by the band, Deep Purple, from across the lake, and inspired their classic track *Smoke on the Water*.

Orientation & Information

Montreux is at the eastern end of Lake Geneva. The train station (with bike rental, money-exchange counters, and Sfr2 luggage lockers) and the main post office are on Ave des Alpes, which down to the left leads to the core of the town, Place de la Paix. From here, the old town (vieille ville) is up the hill, and the main shopping streets, Grand Rue and Ave du Casino, are either side.

The tourist information office (☎ 021-963 12 12) is a few minutes away on the lakefront to the west of Place du Marché; it is open Monday to Friday from 8.30 am to noon and 1.30 to 6 pm, and on Saturday from 9 am to noon. Hours are extended in the summer, when the place is open daily. The tourist office makes free hotel reservations – contact it well in advance if your visit coincides with one of the festivals.

The telephone code for Montreux is 021.

Organised Tours

The tourist office organises a wide variety of programmes, including a full day trip to Mont Blanc (Sfr60), an outing to Gruyères (Sfr40), and tours of local vineyards.

Things to See & Do

Château de Chillon Chillon Castle receives

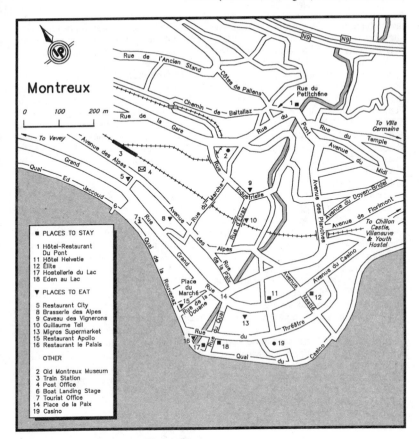

Montreux

0   100   200 m

To Vevey

To Villa Germaine

To Chillon Castle, Villeneuve & Youth Hostel

Rue de l'Ancien Stand
Côtes de Pallens
Rue du Petitchêne
Chemin — de — Baltaliaz
Rue de la Gare
Avenue des Alpes
Quai   Grand   Ed   Jaccoud
Rue du Pont
Rue du
Avenue du Temple
Avenue du Midi
Avenue du Doyen-Bridel
Avenue de Florimont
Rue Industrielle
Rue du Marché
Rue d'Église
Avenue des Planches
Rue des Alpes
Rue du Grand
Quai de la Rouvenaz
Rue de la Paix
Place du Marché
Rue de la Douane
Avenue du Casino
Avenue Théâtre
Théâtre
Quai   du
Casino

■ **PLACES TO STAY**

1 Hôtel–Restaurant Du Pont
11 Hôtel Helvetie
12 Élite
17 Hostellerie du Lac
18 Eden au Lac

▼ **PLACES TO EAT**

5 Restaurant City
8 Brasserie des Alpes
9 Caveau des Vignerons
10 Guillaume Tell
13 Migros Supermarket
15 Restaurant Apollo
16 Restaurant le Palais

OTHER

2 Old Montreux Museum
3 Train Station
4 Post Office
6 Boat Landing Stage
7 Tourist Office
14 Place de la Paix
19 Casino

more visitors than any other historical building in Switzerland. Occupying a stunning position right on Lake Geneva, the fortress caught the public imagination when Lord Byron wrote about the fate of François de Bonivard, who was chained to the fifth pillar in the dungeons for four years in the 16th century. Byron is credited with scratching his own name on the third pillar, though it could equally well be the work of a more recent vandal.

Bonivard's crime was to preach about the Reformation, despite the vehement opposition of the Duke of Savoy who was then resident in the castle. Eschewing intellectual debate, the duke imprisoned Bonivard in his dungeon. Bonivard was only freed when Bernese troops, themselves followers of the Reformation, took over the region in 1536.

The castle is still in excellent condition, and dates from the 11th century. It has undergone much modification and enlargement since then. Allow at least two hours to view the tower, courtyards, dungeons and numerous rooms containing weapons, utensils, frescoes and furniture. Notice particularly the designs on the carved wooden chests and the ceiling in the **Great Hall**. Four models in the museum show how the castle has been altered over the years.

Entry costs Sfr5.50 for adults, Sfr4.50 for students and Sfr2 for children, and the castle opens daily at 10 am (9 am from April to September). The closing time varies through the year: it is 4.45 pm from November to February; 5.30 pm in March and October; 6.30 pm in April, May, June and September; and 7 pm in July and August. The castle is a pleasant 45-minute walk along the lakefront from Montreux (15 minutes from the youth hostel), or it's also accessible by train or trolley bus No 1.

The mild climate allows sub-tropical flora to flourish along the promenade. Take a **walking tour** of the town and pick out locations associated with famous past visitors. These are identified in the tourist office leaflet for Montreux and Vevey, *On the Trail of Hemingway*. In the old town is a small museum, the **Museum of Old Montreux** (Musée du Vieux Montreux), recounting the history of the town and locality. It's open daily from mid-April to mid-October, at 40 Rue de la Gare.

There are several free **swimming spots** on the lake between Vevey and Montreux. Sailing, water-skiing, windsurfing, rowing and boat rental are all available.

Montreux's **casino** (☎ 963 53 31) has several bars and nightclubs on the premises, including the Western Saloon where there's live country music.

Festivals

Montreux's major festivals are in the summer. The best known is the **Montreux Jazz Festival**, lasting for two weeks in early July. The programme is announced at the end of April and tickets are available shortly afterwards from the Montreux tourist office or from branches of the Swiss Bank Corporation throughout Switzerland. You could also write in advance to Festival du Jazz, Service de Location, Case postale 97, CH-1820, Montreux 1, or call the festival office on ☎ 963 46 63. There are sometimes free events during the day, but count on around Sfr50 for one of the big evening gigs.

The week-long **Golden Rose Television Festival** kicks off around a month earlier, and hordes of the industry's professionals hit town.

The **Montreux-Vevey Music Festival** is an extravaganza of classical music lasting from late August to early October. Tickets for performances can cost anything from Sfr20 to Sfr110. Write in advance to Festival de Musique, 5 Rue de Théâtre, Case postale 162, CH-1820, Montreux 2. Branches of the Banque Cantonale Vaudoise sell tickets direct.

Places to Stay

The nearest camping is at the optimistically named *Les Horizons Bleus* (☎ 960 15 47) at Villeneuve. It's by the lake and the harbour, and is open from 1 April to 30 September. Take trolley bus No 1 from Montreux.

The IYHF *youth hostel* (☎ 963 49 34) is at 8 Passage de l'Auberge, Territet, a 30-minute walk along the lake to the south-east from the tourist office. It's nicely situated near the waterfront although the trains clattering overhead will ensure you won't sleep in. It underwent extensive renovations in 1992, and has gleaming new facilities throughout. Dorms are Sfr22 and rooms for couples are Sfr32 per person. The hostel is closed from 23 December to mid-February.

Hotels & Pensions Most hotels raise their prices for the summer season. An exception is *Villa Germaine* (☎ 963 15 28), 3 Ave de Collonge, not far from the station in Territet. Singles/doubles start at Sfr50/80.

In the centre of Montreux, the *Élite* (☎ 963 67 33), 25 Ave du Casino, has singles/doubles from Sfr50/80 using hall shower, or Sfr70/110 with private shower. It's comfortably rundown but the management is eager to please, and there's some free parking round the back. *Hostellerie du Lac* (☎ 963 21 71), 12 Rue du Quai, has rooms with high ceilings, big balconies and views of the lake. Doubles start at Sfr70 using hall shower and Sfr110 with private facilities. Single occupancy gets a discount, and all rooms have TV and radio.

Another budget place to try is *Hôtel-Restaurant du Pont* (☎ 963 22 49), in the old town at 12 Rue du Pont. The rooms are fairly average and cost around Sfr65/110 with private shower/toilet and TV. It's right by the river.

Hôtel Helvetie (☎ 963 25 51), 32 Ave du Casino, is a great place to stay. The large rooms, high ceilings, wide corridors give a wonderful feeling of space and there's also a huge lobby with several different sections. There's also a rooftop terrace, chunky radiators and a great big shaggy dog called Kim. All rooms have bath or shower, toilet, TV, mini-bar and telephone; prices start at Sfr90/140. Parking across the road costs Sfr10 for 24 hours, and there's a quality restaurant.

Eden au Lac (☎ 963 55 51), 11 Rue du Théâtre, occupies a fine site by the lake. The restaurant and lobby areas are very grand but this opulence isn't present to the expected degree in the cheaper rooms. Prices start at Sfr130/190.

Places to Eat

Pick up the list of restaurants from the tourist office. *Migros* supermarket at 49 Ave du Casino has a self-service restaurant, open Monday to Wednesday until 6.30 pm, Thursday and Friday until 7.45 pm, and Saturday until 5 pm. It sometimes has very cheap special offers. *Restaurant City*, 37 Ave des Alpes, is also self-service with meals for around Sfr12. The main advantage of this place is the sunny terrace overlooking the lake; it's open daily from 7 am to midnight (9 pm from October to mid-May). It also gives a 10% discount to students.

Brasserie des Alpes, 23 Ave des Alpes, has a good lunch-time menu du jour for Sfr12 with soup. It's a typical French café environment and is open daily to around midnight. Tasty pizza and pasta start at Sfr11.

Restaurant Apollo, by the lake at 2 Place du Marché, has daily specials from Sfr14, and a good three-course menu for Sfr38. Around the corner on the lake along Rue de Quai, check *Restaurant le Palais*, decked out in ceramic inlays like a low-budget version

of the Taj Mahal. It's fairly pricey, with Oriental and vegetarian food for around Sfr20 to Sfr30, but the weird patio and posey patrons make up for the expense.

Caveau des Vignerons, at 30 Rue Industrielle in the old part of town, is the place to go for fondue (from Sfr17). It also serves filets of perch (Sfr23) and Raclette, and is closed on Sunday. Nearby, *Guillaume Tell* has daily specials with soup for Sfr14 and evening meals from around Sfr29 (closed Wednesday).

Hostellerie du Lac (see Places to Stay) has a mid-price restaurant that is especially good for fish specialities (closed Tuesday). One of the top restaurants for gourmet food in the whole of Switzerland is *Pont de Brent* (☎ 964 52 30), north-west of Montreux in the nearby village of Brent. It has a terrace and is closed on Sunday and Monday.

Getting There & Away

Hourly trains depart to/from Geneva and take one hour 10 minutes to cover the lakeside route. The fare is Sfr26. From Lausanne, there are three trains an hour (Sfr8) which take 19 to 35 minutes. Slow local trains continue eastwards from Montreux to stop at Territet for the youth hostel and Chillon for the castle. Interlaken can be reached via a scenic rail route, with changeovers at Zweisimmen and Spiez. The track winds its way up the hill for an excellent view over Lake Geneva. For boat services, see Getting There & Away in the Geneva and Lausanne sections.

AROUND MONTREUX

Rochers de Naye There is an excellent panorama of the lake and the Alps from this viewing point at 2042 metres. Two restaurants at the top allow you to enjoy the view in comfort, or you can stroll around the grassy plateau and visit the Alpine garden. It's a winding, scenic, 55-minute train journey from Montreux. Trains are run by MOB: the Half-Fare Card is valid and the Swiss Pass is free only up to Caux, and thereafter gets a discount of 25%. Inter-Rail gets 50% off but Eurail is about as useful as a clown costume at a funeral. The full return trip from Montreux costs Sfr48.80, but ask about reduced fares that apply on certain trains in low season. Cars can get as far as Caux, and the return fare from there is Sfr33. The walk up from Montreux takes about 3½ hours.

North-West Vaud

This part of the canton of Vaud is dominated by the Jura Mountains chain and Lake Neuchâtel

YVERDON-LES-BAINS
Yverdon (pronounced Ee-verdon) has been a health centre since Roman times. It's an enjoyable lakeside resort and Vaud's second-largest town after Lausanne (population 22,000).

Orientation & Information
Yverdon is on the southern shore of Lake Neuchâtel at an altitude of 435 metres. The train station has money-exchange facilities daily from at least 5.45 am to 8.40 pm, and new-style Sfr3 or Sfr5 luggage lockers. Close by is the post office. To get to the old town (vieille ville) cross the park (where there is car-parking), turn left and follow the signs. The tourist office (☎ 024-23 62 90) is across the main square, Place Pestalozzi, and is open Monday to Friday from 9 am to noon and 1.30 to 6 pm, and (between June and September only) on Saturday from 9 am to noon.

The telephone code for Yverdon is 024.

Things to See & Do
The centre of town is clustered round the 13th century **castle**, built by Peter II of Savoy. Inside is a **museum** containing local prehistoric artefacts, arms, clothing, and a Ptolemaic Egyptian mummy. The Guard's Tower is devoted to the champion of primary education, Henri Pestalozzi (1746 to 1827), whose educational institution was actually based in the castle for 20 years from 1805. It is open Tuesday to Sunday from 2 to 5 pm, and additionally from 10 am to noon between June and September. Admission costs Sfr4.

Next to the castle is the **House of Elsewhere** (la Maison d'Ailleurs), Place Pestalozzi 14. This is a new museum devoted to science fiction, and contains a mock-up of a spaceship, film stills, a room devoted to the artist H R Giger (of *Alien* fame) and a whole library of books and magazines. It has great potential but is currently underfunded and some of the exhibits are laughably shoddy – almost the museum equivalent of a 'B' movie. It puts on temporary exhibitions: planned for the summer of '94 is a computer games and role-playing games exhibition. It is open Tuesday to Sunday from 2 to 6 pm and entry costs Sfr6 or Sfr4 for students, children and senior citizens.

An interesting feature of Yverdon are the **trotting races** (*trot attelé*) in the hippodrome between the train station and the lake. These mainly take place at weekends between June and November; entry costs around Sfr5 and you can bet anything from Sfr1 up to the shirt off your back.

The lake offers the opportunity for various boat rides (see Getting There & Away) and the usual water sports, including windsurfing, water-skiing and sailing. There are five km of sandy beaches by the town.

Health Spa The water from the 14,000-year-old mineral springs starts off 500 metres below ground. By the time it hits the surface it has picked up all sorts of salubrious properties from the layers of rock, particularly for sufferers of rheumatism and respiratory ailments. It has even spawned a bottled mineral water under the name of *Arkina* which is claimed to be effective in combating obesity.

The **Centre Thermal** (☎ 21 44 56) the health complex to the east of the centre off Ave des Bains, offers a range of treatments. Even if you feel fine you can enjoy bathing in indoor and outdoor pools (temperature 28°

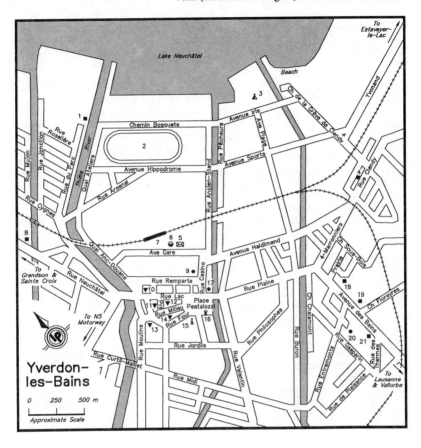

■	**PLACES TO STAY**
1	Youth Hostel
3	Camping des Iris
4	Hôtel de l'Ange
8	Hôtel Industriel
18	Hôtel La Prairie
19	Motel des Bains
21	Grand Hôtel des Bains
▼	**PLACES TO EAT**
10	Manora
11	Don Camillo
12	Placette Supermarket

13	Restaurant des Sports
14	La Couronne
	OTHER
2	Hippodrome
5	Post Office
6	Bus Stop
7	Train Station
9	Casino
15	Tourist Information
16	Castle & Museum
17	House of Elsewhere
20	Health Spa & Centre Thermal

to 34°C, entry Sfr12), take a sauna (Sfr28) or have a massage (Sfr50). It is open Monday to Friday from 8 am to 10 pm, and weekends and holidays from 9 am to 8 pm.

Places to Stay
Camping des Iris (☎ 21 10 89) is by the lake to the north-east of the station (well signposted). It is open from 1 April to late September and costs Sfr per person, Sfr4 per tent and Sfr2 for a car.

The IYHF *youth hostel* (☎ 21 12 33), Rue du Parc 14, is by the Thièle River not far from the lake. Go right from the station and turn right beside the river until you get a chance to cross over (a 10-minute walk). Dorms cost Sfr15, reception is closed from 9 am to 5 pm and the hostel is closed from November to February.

There are no hotels convenient for the station or the old town. Within a 15-minute walk to the west of the station is *Industriel* (☎ 24 20 06), Ave de Grandson 8, with basic rooms for Sfr45/80. At least 20 minutes in the other direction is *De l'Ange* (☎ 21 25 85), Rue Clendy 25, where singles/doubles with hall showers cost from Sfr40/70, or Sfr65/90 with private shower.

The top-quality hotels are on Ave des Bains, near the Centre Thermal. *Motel des Bains* (☎ 23 12 81) at No 21 starts at Sfr95/145, *La Prairie* (☎ 21 19 19), No 9, at Sfr115/170, and *Grand Hôtel des Bains* (☎ 21 70 21), No 22, at Sfr158/220.

Places to Eat
There is a supermarket downstairs in Placette 1, on the corner of Rue Lac and Rue du Pré. Nearby is Placette 2, where there is a buffet-style *Manora* restaurant,Rue de l'Ancienne Poste, open daily to 10 pm. *Don Camillo* (☎ 21 42 82), Rue du Pré 10, is the place to go for Italian food (pizza/pasta from Sfr11; closed Sunday).

Keep an eye out for the many places with lunch-time specials: *La Couronne*, Rue du Milieu, has one for Sfr13 or Sfr18, including soup and salad. The place for those with a discerning palate is *Restaurant des Sports* (☎ 21 27 63), Rue du Milieu 47. The lunch

menu starts at Sfr14 for the main plate and rises to Sfr28 for four courses. Most meat and fish dishes are around the Sfr30 mark, and it's closed on Sunday evening and Monday.

Getting There & Away
Yverdon has direct trains to Lausanne (Sfr11.60, takes 25 minutes), Neuchâtel (Sfr10.60, 20 minutes) and Estavayer-le-Lac (Sfr5.60, 15 minutes). The train to Vallorbe (Sfr14) is awkward (via Cossonay) and takes two hours. By road is much easier as the N9 goes directly there; postbuses depart three to five times daily and the journey takes just 35 minutes.

Several times a day in summer (except Monday), boats sail to Neuchâtel; the journey takes three hours and costs Sfr15. Stops en route include Grandson and Estavayer-le-Lac. You can even get as far as Solothurn by boat, by way of the Zihl canal to Lake Biel then on the Aare River. Call the boat company in Neuchâtel (☎ 038-25 40 12) for information.

Getting Around
All local buses leave from in front of the train station and trips cost Sfr1.20.

GRANDSON
The present **castle** at Grandson dates from the 13th century. Early in 1476 it was taken by Charles the Bold and his Burgundian troops, but they didn't hold it for long. On 2 March the same year the Swiss Confederates returned and easily defeated the Duke's forces. Some were strung up from the apple trees in the castle orchard by the vengeful Swiss, the rest scattered in disarray and left behind much artillery and treasure.

The museum in the castle tells the story of this and other battles with dioramas and displays of weapons. A popular part of the castle is the **Automobile Museum**, the prize exhibit of which is a white Rolls Royce formerly owned by Greta Garbo. From May to October it is open daily from 9 am to 6 pm; the rest of the year hours are reduced to Sunday from 10 am to 5 pm. Admission costs

Sfr7 (children Sfr5.50). There is a tourist office in the castle (☎ 024-24 42 89).

Getting There & Away

Only the slow trains between Yverdon and Neuchâtel stop at Grandson (one every one to two hours). From Yverdon it costs Sfr2 and takes a few minutes. Bus departures from outside Yverdon station are more frequent. Better still, get there by enjoying the five-km stroll around the lake.

SAINTE CROIX

This town has been famous for its music boxes since the mid 19th century. The art of making these expensive items is well documented in the **CIMA Museum** (Centre International de la Méchanique d'Art), Rue de l'Industrie 2.

Some of the larger examples are extremely elaborate, incorporating mini drums, bells, and accordions in addition to the conventional spiked cylinders. Music is produced by the cylinders as they rotate against metal teeth causing the latter to vibrate and hum melodiously upon being released from the spikes. The best exhibits are the musical automata, such as the acrobats, a tiny Mozart, and Pierrot the writer. These and many other ingenious machines are activated by the guide on the 70-minute tour (in French, but English notes are available). There are some good examples of early radios and phonographs, which the town started producing once music boxes became largely superseded by the new technology. Music boxes are still made, however, as the shop on the ground floor demonstrates.

The museum is open Tuesday to Sunday from 1.30 to 6 pm, and entry costs Sfr8 for adults, Sfr7 for senior citizens, Sfr6 for students, Sfr5 for children and Sfr20 for families. The tourist office (☎ 024-61 27 02) is in the same building. In nearby l'Auberson is a similar but smaller display in the **Musée Baud**, open every afternoon from 1 July to 15 September (Sfr6).

The highest point in the area is Le Chasseron (1607 metres). The summit provides a marvellous 360° panorama of the Alps, Lake Neuchâtel and the Jura. There is a car park which is a 45-minute walk from the top. Starting from Sainte Croix it takes under two hours to walk to the summit.

Downhill skiing in the winter is centred on Le Chasseron and the adjoining summits. The one-day pass covers 10 lifts and costs just Sfr22 (Sfr16 for children). The local ski school (☎ 024-61 10 61) can give group lessons (Sfr16 per person for two hours) or individual tuition. There are also 80 km of cross-country trails.

Places to Stay

Sainte Croix has an IYHF *youth hostel* (☎ 024-61 18 10), Rue Centrale 16, which costs Sfr17 and is closed from late October to late December, and for two weeks at the end of April. The town only has a few hotels but they are good value. *Hôtel des Fleurettes* (☎ 024-61 22 94), Chemin des Fleurettes, has singles/doubles for Sfr40/72, or Sfr52/92 with private shower.

Getting There & Away

The only way to get there by train is on the narrow-gauge line from Yverdon (Sfr10.60, takes 35 minutes). There is a fine view of the Alps and Lake Neuchâtel from the hill just outside Sainte Croix. A postbus runs north from Sainte Croix to Buttes, which is connected by rail and bus to the northern Jura. A major road links Sainte Croix to Yverdon and Pontarlier in France.

VALLORBE

This small industrial town has only recently developed its tourist attractions. In 1974 the caves of the Orbe were first open to the public; 1980 saw the opening of the Iron Museum and 1990 the opening of its twin, the Railway Museum. A nearby military fort has been revealing its secrets only since 1988.

Orientation & Information

Vallorbe is a couple of km from the French border and English is not widely spoken. The train station (money-exchange counters, bike rental, Sfr2 lockers) is less than a 10-minute walk from the central street, Grand Rue. A map outside shows the way. The tourist office (☎ 021-843 25 83) is just beyond Grand Rue, in the Musée du Fer. Opening hours are Monday to Friday from 8.30 am to noon and 1.30 to 6 pm, and the same hours daily in the summer high season.

The telephone code for Vallorbe is 021.

Things to See & Do

The Jourgne Pass near Vallorbe acquired strategic importance as war began to threaten in the late 1930s. An underground **fort** was constructed at Pré-Giroud in 1937 to guard this pass and the route along the Vallée de Joux. From the outside it looks like an unremarkable mountain chalet, yet below ground it can accommodate 130 men. There are dormitories, canteens, a kitchen, a telephone exchange, even an infirmary with an operating room. Tunnels connect the living area with the combat zone. As it turned out, the fortress was never used in direct conflict and,

following a period as a training centre, it was allowed to fall into disuse.

It became a tourist attraction after the commune of Vallorbe purchased it from the federal authorities for the princely sum of one franc. The nominal purchase price doesn't stop you from having to pay Sfr8 (Sfr5 for children) to see it, however. Nowadays the fort is populated by plastic dummies instead of flesh and blood personnel, but it still provides a fascinating hint of the myriad military installations that are still hidden away in the Swiss countryside. It is open from 10 am to 5 pm every day in July and August, but only on weekends for the rest of the year between the end of March and the first weekend in November. The guided tour takes around 75 minutes (notes in English). Parking is available nearby. It takes 70 minutes to walk there from Vallorbe or 40 minutes from Le Day train station, the next station in the direction of Lausanne. There is no bus service.

Less than three km outside Vallorbe are stalactite and stalagmite **caves**, caused by the underground course of the Orbe River on

---

Switzerland Goes Green

Swiss households produce nearly as much waste as the leaders in the field, the Americans, accounting for 500 kg per head per year (50% more than in Britain). Around 80% of this is incinerated, and the rest goes into landfill sites or is shunted off to neighbouring France (with France's consent, I presume). None of these methods is environmentally satisfactory. The Swiss are determined to solve the problem and are working towards the aim of 'Reduction, Recovery and Recycling' (a Federal Office for the Environment slogan).

Colour-coded recycling bins are popping up everywhere, accepting glass, aluminium, PET plastic, and used oil. Switzerland already ranks third in the world in terms of bottle recycling: around 60% of non-returnable drinks bottles are recycled, as compared to about 12% in Britain. One-litre beer bottles are invariably deposit-refundable, as are bottles for many of the cheaper cap-topped wines. A returnable bottle may be re-used 50 times. A few years ago, the use of phosphate-containing detergents was banned in Switzerland, and since 1986 battery retailers have had to provide containers for the collection of used batteries.

Many Swiss now take their re-cycling very seriously. A female traveller told me how she was returning from the supermarket in Lauterbrunnen with a couple of bottles of wine and some provisions. The flimsy plastic bag gave way when she was outside and a bottle crashed on to the street. As she lunged to try to save the rest of her shopping she fell over, breaking the other bottle in the process. A Swiss man who observed the scene approached, but it wasn't to help her up or to enquire if she was all right. Instead, he began issuing instructions as to which bins she should use to get rid of the different coloured shattered glass. He stood watching until she had collected up and disposed correctly of every last bit.

The Alp Action Group (tel (☎ 022-735 92 95) is based in Geneva. It was created to try to protect the Alpine environment, which annually receives 100 million visitors. ∎

its way to Lake Brenet. To get there, follow the signs for 'Source Grottos' (free parking outside). The guided tour of the caves takes one hour and costs Sfr12 (children Sfr6). In the entrance hall are displays of rare rocks and minerals, included in the tour price. The caves are open from the end of March to the first weekend in November. It's shut Monday until the end of May, otherwise it's open daily from 9 am to 5 pm (6 pm June to August).

In the town itself, by the tourist office, is an **iron and railway museum**. Iron production and tool manufacturing have been important in the town since the 13th century. The main attraction is the traditional forge where a blacksmith can be seen diligently working away. Power for the furnace is derived from four large paddlewheels turning outside in the Orbe River. The railway section includes models, memorabilia, and a slide show. The museum is open the same days as the caves, but from 9.30 am to noon and 1.30 to 6 pm. Admission costs Sfr8 or Sfr4 for children. If you want to see all three attractions, buy the Clover Card for Sfr24 (children Sfr12), valid for the whole season.

Mont d'Or (across the French border) and the Joux Valley provide opportunities for summer hiking and winter downhill and cross-country skiing. In the pastures at Mont d'Orzeires there is a reservation where North American buffaloes graze. Sailing and windsurfing are just two of the water sports that are popular on Lake Joux. The fishing season (trout) is from March to October. Contact the local tourist office (☎ 021-845 62 57) for more information.

Places to Stay

Camp at *Pré Sous Ville* (☎ 843 23 09), five minutes from the station by the Orbe River and alongside an open-air swimming pool. It is open from 1 May to early October.

The IYHF *youth hostel* (☎ 843 13 49), Rue du Simplon 11, is also just a five-minute walk from Vallorbe train station. Beds cost Sfr16 including breakfast and reception is open from 9 am to 5 pm. The whole hostel is

closed in November and December and for a couple of weeks at the end of April.

There are only two hotels in town. *Hôtel Restaurant l'Orbe* (☎ 843 12 41), on Rue de Lausanne has nine beds for Sfr45 per person using hall shower. *Hôtel des Jurats* (☎ 843 19 91), Rue des Eterpaz, has singles/doubles from Sfr50/70 with private shower or bath.

Places to Eat

There's more choice when eating out. Fish is a speciality of Vallorbe restaurants, especially local trout.

The main street, Grand Rue, has three supermarkets and several places to eat. *Le Rio* draws many people with its tasty and good-value lunch special for Sfr13, including soup. Eat in the room beyond the smoky bar area (closed Sunday). It also has inexpensive pizzas and meat dishes from Sfr14. Towards the train station is the tiny *Mont d'Or*, where pizza start at Sfr9 and filets of perch are Sfr20. The small salad buffet costs Sfr4.50 and Sfr8 (closed Sunday).

Hôtel Restaurant l'Orbe (see Places to Stay) has meals in the café from Sfr16, including trout for Sfr17. It also has a gourmet restaurant where main courses start at Sfr30 and the Menu Dégustation is Sfr60. It is closed in the evening on Sunday and Monday.

Getting There & Away

The high-speed TGV train service from Paris to Lausanne stops at Vallorbe. Border checks are on the train. One regional train an hour goes to Lausanne; it takes 48 minutes and costs Sfr14. By road, the quickest route is the eastwards N9 followed by the southwards N1, but it would be more fun to take the smaller roads across the Jura.

Trains also run along the western shore of Lake Joux and the Orbe River as far as Le Brassus. Roads go either side of the lake, with the quickest route along the eastern shore. A direct bus goes north-east to Yverdon several times a day; the journey takes 40 minutes and costs Sfr15.

Vaud Alps

Only the south-east corner of Vaud extends into the Alps, but it still boasts several interesting resorts and year-round skiing. A regional ski pass for the Vaud Alps (Alpes Vaudoises) costs Sfr42 for one day and Sfr213 for six. You can also ski at Vaud resorts using the Gstaad Super Ski Region (see the Gstaad section in the Bernese Oberland chapter).

Hiking is a popular pastime in the summer, and all the resorts mentioned offer possibilities for circular hikes lasting from two to five hours. Tourist offices can give details.

Only the low season prices are quoted for the hotels listed; prices are usually higher in July and August and peak in the winter high season.

For holiday chalets, write to the local tourist office well in advance, listing requirements. Upon arrival, ask the tourist office about discounts that apply with the local Guest Card.

CHÂTEAU D'OEX

This resort (pronounced Château Day) at 1000 metres is an attractive family resort with limited night life. There's an excellent blue (easy) run that goes all the way from Tête du Grin to Gerignoz, though there's also a good range of more difficult slopes. The ski school (☎ 029-4 68 48) takes children from three years of age. A one-day ski pass for the resort (50 km of runs) costs Sfr32.

A speciality of the resort is **hot air ballooning**, and passenger flights (☎ 029-4 77 88) are available winter and summer. In January it hosts the International Hot Air Ballooning Week where every day there's a special event or competition. Ask the tourist office (☎ 029-4 77 88) for exact dates. **River-rafting** is another possibility. There's also a **museum** highlighting traditional crafts and dwellings of the local Enhaut district. It's closed Monday, Wednesday and for most of October (Sfr3). **Le Chalet** (☎ 029-4 66 77)

is a touristy centre where there's cheese-making (daily except Monday), a model railway (Sfr2), a cheese and crafts shop, and a restaurant specialising in fondues.

Camp year-round by the Sarine River at *Au Berceau* (☎ 029-4 62 34). Accommodation prices are reasonable and prices barely rise in high season. There's even an IYHF *youth hostel* (☎ 029-4 64 04) that's a 10-minute walk from the train station. It costs Sfr17 and is closed from 31 October to mid-December and for a couple of weeks at the end of April. *La Printanière* (☎ 029-4 61 13) has singles/doubles from Sfr32/62 and the three-star *Ermitage* (☎ 029-4 60 03) has rooms from Sfr90/120 with private facilities. It also has some apartments for three or four people (from Sfr180). Both places are central, and nearly all the hotels in the resort have their own restaurant.

Getting There & Away

The resort is on the scenic rail route (the Panoramic Express) run by the private railroad, MOB, that connects Montreux to the Bernese Oberland. Departures are at least hourly. From Montreux it takes one hour and costs Sfr23 (railpasses are valid, except Inter-Rail). National roads run to Château d'Oex from Bulle, Aigle and Gstaad.

LEYSIN

Leysin (1350 metres) started life as a health resort, but it's now a well established skiing area with 60 km of marked runs. It is south-facing and enjoys fine views over the Rhône Valley, especially of the Dents de Midi. Take in the scenery in comfort in the revolving restaurant at the top of **Mt Berneuse** (2048 metres). The cable car up costs Sfr12 (Sfr8 down, Sfr16 return). For the most part, the ski slopes are not too demanding, and a one-day local ski pass costs Sfr31 (Sfr20 for children) with the Visitor's Card. A wide variety of other sports are on offer, including hang-gliding (☎ 025-34 26 02 for the school), tennis, ice-skating and curling.

Every year since 1987 the town has staged a **rock festival** which generally attracts major stars. It lasts for four days in early July and costs around Sfr45 to Sfr60 per day. Get details and tickets from the tourist office (☎ 025-34 22 44).

Leysin has year-round camping at *Semiramis* (☎ 025-34 11 48), one km from the station. At the lower end of the scale, *Club Vagabond* (☎ 025-34 13 21) has rooms from Sfr36/56. It's also a cheap place to eat and drink, and puts on regular special events. Other accommodation options include *Mont Riant* (☎ 025-34 27 01) with rooms from Sfr44/84, all the way up to the *Holiday Inn* (☎ 025-34 27 91), costing Sfr115/150 or more.

Getting There & Away

Leysin is reached from Aigle by a cog railway that departs hourly and takes 35 minutes (Sfr6.60, Sfr13.20 return; railpasses valid). Aigle is a stop on the main rail line between Lausanne and Martigny. By road, it is rather less direct: take highway 11 from Aigle (the road to Château d'Oex) then take a minor road at Le Sépey that doubles back to Leysin.

LES DIABLERETS

This village at 1151 metres is dominated by the mountain of the same name (3210 metres). The **glacier** at 3000 metres allows the opportunity to ski virtually year-round, not to mention offering fantastic views. There are two different cable cars running up to the glacier from the valley floor, and both are linked to the village by bus: starting from either Reusch or Col du Pillon you get to Cabane des Diablerets, where a further cable car whisks you almost to the summit at Scex Rouge. To ski from here all the way back down to Reusch is an exhilarating 2000 metre descent over 14 km.

A one-day summer ski pass costs Sfr46, which although expensive, compares favourably to a simple return fare to the glacier of Sfr42. For winter skiing, use the regional pass or get the Diablerets-Villars pass costing Sfr38 for one day (reduced prices for students and families), which is not valid for the glacier. Les Diablerets is also

known for hosting the **International Alpine Film Festival** at the end of September.

Get more information from the tourist office (☎ 025-53 13 58), which is open daily in season. There's year-round camping at *La Murée* (☎ 021-801 19 08) in the adjoining village of Vers l'Eglise. Places to stay in the centre include *Les Lilas* (☎ 025-53 11 34), just left of the station, with singles/doubles from Sfr50/80 and *Hostellerie les Sources* (☎ 025-53 21 26), near the mini-golf course, starting at Sfr68/112 for rooms with private shower and TV. *Auberge de la Poste* (☎ 025-53 11 24), near the tourist office, costs Sfr45/90. All three places have a restaurant. *Potinière* has a three-course lunch menu for Sfr14.

Getting There & Away

By rail, Les Diablerets is also reached from Aigle: take the hourly train that goes via Le Sépey. Alternatively, there's the postbus from Gstaad (Sfr10.60, takes one hour) which departs every one to two hours. A good road runs from either direction.

VILLARS

Villars (1250 metres) shares the same local ski pass as Les Diablerets, yielding 96 km of runs. It's a bit slow on nightlife with the compensating advantage that it's a good resort for families, with an excellent ski kindergarten (☎ 025-35 22 10). The views across the Rhône Valley are inspiring, encompassing the Dents de Midi, Mont Blanc and the Trient Glacier. The network of mountain transport is efficient and not too crowded. On the slopes, experts have few possibilities as most runs are geared towards beginners and intermediates. The highest skiing area is **Chamossaire** at 2116 metres. The resort's artificial ice-skating rink is a popular feature.

The Villars tourist office is on ☎ 025-35 32 32. The resort has a good choice of hotels boasting at least three stars, such as the central *Alpe Fleurie* (☎ 025-35 34 64), with rooms with private shower from Sfr75/140. Cheap places are harder to find: try *Les Papillons* (☎ 025-35 34 84) starting at

Sfr38/66. Many hotels have their own restaurant, and a few of the top ones even have a private swimming pool.

Getting There & Away

Villars is reached via Bex, 45 minutes away by hourly train. Bex is a stop on the main line from Lausanne to Martigny. There's also a bus that runs from Aigle (Sfr6.80, takes 35 minutes). The road from Villars to Les Diablerets is only open in the summer (bus service).

Valais

The dramatic Alpine scenery of Valais (Wallis in German) once made it one of the most inaccessible regions of Switzerland. The 10 highest mountains in the country – all of them over 4000 metres – are within this canton. Nowadays the mountains and valleys have been opened up by an efficient network of roads, railways and cable cars. It is an area of great natural beauty, and naturally enough, each impressive panorama has spawned its own resort.

The ski resorts in Valais are world-renowned. Zermatt is one of the oldest, and thrives on stupendous views of the Matterhorn. Verbier has a shorter history but is equally famous and gives access to a vast area of exciting and varied skiing. Less-known resorts such as Leukerbad can have perfectly satisfying skiing yet be much cheaper for ski-lift passes. In all there are 47 listed ski centres. In the summer, the mountains yield their treasures to hikers rather than skiers, but many resorts offer a whole host of additional sports, such as angling, swimming, mountaineering, tennis and golf. Just across the Swiss border in France is Mont Blanc.

The extreme mountain terrain has meant that the Swiss have been forced to establish and maintain an incredibly extensive network of pipes and canals, to supply water for homes and irrigation in this remote canton. It has been estimated that this network, if laid end-to-end, could wrap completely around the equator once, although the likelihood of anybody actually wanting to do this is very small. Some of these pipes feed the hydro-electric power installations, including the Grande Dixence Dam – a fantastic engineering feat and a great excursion from Sion. Much of the irrigation system is now very sophisticated, but in some parts the old *bisses*, narrow wooded aqueducts, are still in place.

History

Sion's pre-eminence in Valaisan history started after the Bishop of Valais left Martigny in 580 AD in order to settle in Sion. After 999 AD the Bishop of Sion received the patronage of the Emperor Rudolph III from Burgundy; Sion became an Imperial city and the bishop was able to rule the territory of Valais from Martigny to the Furka Pass. A consistent thorn in the sides of successive bishops were the Dukes of Savoy, and in 1475, an army of Savoyards besieged the city. Sion was liberated at the battle of the Planta with the help of the Swiss Confederation.

The invasion of the French in 1798 saw Valais become the Department of the Simplon. Napoleon was determined to control routes into Italy and he instigated the building of the Simplon Pass road which was opened in 1805. With the exit of Napoleon, Valais was able to join the Swiss Confederation in 1815.

Valais Wine

Valais also is Switzerland's main region for wine-producing, and accounts for 37% of the total land area devoted to this industry. Two-thirds of the wine produced is white wine. Fendant is the name reserved exclusively for Valais white wine. It is dry and fruity, and goes well with cheese dishes, fish, and Valais dried meats. Johannisberg is another well-known Valais white, and comes from the Sylvaner grape. Drink it to accompany fish, shellfish and asparagus. Like Fendant, it is ideal in fondue. Other whites you may come across are Muscat (good with fish) and Ermitage (good with cheese and poached fish). Amigne and Malvoise are dessert wines.

The principal red wine is Dôle, a product of the Pinot Noir and Gamay grapes. It is full-bodied and fruity, and is considered best with red meats, game and cheese; as is the

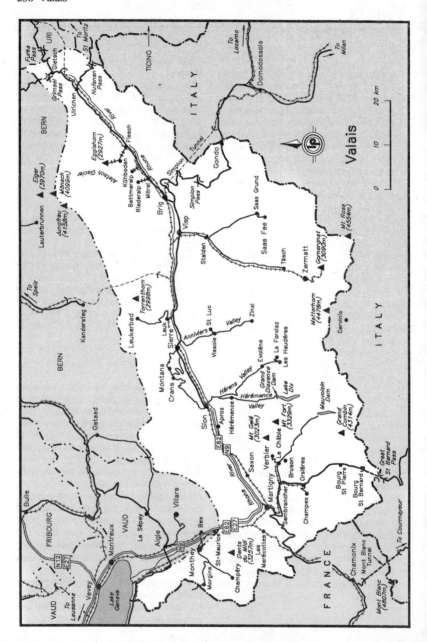

robust red wine, Humagne. Goron is best with white meat and pork.

There are numerous vineyards and wine-growing villages bordering the Rhône between Martigny and Sierre. The regional or local tourist offices can give information about driving itineraries through this area.

Cow Fights

A peculiarity of Valais is the *Combat de Reines* (Kuhkaempfe in German), cow fights which are organised in villages to determine which beast is most suited to lead the herd up to the summer pastures. The cows that take part in these combats are from the Hérens breed, renowned for their fighting instincts. The events have outgrown the traditional *raison d'être*. Breeding is big business: a winner, acclaimed to be the 'queen' of the herd, can be worth as much as Sfr20,000 and much more in terms of prestige. Techniques such as genetic selection and embryo freezing are used to get the most effective contenders to the field of combat. Once selected, they are fed oats concentrate (believed to act as a stimulant), and sometimes even wine.

Contests usually take place on selected Sundays through the summer from the end of March, accompanied by much celebration and consumption of Valaisan wine. The combatants rarely get hurt. There is a grand final in Aproz on Ascension Day and the last meeting of the season is held at the Martigny Fair in October. Aproz is only a 10-minute bus ride from Sion train station.

Orientation & Information

The canton and tourist region of Valais stretches from close to the eastern shore of Lake Geneva to Ticino. It includes the territory south of those points bordering France and Italy, an area of approximately 5220 km. The French/German language divide cuts right through the middle of the canton. The western part of the canton is the Lower Valais (Bas Valais, Unterwallis) and the eastern part the Upper Valais (Haupt Valais, Oberwallis). The Germanisation of the Upper Valais was due to the infiltration of Walser communities from the north in the 6th century.

The regional tourist office (Union Valaisanne du Tourism) is in Sion (☎ 027-22 31 61), 16 Rue de Pré-Fleuri, Sion. Information is available on the first floor; opening hours are Monday to Friday from 8 am to noon and 2 to 6 pm.

Getting There & Away

The chains of mountains strung across the region make north-south progress extremely difficult. See Martigny for routes into France and Italy from west Valais, and Brig for transport routes in east Valais. Brig and Martigny are linked by the east-west N9 which follows the course of the Rhône, turning north from Martigny to Lake Geneva.

Lower Valais

SION

From afar, Sion (Sitten in German) looks fantastic within its cusp of Valaisan peaks. It sits on the mostly flat ribbon of the Rhône Valley, yet rising from the town are two hills, looking (it must be said, though guidebooks never do) like a pair of breasts, each topped by its own 'nipple', a medieval fortification. They lend a sense of history to the town, which is accentuated by the cobbled streets and warren of side-alleys in the centre. Thanks to its status as the cantonal capital, it is the location of several provincial museums.

The bishops of Sion, enjoying the powers of temporal princes, had the habit of dispensing justice with an unecclesiastical ruthlessness and indulging in all sorts of worldly intrigues. The most famous Cardinal-Bishop was Mathieu Schiner who dispatched troops in the early 16th century to aid the papal throne. The political power of the bishops gradually waned until it was removed completely under the 1848 constitution.

Orientation & Information

Sion has a population of 25,100 and lies predominantly on the north bank of the Rhône River. It is French-speaking. The train station is conveniently central and has bike rental and money-exchange counters open daily. The post office is nearby. The old town lies 400 metres to the north. The tourist office (☎ 027-22 85 86), Place de la Planta, sells good city maps for Sfr6.80, but you can get the same map on a smaller scale free from the Swiss Bank Corporation on the corner; its version includes useful bus timetable information. The tourist office is open Monday to Friday from 8.30 am to noon and 2 to 5.30 pm, and Saturday from 9 am to noon. Hours are slightly extended in the summer.

The telephone code for Sion is 027.

Things to See & Do

The **Tourbillon Castle** (Château de Tourbillon) is open daily (except Monday) from 10 am to 6 pm. Little remains to see except the exterior walls, but the view from the top is worth the climb and there's a good picnic area. The grassy hill buzzes with cicadas on the walk up.

The other hill is crowned by the fortress-like **Basilique de Valére**. It dates from the 12th century and has faded frescoes and elaborately carved wooden stalls. Bursting out of the interior back wall, looking like the hull of a ship, is the oldest playable organ in the world. It was constructed in the 15th century and still plays. Next to the church is a museum dealing with history and ethnography, as well as temporary exhibitions (Sfr5, students Sfr2.50, families Sfr10).

On the way up to the castle and the church, spare five minutes for the Town Hall (Hôtel de Ville), which has some fine wooden doors inside on the first floor. Also take a look in the **cathedral** in the old town. It has a wooden triptych above the high altar and a Romanesque belfry dating from the 11th century.

Between Rue de Conthey and Rue de Lausanne is a small covered shopping arcade, and leading from this is the **Maison**

Supersaxo, built in 1505 by Georges Supersaxo (1450-1529). The father of 23 children, his history is tied in with that of the powerful bishop, Mathieu Schiner, a worldly cleric who courted European leaders to an unprecedented degree during his period in power. Between them they plotted the downfall of an earlier bishop, Josse de Silenen, and forced him into exile. But they later fell out, and Supersaxo built this lavish dwelling partly to vex his erstwhile ally. It's an exercise in ostentation. The most impressive remnant is the Baroque rosette on the ceiling in the room on the 2nd floor (free entry, and there are notes in English).

It's open daily from 8 am to noon and (except on Saturday and Sunday afternoon) 2 to 6 pm. Ultimately, Schiner proved the dominant force, as he instigated the arrest of Supersaxo in Rome in 1512. Supersaxo was jailed for two years and eventually exiled to Vevey.

Museums All the museums in the town are closed on Monday. The **Valais Museum of Fine Arts** (Musée Cantonal des Beaux-Arts) is in two sections of the old episcopal residences at the foot of the castle. It concentrates on Valaisan artists, both ancient and modern, and costs Sfr5 (students, children and senior citizens Sfr2.50, families Sfr10) for admission. The **Valais Archaeological Museum** (Musée Cantonal d'Archéologie), on Rue des Châteaux, is of only limited interest to English speakers as all the explanations are in German (Sfr4, students Sfr2). Both are open from 10 am to noon and 2 to 6 pm. The **Valais Museum of Natural History** (Musée Cantonal d'Histoire Naturelle), Ave de la Gare 42, is comparatively small, and has cases full of stuffed animals (Sfr2, students Sfr1, families Sfr4; open 2 to 6 pm).

Places to Stay

The nearest camping is four km west of Sion, at *Les Îles* (☎ 36 43 47), by the Rhône river, off the Route d'Aproz. It has excellent facilities and is closed in November and for most

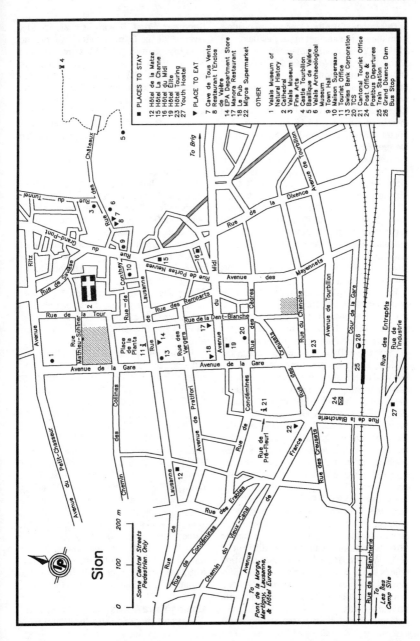

Sion

Some Central Streets
Pedestrian Only

0   100   200 m

To Brig

To Les Iles
Camp Site

To Pont de la Morge,
Martigny, Lausanne,
& Hôtel Europa

■ PLACES TO STAY

12 Hôtel de la Matze
15 Hôtel La Channe
16 Hôtel du Midi
19 Hôtel Elite
23 Hôtel Touring
27 Youth Hostel

▼ PLACE TO EAT

7   Cave de Tous Vents
8   Restaurant l'Enclos
    de Valère
14 EPA Department Store
17 Manora Restaurant
18 Le Pub
22 Migros Supermarket

OTHER

1   Valais Museum of
    Natural History
2   Cathedral
3   Valais Museum of
    Fine Arts
4   Castle Tourbillon
5   Basilique de Valère
6   Valais Archaeological
    Museum
9   Town Hall
10 Maison Supersaxo
11 Tourist Office
13 Swiss Bank Corporation
20 TCS
21 Cantonal Tourist Office
24 Post Office &
    Postbus Departures
25 Train Station
26 Grand Dixence Dam
    Bus Stop

of December. Take the Condémines postbus from the station and get off at Les Îles.

The IYHF *youth hostel* (Auberge de Jeunesse; ☎ 23 74 70), Rue de l'Industrie 2 is behind the station (exit left and turn left under the tracks). It's in a modern building with good showers and costs Sfr19.75. Reception is closed from 10 am to 5 pm and there's an irritating 10.15 pm curfew. The hostel closes from mid-October to mid-December.

Sion has no particularly cheap hotels. If you have your own transport it is easily viable to stay in Pont de la Morge, two km west of Sion, where *Relais du Simplon* (☎ 36 20 30) has rooms for Sfr34 per person and *Auberge des Collines* (☎ 36 20 80) for Sfr40 per person. Both are close to each other on the main road, Rue de Savoie. Postbuses to Aven and Ardon leaving from Sion station stop at the Pont de la Morge post office. Bus No 1 also goes there.

In Sion, the best value hotel is *Hotêl de la Matze* (☎ 22 36 67), Rue de Lausanne 49. It has well-presented rooms of a reasonable size and a cheerful breakfast room. Singles with a shower cubicle in the room are Sfr45, or Sfr55 to Sfr60 with a proper bathroom and toilet. Doubles/triples with private shower/toilet are Sfr90/120. There are usually parking spaces around the back of the hotel on the parallel street. Also good is *Élite* (☎ 22 33 95), Avenue du Midi 6. The turned-down sheets and pillows look like they've been arranged using a protractor but the rooms could be better aired. Singles/doubles/triples with hall shower/toilet are Sfr50/85/120 and there is parking round the back.

La Channe (☎ 22 32 71), Rue des Portes Neuves 9, is in a central pedestrian street so parking can be a problem. Fairly smart singles/doubles using hall showers start at Sfr65/90. Parking can also be difficult at *Hotêl du Midi* (☎ 23 13 31), Place du Midi, which has a busy restaurant and corridors painted an unsettling pink/orange colour. Singles/doubles start at Sfr65/100 with private shower.

Conveniently close to the station is the three-star *Hôtel Touring* (☎ 23 15 51), Avenue de la Gare 6, with free private parking. Singles/doubles are around Sfr90/140 for rooms with private bath or shower, toilet, TV, mini bar, radio and telephone. The most central four-star place, *Europa* (☎ 22 24 23), Rue de l'Envoi 19, is a bit out of the way in the west of Sion. Prices start at Sfr120/160. It has a bar, sauna and restaurants on site, and there is good disabled access.

Places to Eat

There is a huge *Migros* complex, a five-minute walk from the station at Avenue de France. It has two restaurants. An *EPA* department store is opposite the tourist office on Rue de Lausanne, open to 6.30 pm weekdays and 5 pm on Saturday. Its restaurant has a daily menu with soup for Sfr8 and other dishes from Sfr5 to Sfr13. Attached to the Placette department store is a buffet-style *Manora* restaurant, Avenue du Midi, with good, inexpensive food. It is open until 10 pm daily. The salad buffet costs between Sfr3.80 and Sfr9.50 depending upon plate size.

Le Pub, on Avenue de la Gare, offers food either in the bar or in the restaurant section downstairs. Pizza and pasta starts at Sfr 10 and there is a three-course lunch menu for Sfr15. It is open until 1 am daily.

For more authentic eating, explore the small bistros and brasseries in the central pedestrian district. A good mid-price choice is *Restaurant l'Enclos de Valère*, (☎ 23 32 30), Rue de Château 18, a small and quiet French restaurant with meat and fish dishes between Sfr25 to Sfr38 (closed Monday). Valais wines start at Sfr28 a bottle and the three-course menu du jour costs Sfr35. On a sunny day take to the outside tables in the garden. Next door at No 16 is the *Cave de Tous Vents*, under the same ownership, an atmospheric cellar offering fondue from Sfr32 for two. It's open daily from 5 pm to midnight.

Getting There & Away

The airport (☎ 23 64 00) is two km west of

the train station; bus Nos 1 and 2 go there, or you can take a taxi for around Sfr10. Crossair has one or two daily non-stop flights to Zürich which take 50 minutes.

Sion is a major postbus centre, with 29 different routes leaving from outside the train station. A special seven-day pass, valid on all routes, costs Sfr55, or Sfr33 for children and those with the Half-Fare Card.

All trains on the Lausanne-Brig express route stop at Sion. To Lausanne takes 70 minutes and costs Sfr27, and to Brig takes one hour 40 minutes and costs Sfr15.80.

The N9 motorway passes through the south of Sion, with exits on both the west and east side of the city.

Europcar (☎ 22 34 69) is at Garage Delta, Rue de Lausanne 148. Hertz (☎ 22 37 42) is at Garage du Nord, Ave Ritz, and Avis (22 20 77) is at the garage at 23 Ave de Tourbillon.

AROUND SION
Grande Dixence Dam
This dam is hugely impressive by its sheer size. Almost six million cubic metres of concrete went into building it, and it's twice the volume and twice the height (284 metres) of the Great Pyramid of Egypt. It retains 400 cubic metres of water and produces annually 1600 kWh of hydro-electricity. To appreciate the beauty of the surroundings you need to gain some height, and footpaths and a cable car (from Le Chargeur to the lake) allow you to do this. It's at the end of the Hérémence Valley and is circled by towering peaks.

Getting There & Away The road from Sion to the dam is closed in winter and spring. A private bus service runs between the two places two to four times a day from early June to mid-October. The journey takes an hour and costs Sfr26.40 return. Take the blue bus from directly outside the train station in Sion (Swiss Pass valid).

Hérens Valley
This is the other valley heading south from Sion. It promotes itself as the 'true' Valais, where villagers in traditional costumes carry out their traditional lifestyle. Exactly how much of this is tourism-inspired tradition is difficult to gauge. What isn't open to doubt are the many hiking possibilities and the copious wildlife – look out for the Black Woodpecker, the largest in Europe, which has a red marking on its head. The main resorts are south of Evolène. Buses run several times a day from Sion, but only as far as La Forclaz in winter.

MARTIGNY
Martigny (population 11,300) dates back to Roman times and is still unearthing important archaeological finds. The town was seized by the Roman Empire in 15 BC, and in the reign of Emperor Claudius, it was named Forum Claudii Vallensium.

Orientation & Information
French-speaking Martigny is an important junction at the 'L' bend of the Rhône River. The hub of the town is Place Centrale, where you will find the tourist office (☎ 026-21 22 20), open Monday to Friday from 9 am to noon and 2 to 6 pm, and Saturday from 9 am to noon. Summer hours are extended on Saturday to 2 to 6 pm, and in July and August it also open on Sunday from 10 am to noon and 4 to 6 pm. The train station (with bike rental and money exchange) is one km to the northeast of Place Centrale, and most of the Roman remains are to the south.

The telephone code for Martigny is 026.

Things to See & Do
After visiting the tourist office, exit by the interior door leading directly to the stairway of the town hall. There's an impressive stained glass window over three floors (55 sq metres) created by Edmond Bille. Nearby is the church of **Our Lady of the Fields** (Notre Dame des Champs), 17th century and recently renovated, with a Rococo altar and a belfry combining Romanesque and Gothic elements. Also take a look at the chapel of **Our Lady of Compassion Church** (Notre Dame de Compassion), by the Dranse River, noted especially for its ex-voto paintings. Above the chapel is the 13th-century **Bâtiaz**

Castle (Château de la Bâtiaz), thrusting up from the hill. It is is seldom open, but provides a good view of the valley. In this direction are two vineyards within a 50-minute walk (follow signs for Chemin du Vignoble).

Pick up the leaflet from the tourist office which shows a **walking tour** (circuit archéologique) of the main Roman ruins. The **Roman Amphitheatre** can seat 6000 people and is the site for the annual Combat de Reines (see the Festivals section).

The main cultural attraction in the town is the **Foundation Pierre Gianadda**. Not only does it have a Gallo-Roman Museum (the best exhibit is a bronze three-horned bull's head – a Gallic divinity), but it also has a busy programme of classical music concerts, and an art exhibition periodically reviewing major artists. (Rodin is featured from 11 March to 12 June 1994.) In the garden are more archaeological excavations, interestingly juxtaposed with modern art sculptures (by Miró, Moore, Arp, Segal, etc) on the green lawns.

In the automobile museum there's an impressive collection of historic cars, spanning the spectrum from a 1897 Benz (maximum speed 25 km/ph) to a 1929 Mercedes (maximum speed 200 km/ph). A few of the early Swiss cars (like the 1910 and 1911 Turicum) have a horn by the steering wheel, connected by a metal tube to a serpent's head on the front mudguard. When you blow the horn the serpent emits a goose-like honk – who said the Swiss haven't got a sense of humour!

The Foundation is open 15 May to 31 October daily from 9 am to 7 pm, and the rest of the year daily from 10 am to noon and 1.30 to 6 pm. Entry costs Sfr12 for adults, Sfr5 for children (to 10 years) and students, and Sfr25 for families. Ask for the English notes at the ticket desk.

Within 10 km of Martigny are three picturesque **gorges**: Trient, Durnand, and Triège, all accessible by train.

Festivals

The town hosts the **Valais Regional Fair** in early October. Later that month is the traditional event, **Combat de Reines**, the climax of a series of cow-fights conducted in spring and autumn. It's not distasteful (unlike Spanish bullfighting) and the combatants rarely get hurt. See the chapter introduction for background information. Tickets to view the proceedings in the amphitheatre are around Sfr16 for seats and Sfr10 to stand.

In December, the **Bacon Fair** (Foire du Lard), takes place, an annual event dating back to the Middle Ages.

Avenue de la Gare is taken over by a lively **market** every Tuesday morning.

Places to Stay

The TCS *camp site* (☎ 22 45 44), Rue de Levant 68, is reasonably convenient for the centre. It's open year round and reception is open daily from 7 am to 10 pm. Price per person including tax is Sfr5.60 (Sfr5.20 in winter), and double this for a tent and car.

The *youth hostel* (☎ 21 22 60), Rue de Levant 66, has been stripped of its IYHF status, and you can see why when you walk through the underground entrance, below the fire station. It's an old bomb shelter with no windows, no breakfast and cramped bunks. At least it's dirt cheap – Sfr8 including sheets. The hostel is open from April to early October and the doors are locked from 9 am to 5 pm.

Most of the more expensive places raise their prices slightly for the summer season. Not so at *De la Croisée* (☎ 22 23 59), west of the Dranse River at Rue du Léman 51. Prices start at Sfr34 per person. Basic singles/doubles cost Sfr35/55 year-round at *Pension Poste-Bourg* (☎ 22 25 17), Ave du Grand St Bernard 81. Opposite at No 74 is the rather plusher *Du Forum* (☎ 22 18 41), with rooms from Sfr70/120 with private shower/toilet and TV. On the same road towards town, at No 41, is *Du Strand* (☎ 22 95 06), with maze-like, velvety-green corridors and modern rooms with shower/toilet for Sfr60/80.

A five-minute walk from the station by the tracks is *Relais Grand Quai* (☎ 22 20 50), Rue du Simplon 33, offering decent-sized

Top Left: House of Parliament, Lugano, Ticino (TW)
Top Right: Castles Montebello and Sasso Corbaro, Bellinzona, Ticino (MH)
Bottom: Morcote and Lake Lugano, Ticino (MH)

Top Left: Bellinzona from Castel Grande, Ticino (MH)
Top Right: Piazza Cioccaro, Lugano, Ticino (MH)
Bottom Left: Piazza Cioccaro, Lugano, Ticino (MH)
Bottom Right: Train en route to Arosa, Graubünden (MH)

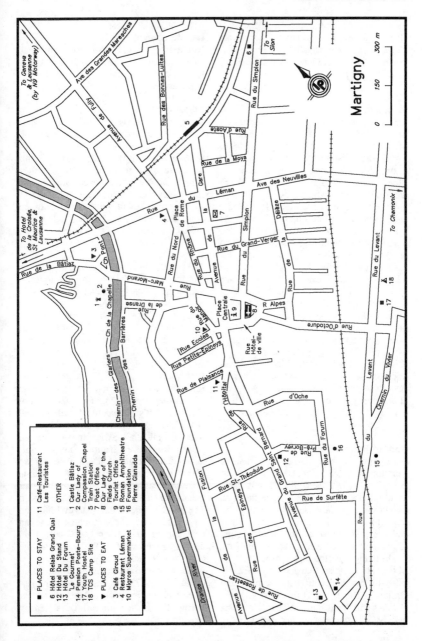

Martigny

To Geneva
& Lausanne
(by N9 Motorway)

To Hotel
de la Croisée,
St Maurice &
Lausanne

To Sion

To Chamonix

0   150   300 m

PLACES TO STAY
6   Hôtel Relais Grand Quai
12 Hôtel Du Stand
13 Hôtel Du Forum
14 'Le Gourmet'
    Pension Poste-Bourg
17 Youth Hostel
18 TCS Camp Site

PLACES TO EAT
3   Café Giraud
4   Restaurant Léman
10 Migros Supermarket

11 Café-Restaurant
    Les Touristes

OTHER
1   Castle Bâtiaz
2   Our Lady of
    Compassion Chapel
5   Train Station
7   Post Office
8   Our Lady of the
    Fields Church
9   Tourist Office
15 Roman Amphitheatre
16 Pierre Gianadda
    Foundation

Ave des Grandes Maresches

Avenue de Fully

Rue des Bonnes-Luites

Rue du Simplon

Rue d'Aoste

Rue de la Moya

Ave des Neuvilles

Gare

du   Léman

Place
de Rome   Rue   de   la   Riche

Rue du Simplon

Rue du Grand-Verger

Rue du Nord

Rue   Marc-Morand

Avenue

Rue

de   la   Délèze

Rue   du   Levant

Rue de la Bâtiaz

Rue   de   la   Dranse

Place
Centrale

R Alpes

Rue d'Octodure

Rue   du   Levant

Chemin   des   Glariers

Chemin   des   Barrières

Ch de la Chapelle

Ch Pont

Rue   du   Manoir

Rue Ecoles

Rue Petits-Epineys

Rue de Plaisance

Rue de l'Hôpital

Rue
Hôtel-
de-ville

Rue   d'Oche

Rue du Forum

Rue de Pré-Borvey

Chemin   du   Vivier

Drance River

Rue   de   la   Fusion

Rue   des   Epineys

Rue St-Théodule

Avenue du Grand Saint Bernard

Rue de Surfête

Rue   du   Levant

Rue de Rossettan

rooms with own bathroom for Sfr58/90. It also has some cheaper rooms without private shower but they're usually full. The restaurant has a good value lunch special for Sfr13 including soup and dessert.

Places to Eat

There is a large *Migros* supermarket with groceries and general goods at Rue du Manoir. The restaurant has meals for Sfr9 to Sfr13 and a comprehensive salad buffet costing Sfr1.60 per 100 grams. It is closed Monday morning and open until 6.30 pm weekdays and 5 pm Saturday.

Café-restaurant *Les Touristes*, Place Plaisance, is not particularly touristy, despite its name, and has pizza/pasta from Sfr9.50 and a daily special with soup for Sfr13. It also has more expensive grills, and snails for Sfr8.50 (closed Wednesday). *Restaurant Léman*, Rue du Léman 19, is a large place specialising in regional cuisine, including fish and game for around Sfr30 (closed Sunday). In contrast, *Café Giroud* is a small place tucked away on Rue de la Bâtiaz, where you can try fondue for Sfr15 and pig's trotters for Sfr12 (closed Sunday).

The best restaurant in Martigny, albeit pricey, is *Le Gourmet* at the Hotel du Forum (see Places to Stay). It offers seasonal specialities and three different set menus. It is closed on Sunday evening and Monday.

Getting There & Away

Martigny is on the main rail route running from Lausanne (Sfr19.80, takes one hour) to Brig (Sfr24, takes one hour). There is also a train departing every one to two hours to Chamonix in France (see the Mont Blanc section for more details). The fare is Sfr24 and the journey takes around two hours, depending upon connections at the border.

Martigny is also the departure point for the St Bernard Express, that goes to Le Châble (Sfr8.40, bus connection for Verbier) and Orsières. Buses go from Martigny via Orsières and the St Bernard Tunnel to Aosta in Italy (Sfr32, at least two departures a day).

AROUND MARTIGNY
Les Marécottes

Not far from Martigny to the west, this small chalet village has a zoo exhibiting Alpine species in their natural habitat (open May to September).

St Maurice

This small town is named after the Roman Christian who, along with many of his followers, was massacred in 302 AD for refusing to worship the gods of Rome. Points of interest are the 11th century Abbey church, the Abbey treasury containing some fine ecclesiastical pieces (call ☎ 025-65 11 81 to enquire about guided tours between April and November), and the castle with a military museum (closed Monday).

Bex

The town of Bex is the next train station in the direction of Monthey from St Maurice and it has the only operational salt mine in Switzerland, producing 150 tons of salt every year. It can be visited daily from 1 April to 15 November by guided tour (Sfr12), but you must telephone in advance on ☎ 025-63 24 62.

Champéry

Running south-west from Monthey is the Illiez Valley, terminating in the ski resort of Champéry. It's a chalet-style village and shares the vast Portes du Soleil ski region with several other Swiss and French ski resorts. Runs near Champéry are predominantly intermediate although experts have plenty of opportunity for off-piste skiing. Prices are reasonable, and are actually better value than on the French side of the border. The resort is beneath the Dents du Midi, and an excellent view of this mountain range can be achieved from **Croix de Culet** (1963 metres), a viewpoint a short walk from the top of the Planachaux cable car.

The tourist office for the Val d'Illiez is on (☎ 025-77 20 77. Another good, inexpensive, and relatively uncrowded resort for skiing the Portes du Soleil is nearby **Morgins**.

Getting There & Away Aigle and St Maurice are on the main rail route from Lausanne to Martigny. From Aigle a train runs hourly to Champéry (takes one hour, Sfr10.60), via Monthey.

Orsières

Winding its way south of Martigny is highway 21 (E27), leading to the Great St Bernard Pass and beyond into Italy. The town of Orsières is as far as you can get by rail. From here you can walk (1¾ hours), take the bus or drive to **Champex** and its attractive lake. A cable car ascends above the lake to **La Breya** (2374 metres). The view from here includes the Grand Combin (4314 metres) to the south-east, and the cable car operates from mid-June to late November (Sfr 12 return).

Bourg St Pierre

South of Orsières is Bourg St Pierre, where Napoleon stayed during one of his incursions over the Alps. Beyond the town, the nine-km St Bernard tunnel, opened in 1964, allows year-round access to Italy. The old road over the **Great St Bernard Pass** is closed in winter and leads to the historic **Hospice**, where the monks have been rescuing travellers stranded in the snows since the 11th century. They have been aided in the task by the famous St Bernard dogs (nowadays Alsatians are used) – it is estimated that over the years, more than 2000 people have been saved by the clerics and their canines.

The first mention of the St Bernard dogs was in 1708. A century later, one of the best-known of the dogs, Barry I, toiled for 12 years in the snow drifts. After his death he was rewarded with a visit to the taxidermist, and now stands in the Natural History Museum in Bern.

A more recent Barry (one of a long line) is in the vestibule of the hospice. Some living specimens can be seen in the kennels. The museum in the hospice tells the history of its rescue work and has church relics and ornaments. It is open from June to October, which coincides with the period the bus runs from Martigny (two a day, takes one hour and

costs Sfr20.80). Buses are more frequent from Orsières. Buses go as far as the hospice, or you can walk the famous path from Bourg St Pierre in under two hours.

MONT BLANC

If there aren't enough mountains in Switzerland to sate your appetite for skiing and scenery, a trip to Mont Blanc makes an excellent and easily arranged excursion. At 4807 metres Mont Blanc is the highest mountain in the Alps, and with the valley floor some 3800 metres below the peak, the views are nothing short of spectacular. Unfortunately, by its sheer massiveness the mountain does tend to attract cloudy weather, so choose your day to visit carefully. The two easiest departure points from Switzerland are Geneva and Martigny.

Orientation & Information

Mont Blanc is on the border with France and Italy. On the French side is the resort of Chamonix, one of the oldest in the Alps, which still retains much of its Victorian architecture. The tourist office (☎ 50.53.00.24) at Place de l'Église is open daily. There is also the Office de Haute Montagne (☎ 50.53.22.08), 2nd floor, 109 Place de l'Eglise, dispensing information for walkers, hikers and mountain climbers.

Across the Italian border is the resort of Courmayeur. For information contact the tourist office (Azienda Autonoma di Soggiorno e Turismo) on ☎ 0165-84 20 60). The two resorts are connected by the Mont Blanc Tunnel. The country telephone code for France is 33 and for Italy is 39.

Things to See & Do

Chamonix Chamonix has exciting if fragmented skiing. A one-day ski pass and equipment rental will cost around 300FF. The most famous area and the world's longest ski run is the **Vallée Blanche**, a 20-km glacier hanging from the shoulder of Mont Blanc. You reach this via the Aiguille du Midi cable railway, and the trip up provides heart-pumping views. There is also the **Mer de Glace Glacier** which can be reached by a cog-wheel railway or by foot from the village. **Le Brévent** peak on the west side of the valley furnishes more hiking opportunities, fine views of Mont Blanc and some fairly gentle skiing. Chamonix's mix of Victorian and more modern buildings makes the village an appealing place in which to stroll around. For more information about Chamonix, refer to Lonely Planet's *France – a travel survival kit.*

Courmayeur The Italian side of the mountain offers a good range of intermediate runs and an excellent ski school. Most of the runs face Mont Blanc (Monte Bianco in Italian) so the views are great. It is also possible to ascend Mont Blanc itself (with a guide) and ski down the other side to Chamonix on the Mer de Glace Glacier, but seek advice before you consider this. The village is atmospheric and reasonably lively, with lots of old buildings to enjoy. For more information about Courmayeur, refer to Lonely Planet's *Italy – a travel survival kit.*

Getting There & Away

The narrow-gauge train line from Saint Gervais-Le Fayet (20 km west of Chamonix) to Martigny (42 km north of Chamonix) stops at 11 towns in the Chamonix Valley, including Chamonix itself. There are nine to 12 return trips a day. You have to change trains on the Swiss border (at Châtelard or Vallorcine) because of differing track gauges. Le Fayet serves as a rail head for long-haul trains to destinations all over France, and this is the easiest route to Geneva, about two hours away.

SAT Autocar (☎ 50.53.01.15) has buses to Annecy, Courmayeur (46FF, takes 40 minutes) and Geneva (135FF, 1½ to two hours).

The road from Chamonix to Martigny follows closely the route of the narrow-gauge railway for much of the distance. From Geneva, the E21 motorway runs all the way to Le Fayet, then an ordinary main road takes over for the last 17 km to Chamonix. There are two ways to get from Martigny to Courmayeur: either via Chamonix and the Mont Blanc Tunnel, or via the E21a and the Great St Bernard Pass (closed in winter) to Aosta, and the E21b from there. This latter route can be duplicated by a combination of train and bus (the bus section over the pass only runs in summer).

VERBIER

Verbier is a trendy, sophisticated resort that receives hordes of weekend visitors from Geneva, 150 km away, yet its history as a tourist centre is extremely short. In 1945 Verbier had just 27 permanent residents, and the first proper ski lift opened as late as 1947. Nowadays it has the largest cable car in Switzerland, Le Jumbo that flies up Mont-

Christian Almer (pioneer mountain guide in the Chamonix region)

Fort holding 150 passengers. But skiers still suffer notoriously slow lift queues at peak times.

Orientation & Information

Verbier is at 1500 metres, on a south-west facing ledge above Le Châble, the terminus of the railway. The resort proper is up the hill from Verbier village. The hub of Verbier is Place Centrale, where you will find the tourist office (☎ 026-31 62 22). Its opening hours are Monday to Saturday from 8.30 am to noon and 2 to 6.30 pm, and Sunday from 9.30 am to noon. In winter, Sunday hours change to 9 am to noon and 4 to 6.30 pm. Just off the square is the post office and postbus terminus. Verbier is mostly shut from late October to early December and in May, and that includes the cable cars.

The telephone code for Verbier is 026.

Activities

Skiing is the primary activity. The ski pass gives access to one of the finest ski areas in the world, comprising 400 km of runs and 100 ski lifts. The pass is also one of the most expensive around, costing Sfr53 for one day, Sfr325 for a week and Sfr1168 for the season. Families get a discount, and more restrictive, slightly cheaper passes are also available.

The skiing is exciting and varied, and there are many opportunities for experts to flaunt their off-piste skills, particularly at Attelas and Mont-Fort. Experienced skiers can also take on the Four Valleys circuit – 80 km of black and red runs which can just about be completed in one day. Mont-Fort at 3330 metres is high enough to allow summer skiing on its glacier. Most of the runs are too difficult for beginners to handle, but there is a ski school (☎ 31 68 25) behind the post office: Sfr23 for one lesson and Sfr115 for seven. Crowds are a definite problem on the less demanding intermediate runs between les Attelas and the village, yet the Savoleyres area on the other side of the resort is less busy and just as good.

Golf There's a new course, offering 18 holes

and fine views. Get information from the tourist office or the golf club (☎ 31 15 66).

Hang-Gliding & Paragliding These sports are becoming increasingly popular. Solo flights or those with an instructor in tandem are possible: contact the Parapente school (☎ 31 68 18) for details. The one-day initiation course costs Sfr190 and a tandem flight costs Sfr390. Verbier hosts a paragliding competition every August.

Ski-Mountaineering The ski school has a Bureau des Guides, where you can organise a guide for ski-mountaineering treks along the Haute Route to Zermatt or Saas Fee. The trip takes three to four days and reaches a maximum altitude of 3800 metres. The charge per day is Sfr170 to Sfr300 per person, depending upon how many people are in the group. Equipment hire and cable cars cost extra.

Hiking The tourist office gives out a map giving brief descriptions (in French) and times of various hiking trails around the resort. From Les Ruinettes, it takes two hours to ascend to the ridge at Creblet, and down into the crater and the lake, Lac des Vaux. For non-skiers, day passes on the lifts cost between Sfr18 and Sfr40 depending upon the validity. For individual tickets, the basic formula is Sfr8 (Sfr12) for each cable station stop.

To get up to **Mt Fort** and enjoy the magnificent view, that includes Mont Blanc, non-skiers need to take a bus or walk from Les Ruinettes to the Jumbo cable car. Allow around an hour each way. The non-skiers day pass costs Sfr40. Mt Gelé gives a better view of the valley below Verbier.

Places to Stay

In Verbier The cheapest option in Verbier are the chalets and private rooms for a minimum one week stay. Check with the tourist office at least four months in advance. Otherwise, prices are quite high (and soar higher in mid and high-season), but you should always get a room with at least a private shower. Some of the more affordable B&B (Garni) hotels in the resort are: *Hotel Rosablanche* (☎ 31 55 55), Rue de la Barmettaz, with singles /doubles from Sfr45/80, *Mont-Gelé* (☎ 31 30 53), by the base of the Les Ruinettes cable car, costing from Sfr54/92, and *Ermitage*, (☎ 31 64 77), Place Centrale, starting at Sfr69/123.

Many places offer half-board as standard. One such place is *De La Poste* (☎ 31 66 81), Rue de Médran, with its own indoor swimming pool and garden terrace. Rooms start at Sfr89/164, or Sfr63/122 using half showers.

One of the best places to stay is *Rosalp* (☎ 31 63 23), a little further along Rue de Médran, with large, well-equipped rooms starting at Sfr180/240 in summer or Sfr260/370 in winter.

Around Verbier The nearest camping is some distance away at Sembrancher (☎ 85 12 54), and it's open year-round.

The nearest IYHF *youth hostel* (☎ 36 23 56) is not very convenient either, as it's on the opposite side of the valley in Bruson. In its favour is the fact that it only costs Sfr7.50 in summer and Sfr8.50 in winter, there's a good kitchen (no meters) and the doors are always open. Blankets but not sheets are supplied, and there's no breakfast and few showers. Bruson is a pleasant, unspoilt village, full of wooden chalets and traditional storage barns on stilts (with circular stones to keep the rats out). The hostel is around the corner from the café-restaurant, but you need to go to the owner's house, 200 metres up from the bus stop, to check-in (before 9 am or after 5 pm). It is closed in May and November. It's a 30-minute walk up to Bruson from Le Châble or take the bus from the train station (Sfr2).

Le Châble is inexpensive for accommodation: *Des Alpes* (☎ 36 14 65) and *l'Escale* (☎ 36 27 07) both have rooms from Sfr30 per person.

Places to Eat

Cheap eating is also fairly problematic in Verbier, unless you're happy resorting to takeaway food from *Harold's Burger* on Place Centrale. There are some supermarkets – the *Denner* on Rue de Verbier is convenient (and it's the cheapest for alcohol!). It has a half-day on Wednesday. Across the road is *Chez Martin*, the most reasonable of several pizzerias in the resort, with prices starting at Sfr11 (closed Monday and Tuesday in low season).

Fondue costs at least Sfr20, in *Channe Valaisanne*, off Place Centrale, which also has daily specials from Sfr14 and a three-course lunch from Sfr17. *La Grotte a Max*, in the Hotel Rosablanche (see Places to Stay), is where you can drink, consume fondue and Valais specialities, and wonder if the pilot on their sign is supposed to be Max himself.

La Pinte in in the Hotel Rosalp (see Places to Stay) offers stylish grills for around Sfr30. The same hotel also has the *Restaurant Pierroz*, one of the top restaurants in Switzerland. Creative cuisine and seasonal specialities may tempt you to extend your mortgage: expect to pay around Sfr30 for a starter and Sfr40 to Sfr60 for a main course. This place also produces its own palatable wine: Gamey and Pinot Noir.

Entertainment

Nightlife is lively, if expensive. *Pub Mont-Ford*, near the base of the Attelas cable car, is a busy and bawdy après-ski bar, particularly popular with English-speakers. *Farm Club*, on Rue de Verbier and near Place Centrale, is a rather aloof and exclusive nightclub. The *Venue*, by the pharmacy off Place Centrale, has more of a common touch; it gets busy around 1 am and entry costs Sfr15 including a drink.

Getting There & Away

From mid-December to mid-April a direct bus goes from Martigny in 45 minutes (Sfr12.80). There are three a day on Saturday, otherwise there's just one bus in the evening. Trains from Martigny run hourly, take 30 minutes, and terminate at Le Châble (Sfr8.40). From there, bus departures are co-ordinated and get you to the resort in 25 minutes (Sfr4.40). In winter, a cable car also ascends from Le Châble. By car or motor-bike is easy; the road from Martigny is good and there are car parks at the entrance to the resort, at the ski lifts, and near Place Centrale.

AROUND VERBIER
Mauvoisin Dam
This dam at the end of the Bagnes Valley reaches a height of 237 metres and walls in a reservoir of 180 million cubic metres. Postbuses depart from Le Châble. Only a few continue as far as Fionnay and thereafter to Mauvoisin, and this section of the journey is completely closed down from early October to mid-June. From Les Ruinettes above Verbier you can walk along the valley to Fionnay in five hours.

Upper Valais

SIERRE
Sierre (Siders in German) is one of the sunniest towns in Switzerland and lies on the French/German language divide. The tourist office (☎ 027-55 85 35) is next to the train station and is open Monday to Friday from 8 am to noon and 2 to 6 pm, and in summer also on Saturday from 9 am to noon.

Things to See & Do
There are several **châteaux** and historic houses in and around the town. Most of these can easily be visited on a walking tour – ask the tourist office for the *Promenade des Châteaux* leaflet. Sierre is surrounded by vineyards and appropriately enough has a **wine museum** (Weinmuseum) in the Château de Villa, north-west of the centre at the end of Ave du Marché. It is open daily except Monday from March to October, and only on Friday, Saturday and Sunday in the winter.

Places to Stay & Eat
East of the centre is an area of protected woodland which contains several camp sites, including the TCS site, *Bois de Finges*

(☎ 027-55 02 84), open from mid-April to early October. *La Poste* (☎ 027-55 10 03) has rooms from Sfr56/95 with private shower and Sfr43/73 without. It's just to the right of the train station and the cheapest place in the centre. *Central* (☎ 027-55 15 66) and *Terminus* (☎ 027-55 04 95) are a better standard and right opposite the station.

There is a *Migros* supermarket and restaurant five minutes to the left of the station on Ave General Guisan. A *Manora* buffet-style restaurant is in the Placette Supermarket to the west of the centre; take bus No 1 from the station.

Getting There & Away
Around two trains an hour stop at Sierre on the main Lausanne-Brig route. The town is the leaping off point for Crans Montana; take the red SMC bus from outside the station (Sfr9.80).

AROUND SIERRE
Anniviers Valley
This valley runs south from Sierre. The inhabitants are known for their nomadic habits, which are gradually dying out. Traditionally, they spend the winter in the mountains and migrate down to homes on the valley floor for the summer.

In the valley there is a novel six-km **planetary walk**, starting at Tignousa (above St Luc) and ending at the Weisshorn Hotel. Along the way are sculptures on pedestals of the planets in the solar system. Information boards alongside give a mass of statistics. The distances between the planets are on the scale of one to 1000 million. The cable car from St Luc to Tignousa stops running from mid-April to mid-June and late October to mid-December. Around six buses a day depart from Sierre and go as far as Zinal, a mountaineering centre at the end of the valley.

CRANS/MONTANA
This resort at 1500 metres claims to be the sunniest ski area in the country. It's fashionable and affluent and boasts the most famous golf course in the Alps.

Orientation & Information

Crans Montana is actually two linked resorts, Crans and Montana (or visa versa), creating a large built-up sprawl amid half a dozen lakes. French is the main language spoken. Crans is to the west, and its tourist office (☎ 027-41 21 32) is on the main street, Route Touristique de Crans. This road joins to Ave du Rawil and thence to Ave de la Gare, Montana's main street. Montana's tourist office (☎ 027-41 30 41) is on this road, backing on to the post office. Local buses are free within this urban area all year. Each tourist office covers both resorts, and they are open daily in high season and weekdays and Saturday morning in low season.

The telephone code for the area is 027.

Activities

Skiing The skiing is good for all ability ranges, with the majority of runs at intermediate level. The Plaine Morte Glacier (3000 metres) allows reasonably testing skiing in the summer. In all, the skiing area offers 160 km of slopes, 44 lifts and 50 km of cross country tracks. Ski passes cost Sfr44 (Sfr26 children) for one day and Sfr222 (Sfr133) for one week.

Golf In the summer there is golf. There is a nine-hole course (Sfr40) and an 18-hole course (Sfr80); contact the Golf Club (☎ 41 27 03). The resort hosts the **European Masters** golf tournament in early September.

Hiking As ever, there are fine views and hiking possibilities if you take the cable cars up into the mountains.

Bridge There's a strong following for bridge games and players meet every afternoon from 3 pm in the Aida-Castel Hotel.

Places to Stay & Eat

There is camping (☎ 41 27 87) by Lake Moubra from mid-June to 30 September. Outside the tourist offices there is an accommodation board with a free telephone. The cheapest place is *Auberge de la Diligence*

(☎ 41 13 28), at the eastern end of Montana in La Comba, starting at Sfr30 per person.

Crans is the more expensive place for accommodation; a good, affordable hotel is *Crans Belvédère* (☎ 41 13 91), five minutes from the Crans tourist office. Rooms start at Sfr61 per person half-board. *Hotel Régina* (☎ 41 35 22), Ave de la Gare, has cheerful singles/doubles from Sfr55/90 with shower and toilet, or Sfr45/80 using hall facilities. Hall lights flick on automatically, which saves the familiar hassle of stumbling around in the dark looking for a luminous switch.

Buy groceries at the *Coop* by Place du Rawil, Montana. Eating is a fairly expensive proposition, unless you stick to the many pizzerias. *Olympic* (☎ 41 29 85), just off Place du Rawil on Ave Louis Antille, has pizzas for Sfr9 to Sfr11 and menus from Sfr15. It also has good, spacious rooms from Sfr61 per person half-pension. Next door is *Le Vieux Moulin*, serving pizza (from Sfr11), fondue (Sfr20), and a daily menu for Sfr14. *Primavera* (☎ 41 42 14), Ave de la Gare, has a good selection of local specialities, meat and fish dishes for around Sfr30. Set menus range from the Sfr12 dish of the day to the Sfr38 four-course special. There are also rooms from Sfr88 per person (half-board) in this three-star hotel.

Getting There & Away

From Sierre the bus takes 45 minutes and departs at least hourly (Sfr9.80). There are two different roads winding up the vineyard-covered hillside to the resort, so you can make it a circular trip either by bus or car.

LEUKERBAD

Leukerbad is the largest thermal centre in Europe and has the hottest springs in Switzerland. The Romans had a settlement here, and in the 19th century, the town was a popular stopover for travellers negotiating the Gemmi Pass to the Bernese Oberland.

Orientation & Information

Leukerbad is 16 km north of Leuk at an altitude of 1411 metres. It is an attractive resort amid a semi-circle of adjacent peaks.

German is the main language. The tourist office (☎ 027-62 11 11) is in the centre, near to where the main street loops over the Dala River. Opening hours are Monday to Friday from 9 to 11.45 am and 2 to 6 pm and Saturday from 9 am to noon and 2 to 5 pm. In the high season it's also open on Sunday from 9 to 11.30 am. The resort has a Guest Card which is good for various discounts, available from hotels. Orient yourself using the brown and yellow hotel signs.

The telephone code for Leukerbad is 027.

Things to See & Do

There are 10 different places to take to the waters, but the biggest and the best is the **Burgerbad** (☎ 61 11 38). It has many different pools, inside and outside, including whirlpools and water massage jets. The temperature ranges from 28°C to 44°C. Entry costs Sfr16 for adults, Sfr11 for students and Sfr8 for children. There are reductions with the Guest Card and for multiple entry tickets. The complex also has a sauna and fitness studio which costs extra. It is open every day until the evening (times vary). The tourist office can give details of training and regeneration programmes and medical treatments that are available in Leukerbad.

The main **skiing** area is the Torrenthorn (2998 metres), yielding mostly medium-difficulty runs, but there are a few easy ones and a demanding run that descends 1400 metres. Ski passes cost Sfr35 (students Sfr29, children Sfr18) for one day and Sfr181 (Sfr145 students, Sfr91 children) for one week. Holders of the Guest Card can get a Thermal Ski Pass Card that is valid for lifts, thermal baths, a fitness programme and other attractions. It's valid for a minimum seven days (Sfr230, students Sfr184, children Sfr115). Activities in the sports centre (☎ 61 10 37) include ice-skating (Sfr8 for half a day), curling and tennis.

A cable car ascends up the sheer side of the northern ridge of mountains to the **Gemmi Pass** (2350 metres). It's a good area for hiking. The cable car costs Sfr18 return, or Sfr12 each way, or it takes two hours to walk up. A six-day summer pass for the cable

cars, baths and other facilities costs Sfr130 (students Sfr104, children Sfr65).

Places to Stay

There is camping (☎ 61 10 37) by the sports arena from 1 May to 31 October. The site has a TV room and a washing machine and it costs Sfr4.50 per adult, Sfr2.50 for a tent and Sfr3 for a car.

Dormitory accommodation is available at *Touristenlager Bergfreude* (☎ 61 17 61), not far from the Gemmi cable car. In the winter, beds are only available at the weekend and cost Sfr16 without breakfast; in the summer they are available daily and cost Sfr24 with breakfast. Showers are Sfr2 extra and there's a café-bar downstairs. The owners are friendly but don't speak English.

Many hotel close in November and early December. *Weisses Rössli* (☎ 61 33 77), off Dorfplatz, has singles/doubles using hall showers for Sfr43/85 and large doubles with own bath for Sfr105. A few doors down is the smaller, slightly cramped *Chamois* (☎ 61 13 57), with rooms for Sfr40/80. Overlooking the Burgerbad is *Viktoria* (☎ 61 16 12), which has smart rooms from Sfr50/86 or Sfr66/104 with private bath and toilet.

The four-star *Badehotel Regina Therme* (☎ 62 11 41) is in the north side of the resort and has its own thermal pools. Rooms start at Sfr122/240.

Places to Eat & Drink

Between the tourist office and Burgerbad is *Römerhof*, with pizza/pasta from Sfr11.50 and fondue for Sfr26 for two. The lunch menu with soup is just Sfr10.50 (Sfr16.50 on Sunday). Down the alleyway is a large *Migros* supermarket. On the same road towards the centre is *Heilquelle*, where vegetarians can choose from a number of dishes between Sfr5.50 and Sfr18. Valais specials cost around Sfr20.

Walliser Kanne, off Dorfplatz, has tasty pizzas from Sfr10 and an excellent if expensive selection of desserts. It also serves cheese and Valaisan dishes (closed Monday). *Hotel Derby*, on the road towards the Gemmi cable car, has a good restaurant where main courses cost Sfr20 to Sfr30. The salad buffet costs Sfr6.50/12 for a small/large plate.

Leukerbad is not really a partying town, although the Burgerbad complex has the *Face* disco. Entry costs Sfr5 and drinks are usually cheaper before 11 pm (closed Monday).

Getting There & Away
Leuk is on the main rail route from Lausanne to Brig. A blue postbus goes from outside Leuk train station to Leukerbad every hour until 7.43 pm (Sfr7.80, Sfr15.60 return; takes 33 minutes). The road winds a bit but is in good condition.

BRIG
Brig is at the crossroads for various major transport routes, meaning an overnight stay may be necessary at some point. Stockalper Castle and the thermal pools at Brigerbad are reasons to extend your visit.

Orientation & Information
Brig (population 9600) is the main town in the Upper Valais. The Rhône River runs from east to west and passes just north of the centre. The train station has money-exchange counters and Visa cash advances. It is open Monday to Saturday from around 6 am to 9.30 pm and Sunday from 8 to 11.30 pm and 1.20 to 7 pm. The tourist office (☎ 028-23 19 01) is on the 1st floor of the station, open Monday to Friday from 8.30 am to noon and 2 to 6 pm, and Saturday from 9 am to noon and 2 to 5 pm. It makes free hotel reservations. Postbuses leave from just outside the train station. Directly ahead is Bahnhofstrasse, leading to the core of the town.

The telephone code for Brig is 028.

Stockalper Castle
Made out of granite and volcanic rock, this building (☎ 23 25 67) was formerly Switzerland's largest private residence. It stands on Alte Simplonstrasse and is instantly recognisable by its three onion domes. The central courtyard is particularly attractive. There are hourly guided tours of the interior in summer, lasting 50 minutes (in English if there's the demand). The museum section is interesting, provided you can get the guide to translate the German signs. It is open from May to October and the tour costs Sfr4 or Sfr1 for children.

The main fascination of the castle derives from the man who built it, Kaspar Jodok von Stockalper (1609-91), self-dubbed the Great Stockalper. He made a vast amount of money from salt and other products by controlling trade with Italy over the Simplon Pass. Probably a greater fortune was made from dealing in mercenaries, especially to France. His success allowed him to mix with royalty and helped to build up the reputation and prosperity of Brig itself. He built most of the centre of the town and at one stage owned half of the Upper Valais. In those days a humble person had to work 10 years to buy a single cow. With only part of his fortune Stockalper could have bought cows stretching from the Furka Pass (the eastern border of Valais) all the way to Geneva.

Small wonder the people of Brig found him and his ostentatious wealth unbearable, and he was overthrown. Much of his wealth was confiscated, and he was eventually forced to flee in fear across the border into Italy. It was six years before he was able to return, to die unmourned shortly afterwards.

Places to Stay
Campingplatz Brigerbad (☎ 46 46 88) is part of the thermal complex so campers get reduced admission to the pools. It's open from mid-May to mid-October and costs Sfr6 per person plus Sfr8 per site. Motorcyclists are not allowed to park their motorbikes by their tents and must leave them in the car park. There is a restaurant and shop on site, and good washing machines.

Hotel prices in Brig are comparatively low, and they only rise marginally in the summer high season. *Café Suisse* (☎ 23 15 33), off Bahnhofstrasse at Rhonesandstrasse 6, has singles/doubles for just Sfr30/56, but the rooms are depressingly bare and there's no shower in the house. No check-in is possible on Sunday. *Café la Poste* (☎ 23 12 39),

Furkastrasse 23, has basic but quite acceptable rooms using hall shower for around Sfr40 per person. You can use their washing machine for Sfr3. To get there, turn right from the station and left on Furkastrasse. *Matza* (☎ 23 15 22), Alte Simplonstrasse 18, near the castle, is the same price.

At Gliserallee 50, over the Saltina River from the old town, is the three-star *Hotel Central* (☎ 23 50 20), featuring rooms with private shower and TV from Sfr65/100. *Schlosshotel* (☎ 23 64 55), Kirchgasse 4, offers the best perspective possible of the castle's triple onion domes, and its curved design gives rooms a novel shape. All rooms have shower/toilet and TV and singles cost Sfr80. The doubles for Sfr160 are vast, and it's worth paying the extra compared to double occupancy of a single for Sfr140.

Places to Eat

There is a *Migros* supermarket and self-service restaurant 50 metres from the station to the left. The restaurant is open Monday to Friday from 7.30 am to 6.30 pm and Saturday until 4 pm, but the supermarket section is closed lunch times and Monday morning.

Café la Poste (see Places to Stay) has filling if simple fare, such as the Tagesteller for Sfr12. A large bowl of soup with bread is just Sfr2.50 and fondue is Sfr15. Just 50 metres down the road towards the old town is the *Mascotte* bar and restaurant, with pizza and pasta from Sfr11 (closed Monday). Look out for several other bars in the centre that offer cheapish snacks.

Restaurant zum Eidgenossen, Schulhausstrasse 2, off Bahnhofstrasse, has Valais meat plates (air-dried cold meat cut into thin slices) for Sfr18 and Sfr19, fondue for Sfr15 and a daily special with soup for Sfr14. The ground floor is a bar area and upstairs is a plusher area only for grills. *Hotel du Pont*, Marktplatz 1, has a similar refined section beyond the bar area. Grills, fish, and house specialities are upwards of Sfr20 and a four-course menu costs Sfr48.

Getting There & Away

Hourly buses leave for Saas Fee (Sfr30

return, valid one month) and call at Visp en route.

Brig is an important junction for train users. It is a stop on the Glacier Express line from Zermatt to St Moritz, and it connects the route to Locarno through Italy with the service to Interlaken via Spiez. BVZ trains to Zermatt depart hourly (Sfr55 return, valid for one month) from the track outside the main station entrance. To St Moritz costs Sfr92 and takes over six hours.

The Spiez-Locarno rail route is of interest to drivers as it includes vehicle-carrying trains. The Brig-Spiez section passes through the Lötschberg Tunnel and is particularly crucial as there is no corresponding road route. To transport a car or camper van through the tunnel section (Goppenstein to Kandersteg) costs Sfr23 (motorbikes Sfr15, bicycles Sfr7) including occupants. Trains run every 30 minutes from 5.35 am to 11.05 pm (plus a last train at midnight) and the journey takes 15 minutes.

The Simplon Tunnel & Pass The tunnel extends 20 km (the longest in the world) from Brig to Iselle in Italy. From Brig to Locarno via the tunnel takes under 2½ hours and costs Sfr47. A passport must be shown, and you need to change trains at Domodossola.

Vehicles are no longer transported by train through the tunnel; the only option is taking the Simplon Pass (open in winter) at 2005 metres. This road is steep, winding and time-consuming but does provide excellent views as it passes through the Gondo gorge, and on one stretch the Aletsch Glacier is visible. It was Napoleon Bonaparte who was responsible for building the first proper road through here; it was the strategic importance of this pass that he had on his mind when he set 30,000 men to work upgrading the original track after the battle of Marengo (1800).

There is a cycling track along the north bank of the Rhône, and bikes can be rented from Brig or Visp train station.

BRIGERBAD

Six km west of Brig, Brigerbad has the

largest collection of open-air thermal swimming baths in Switzerland. Some pools are curative and others are ideal for just swimming and frolicking, particularly the one with underwater jet propulsion. There are five pools in the open air with a water temperature of 27°C to 37°C. Entry costs Sfr10 (children Sfr6 or Sfr3) for the whole day and it's open late May to late September, daily from 9.30 am to 6 pm. There's also a unique grotto pool (Sfr8).

VISP
Like its neighbour Brig, you may have to stay overnight here on your way to somewhere else, but unlike Brig, there's nothing much to make you prolong your stay.

Orientation & Information
Visp stands at the entrance to the valley leading to Zermatt and Saas Fee. The post office and tourist office (☎ 028-46 61 61) are side by side on Kantonsstrasse. They are just a five-minute walk down Bahnhofstrasse from the train station, which has money-exchange counters open daily from 5.15 am to 10 pm. Tourist office opening hours are Monday to Friday from 8 to 11.45 am and 1.45 to 6 pm, and Saturday from 8 am to noon. Postbuses depart from outside the post office.

Things to See & Do
A popular activity for visitors is to go to bed early. Either that or stay awake wondering how on earth they managed to get stuck somewhere where there's nothing to do. At least this town does provide a good opportunity to catch up on holiday reading.

I'm being a little unfair, I suppose, as the old centre is fairly attractive with its cobbled streets and shuttered windows. You could also make for the cinema on Napoleon-strasse, or the swimming pool near the Mühleye camp site, open June to September. Alternatively, there's the three-hour hike up the hill to the wine-growing village of Visperterminen.

Places to Stay & Eat
On Kantonsstrasse, head east for camping *Seewijni* (☎ 028-46 20 86), open April to October, or west then right once over the river for *Mühleye* camp site (☎ 028-46 32 98), open June to September.

Hotel Bristol (☎ 028-46 33 23), at the junction of Kantonsstrasse and Napoleon-strasse, has singles/doubles from Sfr38/70 with use of hall showers. More convenient for the station is *Hotel Adler* (☎ 028-46 34 62) on Brückenweg, off Bahnhofstrasse. It has rooms from Sfr45/80 with private shower, toilet and TV. *Hotel Touring* (☎ 028-46 47 77) is slightly more comfortable (Sfr60/110) and right next to the station.

Opposite the post office is a *Migros* supermarket. There are several places to eat on Bahnhofstrasse, including the good-quality *Gasthaus zur Traube* at No 22, with main courses around Sfr30 (closed Sunday and Monday). Continue along Bahnhofstrasse for Martinistrasse. At No 2 is *Pizzeria Wiwanni*, offering pizza/pasta from Sfr9. Farther along at No 1 is *Martini-keller*. It has a first floor terrace, fondue for Sfr17 and other meals for Sfr13 to Sfr35.

Getting There & Away
See the previous Brig section for more details. Frequent buses and trains traverse the 10 km to Brig, and the fare is just Sfr2.40. Services to/from Zermatt and Saas Fee stop at Visp, but when leaving those resorts you may need to continue to Brig for the quickest onward connection. Parking is free in Visp if you take the Zermatt train (for details call ☎ 028-23 13 33). There's a brand new multi-storey car park by the train station.

ZERMATT
This skiing and mountaineering resort bathes in the reflected glory of one of the most famous peaks in the Alps, the Matterhorn. On Friday 13 July 1865, a party of seven led by Edward Whymper set out on the first successful ascent of this mountain. The climb up took 32 hours and was completed without problems. But on the way down, one of the team slipped and sent himself and

three others crashing to their deaths in a 1200-metre fall down the North Wall. Only Whymper and two Swiss guides survived to tell the tale.

Mountaineers still flock here, and some never leave; their names end up inscribed in stone in the town cemetery. Skiers come here to enjoy virtually year-round skiing. The more sedentary come simply to enjoy the awe-inspiring views.

Zermatt doubled in size during the skiing boom of the 1960s and 1970s, but not without its problems along the way – in February 1963 it suffered a wave of typhoid infections and it was a month before the source of the problem was discovered in the water supply. Things have long since settled down. For the rich and stylish, Zermatt is a place to see and be seen. The water is perfectly safe, although the élite seem content instead to drink alcohol at 'peak' prices in the plusher clubs. The size of the resort has now stabilised; under pressure from environmentalists, the present policy is to replace rather than expand existing facilities.

Orientation & Information

The massive Matterhorn stands sentinel at the end of the valley. Zermatt (1620 metres) is car-free except for electric taxis, and street names are rarely used. The centre of the resort is to the right of the train station.

The tourist office (☎ 028-66 11 81), beside the train station on the right, is open Monday to Friday from 8.30 am to noon and 1.30 to 6.00 pm, and Saturday from 8.30 am to noon. During the summer and winter high season it is open weekdays from 8.30 am to noon and 2 to 7 pm, Saturday from 8.30 am to 7 pm, and Sunday from 9.30 am to noon and 4 to 7 pm. Inside and in the station are accommodation boards with a free telephone. Next to the tourist office is a travel agent which changes money daily until 6 pm (no commission, same rates as banks).

The Mountain Guides office or Bergführerbüro (☎ 028-67 34 56), on the main street in the same building as the ski school, is another good information source.

It is open all day from July to mid-

October, and 5 to 7 pm only from mid-February to mid-May. Enquire here about climbing (for climbing the Matterhorn they recommend previous experience, one week's preparation, and the small matter of a Sfr610 guide fee), Haute Route ski-touring, and heli-skiing.

Some hotels and restaurants close for at least part of the low season, which falls in May, June, and mid-September to mid-November. The post office is on the main street, and the telephone code for Zermatt is 028.

Telephone ☎ 67 20 00 for emergency helicopter rescue and ☎ 187 for avalanche information (winter only).

Activities

Skiing Zermatt has many demanding slopes to test the experienced and intermediate skier in three different skiing areas: Rothorn, Stockhorn and Klein Matterhorn. In all there are 230 km of ski runs, although transferring between the areas can be a bit of a hassle. Beginners have fewer options on the slopes, and what makes it worse for them is that the ski school (☎ 67 54 44) has a reputation for unreliability and impatience. Spring is a popular time as the higher runs are opening up, but in early summer the snow is still good and the lifts are much less busy.

The Klein Matterhorn is topped by the highest cable station in Europe (3820 metres), and provides access to summer skiing slopes (the highest skiing in Europe). It is also the starting point for skiing to Italy (see the following Cervinia section). With 25 km of runs, Zermatt has the most extensive summer skiing in Switzerland.

A day pass for all rides in Zermatt (not including Cervinia) costs Sfr58, or Sfr290 for one week. Ski coupons are available (Sfr64 and Sfr128). Summer skiing is Sfr50 or Sfr176. Ski shops open daily for rental – allow Sfr30 per day for skis and stocks and Sfr14 per day for boots.

Heli-skiing is a possibility, if you can afford to lay out at least Sfr280.

Cervinia This Italian ski resort is a good day

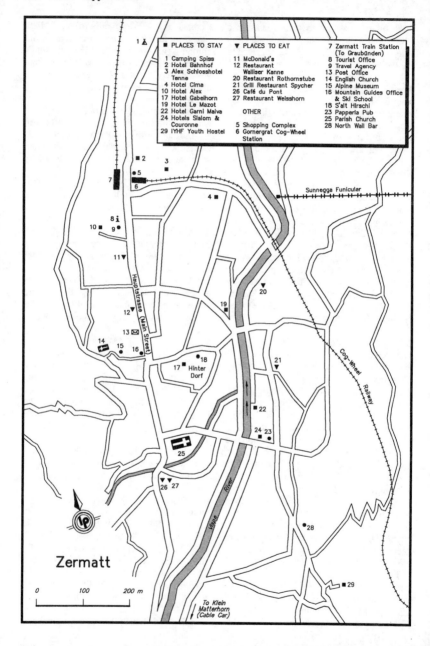

PLACES TO STAY
1 Camping Spiss
2 Hotel Bahnhof
3 Alex Schlosshotel Tenne
4 Hotel Cima
10 Hotel Alex
17 Hotel Gabelhorn
19 Hotel Le Mazot
22 Hotel Garni Maiva
24 Hotels Slalom & Couronne
29 IYHF Youth Hostel

PLACES TO EAT
11 McDonald's
12 Restaurant Walliser Kanne
20 Restaurant Rothornstube
21 Grill Restaurant Spycher
26 Café du Pont
27 Restaurant Weisshorn

OTHER
5 Shopping Complex
6 Gornergrat Cog-Wheel Station
7 Zermatt Train Station (To Graubünden)
8 Tourist Office
9 Travel Agency
13 Post Office
14 English Church
15 Alpine Museum
16 Mountain Guides Office & Ski School
18 S'alt Hirschi
23 Papperla Pub
25 Parish Church
28 North Wall Bar

Sunnegga Funicular

Hauptstrasse (Main Street)

Hinter Dorf

Cog-Wheel Railway

Vispa River

Zermatt

0   100   200 m

To Klein Matterhorn (Cable Car)

trip from Zermatt. Intermediate skiers can handle the route from Klein Matterhorn (don't forget your passport). A one-day pass to ski Klein Matterhorn and Cervinia costs Sfr58, or if you have a longer-term general pass, just pay a supplement of Sfr29 to use Cervinia's ski area for one day.

Getting back to Zermatt at the end of the day has been made easier, thanks to a 150-person gondola on the Italian side, installed in the winter of 1992. Cervinia offers good, long runs for beginners and intermediates. Food and drink prices in the village are reasonable, too. It's just a pity that visually the resort is a bit of an eyesore, with too many concrete-block constructions looking like building site leftovers. Non-skiers can't get down to Cervinia purely by cable car, and glacier crevasses make attempts to hike down hazardous.

Things to See & Do

There are excellent views from any of the cable cars and gondolas. The cog-wheel railway to **Gornergrat** (3100 metres) is a particular highlight. This mountain railway is the most popular in the country and every year 3.3 million people take the trip. The trip up takes 25 to 43 minutes and there are two to three departures an hour from the train station. The fare is Sfr33 to go up and Sfr53 return; Inter-Rail and the Half-Fare Card get 50% off and the Swiss Pass 25% off, but a Eurail pass would be more use if you folded it into the shape of a glider and tried to float to the top.

Along the way you're rewarded with magical views of the Matterhorn (sit on the right-hand side) and the surrounding peaks. The view from the mid-way station of Riffelalp to the north is a fine composition of swathes of trees (yellow and green in the autumn) and the mountains ringing the valley. From Gornergrat you get a different perspective of the Matterhorn (but not superior to the view from the village, in my opinion) and a marvellous panorama of the peaks round Mt Rosa. It takes around five hours to walk up from the village.

The village itself is well worth exploring.

Glance inside the **Parish church**, where there are good altar pieces and an unusual ceiling mural. **Hinter Dorf**, off the main street, is the oldest part. It's crammed with traditional, tumble-down wooden Valais homes, a world away from the flashy boutiques by the church selling glass ornaments, figurines and expensive knick-knacks. Notice the stone discs on the stilts of the storage barns in Hinter Dorf: they're intended to keep out rodents.

A walk in the **cemetery** is a sobering experience for would-be mountaineers, as numerous monuments tell of deaths on Mt Rosa and the Matterhorn. The **Alpine Museum** has exhibits on mountain ascents, local fauna, the development of Zermatt, and famous visitors. It's open daily except Saturday and entry costs Sfr3 (children Sfr1). Around the back is the **English church**, where there are more mountaineering epitaphs. A pair from Cambridge University in England were lost in in the mountains in August 1959. Their bodies were only found 30 years later.

Helicopter rides (☎ 67 34 87) cost Sfr160 per person for a 20-minute flight.

Festivals

On 15 or 16 August there's an Alpine Folklore parade and music involving 1200 participants.

Places to Stay – bottom end

Camping *Camping Spiss* (☎ 67 39 21), to the left of the train station, is open from June to September and charges Sfr7 per day, all inclusive.

Hostels & Hotels The IYHF *youth hostel* (Jugendherberge in German: ☎ 67 23 20) is rather rule-orientated but has an excellent view of the Matterhorn. Dorm beds including breakfast and a compulsory dinner or lunch packet costs Sfr32. Laundry loads cost Sfr8. The doors stay open during the day, but a curfew comes into effect at 11.30 pm. The hostel is shut during May, and from the beginning of November to mid-December.

Opposite the train station and popular with

mountaineers is *Hotel Bahnhof* (☎ 67 24 06), with dorms for Sfr22 singles/doubles for around Sfr40/70. There's no breakfast but guests have use of a communal kitchen and the doors are open for access day and night. It is closed from mid-October to the beginning of December. Hotel prices vary about 40% depending upon the season, but the price difference at the Hotel Bahnhof is minimal.

Hotel Gabelhorn (☎ 67 22 35) is a fine budget choice in the Hinter Dorf area of the village. It's a friendly, family-run place with smallish but comfortable rooms from Sfr36, with use of hall showers. On the same lane by the river is *Le Mazot* (☎ 67 27 77), offering rooms of a similar scale and price.

Places to Stay – middle

Hotel Garni Malva (☎ 67 30 33), overlooking the east side of the river, is open year-round. It costs from Sfr45 per person or from Sfr55 with private shower, and all rooms have a balcony. *Cima* (☎ 66 23 37), in front of the station and halfway to the river, is slightly smaller and has rooms all with private shower for Sfr48 per person in the summer and Sfr58 in the winter.

Slalom (☎ 67 19 77), has an excellent location over the river, and rooms with private shower from Sfr61 per person. Its twin in the same building is *Couronne* (☎ 67 26 81), and gives the option of half or full pension from Sfr91 per person.

Places to Stay – top end

Zermatt offers a wide choice of four-star hotels. *Alex Schlosshotel Tenne* (☎ 67 18 01) is architecturally interesting and conveniently situated near the train station. Many rooms have art nouveau features. *Alex* (☎ 67 17 26), owned by the same family, is behind the tourist office. It also has creative touches in the decor department, and there's an indoor swimming pool and sauna (free for guests, Sfr25 for others) and many other facilities. The bar and disco gets busy with people of all ages. Both hotels start at around Sfr130 per person with appetising multi-course dinners included as standard.

Places to Eat & Drink

Get supplies from the *Coop* in the shopping complex opposite the train station. The *Big Shop* in the high street is one of the cheapest places for hot food, with takeaways for under Sfr10. Unusually for a ski resort, there's also a *McDonald's*, pretending to be inconspicuous in a chalet on the main street.

Beyond the church on the main street, the *Café du Pont* is a rustic place, exuding a red glow from the lampshades. Raclette snacks are Sfr6 and other meals start at Sfr12. Valais plates are Sfr18 and Sfr19. The next door *Restaurant Weisshorn*, is similar, except that the lampshades throw out yellow light. It's roomier and the menu wider. Both places are open daily. Also recommended is *Walliser Kanne*, by the post office, which has pizzas, fondue, fish dishes and Valais specialities from Sfr10 to Sfr20. Valais masks grimace from the wall.

Grill Restaurant Spycher, on the east side of the river by the Hotel Aristella, has interesting and varied dishes (English menus) from Sfr18 to Sfr40. It's in a small chalet and has an extensive wine list. It closed from May to mid-June and in November; at other times it's open daily. Another quality place is *Rothornstube* in the Perrin hotel on the west side of the river. It has grilled dishes from Sfr15 to Sfr25 and several three-course menus for Sfr20 (closed Monday).

Entertainment

North Wall Bar, near the youth hostel, is about the cheapest and best bar in the village, and popular with resort workers. It has ski videos, music, good pizzas from Sfr9 and beer at Sfr4 for half a litre. The bar is closed during the low season, otherwise it's open daily from 6.30 pm to midnight.

Just down the hill, the more expensive *Papperla Pub* is also popular, and has pizzas from Sfr11. *S'alt Hirschi*, in the old part of the village, is a good place for a beer (Sfr4.20 for half a litre) and a snack in a less hectic environment (closed Monday and Tuesday). There are many other bars and clubs where you drink, dance and unwind. Just follow your eyes and ears.

Getting There & Away

Train Hourly trains depart from Brig at 23 minutes past the hour up to 8.23 pm, calling at Visp en route. The steep and scenic journey takes 80 minutes and costs Sfr33 one way, or Sfr53 return. It is a private railway; Inter-Rail earns 50% off and the Swiss Pass is good for free travel. Eurail Pass offers no discounts. The only way out is to backtrack, but if you're going to Saas Fee you can divert there from Stalden Saas.

Zermatt is the start of the famous Glacier Express to Graubünden, one of the most spectacular train rides in the world. It takes nearly eight hours to reach St Moritz, and costs Sfr112 in 2nd class and Sfr182 in 1st class. This includes a compulsory Sfr6 reservation fee which must be paid whether it's needed or not (even if you have a railpass). This fee isn't payable on normal trains following the same route, and it doesn't apply on the Glacier Express if you're only going to/from Brig or Visp.

Car As Zermatt is car-free, you need to park cars at Täsch (Sfr4.50 per day) and take the train from there (Sfr5.60). There is a road from Täsch, but it's private and tourists are never granted permits to use it. Parking is free in Visp if you take the Zermatt train (for details (☎ 028-23 13 33).

SAAS FEE

The self-styled Pearl of the Alps is in the valley adjoining its more famous neighbour, Zermatt. It may not have the Matterhorn, but there are plenty of other towering peaks to overwhelm the senses, and after a hard day's hiking or skiing there are various nightspots to help you unwind. But at night you have to rein yourself in even as you're letting yourself go. A humourless notice in the Hotel Walliserhof warns:

Singing, whistling, yelling and any other disturbance of the night's rest is strictly prohibited after 10 pm in the entire village, including on public squares and streets. Fines of up to Sfr200 are imposed for violations.

Orientation & Information

Saas Fee (1800 metres) is spread out in a long line. The village centre and ski lifts are to the left of the bus station. The village extends at least as far to the right-hand side as well; in this direction there are a few hotels and many holiday chalets.

The tourist office (☎ 028-57 14 57) is opposite the bus station. High season opening hours are Monday to Friday from 8.30 am to noon and 2 to 6.30 pm, Saturday from 8.30 am to 7 pm, and Sunday from 4 to 6 pm. During the low season, weekend opening is reduced depending on demand. The hotel list from the tourist office has a functional map. The resort has a Guest Card system, available from hotels. High season is from mid-December to mid-April, and many places shut in November and May.

There is a post office in the bus station and the telephone code for Saas Fee is 028.

Things to See & Do

Saas Fee is on a ledge above Saas Grund, and is surrounded by an impressive panorama of 13 peaks exceeding 4000 metres. Skiing is the primary activity and winter is the most important season. About 80 km of ski runs favour beginners and experts but with fewer runs geared towards intermediates. A general lift pass costs Sfr50 (Sfr30 children) for one day and Sfr270 (Sfr160 children) for one week. Ski rental prices are about Sfr30 per day for skis and stocks and Sfr14 per day for ski boots. The village has two natural ice rinks.

The tourist office has a map of summer walking trails in the region which cover a total of 280 km. Even in winter, 30 km of marked footpaths remain open. The highest underground funicular (metro) in the world operates all year to Mittelallalin at 3500 metres, giving access to the Feegletscher. This is the centre of summer skiing, with 15 km of runs above 2700 metres. The funicular was opened in 1984 and ascends 500 metres in 2½ minutes. Under the top station is the **Ice Pavilion**, 10 metres below the surface of the ice. It gives an excellent if slightly erudite explanation of glaciers and the difficulty and

Glaciers

With fears of global warming, glaciers are coming increasingly under scrutiny. Of the world's total supply of fresh water, 80% is stored in ice and snow, and 97% of this is in Antarctica and Greenland. But glaciers are important in the rest of the world, too. Without glacier meltwater, many areas (including Valais) at the foot of high mountain ranges would be desert or steppes. Within Switzerland, the most extensive and highest glacial regions are in Valais and the Bernese Alps.

There's much more to glaciers than lumps of ice. They start off as snow, which over the course of years gets compressed to firn. About 10 metres of fresh snow makes one metre of firn. Ice eventually evolves from firn. Surprisingly, it takes longer to get to ice in 'cold' glaciers (ie those below 0°C, such as the one at Titlis) than in 'temperate' glaciers (like the Obere Glacier in Grindelwald). Glaciers are filled with air bubbles, formed during the transformation of snow to ice, and the gas content of these bubbles may be modified by water-flows in a temperate glacier.

The ice at the bottom of glaciers (in the abalation zone) may be centuries old, and makes it possible to measure past environmental pollution. The eruption of Krakatau in 1883 can be measured in glacial ice, and there are traces of the 1977 Sahara dust storms in Alpine glaciers. The peak of nuclear testing and fallout, 1963, is a benchmark year in dating glacial ice.

Ice avalanches from glaciers account for an average of nearly two deaths per year in Switzerland. The worst recent disaster was at Allalin on 30 August 1965, when 88 people died. Glaciers are always moving. You may think that the movement is so slow as to be insignificant, but owing to the movement of the Titlis glacier, the masts of the ski lifts there have to be repositioned three to four times a year. In the course of the summer huge crevasses are opened up in the ice which have to be filled in before skiing starts again in the winter. But they can still be hazardous – never leave the marked trails when skiing on glaciers.

(Much of the information in this passage is based on the displays in the ice pavilions in Saas Fee and Titlis.) ∎

importance of surveying them. Dummies enact some of the scenarios expounded. Entry costs Sfr5 (children Sfr3) and it's open during metro running times.

Above ground there's a revolving restaurant which is quite expensive (meals from Sfr20) but the views are wonderful. Alternatively, you could try the cheaper self-service restaurant (meals from Sfr12) and take in the view from the stationary terrace. From Saas Fee to Mittelallalin by cable car then funicular costs Sfr40 up, Sfr30 down, and Sfr48 return (children half-price).

Back down in the village there is the **Saaser Museum**, that tells the history of the resort and gives details about local folklore and building interiors (entry Sfr3). It's open weekday afternoons in winter and daily except Monday in summer. There's also a sports centre near the bus station with swimming, tennis, a gymnasium and a sauna, and a mountaineering school (☎ 57 23 48 in summer and (☎ 57 22 68 in winter). Ski-mountaineering is possible along the famous Haute Route all the way to Chamonix.

Places to Stay – bottom end

Camping The camp site *Terminus* (☎ 57 14 57), right of the bus station, costs Sfr4 per person plus Sfr3 for a tent. It is open from late May to late September.

Hotels The *Albana*, five minutes to the right of the bus station, is an excellent deal. Two to five-bed rooms (they mix and match) cost Sfr22 to Sfr40 per person, and each has a shower, toilet and balcony as well as great breakfast-buffets. Half-pension costs Sfr10 extra. It shuts at the end of April and reopens in early July. It's a good idea to book in advance in winter.

Reception is in the adjoining *Hotel Mascotte* (☎ 57 27 24), which has rooms from Sfr40 per person with private toilet and shower. Also ask here about the *Chalet Alba*, starting at Sfr20 per person.

Places to Stay – middle

In the south of the village, convenient for the ski lifts, is *Garni Feehof* (☎ 57 33 44), with good singles/doubles for around Sfr40/80.

There's a sun terrace and several small TV rooms and kitchens.

Even closer to the lifts is *Rendez-Vous* (☎ 57 20 40), with rooms for Sfr63/116, or Sfr83/156 with half-pension. It has some dorms (Sfr35) but they're nowhere near as good value as the Albana, and some apartments (Sfr25 per person). By the tourist office, try the friendly *Hotel Bergheimat* (☎ 57 20 30), starting at Sfr70 per person for half-pension.

In the extreme north of the village, *Alp Hitta* (☎ 57 10 50) has two to four-person apartments, each with a small kitchen, which are available all year. The price of Sfr35 per person (Sfr32 in summer) includes breakfast in the restaurant.

Zurbriggen (☎ 57 20 50), just left of the bus station, has rooms from Sfr57 per person. This place has a fantastic garden, with a huge rock covered in various implements and carved tree trunks.

Places to Stay – top end

Walliserhof (☎ 57 20 21), just down the road, has comfortable rooms finished in wood and floral fabric, with large balconies. As in many other hotels, rooms facing south are more expensive. Prices start at Sfr176/312 (half-pension) for rooms with all the expected amenities, and dinners approach gourmet standard.

Places to Eat

The cheapest eating is at the various *Metzgerei* (butcher shops) where you can get hot takeaways. The best is *Charly's Metzg*, round the corner from the tourist office, which has chips for Sfr2, whole chickens for Sfr8, and a Tagesmenu for Sfr8. There's a supermarket opposite.

Eat pizza from Sfr11 at *Boccalino* near the ski lifts. The kitchen closes at 9.45 pm and it's open daily in season. *Restaurant Vieux Chalet*, off the main street near the tourist office, is good for snacks of Raclette (Sfr5.50) and ravioli (Sfr6.50), as well as main meals such as fondue (Sfr20). It's a small cosy place with live music some evenings. *Restaurant Alp Hitta* (see Places to

Stay) has a relaxed atmosphere, Raclette for Sfr5, fondue from Sfr18 and other dishes from Sfr12. It is open daily from 8 am to 1.30 am, except from mid-April to mid-June and mid-October to mid-December when it closes down.

La Ferme, on the main street near the tourist office, has a satisfying three-course lunch and evening menu for Sfr25. Other main courses are Sfr20 to Sfr30 and beer is Sfr3 for 0.3 litre. Farm implements hang from walls and ceiling and sledges are used as coat hangers. On the same road towards the ski lifts is *Gletschergarten*, with a wide selection of meals ranging from Sfr11 to Sfr40.

Fletschhorn (☎ 57 21 31) is one of the top 20 restaurants in Switzerland. It's in a quiet location beyond the northern part of the village, about a 10-minute walk from Alp Hitta (or get them to pick you up in their electric car). Special menus cost Sfr100 and Sfr150. It is closed from the end of April to mid-June and mid-October to mid-December.

Getting There & Away

Up until 1951, the only transportation available to Saas Fee from Saas Grund was by foot or mule-train. Things are a little easier now, although you still can't get there by train. Hourly buses depart from Brig via Visp, take one hour and cost Sfr30 for a one-month return. You can transfer from the Zermatt train at Stalden Saas.

Like Zermatt, Saas Fee is car-free. Park at the entrance to the village, where daily charges are Sfr12 in the garage or Sfr10 outside. Get a Sfr4 per day reduction thereafter with the Guest Card by validating it at the tourist office.

ALETSCH GLACIER

This vast river of ice is an inspiring sight. It's the longest glacier in the Alps, stretching from the Jungfrau (4158 metres) in the Bernese Oberland to a plateau above the Rhône River. Its southern expanse is fringed by the Aletschwald, one of the highest pine forests in Europe (2000 metres).

Orientation & Information

There are two resorts on the southern rim, separated from the forest by a ridge of hills. The westernmost is Riederalp at 1925 metres. Its tourist office (☎ 028-27 13 65) is open Monday to Saturday from 8 am to noon and 2 to 6 pm. A easy walk to the east is the largest resort, Bettmeralp (1939 metres). It's tourist office (☎ 028-27 12 91) is open similar hours. Further east is tiny Kühboden (2212 metres). All these places are car-free. Ask for the Guest Card (Gästekarte) giving useful discounts.

The telephone code for the area is 028.

Things to See & Do

Summer hiking is excellent in the Aletsch forest along numerous marked trails. The tourist office in either Riederalp and Bettmeralp can give details of guided walks around and across the glacier. Riederalp also has an Alpine dairy and an Alpine museum. Kühboden gives access to the Eggishorn (2927 metres), providing possibly the best view of the glacier. In the Aletsch region there are 75 km of ski runs and 25 lifts. The skiing is mostly intermediate or easy. There are several versions of ski passes costing between Sfr30 and Sfr46 per day.

Places to Stay & Eat

There is a non-IYHF hostel, the *Familien und Jugendherberge* (☎ 71 13 77), at the Kühboden cable station. It's closed from late April to the end of May and late October to

early December, and costs from Sfr20, or from Sfr36 with half-pension.

In Riederalp, the *Hotel Bergdohl* (☎ 27 13 37), by the Blausee chairlift, has rooms from Sfr60 per person with private shower, or Sfr50 without (for bed and breakfast).In winter, half-pension starts at Sfr80 per person.

In Bettmeralp, try *Garni Sporting* (☎ 27 22 52), not far from the Bettmerhorn lift, with bed and breakfast from Sfr50 per person (Sfr65 in winter), or the nearby and comfortable *Alpfrieden*, starting at Sfr100 per person (Sfr120 in winter) for half-pension.

Both Riederalp and Bettmeralp have a *Coop*. Also look for the bakeries (Bäckerei) and butcher shops (Metzgerei) for cheap snacks. Eat pizzas in *Postillon* in Bettmeralp or at *Boccalino* in the Hotel Alpenrose in Riederalp. The Alpenrose also has *Walliser Kanne*, a restaurant with theme evenings ranging from Italian food to cheese specialities.

Getting There & Away

The base stations for these resorts are on the Glacier Express route, between Brig and Andermatt. Cable car departures are linked to train arrivals. Mörel up to Riederalp costs Sfr6.80 one way or Sfr13.60 return, the same as from Betten up to Bettmeralp. From Fiesch all the way up to Eggishorn via Kühboden costs Sfr34.60. The Swiss Pass gives you a 25% reduction on these fares.

Ticino

Situated south of the Alps and enjoying a Mediterranean climate, Ticino (Tessin in German) gives more than just a taste of Italy. Indeed, it once belonged to Italy. Como and Milan contested control for many years until the Dukes of Milan gained the ascendancy. Swiss encroachment on the area began in 1478 when the canton of Uri annexed the Leventina Valley (Valle Leventina), on the southern side of the St Gotthard Pass.

The Swiss Confederation gradually expanded southwards until by 1513 it had control of the whole area. Except for Bellinzona, which was under the authority of Uri, Schwyz and Unterwalden, Ticino became the joint property of the then member cantons. But the Confederation did little to develop its new acquisition and the region languished. Ticino remained politically tied (and subservient) to the Confederates until 1798 when France imposed its Helvetian Republic. Ticino then became a free canton, and despite the years as a subject territory, opted to officially join the Confederation in 1803, this time on equal terms.

Although Swiss order and efficiency pervades the canton's mediterranean flavour, the native people are darker skinned than their compatriots in other regions, and the cuisine, architecture and vegetation reflect that found farther south. Italian is the official language in this Catholic canton. Many people also speak French and German but you will find English less widely spoken than in the rest of Switzerland. The region offers mountain hikes and dramatic mountain valleys in the north; water sports and relaxed, leisurely towns in the south.

Orientation & Information

Ticino is the fourth largest Swiss canton. Winters are mild but the best time to visit is spring to autumn, when the flowers bloom, the lakes come alive, and the piazzas become places to watch the world drift by. Average afternoon temperatures for Lugano are around 28°C in July and August, 17°C in April and September, and 7°C in December and January. Locarno gets over 2300 hours of sunshine per year, with an average yearly temperature of 15.5°C.

The regional tourist office is in Bellinzona (Ente ticinese per il turismo; ☎ 092-25 70 56) at Villa Turrita, Via Lugano 12, Bellinzona. Opening hours are Monday to Friday from 8 am to noon and from 2 to 6 pm. Postal enquiries can be addressed to the same office via its box number: Casella postale 1441, CH-6501 Bellinzona.

Food & Drink

Pizza and pasta are ubiquitous, but there are many other dishes to try. *Risotto con funghi* is liquidy rice with saffron and mushrooms. It is often served with *osso bucco*, a circular slab of veal or (less expensively) pork, with the bone marrow in the centre. *Polenta* is an accompaniment to all sorts of dishes, particularly braised meat. It's made from maize and looks a bit like yellow mashed potato. *Cazzöla* is a selection of meats with cabbage and potatoes.

For authentic eating in rural areas, search out a *grotto* (country inn), and wash down your meal with a Ticinese Merlot. Over 75% of local wine produced is Merlot, a red characterised by its full-bodied taste. 'VITI' on the label is a seal of very high quality.

Getting Around

There are two regional travel passes for Ticino. The Locarno/Ascona Region pass costs Sfr70 (Sfr60 for holders of Swiss rail passes) in 2nd class only. It gives seven days free travel on boat, train and bus routes around Locarno and the lake, and 50% off trains to Bellinzona and Lugano, and boats on Lake Maggiore. The Lugano Region pass gives free travel on Lake Maggiore, and on

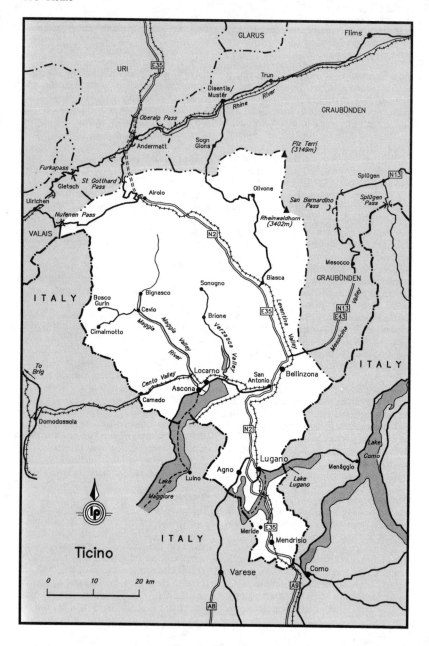

regional public transport around Lugano. It also gives 50% off a number of other routes, including transport on land and water around Locarno. Available in 2nd class only, it costs Sfr78 (Sfr68 pass-holders, Sfr39 children) for seven days, or Sfr60 (Sfr50 and Sfr30) if you travel free for only three days out of the seven. These passes are issued between 1 March and 31 October.

Bellinzona

The capital of Ticino (population 16,900) is a city of castles. It is set in a valley of lush mountains, and stands at the southern side of two important Alpine passes, San Bernardino and St Gotthard.

Orientation & Information

Postbuses arrive one block away from the train station on Via C Molo. The train station has a money-exchange counter, open daily from 5.20 am to 9.40 pm, and bike rental. The tourist office (☎ 092-25 21 31), Via Camminata 2, Palazzo Civico, is open Monday to Friday from 8 am to noon and 1.30 to 6.30 pm, and (from 1 March to 30 November) Saturday from 9 am to noon. To get there, turn left out of the station and walk for 10 minutes, passing the main post office on Viale Stazione (6500 Bellinzona 1) on the way. The tourist office sells a hiking map for the surrounding area (Sfr7), detailing routes and durations.

The telephone code for Bellinzona is 092.

Things to See & Do

The three medieval castles which dominate the town are testimony to Bellinzona's historical importance, based on its key location at the crossroads of the major routes through the Alps. All the castles are well preserved and offer marvellous views of the town and surrounding mountains. The central **Grand Castle** (Castel Grande) dates from around the 6th century. Entry is free and it's open daily for visits to the grounds. The **Archae-**

ological Museum in the castle is closed on Monday (admission Sfr2, students Sfr1).

Montebello Castle (Castello di Montebello), slightly above the town, is open daily from 8 am to 6 pm with free entry. It houses a small museum which is closed on Monday and costs Sfr2 (students Sfr1) for admission. Inside are historical and archaeological displays. Quite a trek up the hill is the smaller **Sasso Corbaro Castle** (Castello di Sasso Corbaro), open from 1 April to 31 October from 9 am to noon and 2 to 5 pm, except on Monday when it's closed. It also has a small museum in the dungeon, which costs Sfr2 (students Sfr1) to get in. Exhibits include historical clothing, tools and crafts. There are no buses up there but it's easy to beg a lift back down again from the car park. Combined museum tickets for the three castles cost Sfr4 (students Sfr2). The castles are often respectively referred to as that of Uri, Schwyz and Unterwalden, after the bailiffs of the cantons who ruled the town from the 16th century.

The **Santa Maria delle Grazie Church**, Via Lugano, features an impressive 15th century fresco of the crucifixion, comparable to the more famous version of the scene in the Santa Maria Church in Lugano. The artist who produced this impressive fresco is unknown.

Every Saturday morning there's a **market** that sprawls across the main street either side of the tourist office. There are stalls selling fruit and vegetables, clothes and crafts, plus there's usually a couple of buskers (street musicians) to liven things up. It's very much a social occasion, with locals standing around chatting rather than indulging in any frenzied buying. This relaxed approach to life becomes rather more animated during the **Rabadan Carnival**, that stretches over several days in February (starts always on Thursday, 8½ weeks before Easter Sunday).

Places to Stay

The *camp site* (☎ 29 11 18), Bosco di Molinazzo, costs from Sfr4.60 per person, Sfr4 per tent and Sfr8 for a camper van. It is open from May to early October, and is by

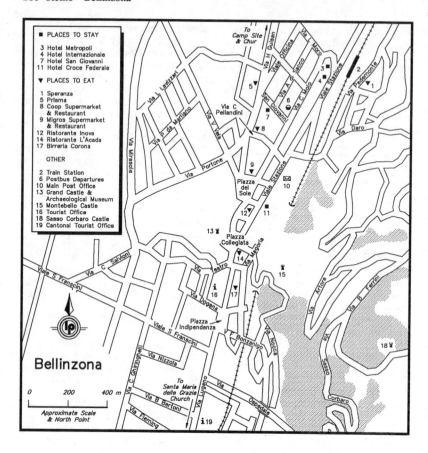

PLACES TO STAY

3 Hotel Metropoli
4 Hotel Internazionale
7 Hotel San Giovanni
11 Hotel Croce Federale

PLACES TO EAT

1 Speranza
5 Prisma
8 Coop Supermarket & Restaurant
9 Migros Supermarket & Restaurant
12 Ristorante Inova
14 Ristorante L'Acada
17 Birreria Corona

OTHER

2 Train Station
6 Postbus Departures
10 Main Post Office
13 Grand Castle & Archaeological Museum
15 Montebello Castle
16 Tourist Office
18 Sasso Corbaro Castle
19 Cantonal Tourist Office

Bellinzona

0   200   400 m

Approximate Scale & North Point

the river in the northern suburb of Molinazzo.

Bellinzona hasn't got a very wide choice of hotels so book ahead if you can. Convenient for the station is *Metropoli* (☎ 25 11 79), Via Ludovico il Moro. The rooms are pretty basic but a decent size, and there is a bath/shower in the hallway. The café/bar downstairs has TV, pool and pinball machines and can get quite busy. Singles/doubles start at Sfr38/76. Also conveniently placed and of a similar standard is *San Giovanni* (☎ 25 19 19), Via San Giovanni 7, with singles/doubles for

Sfr40/80. The rooms are slightly smarter than those at Metropoli, and the café is quieter.

Ideally situated in the centre is *Croce Federale* (☎ 25 16 67), Viale Stazione 12, with singles/doubles/triples for Sfr90/120/150. All rooms have shower, toilet and TV. Top-of-the-range in Bellinzona are two three-star hotels. One of them is the *Internazionale* (☎ 25 43 33), opposite the station on Piazza Stazione. It's hardly plush, although the stained-glass windows over the stairs are eye-catching. Rooms with private bathroom, TV and radio are around

Sfr95/150 for singles/doubles. There are a few cheaper doubles without private shower.

Places to Eat

The *Migros*, Piazza del Sole, and the *Coop*, Via H Guisan, supermarkets both have a restaurant. Hot food is available until around 6 pm weekdays and 5 pm Saturday. There is also a supermarket and the cheap, self-service *Ristorante Inova* downstairs in the Innovazione department store on Viale Stazione. Opening hours are Monday to Friday from 8.30 am to 6.30 pm and Saturday from 8 am to 5 pm.

The food is good in *Ristorante l'Arcada*, Piazza Collegiata 1. Pasta starts at Sfr10, salads at Sfr4.50, and meat and fish dishes are Sfr18 to Sfr30. Similarly priced and also good is *Birreria Corona*, opposite the tourist office at Via Camminata 5. Like the self-service places, these restaurants are closed on Sunday, so that might be a good day to consider going on a diet.

If you don't fancy making Sunday a day of rest for your stomach, look in at *Speranza* (☎ 26 19 39), Via Pedemonte 12. It's popular with locals and not many tourists find this place as it's on the inaccessible side of the station. You really get personal service in this small place – there's no written menu; instead, the chef comes out of the kitchen to tell you what's cooking tonight. Ordering can be a bit disconcerting as they don't speak much English so you may not be 100% sure what you're going to end up with, but the food is tasty, well prepared, and you're usually offered refills. Expect to pay around Sfr10 to Sfr15 for a starter and Sfr20 to Sfr40 for a main course. It's closed on Monday and Tuesday and in July and August.

Quality food can also be savoured at *Prisma* (☎ 26 34 46), Via H Guisan 5c, in the same large building as the bank (closed Sunday), and at the restaurant in the Castel Grande (☎ 26 23 53), which is closed on Mondays.

Getting There & Away

Bellinzona is on the train route connecting Locarno (Sfr6.20) and Lugano (Sfr9). The journey takes 25 to 35 minutes in either direction, with two trains an hour. It is also on the Zürich-Milan route. Postbuses head north-east to Chur. You need to reserve your postbus seat the day before on ☎ 25 77 55. There is a good cycling track along the Ticino River to Lake Maggiore and Locarno.

Car Rental Hertz (☎ 26 10 33) is at Via F Zorzi 40 and Budget (☎ 62 15 10) is at Via Cantonale. Avis has no local office.

Lugano

Switzerland's southernmost tourist town offers an excellent combination of lazy days, watery pursuits and hillside hikes. It's the largest city in Ticino (28,200 inhabitants) and the fourth most important financial centre in Switzerland.

Before the Swiss arrived on the scene in 1512, Lugano was successively under the jurisdiction of the Bishop of Como and the Duke of Milan. In the days of France's Helvetic Republic it was the citizens of Lugano who started the move for Ticino to officially join the Swiss Confederation, proclaiming themselves 'Liberi e Svizzeri' (Free and Swiss).

Orientation

Lugano is 270 metres above sea level on the shores of Lake Lugano. The train station is above and to the west of the old town. Take the stairs or the funicular (Sfr0.60) down to the centre which is dominated by piazzas. The most important one, the Piazza della Riforma, contains the Neo-Classical Municipio building. Paradiso is a suburb to the south; hotels here are slightly better value than in the centre, and it is the departure point for the funicular up to Mt San Salvatore. The other mountain that looms over the town, Mt Brè, is to the east. The airport is three km west of the train station.

Information

Train Station The station has an efficient

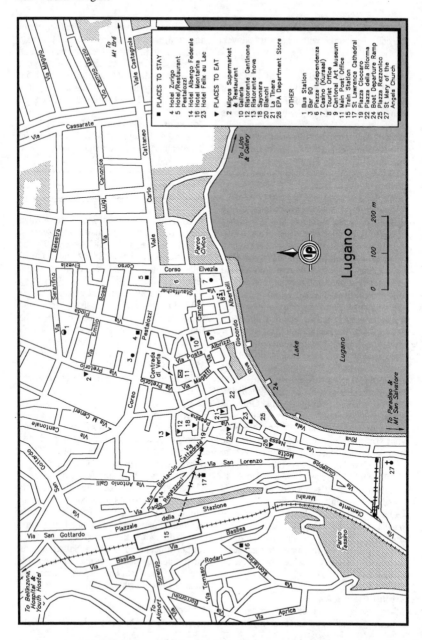

PLACES TO STAY

4 Hotel Zurigo
5 Hotel/Restaurant
   Pestalozzi
14 Hotel Albergo Federale
16 Hotel Montarina
23 Hotel Felix au Lac

▼ PLACES TO EAT

2 Migros Supermarket
   & Restaurant
10 Galleria
12 Ristorante Cantinone
13 Ristorante Inova
18 Sayonara
20 Bianchi
21 La Tinera
26 EPA Department Store

OTHER

1 Bus Station
3 Bar 90
6 Piazza Independenza
7 Casino (Kursaal)
8 Tourist Office
9 Cantonal Art Museum
11 Main Post Office
15 Train Station
17 St Lawrence Cathedral
19 Piazza Cioccaro
22 Piazza della Riforma
24 Boat Departure Ramp
25 Piazza Rezzonico
27 St Mary of the
   Angels Church

Lugano

Lake
Lugano

train information office, open daily from 8.30 am to 6.30 pm (5.30 pm Saturday, 6 pm Sunday). The Swissair check-in is for Zürich and Basel airports, and also deals with bike rental (open daily from 6.30 am to 7.30 pm). The money-exchange office is open Monday to Saturday from 6.30 am to 7.45 pm, and Sunday from 8 am to 6.45 pm. There is also a hotel information and reservation office (Sfr3 fee). It only handles hotels in the Swiss Hotel Association, and it's open Monday to Saturday from 10 am to 8 pm (6 pm in winter).

Tourist Office The tourist office (☎ 091-21 46 64) overlooks Lake Lugano, on Riva Giocondo Albertolli 5. Opening hours are Monday to Friday from 9 am to 6 pm (6.30 pm between 1 July and 30 September). From April to October it is also open on Saturday from 9 am to 5 pm. These hours are subject to change depending on demand. Ask about the Guest Card if you're staying more than three days in the region, and pick up the *Regione Lago di Lugano* official guide which is in four languages.

Post & Telecommunications The main post office is in the centre of the old town at Via Della Posta, on the corner of Contrada di Verla. Opening hours are Monday to Friday from 7.30 to noon and 1.45 to 6.30 pm, and Saturday from 8 am to noon. Services are available additional hours subject to a surcharge.

The telephone code for Lugano is 091.

Consulates There are a number of consulates in town, including those for Britain (☎ 23 86 06), Via Motta 19, and Italy (☎ 22 05 13), Via Monte Ceneri 16.

Emergency Call the police on ☎ 117, and dial ☎ 111 for a doctor or dentist. The hospital, Ospedale Civico (☎ 58 61 11), is at Via Tesserete.

Walking Tour

Old Town Winding alleyways, pedestrian-only piazzas and colourful parks make

Lugano an ideal town for walking around. On Tuesday morning from March to October, the tourist office conducts a free guided walk of the centre; make a reservation the day before. Spend some time in the **Parco Civico**, near the tourist office. Magnolias and camellias flower in March, and a month later rhododenrons and azaleas burst forth.

The **St Mary of the Angels Church** (Santa Maria degli Angioli), Piazza Luini, has a pair of frescoes by Bernardino Luini dating from 1529; the most powerful depicts the Crucifixion. Below the train station is the **St Lawrence Cathedral** (Cathedral of San Lorenzo), noted for the Renaissance façade (1517), particularly the three fine doorways that overlook the lake. Inside are frescoes dating from a similar era, and choir stalls with a mini statue protruding from each armrest. The tabernacle at the end of the aisle is 16th century.

Museums & Galleries The **Thyssen-Bornemisza Gallery**, Villa Favorita, Castagnola, is a famous private art collection. In 1993 the old masters of the collection were transferred to Spain on a 10-year loan, but what's left behind is extremely impressive. It constitutes 150 works by American and European artists from the 19th and 20th century, covering all major styles from abstract to photorealism.

The wealthy Baron von Thyssen-Bornemisza (the family amassed its fortune from steel) can only get richer, as the gallery charges as much as Sfr12 (Sfr8 for students) for admission, or more if there's a special exhibition. At the head of the collection is a portrait of the baron by Lucian Freud, completed in 1985. The composition is dominated by the baron's large, veined hands, gnarled, no doubt, from handling so much cash. Opening hours are Friday to Sunday from 10 am to 5 pm between April and late June, and thereafter daily except Monday the same hours up to the end of October. Take the boat from the departure ramp or bus No 2 from Lugano.

Five-minutes' walk east is the **Museum of**

Extra-European Cultures (Museo delle Culture Extraeuropee), Via Cortivo. It lacks signs in English, but the statues, fertility symbols, masks and photographs are extremely evocative of ancient tribal lifestyles without needing words. Entry costs Sfr6 (Sfr3 for students), and it's open Tuesday to Sunday from 10 am to 5 pm. If you walk back from Gandria (see the Lake Lugano section) you pass by this museum.

The **Cantonal Art Museum** (Museo cantonale d'Arte), Via Canova 10, has a worthwhile modern art collection from the 19th and 20th centuries. Ticinese artists are well represented. It costs Sfr5 or Sfr8 (students Sfr3) to get in, depending upon special exhibitions. Opening times are Wednesday to Sunday from 10 am to 5 pm, and Tuesday from 2 pm to 2 pm.

The **Modern Art Museum** (Museo d'Arte Moderna) is at Riva Antonio Caccia 5, towards Paradiso (closed Monday). You can walk or take bus No 1 or 10 from Piazza Rezzonico.

Activities

The Lido, just east of the Cassarate River, offers a swimming pool and sandy beaches for Sfr5 a day, and it's open daily from 1 May to mid-September (9 am to at least 6 pm). A tourist fishing permit for Lake Lugano and the rest of Ticino costs Sfr50 and is valid for 10 days. Buy it from the tourist office.

Places where you can water-ski, sail and windsurf are listed in the official guide. The cheapest place for all these activities is the Club Nautico Sassalto (☎ 71 12 45), Caslano, where prices respectively are Sfr1.70 per minute, Sfr15 for two hours, and Sfr10 for two hours. Caslano is reached by the Ferrovia Ponte Tresa from in front of the train station (Sfr5). Pedalos near the boat landing stage can be peddled for Sfr12 an hour or Sfr6 for 30 minutes.

Courses

The Migros scuola club (☎ 22 76 21), for languages and other courses, is in the same building as the supermarket at Via Pretorio 15.

Places to Stay – bottom end

Camping There are six camp sites by the arm of the lake that loops up near Agno airport. All are open from approximately Easter to the end of October. The Ferrovia Ponte Tresa train from in front of the main station gets you to the vicinity. The cheapest site is *La Palma*, (☎ 59 23 38), costing from Sfr4 per adult and Sfr3 per tent, but the TCS site, *La Piodella* (☎ 54 77 88), has many more facilities and is only marginally more expensive.

Youth Hostel The relaxed IYHF *youth hostel* (☎ 56 27 28), Via Cantonale 13, is a hard 20-minutes' walk uphill from the train station (signposted), or take bus No 5 to Crocifisso (Sfr1.50). Beds are Sfr12 plus Sfr2 for sheets and Sfr5 for breakfast. It's a refreshing family-run place, with classical music wafting through the reception and breakfast area, CNN (the American news channel) on the TV, and its own extensive grounds, including an outdoor swimming pool. Pity about that 10 pm curfew, though. Reception is shut from 1 to 3 pm and but the dorms stay open throughout the day. The hostel closes from 31 October to mid-March.

Hotels Around the back of the train station is *Hotel Montarina* (☎ 56 72 72), Via Montarina 1, which has beds in large dorms for Sfr16 to Sfr20 per night, depending upon the length of stay. Singles/doubles start at Sfr45/70 and triples/quads at Sfr96/128, all without breakfast. It's a nice building but watch out for the resident ants. Reception is open from 9 am to 9 pm and there is no daytime closing or curfew. The hotel is closed from 31 October to about a week before Easter.

Zurigo (☎ 23 43 43), Corso Pestalozzi 13, is conveniently central and has plenty of parking. Rooms are functional and start at Sfr40/65 using hall shower or Sfr70/110 with private shower. The hotel is closed in December and January.

Hotel Restaurant Pestalozzi (☎ 22 95 95), Piazza Indipendenza 9, has singles/doubles/triples from Sfr42/82/112 using hall showers, or you can pay more for a private shower or bath. The rooms vary greatly in style depending on which floor you're on. On the newer top (fourth) floor, the brash red paintwork, large door numbers and small modern desks are reminiscent of a student hall of residence. The rooms on the lower floors with their old, solid brown furniture are more like your grandparents' spare bedroom. Some rooms are an idiosyncratic hybrid of the two.

Around the bay in Paradiso is *Victoria au Lac* (☎ 54 20 31), Via General Guisan 3, which sometimes has space when places in town are full. It's slightly ageing but comfortable enough and very atmospheric; singles/doubles start at around Sfr45/70, or Sfr80/110 with shower. Parking is no problem, and it's open from April to October.

Places to Stay – middle
The hotel *Felix au Lac* (☎ 23 97 33), Piazza Rezzonico 6, is very centrally situated near Piazza Riforma. Singles/doubles with shower start at Sfr60/110.

Albergo Federale (☎ 22 05 52), Via Paolo Regazzoni, is midway between the station and the old towh. Singles/doubles with private shower/toilet and radio in this comfortable three-star place start at Sfr95/164. It closes from mid-December to 1 February.

Places to Stay – top end
In four-star hotels, you tend to get more facilities for your money in Paradiso rather than in Lugano itself. *Admiral* (☎ 54 23 24), Via Geretta 15, near the Paradiso funicular, has large, standardised rooms decked out in shades of blue. The indoor and roof-top swimming pools and the fitness room are free for guests but the massage and sauna cost extra. Singles/doubles start at Sfr140/210.

Places to Eat
There is a large *Migros* supermarket and restaurant on Via Pretorio opposite Via Emilio Bossi. The restaurant is on the 5th floor and is open to 10 pm from Monday to Saturday. It has a salad and dessert buffet, as well as main meals from Sfr6. An *EPA* self-service restaurant in the department store is similarly priced and can be found on Piazzetta San Carlo.

Any number of restaurants around town offer pizza and pasta from about Sfr10. *Ristorante Cantinone* (☎ 091-23 10 68) on Piazza Cioccaro has a vast selection of good-sized pizzas from Sfr10 and is open daily from 7 am to midnight. Up the stairs near either the main or back entrance is *Ristorante Inova*, a buffet-style place where the food is cooked in front of you. An excellent deal is the pasta for Sfr7.90 where you can select the ingredients for the sauce yourself from the counter. Salad plates are Sfr3.80 to Sfr9.50, and it's open daily to 10 pm.

Also good and cheap for Italian and vegetarian food is *Hotel Restaurant Pestalozzi* (see Places to Stay), open daily from 6 am to 11 pm. It's an alcohol-free restaurant with a wide choice of daily specials from Sfr9.50 to Sfr14.50

Across Piazza Cioccaro from Ristorante Cantinone is the large *Sayonara*. It has the usual pizza/pasta, and, in season, a strangely comprehensive selection of asparagus (Sfr10 to Sfr30). *La Tinera*, Via dei Gorini, off Piazza della Riforma, has a typical Ticinese ambience and daily specials between Sfr10 to Sfr17. Local wines start at Sfr22 a bottle. It's closed on Sunday and it's not unusual to have to queue before you can be seated.

In Paradiso, the *Ristorante Bar Paradiso*, on Via San Salvatore by the funicular station, offers pasta and gnocchi from Sfr11 and meat and fish dishes from Sfr19. Middle of the road music tinkles in the background, except on Sunday when it's closed.

Expensive Restaurants Eating in Lugano can be a superb if asset-stripping experience. *Bianchi* (☎ 22 84 79), Via Pessina 3, is opposite the elegant shops in the old town and is suitably elegant itself. Waiters dressed in black hover like vultures in reverse – waiting to dispense rather than devour the feast. The chef's recommendations cost Sfr25 to Sfr50 and there's a five-course gastronomic menu for Sfr78. Similarly priced is the ultimately civilised *Galleria* (☎ 23 62 88) at Via

Vegezzi 4, where *sotto voce* waiters whisper over soft music (closed Sunday).

Also excellent (they're both high up in Switzerland's 'top 100') and similarly expensive are *Santabbondio* – (☎ 54 32 37), Via Fomelino 10, near Agno airport (closed Saturday lunch, Sunday evening, and Monday), and *Al Portone* (☎ 23 59 95), Viale Cassarate 3.

Entertainment

Lugano has plenty of options for a night out although not much within reach of the budget traveller. The tourist office has a list of discos, nightclubs and piano bars. The *Kursaal* (casino) near the tourist office on Via Stauffacher, has a cinema. *Bar 90*, Corso Pestalozzi 9, is a bingo hall most nights, but transforms into a live blues venue on Wednesday (cover Sfr10) and a disco on Friday (free entry). A beer costs around Sfr6.

In April and May there is a series of classical music concerts under the banner, Primavera Concertistica, which are performed in the *Palazzo dei Congressi*, in the Parco Civico. Tickets cost Sfr30 to Sfr60, and you can buy them at the tourist office. Other music festivals occur later in the summer, such as the jazz festival in July.

Getting There & Away

Agno airport has Crossair flights nonstop to/from Basel, Bern, Geneva and Zürich, with departures several times a day. There are also direct connections to Rome and Munich. Crossair can be contacted on ☎ 50 50 01.

Lugano is on the same road and rail route as Bellinzona. There is a daily postbus service direct to St Moritz (one in winter, two in summer), which costs Sfr53 and takes four hours. You need to reserve your seat the day before at the train information counter in the station, or by phoning ☎ 091-21 95 20. All postbuses leave from the main bus depot at Via Serafino Balestra, but you can pick up the St Moritz bus and many others outside the train station five minutes later.

In the summer there's also the Palm Express to St Moritz, a bus originating in Locarno and calling only at the train station in Lugano centre (reserve ahead).For train and boat information see the Bellinzona and Lake Lugano sections.

Car Rental Hertz (☎ 23 46 75) is at Via San Gottardo 13 and Europcar (☎ 22 88 44) is at Via Ciani 5. Avis (☎ 22 62 56) is at Via Clemente Maraini 8. Just down the road at No 14 is Budget (☎ 54 17 19), in the same place as a local operator, Sud (☎ 54 98 73). All the international companies have airport offices.

Getting Around

Getting to the airport involves taking the small train in front of the train station, the Ferrovia Ponte Tresa (every 20 to 30 minutes), getting off at Agno (Sfr3.80), and walking for 10 minutes. A taxi from the town centre costs around Sfr25 to Sfr30.

Pick up a bus map from the tourist office. A single trip costs Sfr0.80 to Sfr1.50 (ticket dispensers indicate the appropriate rate) or it's only Sfr4 for a one-day pass and Sfr18 for one week. The Lugano Region pass (see Getting Around at the beginning of the chapter) is valid on the funiculars up to San Salvatore and Mt Brè. It also gets 25% off the trip up to Mt Generoso, as does the Swiss Pass.

You can park all day at the multi-storey car park opposite Migros (entrance Via Pioda); fees are Sfr1 per hour. Call ☎ 51 21 21 for a taxi.

AROUND LUGANO

The tourist office has free guides detailing walks of up to three hours' duration heading south along the lake, or north towards Locarno. Touring the lake itself by boat is an unmissable pleasure on a sunny day (see the following section). Also unmissable – quite literally – are the two peaks soaring over the town, **Mt San Salvatore** and **Mt Brè**. Lugano has dubbed itself the 'Rio de Janeiro of the Old Continent' for the resemblance that Mt San Salvatore (912 metres) bears to Rio's Sugarloaf Mountain. The funicular from Paradiso up Mt San Salvatore operates from March to November only and costs Sfr10 to go up or Sfr14 return. From the top you get an excellent perspective of the meandering contours of the lake. The walk down takes a little over an hour back to Paradiso or Melide.

To ascend Mt Brè, you can take the year-round funicular from Cassarate which costs Sfr10 to go up or Sfr15 return (often closed for maintenance in January). Mt Brè (925 metres) offers a clearer view of the curve of the bay round Lugano. A cheaper way to get up Mt Brè is to drive, or take bus No 12 from the main post office to Brè village, and walk about 15 minutes from there.

Lake Lugano

There are many points of interest around the lake, easily visited on a day tour if you don't fancy a longer excursion. Boats are operated by the Società Navigazione del Lago di Lugano (☎ 51 52 23). Examples of return fares from Lugano are Gandria (Sfr18), Melide (Sfr13) and Morcote (Sfr20). If you want to visit several places, buy a pass: one day costs Sfr30 (Sfr19 for children), three days costs Sfr44 (Sfr37) and one week costs Sfr50 (Sfr40).

The departure point from Lugano is by the Piazza della Riforma. Boats sail year-round, but the service is more frequent and extensive from the end of May to late October. Circular cruises cost Sfr12.20 to Sfr26.40 (reductions apply). See the later Ceresio section for other places to visit round the lake. The Swiss Pass is valid and the Half-Fare Card gets reductions.

Gandria

Gandria is an attractive village where the houses tumble down the hill right to the water's edge. Piers and boathouses, with small craft dangling from pulleys, stand in lieu of garages as no cars can get near most of these houses; only alleys and stairways separate the compact dwellings. A popular round trip is to take the boat from Lugano

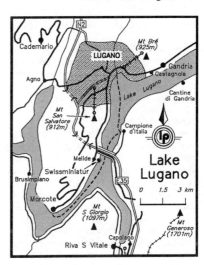

and to walk back along the shore to Castagnola (around 40 minutes), where you can visit the Villa Favorita, or simply continue walking or take the bus back into Lugano.

From Gandria, take the path by the church. A few minutes after leaving the village you reach a small cove where the main road can be seen winding its own course above. The bare rock here reveals wonderful patterns in its curved fault lines.

There are a couple of hotels in Gandria. Just above the boat landing stage awaits *Miralago* (☎ 091-51 43 61), open from 1 April to 31 October. It costs Sfr30 per person (Sfr35 in peak season) with showers on the floor. The restaurant offers spaghetti from Sfr10.80, and meat dishes ranging from simple cutlets (Sfr13.50) to giant fillets (Sfr74 for two).

Across the lake from Gandria is the **Customs Museum**, at Cantine di Gandria, accessible by boat. It tells the story of the development of customs in the area, using documents, dummies, and confiscated exhibits. An interesting section reveals the ploys used by smugglers over the years. Common tricks include false-bottomed shoes, hollowed out books and modified fuel tanks.

The museum is open from mid-April to late October, daily from 1.30 to 5.30 pm, and entry is free. As there are only minimal notes in English you can get around in 30 to 40 minutes.

Campione d'Italia

This really is part of Italy – a forgotten anomaly surrounded by Switzerland. It's not immediately obvious you're in another country: there are no border formalities, nearly all the cars in the village have Swiss number plates and they still use Swiss money and Swiss telephones. Not everything is the same, though – the post boxes are red, not yellow as in Switzerland, and the policemen and police cars bear Italian livery. But the main difference is in the gambling laws: there are none of those Swiss restrictions so the casino does brisk business especially, ironically, with Swiss visitors. It is open from 4 pm to 2 am daily and smart dress is required for entry. In the evening there is a special private bus service from Piazza Rezzonico in Lugano to the casino (travel passes not valid). The casino might lose its appeal when the liberalisation of the Swiss gambling regulations comes into effect (no fixed date yet).

There are no customs formalities, but it is a wise precaution to take your passport. The tourist office (☎ 091-68 81 82) and the post office are both near the boat landing stage. Go slightly to the right upon alighting and about 50 metres up the hill.

If you want to eat lunch in Italy, there's the *Pizzeria Rally* right next to the boat landing stage, with pizza starting at Sfr9.50 and daily specials from Sfr10. They want Swiss money but you know you're not in Switzerland when you go to the 'gents' and find a squat-over-the-hole lavatory instead of the usual pristine Swiss porcelain with electronic sensors. Those seeking more elegance and higher quality (and prices) can saunter across the road to *Ristorante Taverna*.

Mt Generoso

The panorama provided by this summit

(1701 metres) includes the lakes, the Alps, and even the Apennines on a clear day. It can be reached by taking the boat, train or car to Capolago, and then the funicular (approximately hourly, Sfr28 up or Sfr39 return, with reductions for children). The funicular and the boat only operate from early April to mid-November.

CERESIO

This is the area south of Lugano, a peninsular created by the looping shoreline of Lake Lugano. There are walking trails dissecting the interior and small villages dotting the lakeside. The main tourist attraction is the **Swissminiatur fun park** in Melide. The tourist office in Melide (☎ 091-68 63 83), Via Pocobelli 14, covers the whole region. Opening hours are Monday to Friday from 8 am to noon and 2 to 6 pm, and from Easter to October also on Saturday morning.

It has a list of holiday apartments in the area; nearly all are available on a weekly basis, although a few allow shorter stays, starting from Sfr25 per person.

There is one IYHF *youth hostel* (☎ 091-60 11 51), in Fignio, open from March to the end of October. Dorm beds cost Sfr18 with breakfast and you can reach Fignio by postbus (several a day from Lugano) or in the summer by boat. Buses and boats (year-round) also connect Morcote and Melide to Lugano.

Some of the roads in Ceresio afford excellent views, particularly the upper road from Melide to Lugano, passing through Carona at 602 metres. Carona is also a suitable starting point for a number of hikes, and it can be reached from Melide by funicular.

Melide

Melide is on the bulge of the shore from which the N2 motorway slices across the lake. The main attraction of this village is **Swissminiatur** (☎ 091-68 79 51), where you'll find 1:25 scale models of over 100 national attractions. Children and adults can spend a great couple of hours wondering around the faithfully reproduced replicas. The models are so good that it can help you

Top: Arosa, Graubünden (MH)
Bottom Left: St Martin's Church, Chur, Graubünden (MH)
Bottom Right: Fountain near St Martin's Church, Chur, Graubünden (MH)

Top: Soglio village, Graubünden (MH)
Bottom: Pontresina, Graubünden (MH)

decide if you want to go on to see the real thing, and there are many boats, cable cars and trains whizzing about the place to complete the picture.

The park is open from mid-March to the end of October, daily from 8.30 to at least 6 pm. If the weather is fine it's also open in the afternoons from November to mid-December. Admission costs Sfr9 for adults and Sfr5 for children, and the programme for Sfr2 is essential as there are no other signs. Take advantage of cheap self-service restaurant on the site.

Places to Stay & Eat The newly renovated *Hotel Del Lago* (☎ 091-68 70 41), Lungolago G Motta 9, is gleaming white with lino floors. Singles/doubles with shower, toilet and TV start at Sfr70/120 including breakfast-buffet. The restaurant is mid-price and has a good choice of fish, grills and house specialities. There's also a salad buffet (Sfr4.50 to Sfr9 per plate).

Opposite is *Bellavista* (☎ 68 98 35) with rooms with shower from Sfr45/90, and pizza and pasta in the restaurant from Sfr9. On the edge of the village on the far side of the boat landing stage is *Generoso* (☎ 091-68 70 71), Via Lungolago G Motta 60, has singles/doubles with private shower from Sfr60/90 and Sfr35/70 without.

Morcote

This photogenic fishing village clusters at the foot of Mt Abostora. It is graced with houses with arcades and narrow stairways that lead up to the church of **Santa Maria del Sasso** (15-minutes' climb). The views are excellent, and the church itself has frescoes (16th century), busts of bishops, and carved faces on the organ. Nearby, the cemetery is typically Italian in the way that the faces of the deceased are displayed amid bouquets at their final resting place.

In the village is the **Parco Scherrer**, offering an eclectic collection of architectural styles from around the world, including copies of famous buildings and generic types (eg Temple of Nefertiti, Siamese tea-house). It's all set in subtropical parkland, open 15

March to 31 October, daily between 9 am and 5 pm. Admission costs Sfr4 (children Sfr1).

By the boat landing stage is a covered arcade where shops offer souvenirs and unusual odds and ends. The walk along the shore to Melide takes around 50 minutes.

Places to Stay & Eat Morcote lacks a budget hotel. The cheapest rooms are at *Oasis* (☎ 091-69 11 61), which has singles/doubles for Sfr45/80. The restaurant has pasta dishes starting at Sfr10. It's not far from the boat landing stage in the direction of Melide. A little farther on is the *Coop* (early closing on Wednesday).

Della Posta (☎ 091-69 11 27), right by the post office, has rooms with private shower from Sfr80/136. It is also a reasonable place to eat, with pizza and pasta starting at Sfr10.50 and meat and fish dishes nudging Sfr30. It has the advantage of a sunny first-floor terrace and a section on the edge of the lake. The restaurant is open daily but closed from November to March. Nearby is the more expensive *Carina Carlton*, but there are plenty of other restaurants queuing for your custom along the quayside.

MENDRISIO

South of Lake Lugano is Mendrisiotto and Lower Ceresio. It is a fine area for walking tours around the rolling valleys and unspoilt villages. Mendrisio is the district capital (population 6500) and has a tourist office (☎ 091-46 57 61). It has several interesting old churches and buildings, and is especially worth a visit for the Maundy Thursday Procession or the Wine Harvest in September.

MERIDE

The Fossil Museum in Meride, to the northwest, displays vestiges of the first creatures to inhabit the region – reptiles and fish dating back 200 million years. (The museum is open daily from 8 am to 6 pm, free entry). Near the town is a circular nature trail, complete with periodic information panels.

Locarno

Locarno lies at the northern end of Lake Maggiore. Switzerland's lowest town, at 205 metres above sea level, Locarno enjoys the country's best climate. This status is based upon the calculation that it receives more hours of sunshine than anywhere else; strange, therefore, that several other towns (especially in Valais) stake rival claims to having the sunniest climate. Locarno achieved prominence when it hosted the 1925 Peace Conference which intended to bring stability to Europe in the aftermath of WW I.

Orientation & Information

The centre of town is the Piazza Grande where the main post office can be found. The tourist office (☎ 093-31 03 33) is nearby at Largo Zorzi, adjoining the Kursaal. It has brochures on many parts of Switzerland. From April to October, it's open Monday to Friday from 8 am to 7 pm, and Saturday and Sunday from 9 am to noon and 1 to 5 pm.

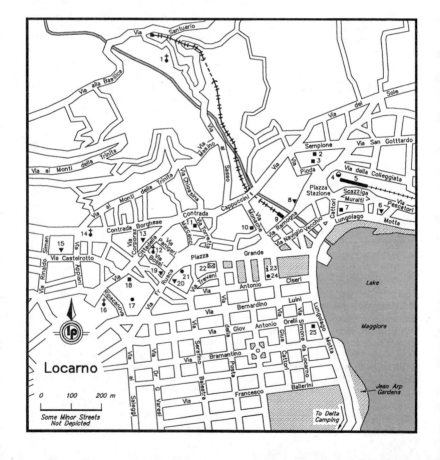

From November to March, opening hours are Monday to Friday from 8 am to noon, and 2 to 6 pm.

North and west of Piazza Grande is the old part of town (Città Vecchia), where the streets are small (too small to be shown on our map) and sometimes confusing. But getting lost in this area is fun rather than frustrating. Five-minutes' walk away is the train station, where money-exchange counters are open daily from 5.10 am to 9.30 pm, and bike rental and left-luggage are available daily from 5.10 am to 11.30 pm.

The telephone code for Locarno is 093.

Things to See & Do

Madonna del Sasso This sanctuary overlooks the town and lake from a prominent position on the hillside. It was built after the Virgin Mary appeared in a vision to a monk, Bartolomeo d'Ivrea in 1480. There's a small museum (Sfr2.50, children and students Sfr1), a church (chiesa) and several very distinctive statue groups on the stairway. The best-known painting in the church is *la fuga in egitto* (Flight to Egypt) (1522) by Bramantino. Also don't miss *il transporto al sepolcro* by Antonio Ciseri (1821-91), with the haunting, mournful face of the central bearer. His silent grief comes across with all the greater intensity by being juxtaposed with the melodramatic swoonings of the women behind him (no matter if one of the women is Mary herself).

Something of a contrast in style are the many naive votive paintings by the church entrance, where the Madonna and Child appear as ghostly apparitions in life-and-death situations. There is a funicular from the town centre to the sanctuary (Sfr5 return), but the 20-minute walk up is not demanding (take Via al Sasso off Via Cappuccini). At least take the walk down, as you pass some ancient shrines on the way. On the Via Crucis route you're accompanied by the Stations of the Cross.

Other Attractions From the sanctuary, a cable car flies up to **Cardada** (Sfr15.50 return), and thereafter a chair lift soars to **Cimetta** (Sfr20 combined return fare) at 1672 metres. The Swiss Pass gets a reduction but the Half-Fare Card doesn't. From either stop there are fine views and several walking trails, and the transport up runs year round (there's some skiing in winter). Paragliding is possible up here; call ☎ 35 22 38 for information.

In the town, explore the Italianate piazzas and arcades, and admire the Lombardic houses. At one time the Piazza Grande curved round the actual shoreline of the lake.

There are a couple of interesting churches worth peeking inside. The 17th century **Chiesa Nuova** on Via Cittadella, has an ornate ceiling complete with frolicking angels, and a giant St Christopher with disproportionately tiny feet outside. The **Sant'**

■ PLACES TO STAY

2   Hotel Stazione
3   Hotel Garni Montaldi
7   Hotel Ristorante Zurigo
10 Hotel Zingara
11 Pensione Città Vecchia
18 Schloss Hotel & Visconti
25 Treff Hotel Arcadia

▼ PLACES TO EAT

6   Ristorante Centenario
8   Ristorante Inova
13 Ristorante Cittadella
15 Trattoria Campagna Ristorante
19 Coop Supermarket & Restaurant
20 Migros Supermarket & Restaurant

OTHER

1   Madonna del Sasso
4   Bus Departures
5   Train Station
9   Funicular Station
12 Nuova Church
14 St Antonio Church
16 San Fransesco Church
17 Castello Visconti
21 Bar Cantina
22 Main Post Office
23 Tourist Office
24 Kursaal

Antonio Church has paintings by Orelli, as does the **San Francesco Church.**

Off Piazza Grande is the **Castello Visconti**, dating from the 15th century and now housing a museum with Roman and Bronze Age exhibits, and modern art (Sfr3, open Tuesday to Sunday from 10 am to noon and 2 to 5 pm). Locarno was believed to be a glass manufacturing town in Roman times, which accounts for the strong showing of glass artefacts in the museum.

Locarno's climate is perfect for strolls round the lake. Wistaria, mimosa, azaleas, camellias and magnolias blossom as early as March. **Giardini Jean Arp** (Jean Arp Gardens) is a small lakeside park off Lungolago Gius Motta, where sculptures by the surrealist artist are scattered among the palm trees and tulips. There are various free swimming spots around the lake, and sailing is another popular activity. The tourist office has a list of hiring outlets as well as selling fishing permits, valid for the whole canton (Sfr50 for 10 days).

Organised Tours
Various guided tours are offered from Locarno, such as to Milan (Sfr50), Lake Como (Sfr55), the Italian part of Lake Maggiore (Sfr50). The tourist office has details. Locarno is also an ideal base for exploring the northern valleys (see the end of this chapter).

Places to Stay
From March to October, many hotels participate in a special scheme, where if you take three night's accommodation a free three-day transport pass is thrown in. It is valid for local trains, buses, boats, and mountain transport up to Cimetta. Enquire directly at hotels. There is a hotel board and free telephone at the train station.

Places to Stay – bottom
Camping *Delta Camping* (☎ 31 60 81) is expensive at Sfr30 minimum per site (for two people), rising to Sfr39 from 1 June to 31 August. But it is a five-star site with copious facilities, and it's open from late March to mid-October.

Hostel *Pensione Città Vecchia* (☎ 31 45 54), Via Toretta 13, off Piazza Grande (head up the hill by the sign for 'Innovazione'), is a friendly, private hostel without curfew or daytime closing. Beds are Sfr20 with your own sleeping bag, or Sfr24 if you need sheets. Dorms vary in size but the price doesn't change. Hall showers are free, and breakfast is Sfr4 including refills. It is only open from 1 March to 31 October, and getting a bed here can be a problem in the peak of summer (telephone reservations are accepted).

Hotels *Zingara* (☎ 31 12 19), off Piazza Grande at Via delle Monache 1, has singles/doubles from Sfr25/50 and triples/quads for Sfr85/100. Triples have a private shower/toilet; if staying in the rest of the rooms, use those in the hall. It's a bit basic and some of the furniture looks like discards from a brothel, but you can't complain at the price. Reserve ahead, especially for singles. Things can get noisy from the bar downstairs and most of the clientele are young revellers.

Convenient for the station is *Garni Montaldi* (☎ 33 02 22), Piazza Stazione, with singles/doubles from Sfr42/82. Reception is also here for *Stazione*, an older, noisier building to the rear where singles/doubles start at Sfr38/76 with shower. Both hotels are open from mid-March. Stazione closes again at the end of October, and Garni Montaldi at the beginning of January.

Places to Stay – middle
Hotel Ristorante Zurigo (☎ 33 16 17), Viale Verbano 9, offers comfortable accommodation overlooking the lake. Gold-coloured metal bedsteads, tastefully arranged pictures and patterned tiled floors give the rooms some style. Prices start at Sfr80/112 for a single/double in winter, rising to Sfr138/168 in summer. All rooms have cable TV and private shower/toilet. The restaurant serves good, low to mid-price food, with various vegetarian choices.

Schloss Hotel (☎ 31 23 61), Via B Rusca in the old town, is a place with character and a slightly regal air, in its own grounds with ample parking. Singles/doubles start at Sfr75/130 and it's open from March to October.

Places to Stay – top end
Treff Hotel Arcadia (☎ 31 02 82) Lungolago Motta, is a four-star family hotel overlooking the lake. It has modern spacious rooms, all with a large balcony, satellite TV, private bathroom, mini bar, and telephone. Prices start at Sfr128/220 for single/double occupancy and there are larger apartments suitable for families. The hotel has a roof terrace and an outdoor swimming pool.

Places to Eat
Lake Maggiore yields many different varieties of fish, particularly perch (*persico*) and whitefish (*corigone*).

Both the *Migros* and *Coop* supermarkets on Piazza Grande have a self-service restaurant, with meals for around Sfr6 to Sfr13. *Inova*, Via Stazione 1, by the train station, has good self-service dishes from Sfr6.90 and help-yourself salad plates from Sfr3.80 to Sfr9.50. It is open daily to 10 pm.

The popular *Trattoria Campagna Ristorante* (☎ 31 99 47), Via Castelrotto near St Antonio Church, has *piatti del giorno* (dishes of the day) from Sfr12, and pizza and pasta from Sfr9.50. It is open every day until midnight. The restaurant adjoining the Schloss Hotel, *Visconti*, is atmospheric, with main courses starting at around Sfr25.

The place to go for fish specialities is *Ristorante Cittadella* (☎ 31 58 85), Via Cittadella 18 – its upstairs section serves nothing else. Main dishes are around Sfr25 to Sfr40, although downstairs you can also tuck into pizzas from Sfr10.50 (open daily).

For a good, gastronomic feast, where the food is served on sparkling silver salvers, go to *Ristorante Centenario* (☎ 33 82 22), Lungolago 17. It's widely acknowledged as the best restaurant in Ticino, but the prices might make you flavour its French cuisine with the salt of your own tears. Three small

courses in the business lunch cost Sfr48, the eight-course evening menu is Sfr128, and à-la-carte eating is around Sfr38 to Sfr48. The restaurant is closed on Sunday and Monday.

Entertainment
Downstairs in Zingara (see Places to Stay) there's a bar which every night turns into a disco from 8 pm to 1 am, and prices are hiked accordingly (beer Sfr8). The *Kursaal* by the tourist office offers a choice of theatre, cinema, gambling (Boule), drinking and dancing. Classical concerts are held at the Castello Visconti, a couple of churches, and especially at Sopra Cenerina on Piazza Grande. The tourist office sells tickets for all venues.

Next to Migros on Piazza Grande is *Bar Cantina* with a large selection of different wines stacked up on the shelves, and a brightly-lit, lively ambience. There's usually live music on a Saturday of a dance-along accordion-based variety. It attracts mainly an older clientele and somehow veers between the authentic and the excruciating. Check if it's your style from the window.

Locarno hosts an international film festival in the first two weeks in August: at night, films are screened in the open-air in the Piazza Grande.

Getting There & Away
Train There are trains every two hours from Brig, passing through Italy en route. The cost is Sfr47 and it takes around three hours. You change trains at Domodossola across the border, so bring your passport.

Bus Postbuses to the surrounding valleys leave from outside the train station. From the end of May to mid-October the Palm Express bus goes to St Moritz via Lugano, once a day. Reserve a seat in advance on ☎ 091-21 95 20.

Car The St Gotthard pass provides the road link (N2) to central Switzerland. Hertz (☎ 33 50 50) is at Via Sempione 12 and Europcar

(☎ 31 88 44) is at Via Trevani. Avis (☎ 35 44 55) is at Via Cantonale in nearby Ascona.

Boat One-day travel passes for boats on Lake Maggiore cost Sfr9 or Sfr17 depending upon the area they're valid for on the Swiss part of the lake. More extensive cruises around the Italian part of the lake are also available. Boats sail from early April to late September. For more information, contact Navigazione Lago Maggiore on ☎ 31 18 65. There are several boats and hydrofoils departing Locarno daily for Italian resorts. Examples of fares are Luino Sfr16.60, Stresa Sfr22.80, and Arona Sfr25.80. Reservations are essential for hydrofoils and cost Sfr1. The only car ferry across the lake is in Italy, from Intra to Laveno. The Swiss Pass is not valid on any boats.

Getting Around
There are parking spaces on and under Piazza Grande. Local buses (including to Ascona) are run by a private company called 'Fart'. This derogatory name is rather appropriate because the company has the cheek to charge for its schedules. (I know of none other in Switzerland that does this.) Single trips cost Sfr1 to Sfr2, or it's Sfr5.60 for a day pass. The Swiss Pass is valid.

AROUND LOCARNO
South-west of Ascona are the **Isles of Brissago**, famous for the botanical gardens (Sfr5, open early April to late September) where subtropical flora thrive. The boat trip, departing from the corner of Piazza Grande, costs Sfr17 (children half-price), or Sfr9 if you embark from Ascona. **Ronco**, beautifully situated opposite the islands, is a great drive from Locarno.

ASCONA
Ascona is Locarno's smaller twin on the opposite side of the delta of the Maggiore River. The village is known as a centre for arts – the backstreets are filled with art galleries and craft shops, and it hosts an international music festival from the end of August to early October, and a New Orleans jazz festival at the end of June. The community of artists and intellectuals embraced the 'back to nature' movement at the beginning of the century, and welcomed the exiled Lenin for a time.

The Ascona tourist office (☎ 093-35 00 90) is by the church tower near the waterfront. Winter opening hours are Monday to Friday from 9 am to noon and 2 to 5.30 pm. In the summer it is open daily for longer hours.

The town still pursues an independent course, to the extent that there is scant cooperation between its tourist office and that in Locarno. Ascona has the **Museo comunale d'arte moderna** in the Palazzo Pancaldi, Via Borgo 34, which includes paintings by artists connected with the town, among them Paul Klee, Hans Arp, Ben Nicholson and Alexej Jawlensky. The museum is open Tuesday to Saturday from 10 am to noon and 3 to 6 pm, and Sunday from 10 am to noon, and entry costs Sfr3.

Places to Stay & Eat
There's a cheap camp site near Ascona, *Segnale* (☎ 35 29 70), that's open from Easter to the end of October.

The waterfront is one long parade of mid-price hotels and restaurants with outside tables. *Al porto* (☎ 093-35 13 21) is typical of these, with singles/doubles starting at Sfr68/136 or Sfr78/156 with lake view. All rooms have private shower, toilet, TV and direct-dial telephone, and are located in four different buildings. The restaurant has fish dishes from Sfr23 and a good choice of vegetarian food (Sfr7 to Sfr14.50); in winter it is closed on Monday and during January.

Garni Silvia (☎ 093-35 13 14) Via Circonvallazione 7, near the Mobil petrol station, has large, fresh rooms with hall showers and there's plenty of foliage on the stairway to keep you company. Singles/doubles start at Sfr38/72, except for a single night's stay, when a surcharge of Sfr3 per person applies. Just down the road is a *Coop* supermarket and restaurant.

Getting There & Away

Take bus No 31 from the train station or Piazza Grande in Locarno, which stops at Ascona post office with departures every 15 minutes.

Northern Valleys

The two valleys north of Locarno are dead-ends, but they make fine day trips and allow you to explore areas relatively untainted by tourism. Take refreshment in rustic *grotti* (country inns). Both the Maggia and Verzasca valleys can be visited on a special tour (Sfr30) from mid-March to the end of October; reserve at the Locarno tourist office.

All these northern valleys proffer scenic delights, although the minor road winding over the San Bernardino is perhaps the most spectacular (closed from November to May). The motorway is open year-round.

Maggia Valley

The valley (valle in Italian) follows the Maggia River, passing small villages, until at Cevio it splits, the first of many divisions into smaller valleys. Take the left branch then a right into the valley that terminates at **Bosco Gurin**. This village was settled by folk from the Valais in the 12th century, and it is the only place in Ticino where German is the principal language spoken. Bus No 10 runs hourly from Locarno to Cevio (takes 50 minutes), but buses are less frequent for the 40-minute trip on to Bosco Gurin. The total

same day return fare is Sfr25; if you stay overnight the fare leaps to Sfr40.40.

Verzasca Valley

This valley (Val Verzasca) is wilder and less developed than Maggia. Brione, where the valley forks, has a castle and a 14th century church. The right-hand fork goes to **Sonogno**, noted for its simple, stone-built houses. Postbuses run from Locarno only every two hours or so; the journey takes 70 minutes and costs Sfr29 return.

Cento Valley

Centovalli (literally 'a hundred valleys') heading west, is the route to Domodossola in Italy. At Rè, on the Italian side, there is a procession of pilgrims on 30 April each year, a tradition that originated after a painting of the Madonna was reported to start bleeding upon being struck by a ball.

Leventina Valley

From Bellinzona, the Valle Leventina is the rail and road route to Andermatt and Zürich. There is the choice of taking the motorway (N2/E35) or a smaller parallel road. En route, the town of Biasca has a 12th-century Romanesque church with a tall belfry and some fading frescoes. At Biasca, the valley splits: Val Blenio is the route to Disentis, on the Vorder-Rhein.

Mesolcina Valley

North-east of Bellinzona is the Valle Mesolcina, leading to the San Bernardino Pass and the Hinter-Rhein. Again, there is a choice of taking a motorway (N13/E43) or a smaller road (highway 13).

Graubünden

Once upon a time, tourists in Switzerland were a summer phenomenon. Then, in 1864, the owner of the Engadiner Kulm Hotel in St Moritz offered four English summer guests free accommodation if they returned for the winter. He told them they were missing the best time of the year. Although dubious, the English were unable to refuse a free offer. They returned, enjoyed themselves, and winter tourism was born.

Today Graubünden (Grisons, Grigioni, Grishun) has some of the most developed and best known winter sports centres in the world, including Arosa, Davos, Klosters, Flims, and, of course, St Moritz. Tourism is a major earner for the canton; around 50% of the population are directly or indirectly employed in the sector, and it accounts for 20% of overnight stays in Switzerland as a whole.

Away from the international resorts, Graubünden is a relatively unspoiled region of rural villages, Alpine lakes and mountain vistas. In addition to tourism, the generation of hydro-electric power is important to the local economy. It has the lowest unemployment rate (1.7%), yet is only the 12th-richest canton, earning Sfr37,132 per capita.

In medieval times the region was known as Rhaetia, and was loosely bound together by an association of three leagues. The modern name for the canton was derived from the *Grauer Bund*, or Grey League. Conquest of the area by an outsider was virtually impossible because of the mountainous terrain – 221 separate communities were scattered within 150 distinct valleys. Graubünden joined the Swiss Confederation in 1803.

Orientation & Information
Graubünden is the largest Swiss canton, covering an area of 7106 sq km, ranging in altitude from 270 metres (Misox) to 4049 metres (Piz Bernina). There are two major rivers in this canton; the Rhine and the Inn.

The Alps cover most of the terrain, accounting for the fact that it is also the most sparsely populated canton, with just 25 inhabitants per sq km. The Septimber Pass, Julier Pass and Maloja Pass are transit routes through the Alps that have been important since Roman times.

Chur is the cantonal capital, and has the regional tourist office (☎ 081-22 13 60), 2nd floor, Alexanderstrasse 24, with information on the whole canton. It's open Monday to Friday from 8 am to noon and from 1.30 to 5.30 pm. The office is in the building marked 'Publicitas' and is visible from the train station. A better number to ring for information is the new office (☎ 081-302 61 00) at the Heidiland Restaurant on the N13 autobahn, the route south from Sargans.

Holiday apartments abound in Graubünden and are usually better value than hotels and pensions. A minimum stay of three days to one week is usually required and they generally need to be booked up well in advance. Tourist offices compile lists of these, and can inform you about another cheap option; private rooms.

Language
The extent to which the mountains have dominated and isolated the region can be heard in the language. In the north (around Chur and Davos) the people speak German, in the south, Italian, and in between (St Moritz, Lower Engadine, Vorderrhine Valley) mostly Romansch. Yet even between neighbouring valleys there can be significant linguistic differences. Take the word 'cup' as an example. In German it's *Tasse*, Italian it's *tazza* and Romansch it's *cuppina*. None of these words for cup are used in the Hinter-Rhine Valley where they say *(scariola)*, the Albula Valley *(cuppegn)* or the Müstair Valley *(cupina)*.

The use of Romansch is gradually in decline, and linguists fear it may disappear altogether. Already, German speakers

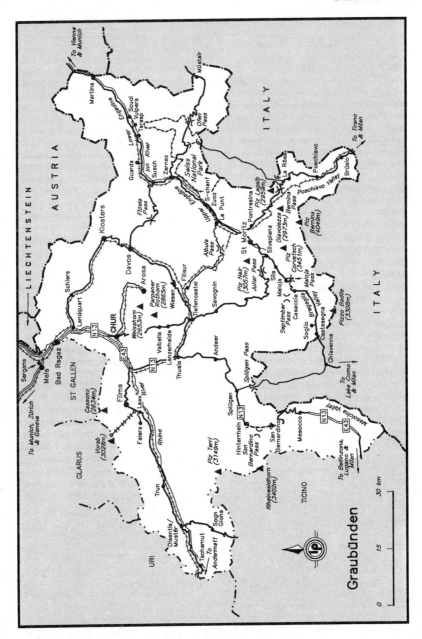

Graubünden

account for 60% of the Graubünden population, with Romansch down to 22 %.

When to Go
Most of the resorts mentioned in this chapter virtually close down in May and November and for one or two weeks either side. It's a fine time to go if you hate crowds and just want to do a lot of walking, but bear in mind that most if not all of the cable cars will shut down. Tourist offices will be able to provide exact running times. There will always be a fair selection of restaurants and hotels still open, and the restaurants you find are likely to be pretty good, as they're the ones that can attract the local trade. Hotels may even be inclined to negotiate on rates.

Peak season is approximately Christmas to the end of February and July and August.

Activities
Museums and galleries are not the main reason to visit Graubünden. Instead, it is an area for enjoying the majestic scenery and outdoor activities. There are 10,500 km of footpaths, 1500 km of ski slopes and 870 km of cross-country ski trails. Graubünden has over 600 lakes, and those offering the greatest choice of water sports are the lakes at Lenzerheide-Valbella, St Moritz, Sils/Maloja, and Silvaplana. Average costs are: Sfr250 for one week at a sailing school, Sfr80 to Sfr140 for one day's sailing boat rental, and Sfr9 for 30 minutes' windsurfing.

Getting Around
Public Transport Graubünden has a regional transport pass issued between 1 May and 31 October and valid for 15 days. It is good for a 50% discount on main transport routes throughout the region (extending to Bellinzona, Andermatt and Samnaun) and for free travel in five days on selected lines, encompassing Tirano (in Italy), St Moritz, Scuol, Davos, Arosa, Disentis/Mustér and Chur. The price is Sfr110 in 2nd class (Sfr90 with Swiss railpasses, Sfr55 for children) and Sfr175 (Sfr140 or Sfr87.50) in 1st class. Buy them from SNTO abroad, stations of the

Rhätische Railway or Graubünden post offices.

Car & Motorbike Motorways barely invade Graubünden's territory, but the roads are excellent given the difficulties of the terrain. There are three main passes from northern Graubünden to the southern valleys of Bregaglia and Engadine; from west to east they are: Julier (open year-round), Albula (summer only) and Flüela (year-round, but may close in bad weather). These approximately correspond to three exit points into Italy: Maloja, Bernina and Ofen (all open year-round). The Oberalp Pass, the route west to Andermatt, is closed in winter, but as at Albula, there is the option of taking the car-carrying train instead. It is advisable to carry snow chains in winter.

Chur

Chur is the cantonal capital, yet retains a small-town feel with its population of 32,000. It has been continuously inhabited since 3000 BC. The city was virtually destroyed by fire in 1464, and German-speaking artisans poured in to carry out the rebuilding. They rebuilt the linguistic landscape too, for the city had previously been Romansch-speaking. Chur is pronounced *khoor*; to sound like the locals, rasp it out as if you're clearing your throat preparatory to spitting.

Orientation & Information
The old town is situated between the train station and the cathedral. The train station has luggage lockers, bike rental and money-exchange counters (5.45 am to 9.15 pm daily). Five minutes' walk straight ahead down Bahnhofstrasse is Postplatz. To the right is a post office (PTT 7002, Chur 2) and to the left is the tourist office (☎ 081-22 18 18), Grabenstrasse 5, open Monday to Friday from 8 am to noon and 1.30 to 6 pm, and

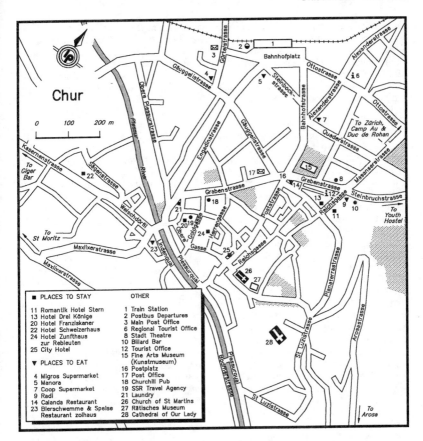

Chur

0   100   200 m

PLACES TO STAY

11 Romantik Hotel Stern
13 Hotel Drei Könige
20 Hotel Franziskaner
22 Hotel Schweizerhaus
24 Hotel Zunfthaus
   zur Rebleuten
25 City Hotel

▼ PLACES TO EAT

4 Migros Supermarket
5 Manora
7 Coop Supermarket
9 Radl
14 Calanda Restaurant
23 Bierschwemme & Speise
   Restaurant zolhaus

OTHER

1 Train Station
2 Postbus Departures
3 Main Post Office
6 Regional Tourist Office
8 Stadt Theatre
10 Billard Bar
12 Tourist Office
15 Fine Arts Museum
   (Kunstmuseum)
16 Postplatz
17 Post Office
18 Churchill Pub
19 SSR Travel Agency
21 Laundry
26 Church of St Martins
27 Rätisches Museum
28 Cathedral of Our Lady

Saturday from 9 am to noon. Pick up a free copy of the two walking tours of the centre of town. The office makes hotel reservations for Sfr2 commission.

Many shops in the centre have late opening on Friday nights until 9 pm. SSR (☎ 081-22 97 76), the budget travel agency, is at Untere Gasse. Nearby on Grabenstrasse is a self-service laundry, open daily to midnight. It costs from Sfr6 to wash and Sfr3 to dry.

The main post office (Hauptpost, Chur 1), is by the train station.

The telephone code for Chur is 081.

Things to See & Do

Chur has an attractive old town with 16th century buildings, fountains and alleyways. Follow the green and red footprints on the pavement that correspond to the tourist office walking tours. At various points you come across amusing murals of ordinary people painted on walls and building façades by Robert Indermaur. Arcas (green walking route) is a pleasing square with the church spire rising in the background.

Augusto Giacometti designed three of the windows in the 1491 **Church of St Martin**. By the church is the **Rätisches Museum**,

Hofstrasse 1, displaying a standard provincial collection relating to local history, furniture, crafts and costumes, although the odd Egyptian sarcophagus is an unexpected addition (German signs only). It is open Tuesday to Sunday from 10 am to noon and 2 to 5 pm, and admission costs Sfr3 (students Sfr1.50).

In the impressive **cathedral**, built from 1150, are a number of interesting features, including the carved heads on the choir stalls. The particularly fine **high altar**, made by Jakob Russ from 1486-92, is the largest Gothic triptych in Switzerland. It's just a pity that it's so dark and distant that you can't appreciate it properly. (There are two tiers of alarms to keep you away.) The crypt contains valuable religious reliquaries from the Middle Ages. It can be viewed Monday to Saturday from 10 am to noon and 2 to 4 pm, but you need to get the key from the 1st floor of Hofstrasse 2.

The **Kunstmuseum** on Postplatz contains modern art, including a generous gathering of work by the three Giacomettis: Alberto, Augusto and Giovanni. Note also the sci-fi designs by local artist, H R Giger. If you think there's a resemblance between his work and the monster in the film *Alien*, you're right. That beastie with its metallic grin was his brainchild. And speaking of brains, devotees of progressive rock will recognise his distinctive style from the cover of Emerson Lake & Palmer's album, *Brain Salad Surgery*. If you like his stuff, check out his bar (see the Entertainment section). Entry to the museum costs Sfr5 (students Sfr3), and it's open the same hours as the Rätisches Museum.

Places to Stay – bottom end
Camping *Camp Au* (☎ 081-24 22 83), to the north of town by the sports centre, costs Sfr5 per person and from Sfr4 for a tent, and it is open year-round.

Hostel The IYHF *youth hostel* (☎ 081-22 65 63), Berggasse 28, is up the hill to the east, a 15-minute walk from the tourist office. This rustic hostel is very intimate: each bunk comprises at least five mattresses side by side. Beds cost Sfr16.40 including breakfast. Curfew is at 11 pm, and reception shuts from 10 am to 5 pm during which time the doors are locked. The hostel is closed at Christmas and during January and February. Take bus Nos 1 or 8 from the train station.

There are no particularly cheap hotels in town. *Franziskaner* (☎ 081-22 12 61), Untere Gasse, has adequate singles/doubles including breakfast for Sfr45/90, with free use of the hall shower; doubles with shower and toilet are Sfr120. *Schweizerhaus* (☎ 22 10 96) on Kasernenstrasse, is a bar/café with singles/doubles for Sfr45/85 or Sfr58/90 with a shower cubicle built into the corner of the room. The peeling paint on the doors is off-putting but the rooms are fine.

More conveniently located for the centre, *City Hotel* (☎ 22 54 44) on Obere Gasse, offers similar shower cubicles in singles/doubles for Sfr55/80. The rooms are smallish but nicely decorated and have an ancient radio that takes about 10 years to warm up. The hotel also runs the bar and restaurant at ground level.

Places to Stay – middle
Greater comfort can be found at *Hotel Drei Könige* (☎ 081-22 17 25), Reichsgasse 18. Singles/doubles are Sfr85/135 with shower or Sfr65/110 without. Garage parking is available and it also stages occasional concerts. *Hotel Zunfthaus zur Rebleuten* (☎ 22 17 13), Kupfergasse 1, is similarly priced. It's in a 500-year-old building with a striking front fresco; the rooms are fine but somehow don't quite live up to expectations. *Romantik Hotel Stern* – with a name like that it also inspires certain expectations – opposite Drei Könige on Reichsgasse, offers three-star comfort from Sfr100/175.

Top of the range is the four-star *Duc de Rohan* (☎ 22 10 22) on Masanserstrasse, where prices start at Sfr110/180. It offers a swimming pool and sauna among its facilities.

Places to Eat
There is a *Coop* with a restaurant on the

intersection of Bahnhofstrasse and Alexanderstrasse, open to 6.30 pm Monday to Thursday, 9 pm on Friday and 5 pm on Saturday. Opposite the train station on Steinbockstrasse there's one of the always reliable *Manora* buffet restaurants. Main dishes are Sfr8 to Sfr11. It's open from 7 am (8 am Sunday) to 10.30 pm every day. Not far away on Gürtelstrasse is a *Migros* supermarket and restaurant.

Calanda Restaurant on Postplatz has a variety of cheap menus from Sfr12.50, including vegetarian choices. It's also popular with evening drinkers. *Radi*, Steinbruchstrasse 2, is a simple restaurant/bar with daily specials for Sfr11, or Sfr13 with soup. It's open daily from 8 am to midnight. Finish off with a game of pool in the *Billiard Bar* next door.

Chur has its own mini red light district on Welschdörfli, which is also a cheap place to eat. A pizzeria and a snack bar are opposite each other on the main road. On the fringes is *Bierschwemme*, Maxlixerstrasse 1, a bar with hot meals from just Sfr7.50, and fondue for Sfr12.80. The daily special with soup is Sfr9.80 and beer is Sfr3.40 for half a litre. Upstairs is the more expensive *Speise Restaurant Zollhaus*.

For well-prepared food in a wooden environment (the décor, not the company), go to *Hotel Stern* (see Places to Stay). Main dishes are around Sfr30, or you can splash out on the eight-course gourmet menu at Sfr130 for two. Lunch-time eating is cheaper, with three menus (one vegetarian) from Sfr14 including soup. The restaurant is open daily. Also good is the restaurant in *Hotel Zunfthaus zur Rebleuten* (see Places to Stay), with main dishes from Sfr18 and multi-course menus (closed Saturday lunch time and Monday).

Entertainment

The *Stadt Theatre* is opposite the tourist office, which sells tickets for most events. Theatre productions are very occasionally in English, and a variety of musical events are staged. Buskers or street musicians are usually to be found chanting and playing South American rhythms in the station or on Bahnhofstrasse.

At night the hectic, crowded *Churchill Pub* on Grabenstrasse is where the local youth go to drink, pose and play pool.

The silver and black *Giger Bar*, (☎ 23 75 06), Comercialstrasse 23, owned by the artist H R Giger, is a must for anyone interested in sci-fi themes. The whole place looks like something out of a space movie, with particularly wacky front doors and an intricate design on the floor. You half expect those skeletal chairs that curve above your head to ingest you at any moment. Beers cost Sfr3.60 for 0.3 litre. It's open daily except Sunday from 7.30 am to midnight, and it's in southwest Chur. Take bus No 1 from the station, get off at the 'Freifeld' stop and turn left by the 'Möbelmarkt' shop sign. It's 50 metres down, by the statue of a (sort of) female.

Getting There & Away

There are rail connections to Davos, Klosters and Arosa, and fast trains to Sargans (the station for Liechtenstein, only 22 minutes away) and Zürich (85 minutes, Sfr36). Chur can be visited on the Glacier Express route (see Getting There & Away in the St Moritz section). Postbuses leave from in front of the train station, including the express service to Bellinzona.

Graubünden's one motorway, the N13 (E43), goes north from Chur to Zürich and Lake Constance.

Car Rental Avis (☎ 22 39 73) is at Kasernenstrasse 88, and Hertz (☎ 22 32 22) is nearby at No 92.

Getting Around

The train station is the hub for all local buses, which cost Sfr2 per journey. A strip of 12 tickets costs Sfr12. Last buses are around 11 pm, but a hint that Chur is not really a partying town is given in the fact that buses combine schedules and reduce frequencies as early as 8 pm. The Swiss Pass is valid on city transport.

Car parking is not possible in the streets of the old town at night. Instead, look for signs for several garages on the edge of the old quarter.

AROUND CHUR
Lenzerheide & Valbella

These twin-resorts at 1480 metres are beautifully situated on either side of Lake Heidsee, with surrounding woodland and soaring peaks. It attracts few foreign visitors, but it's a great place for relaxation and sports. It offers a quiet nightlife, and skiing mainly geared towards beginners and intermediates. A one-day ski pass costs Sfr42 for adults, Sfr34 for youths and senior citizens, and Sfr25 for children. Ski coupons are available for Sfr58 and Sfr110.

The Parpaner Rothorn (2865 metres) is the highest point that can be reached by cable car, and has several walking trails radiating from the summit. Contact the tourist office (☎ 081-34 34 34) for more information.

Getting There & Away

The resort is easily reached by bus (hourly from Chur, Sfr8.40, takes 40 minutes) or car. It is on highway 3, the route from Chur to St Moritz that goes over the Julier Pass.

Rhine River

The Rhine (Rhein in German) is one of Europe's most important rivers. The Rhine has two sources in Graubünden – the Vorderrhein and the Hinterrhein. In the 1980s Swiss companies in Basel badly polluted the river by accidentally discharging chemical waste products into it. Germany and the Netherlands, which suffered the consequences down-river, were not pleased. The Swiss have long since cleaned up their act. ·

FLIMS

This well-established ski resort at 1050 metres is favoured more by the Swiss than by foreign visitors.

Orientation & Information

The resort is divided into two localities,

about one km apart. Flims Dorf is larger, more residential, and slightly closer to the ski lifts. Flims Waldhaus is nicely situated between two areas of woodland and has most of the hotels. It also has the tourist office (☎ 081-39 10 22), open Monday to Friday from 9 am to noon and 2 to 6 pm, and Saturday from 9 am to noon. In the summer and winter high season it is additionally open on Saturday from 2 to 5 pm. A Guest Card system operates in the resort. Postbuses stop at the tourist office and at the post office in Flims Dorf.

The telephone code for the area is 081.

Activities

Skiing The skiing area is grouped under the name 'the White Arena' and includes the adjoining villages of Laax and Falera. Most of the runs are intermediate or easy and are centred on four mountains: Crap Masegn (2477 metres), Vorab (3018 metres), La Siala (2810 metres) and Cassons (2634 metres). A one-day ski pass costs Sfr50 (Sfr4 supplement for weekends and holidays), covers 220 km of runs and includes a free ski bus between lifts. Children's passes are half-price. Other winter activities encompass cross-country skiing, 60 km of winter footpaths, curling and tobogganing.

Hiking In summer, the hiking network extends to 200 km, including to the Rhine Gorge (dubbed the Swiss Grand Canyon). At the summit of the Cassons there is a circular walking route, the *Naturlehrpfad*, that yields delights of flora, fauna and geology. It takes up to three hours to complete the circuit; take the cable car from Flims to Cassonsgrat (Sfr24 one way, Sfr36 return).

River-Rafting River-rafting on the Rhine River is fast and furious on the stretch of the Vorderrhein between Ilanz and Reichenau, near Flims. Swissraft Flims-Laax (☎ 081-921 41 41), CH-7032 Laax-Murschetg, has two itineraries; one trip lasting around three hours over 17 km for Sfr72 and another lasting up to six hours over 20 km and costing Sfr113 (both trips May to September only). It also has trips combining boating and mountain biking.

Other Activities The best lake for boating and swimming is Lake Cresta, open from late May to mid-October (Sfr5.50 with Guest Card, Sfr7.50 without). Fishing on the Rhine River is also possible (permits from the tourist office). Para-gliding (☎ 921 33 55) courses are available year-round, as are accompanied flights and hot air ballooning (☎ 921 41 41 for both).

Places to Stay

Many, many apartments are available ranging from Sfr30 to Sfr240 per person; contact the tourist office well in advance.

There is camping at *Prau* (☎ 39 15 75), just outside Flims Waldhaus on the road to Laax. It is open year-round and costs Sfr5 per person and Sfr3 for a tent.

To find somewhere to stay, check the tourist office or the hotel board and free telephone outside the post office in Flims Dorf. The cheapest option is at the *Insti Garni* (☎ 39 12 08), a student residence where rooms are only available in the holidays. There are plenty of showers either in the hall or in rooms and singles/doubles start at Sfr30/45. It is halfway between Dorf and Waldhaus.

An excellent and inexpensive choice is *Guardaval* (☎ 39 11 19) in Waldhaus. The rooms are a good size, many with a balcony, and the owner is solicitous. Parking is ample and there's a garden with a summer house. Singles/doubles start at Sfr44/80 with private shower and there are a few slightly cheaper rooms using the shower in the hall.

By the tourist office is the *Schlosshotel* (☎ 39 12 45), with an easily identifiable pointed tower. It has a welcoming large lounge, with an open fire and hunting trophies on the wall. Rooms were newly renovated in the summer of 1993 and prices start at Sfr65 per person (add Sfr15 for half-pension).

One of several four-star hotels, *Crap Ner* (☎ 39 26 26) is immune to puns about its name (*crap* means stone in Romansch). It's near the postbus stop in Flims Dorf and offers a free shuttle to the ski lifts. Good facilities include a sauna and indoor swimming pool, and rooms start at Sfr80/126 in summer and Sfr115/184 in winter.

Places to Eat

Near the Dorf bus stop are both a *Denner* and *Coop* supermarket. The best budget eating deal is at the *Hotel Albana*, by the cable car station. It has a self-service restaurant on the 1st floor in comfortable and relaxed surroundings, with a bar area. The Tagesteller costs Sfr8.50 and pizzas start at the same price. Plates from the salad buffet cost Sfr3.50 or Sfr8.50. Hot food is served between 11 am and 11 pm daily. There's another inexpensive self-service restaurant at the Naraus cable station.

Towards Waldhaus is *Grischuna*, offering a daily menu with soup for Sfr16.50 and house specialities for Sfr30 to Sfr40 (closed Tuesday and Wednesday in summer). It has rooms as well but they are rather cramped for the price. *Restaurant Giardino* is in the hotel Crap Ner (see Places to Stay), with tempting choices for Sfr18 to Sfr40. There's a salad buffet (Sfr7 or Sfr9) and vegetarian dishes for Sfr15.

In Flims Waldhaus there are a couple of pizzerias. Try *Pomodor* on the main road, with pizzas from Sfr12 and pasta and risotto from Sfr12.50.

Getting There & Away

The nearest train station is at Reichenau or Ilanz. Postbuses run to Flims (and the other villages in the White Arena area) approximately hourly from Chur. The trip takes less than an hour and costs Sfr10.60, stopping at Reichenau. Buses also run frequently to Ilanz (takes 30 minutes), but the service stops around 6.30 pm.

Arosa

Arosa is a relaxing resort at 1800 metres, spread out in the Schanfigg Valley amid lakes and woodland.

Orientation & Information

Arosa has two parts; Ausserarosa (Outer Arosa), is the main resort, and Innerarosa is the older part of the village. Ausserarosa is grouped around the shores of the Lake Obersee. This is the terminus for the train, and in the station are money-exchange counters, luggage storage, and bike rental.

From Oberseeplatz, take Poststrasse, heading uphill in the direction of Innerarosa. After five minutes you'll reach the tourist office (☎ 081-31 16 21), open in summer Monday to Friday from 8 am to noon and 2 to 6 pm, and Saturday from 8 am to noon and (July to mid-August) 2 pm to 4 pm. Winter hours are Monday to Friday from 8 am to 6 pm, Saturday from 9 am to 5.30 pm, and Sunday from 10 am to noon and 4 to 5.30 pm. Contact the office several months in advance (Kurverein Arosa, CH-7050) if you're interested in renting a holiday apartment. Buses in the resort are free for everybody until around 7 pm; they cost Sfr3 thereafter.

The main post office is at Oberseeplatz, and the telephone code for Arosa is 081.

Activities

Arosa has over 70 km of **skiing** for mixed abilities based on three main mountains. In particular, beginners have a good choice of runs, and the ski school can be contacted on ☎ 31 19 96. The highest skiing point is the Weisshorn at 2653 metres. Ski passes cost Sfr46 for one day and Sfr215 for one week (children half-price). As well as cross-country skiing, Arosa features several ice-skating rinks (natural and artificial), curling, and tobogganing (from Tschuggen down to the village). Hot air balloon flights (☎ 31 18 43) last about an hour and cost Sfr330 per person (December to April).

In the summer, there is a free bathing beach at **Untersee**, open daily from 9 am to 11 pm. The larger **Obersee** is used for rowing boats and pedalos (Sfr8 to Sfr15 per hour). Permits for trout fishing in both lakes can be obtained from the tourist office.

There are 200 km of maintained **hiking** trails, and the opportunity to go on a guided nature observation walk (Sfr5, reserve in advance from tourist office). The walk up to Weisshorn from the village takes about 3½ hours. The cable car to the top costs Sfr22, or Sfr28 return (30% off with Swiss Pass, half-price with Half-Fare Card, no reduction with Eurail or Inter-Rail). The view is extensive and elevating (viewing table).

Other activities include horse-riding, tennis and golf (nine-hole course).

Places to Stay – bottom end

Camping The *camp site* (☎ 31 17 45), is in a quiet location on the edge of the village, down from the tourist office. It is open year-round and costs Sfr6.50 per adult, Sfr4 for a tent and Sfr2 for a car.

Hostel For the IYHF *youth hostel* (☎ 31 13 97), Seewaldstrasse, take a left just beyond the tourist office. Like many hotels, it is closed from late April to early June and from mid-October to early December. Dorms cost Sfr20 in summer and Sfr30 in winter, when dinner is included. The reception is closed from 10 am to 5 pm but the doors stay open, and a key is available for late entry. Don't take the draconian notices in the entrance (eg, re-entry will be refused to anyone under the influence of alcohol) too seriously. Double rooms for couples cost an extra Sfr7 per person in summer and Sfr10 in winter.

Hotels & Pensions Many hotels and pensions have a surcharge for short stays (one or two nights), particularly in winter. One of the cheapest places is *Bündnerhof & Rössli* (☎ 31 16 32), on the opposite side of the Obersee from the station and open year-round. Singles/doubles in summer start at Sfr57/114 with private shower and Sfr45/90 without, and in winter from Sfr95/180 and

Sfr80/150. *Regula* (☎ 31 27 06), on Oberseeplatz, is convenient and cheap (from Sfr43/76), but it is doubtful whether it will stay open in 1994.

Pension Mezzaprada (☎ 31 12 70), by the children's ski school in Innerarosa, is open from 1 December to one week after Easter and has good-sized rooms with own shower from Sfr60 per person. There's one room only using hall shower from Sfr45. Also near the Brüggli bus stop is *Sonnenhalde* (☎ 31 15 31), starting at Sfr42 per person in summer and Sfr46 in winter. Rooms with private shower are also available.

Hotel Quellenhof (☎ 31 17 18) has fresh and light, if not overly huge, rooms near to the tourist office. They all have shower, toilet and TV. Prices start at Sfr60 per person in the summer and Sfr85 in the winter, when a Sfr8 supplement applies for short stays. Half-pension is available.

Places to Stay – middle

Hotel Alpensonne (☎ 31 15 47) is up the hill not far from the Brüggli lifts. The rooms are reasonably spacious, with private shower/toilet, and the south-facing ones have a big balcony with a fine view. Prices start at Sfr65/120 in summer and Sfr120/200 in winter when there's normally a minimum three-day stay in busy periods. For half-pension add Sfr20 per person; the hotel shuts in May and June.

The top hotels usually offer rooms on a minimum half-pension basis. Try *Hohenfels* (☎ 31 01 01), near the Catholic church, starting at Sfr100/180 in summer and Sfr158/266 in winter, or the marginally moe expensive *Posthotel* (☎ 31 01 21), right by the train station.

Places to Eat

There's a *Denner* supermarket (shut Thursday) near to the train station and a *Coop* (open weekdays and Saturday) by the tourist office.

Between the tourist office and Oberseeplatz is the *Café-Restaurant Oasis*, where you can get simple meals from Sfr7.50 to Sfr16. It is open to 7 pm except on Tuesday.

Opposite is the alcohol-free *Orelli's Restaurant*, offering good vegetarian dishes for around Sfr14 and a salad buffet for Sfr8 to 13 per plate. It has a wide selection of other meals between Sfr6.50 and Sfr28, and it's open daily from 7.30 am to 9 pm. Rooms are also available from Sfr65 per person (half-pension).

By the Obersee, anticlockwise from Oberseeplatz, is the *Hotel Carmenna*, which has a pizzeria open in the evenings from 6 pm to 1 am. Prices are in the range of Sfr11.50 to Sfr17.50. There's often live piano music in the bar in the evening.

Quellenhof (see Places to Stay) has a good restaurant, where most dishes cost between Sfr16 and Sfr28. It has a daily menu with soup for Sfr16. Also worth considering is the restaurant in *Alpensonne* (see Places to Stay), where meals cost from Sfr14.50 to Sfr43. There's a four-course menu for Sfr36. *Hotel Anita* (☎ 31 11 09), near the Catholic church, has a gourmet restaurant.

Entertainment

Daily events are listed in the *Wochenbulletin* from the tourist office. There are occasional musical events in the village church. Pool can be played at *Rondo* in the Kursaal, daily from 1.30 pm to 3 am. The Kursaal also features a cinema and a nightclub.

Getting There & Away

The only way to get there is from Chur; take the narrow-gauge train from in front of the train station (Sfr10.60). Departures are hourly and the trip takes an hour. It's a winding, scenic journey with views of mountains, pine trees streams and bridges (sit on the right). The road follows the same route. Snow chains are recommended in winter.

Davos

Originally known as a health resort, Davos (1560 metres) is simply one of the best skiing areas in the world. It includes the legendary

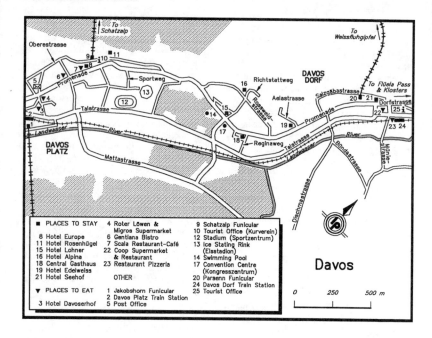

PLACES TO STAY

8 Hotel Europe
11 Hotel Rosenhügel
15 Hotel Lohner
16 Hotel Alpina
18 Central Gasthaus
19 Hotel Edelweiss
21 Hotel Seehof

▼ **PLACES TO EAT**

3 Hotel Davoserhof

4 Roter Löwen &
   Migros Supermarket
6 Gentiana Bistro
7 Scala Restaurant–Café
22 Coop Supermarket
23 Restaurant Pizzeria

OTHER

1 Jakobshorn Funicular
2 Davos Platz Train Station
5 Post Office

9 Schatzalp Funicular
10 Tourist Office (Kurverein)
12 Stadium (Sportzentrum)
13 Ice Stating Rink
   (Eisstadion)
14 Swimming Pool
17 Convention Centre
   (Kongresszentrum)
20 Parsenn Funicular
24 Davos Dorf Train Station
25 Tourist Office

Davos

0   250   500 m

Parsenn-Weissfluh area, where ski runs are a vertical mile long.

Orientation & Information

With a population exceeding 10,000, Davos is more of a town than a village. It is a four km-long conurbation stretched beside the railway line and the Landwasser River. It comprises two contiguous areas, each with its own railway station, Davos Platz and Davos Dorf. Both stations have money-exchange counters and lockers but only Davos Dorf has bike rental.

Davos Platz, to the south-west, is more built up than Dorf and the centre of most of the activity. From the Davos-Platz station, climb the hill to the right until you get on the Promenade, the main street, where there is a post office (on Postplatz). Turn right on the Promenade and continue for 300 metres for the Platz main tourist office. The Kurverein (☎ 081-45 21 21) at No 67, open Monday to Friday from 8.30 am to noon and 1.45 to 6

pm, and Saturday from 8.30 am to noon. During the high season, additional hours are Saturday from 4 to 6 pm and Sunday from 9 to 11 am.

The Promenade continues all the way to Dorf where it becomes Dorfstrasse. There is another tourist office (open the same hours) and a post office close to the Dorf train station. Both tourist offices make room reservations without commission. The Visitor's Card, given to guests by hotels, allows free travel on local buses and trains, as does the general ski pass (and the Swiss Pass).

The telephone code for Davos is 081.

Activities

Skiing Davos offers tremendous variety for experienced and intermediate skiers. The Weissfluh ski area goes as high as 2844 metres, and from here you can ski all the way to Kublis, over 2000 metres lower and 12 km distant. Alternatively, you can take the demanding run down to Wolfgang (1629 metres) or the scenic slopes down to Klosters. Across the valley, Brämabüel and Jakobshorn offer equally good skiing for all abilities, and the nearby areas of Pischa and Rinerhorn are also easily within reach of Davos. See also the Klosters section for further skiing areas.

In all there are 320 km of ski runs in the Davos/Klosters region, which are covered by the general REGA pass costing Sfr107 (Sfr64 children) for a minimum two days. Six days cost Sfr244 (Sfr146), but for low season weeks in January, late March and early April this price is reduced by 20%. In the pre-Christmas low season this discount applies on REGA passes of two to 21 days' validity. Daily passes for specific areas cost between Sfr22 (Sfr19) and Sfr51 (Sfr31).

The Davos ski school (☎ 43 71 71), Promenade 83, costs Sfr48 for a day and Sfr180 for five days. There are 75 km of cross-country trails open from December to April.

Hiking The mountains provide extensive hiking options. The views of the Alps are excellent from Weissfluh, and you can walk to the top in about 3½ hours in summer. The easy way is to take the Parsenn funicular from near Dorf station up to Weissfluhjoch, and the cable car from there up to Weissfluhgipfel. The combined fare is Sfr24 up, Sfr22 down, and Sfr30 return (25% off with Swiss Pass, half-price with Half-Fare Card. Getting a discount with Eurail or Inter-Rail is as likely as stopping a runaway train with a pocket magnet.

On the other side of the valley, get to Pischa (2465 metres) by bus and cable car. The walk from there, along the mountain ridge and back down to Dorf, takes about three hours.

Other Activities Davos Platz has a large natural ice rink where **ice hockey** games are staged in the winter. It is complemented by an artificial rink, open all year except in May. Ice-skating costs Sfr4.50 for adults and Sfr3 for children. There's a sports stadium next door. Schatzalp is the place for **tobogganing**, and toboggans can be hired at the lower

Schatzalp funicular station (☎ 43 57 26). Contact the Flugschulcentre (☎ 46 56 56), Promenade 111, for **paragliding**. A 'taxi' flight with a pilot costs Sfr130, and tuition costs Sfr100 per day. The indoor **swimming pool** is midway between Platz and Dorf. Entry costs Sfr4.50 (Sfr2.50 students, Sfr2 children) or Sfr11 including the sauna.

There are three small **museums** in and around Davos which can claim the attention if the weather is poor. North of Dorf is **Davoser See**, a lake where there is a beach, swimming and water sports.

Davos hosts an International **Music Festival** from late July to mid-August, featuring a variety of classical works, held in the Convention Centre (Kongresszentrum). Get information and tickets from the main tourist office.

Places to Stay – bottom end
Camping Camp at *Färich* (☎ 46 10 43), just outside Davos Dorf on the road to the Flüela Pass. It is open from mid-May to late September.

Hostel The IYHF *youth hostel* (☎ 46 14 84) is nicely situated by the woods on the far side of Davoser See (in the direction of Klosters). The nearest train station is Davos Wolfgang. Dorms cost Sfr16 and reception is shut from 9.30 am to 5 pm. The hostel is closed in November and May. Other places with dormitory accommodation are shown in the hotels booklet from the tourist office.

Hotels & Pensions Most of the cheaper hotels and pensions in are in Dorf, about halfway towards Platz. *Edelweiss* (☎ 46 10 33) is less than one km from Dorf station on Promenade, above a flower shop. The rooms are old fashioned but fine. Doubles with private shower start at Sfr88 in the summer and Sfr100 in the winter. Singles/doubles using hall showers start at Sfr40/68 in the summer and Sfr48/80 in the winter, and triples and quads are also available.

Nearer to Platz on Promenade is *Central Gasthaus* (☎ 46 11 44), with reasonable rooms from Sfr35 per person in summer and

Sfr45 per person in winter, some with private shower. It also has a restaurant. Unlike most places, it doesn't close in November or May.

Continuing towards Platz on Promenade is *Lohner* (☎ 46 44 45), a greyish building with bed and breakfast per person from Sfr38 in summer and Sfr57 in winter, and half-pension for Sfr10 extra. Leading off from Lohner is Richstattweg, along which you'll find *Alpina* (☎ 46 47 67) where winter bed & breakfast prices start at Sfr44, and half-board is Sfr14 extra. Summer prices start at Sfr32.

Places to Stay – middle

Up on the hill behind the tourist office in Platz is *Hotel Rosenhügel* (☎ 43 54 25). It is instantly recognisable by its giant (fake) roses growing up the side of the building. The interior is decorated with similar flair, with the rose motif constantly reappearing. There is a good view across the town, a comfortable, welcoming ambience, and it's open year-round. In the summer, prices start at Sfr64/112 with private shower or Sfr47/86 using one in the hall. In the winter prices jump to at least Sfr70 per person. Add Sfr10 per person for half-pension.

Places to Stay – top end

There are over a dozen four-star hotels with stacks of facilities. *Seehof* (☎ 47 61 10), Dorfstrasse in Davos Dorf, has a sauna, whirlpool, solarium and fitness room, as well as easy disabled access. Winter prices start at Sfr150 per person. *Europe* (☎ 43 59 21), Promenade 63, Davos Platz, lacks the whirlpool but makes up with an indoor swimming pool. It also has many brochures in a room off the lobby, so it's a good place to pick up information if the tourist office is shut. Winter prices start at Sfr140 per person. Both places offer half-pension terms and reduce their prices around 30% in summer.

If you prefer more of a village environment, consider staying in nearby Klosters.

Places to Eat

There is a *Coop* supermarket with a restaurant in Dorf less than 100 metres to the left of the Davos Dorf station. The restaurant is open daily to 7.30 pm (7 pm on Sunday). Right by Dorf station is *Restaurant Pizzeria*, where prices for pizza/pasta start at Sfr10.

There is also inexpensive eating at Davos Platz station in the *Express Buffet*; meals start at Sfr11.50. Just up the hill is the Rafia Centre on Postplatz. Inside is a *Migros* without a restaurant, but you can get hot meals at *Roter Löwen* (the Red Lion Bar) adjoining the centre. It has a daily menu with soup for Sfr14.50 and a vegetarian dish for the same price. Pasta starts at Sfr11.50 and the salad buffet costs Sfr7.50 or Sfr11 plate. It is open daily, except on Sunday between August and November.

By the Hotel Europe on Promenade is *Scala Restaurant-Café*, with outside seating. The décor inside includes modern art and a giant portrait of Gorbachev on one wall. Pizza/pasta starts at Sfr12 and other main courses are around Sfr30. The three-course menu for Sfr15 is available at lunch time only. Upstairs are other, plusher restaurants open evenings only, and a piano bar. *Gentiana Bistro*, Promenade 53, is a specialist in snail dishes (Sfr10 to Sfr22.50) and meat and

Alpine chapel near Davos

cheese fondues (Sfr19 to Sfr49). It is open daily.

The best place to eat is in *Hotel Davoserhof* (☎ 43 68 17), Postplatz, near Davos Platz station. It specialises in Italian food, with main dishes around Sfr35 to Sfr60. The business lunch costs Sfr45 and evening menus are around Sfr100. The hotel also has a bar where there is live music nightly in the season. Another top-notch place is the restaurant in *Hubli's Landhaus* (☎ 46 21 21), midway between Davos Dorf and Klosters at Davos Laret.

Getting There & Away

Davos is on the Rhätische Railway line between Landquart and Filisur, with trains running hourly. Change at Landquart for Chur; the total journey takes up to two hours and costs Sfr26. Landquart is also the junction for trains north and to Zürich. Change at Filisur for St Moritz; the total journey takes 1½ hours and costs Sfr25. En route you might be tempted to alight at Wiesen station, where there's a precipitous gorge and hiking paths.

Postbuses connect Davos to eastern Graubünden and the lower Engadine. Highway 28 follows the same route to/from Davos as the railway. Snow chains are most likely to be needed in winter on the stretch between Klosters and Davos.

KLOSTERS

Favourite resort of Britain's Prince Charles, Klosters (1194 metres) provides the atmosphere of a traditional skiing village that is lacking in neighbouring Davos. Expect fewer diversions in the evening.

Orientation & Information

Like Davos, Klosters is split into two. Klosters Platz is the most important part, and is compactly grouped around the train station. Exit right and turn right for the tourist office, or Kurverein (☎ 081-69 18 77), open Monday to Friday from 8 am to noon and 2 to 6 pm, and Saturday from 8 am to noon. Additional high-season hours are Saturday from 2 to 4 pm in summer, Satur-

day from 2 pm to 5 pm and Sunday from 4 to 6 pm in winter. The post office is opposite the station.

Two km to the left of the station is the smaller enclave of Klosters Dorf, with several hotels, a tourist office (☎ 081-69 19 78), and the Madrisa cable car. Hotels (including the youth hostel) provide a Guest Card. Klosters buses are free for hotel guests.

The telephone code for Klosters is 081.

Activities

The same **skiing** passes are available as mentioned in the Davos section. Above the village at 2300 metres is the Gotschnagrat, accessible from the cable car by the train station. It gives access to the fearful Gotschnawang, one of the hardest runs in the world. One of Prince Charles' companions had an accident here a few years back, and they now only open it if conditions are perfect. On the other side of the valley, the Madrisa region has runs favouring beginners and intermediates; a day pass just for this region costs Sfr39 (Sfr22 children). Forty km of cross-country skiing trails run east from the village. Cross-country rental costs Sfr18 for one day, and the school (☎ 69 18 77) gives lessons from Sfr75 (Sfr67 children) for three half-days.

The village also boasts an ice rink, swimming pools and tennis courts. The tourist office has a leaflet giving times and descriptions (in English) of nearby hikes.

Places to Stay

The tourist office can supply lists of the many apartments and private rooms (minimum stay of seven days). Request details as early as July for the popular winter season.

The IYHF youth hostel is called *Soldanella* (☎ 69 13 16) and it's at Talstrasse 73, at least a 10-minute walk from the station (head right, turn left at the junction and look for the signs). Dorms cost Sfr19.70 (including tax), and dinners (Sfr9.50) are sociable, help-yourself affairs. Doubles are Sfr55.40. There's a games room but few showers except for the 'open plan' shower room downstairs. Reception is shut from 9.30 am to 5 pm but the doors remain open, and there's no curfew. The hostel closes from mid-May to mid-June and in November.

Minerva (☎ 69 15 62) is a tiny place near the tourist office with rooms from Sfr40 per person. Towards Klosters Dorf is *Malein* (☎ 69 10 88), a cosy place with rooms using hall showers starting at Sfr33. *Rufinis* (☎ 69 13 71) is a pretty chalet with a restaurant close to the Dorf tourist office. Rooms start at Sfr25 to Sfr48 per person, depending upon the season. *Bündnerhof* (☎ 69 14 50), beyond the Platz tourist office, gives more comfort and is family-oriented. Prices start at Sfr60 per person.

Hotel Alpina (☎ 69 41 21) opposite the station has good rooms from Sfr95/170 (Sfr165/250 in winter) and a special guesthouse section where prices start at Sfr110/200 (Sfr195/300). The bathrooms are a treat in this place, and are fitted with a jacuzzi and an extremely sophisticated toilet. Breakfast-buffet and admission to the swimming pool, sauna and fitness room are included. Apartments are also available for Sfr110/300 (Sfr160 to Sfr500) with breakfast excluded. See also Places to Eat for more suggestions.

Places to Eat

Fifty metres to the right from the train station is a *Coop* restaurant and supermarket, where hot food is available until 6 pm on weekdays and 4 pm on Saturday. Daily menus cost Sfr9 and Sfr10. This is really the only budget option in the village, other than eating in the youth hostel.

The most affordable place is *à Porta*, to the right of the station on Bahnhofstrasse. Pizza starts at Sfr11.50, and it also has pasta, risotto, grills, and a three-course menu for Sfr26. It is open daily, except in November and on Monday in the low season. Nearby at No 12 is *Chesa Grischuna*, offering varied mid-price to expensive food, such as lunch menus from Sfr18 and four-course dinners from Sfr50.

Gasthaus Casanna (☎ 69 12 29) on Landstrasse has spaghetti bolognese for Sfr11, but most dishes top Sfr20 in the unpretentious restaurant. It also has standard rooms for Sfr50 per person using hall shower. The restaurant (and reception) is closed Monday, and Sunday in summer. Just along the road towards Dorf is *Sonne* (☎ 69 13 49), with tempting smells issuing from the restaurant. There is a Tagesteller from Sfr14, otherwise main courses are mostly Sfr25 to Sfr50. Rooms cost Sfr55 per person.

The best restaurant is the *Walserstube* in the Hotel Walserhof (☎ 69 42 42), Landstrasse 141. It serves seasonal specialities and regional dishes. You could easily spend Sfr100 per head in this place (including wine) but the food is superb. It's run by the Bollingers: Mr is in charge of the kitchen and Mrs circulates amongst the guests. Reserve ahead, especially for weekends.

Getting There & Away

See Getting There and Away for Davos, as Klosters is on the the same rail route between Landquart and Filisur. Klosters to Davos Platz takes 30 minutes and costs Sfr7.80.

Engadine Valley

This valley gets its name from the Inn River (En in Romansch) that meanders along its length. It is divided into two sections, the Upper Engadine (Ober-Engadin) from Maloja to Zernez, and the Lower Engadine (Unter-Engadin), stretching from Zernez to Martina, by the Austrian border. The scenery is tremendous, but the mountains don't have the same vertical impact as they do in some other parts of the Alps as the valley floor is so high, averaging around 1500 metres. The valley is Romansch-speaking, although most of the people you'll encounter as a visitor will also speak English and/or German. Turn to the Facts about the Country chapter for translations of key words.

The Engadine is an excellent valley for exploration by car, bus or train, in part because the contrast between the sophisticated international resorts and the unpretentious rural villages is so marked. In the latter category, many houses display the traditional *sgraffito* design that runs like a floral trim around the edges of building exteriors. These designs, often incorporating arabesques, scrolls and rosettes, are made by scratching off a plaster covering to reveal a different colour underneath. This method of decoration is unique to the Engadine.

There is a low, middle and high season in both summer and winter. Hotel prices peak in the winter season; the change can be quite significant for middle-range to top-end hotels or very minimal in budget places. Prices quoted here are for the low season in winter, except for St Moritz where an indication of summer prices is also given.

Chalandamarz, a spring and youth festival, is celebrated in the Engadine on 1 March. The **Schlitteda**, an ancient custom involving a procession of colourful horse-drawn sledges, can be seen in St Moritz, Pontresina and Silvaplana in January.

Activities

Skiing The regional ski pass for the Upper Engadine covers 350 km of downhill runs serviced by 59 cable cars and lifts. It includes skiing in St Moritz and the surrounding resorts like Sils, Silvaplana, Celerina, Pontresina, Diavolezza and Zuoz. Most of the skiing is too daunting for beginners, but intermediates have endless possibilities. The general pass costs Sfr47 (Sfr37 children) for one day and Sfr261 (Sfr195 children) for one week. Cheaper, more restrictive passes are available but the general pass is the best deal if you want to do any serious skiing. It even includes train and postbus transport between the different areas and entry for the indoor swimming pools in St Moritz and Pontresina. Rental for skis, boots and sticks is about Sfr39 per day.

The region also boasts 160 km of cross-country trails (equipment rental Sfr18). The famous **Engadine Ski Marathon** takes place on the second Sunday in March. It starts at Maloja, crosses over the frozen lakes at Sils and Silvaplana, passes by the south-east side of Lake St Moritz, and finishes between Zuoz and S-chanf, a distance of some 42 km. It's a great spectacle, with around 12,000 professional and amateur skiers taking part. The elite take around one hour 20 minutes to complete the course, but the 'fun' contestants make it last most of the day. If you don't want to join the crowds at the beginning or end of the race, a good place to watch is the approach to Pontresina. There's a tricky bit as they leave the woods where many amateurs are sent tumbling (to sympathetic laughter from spectators), and then a downhill section where they can regain their composure.

Alternatively, the Stazersee is a pleasant 35-minute walk from St Moritz (anticlockwise round the lake) and a place where you can get a clear view of the skiers.

Getting Around

See St Moritz for getting to the Engadine. From St Moritz, Rhätische railway trains go every hour as far as Scuol (Sfr24, takes 1½ hours). Stops en route include Zuoz (Sfr6.80, 45 minutes), Zernez (Sfr13.20, one hour) and Guarda (Sfr18.60, 1¼ hours). In the other direction you need to take the Castasegna bus, that leaves approximately hourly and stops at the Hotel Sonne in St Moritz Bad. It also stops at Silvaplana (Sfr3.40, takes 15 minutes), Sils (Sfr5.60, 20 minutes), and Maloja (Sfr8.40, 35 minutes).

MALOJA

At its northern end, Maloja (1809 metres) has Lake Segl, and at its southern end the Maloja Pass, which barely rises above the village yet falls away sharply on the far side. The tourist office or Kurverein (☎ 082-4 31 88) is on the main street, and open Monday to Friday from 8.30 am to noon and 2 to 6 pm, and Saturday morning in the high season. It can give advice about all day hikes over nearby passes, such as the historic September Pass to the north or the Muretto Pass south to Italy. It even organises excursions itself: hiking out with a guide and returning by bus will cost around Sfr45.

The artist, Giovanni Segantini, lived in the

village from 1894 until his death in 1899, and his studio can be viewed in the summer.

Places to Stay & Eat

Camp by the lake at *Plan Curtinac* (☎ 082-4 31 81), open from the end of May to late September. The IYHF *youth hostel* (☎ 082-4 32 58) is on the main street, in two barn-like buildings on either side of the garage. It's comfortable enough inside, with a kitchen, a games room, and dinners for Sfr9. Dorms cost Sfr17 and there are some doubles for Sfr44. Reception is only open from 8 to 9.30 am, 4.30 to 6 pm, and 8 to 9 pm; the hostel is closed in June and from mid-November to mid-December.

Nowhere else to stay is particularly cheap: try *Pension Bellavista* (☎ 082-4 31 95), near the lake, with singles/doubles for Sfr52/100 using hall showers, or *Longhin* (☎ 082-4 31 31), on the main street, starting at Sfr70/150 (half-pension) using private shower.

Eat at hotels or make use of the garden of *Restaurant Chesa Alpina*, where main courses start at Sfr18. There is a supermarket opposite the post office (closed Wednesday).

SILS

Peaceful Sils has two parts: Baselgia by the lake, and Maria at the foot of the mountains, where most of the amenities are located. Postbuses stop at both parts. A cable car ascends to Furtschellas (Sfr10 up, Sfr8 down, Sfr15 return; children half-price) at 2312 metres, where there is a network of hiking trails and ski slopes. Water sports are also major attractions.

The philosopher, Friedrich Nietzsche, spent his summers in the resort from 1881 to 1888, and you can look around the **Nietzsche Haus** (Sfr4, students Sfr2) in summer and winter from 3 to 6 pm, daily except Monday. He wrote several important works here, such as *Also Sprach Zarathustra*. You won't learn much about the man's life unless you can read German, but the many photos are interesting; it's amusing to see how his moustache grew in stature during the course of his life, from a skimpy floss fringing his upper lip in his student days

to a bloated hedgehog bristling under his nose at the time of his death.

The tourist office (☎ 082-4 52 37) is just around the corner, in the same building as the bank. Its opening hours are Monday to Friday from 8.30 am to noon and 2 to 6 pm, and in the high season on Saturday from 9 to 1 am and 3 to 5 pm.

Places to Stay & Eat

Baukantine Kuhn (☎ 082-4 52 62) provides cheap beds from Sfr15 to Sfr30 per person, and there is a kitchen. It is by the river (on the south bank) about halfway towards Lake Silvaplana.

Close to the tourist office is *Pension Schulze* (☎ 082-4 52 13), with singles/doubles for Sfr55 per person with private shower or Sfr45 without. On the other side of the main road is *Restorant Survial*, serving pasta from Sfr9, daily specials for Sfr14, and grills and fish from Sfr20. It's open daily from 8.30 am to 10 pm, except Saturday. A *Volg* supermarket is nearby.

Close to the post office is *Maria*, which smells of pine and offers rooms with private shower from Sfr92 per person (half-pension). The restaurant has cheap lunch specials from Sfr7.50 to Sfr13, although evening dining is fairly pricey.

SILVAPLANA

On a bay jutting between the two lakes, Silvaplana is a centre for water sports, especially windsurfing. The tourist office (☎ 082-4 81 51) can give details. Across the causeway is Surlej, providing access to skiing slopes and marvellous views from Piz Corvatsch (3451 metres). The cable car costs Sfr19 up, Sfr13 down and Sfr27 return. Skiing is possible even in the summer (day pass Sfr32 for adults or Sfr24 for children).

Places to Stay & Eat

Lakeside *camping* (☎ 082-4 84 92) is available from late May to late October. Silvaplana is an easy and pleasant walk around Lake Campfèr from St Moritz Bad, but if you want to stay in the village the best value is *Engiadina* (☎ 082-4 81 15). This family hotel has singles/doubles with private shower from Sfr79/148, or Sfr65/120 without (for half-pension).

There is a *Volg* supermarket by the campsite. *Restaurant Margun* serves pizzas until midnight.

ST MORITZ

In Peter Sarstedt's 1960s tune *Where do you go to my Lovely*? he sings about the beautiful people (reputedly inspired by Sophia Loren) in St Moritz. The image conveyed by the lines in this song still applies in the resort today.

Despite being at the forefront of the winter sports scene in the 19th century, St Moritz hasn't become a mass-market holiday destination in the way that many other resorts have. The main reason for this is its enduring air of exclusivity – one feels the wealthy want to enjoy the facilities without the bother of having to barge the proles out of their path. Average mortals who meander into the rarefied atmosphere of St Moritz Dorf almost feel compelled to apologise that they don't own a wardrobe full of fur coats and a fleet of flashy sports cars. Just about anything you do here costs a pile of money; even window shopping makes you feel nervous about your budget.

People who want to linger on the fringes of the elite can stay around the lake in St Moritz Bad. Here you can eat and sleep without taking out a mortgage – there's even a youth hostel (gleaming and expensive, but a youth hostel nonetheless).

People come here to enjoy a huge variety of winter and summer sports. There is diverse downhill skiing, and probably the best cross-country skiing in the Alps. The Cresta Run is one of the resort's big draws. Health treatments are also part of the St Moritz package. The curative properties of its waters have been known for 3000 years.

Orientation & Information

St Moritz (San Murezzan in Romansch) exudes health and wealth from the slopes overlooking the lake that shares its name (St Moritzersee in German, Lej da San Murezzan in Romansch). The train station near the lakeside rents bikes and changes money from 6.45 am to 7.45 pm daily. Just up the hill is the post office and five minutes farther on is the tourist office (☎ 082-3 31 47) at Via Maistra 12. It's open Monday to Friday from 9 am to noon and 2 to 6 pm, on Saturday morning, and also on Saturday afternoon during the high season. St Moritz Bad is about two km south-west from the main town, St Moritz Dorf.

Not much stays open during November, May and early June. In winter, St Moritz has plenty of sun and snow, but is colder than might be expected for its altitude (1856 metres). Guests in the resort get a Holiday Pass that earns some useful privileges.

The telephone code for St Moritz is 082.

Activities

Skiing The downhill skiing area adjacent to St Moritz is centred around Corviglia (2486 metres), accessible by funicular from Dorf. From Bad a cable car goes to Signal (shorter queues), giving access to the slopes of Piz Nair. If you ski on Piz Corvatsch, above nearby Silvaplana, you can ski back down to Bad via the demanding Hahnensee run.

Hiking There are 120 km of marked hiking paths you can tramp along, and many are open in winter. The tourist office has a map giving suggestions (in English) for walking throughout the Upper Engadine. Above St Moritz soars the Piz Nair (3057 metres), and the summit provides a marvellous perspective of Alpine peaks and the lakes and valley below. Walking to the top in summer from the village will take around three hours. The easy way to get up is by funicular then cable car; the complete trip costs Sfr20 each way and Sfr30 return (25% reduction with Swiss Pass, 50% off with Half-Fare Card, no reduction with Inter-Rail or Eurail).

Other Activities Numerous other sporting activities are on offer: tennis, squash, fishing, horse riding, sailing and windsurfing, to mention just a few. Inevitably,

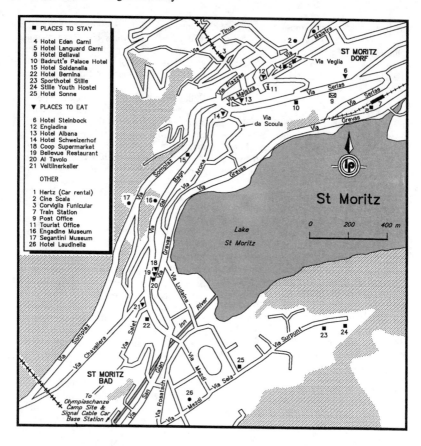

however, they are expensive. A 'taxi' ride by hang-glider (☎ 3 24 16), for example, costs Sfr200. Get other prices from the tourist office. Golf is played on the frozen lake in winter, and in the summer at the 18-hole Samedan course (☎ 6 52 25). For fishing in the lake you need a permit; contact the Gemeindepolizei (☎ 3 30 17).

Buying a **health treatment** in the spa is another way to spend money. The Holiday Pass gets reduced entry to the Health Spa Centre in St Moritz Bad and a free mineral drink. For information on treatments available there, telephone ☎ 3 30 62.

Things to See & Do

The **Engadine Museum** gives a good introduction to the style of dwellings and simple interiors you may encounter if you explore the Engadine Valley, and some rather patrician interiors you probably won't encounter. The building itself is typical, featuring sgraffito designs on the façade. Traditional stoves and archaeological finds complete the collection. It is open from Monday to Friday from 9.30 am to noon and 2 to 5 pm, and Sunday from 10 am to noon. Entry is Sfr4 for adults and Sfr2.50 for children.

The **Segantini Museum** is devoted to the

local 19th century artist of the same name, who specialised in mountain scenes. The most powerful piece here is the three-part *To Be, To Pass, To Become*. Opening hours are Tuesday to Saturday from 9 am to 12.30 pm and 2.30 to 5 pm, and Sunday from 10.30 am to 12.30 pm and 2.30 to 4.30 pm. Admission costs Sfr5 for adults, Sfr3 for students, and Sfr1.50 for children.

Places to Stay – bottom end
Hotel prices peak at around mid-December to mid-February. The summer high season, July and August, isn't quite so expensive.

Camping The *Olympiaschanze* camp site (☎ 3 40 90) is one km south-west of St Moritz Bad; it is open from late May to early October and costs Sfr4 per adult and from Sfr5 per tent.

Hostel The IYHF *Stille Youth Hostel* (☎ 3 39 69), Via Surpunt 60, St Moritz Bad, is 35 minutes' walk around the lake from the tourist office.

It's in a new building with excellent facilities. Beds in four-bed dorms are Sfr31.30, and double rooms are Sfr41.30 per person. That sounds expensive but the price does include breakfast and dinner. Laundry costs Sfr4 per load. Reception is closed from 9 am to 4 pm (but the downstairs doors stay open), curfew is 10 pm and the hostel closes from May to mid-June, and from November to mid-December. Buses from the station stop at the Hotel Sonne (Sfr2).

Hotels The nearest thing to a budget hotel, closest to the centre of Dorf is *Bellaval* (☎ 3 32 45), right by the train station on the south side of the tracks. Singles/doubles start at Sfr50/96 in summer or winter using hall showers. Doubles with own shower and toilet (from Sfr130) are reasonably large, if slightly bare. The *Sporthotel Stille* (☎ 3 69 48), by the youth hostel, attracts a young and sporty crowd; it has its own bar, and sometimes a disco and live music. Prices per person are Sfr45 for bed and breakfast in the summer, and Sfr69 for half-pension in the

winter, in doubles only (single people can be mixed, or pay extra).

Nearby is the *Hotel Sonne* (☎ 3 35 27), Via Sela 11, which has singles/doubles with a range of amenities starting at Sfr60/100 with very little variation in price through the year. Also in Bad, but north of the Inn River on Via dal Bagn, is *Hotel Bernina* (☎ 3 60 22), with reasonable rooms starting at Sfr45 per person using hall showers or Sfr60 with one in the room. The food is not bad in the restaurant, either.

Places to Stay – middle
Staying in the centre of St Moritz Dorf involves splashing out on at least a three-star hotel. Two good family hotels are close together on Via Veglia, around the back of the tourist office: *Hotel Eden Garni* (☎ 3 61 61) starts at Sfr80/160 and *Hotel Languard Garni* (☎ 3 31 37) at Sfr80/150. There's little to choose between them in the standard of rooms. Eden has a nice central atrium although Languard's prices rise less in winter. Also worth considering is *Soldanella* (☎ 3 36 51), with rooms starting at Sfr85 per person in summer or Sfr110 in winter. It's a few minutes' walk south from the centre of town at Via Somplaz 17.

Places to Stay – top end
The place to see and be seen is the renowned *Badrutt's Palace Hotel* (☎ 2 11 01) on Via Serlas. Of course, you have to pay for the privilege, with rooms with half-board costing at least Sfr230/400 in summer and Sfr340/620 in winter. The public areas reek of class and taste (men must wear a jacket and tie after 7 pm), but the cheaper rooms aren't as lavish as you might expect.

Places to Eat
The cheapest restaurants are in St Moritz Bad. There is a *Coop* in Via dal Bagn. It has a self-service restaurant next door under the name of *Bellevue*, where there are menus for Sfr8.50 and a special with salad for Sfr10.50. It is open until 7 pm on Monday to Thursday, 8 pm on Friday and 5 pm on Saturday. Beside it is *Al Tavolo*, with light meals from Sfr10,

although à la carte dishes are mostly above Sfr20. It is open daily until 11 pm (kitchen until 9 pm).

Veltlinerkeller, nearby at Via dal Bagn 11, features Engadine sgraffito outside and beheaded animals inside. If the hunting trophies don't put you off your food, tuck into pasta, grills, omelettes, fish or schnitzels in the range of Sfr9 to Sfr36 (closed Sunday). The popular *Hotel Sonne*, (see Places to Stay) serves pasta, salads and tasty pizzas from Sfr11. It is open daily from 7 am to midnight, and has a bar area.

Eating in Dorf is not necessarily an asset-stripping experience if you stick to lunch-time specials, which many good-quality restaurants offer. *Hotel Albana*, Via Maistra 6, has lunch with soup for Sfr14 or for Sfr18 including a starter. The three-course evening menu is around Sfr35, and main courses top Sfr20 (open daily). The restaurant of the *Hotel Schweizerhof*, Via dal Bagn 54, has a lunch menu with starter for Sfr15. In the Stübli (bar area) there is live music nightly (from 10.30 pm); it is open daily from around 8 pm to 2 am.

The restaurant of the *Hotel Steinbock*, opposite the post office at Via Serlas 12, is good value and popular with locals. Light meals start at Sfr14 but most dishes are around Sfr25 to Sfr40, and it's open daily during the season. *Engiadina*, around the corner from the tourist office at Plazza da Scuola 2, is famous for fondue, and that's the best thing to eat here (from Sfr23.50 per person). It is closed on Sunday.

Try an expensive taste of the high life at the top of the Corviglia funicular by sampling the truffles, caviar and desserts at *la Marmite* (☎ 082-3 63 55). Queue or reserve ahead in season, when it's open daily. The adjoining self-service section is reasonably cheap.

Entertainment

Nightlife is lively and varied, but unless you have plenty of money, forget it! Over 20 bars and clubs have dancing and/or music. One of the most elegant places is the *King's Club* in Badrutt's Palace Hotel. This disco is open

nightly from 9.30 pm and entry costs Sfr30 including a drink. *Cine Scala* by the Schiefer Turm (the Leaning Tower) shows films in the original language.

Concerts, theatre and other events are staged by Pro Cultura (☎ 2 21 31), based in the Laudinella Hotel in St Moritz Bad.

Getting There & Away

Train Nine daily trains travel south to Tirano in Italy with connections to Milan. The famous Glacier Express links St Moritz to Zermatt via the 2033-metre Oberalp Pass. The wonderful, scenic route takes 7½ hours to cover the 290 km and crosses 291 bridges. Drink glasses in the dining car have sloping bases to compensate for the hills – but you must remember to keep turning them around! There is a Sfr6 reservation fee (not covered by rail passes) payable on these trains, which is not required for normal trains following the same route.

Bus To Lugano, two postbuses run daily in summer, one in winter. The seat must be reserved the day before; ☎ 3 30 72. There's also the Palm Express bus in the summer to Lugano and Locarno; seats must be reserved on ☎ 091-21 95 20. A train-and-bus combination will get you to Landeck in Austria for Sfr45. In summer there is also a direct bus.

Car & Motorbike The roads around St Moritz are good, if winding. See the chapter introduction for details of which passes are open in winter.

Car Rental Hertz (☎ 3 27 84) is at Via Maistra 46 and local firm Auto Mathis (☎ 3 12 13) is at Via Somplaz 33. Budget (☎ 3 80 25) is at nearby Celerina.

AROUND ST MORITZ
Celerina

This resort (Schlarigna in Romansch) by the Inn River is 45 minutes' walk from St Moritz and shares the same ski slopes. In the winter it is known for its famous Olympic **bob-run** and **cresta run** (a toboggan course enticingly known as the skeleton run). These skim their way through the snow at the St Moritz end of the village.

The tourist office (☎ 082-3 39 66) is in the centre of the village at the intersection of Via Maistra and Via da la Staziun. It is open Monday to Friday from 8.30 am to noon and 2 to 6 pm, and Saturday from 9 to 11 am and 3 to 5 pm.

Places to Stay & Eat Except for apartments and two private rooms (details from the tourist office), the cheapest lodgings is at *Hotel Trais Fluors* (☎ 082-3 88 85). It's grimy and decaying on the outside, but acceptable inside, and singles/doubles start at Sfr48/84. The hotel is north-east of the tourist office on Via Samedan. Between the two is the comfortable *Arturo* (☎ 082-3 66 85) on Via Maistra. Prices start at Sfr65/130 and all rooms have private shower and toilet. There's an interesting priority in the restaurant – small selection of food (around Sfr30) and large selection of wine.

Demont Garni (☎ 082-3 65 44), on Via Maistra in the direction of the cresta run, has smallish but pleasant rooms from Sfr55/90 with shower in the hall, or Sfr75/130 with private shower. Two doors away is *Veltlinerkeller*, where pasta starts from Sfr9.50 and other dishes from Sfr18 (closed Sunday). There are two *supermarkets* near Arturo and one opposite the tourist office.

Getting There & Away Celerina is easily reached by train or postbus from St Moritz (Sfr2). You can get off the bus by the cresta run or in the centre; the train takes you to the centre of the village.

ZUOZ

Zuoz has some undemanding skiing (day pass Sfr31, or Sfr23 for children), but a greater attraction are the beautiful Engadine houses sporting traditional sgraffito designs. The main square looks suitably immune to contamination by modern life, and features a fountain bearing the coat of arms of the influential Planta family. The bear's paw motif reappears in the church, which also has windows in the chancel designed by Augusto

Giacometti. The small prison tower next door contains some torture implements – don't annoy the tourist office (☎ 082-7 15 10) staff, because they look after the key. Office opening hours are Monday to Friday from 9 am to noon and 2 to 6 pm, and Saturday from 9 to 1 am. In the low season it closes at 5 pm and on Saturday. There is a post office by the train station.

Places to Stay & Eat
The tourist office has lists of over 100 apartments and four private rooms (from Sfr24 per person). Near the main square, *Pension Albanas* (☎ 082-7 12 18) has doubles from Sfr86. Meals in the restaurant start at Sfr9.50 (closed Tuesday in low season). Virtually opposite is *Crusch Alva* (☎ 082-7 13 19), where singles/doubles start at Sfr70/140, and tasty meals start at around Sfr20.

There is a *Volg* supermarket by the tourist office. *Restaurant Dorta*, on the far side of the train station, has occasional live music and inexpensive food. Also cheap is *Cafeteria Resgia*, a little farther on.

ZERNEZ

Zernez is another attractive Engadine village, but its main claim to fame is as the headquarters of the **Swiss National Park**. This is 169 sq km of woodland and mountains where flora and fauna flourish in a stringently protected natural environment. Ibexes, chamois and marmots are left to roam at will. You can roam the park too, but not at will, as deviating from the paths is not permitted. Numerous other regulations prohibit camping, littering, lighting fires, cycling, picking flowers, bringing dogs into the park, or disturbing the animals in any way. Less relevantly, you also may not allow cattle to graze. Fines of up to Sfr500 are imposed for violations.

By the Zernez entrance to the park is the National Park House (☎ 082-8 13 78), open from June to October, when the park itself is open. It can give details of hiking paths, route descriptions, the best locations to see particular animals, and other information. A similar low-down can be picked up at the

Zernez tourist office (☎ 082-8 13 00), on the main street leading from the train station. Look for the *infuormazium* sign; opening hours are Monday to Friday from 8.30 to noon and 2 to 6.30 pm, and Saturday from 2 to 4 pm. Winter opening reduces to four hours per weekday.

Places to Stay & Eat

Camping *Cul* (☎ 082-8 14 62) is around the back of the station and open from mid-May to the end of September. Walk along the main street and turn left at the first crossroads for *Hotel Bär-Post* (☎ 082-8 11 41), which has dormitory accommodation for Sfr15 per night or Sfr25 including breakfast. It is closed in winter.

Not far from the station on the main street is *Filli* (☎ 082-8 10 72), where rooms with private shower start at Sfr48 per person or Sfr36 using one in the hall. It has a restaurant where basic meals start at Sfr11. *Adler* (☎ 082-8 12 13), towards the park, has rooms for a similar price.

Alpina (☎ 082-8 12 33), and the next door *Spöl* (☎ 082-8 12 79), in the centre of the village, are both fresh, attractive buildings where rooms with private facilities including TV start at Sfr60 per person. Both have decent restaurants. Across the street is *Pizzeria Mirta*, where prices start at Sfr12. There is a *Coop* opposite the tourist office, with no half-day closing.

Il Fuorn (☎ 082-8 12 26), in the middle of the national park by the main road, has rooms from Sfr50/75.

Getting There & Away

From Zernez, the train fare is Sfr7.20 to Zuoz (takes 25 minutes) and Sfr7.80 to Scuol (takes 30 minutes).

The main road through the park, highway 28, goes from Zernez, over the Ofen Pass (2149 metres; Pass dal Fuorn in Romansch), and into Italy. This route is covered by postbus: there are five to eight departures a day between Zernez and Müstair. The park can also be entered on foot from close to S-chanf and Scuol.

MÜSTAIR

The village of Müstair, at the far side of the park by the Italian border, has the Abbey of St John the Baptist, founded in the 8th century. Inside there is a unique series of wall paintings from the Carolingian period (around 800 AD), and a statue of Charlemagne from the 12th century.

GUARDA

This is one of the best preserved villages in the Engadine, with tiny, cobbled streets, fountains, and many houses bearing sgraffito engravings. It easily merits an hour or so exploring its confines. Guarda is 20 minutes' walk from the train station by the footpath (40 minutes by road), or you can take the fairly infrequent postbus. The train station is 15 minutes from either Zernez or Scuol-Tarasp. Contact the tourist office (☎ 081-862 23 42) for information on accommodation.

SCUOL

The valley gets wilder and more scenic towards Scuol (Schuls in German), and you pass Tarasp Castle rising impressively on a ridge. Scuol includes the smaller resorts of Vulpera and Tarasp, which are on the south side of the Inn River.

Orientation & Information

Scuol is the main resort in the Lower Engadine. The train station is west of the main village. Take the postbus or walk down to the centre in around 15 minutes. The tourist office (☎ 081-862 94 94) is on the main street (Via Maistra). It is open Monday to Friday from 8 am to noon and 2 to 6 pm, and in the high season on Saturday from 9 am to noon and 2 to 5 pm. The post office is halfway between the station and the tourist office.

The telephone code for the three resorts is 081.

Things to See & Do

There is skiing above Scuol between 280 and 1250 metres, offering a total of 80 km of runs, the longest of which exceeds 10 km. A one-day pass costs Sfr39 for adults, Sfr30 for youths or senior citizens, or Sfr23 for children. Swissraft Engadin (☎ 081-921 41 00) offers rafting excursions down the river to Martina (18 km); prices start at Sfr85. Lower Scuol displays some typical Engadine dwellings, and has a museum devoted to the Lower Engadine which is open only a few days a week between June and October.

Scuol is a health spa, and there are around 25 mineral springs in the vicinity. A new health centre, Bogn, opened in 1993 near the tourist office. Telephone the tourist office number for information. Tarasp also offers health treatments. **Tarasp Castle** (☎ 9 07 73) is open from June to mid-October; it was controlled by the Austrians until 1803.

Places to Stay & Eat

There is camping at *Gurlaina* (☎ 864 15 01), by the southern banks of the Inn. It's open year-round and costs from Sfr4.60 per adult and Sfr4 for a tent.

Contact the tourist office about the many holiday apartments. *Hotel Garni Grusaida* (☎ 864 14 74) is on the far side of Scuol and has rooms starting at Sfr40 per person. *Hotel Garni Engiadina* (☎ 864 14 21) is a typical Engadine building in Lower Scuol and has rooms with private shower from Sfr50 per person.

Café Collina (☎ 864 03 93), opposite the post office, costs Sfr55 per person for pleasant, non-standardised rooms, using private or hall shower. The owner is rather casual about prices and may be amenable to negotiation. The restaurant serves pizza and pasta from around Sfr10 and has a daily menu with soup for about Sfr15. *Hotel Traube* (☎ 864 12 07), on the main street, has rooms including TV from Sfr71 per person. Half-pension is Sfr15 to Sfr25, and its restaurant serves good, mid-price food.

There is a *Coop* on the main street, with no half-day closing. In the same arcade as the tourist office is *Café Benderer*, with lunch menus for around Sfr13 (closed Sunday). On the opposite side of the road is *Quellenhof*, with a Tagesmenu for Sfr12 and steaks and grills from Sfr16.

Getting There & Away

The train from St Moritz terminates at Scuol-Tarasp. Postbuses from the station continue to Martina, Samnaun (a duty-free area in Switzerland), and Austria. From the end of May to late October, several buses a day run to/from Davos, and the journey takes under two hours (Sfr18.60). Buses run year-round to Landeck in Austria.

Bernina Pass Road

This road runs from Celerina in a south-easterly direction, leading to Tirano in Italy. It links the Bernina and the Poschiavo Valleys by way of the Bernina Pass at 2323 metres. There are some great hiking trails in the surrounding mountains, and these are identified and described in the *Summer Panorama Map* available from the tourist office in Pontresina. This map also details winter skiing in the valley. The ski lifts are covered by the Upper Engadine ski pass (see the Engadine section).

Getting There & Away

Trains run every one to two hours from St Moritz to Tirano, stopping at all stations en route. Postbuses operate either side of the Bernina Pass but there's no through service, even though the pass is open for traffic year-round.

PONTRESINA

Pontresina (1800 metres) is at the mouth of the Bernina Valley, close enough to the Engadine for the Engadine Ski Marathon to loop down to the village en route to Zernez. Interesting features in the village are the pentagonal Moorish tower and the Sta Maria chapel with frescos dating from the 13th and 15th centuries.

Orientation & Information

The train station is to the west of the village, and changes money. Cross over the two rivers, Rosegg and Bernina, for the centre and the tourist office, open Monday to Friday from 8.30 am to noon and 2 to 6 pm, and Saturday from 8.30 am to noon and (in the high season) from 2 to 5 pm.

Activities

Skiing Like most of the resorts in the vicinity, Pontresina has plenty of sports facilities to offer the visitor. There's not very much skiing from Pontresina's own mountain, Alp Languard (2261 metres), but it's feasible to use the resort as a base for exploring the slopes farther down the valley, at Piz Lagalb and especially Diavolezza (summer skiing possible). A one-day ski pass to cover these areas costs Sfr39 (children Sfr31).

Hiking In the summer, hiking trails wind away from Alp Languard in all directions; the chair lift to the summit runs from the end of May to mid-October and costs Sfr11 each way and Sfr17 return (children half-price). It takes 2½ hours to walk to Muottas Muragli (2453 metres), overlooking the junction of the Bernina and Engadine Valleys. This is the best spot for a view of the course of the Inn River.

Mountaineering Pontresina is well known as a mountaineering centre. Its mountaineering school (☎ 082-6 64 44) has a programme of touring weeks between February and October, either on skis or on foot. Prices for the week including half-pension are typically around Sfr750, and one-day excursions are also available from Sfr65. For details, write to the Schweizer Bergsteigerschule Bernina-Bergell, CH-7504, Pontresina.

Places to Stay & Eat

There is camping at *Plauns* (☎ 082-6 62 85), open from early June to mid-October.

The IYHF *youth hostel* (☎ 082-6 72 23) is right next to the train station. The hostel is closed from late April to early June and from mid-October to 1 December, and reception closes at 9 am and re-opens from 4 to 9 pm. Dorms cost as much as Sfr32.25 because breakfast and dinner are compulsory. The hostel runs the *Restaurant Tolais* from the same premises which has meals starting

around Sfr11 (open until 8 pm daily except 6 pm on Sunday).

In the centre, the cheapest place to stay is *Pension Valtellina* (☎ 6 64 06), where old-fashioned rooms with hall shower cost between Sfr44 to Sfr50 per person, depending on the season. It's on the main street between the tourist office and the post office.

There are many places to eat along the main street, but the only inexpensive option is searching for daily specials, or compiling a snack at the *Coop* supermarket near the post office (no half-day closing). *Bahnhof* (☎ 6 62 42), by the station, has menus from about Sfr12 and rooms at half-board from Sfr70, using the hall shower. The *Sportpavilion* has an inexpensive pizzeria.

Steinbock (☎ 6 63 71), beyond the post office, is a good choice for mid-price food. It also has singles/doubles from Sfr105/200 with private shower, including half-pension. Some cheaper singles are available from Sfr80. Good hotel facilities include an indoor swimming pool and a sauna.

Getting There & Away

Trains from St Moritz take 11 minutes and cost Sfr2. Postbuses leave from the centre of Pontresina by the post office, and run about every 30 minutes to St Moritz.

CHÜNETTA

This is a well-known belvedere above the Morteratsch train station and below the Morteratsch Glacier. It can be reached in only about a 30-minute walk from the station and the views are more than worth the effort.

DIAVOLEZZA

Diavolezza (2973 metres) offers testing skiing on the glacier and inspiring views of the Bernina Massif. Take the train to Bernina Diavolezza and then the cable car (Sfr16 up, Sfr12 down or Sfr24 return). Alternatively, get off the train at the previous stop, Bernina Suot, and take the trail up, which gets steep after a gentle start (takes 2¾ hours). A summer ski pass to cover the cable car and ski lift costs Sfr30 (children Sfr23) for one day.

Top Left: Guards at Landsgemeinde, Appenzell, North-East Switzerland (MH)
Top Right: Abbey church, Einsiedeln, Central Switzerland (MH)
Bottom Left: Landsgemeinde, Appenzell, North-East Switzerland (MH)
Bottom Right: Oriel window, Rorschach, North-East Switzerland (MH)

Top: Rathausplatz, Stein am Rhein, North-East Switzerland (MH)
Bottom Left: Baroque altarpiece in church, Appenzell, North-East Switzerland (MH)
Bottom Right: Children in traditional dress parade, Vaduz, Liechtenstein (MH)

PIZ LAGALB

This peak (2898 metres) is on the opposite side of the valley and gives comparable views of a landscape of mountains, glaciers and lakes. Take the cable car from the Bernina Lagalb station which costs Sfr14 up, Sfr10 down and Sfr19 return (children half-price). The walk down from the peak to the next station along, Ospizio Bernina, takes 1½ hours.

ALP GRÜM

This viewing point at 2019 metres provides a tremendous view over the Poschiavo Valley to the south, with the lake shimmering below and the mountains glowering above. The *Hotel Ristorante Belvedere* provides refreshment. From here you can walk down to Caviglia in one hour or back to Ospizio Bernina in 1½ hours.

Getting There & Away.

The train from St Moritz takes one hour and costs Sfr23.20 return. From the end of May to late October there's a special excursion fare costing Sfr34 (Sfr23 children or with Half-Fare Card) which includes a midday meal at Alp Grüm. On the menu is *pizzoccheri*, a type of dumpling that is a speciality of this valley.

The closest you can get by car is Ospizio Bernina; walk or take the train from there.

Bregaglia Valley

From the Maloja Pass (1815 metres), the road spirals downwards to the Bregaglia Valley (Bergell in German), cutting a course running south-west into Italy. The road then splits: one arm leads north and back into Switzerland via the Splügen Pass, and the other goes south to Lake Como and on to Milan. The postbus from St Moritz to Lugano branches off from the Milan road to circle the western shore of the lake.

As the valley proceeds in a south-westerly direction, the villages betray an increasing Italian influence. **Stampa** was the home of

the artist Alberto Giacometti (1901-66), and is now the location of the tourist office (☎ 082-4 15 55) for the Bregaglia.

SOGLIO

This is a tiny (220 inhabitants), idyllic village (La Soglina in Italian) close to the Italian border. It commands excellent views over the valley, and faces the smooth-sided Pizzo Badile (3308 metres). Soglio rests on a south-facing ledge, reached from the valley floor by a narrow, winding road.

The village is a warren of small lanes and alleys overlooked by picturesque houses, and there is a church with an Italianate bell tower. Soglio is the starting point for several **hiking** trails, most notably the historic **Panorama Hochweg**, which easily lives up to its name. It takes around four hours to reach Casaccia, 11 km distant. Stampa, also on the valley floor, takes 1½ hours.

Places to Stay & Eat

It is worth visiting Soglio if only to stay in the *Palazzo Salis* (☎ 082-4 12 08). This place really is like a palace, with paintings and portraits on the walls, suits of armour, hunting trophies and fine old furniture. There are several lobbies, an open fire, and a private garden. The rooms are grand, too, with porcelain stoves and stucco or wooden ceilings. The amazing thing is that this place isn't expensive. Singles/doubles using hall showers start at Sfr40/80, and doubles with private shower start at Sfr100.

The hotel is only open from Easter to 31 October. It is 50 metres up from the post office, and has parking places at the front. The restaurant has pasta from Sfr15 and grills from Sfr26.

The other accommodation is more expensive (starting at Sfr47 per person) and has much less character. There are three places, all owned by the same family. Enquire in the hotel/restaurant *Stüa Grande* (☎ 082-4 16 08) by the church, which is open daily in summer and closed on Wednesday in winter (and for all of November). Meals cost Sfr11 to Sfr40. It has a good wine selection and beer is Sfr3.80 for half a litre.

Getting There & Away

Buses from St Moritz to Castasegna run along the Bregaglia Valley. Alight at the post office at Pomontogno and take the bus to Soglio from there (Sfr2 one way, Sfr4 return, Six to 10 departures per day).

North-East Switzerland

The north-east of Switzerland is often over-looked by visitors. That's a pity, because although it doesn't have the scenic grandeur of the southern areas, the rolling green hills are equally enticing. The region is over-loaded with castles (most of them private) and attractive town centres. Stein am Rhein has probably the prettiest main square in all Switzerland. Lake Constance (Bodensee) is another big draw, providing summer recre-

ation possibilities and access to attractions in neighbouring Germany and Austria.

History

Glarus was one of the earliest converts to the Swiss Confederation, joining in 1352. Schaffhausen joined in 1501 after the Swabian War, and Appenzell in 1513 during the Swiss attempts to subjugate Milan. During this period of expansionist policies

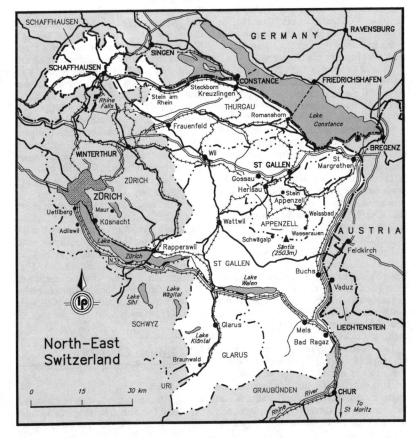

North-East Switzerland

by the Confederation, Thurgau became a sovereign territory and St Gallen an 'allied canton' (with inferior rights). Both became full cantons in Napoleon's 1803 reorganisation of the Helvetic Republic.

The north-east could easily have become larger than it is; in 1510 the German town of Constance would have been admitted, had not the confederates shied away from altering the urban/rural balance, and in 1918 the Austrian state of Vorarlberg wanted to join the Confederation, a request turned down by the great powers in 1919.

Orientation & Information

The north-east tourist region includes the cantons of Schaffhausen, Thurgau, St Gallen, Appenzell and Glarus. It also takes in the Principality of Liechtenstein which is dealt with in a separate chapter.

Most of the land is fairly flat, making it suitable for dairy and arable farming. The Appenzell region is famous for the production of the cheese of the same name. Textiles are also important, particularly in St Gallen, where embroidered lace has an international reputation. The metal and machine industries also make a significant contribution to the local economy.

The north-east is also noted for the high concentration of small and medium-size breweries. Liquid assets to look out for include *Falkenbier* (brewed in Schaffhausen), *Löwengarten Bier* (Rorschach) and *Locher Bräu* (Appenzell).

The region's best-known mountain is Säntis (2503 metres), although there are some higher peaks in the southern part. Aside from Lake Constance, which it shares with Germany and Austria, the largest lake in the north-east is the Walensee. The Rhine Falls, near Schaffhausen, are a noisy, often dramatic spectacle.

The local people in rural parts have a reputation for being traditional, parochial folk. This is reflected in the fact that the ancient practice of the Landsgemeinde (open-air parliament) is still conducted in two cantons. This annual open-air meeting, where citizens vote by show of hands on

local matters, is well worth viewing. Citizens in Glarus vote on the first Sunday in May. Appenzell is split into two half-cantons so there is a meeting at two locations on the last Sunday in April: in Appenzell village and either in Trogen (even years) or Hundwill (odd years).

Information for the north-east is covered by the St Gallen tourist office (see the following St Gallen Canton section). Unfortunately they're not particularly helpful in promoting the region and you have to work hard to find out anything at all.

Getting Around

The canton of Thurgau has a regional one-day pass, the *Thurgauer Tageskarte*. It covers a 1000-km network of rail, bus and boat travel, and costs Sfr24, or Sfr15 for children (six to 16 years) and those with the Half-Fare Card. This is bound to save you money, particularly if you're planning a boat trip on the Rhine River or Lake Constance. Just the fare from Kreuzlingen to Schaffhausen, for example, would otherwise cost you Sfr23. Towns bordering Thurgau, like St Gallen, Winterthur and Schaffhausen are covered, and the pass is issued year-round. Parents travelling with children should buy a Family Card (see the Getting Around chapter).

Another regional pass covers some of the routes in the Säntis region, including Appenzell, Ebenalp, Gamsalp and Buchs. This pass is worth it if you really want to spend seven days (the period of validity) in this small area, or simply intend to do a lot of mountain-hopping within a couple of days. The fare is Sfr85 or Sfr70 for those with the main Swiss rail passes, and it's issued from May to October.

St Gallen Canton

ST GALLEN

In 612 AD, an itinerant Irish monk called Gallus fell into a briar. Relying on a peculiar form of Irish logic, the venerable Gallus interpreted this clumsy act as a sign from God and decided to stay put and build a hermitage. He was helped in this task, according to legend, by a bear. From this inauspicious beginning, the town of St Gallen evolved and developed into an important medieval cultural centre, reaching the peak of its influence in the 10th century. The Reformation was brought to St Gallen in 1524 by Vadian, the mayor of the town, whose statue stands in Marktgasse.

Orientation & Information

St Gallen has a population of 73,000, the seventh largest city in Switzerland. The train station has the usual facilities, including train information, lockers, money-exchange counters and bike rental. The main post office (Bahnhofplatz, CH-9001 St Gallen) is opposite the train station, and is also the departure point for postbuses. The transport hub for city buses is also by the station.

Two minutes away is the tourist office (☎ 071-22 62 62), Bahnhofplatz 1a, which is open Monday to Friday from 9 am to noon and 1 to 6 pm, and on Saturday from 9 am to noon. Its hotel guide has a detailed map of the centre. A few minutes to the east is the pedestrian-only old town, dominated by the twin spires of the cathedral. Most of the main sights are clustered in this area.

The budget travel agency, SSR (☎ 071-23 34 47) is at Frongartenstrasse 15, open from Monday afternoon to Saturday morning.

The telephone code for St Gallen is 071.

Things to See & Do

St Gallen has one of the best city centres in Switzerland. It's full of interesting buildings with colourful murals, carved balconies and relief statues. The most striking feature of the centre are the oriel windows. Some of the best are on Gallusplatz, Spisergasse and Kugelgasse. Look out also for the colourful market on Marktplatz on Wednesday and Saturday.

The twin-tower **cathedral** cannot and should not be missed. It's the final incarnation of Gallus' original hermit's cell and the subsequent monastery. Work was begun in 1755 and the 68-metre-high towers were erected in 1766. Completed in 1768, it's immensely impressive and impressively immense. Forget the Sistine Chapel in Rome – a lot more paint went onto this ceiling! Most of this paint was applied by Joseph Wannenmacher. The stucco embellishments are the work of the Gigi brothers. Look out also for the pulpit, arches, statue groups and woodcarvings around the confessionals. It's open daily except during services.

Adjoining the church is the **Stiftsbibliothek** (Collegiate Library), containing some beautifully etched manuscripts from the Middle Ages and a splendidly opulent Rococo interior. The graceful lines of the wooden balustrades in the main hall show rare artistry. In total, the library contains 130,000 volumes. There's even an Egyptian mummy dating from 700 BC. Entry costs Sfr3 or Sfr2 for students and children. Opening times are: May to October, Monday to Saturday from 9 am to noon and 2 to 5 pm and Sunday from 10.30 am to noon and (June to August only) 2 to 4 pm; December to March, Tuesday to Saturday from 9 am to noon and 2 to 4 pm; April, Monday to Saturday from 9 am to noon and 2 to 5 pm.

St Gallen has several museums vying for the attention in the Stadtpark, off Museumstrasse to the east of the old town. The most significant is probably the **Historical Museum**. Of particular note are the models and maps of the town, illustrating the successive versions of the monastery-turned-abbey. Elsewhere in the museum there are some excellent tiled stoves and panelled state rooms, as well as portraits, uniforms, ceramics and ethnological exhibits. Entry costs Sfr4 (children Sfr2) and it's open Tuesday to Saturday from 10 am to noon and 2 pm to 5 pm, and Sunday from 10 am to 5 pm.

The **Textile Museum**, Vadianstrasse 2, displays an extensive collection of intricately-worked lace and embroidery, spanning three centuries. It's open Monday to Saturday from 10 am to noon and 2 to 5 pm (closed Saturday from November to

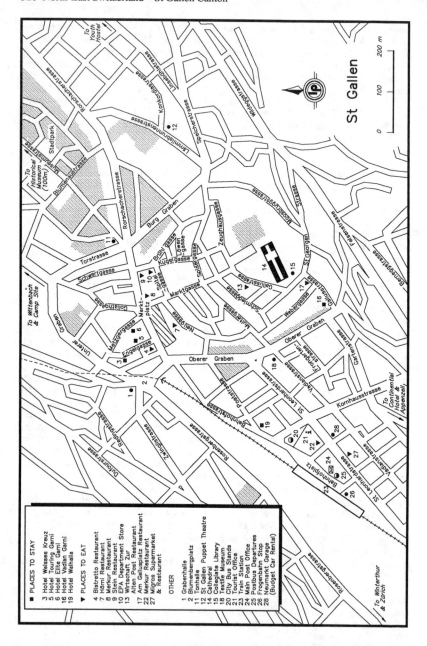

St Gallen

0   100   200 m

PLACES TO STAY
3 Hotel Weisses Kreuz
5 Hotel Touring Garni
6 Hotel Elite Garni
16 Hotel Vadian Garni
19 Hotel Walhalla

▼ PLACES TO EAT
4 Bistretto Restaurant
7 Hörnli Restaurant
8 Merkur Restaurant
9 Stein Restaurant
10 EPA Department Store
13 Wirtschaft Zur
   Alten Post Restaurant
17 Am Gallusplatz Restaurant
22 Merkur Restaurant
27 Migros Supermarket
   & Restaurant

OTHER
1 Grabenhalle
2 Blumenbergplatz
11 Tonhalle
12 St Gallen Puppet Theatre
14 Cathedral
15 Collegiate Library
18 Textile Museum
20 City Bus Stands
21 Tourist Office
23 Train Station
24 Main Post Office
25 Postbus Departures
26 Frogenbahn Stop
28 Neumarkt Garage
   (Budget Car Rental)

March) and costs Sfr4 (free for children and students).

Places to Stay

Exhibitions and conferences can make beds scarce and prices high; busy times are usually April and October.

Camping The nearest camping is north of St Gallen at *Leebrücke* (☎ 071-38 49 69) in Wittenbach.

Hostel The IYHF *youth hostel* (☎ 25 47 77) is a signposted, 15-minute walk east of the old town at Jüchstrasse 25 (once you get into Linsebühlstrasse, follow only the hostel signs with the adult and child – turning right with the other hostel signs makes the walk much longer). However, it's easier to take the orange Trogenbahn from outside the station to 'Schülerhaus' (Sfr2) and walk a few minutes up the hill, until you see the hostel on the left. Beds are Sfr19 in a dorm or Sfr29 in a double room. Reception is closed from 9 am to 5 pm although the front doors usually stay open. Reception closes again at 10 pm and curfew is at midnight (keys are available). You may be lumbered with the occasional chore while staying here. The hostel closes for two weeks at Christmas and from 1 February to the end of March.

Hotels & Pensions *Weisses Kreuz* (☎ 23 28 43) on Engelgasse is the best value; it has reasonable singles/doubles for Sfr42/76 with free use of the hall shower. There are also four good-sized doubles with shower for Sfr90. The reception is in the cosy bar downstairs. If you can't get in there, *Touring Garni* (☎ 22 58 01) is virtually opposite. Rooms are of varying quality, so ask to see several; those with a proper en suite bathroom are a good deal. Singles/doubles are around Sfr55/95, and there are cheaper rooms with no shower facilities available. *Elite Garni* (☎ 22 12 36), Metzgergasse 9-11, is a similar standard but slightly more expensive. The alcohol-free *Vadian Garni* (☎ 23 60 80), Gallusstrasse 36 is another cheapish option, with rooms starting at Sfr50/80.

The best mid-price deal is *Continental* (☎ 27 88 11), Teufener Strasse 95. It's a little bit out of the way, but bus No 5 stops out the front (stop: Ruhbergstrasse) and goes to Bahnhofplatz every 10 minutes. Comfortable rooms with TV and bath or shower start at Sfr90/170. The cheaper rooms face the main street and there is garage parking for Sfr9. The restaurant is reasonable, too, with meat and vegetarian dishes for Sfr8.50 to Sfr36.

The Best Western *Hotel Walhalla* (☎ 22 29 22) is conveniently situated on Bahnhofplatz, but the rooms are a bit pokey for a four-star, and the TVs aren't even remote control. Prices start at Sfr150/230.

Places to Eat

Eating can be pretty good in St Gallen across the range. At the basic level, look out for various fast-food stalls selling St Gallen sausage and bread for around Sfr3.50. Alternatively, make for the *Migros* supermarket and restaurant near the tourist office on St Leonhardstrasse. Both sections are open until 6.30 pm weekdays (9 pm on Thursday) and 5 pm on Saturday. Self-service food is also available in the restaurant of the EPA department store at Bohl 6.

Hörni, Marktplatz 5, has a restaurant on the first floor, where daily specials (lunch and evening) start at Sfr11.50. A wide selection of imported beers is on offer, but the cheaper draught beer is only available in the bar downstairs. *Bistretto*, off Marktplatz on Augustinergasse, has good, cheap pasta and pizzas (if smallish servings), and a self-service salad bar with plates from Sfr4.30. Both restaurants are open daily.

Merkur Restaurant, on the corner of Gutenbergstrasse and St Leonhardstrasse, offers vegetarian and meat dishes from Sfr10.50. There's another branch open longer hours in Bohl, off Marktplatz (both closed Sunday). Also on Bohl is *Stein*, with a good range of pasta, meat dishes, salad and Indonesian food (Sfr6.50 to Sfr15). The lunch and evening Tagesteller with soup is Sfr12 and the vegetarian special is Sfr13.50.

It's open daily but closes early at 6.30 pm on Saturday and Sunday.

A good mid-price place is *Wirtschaft Zur Alten Post* (☎ 22 66 01), Gallusstrasse 4. The food is typically Swiss, with meat and fish dishes starting at Sfr29. Lunch menus (Sfr12.50 to Sfr25) are more affordable. Small and cosy, this restaurant fills quickly, so reserve ahead. It's closed on Sunday and Monday.

Top-of-the-range in prices and quality is *Am Gallusplatz* (☎ 23 33 30), Gallusstrasse 24. You can construct your own multi-course feast from a number of options (Sfr60 to Sfr93), or go with one of the set menus (Sf:82 to Sfr165). The style is French nouvelle cuisine and it's closed Saturday lunch time and all day Monday.

Entertainment

The *Grabenhalle* (☎ 22 82 11), Blumenbergplatz, is a major venue for rock and jazz concerts. *Bavaria* (☎ 24 59 39), Speichser-strasse 54, near the youth hostel, has live rock music once a week, usually on Friday or Saturday. Entry is free and there is also hot food for Sfr8 to Sfr24. Beer costs Sfr4, or Sfr4.50 on music nights (half a litre).

There are several theatres in the city, including the *Puppet Theatre* at Lämmlisbrunnenstrasse 34. Classical concerts are often performed at the *Tonhalle*, Museumstrasse 25. The tourist office has details.

Getting There & Away

St Gallen is the transport hub for the northeast. It's just a short train or bus ride to/from Lake Constance. There are also regular trains to Bregenz in Austria (Sfr12), Constance (Sfr15), Chur (Sfr32) and Zürich (Sfr24.20).

By car, the main link is the N1/E60 motorway, which runs from Zürich and Winterthur through to the Austrian border. It gets almost to the centre of town, just slightly to the north.

For car hire, go to Avis (☎ 27 35 77), Züricherstrasse 246, Hertz (☎ 28 84 74), down the road at No 63, or Budget (☎ 22 11 14) at the Neumarkt garage.

Getting Around

Journeys on the bus cost Sfr1.70, though you could also pay Sfr17 for 12 tickets, Sfr6 for a day pass, or Sfr19 for one week. Buy tickets from dispensers; there's a fine of Sfr50 if you're caught without one. Bus tickets are not valid on the Trogenbahn, where the fare depends upon distance, but the general day passes *are* valid.

RAPPERSWIL

This small town on the north bank of Lake Zürich is in the canton of St Gallen. The tourist office (☎ 055-27 70 00) is five minutes from the train station on Seequai, and is open Monday to Friday from 8.15 am to noon and 1 to 5.15 pm. The town has a castle which dates from the 13th century and provides a fine view from its terrace.

But the main reason to stop off is for the **Knie Kinderzoo** (children's zoo), situated behind the station (signposted). There are animal rides and other attractions such as a Noah's Ark. Best of all are the performing dolphins who show off their stunts several times a day. Entry costs Sfr7 for adults and Sfr3 for children, and it is open mid-March to early November, from 9 am to 6 pm (7 pm July and August). The Knie circus is a travelling show that visits many Swiss towns.

Places to Stay & Eat

The IYHF *youth hostel* (☎ 055-27 99 27), Hessenhofweg 10, is close to the lake in the suburb of Jona. It costs Sfr21 and it is closed from 1 November to the end of January. In the sports complex near the children's zoo is the *Familien Herberge Lido* (☎ 055-27 33 98). Beds in two, four or eight-bed rooms with shower cost Sfr17 (children to age 12 Sfr13), and you also get reduced entry to the swimming pool. Breakfast costs Sfr9.

Du Lac Mövenpick (☎ 055-27 19 43), near the tourist office, has singles/doubles with private shower/toilet for Sfr60/95, and some cheaper doubles for Sfr70. It also has a *Bistro* with a fairly ordinary salad buffet (Sfr5.90 to Sfr12.80) and a fair selection of vegetarian, pasta and meat dishes from Sfr12.50. It's open daily to at least 11.30 pm.

Opposite the station is a large *Migros* with meals from Sfr8.20. The supermarket is open until 6.30 pm weekdays (9 pm Wednesday) and 4 pm Saturday; the restaurant is open in addition on Sunday from 9 am to 6 pm.

Getting There & Away
By train, Rapperswil is 40 minutes from Zürich and 50 minutes from St Gallen (Sfr21). It is within the boundary of the canton of Zürich transport (S-Bahn lines S5 and S7) and can also be reached by boat (Swiss Pass valid on services from Zürich).

Appenzellerland

If you ever hear a joke in Switzerland, the inhabitants of Appenzellerland are likely to be the butt. They are known for their parochialism and are considered (a little unfairly) to be several stages lower on the evolutionary ladder than the rest of humanity. Politically, Appenzellerland is divided into two half-cantons, Innerrhoden and Ausserrhoden. Appenzell itself is in Innerrhoden. Women were finally allowed to vote for the first time in Innerrhoden cantonal affairs in 1991, and then only after the supreme court ruled their exclusion by the men unconstitutional. The men of Ausserrhoden, reluctantly but without coercion, allowed the women to have their say the year before.

Such resistance to change has its advantages for the tourist in that Appenzellerland has a quaint air of being unaffected by modern life. It is a region of farms, verdant hills and villages with characteristic gabled houses. Several mountains enliven the hiking possibilities.

Activities
Hiking Pick up the free hiking map from one of the local tourist offices, which gives a summary of routes and average walking times. All the peaks in the region can be ascended by foot if you don't want to take the cable car. There's a **geological walk**

(geologischer Wanderweg) running from Hoher Kasten to Stauberen, on to Saxerlücke and the lake of Sämtisersee, and back down to Brülisau. It takes about 5½ hours and there are 14 information boards along the way, detailing geological features. Get to the start by taking the train to Weissbad, the bus to Brülisau, and the cable car to Hoher Kasten (Sfr16 up, Sfr11 down, Sfr20 return). See the Säntis section for more walking suggestions.

Skiing Skiing is not a major activity, but it's still possible. The main area for downhill is the **Kronberg** (1663 metres) with 10 km of runs, reached by cable car or ski lift from Jakobsbad. There are also some slopes on Ebenalp and above Appenzell. A three-day lift pass costs Sfr45, available from the Appenzell tourist office. There are also some ski schools and cross-country skiing trails.

APPENZELL
The smell of the countryside – cows and their waste products – permeates the air in pastoral Appenzell. The village is a delight to wander around, with traditional old houses, painted façades and lush surrounding pastures.

Orientation & Information
The train station is five minutes from the centre of town and changes money daily. The tourist office (☎ 071-87 41 11) is on the main thoroughfare, Hauptgasse, and has information on all of Appenzellerland. It is open Monday to Friday from 8 am to noon and 2 to 5 pm, and Saturday from 9 am to noon and (summer only) from 2 to 4 pm.

Things to See & Do
Hauptgasse is an attractive main street, with wrought-iron hanging signs, and souvenir shops selling locally-made wares, such as embroidery and decorated confectionery. Take a look inside the village **church** on Hauptgasse and admire the gold and silver figures flanking the Baroque altar. Over the river lies the **Alpenbitter Distillery** (☎ 071-87 17 17). It offers free tours for groups from

Monday to Saturday; telephone ahead and ask if you can tag on to an existing group.

The streets are bedecked with flags and flowers on the last Sunday in April. This is when the locals vote on cantonal issues by a show of hands in the open-air parliament, the Landsgemeinde. It takes place, not surprisingly, in Landsgemeindeplatz. Everyone wears traditional dress for the occasion and many of the men carry swords or daggers as proof of citizenship.

Places to Stay & Eat

There is year-round camping at *Eischen* (☎ 071-87 14 97). *Gasthaus Hof* (☎ 071-87 22 10), off Landsgemeindeplatz, has good dorms in a building behind its restaurant. Prices are Sfr16.50 with breakfast, Sfr12.70 without, and Sfr4 for sheets if required.

Hotel Traube (☎ 071-87 14 07), by the corner of Postplatz, has singles/doubles for Sfr55/90 using hall shower, and doubles for Sfr110 with private shower. *Gasthaus Traube* (different place), just off Hauptgasse, is probably the cheapest place to eat, out of an expensive bunch. Light meals cost Sfr10.50 but most dishes top Sfr16 (closed Monday).

Restaurant Sonne, on Landsgemeindeplatz, has daily specials from Sfr13 (closed Thursday and Friday). *Hotel Säntis* (☎ 071-87 10 26), also on Landsgemeindeplatz, provides more expensive options for both eating and sleeping.

Getting There & Away

The red, narrow-gauge Appenzell train leaves from outside the St Gallen station. It careers along, criss-crossing the course of the road, and takes around 40 minutes. There are two alternative routes so you can go back a different way. Departures from St Gallen are approximately every half hour, via Gais (Sfr6.80) or Herisau (Sfr11.60).

STEIN

Appenzell culture and crafts are highlighted in this small village. The **Appenzell Showcase Cheese Dairy** (Appenzeller Schaukäserie) provides the opportunity to see the famous cheese undergo a 10-stage progress from pure milk to a ripened cheese wheel. A viewing gallery allows you to watch every move made by the white-clad workers as they rush around manipulating gleaming metal vats and presses. (There's no sneaking a quiet fag behind the churns for these people.)

It's free and open daily from 8 am to 7 pm, but it's more interesting to go when the various processes are instigated, from 9 to 11 am and 1 to 3 pm. A brochure in English explains the different stages and contains cheese recipes on the reverse. There's a restaurant on site.

Next door is the **Folklore Museum** (Volkskunde Museum). In addition to the periodic weaving demonstrations, displays include furniture, cowbells, decorated harnesses and traditional pipes. The best exhibit is the collection of simple, childlike, yet evocative pictures of village life, usually showing herders leading lines of cattle. Cows in the foreground are often the same size as those in the distance – the newfangled notion of artistic perspective obviously hadn't reached Appenzellerland at the time (19th century!).

It takes only an hour or so to get round, and costs Sfr7 (Sfr6 students, Sfr3.50 children). Opening times are: January, Sunday from 10 am to 5 pm on Sunday; February, March, November and December, 10 am to 5 pm on Sunday plus 1.30 to 5 pm from Tuesday to Saturday; April to October, 10 am to noon and 1.30 to 5 pm from Tuesday to Saturday, and 10 am to 6 pm on Sunday.

Getting There & Away

The St Gallen bus (direction: Herisau) passes through woodland and rolling countryside, takes 15 minutes, and drops you right opposite the cheese dairy. The fare is Sfr4.40 and departures are every one to two hours.

SÄNTIS

Although a mere tiddler in Swiss terms, the Säntis mountain (2502 metres) is the highest peak in the vicinity, and accordingly offers a marvellous panorama that encompasses

Lake Constance, Lake Zürich, the Alps and the Vorarlberg Mountains. To get there, take the train to Urnäsch (on the Appenzell to Herisau line) and transfer to the bus (approximately hourly) to Schwägalp. From Schwägalp, a cable car ascends to the summit every 30 minutes (7.30 am to 6.30 pm in summer, 8.30 am to 5 pm in winter). The fare is: Sfr16.40 up, Sfr14 down, and Sfr23 return.

From Säntis, you can walk along the ridge to the neighbouring peak of **Ebenalp** (1640 metres) in about 2½ hours (3½ hours going the other way). On Ebenalp there are prehistoric caves at Wildkirchli, showing traces of Stone Age habitation. The descent to Lake Wasserauen on foot via the lake of Sämtisersee takes 1½ hours. Alternatively, a cable car runs between the summit and Wasserauen approximately every 30 minutes (Sfr15 up, Sfr10 down, Sfr19 return). Wasserauen and Appenzell are connected by rail.

Schaffhausen Canton

SCHAFFHAUSEN

The capital of the canton that bears its name, Schaffhausen, joined the Swiss Confederation in 1501. It is known as a heavy industry, communications and arms centre. During WW II, in 1944 and 1945, it was accidentally bombed by the USA. A few people believe that this was not quite the accident the Americans claimed, as some of the arms then produced by the town ended up in German hands. Thankfully its medieval town centre survived the shelling, and today merits a leisurely exploration.

Orientation & Information

Schaffhausen is in a bulge of Swiss territory surrounded by Germany on the north bank of the Rhine. The train station is adjacent to the old town, and has lockers, bike rental, and money-exchange counters (open daily from 6.50 am to 7.10 pm). There are also information offices for both Swiss and German trains. The tourist office (☎ 053-25 51 41) is in the heart of the old town at Vorstadt 12. It is open Monday to Friday from 9 am to noon and 2 to 6 pm, and Saturday from 9 am to noon. Postbuses depart from the rear of the station and local buses from the front. The main post office is also opposite the station.

The telephone code for Schaffhausen is 053.

Things to See & Do

The attractive old town is bursting with oriel windows, painted façades and ornamental fountains. The best streets are Vordergasse and Vorstadt, which intersect at Fronwagplatz. From April to October the tourist office organises a guided walking tour of the centre on Monday, Wednesday and Friday afternoons (Sfr8, children Sfr4).

Vordergasse has the most distinctive house in the centre, the 16th century **Haus zum Ritter**, decorated in scenes from mythology and Roman history. These drawings are a relatively recent copy of work done by Tobias Stimmer in 1570. Fragments of the originals can be seen in the **Allerheiligen Museum**, by the cathedral in Klosterplatz. The rest of the collection ranges from ancient bones to modern art. Entry is free and it's open from Tuesday to Sunday from 10 am to noon and 2 to 5 pm.

Get an overview of the town from the **Munot**, a fortification atop a vine-covered hill. The summit can be attained in just 15 minutes from the centre. Aside from the impressive view, this 16th century keep boasts a couple of old canons. It's free and open daily: 9 am to 8 pm in summer and 9 am to 5 pm from November to April.

The Rhine Falls (see the Around Schaffhausen section) is an easy excursion from the town. Another essential excursion while in the area is a trip along the river. The 45 km from Schaffhausen to Constance is considered one of the Rhine's most beautiful stretches, passing by meadows, castles and ancient villages. See Stein am Rhein and the Lake Constance Getting Around sections for more details.

The Second World War

Quite how Switzerland managed to avoid getting sucked into the 1939-45 war is a question without an easy answer. The country's civil defence was not so developed in those days, and it would have been relatively easy for Hitler to sweep in and take the northern cities, if not the Alpine regions. Indeed, in July 1940 General Guisan realised that the borders could not be held against attack, and re-deployed the army from frontier posts to entrenched positions in the Alps. There was even some support for Nazi Germany (not least from the president of the Federal Council) boosted by the common border and language, which would have made Hitler's task easier. Nazi party members numbered 4000 in Basel alone.

Switzerland was undeniably an irritation to Hitler. Swiss pilots were by no means reluctant to shoot down German planes which violated their air-space. When Paris fell in 1940 the Nazis discovered a secret agreement for the exchange of military information between Switzerland and France. This could easily have been used as a pretext for invasion.

To keep Germany at bay, Switzerland resorted to negotiation and bluff. In a famous (and probably aprocryphal) conversation between a member of the German military and General Guisan, the German asked what would happen if the Nazis sent down a force to take Switzerland. Guisan told him that he could have over 600,000 men mobilised to defend the country within a few hours. 'And what would happen if we sent down a force double that size?' probed the German. Guisan replied simply, 'Then each man would have to shoot twice.'

In practical terms, Switzerland was also at pains to ensure that its neutrality would be useful to both sides, to make it less advantageous for anyone to consider violating that status. Diplomatic relations were kept open with both the Allies and the Nazis, allowing Switzerland to be a conduit through which the belligerents could communicate, and the country undertook tasks like exchanges of prisoners of war. Exactly how far Switzerland had to go to pacify Hitler is not in the public domain, but it is accepted that some arms (tank parts, etc) produced by the town of Schaffhausen ended up in Germany. Whether this was by intent or 'accident' is also not clear.

Strange and secretive things happen in wartime. Perhaps it is a coincidence that American bombers, on a mission to southern Germany on 1 April 1944, 'mistakenly' identified Schaffhausen as a German target and unloaded their bombs. The town suffered about 100 casualties, with most bombs falling around the train station and in the nearby woods. The Americans' excuse to the outraged Swiss for this error was that there were navigational difficulties induced by bad weather. Swiss outrage was merely inflamed by this explanation, as weather conditions on the day in question were extremely clear.

The Americans later supplemented their account of the incident with the information that the divisional leader had been shot down earlier, and the winds they encountered were much stronger than expected. The USA paid full compensation to Switzerland, and created guidelines that no target would be bombed within 50 miles of the Swiss frontier, unless positively identified. Curious, therefore, that on 22 February 1945 Schaffhausen again suffered 'accidental' bombing, this time leaving 16 dead. ■

Places to Stay

Camp by the river at *Rheinwiesen* (☎ 29 33 00), just east of the town in Langwiesen. It's open from 1 May to mid-September.

The IYHF *youth hostel* (☎ 25 88 00) is 20 minutes' walk west of the train station (or take bus No 3), at Randenstrasse 65. Dorms cost Sfr16 with breakfast, and the reception is closed from 10 am to 5.30 pm. The hostel closes from 1 November to the end of February.

The best budget deal in the town centre is *Steinbock* (☎ 25 42 60), Webergasse 47, with singles/doubles for Sfr43/70, and triples for Sfr90, all without breakfast. It's above a fairly noisy café but the rooms are clean, reasonably sized, and there are free hall showers. *Tanne* (☎ 25 41 79), Tanne 3 off Fronwagplatz, is cheaper, with singles/doubles for Sfr40/80, but there are no showers at all.

Park Villa (☎ 25 27 37), is south of the station by the west side of the tracks, and costs from Sfr65/100 for comfortable rooms with hall shower, or Sfr98/130 with private shower. The best hotel is the convenient *Hotel Bahnhof* (☎ 24 19 24), Bahnhofstrasse 46. Rooms are quiet and large with all amenities, and cost from Sfr85/145. The radio picks up the BBC world service.

Places to Eat

You can eat for under Sfr10 at either the *Migros* supermarket and restaurant at Vorstadt 39, or the *EPA* department store and restaurant at Vordergasse 69. The food is self-service and good value. Both places are open until 6.30 pm on weekdays and 4 pm on Saturday. The Vilan department store by Fronwagplatz has a *Manora* self-service restaurant, which has great salad and dessert buffets (open same hours).

A comfortable ambience, despite the glowering masks on the wall, can be found at *Walliser Kanne*, Webergasse 27, which specialises in fondues (from Sfr17.50) and other cheese concoctions, plus various steaks and schnitzels. It's closed Tuesday. There are also several reasonable cafés with outside seating on Fronwagplatz, that are ideal on a sunny day.

For a taste treat, go to *Rheinhotel Fischerzunft* (☎ 25 32 81), Rheinquai 8. It is acclaimed as one of the top 10 restaurants in Switzerland (based on the results of an annual survey), a justification for spending around Sfr50 per main dish. It serves Oriental and Swiss food, particularly fish dishes, and it's open daily. Rooms (also expensive) are available, too.

Getting There & Away

There are hourly IC (Intercity) trains to Zürich and Constance (via Singen, Sfr12.60). Basel can be reached by either Swiss (Sfr39, via Zürich) or German (Sfr19.40) trains. Schaffhausen is within range of Zürich's S-Bahn bus system (lines S22 and S33; fare Sfr14). Steamers travel to Constance several times a day in summer, and the trip takes four hours; they depart from Freier Platz (☎ 25 42 82 for information). Schaffhausen has excellent road connections radiating out in all directions.

THE RHINE FALLS (RHEINFALL)

This is the largest waterfall in Europe, and makes a tremendous racket as the Rhine

crashes down a 23-metre drop. The average flow of water is 600 cubic metres per second in summer and 250 cubic metres in winter. The highest ever recorded was 12,250 cubic metres per second in the summer of 1965. Impassable to shipping, the falls contributed greatly to the past expansion of Schaffhausen, three km up-river, as boats were forced to unload cargo there.

From the north bank of the river the falls are less steep and less violent. You need to cross the bridge to the south side to get a true impression of the power of the water flow. The viewpoint from the Schloss Laufen is best. A stairway leads right down to the edge, where the water leaps and boils and sprays the edge of the platform. You need to pay Sfr0.50 to the Schloss souvenir shop to gain access to the staircase. It seems surprising that they should bother to charge, because when the shop shuts in the evening you can walk down for nothing.

Places to Stay & Eat

Within the Schloss is an ageing *youth hostel* (☎ 053-29 61 52) where the doors are locked from 10 am to 5 pm and there's a 10 pm curfew. Dorms cost Sfr17 and the hostel is closed in January and February. Kitchen facilities are available for a Sfr2 charge. Stock up or eat in the *Migros* supermarket/restaurant in Neuhausen. It has good salad and dessert buffets (Sfr1.70 per 100 grams) and no half-day closing. The Schloss also has a restaurant, where main courses cost Sfr15 to Sfr32 (closed Monday and Tuesday)

Getting There & Away

From Schaffhausen, the falls can be reached by a 40-minute stroll westward along the river. Alternatively, take bus Nos 1 or 9 to Neuhausen and get off by the Migros in the centre; then follow the brown signs leading to the north bank of the river (three minutes).

STEIN AM RHEIN

Stein is quite simply delightful, its medieval centre completely captivating. Unused film in your camera stands no chance – the

Rathausplatz will claim it before you have time to draw breath. Inevitably, such beauty has its down side. Stein receives 45,000 overnight visitors annually – quite manageable for a population of just 2500. However, over *one million* people per year visit on day trips. The tour buses rolling through are in danger of choking the place to death. If possible, try to visit outside the summer crush.

Orientation & Information

Stein reclines on both sides of the Rhine River. The train station is on the south side, and has money-exchange, bike rental and left luggage facilities. Take Bahnhofstrasse and turn right then left to cross the river for the old town (a 10-minute walk). Leading off the pivotal Rathausplatz is Oberstadt, where awaits the tourist office (☎ 054-41 28 35) at No 10. Its opening hours are Monday to Friday from 9 to 11 am and 2 to 5 pm. The small post office is on Brodlaubegasse. The telephone code for Stein is 054.

Things to See & Do

The first thing to do is to admire the splendid façades of the buildings all around the **Rathausplatz**. It is the most photogenic square in Switzerland. Many of the murals depict the animal or object after which the house is named, such as the Sun, Red Ox or White Eagle. A particularly good pairing of pictorial scenes is at Nos 14 and 15. The former was painted by Thomas Schmid from 1520-25; it is the oldest fresco in Rathausplatz. No 15 displays the most recent work, painted by Alois Carigiet in 1956. The town hall opposite has some historical exhibits on the second floor. No 17 contains a small museum of phonographs (Sfr2 entry).

The streets round the square are worth exploring, too. There are several gate towers dating from the 14th century, including one at the end of Understadt. **Kloster St Georgen** is a well-preserved former Benedictine monastery dating from the 12th century. It houses a museum of local history and art, open March to October from 10 am to noon and 1.30 pm to 5 pm (closed Monday; Sfr3, children and students

Sfr1.50). The **Puppet Museum**, Schwarzhorngasse 136, features 500 antique puppets going back 150 years. It's open mid-April to mid-October from 11 am to 5 pm (closed Monday) and costs Sfr5, with reductions for students.

On the hill above the town, the **Hohenklingen Castle** offers a commanding view of the town and river, and a restaurant (closed Monday and the months of January and February).

Places to Stay

Stein camp site, *Grenzstein* (☎ 41 23 79), is about two km from the village by the Rhine. It is open year round and costs Sfr5 per adult, Sfr3 per child, Sfr4 for a tent and Sfr2 for a car. Good facilities on site include a new ablutions block, washing machines, camp shop and restaurant.

The IYHF *youth hostel* (☎ 41 12 55) is 1½ km out of the centre at Hemishoferstrasse 711. This road is the continuation of Understadt to the west, and the hostel is two minutes from the beach. It's closed from 1 November to the end of February (reception closed 9 am to 5.30 pm; beds cost Sfr16.)

Gästehaus Garni Bleichehof (☎ 41 22 57) costs Sfr40/70 but it's not really viable unless you have your own transport or don't mind walking over two km; head towards the Hohenklingen castle then follow the brown signs (no street name).

Staying in the centre is a budget-busting proposition. *Gasthaus Zur Ilge* (☎ 41 22 72) on Rathausplatz is one of the cheapest, with singles/doubles for Sfr65/95. *Hotel Adler* (☎ 42 61 61), Rathausplatz 15, has comfortable rooms for Sfr100/140 with own shower, toilet, TV and telephone. It is also the reception for the *Motel Roseberg*, on the south side of the river. Rooms here are slightly smaller and lack the TV; prices start at Sfr80/100 and use of the garage costs Sfr10.

Places to Eat

As if to deliberately counterbalance the splendour of the old centre, the *Migros* supermarket and restaurant is housed in the ugliest modern building imaginable. Look for the dreary concrete block with all the flair of a bombshelter that defaces Di Gross Schanz, a couple of minutes north of the Obertor gate tower. Meals start at Sfr9 and opening times are Monday to Friday from 9 am to 6.30 pm and Saturday from 7.30 am to 4 pm.

Most of the other restaurants are on the pricey side. Fish dishes are a speciality at a number of places in the centre, including at *Salmenstübli*, Understadt 10. Prices are in the range of Sfr18 to Sfr30 and it is closed Monday. *Adler*, Rathausplatz 15, likewise has many fishy options, plus game in season (Sfr20 to Sfr40, closed Tuesday).

For top quality, look to *Sonne* (☎ 41 21 28) also on Rathausplatz. It's the oldest restaurant in town (the building dates from 1463) and it is closed on Wednesday and (in winter) Tuesday. It serves fish dishes and seasonal specialities for around Sfr35 to Sfr50, and open (decanted) wines.

Getting There & Away

Stein am Rhein is just within the range of Zürich's S-Bahn network (line S29) and the fare is Sfr19.60. It is also on the Schaffhausen-Rorschach line (Sfr6.20), with trains departing every hour. The easiest way to St Gallen (Sfr22) is via this route, changing at Romanshorn. Regular buses to Singen (in Germany) depart from the train station.

A boat trip along this stretch of the Rhine is a real pleasure (see Getting Around in Lake Constance section). The same sights can be perused by car on highway 13, which runs along the south bank of the river. Although the other towns and villages en route aren't as perfectly preserved as Stein am Rhein, many feature attractive church spires, half-timbered houses and hilltop castles. Places to look out for, and perhaps linger a while, are Ermatingen and especially Steckborn to the east, and Diessenhofen to the west.

Lake Constance

Lake Constance (or Bodensee in German) is a giant bulge in the sinewy course of the Rhine and offers a choice of water sports, relaxation or cultural pursuits. Constance (Konstanz) the town achieved historical significance in 1414 when the Council of Constance was called to try to heal huge rifts in the Catholic Church. The consequent burning at the stake of the religious reformer, Jan Hus, as a heretic, and the scattering of his ashes over the lake, failed to halt the impetus towards the Reformation.

Lake Constance is a summer area, too often foggy or at best hazy in winter. On the German side of the lake, the pre-Lent Fasnacht celebrations can be lively, helped along by Constance's large student population.

Orientation

The lake is shared by three countries. The southern shore is Swiss, the northern shore is German and the eastern corner is Austrian. Constance is the largest town on the lake and sits on the end of the peninsula between the two western arms, the Überlinger See and the Unter See. Constance proper is in Germany, although the adjoining town of Kreuzlingen is Swiss and really all part of the same conurbation. Border controls between the two are minimal. Romanshorn and Rorschach are the other two main towns on the Swiss side, but plenty of other enjoyable resorts dot the shoreline in between.

In addition to Constance, the German stretch of the lake features two other main tourist centres, Meersburg and the island of Lindau. The only town of note in the Austrian part of the lake is Bregenz.

Resorts in all three countries are covered in this section. Prices listed are given in the local currency. One Swiss Franc is worth around DM1.1 (Deutschmarks) and 7.5AS (Austrian schillings). In Germany and Austria, post offices provide the most cost-effective money-exchange facilities. Most shops and restaurants will accept neighbouring currencies. Accommodation and food are cheaper in Germany and Austria than in Switzerland, so it could make sense to use

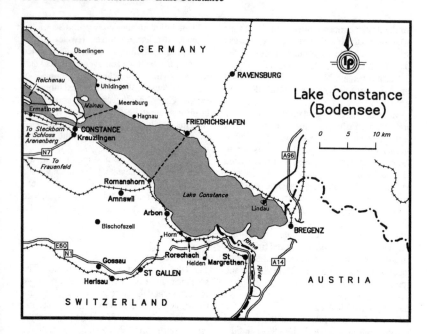

Lake Constance
(Bodensee)

one of those two countries as a base for exploring the whole lake.

Information

Switzerland Kreuzlingen has a tourist information counter in a travel agent (☎ 072-72 38 40), Hauptstrasse 39. Opening hours are Monday to Friday from 8.30 am to noon and 1.45 to 6 pm. Tourist information is also available via a travel agent in Romanshorn (☎ 071-63 32 32), directly opposite the train station, and in Arbon (☎ 071-46 33 37), just to the left of the station at Bahnhofstrasse 26.

Rorschach has its own tiny tourist office (☎ 071-41 70 34), opposite the Hafen train station and near the post office. It sells a hiking map for Sfr5 and it's open weekdays (except Monday morning) from 9 am to noon and 2 to 5 pm. Winter hours are reduced to Monday to Friday from 9 am to noon.

Germany In Constance, the tourist information office (☎ 07531-28 43 76) is to the right

from the train station and is not overly helpful. The Bodensee-Verkehrsdienst (☎ 07531-28 13 98), Hafenstrasse 6, by Platz 4 on the lake, is the information and sales office for ship travel, and is much more enthusiastic about helping you plan outings (closed in winter). The SBB counter in Constance train station changes money without charging commission.

Meersburg's friendly tourist information office (☎ 07532-8 23 83) is up the steep hill on the Schlossplatz at Kirchstrasse 4. It's open Monday to Friday from 9 am to noon and 2.30 to 5 pm. Lindau is just inside Bavaria in the east, near the Austrian border. Tourist information (☎ 08382-2 60 00) for the island and environs is directly opposite the station, open weekdays, and Saturday mornings in summer.

The country telephone code for Germany is 49.

Austria Bregenz is the provincial capital of

Vorarlberg, Austria's smallest state. Turn left down Bahnhofstrasse as you exit the station for the town centre and the tourist office (☎ 05574-433 910), which is on Anton Schneider Strasse 4A. It is open Monday to Friday from 9 am to noon and 2 to 6 pm and Saturday from 9 am to noon, except in July and August when hours are extended. The post office is on Seestrasse (Postamt 6900).

The country telephone code for Austria is 43.

Things to See

The lake itself is the major attraction of most of the resorts; explore its shores by boat and foot. Boat tours taking in all three countries are frequent and fun. See the Getting Around section for details.

Rorschach The main points of interest are around the Rorschach Hafen train station. The station itself is quaint, with a line of cafés and bars alongside the tracks. It is also the departure point for the hourly cogwheel train which climbs a scenic route to the health resort of **Heiden**. Exit the station and turn left down Hauptstrasse to see some fine oriel windows, particularly at No 33 and around the town hall (Rathaus). The main Rorschach station, which is on the St Gallen-Bregenz route, is a couple of km to the east of the centre.

Also by the Hafen station is the **Heimat Museum**, housed in the old Kornhaus and featuring a good scale model of the town in 1797, lace and embroidery displays, and temporary exhibitions. It is open daily except Monday from mid-April to mid-November. Entry costs Sfr3 or Sfr1 for students and children. Continue along the promenade for a pleasant 50-minute amble to the resort of **Horn**.

Arbon The historic centre of town, with its castle and old churches, certainly merits a stroll. The castle was built in the 16th century and home to an historical museum that is open daily from May to September. There are also a number of eye-catching, half-timbered houses in the centre, particularly

around the back of the Stadthaus on Hauptstrasse. From the train station, turn left and walk down Bahnhofstrasse for 10 minutes.

About 15 km north-west of Arbon along the coast is **Romanshorn**. This industrial town is of minimal sightseeing interest, but is nevertheless a convenient base, thanks to the direct ferry service to Friedrichshafen (see the Getting Around section for details).

Kreuzlingen There's not very much to see in the town, except perhaps the 17th century **St Ulric's Church** on Hauptstrasse. Most of the attractions are on the German side of the border. The main crossing points are at Hauptstrasse and Konstanzerstrasse. There's a smaller crossing by the east side of the railtracks that is usually unattended in the evening; using this route you can walk to the centre of Constance from Kreuzlingen youth hostel in 20 minutes, rather than messing around taking two trains.

A possible excursion when the weather is poor is to nearby **Frauenfeld**, where the cantonal museums of Thurgau are located: the Historisches Museum in the Schloss, the Naturmuseum in the Luzernerhaus, and the (Fine Arts Museum) Kunstmuseum in Warth, a village adjoining Frauenfeld. Even closer to Kreuzlingen is the Napoleon Museum in Schloss Arenenberg.

Constance The town's most visible feature is the Gothic spire of the **cathedral**, added only in 1856 to a church that was started in 1052. The views from the top are excellent. Follow the walking tour of the historic centre prescribed in the tourist office leaflet, lingering in the **Stadtgarten** and the Bohemian **Rheingasse** quarter. If you have time, head across the footbridge to **Mainau Island**, a peaceful tropical garden that was established by the royal house of Sweden (entrance DM13). Constance has a casino, where Swiss gamblers can lose the large amounts of money that restrictive laws (soon to be changed) prevent them from losing in their own country.

Meersburg Meersburg is the prettiest town on the lake, with terraced streets and vineyard-patterned hills. The **Marktplatz** offers great vistas and leads to **Steigstrasse**, one of the classic streets of Germany, with two lines of beautiful half-timbered houses. The 17th century **Altes Schloss** is the oldest inhabited castle in Germany and houses ancient weaponry (open daily; DM6, students DM5). The adjacent **Neues Schloss** is classic Baroque and contains a wonderful staircase (open daily April to October; DM3, students DM1.50).

Lindau This island village spills over onto the adjoining north shore. If you decide to join the crowds, take a walking tour along **Maximilianstrasse**, **Ludwigstrasse**, and the **harbour** with its Bavarian Lion monument and lighthouse. Also note the muralled **Altes Rathaus** at Reichsplatz. There's a great **model railway** (Modelbahn) at Seeparkplatz Insel with 500 metres of track, but unfortunately it's due to close in 1994 unless attempts to save it are successful.

Friedrichshafen Graf Zeppelin was born in Constance but first built his overgrown balloons in this town, an endeavour commemorated in the **Zeppelin Museum** in the town.

Überlingen This town features the astonishing **Cathedral of St Nicholas** which boasts a dozen side altars and a wooden four-storey central altar dating from the 17th century, bedecked in intricate carvings. Another impressive Baroque church can be found at **Birnau**.

Bregenz The old town is worth a stroll. Its centrepiece and the town emblem is the bulbous Baroque **St Martin's Tower** built in 1599. Follow the walking route described in the tourist office leaflet. The **Pfänder** Mountain offers an impressive panorama over the lake and beyond. A cable car to the top operates daily except during maintenance in November. Fares are: up 44AS, down 31AS, and return 63AS. The tourist office sells

tickets for the **Bregenz Festival** which takes place from late July to late August. Operas and classical works are performed from a vast water-bourne stage on the edge of the lake. Like Constance, Bregenz has a casino that attracts many gamblers from Switzerland.

Activities

Water Sports In season, the lake buzzes with possibilities. There are numerous locations for swimming in swimming pools, private beaches or free public beaches.

In Switzerland, there are sailing schools at Kreuzlingen (☎ 072-75 25 95), Romanshorn (☎ 071-63 51 21) and Rorschach (☎ 071-41 96 91). Horn has the Shipper's Shop (☎ 017-41 56 68), Seestrasse 64, which has a sailing school, boat and yacht charter, and sells all sorts of gear for water sports.

In Constance, head to the hot little sports shop, 3 UP (☎ 07531-2 31 17), at Münzgasse 10, for gear, information and instruction packages. Constance has a public beach at **Strandbad Horn**, open May to September.

Overall, Meersburg is a better base for water pursuits. The active windsurfing school (☎ 07532-53 30) at Uferpromenade 37 is one of the best organised on the lake, and some of the best windsurfers hang out here. In nearby Hagnau, there's another school called RePa Yachtschule-Windsurfing Hagnau (☎ 07545-62 93). It offers an unhurried, seven-day beginner's windsurfing course for DM220. For sailing, contact the Bodensee-Yachtschule on ☎ 07532-55 11. Rudi Thum and his crew run lots of courses, starting at DM250 for one week. Call Motorboot-Charter (☎ 07532-3 64) for sailing boat and motorboat rental.

Lindau's water isn't as crowded as the land; Hermann Kreitmeir (☎ 08382-2 33 30) has windsurfing schools and equipment rental at Strandbad Eichwald.

Cycling Constance is a good base for cycling. Aktiv-Reisen Velotours (☎ 07531-5 20 85), at Mainaustrasse 34, rents good bikes (DM20 per day or DM100 per week) and runs popular bike trips around the lake. Constance, Lindau and Bregenz train stations also rent bikes, as do the stations of all the places mentioned on the Swiss side (except Horn).

The Cyclists' Touring Club in Britain produces useful notes to accompany a circular tour of the lake.

Places to Stay
The thriving tourist industry means hotels and pensions can be a bit pricey; fortunately there are excellent hostel and camping facilities around the lake. Tourist offices have lists of holiday apartments and cheap private homes (usually a three-day minimum stay is required).

Camping Many sites dot the shores of the lake. *Strandbadcamping Buchhorn* (☎ 071-46 65 45), Arbon, *Strandbad Amriswil* (☎ 071-63 47 73), west of Romanshorn at Uttwil, and *Fischerhaus* (☎ 072-75 49 03), Kreuzlingen, are all reasonably situated. Opening times for these sites vary slightly, but they are all closed from November to March.

Recommended camping grounds in Germany include: *Camping Hagnau* (☎ 07545-64 13), four km east of Meersburg (one of three camping grounds side-by-side); *Camping Seeperle* (☎ 07556-54 54) in Uhldingen-Seefelden, five km west of Meersburg; and *Campingplatz Lindau-Zech* (☎ 08382-7 22 36), three km south-east of Lindau proper.

Seecamping (☎ 05574-31 895/6), Bodangasse 7, offers a lakeside site 3 km west of Bregenz train station. It is open mid-May to mid-September and prices are 50AS per person, 45AS per tent and 45AS per car.

Hostels Prices in Germany are lower for people under 27 (so-called juniors). There is no junior/senior distinction in Bregenz or the Swiss hostels. All the hostels listed are IYHF affiliated and include breakfast.

Switzerland Kreuzlingen's *youth hostel* (☎ 072-75 26 63), Promenadenstrasse 7, is 10 minutes' walk from Kreuzlingen Hafen station (turn left, then left again over the tracks). It features communal showers and good buffet breakfasts in a fine old building situated in parkland. Dorms cost Sfr15.20 and it is closed from mid-December to early March.

The *youth hostel* at Romanshorn (☎ 071-63 17 17), Gottfried Keller Strasse 6, is just five minutes from the station. Beds start at Sfr16 and it is closed from November to mid-February. Rorschach's *youth hostel* (☎ 071-41 54 11) is for groups only.

Germany The *youth hostel* (☎ 07531-3 32 60) at Allmannshohe 18 in Constance is closed during winter and costs DM15.50/20.50 for juniors/seniors. Take bus Nos 1 or 4 from the station. The *youth hostel* (☎ 07551-42 04), Alte Nussdorfer Strasse 26, in Überlingen, 15 km west of Meersburg, costs DM17/22.50. The *youth hostel* (☎ 08382-58 13) at Herbergsweg 11 in Lindau is closed until 1994, and as it's in Bavaria, only juniors may stay there. Friedrichshafen's *youth hostel* (☎ 07321-420 45) is at Liststrasse 15 (DM16.50/21).

Austria The IYHF *youth hostel* (☎ 05574-22 867), Belruptstrasse 16A, Bregenz, is open April to September. Curfew is 10 pm and dorms shut from 9 am to 5 pm but you can leave your bags in reception during the day. Beds cost 98AS.

Hotels & Pensions Most places round the lake are smaller-scale establishments, so book ahead in season. Contact tourist offices well in advance for lists of holiday apartments.

Switzerland The cheapest place in the centre of Rorschach is *Hotel Löwen* (☎ 071-41 38 98), Hauptstrasse 92, with fair-sized singles/doubles for Sfr40/70. Each has a shower cubicle in the room. Downstairs there's a British-style pub with lots of foliage and live piano music nightly. A couple of doors along the road at No 88 is *Hotel Jud* (☎ 071-41 76 44), with nicely proportioned rooms for Sfr70/120 with own shower, toilet and TV.

At Horn, the next resort along the shore, there are private rooms available from Frau Baumann (☎ 071-41 26 52) at the bakery (Bäckerei), Seestrasse 72. They're usually only available in the summer and cost Sfr20 per person without breakfast.

Hotel Krone (☎ 071-46 10 87), Bahnhofstrasse 20, Arbon, requires a four-day minimum stay for its rooms at Sfr25 per person. Also conveniently central is *Pension Garni Sonnenhof* (☎ 071-46 15 10), Rebenstrasse 18, which costs from Sfr40 per person. *Hotel Park*, (☎ 071-46 11 19), Parkstrasse 7, off Bahnhofstrasse in the centre, has rooms painted in gentle colours for Sfr80/130, all with shower, toilet and TV.

Romanshorn has several hotels close to the train station but they're all rather pricey. An exception is *Bodan* (☎ 071-63 15 02), opposite and to the right, which has singles/doubles for Sfr35/70 using showers in the hall. Doubles with private shower/toilet are Sfr90.

In Kreuzlingen, try *Schweizerland* (☎ 072-72 17 17), near the border at Hauptstrasse 6. Basic singles/doubles are Sfr43/77, rising to Sfr53/97 with private bathroom. To get there from the main station, walk left then first left. *Bahnhof-Post* (☎ 072-72 79 72), Bahnhofstrasse, has more facilities and is right opposite the main station. Singles/doubles cost Sfr48/90 or Sfr75/116.

Germany In Constance, check the accommodation board outside the tourist office. The central *Pension Gretel* (☎ 07531-2 46 35) at Zollernstrasse 6-8, has rooms for DM40 per person. Unfortunately the management is unreliable and unfriendly; telephone reservations may not be honoured. Also central and more amenable is *Pension Graf* (☎ 07531-2 14 86), Wiesenstrasse 2, with singles/doubles for DM47/70 and triples/quads for DM99/105.

In Meersburg, head up the steep hill to *Gasthaus zum Letzten Heller* (☎ 07532-61 49), Daisendorfer Strasse 41, for singles/

doubles at DM35/65 (great food, too). For splurging windsurfers who want to stay where they can overlook the action, the hot spot to sleep and eat is the *Hotel-Café Off* (☎ 07532-3 33) by the water at Uferpromenade 51. At DM90/140 for singles/doubles it's not cheap, but the people, location and balconies are great.

In Lindau, the best deal on the island is at *Gästehaus Limmer* (☎ 08382-58 77), In der Grub 16, with singles/doubles for DM32/60. *Gästehaus Tannheim* (☎ 08382-37 36) is near the water on the mainland at Bregenzer Strasse 16. Singles/doubles are DM40/70.

Austria In Bregenz, lists of private rooms (from 140AS per person), apartments (from 450AS) and pensions (from 170AS per person) are supplied by the tourist office. A surcharge normally applies for a single night's stay. Cheap and in the centre is *Pension Günz* (☎ (05574) 43 657), Anton Schneider Strasse 38, with rooms from AS190 per person. It's only open from Easter to 1 October. *Pension Traube* (☎ 05574-424 01), Anton Schneider Strasse 34, has rooms from AS240 per person.

Places to Eat

If you eat anywhere overlooking the water, including a ship, you're paying for the view and the food rarely lives up to the prices. Fresh fish from the lake is widely available.

Switzerland Rorschach has a better than average, licensed *Coop* restaurant with menus from Sfr10 and a salad buffet from Sfr3.80. It's around the back of the post office on Poststrasse, and is open weekdays until 6.30 pm, Saturday to 4 pm and Sunday to 7 pm. The supermarket section stays open until 9 pm on Friday but it's closed on Sunday.

Across the road is *Pizzeria Krone*, with prices starting at Sfr9.50 (open daily). *Jud* (see Places to Stay) offers well-prepared platefuls of fish, schnitzel or steak for Sfr15 to Sfr25. In Horn, the *Hotel Schiff*, Seestrasse 74, offers a welcome change from the usual with its South American and Spanish specialities (Sfr12.50 to Sfr25). It's closed on Tuesday in the off-season.

The cheap choice in Arbon is the *Migros* restaurant and supermarket, opposite and to the left of the train station. Also for the budget-conscious is *Hotel Krone* (see Places to Stay), offering inexpensive pizzas and a Tagesmenu for Sfr9. Those on a spending spree can wander into *Wirtschaft zum Römerhof* (☎ 071-46 17 08), Hauptstrasse, in a distinctive old building attached to the ancient town fortifications. Main courses are around Sfr30 and it is closed on Wednesday. *Hotel Park* (see Places to Stay) is a good place for fish from the lake for around Sfr20.

A choice of eateries awaits opposite the train station in Romanshorn. *Bodan* (see Places to Stay) sometimes has interesting daily specials for around Sfr17. *Hotel Bahnhof* has hot food daily from Sfr7 to Sfr38, and *Pizzeria Mona Lisa* has pizza and pasta from Sfr9.50 (closed Tuesday).

In Kreuzlingen there's a *Coop* supermarket five minutes' from the main station with two restaurants; head left then look for the shop sign down the sidestreet. Ultra-cheap is the self-service restaurant in the *EPA* department store, on the corner of Hauptstrasse and Parkstrasse. Nearby at Hauptstrasse 82 is the *Park Café*, with a good selection of dishes for vegetarians for Sfr8 to Sfr15.50 (closed Monday). *Restaurant Seeburg* (☎ 072-75 47 75), by the youth hostel, offers quality cuisine in a fine setting. Main dishes start at Sfr15 (closed Tuesday and Wednesday).

Germany In Constance, make a habit of eating and drinking at *Seekuh* at Konzilstrasse 4, a student-type bar that dishes up great food and company. Salads, pasta and pizza cost DM5 to DM10 and the conversation is free and easy. It's open every evening until 1 am. Another good place in a similar mould is *Sedir*, Hofhalde 11, serving tasty bowls of pasta for around DM8 (open daily). Also visit the university (Mensa) for cheap lunches. *Gasthaus Burengeneral*, Brotlaube 4, is the place to try fish from the lake for around DM20 (closed Thursday).

One of the best places to eat in Meersburg is *Gasthof zum Bären*, at Marktplatz 11 in the story-book centre of town. The Gilowsky-Karrer clan prepares huge portions of food (and has singles/doubles for DM58/110). *Winzerstube zum Becher* (☎ 07532-60 19), Höllgasse 4, is highly recommended if you can afford to pay for top quality. Main dishes start at DM30 and it's closed on Monday; reserve ahead for the balcony seating. In nearby Hagnau, try the cheerful *König-Stüble* at Seestrasse 10, for creative personal pizzas from DM7.50 to DM13.50.

Life in Lindau isn't easy when it comes to food, but the friendly *Früchtehaus Hannes*, at In der Grub 36, makes up for all of the bland tourist eateries. It offers fruit, vegetables, meats, fish, pastas and prepared salads, all sold by weight. Put together a picnic to eat outside or in the small café in the rear (open weekdays to 6 pm and Saturday to 1 pm). The touristy *Goldenes Lamm Restaurant* on Paradiesplatz has a good three-course menu for DM20, other specialities from DM16 and occasional live music.

Austria One of the cheapest eating-houses in Bregenz is *Restaurant Charly*, Anton Schneider Strasse 19, which serves pizza and pasta from 55AS. It is open daily to 11.30 pm except on Sunday when it shuts at 2 pm. For Austrian food, try *Gasthaus Maurachbund*, Maurachgasse 11, with main dishes from AS80 to AS190, or the more expensive but atmospheric *Alte Weinstube Zur Ilge*, Maurachgasse 6. Both are closed Sunday.

Getting There & Away

Direct trains run hourly from Schaffhausen to Kreuzlingen and the journey takes one hour. Excursions to the lake are easy from St Gallen: direct trains go to Romanshorn and Rorschach, and a direct bus to Arbon and Rorschach (Sfr6.80). Constance has train connections every one to two hours to Zürich and Donaueschingen (DM21). Trains from Munich go to Lindau (2½ hours). Trains from Switzerland to Bregenz go via St Margrethen. Bregenz is on the main express rail route through Austria, with regular direct trains to Innsbruck, Salzburg and Vienna.

Access to the lake by road is good on all sides. From Zürich, the N1 (E60) motorway runs north-east via Winterthur and St Gallen, to the Austrian border near Rorschach. The N7 branches off just after Winterthur and leads to Kreuzlingen.

Getting Around

Train & Bus Although trains link Bregenz, Lindau, Friedrichshafen and Constance, buses often provide the easiest land connections between these places. Meersburg isn't even on the railway line, and can be reached by bus from Friedrichshafen or by car ferry from Constance (see the following Boat section). On the Swiss side, train or bus is equally convenient. Single rail fares from Rorschach Hafen are: Horn Sfr2, Arbon Sfr2.80, Romanshorn Sfr5 and Kreuzlingen Sfr10.60.

Car The B31 hugs the northern shore of the lake but it can get busy. Likewise on the southern shore, where highway 13 shadows the course of the railway line around the lake, linking all the Swiss resorts mentioned in this section.

Boat The most enjoyable way to get around is by boat. Ferries follow a number of routes, travelling across, along, or around the lake from late April to early October, with the more frequent services starting in late May. Eurail and Interrail passes get 50% off. The Swiss Pass and the Thurgau day pass (see Getting Around in the chapter introduction) are valid only for the Swiss side of the lake. For boat information in Romanshorn ring ☎ 071-63 14 23, in Bregenz ring ☎ 05574-42 868 and in Constance ring ☎ 07531-28 13 98.

Bregenz to Constance by boat (via the German shore) takes three hours 30 minutes with up to six departures per day (DM18.60). Boats also cruise along the Rhine from Kreuzlingen and Constance all the way to Schaffhausen, via the island of Reichenau and Stein am Rhein. The total journey takes three hours 40 minutes heading downstream to Schaffhausen and 4½ hours going the other way (Sfr23 in either direction).

Between Meersburg and Constance there's a car ferry that sails all year-round; every 15 minutes in the day, every 30 minutes in the evening and hourly all through the night. The fare is only DM2, plus DM9 per car. In Meersburg, boats depart only a few minutes' walk from the centre, but in Constance, you need to get to/from Staad (bus No 1 from the Bahnhof). Another car ferry sails during the day between Romanshorn and Friedrichshafen. Departures are hourly in the summer and every two hours from November to March. The fare is Sfr6.40 plus from Sfr21 per car, and the journey takes 40 minutes. The boat landing stage in Romanshorn is directly outside the train station.

Liechtenstein

In some ways you could be forgiven for thinking Liechtenstein is part of Switzerland. The Swiss franc is the legal currency, all travel documents valid for Switzerland are also valid for Liechtenstein, and the only border regulations are on the Austrian side. Blink and you might miss it, the country measures just 25 km from north to south, and an average of six km from west to east. Switzerland also represents Liechtenstein abroad and in foreign policy (subject to consultation).

But a closer look reveals that Liechtenstein is quite distinct. The ties with Switzerland began only in 1923 with the signing of a customs and monetary union. Before that, it had a similar agreement with Austria-Hungary from 1852 to 1919. Unlike in Switzerland, there is no military service and no army. In fact, the country last went to war in 1866; soldiers guarded an Alpine pass, and never once made contact with the enemy. The armed might of Liechtenstein, numbering 80 men, was disbanded in 1868.

It also has its own reigning monarch. The present dynasty of rulers has controlled lands here since 1699, mostly by remote control from their estates in the former Czechoslovakia. Prince Franz Josef II was the first ruler to actually live in Liechtenstein, in the castle above Vaduz, the capital and seat of government. He died in 1989 after a reign of 51 years and was succeeded by his son, Prince Hans Adam II.

Although it shares the Swiss telephone and postal system, Liechtenstein issues its own postage stamps. It is a prosperous country and the people are proud of their independence.

Facts about the Country

Liechtenstein was colonised by the Rhaetians after 800 BC and conquered by the

Liechtenstein's Coat of Arms

Romans in 15 BC. Christianity appeared in the region in the 4th century. The country's modern history began when Prince Johann Adam of Liechtenstein purchased the Lordship of Schellenberg (1699) and the County of Vaduz (1712) from the impoverished German nobles who had previously governed them. Although he already owned vast tracts of land in Austria, Hungary, Bohemia and Moravia, the purpose of this purchase was to qualify for a vote in the Diet of Princes. It became a principality on 23 January 1719 by decree of the Holy Roman Emperor, Charles VI.

Liechtenstein remained a principality under the Holy Roman Empire until 1806, when Napoleon drafted it into his Confederacy of the Rhine as part of his machinations against Prussia. Following Napoleon's fall and the Congress of Vienna in 1815, it joined the German Confederation, before achieving full sovereign independence when that fell apart in 1866. The modern constitution was drawn up in 1921. Even today the prince retains the power to dissolve parliament and must approve every act before it becomes law.

Prince Hans Adam (full title: His Serene Highness Prince Johannes Adam von und zu Liechtenstein) succeeded Franz Josef II in November 1989, although he had effectively been running the state since 1984. He has always tried to stamp his own authority on the government, going as far as to dissolve parliament in 1989 when politicians failed to give support to his plan to build a new museum for his art collection. The prince is also keen to ensure that the country doesn't blindly follow Switzerland's lead in international affairs, and campaigned actively for EEA (European Economic Area) membership, even threatening to renew the family tradition of living abroad if this policy was rejected. In December 1992, shortly after the Swiss 'No' to the same issue, 55% of Liechtensteiners voted in favour of EEA membership. The government is currently negotiating with Switzerland about the ramifications for the open border between the two countries.

Despite its small size, Liechtenstein has two political regions, Upper and Lower, yielding a total of 25 parliamentary members. As in Switzerland, local communities (11 in number) have a fair degree of autonomy. There are three distinct geographical areas: the Rhine valley in the west, the edge of the Tirolean Alps in the south-east, and the northern lowlands. The current population is under 30,000, with a third of that total made up of foreign residents.

Liechtenstein is well known as a tax haven, and a significant proportion of national income is derived from this status. The late infamous entrepreneur Robert Maxwell was one person who took advantage of the discretion and secrecy of the banking services. The government is understandably sensitive about bad press from acceptance of funds from dubious origins. Although the banks have agreed to tighter controls, there are no plans to do away with numbered bank accounts.

Wine production is also important to the economy. Liechtenstein is one of the richest countries per capita in the world, and unemployment is only an isolated phenomenon. Such is its economic strength, that it even employs guest workers from affluent Switzerland!

The abbreviation for the country is FL, which is used on vehicle registration plates. Nearly 90% of the population are Catholic. The official language is German, although most people also speak French and English. The German/Austrian greeting *Grüss Gott* is more common than the Swiss *Grüezi*. Women were given the vote only as recently as 1984 (the men claim they didn't want it). In September 1990, Liechtenstein became a member of the United Nations.

Facts for the Visitor

See the Switzerland Facts for the Visitor chapter for practical details not covered here.

Tourist information abroad is distributed through Swiss National Tourist Offices. Local offices in Liechtenstein are well organised and you can pick up the excellent *Tourism Handbook* which tells you everything you might want to know about the country. A hotel and pension list is given out that covers the whole country.

Prices are comparable to those in Switzerland, but budget travellers will lament the lack of cheap self-service restaurants. Shops are usually open Monday to Friday from 8 am to noon and 1.30 to 6.30 pm, and Saturday from 8 am to 4 pm. Banks share the same weekday hours except they shut around 4.30 pm.

Liechtenstein does not celebrate Switzerland's National Festival (1 August), but it makes up by having a public holiday on all the main Catholic feast days, as well as on Labour day on 1 May. The birthday of Franz Josef II on 15 August is also celebrated. Although the stamps are different,

Liechtenstein

To St Gallen
& Lake
Constance

To
Vienna

Sennwald   Ruggell

0   2.5   5 km

Schellenberg Feldkirch
Mauren

Eschen
Haag   Benderrn   Schaanwald

Nendeln

N13   16   Planken   AUSTRIA

Buchs   Schaan   Youth
Hostel

SWITZERLAND   VADUZ
Gaflei
Silum
Sevelen   Triesenberg

Steg

Triesen   Malbun

Trübbach

Balzers

To Zürich

Sargans

postal rates are the same as for Switzerland. The telephone code for all Liechtenstein is 075.

It would be slightly unfair – but not very far removed from the truth – to say that if Liechtenstein was not a separate country, few people would bother to visit. As it is, many people just come here for stamps – a stamp in the passport and stamps on a postcard for the folks back home. But it's worth lingering to appreciate the prince's art collection, and to enjoy the scenery.

Getting There & Away

There is no airport (the nearest is in Zürich), and only a few trains stop within the country at Schaan. Getting there by postbus is easiest. There are approximately two buses an hour from the Swiss border towns of Buchs and Sargans which stop in Vaduz (Sfr3 single fare).

By road, route 16 from Switzerland passes through Liechtenstein via Schaan and terminates at Feldkirch in Austria. The N13 follows the Rhine along the Swiss/Liechtenstein border; minor roads cross into Liechtenstein at each motorway exit.

Getting Around

Postbus travel within Liechtenstein is cheap and reliable; fares cost Sfr2 or Sfr3, the higher rate is for journeys exceeding 13 km (such as Vaduz to Malbun). The only drawback is that some services finish early: for example, the last of the hourly buses from Vaduz to Malbun leaves at 5.10 pm (6.10 pm in summer). Get a timetable from the Vaduz tourist office.

For car hire, contact Hertz (☎ 232 02 22), Gewerbeweg 13, Vaduz, or Autovermietung Nolo AG (☎ 232 94 66), Landstrasse 45, Vaduz. There are eight taxi companies in the country; in Vaduz, ring (☎ 233 35 35 or ☎ 232 18 66.

For bicycle hire, go to the Swiss train station in Buchs or Sargans, or try Hans Melliger (☎ 232 16 06), Kirchstrasse 10, Vaduz. Prices are Sfr20 per day, and bikes can be picked up the evening before. It is open weekdays to 6.30 pm (except half-day closing on Tuesday) and Saturday to 2 pm.

Vaduz

The capital of Liechtenstein, with less than 5000 inhabitants, is really no more than a village. But it still contains most of the points of interest in the country.

Orientation & Information

Vaduz is the geographical and political centre of the country. Two one-way streets, Städtle and Äulestrasse, diverge and then rejoin, thereby enclosing the centre of town.

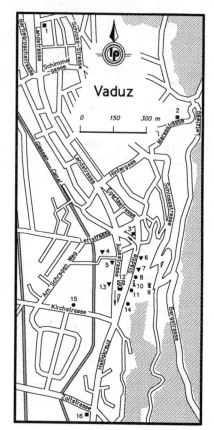

Vaduz

0   150   300 m

■ **PLACES TO STAY**

1   Hotel Falknis
2   Parkhotel Sonnenhof
3   Hotel Engel
16 Gasthof Au

▼ **PLACES TO EAT**

4   Denner Supermarket
5   Old Castle Inn
6   Au Premier
7   Café Wolf
13 Café Amann

OTHER

8   Liechtenstein State Art Collection
9   Vaduz Castle
10 Tourist Office
11 Postage Stamp Museum
12 Post Office & Postbus Departures
14 Liechtenstein National Museum
15 Hans Melliger (Bike Rental)

Everything of importance is near this small area, including the bus station.

The Vaduz tourist office (☎ 075-232 14 43), Städtle 37, has a free room-finding service and information on the whole country. It is open Monday to Friday from 8 am to noon and 1.30 to 5.30 pm. The office is also open May to September on Saturday from 9 am to noon and 1.30 to 4 pm; and July and August on Sunday from 9 am to noon and 1.30 to 4 pm. Staff members are kept busy putting souvenir stamps in people's passports (Sfr1).

The main post office, Äulestrasse 38, is open Monday to Friday from 8 am to 6.30 pm, and on Saturday from 8 to 11 am. The post office has an adjoining philatelic section that is open similar hours.

Things to See & Do
Although the **castle** is not open to the public, it is worth climbing up the hill for a closer look. There's a good view of Vaduz and the mountains, and a network of marked walking trails along the ridge. The **National Museum** (Landesmuseum), Städtle 43, has coins, weapons, folklore exhibits and an informative slide show in English of the history of Liechtenstein. The museum is open daily from 10 am to noon and 1.30 to 5.30 pm between May and October. The rest of the year it's open Tuesday to Sunday from 2 to 5.30 pm, and entry costs Sfr2 (students Sfr1).

The **State Art Collection** (Staatliche Kunstsammlung) at Städtle 37 is wholly devoted to temporary exhibitions that invariably contain something special. It includes parts of the art collection that the princes of Liechtenstein have acquired over the centuries. It is open daily from 10 am to noon and 1.30 to 5.30 pm (5 pm November to March). Admission costs Sfr3 (students Sfr1.50).

The **Postage Stamp Museum**, next to the tourist office, contains 300 frames of national stamps issued since 1912. Located in just one room, it is free and open daily the same hours as the state art collection. Look out for processions and fireworks on 15 August, Liechtenstein's national holiday.

It is possible to sample the wines from the prince's own vineyard, but only for groups of 10 or more people. Advance reservations are essential; contact the Hofkellerei (☎ 232 10 18), Feldstrasse 4.

Places to Stay

Vaduz has no camping. The only sites are at Bendern (☎ 373 12 11), by the river in the north, and *Camping Mittagspitze* (☎ 392 26 86), south of Triesen. Both are open year-round.

The IYHF *Schaan-Vaduz Youth Hostel* (☎ 232 50 22; see the Liechenstein map), Untere Rütigasse 6, is open from January to mid-November, except for two weeks' closure around the end of February. It's newly renovated, and dorm beds cost from Sfr16.30. Reception is closed from 10 am to 5 pm, when the doors are also locked. It is 20 minutes' walk from Buchs or 10 minutes' walk from Schaan railway stations. Take the road to Vaduz and turn right at Marianumstrasse.

Hotel Falknis (☎ 232 63 77), Landstrasse, is a 15-minute walk from the centre of Vaduz towards Schaan. Reasonable singles/doubles are Sfr40/80 with a shower on each floor. *Gasthof Au* (☎ 232 11 17), Austrasse 2, south of the centre, is the only other budget option in Vaduz. Doubles with shower start at Sfr90, or Sfr70 without. Eating is pleasant and inexpensive in its garden restaurant.

Hotel Engel (☎ 232 03 13), Städtle 13, has singles/doubles with private shower and TV starting at Sfr98/120, or Sfr120/145 if you want a bath and balcony. *Parkhotel Sonnenhof* (☎ 232 11 92) is more luxurious and has an indoor swimming pool (free) and sauna (Sfr25). There are fine views from its

elevated perspective and the rooms are bright and cheerful. Prices start at Sfr150/260 and it has a guests-only restaurant. It's in the north-east of the village on Grasiger Weg.

Places to Eat & Drink

Restaurants are expensive in Vaduz, so look out for lunch-time specials. Opposite the car park on Äulestrasse is *Denner* supermarket, open to 6.30 pm weekdays and 4 pm on Saturday.

The best choice at the lower end of the scale for a sit-down meal is *Hotel Engel* (see Places to Stay). It has meals from Sfr13 and house specialities for around Sfr25. A tasty dish is *Schwingerhörnli* for Sfr13.50. This pasta carbonara-style concoction comes with a bowl of crushed apples that you can eat simultaneously or treat as a dessert.

Old Castle Inn, on Äulestrasse, has main meals starting from Sfr14.50 and a lunch menu with soup for Sfr15.50. It's like an English pub inside, and has an outside terrace (open daily). Another good place to try is *Café Amann* at No 56. Its daily lunch menu with soup is Sfr14.50, and other meals and snacks cost Sfr4 to Sfr18.50. It is open until 7 pm on weekdays and 1 pm on Saturday.

Café Wolf, Städtle 29, has lunch menus with soup for Sfr18.50. In the shop on the ground floor you can gorge on quality confectionery. One of its specialities is

Vaduz Castle

cognac-filled chocolate snail-shapes (Sfr11 for seven). It's closed on Monday. Hotel Real, Städtle 21, has *Au Premier* (☎ 232 22 22), the best restaurant in Liechtenstein. Enjoy seasonal specialities and locally produced wine in an interior where the lighting comes from dozens of shimmering cylinders. Main courses top Sfr40 and it is open daily.

Below ground at Hotel Falknis (see Places to Stay) is *Caruso* a lively, expensive bar packed with bright young things in a dark, mirrored environment.

Around Vaduz

The lowland (Unterland) of northern Liechtenstein is dotted with small communities. There's little to do except enjoy the quiet pace of life and view the village churches. Pottery-making is demonstrated at Schaedler Keramik (☎ 373 14 14) in **Nendeln**. Admission is free and opening hours are Monday to Friday from 8 am to noon and 1.30 to 5 pm. The Rofenberg in **Eschen-Nendel** was formerly a place of public execution and is now the site of the Holy Cross Chapel. **Schellenberg** has a Russian monument, commemorating the night in 1945 when a band of 500 heavily armed Russian soldiers crossed the border. They had been fighting for the German army, but they came to defect, not attack.

Triesenberg, on a terrace above Vaduz, commands an excellent view over the Rhine valley and has a pretty, onion-domed church. There's also a museum devoted to the Walser community which journeyed from Valais to settle here in the 13th century. It is open every afternoon except Monday and admission costs Sfr2 or Sfr1 for students. The Walser dialect is still spoken in this community.

In the extreme south of the country is **Balzers**, which is dominated by the soaring sides of Gutenberg Castle. The interior of the castle is closed for long-term renovations.

Malbun

Nestled amid the mountains in the southeast, Malbun is Liechtenstein's ski resort. The skiing is inexpensive if not too extensive. Runs are for beginners and intermediates, with just a couple of stretches for experts. There are two ski schools in the resort. A pass for all ski lifts and chair lifts costs Sfr19 (children Sfr12) for half a day, Sfr29 (Sfr19) for a day or Sfr120 (Sfr75) for one week. Equipment rental costs Sfr37 including skis, shoes and poles, from the sports shop (☎ 263 37 55) or ski school (☎ 262 29 34). The sports shop changes money but charges Sfr5 commission, so change in Vaduz or use the bankomat for Eurocheque cards. Two km from Malbun is the Väluna Valley, the main area for cross country skiing. The road from Vaduz terminates at Malbun. The tourist office (☎ 2 65 77) is by the bus stop and is open daily (except Thursday and Sunday) from 9 am to noon, and 1.30 to 5pm (1 to 4 pm on Saturday). It's closed during the low season from the end of April to early June, and mid-October to mid-December. For recorded snow reports in German, call ☎ 232 80 80.

Places to Stay & Eat There are nine hotels in this small village, nearly all with restaurants. By the bus stop is *Alpenhotel Malbun*(☎ 232 11 81), which is under the same management as the nearby *Galina* (☎ 232 34 24). Prices per person start at Sfr40 for a (☎ 232 11 81), which is under the same management as the nearby *Galina* (☎ 232 34 24). Prices per person start at Sfr40 for a basic room or Sfr70 for one with private bath. Half and full-pension are available at favourable rates, and there is an annex with a swimming pool.

Turna (☎ 232 34 21), by the Sareis ski lift, has doubles starting at Sfr70 in summer and Sfr80 in winter, or Sfr90/100 in summer/winter with private shower and toilet. All three places have inexpensive restaurants with sunny outside terraces, and Turna also has a bar and disco.

Index

MAPS

TEXT

Map references are in **bold** type.

PLANET TALK
Lonely Planet's FREE quarterly newsletter

We love hearing from you and think you'd like to hear from us.

When...is the right time to see reindeer in Finland?
Where...can you hear the best palm-wine music in Ghana?
How...do you get from Asunción to Areguá by steam train?
What...is the best way to see India?

For the answer to these and many other questions read PLANET TALK.

Every issue is packed with up-to-date travel news and advice including:

- *a letter from Lonely Planet founders Tony and Maureen Wheeler*
- *travel diary from a Lonely Planet author - find out what it's really like out on the road*
- *feature article on an important and topical travel issue*
- *a selection of recent letters from our readers*
- *the latest travel news from all over the world*
- *details on Lonely Planet's new and forthcoming releases*

To join our mailing list contact any Lonely Planet office (address below).

LONELY PLANET PUBLICATIONS
Australia: PO Box 617, Hawthorn 3122, Victoria (tel: 03-819 1877)
USA: Embarcadero West, 155 Filbert St, Suite 251, Oakland, CA 94607 (tel: 510-893 8555)
TOLL FREE: (800) 275-8555
UK: 10 Barley Mow Passage, Chiswick, London W4 4PH (tel: 081-742 3161)
France: 71 bis rue du Cardinal Lemoine – 75005 Paris (tel: 1-46 34 00 58)

Also available: Lonely Planet T-shirts. 100% heavyweight cotton (S, M, L, XL)

Lonely Planet guides to Europe

Eastern Europe on a shoestring
This guide has opened up a whole new world for travellers – Albania, Bulgaria, Czechoslovakia, eastern Germany, Hungary, Poland, Romania and the former republics of Yugoslavia.
'...a thorough, well-researched book. Only a fool would go East without it.' – *Great Expeditions*

Mediterranean Europe on a shoestring
Details on hundreds of galleries, museums and architectural masterpieces and information on outdoor activities including hiking, sailing and skiing. Information on travelling in Albania, Andorra, Cyprus, France, Greece, Italy, Malta, Morocco, Portugal, Spain, Tunisia, Turkey and the former republics of Yugoslavia.

Scandinavian & Baltic Europe on a shoestring
A comprehensive guide to travelling in this region including details on galleries, festivals and museums, as well as outdoor activities, national parks and wildlife. Countries featured are Denmark, Estonia, the Faroe Islands, Finland, Iceland, Latvia, Lithuania, Norway and Sweden.

Western Europe on a shoestring
This long-awaited guide covers all of Western Europe's well-loved sights and provides routes for cycling and driving tours, plus details on hiking, climbing and skiing. All the travel facts on Andorra, Austria, Belgium, Britain, France, Germany, Ireland, Italy, Liechtenstein, Luxembourg, Netherlands, Portugal, Spain and Switzerland.

Baltic States & Kaliningrad – travel survival kit
The Baltic States burst on to the world scene almost from nowhere in the late 1980s. Now that travellers are free to move around the region they will discover nations with a rich and colourful history and culture, and a welcoming attitude to all travellers.

Dublin – city guide
Where to enjoy a pint of Guinness and a plate of Irish stew, where to see spectacular Georgian architecture or experience Irish hospitality – Dublin city guide will ensure you won't miss out on anything.

Finland – travel survival kit
Finland is an intriguing blend of Swedish and Russian influences. With its medieval stone castles, picturesque wooden houses, vast forest and lake district, and interesting wildlife, it is a wonderland to delight any traveller.

France – travel survival kit
Stylish, diverse, celebrated by romantics and revolutionaries alike, France is a destination that's always in fashion. A comprehensive guide packed with invaluable advice.

Greece – travel survival kit
Famous ruins, secluded beaches, sumptuous food, sun-drenched islands, ancient pathways and much more are covered in this comprehensive guide to this ever-popular destination.

Hungary – travel survival kit
Formerly seen as the gateway to eastern Europe, Hungary is a romantic country of music, wine and folklore. This guide contains detailed back-

ground information on Hungary's cultural and historical past as well as practical advice on the many activities available to travellers.

Ireland – travel survival kit
Ireland is one of Europe's least 'spoilt' countries. Green, relaxed and welcoming, it does not take travellers long before they feel at ease. An entertaining and comprehensive guide to this troubled country.

Italy – travel survival kit
Italy is art – not just in the galleries and museums. You'll discover its charm on the streets and in the markets, in rustic hill-top villages and in the glamorous city boutiques. A thorough guide to the thousands of attractions of this ever-popular destination.

Poland – travel survival kit
With the collapse of communism, Poland has opened up to travellers, revealing a rich cultural heritage. This guide will help you make the most of this safe and friendly country.

Turkey – a travel survival kit
This acclaimed guide takes you from Istanbul bazaars to Mediterranean beaches, from historic battlegrounds to the stamping grounds of St Paul, Alexander the Great, Emperor Constantine and King Croesus.

USSR – travel survival kit
Invaluable advice on getting around and beating red tape for individual and group travellers alike. This comprehensive guide includes an unsanitised historical background and complete information on art and culture. Over 130 reliable maps, and all place names are given in Cyrillic script. Includes the independent states.

Trekking in Greece
Mountainous landscape, the solitude of ancient pathways and secluded beaches await those who dare to extend their horizons beyond Athens and the antiquities. Covers the main trekking regions and includes contoured maps of trekking routes.

Trekking in Spain
Aimed at both overnight trekkers and day hikers, this guidebook includes useful maps and full details on hikes in some of Spain's most beautiful wilderness areas.

Also available:
Eastern Europe phrasebook
Discover the most enjoyable way to get around and make friends in Bulgarian, Czech, Hungarian, Polish, Romanian and Slovak.

Mediterranean Europe phrasebook
Ask for directions to the galleries and museums in Albanian, Greek, Italian, Macedonian, Maltese, Serbian & Croatian and Slovene.

Scandinavian Europe phrasebook
Find your way around the ski trails and enjoy the local festivals in Danish, Finnish, Icelandic, Norwegian and Swedish.

Western Europe phrasebook
Show your appreciation for the great masters in Basque, Catalan, Dutch, French, German, Irish, Portuguese and Spanish (Castilian).

Lonely Planet Guidebooks

Lonely Planet guidebooks cover every accessible part of Asia as well as Australia, the Pacific, South America, Africa, the Middle East, Europe and parts of North America. There are five series: *travel survival kits*, covering a country for a range of budgets; *shoestring guides* with compact information for low-budget travel in a major region; *walking guides*; *city guides* and *phrasebooks*.

Australia & the Pacific
Australia
Australian phrasebook
Bushwalking in Australia
Islands of Australia's Great Barrier Reef
Outback Australia
Fiji
Fijian phrasebook
Melbourne city guide
Micronesia
New Caledonia
New South Wales
New Zealand
Tramping in New Zealand
Papua New Guinea
Bushwalking in Papua New Guinea
Papua New Guinea phrasebook
Rarotonga & the Cook Islands
Samoa
Solomon Islands
Sydney city guide
Tahiti & French Polynesia
Tonga
Vanuatu
Victoria

South-East Asia
Bali & Lombok
Bangkok city guide
Cambodia
Indonesia
Indonesia phrasebook
Laos
Malaysia, Singapore & Brunei
Myanmar (Burma)
Burmese phrasebook
Philippines
Pilipino phrasebook
Singapore city guide
South-East Asia on a shoestring
Thailand
Thai phrasebook
Vietnam
Vietnamese phrasebook

North-East Asia
China
Beijing city guide
Cantonese phrasebook
Mandarin Chinese phrasebook
Hong Kong, Macau & Canton
Japan
Japanese phrasebook
Korea
Korean phrasebook
Mongolia
North-East Asia on a shoestring
Seoul city guide
Taiwan
Tibet
Tibet phrasebook
Tokyo city guide

Middle East
Arab Gulf States
Egypt & the Sudan
Arabic (Egyptian) phrasebook
Iran
Israel
Jordan & Syria
Middle East
Turkish phrasebook
Trekking in Turkey
Yemen

Indian Ocean
Madagascar & Comoros
Maldives & Islands of the East Indian Ocean
Mauritius, Réunion & Seychelles

Mail Order

Lonely Planet guidebooks are distributed worldwide. They are also available by mail order from Lonely Planet, so if you have difficulty finding a title please write to us. US and Canadian residents should write to Embarcadero West, 155 Filbert St, Suite 251, Oakland CA 94607, USA; European residents should write to 10 Barley Mow Passage, Chiswick, London W4 4PH; and residents of other countries to PO Box 617, Hawthorn, Victoria 3122, Australia.

Indian Subcontinent
Bangladesh
India
Hindi/Urdu phrasebook
Trekking in the Indian Himalaya
Karakoram Highway
Kashmir, Ladakh & Zanskar
Nepal
Trekking in the Nepal Himalaya
Nepali phrasebook
Pakistan
Sri Lanka
Sri Lanka phrasebook

Africa
Africa on a shoestring
Central Africa
East Africa
Trekking in East Africa
Kenya
Swahili phrasebook
Morocco, Algeria & Tunisia
Arabic (Moroccan) phrasebook
South Africa, Lesotho & Swaziland
Zimbabwe, Botswana & Namibia
West Africa.

Central America & the Caribbean
Baja California
Central America on a shoestring
Costa Rica
Eastern Caribbean
Guatemala, Belize & Yucatán: La Ruta Maya
Mexico

Europe
Baltic States & Kaliningrad
Dublin city guide
Eastern Europe on a shoestring
Eastern Europe phrasebook
Finland
France
Greece
Hungary
Iceland, Greenland & the Faroe Islands
Ireland
Italy
Mediterranean Europe on a shoestring
Mediterranean Europe phrasebook
Poland
Scandinavian & Baltic Europe on a shoestring
Scandinavian Europe phrasebook
Switzerland
Trekking in Spain
Trekking in Greece
USSR
Russian phrasebook
Western Europe on a shoestring
Western Europe phrasebook

North America
Alaska
Canada
Hawaii

South America
Argentina, Uruguay & Paraguay
Bolivia
Brazil
Brazilian phrasebook
Chile & Easter Island
Colombia
Ecuador & the Galápagos Islands
Latin American Spanish phrasebook
Peru
Quechua phrasebook
South America on a shoestring
Trekking in the Patagonian Andes
Venezuela

The Lonely Planet Story

Lonely Planet published its first book in 1973 in response to the numerous 'How did you do it?' questions Maureen and Tony Wheeler were asked after driving, bussing, hitching, sailing and railing their way from England to Australia.

Written at a kitchen table and hand collated, trimmed and stapled, *Across Asia on the Cheap* became an instant local bestseller, inspiring thoughts of another book.

Eighteen months in South-East Asia resulted in their second guide, *South-East Asia on a shoestring*, which they put together in a backstreet Chinese hotel in Singapore in 1975. The 'yellow bible' as it quickly became known to backpackers around the world, soon became *the* guide to the region. It has sold well over half a million copies and is now in its 8th edition, still retaining its familiar yellow cover.

Today there are over 140 Lonely Planet titles in print – books that have that same adventurous approach to travel as those early guides; books that 'assume you know how to get your luggage off the carousel' as one reviewer put it.

Although Lonely Planet initially specialised in guides to Asia, they now cover most regions of the world, including the Pacific, South America, Africa, the Middle East and Europe. The list of *walking guides* and *phrasebooks* (for 'unusual' languages such as Quechua, Swahili, Nepali and Egyptian Arabic) is also growing rapidly.

The emphasis continues to be on travel for independent travellers. Tony and Maureen still travel for several months of each year and play an active part in the writing, updating and quality control of Lonely Planet's guides.

They have been joined by over 50 authors, 90 staff – mainly editors, cartographers & designers – at our office in Melbourne, Australia, at our US office in Oakland, California and at our European office in Paris; another five at our office in London handle sales for Britain, Europe and Africa. Travellers themselves also make a valuable contribution to the guides through the feedback we receive in thousands of letters each year.

The people at Lonely Planet strongly believe that travellers can make a positive contribution to the countries they visit, both through their appreciation of the countries' culture, wildlife and natural features, and through the money they spend. In addition, the company makes a direct contribution to the countries and regions it covers. Since 1986 a percentage of the income from each book has been donated to ventures such as famine relief in Africa; aid projects in India; agricultural projects in Central America; Greenpeace's efforts to halt French nuclear testing in the Pacific and Amnesty International. In 1993 $100,000 was donated to such causes.

Lonely Planet's basic travel philosophy is summed up in Tony Wheeler's comment, 'Don't worry about whether your trip will work out. Just go!'.